T0338664

Handbook of Research on Pattern Engineering System Development for Big Data Analytics

Vivek Tiwari
International Institute of Information Technology, India

Ramjeevan Singh Thakur
Maulana Azad National Institute of Technology, India

Basant Tiwari
Hawassa University, Ethiopia

Shailendra Gupta
AISECT University, India

A volume in the Advances in Systems Analysis,
Software Engineering, and High Performance
Computing (ASASEHPC) Book Series

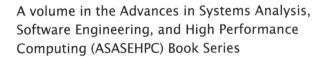

Published in the United States of America by
    IGI Global
    Engineering Science Reference (an imprint of IGI Global)
    701 E. Chocolate Avenue
    Hershey PA, USA 17033
    Tel: 717-533-8845
    Fax: 717-533-8661
    E-mail: cust@igi-global.com
    Web site: http://www.igi-global.com

Library of Congress Cataloging-in-Publication Data

Names: Tiwari, Vivek, 1982- editor.
Title: Handbook of research on pattern engineering system development for big
  data analytics / Vivek Tiwari, Ramjeevan Singh Thakur, Basant Tiwari, and
  Shailendra Gupta, editors.
Description: Hershey, PA : Engineering Science Reference, [2018] | Includes
  bibliographical references.
Identifiers: LCCN 2017022957| ISBN 9781522538707 (hardcover) | ISBN
  9781522538714 (ebook)
Subjects: LCSH: Big data. | Pattern recognition systems.
Classification: LCC QA76.9.B45 H38 2018 | DDC 005.7--dc23 LC record available at https://lccn.loc.gov/2017022957

This book is published in the IGI Global book series Advances in Systems Analysis, Software Engineering, and High Performance Computing (ASASEHPC) (ISSN: 2327-3453; eISSN: 2327-3461)

British Cataloguing in Publication Data
A Cataloguing in Publication record for this book is available from the British Library.

Advances in Systems Analysis, Software Engineering, and High Performance Computing (ASASEHPC) Book Series

Vijayan Sugumaran
Oakland University, USA

ISSN:2327-3453
EISSN:2327-3461

MISSION

The theory and practice of computing applications and distributed systems has emerged as one of the key areas of research driving innovations in business, engineering, and science. The fields of software engineering, systems analysis, and high performance computing offer a wide range of applications and solutions in solving computational problems for any modern organization.

The **Advances in Systems Analysis, Software Engineering, and High Performance Computing (ASASEHPC) Book Series** brings together research in the areas of distributed computing, systems and software engineering, high performance computing, and service science. This collection of publications is useful for academics, researchers, and practitioners seeking the latest practices and knowledge in this field.

COVERAGE

- Software Engineering
- Performance Modelling
- Engineering Environments
- Computer System Analysis
- Network Management
- Parallel Architectures
- Computer Networking
- Enterprise Information Systems
- Distributed Cloud Computing
- Computer graphics

IGI Global is currently accepting manuscripts for publication within this series. To submit a proposal for a volume in this series, please contact our Acquisition Editors at Acquisitions@igi-global.com or visit: http://www.igi-global.com/publish/.

Titles in this Series

For a list of additional titles in this series, please visit: www.igi-global.com/book-series

Formation Methods, Models, and Hardware Implementation of Pseudorandom Number Generators Emerging Research and Opportunities
Stepan Bilan (State Economy and Technology University of Transport, Ukraine)
Engineering Science Reference • copyright 2018 • 301pp • H/C (ISBN: 9781522527732) • US $180.00 (our price)

Aligning Perceptual and Conceptual Information for Cognitive Contextual System Development Emerging Research and Opportunities
Gary Kuvich (IBM, USA)
Engineering Science Reference • copyright 2018 • 172pp • H/C (ISBN: 9781522524311) • US $165.00 (our price)

Applied Computational Intelligence and Soft Computing in Engineering
Saifullah Khalid (CCSI Airport, India)
Engineering Science Reference • copyright 2018 • 340pp • H/C (ISBN: 9781522531296) • US $225.00 (our price)

Enhancing Software Fault Prediction With Machine Learning Emerging Research and Opportunities
Ekbal Rashid (Aurora's Technological and Research Institute, India)
Engineering Science Reference • copyright 2018 • 129pp • H/C (ISBN: 9781522531852) • US $165.00 (our price)

Solutions for Cyber-Physical Systems Ubiquity
Norbert Druml (Independent Researcher, Austria) Andreas Genser (Independent Researcher, Austria) Armin Krieg (Independent Researcher, Austria) Manuel Menghin (Independent Researcher, Austria) and Andrea Hoeller (Independent Researcher, Austria)
Engineering Science Reference • copyright 2018 • 482pp • H/C (ISBN: 9781522528456) • US $225.00 (our price)

Large-Scale Fuzzy Interconnected Control Systems Design and Analysis
Zhixiong Zhong (Xiamen University of Technology, China) and Chih-Min Lin (Yuan Ze University, Taiwan)
Information Science Reference • copyright 2017 • 223pp • H/C (ISBN: 9781522523857) • US $175.00 (our price)

Microcontroller System Design Using PIC18F Processors
Nicolas K. Haddad (University of Balamand, Lebanon)
Information Science Reference • copyright 2017 • 428pp • H/C (ISBN: 9781683180005) • US $195.00 (our price)

Probabilistic Nodes Combination (PNC) for Object Modeling and Contour Reconstruction
Dariusz Jacek Jakóbczak (Technical University of Koszalin, Poland)
Information Science Reference • copyright 2017 • 312pp • H/C (ISBN: 9781522525318) • US $175.00 (our price)

701 East Chocolate Avenue, Hershey, PA 17033, USA
Tel: 717-533-8845 x100 • Fax: 717-533-8661
E-Mail: cust@igi-global.com • www.igi-global.com

Editorial Advisory Board

List of Contributors

Table of Contents

Section 1
Applications and Approaches to Big Data

Section 2
Data Mining and Computing

Section 3
Data-Oriented Security and Networking

Detailed Table of Contents

Section 1
Applications and Approaches to Big Data

Chapter 1

Ramgopal Kashyap, Sagar Institute of Science and Technology, India
Albert Dayor Piersson, University of Cape Coast, Ghana

Big data today is being investigated to find the bits of knowledge that prompt better choices and vital business moves. The data innovations are developing to a point in which an ever-increasing number of associations are set up to pilot and embrace big data as a center part of the data administration and examination framework. It is a range of research that is blasting yet at the same time confronts many difficulties in utilizing the esteem that information brings to the table. The battle against "spam information" and information quality is a pivotal issue. Big data challenges are discussed and some solutions are proposed because the volume of made information will surpass the capacity limits and will require cautious determination.

Chapter 2

Dharmendra Singh Rajput, VIT University, India
T. Sunil Kumar Reddy, Sri Venkateswara College of Engineering and Technology, India
Dasari Naga Raju, Sri Venkateswara College of Engineering and Technology, India

In recent years, big data analytics is the major research area where the researchers are focused. Complex structures are trained at each level to simplify the data abstractions. Deep learning algorithms are one of the promising researches for automation of complex data extraction from large data sets. Deep learning mechanisms produce better results in machine learning, such as computer vision, improved classification modelling, probabilistic models of data samples, and invariant data sets. The challenges handled by the big data are fast information retrieval, semantic indexing, extracting complex patterns, and data tagging. Some investigations are concentrated on integration of deep learning approaches with big data analytics which pose some severe challenges like scalability, high dimensionality, data streaming, and distributed computing. Finally, the chapter concludes by posing some questions to develop the future work in semantic indexing, active learning, semi-supervised learning, domain adaptation modelling, data sampling, and data abstractions.

Chapter 3

Rajit Nair, Maulana Azad National Institute of Technology, India
Amit Bhagat, Maulana Azad National Institute of Technology, India

Data is being captured in all domains of society and one of the important aspects is transportation. Large amounts of data have been collected, which are detailed, fine-grained, and of greater coverage and help us to allow traffic and transportation to be tracked to an extent that was not possible in the past. Existing big data analytics for transportation is already yielding useful applications in the areas of traffic routing, congestion management, and scheduling. This is just the origin of the applications of big data that will ultimately make the transportation network able to be managed properly and in an efficient way. It has been observed that so many individuals are not following the traffic rules properly, especially where there are high populations, so to monitor theses types of traffic violators, this chapter proposes a work that is mainly based on big data analytics. In this chapter, the authors trace the vehicle and the data that has been collected by different devices and analyze it using some of the big data analysis methods.

Chapter 4

Misbahul Haque, Aligarh Muslim University, India
Mohd Imran, Aligarh Muslim University, India
Mohd Vasim Ahamad, Aligarh Muslim University, India
Mohd Shoaib, Aligarh Muslim University, India

In today's world, humungous and heterogeneous data are being generated from every action of researchers, health organizations, etc. This fast, voluminous, and heterogeneous generation leads to the evolution of the term big data. Big data can be computationally analyzed to uncover hidden trends and patterns that help in finding solutions to the problems arising in various fields. Analysis of big data for manufacturing operational acquaintance at an unparalleled specificity and scale is called big data analytics. Proper utilization of analytics can assist in making effective decisions, improved care delivery, and achieving cost savings. Recognizing hidden trends and useful patterns can lead us to have a clear understanding of the valuable information that these data holds. This chapter presents a quality overview of big data and analytics with its application in the field of healthcare industries as these industries requires their stream of data to be stored and analyzed efficiently in order to improve their future perspective and customer satisfaction.

Chapter 5

Mohd Vasim Ahamad, Aligarh Muslim University, India
Misbahul Haque, Aligarh Muslim University, India
Mohd Imran, Aligarh Muslim University, India

In the present digital era, more data are generated and collected than ever before. But, this huge amount of data is of no use until it is converted into some useful information. This huge amount of data, coming from a number of sources in various data formats and having more complexity, is called big data. To convert the big data into meaningful information, the authors use different analytical approaches. Information extracted, after applying big data analytics methods over big data, can be used in business decision making, fraud detection, healthcare services, education sector, machine learning, extreme personalization, etc. This chapter presents the basics of big data and big data analytics. Big data analysts face many challenges in storing, managing, and analyzing big data. This chapter provides details of challenges in all mentioned dimensions. Furthermore, recent trends of big data analytics and future directions for big data researchers are also described.

Chapter 6

Mohd Imran, Aligarh Muslim University, India
Mohd Vasim Ahamad, Aligarh Muslim University, India
Misbahul Haque, Aligarh Muslim University, India
Mohd Shoaib, Aligarh Muslim University, India

The term big data analytics refers to mining and analyzing of the voluminous amount of data in big data by using various tools and platforms. Some of the popular tools are Apache Hadoop, Apache Spark, HBase, Storm, Grid Gain, HPCC, Casandra, Pig, Hive, and No SQL, etc. These tools are used depending on the parameter taken for big data analysis. So, we need a comparative analysis of such analytical tools to choose best and simpler way of analysis to gain more optimal throughput and efficient mining. This chapter contributes to a comparative study of big data analytics tools based on different aspects such as their functionality, pros, and cons based on characteristics that can be used to determine the best and most efficient among them. Through the comparative study, people are capable of using such tools in a more efficient way.

Section 2
Data Mining and Computing

Chapter 7

Gaganmeet Kaur Awal, Jawaharlal Nehru University, India
K. K. Bharadwaj, Jawaharlal Nehru University, India

Due to the digital nature of the web, the social web mimics the real-world social dynamics that manifest themselves as data and can be easily mined as patterns, making the web a fertile ground for business and research-oriented analytical applications. Collective intelligence (CI) is a multifaceted field with roots in sociology, biology, and many other disciplines. Various manifestations of CI support the successful existence of large-scale social systems. This chapter gives an overview of the principles of CI and the concept of "wisdom of crowds" and highlights how to maximize the potential of big data analytics for CI. Also, various techniques and approaches have been described that leverage these CI concepts across a diverse range of ever-evolving social systems for commercial business applications like influence mining, expertise discovery, etc.

Chapter 8

Stock investors always consider potential future prices before investing in any stock for making a profit. A large number of studies are found on the prediction of stock market indices. However, the focus on individual stock closing price predictions well ahead of time is limited. In this chapter, a comparative study of machine-learning-based models is used for the prediction of the closing price of a particular stock. The proposed models are designed using back propagation neural networks (BPNN), support vector regression (SVR) with SMOReg, and linear regression (LR) for the prediction of the closing price of individual stocks. A total of 37 technical indicators (features) derived from historical closing prices of stocks are considered for predicting the future price of stock in a time window of five days. The experiment is performed on stocks listed on Bombay Stock Exchange (BSS), India. The model is trained and tested using feature values extracted from the past five-year closing price of stocks of different sectors including aviation, pharma, banking, entertainment, and IT.

Chapter 9

E-commerce has become a daily activity in human life. In it, the opinion and past experience related to particular product of others is playing a prominent role in selecting the product from the online market. In this chapter, the authors consider Tweets as a point of source to express users' emotions on particular subjects. This is scored with different sentiment scoring techniques. Since the patterns used in social media are relatively short, exact matches are uncommon, and taking advantage of partial matches allows one to significantly improve the accuracy of analysis on sentiments. The authors also focus on applying artificial neural fuzzy inference system (ANFIS) to train the model for better opinion mining. The scored sentiments are then classified using machine learning algorithms like support vector machine (SVM), decision tree, and naive Bayes.

Chapter 10

Customized web services are offered to users by grouping them according to their access patterns. Clustering techniques are very useful in grouping users and analyzing web access patterns. Clustering can be an object clustering performed on feature vectors or relational clustering performed on relational data. The relational clustering is preferred over object clustering for web users' sessions because of high dimensionality and sparsity of web users' data. However, relational clustering of web users depends on underlying dissimilarity measures used. Therefore, correct dissimilarity measure for matching relational web access patterns between user sessions is very important. In this chapter, the various dissimilarity measures used in relational clustering of web users' data are discussed. The concept of an augmented user session is also discussed to derive different augmented session dissimilarity measures. The discussed session dissimilarity measures are used with relational fuzzy clustering algorithms. The comparative performance binary session similarity and augmented session similarity measures are evaluated using intra-cluster and inter-cluster distance-based cluster quality ratio. The results suggested the augmented session dissimilarity measures in general, and intuitive augmented session (dis)similarity measure, in particular, performed better than the other measures.

Chapter 11

Arvind Kumar Kourav, BITS Bhopal, India
Shilpi Sharma, BIT, India
Vimal Tiwari, BIT, India

Digital image processing has an enormous impact on technical and industrial applications. Uncompressed images need large storage capacity and communication bandwidth. Digital images have become a significant source of information in the current world of communication systems. This chapter explores the phenomenon of digital images and basic techniques of digital image processing in detail. With the creation of multimedia, the requirements for the storage of a larger amount of high quality pictures and data analysis are increasing.

Chapter 12

Dilip Singh Sisodia, National Institute of Technology Raipur, India

Web robots are autonomous software agents used for crawling websites in a mechanized way for non-malicious and malicious reasons. With the popularity of Web 2.0 services, web robots are also proliferating and growing in sophistication. The web servers are flooded with access requests from web robots. The web access requests are recorded in the form of web server logs, which contains significant knowledge about web access patterns of visitors. The presence of web robot access requests in log repositories distorts the actual access patterns of human visitors. The human visitors' actual web access patterns are potentially useful for enhancement of services for more satisfaction or optimization of server resources. In this chapter, the correlative access patterns of human visitors and web robots are discussed using the web server access logs of a portal.

Chapter 13

Vinod Kumar, Maulana Azad National Institute of Technology, India
R. S. Thakur, Maulana Azad National Institute of Technology, India

Websites have become the major source of information, and analysis for web usage has become the most important way of investigating a user's behaviour and obtaining information for website owners to use to make any strategic decisions. This chapter sheds light on the concept of web usage mining, techniques, and its application in various domains.

Chapter 14

Ramgopal Kashyap, Sagar Institute of Science and Technology, India
Pratima Gautam, AISECT University, India
Vivek Tiwari, International Institute of Information Technology, India

Extricating information from expansive, heterogeneous, and loud datasets requires capable processing assets, as well as the programming reflections to utilize them successfully. The deliberations that have risen in the most recent decade mix thoughts from parallel databases, dispersed frameworks, and programming dialects to make another class of adaptable information investigation stages that shape the establishment of information science. In this chapter, the scene of important frameworks, the standards on which they depend, their tradeoffs, and how to assess their utility against prerequisites are given.

Section 3
Data-Oriented Security and Networking

Chapter 15

Harsha Vasudev, Birla Institute of Technology and Science, India
Debasis Das, Birla Institute of Technology and Science, India

More study is needed to make VANETs more relevant. Opportunistic routing (OR) is a new model that has been proposed for wireless networks. OR has emerged from the research communities because of its ability to increase the performance of wireless networks. It benefits from the broadcast characteristic of wireless mediums to improve network performance. The basic function of OR is its ability to overhear the transmitted packet and to coordinate among relaying nodes. In this chapter, an exhaustive survey of existing OR protocols is done by considering various factors. More precisely, existing secure OR protocols are deliberated. Future directions of research are also included, which provide a superior way to overcome some of the limitations of these existing protocols. Through this detailed survey, an outline and in-depth knowledge of existing OR protocols can be acquired.

Chapter 16

Rachnana Dubey, LNCT, India
Jay Prakash Maurya, LNCT, India
R. S. Thakur, Maulana Azad National Institute of Technology, India

The internet has become very popular, and the concept of electronic mail has made it easy and cheap to communicate with many people. But, many undesired mails are also received by users and the higher percentage of these e-mails is termed spam. The goal of spam classification is to distinguish between spam and legitimate e-mail messages. But, with the popularization of the internet, it is challenging to develop spam filters that can effectively eliminate the increasing volumes of unwanted e-mails automatically before they enter a user's mailbox. The main objective of this chapter is to examine and identify the best detection approach for spam categorization. Different types of algorithms and data mining models are proposed, implemented, and evaluated on data sets. For improvement of spam filtering technique, the authors analyze the methods of feature selection and give recommendations of their use. The chapter concludes that the data mining models using a combination of supervised learning algorithms provide better results than single data models.

Chapter 17

Secured text data transmission plays an important role in communications. Discrete wavelet transform (DWT) is a time variant transform. The drawback of DWT can be overcome by stationary wavelet transform (SWT). SWT is designed to achieve the translation invariance. This chapter presents a novel secured text data transmission through video steganography using two-level stationary wavelet transform (SWT) and singular value decomposition (SVD). SVD of an image can be factored into its three components. In this chapter, text data is encrypted in cover video file using SWT and SVD techniques. First, the cover video is split into frames and each frame of the video acts as an image. Each character in the text data is encrypted with appropriate key value in each frame of the image using two-level SWT and SVD. The encrypted images are converted into video files that are called stego-video files. The text data can be recovered from the stego-video files after converting these files into frames by applying suitable key values, two-level SWT and SVD techniques.

Chapter 18

Real-time online applications and mobile data generate huge volume of data. There is a need to process this data into compact data structures and extract meaningful information. A number of approaches have been proposed in literature to overcome the issues of data stream mining. This chapter summarizes various issues and application techniques. The chapter is a guideline for research to identify the research issues and select the most appropriate method in order to detect and process novel class.

Chapter 19

Fractal algorithms are used to represent similar parts of images into mathematical transforms that can recreate the original image. This chapter presents a fast fractal image compression technique via domain kick-out method, based on averaging of domain images to discard redundant domain images. It accelerates the encoding process by reducing the size of the domain pool. Results of a simulation on the proposed speedup technique on three standard test images shows that performance of the proposed technique is far superior to the present kick out methods of fractal image compression. It has reported a speedup ratio of 31.07 in average while resulting into compression ratio and retrieved image quality comparable to Jacquin's full search method.

Chapter 20

Sreerama Murthy Kattamuri, Sreenidhi Institute of Science and Technology, India
Vijayalakshmi Kakulapati, Sreenidhi Institute of Science and Technology, India
Pallam Setty S., Andhra University, India

An intrusion detection system (IDS) focuses on determining malicious tasks by verifying network traffic and informing the network administrator for restricting the user or source or source IP address from accessing the network. SNORT is an open source intrusion detection system (IDS) and SNORT also acts as an intrusion prevention system (IPS) for monitoring and prevention of security attacks on networks. The authors applied encryption for text files by using cryptographic algorithms like Elgamal and RSA. This chapter tested the performance of mail clients in low cost, low power computer Raspberry Pi, and verified that SNORT is efficient for both algorithms. Within low cost, low power computer, they observed that as the size of the file increases, the run time is constant for compressed data; whereas in plain text, it changed significantly.

Foreword

The fields of computer science have given us much to think and work with. Data analysis and Mining might not have satisfied all its buildup, but rather it had an exceptionally solid role in stimulating thought about what knowledge can and cannot be demonstrated.

The whole book dedicated to Bigdata, data analysis, pattern and their utility. Data analysis is not just about having more insight into the data, but far more. There are various aspects and dimensions to see the same data and the utility of the outcome depends on this. I think, the medical sector is one of the most promising and challenging dimensions of data analysis. It is promising because having direct impact on our society and livelihood and challenging because of having complex data, variety of formats, data confidentiality, and many more. I think, this book provides enough information and necessary components for aforesaid issues.

Reviewing the contents of this book, I am struck by the different and diverse nature of the field as well as how much convergence and coherence has emerged in such a short time. This book figures out with every aspect of the field without turning into an immense awkward black box of a thing concentrated on data, information, knowledge and everything else under the sun. It is interesting to see just how much agreement there exists among researchers and practitioners as to what data analysis, security and mining are. This book is a decent stride in that heading.

R. K. Pateriya
Maulana Azad National Institute of Technology, India

Preface

Nowadays, many applications are generating huge quantities of data (agriculture, weather, medical, clinical, reports, stock, logs, etc.) and it becomes difficult to manage efficiently. Instant and correct decisions are always key factors in business and health care industries. However, there are numbers of approaches have been discovered such as data warehousing, databases, Bigdata, cloud, etc., but, all are concentrating on only data management and it can be viewed as two ways, daily transaction data management and historical data management. Transaction data are managed and maintained by operational database which is also known as Database Management Systems (DBMS). Historical data are managed by data warehouses and it is used for analysis and decision making. These both approaches are the best for data management, but they do not allow to facilitate *knowledge on-demand*. Noteworthy, Users have to do analysis repeatedly whenever the need arises. Nowadays, databases are huge and dynamic because it comes from various application domains and a variety of patterns can be extracted. It is clear that business users do not have an interest in data, but they are striving for trends hidden within the data. So, more elaborated and advanced techniques are needed to be investigated to mine the hidden trends and let them available for further analysis. Many techniques are developed to extract patterns, especially in the context of data mining and the results of such techniques are abstract and compact representations of the original data. The data processing methods such as data mining produce the results such as clusters, association rules, decision trees and others. The output of all the data mining and knowledge discovery techniques represent big portions of the raw data by a few number of knowledge-carrying representatives, which call *patterns*. The pattern is useful because it describes a recurrent behavior and trends. The pattern is a compact representation of raw data, but, usually, in a form that cannot lead us significant meaning directly to real life use. The volume of extracting patterns from various knowledge discovery applications is increasing exponentially, so there requires an effective pattern analysis system that will permit us to compare, query and store the patterns.

The beginning of 90s, it was considered that huge amount of data is available and data warehousing was getting tremendous success as a central data repository system. The working of a Bigdata/Hadoop is represented as multiple layers of data and their processing unit, where, data move from one layer to another. A Bigdata/Hadoop is a distributed data repository system where data comes from external data sources. Basically, data coming from external source are heterogeneous in nature. Often, external data sources are transaction and production system so data are frequently changed. Moreover, these systems may suffer with one major problem of schema changes. So, there is need a system that works as a facilitator for data analysis on the fly. Bigdata/Hadoop can be considered as a separate and dedicated repository of data and further analysis. Furthermore, Bigdata/Hadoop provides a basic framework for analytical processing, decision making, and data mining applications. Several benefits exist when Bigdata/Hadoop is used together with diverse applications. First, Bigdata/Hadoop combine data from many disparate sources—including legacy and retired systems—obviating the need for time-consuming manual extraction (schema preparation) and assimilation of data from multiple systems. Furthermore, as data are combined, they are often standardized to allow comparisons to be made (e.g. gender of "male," "M," and "1" might be converted into a uniform value). Second, the integration with tools to perform data mining and statistical analyses allows a wide variety of exploratory analyses to be rapidly performed. Third, because Bigdata/Hadoop is distributed that hold the source data, performing analyses does not result in additional load and a concomitant reduction in response time. Finally, unlike conventional databases that typically store data in a entity centric manner, data Bigdata/Hadoop store data in a format that easily allows cross entity searches (e.g., "find all patients with systolic blood pressure greater than 140").

Basically, data mining is able to extract the knowledge from a variety of data. Furthermore, underlying methods and algorithms may differ with the view of different types of data. Data mining techniques should be able to handle the challenges carried by data due to their diversity. All pattern generating methods produce knowledge in the form of patterns and most importantly, these patterns are not persistent by nature. Means, the pattern gets lost when it goes out of memory in spite of having long and complex process behind the pattern generation and It is time and resource consuming as well. The major drawbacks with these pattern generating methods are:

1. Patterns are not persistent, i.e. each time when patterns are in need, it is necessary to execute pattern generating method again and again.
2. Patterns have become stale when data source is updated i.e., as source of data or data warehouse is updated then the same pattern extracting method may give different patterns as compared to earlier.
3. In some cases, patterns are huge itself and it is hard to manage in main memory because the algorithm which generates patterns itself resides in memory and occupy major portion. This situation makes the whole process slow.
4. In some cases, the data warehouse is not maintained by the organizations, i.e. data need to be accessed from various locations on-demand. It may face some authentication and authorization issues because there is a need to make connection with various data sources on the fly and even this complex process is required to be repeated again and again to get the patterns on different moments.
5. The process of collecting the data every time is not a single issue, but further preprocessing of data (cleaning, transformation, etc.) is required to make it suitable for analysis.

Due to all above said issues data management through data warehousing and pattern generation through data mining is still suffering from many problems. So, this kind of data management and decision-making process is not full proof, suitable in critical business application and health care decision making.

This book aims to investigate all the approaches which help with efficient and flexible data analysis specially in medical and bioinformatics domain. Through this book, we are looking forward new approaches or existing methods which can modify to accommodate in on-demand bioinformatics knowledge retrieval concept. There is found little investigation on pattern management for business and health care industries. Healthcare practices have been enhanced through the use of information technologies and analytical methods. Nowadays, there is a need to optimize health care data or trends management through knowledge on-demand concept. This book investigates the incorporation of pattern management into business technologies and health care for the decision making and prediction process. This book brings together the common issues of business and health care pattern management. These two areas have not been tackled collectively till date. This book tries to uncover the various strategies, techniques and approaches which may improve the organization's pattern management power and helps for quick and efficient decision making. Instant and correct decisions are always key factors in business and health care industries. There need a separate system which helps to organize, store, manipulate and retrieval of patterns. This book will spread an awareness about bioinformatics pattern management, its need and applications. We are looking forward attention on business applications health care data management, but is not limited to.

So as to give the most thorough, in-depth, and current scope of every single related subject and their applications, and also to offer a solitary reference source on all conceptual, methodological and technical, We are satisfied to offer a rich collection on this quickly developing discipline. This collection intends to enable specialists, researchers, understudies, and professionals by encouraging their extensive comprehension of the most basic data analysis in medical territories inside this field of study.

This collection, entitled *Handbook of Research on Pattern Engineering System Development for Big Data Analytics* is organized into three distinct sections, which are as follows: (1) Applications and Approaches to Big Data, (2) Data Mining and Computing, (3) Data-Oriented Security and Networking. The following paragraphs provide a summary of what is covered in each chapter.

- **Chapter 1 (Big Data Research Challenges and Solutions in Medical Industries):** The appearance of advances like versatile processing, distributed computing, web of things, sensor based systems and the accessibility of web in handheld gadgets has brought about an era of extensive measure of information, both organized and unstructured, which is called "Big Data". New apparatuses, innovations, models and systems are utilized to deal with huge information. Huge Data will enable customary cases and methodology information to be coordinated with information made outside of human services to separate simulated boundaries between social insurance. For instance, information from market buys, online networking, and individual inclinations can be incorporated to better comprehend what impacts individual and populace health. This chapter discussed various challenges and approaches for implementing medical oriented stuff in Big Data scenario.

- **Chapter 2 (Investigation on Deep Learning Approach for Big Data - Applications and Challenges):** Big data plays crucial role in public and private organizations for collecting the huge volumes of data contains useful information about some domains such as cyber security, medical informatics, marketing, fraud detection and National intelligence. For development of existing and future technology, some of the companies like Microsoft, Amazon and Google are analysing the huge volumes of data for decision making and business analysis. Deep learning techniques are the new development for extracting the high level complex structures in the data analysis using the superior learning approach. This chapter plots some investigations on integration of deep learning approaches with big data analytics which pose some severe challenges like scalability, high dimensionality, data streaming and distributed computing. Finally, the research work concludes by posing some questions to develop the future work in semantic indexing, active learning, semi-supervised learning, domain adaptation modelling, data sampling and data abstractions.

- **Chapter 3 (An Application of Big Data Analytics in Road Transportation):** An important concern today in India is vehicle population which spurs due to rise in population and economic recovery creates a severe pressure on traffic management in the major urban areas of the country. Large amount of data has been collected exponentially which are detailed, fine-grained and of greater coverage that helps us to allow traffic and transportation to be tracked to an extent which was not possible in the past. It has been observed that so many individuals are not following the traffic rules properly, especially a place where there is high population, so to monitor theses type of traffic violators this chapter proposes a work which is mainly based on big data analytics. In this chapter the authors will trace the vehicle and the data which has been collected by different devices will be analysed by using some of the big data analysis method.

- **Chapter 4 (Big Data and Analytics - Application to Healthcare Industry):** This chapter presents a quality overview of Big Data and analytics with its application in the field of healthcare industries as these industries require their stream of data to be stored and analyzed efficiently in order to improve their future perspective and customer satisfaction. The traditionally structured databases create a big chaos in dealing with the challenges that the humongous data creates. Big Data analytics has very much efficiently garnered a favor for these industries to accomplish their goal of analyzing, identifying and exploring the underlying knowledge in order to improve the health condition of patients when used wisely in healthcare industries while achieving customer satisfaction in business industries.

- **Chapter 5 (Insight Into Big Data Analytics: Challenges, Recent Trends, and Future Prospects):** In the present digital era, data are generated and collected more and more than ever before. But, this huge amount of data is of no use until it is converted into some useful information. This huge amount of data, coming from a number of sources in various data formats and having more complexity, is called as big data. To convert the big data into meaningful information, we use different analytical approaches. Information extracted, after applying big data analytics methods over big data, can be used in business decision making, fraud detection, healthcare services, education sector, machine learning, extreme personalization, etc. This chapter presents basics of big data and big data analytics. Big data analyst faces many challenges in storing, managing and analyzing the big data. This chapter provides details of challenges in all mentioned dimensions. Furthermore, recent trends of big data analytics and future directions for big data researchers are also described.

- **Chapter 6 (Big Data Analytics - Tools and Platforms in Big Data Landscape):** Each one of analytics tool has certain ups and downs in their environment. It is not necessary that one analytics tool used and exclusively designed for a special dataset containing terabytes to petabytes of data; have the capability of same performance while interaction with separate dataset in a different environment. So we need a comparative analysis of such analytical tools to choose best and simpler way of analysis to gain more optimal throughput and efficient mining. This chapter contributes to a comparative study of big data analytics tools based on different aspects as their functionality, pros, and cons based on characteristics which can be used to determine the best and efficient among them. It also explains different characteristics and features of BDA both in tabular and well explained manner. By learning the comparative study, people are capable of learning usability of such tools in more efficient way.

- **Chapter 7 (Harnessing Collective Intelligence Through Pattern Mining in Social Computational Systems):** Due to the digital nature of the web, the social Web mimics the real-world social dynamics that manifest themselves as data and can be easily mined as patterns, making the Web a fertile ground for business and research-oriented analytical applications. Collective intelligence (CI) is a multifaceted field with roots in sociology, biology and many other disciplines. Various manifestations of CI support the successful existence of large-scale social systems. This chapter gives an overview of the principles of CI and the concept of "wisdom of crowds" and will highlight how to maximize the potential of big data analytics for CI. Also, various techniques and approaches have been described that leverage these CI concepts across a diverse range of ever-evolving social systems for commercial business applications like influence mining, expertise discovery, etc.

- **Chapter 8 (Machine Learning Models for Forecasting of Individual Stocks Price Patterns):** Stock investors always consider potential future price before investing in any stock for making a profit. A large number of studies are found on the prediction of stock market indices. However, the focus on individual stocks closing price prediction well ahead of time is limited. In this chapter, a comparative study of machine learning-based models is used for the prediction of the closing price of a particular stock. The proposed models are designed using back propagation neural networks (BPNN), support vector regression (SVR) with SMOReg and linear regression (LR) for the prediction of the closing price of individual stocks. The performance of prediction model is compared using error measures including the mean absolute error (MAE), mean absolute percentage error (MAPE) and root mean squared error (RMSE). The comparative analysis of error measures shows that BPNN outperforms SVR with SMOReg and LR and performs the more accurate prediction of stock prices.

- **Chapter 9 (Sentiments Analysis Using Artificial Neural Fuzzy Inference System):** We also focus on applying Artificial Neural Fuzzy Inference System (ANFIS) to train the model for better opinion mining. The scored sentiments are then classified using machine learning algorithms like: Support Vector Machine (SVM), Decision tree and Naive Bayes. Experiments are carried out on different big data analytics platform like: Hadoop and spark, to measure the accuracy of the such model using F-score obtained from precision and recall parameters. Finally, the obtained user opinions are visualized, by which user can save their time and money in getting introduced to new product.

- **Chapter 10 (A Relative Performance of Dissimilarity Measures for Matching Relational Web Access Patterns Between User Sessions):** In this chapter, the various dissimilarity measures used in relational clustering of web users' data are discussed. The concept of an augmented user session is also discussed to derive different augmented session dissimilarity measures. The session dissimilarity measures are used with relational fuzzy clustering algorithms. The comparative performance binary session similarity and augmented session similarity measures are evaluated using intra-cluster and inter-cluster distance based cluster quality ratio. The results sugested the augmented session dissimilarity measures in general, and intuitive augmented session (dis)similarity measure, in particular, performed better than the other measures.

- **Chapter 11 (Discrete Wavelet Transform [DWT] - A Comparative Analysis of DFT Algorithms to Improve Image Quality):** Digital image processing has an enormous impact on technical and industrial applications. Wavelets analysis is functions defined in a finite interval and set the having average tends to zero. Wavelet transform algorithms are explained and implemented for comparative performance analysis in the field of image compression. Comparative result analysis of EZW, WDR, SPIHT, and STW are produce, these algorithms are implemented by the MATLAB Software using wavelet tool box. This comparative performance analysis of images is analyzed for the value of PSNR, MSE, CR, and BPP for the better quality of compressed image.

- **Chapter 12 (Web Access Patterns of Actual Human Visitors and Web Robots - A Correlated Examination):** Web robots are autonomous software agents used for crawling websites in a mechanized way for non-malicious and malicious reasons. With the popularity of Web 2.0 services, web robots are also proliferating and growing in sophistication. The Web servers are flooded with access requests from Web robots. The web access requests are recorded in the form of web server logs which contains significant knowledge about Web access patterns of visitors. The presence of web robots access requests in log repositories distorted the actual access patterns of human visitors. The human visitor's actual Web access patterns are potentially useful for enhancement of services for more satisfaction or optimization of server resources. In this Chapter, the correlative access patterns of human visitors and Web robots are discussed using Web server access logs of a portal.

- **Chapter 13 (Web Usage Mining Concept and Applications at a Glance):** With the exponential growth in the World Wide Web, the gigantic number of websites is running over the internet. It is still continuously growing with a great pace. Websites have become inevitably the major source of information accessing for the people. Now, analysis for the web usage has become the most important way of investigating the user's behaviour for website owner to make the any strategic decision. This chapter will shed light on the concept of web usage mining, techniques and its application in various domains.

- **Chapter 14 (Management and Monitoring Patterns and Future Scope):** Extricating information from expansive, heterogeneous, and loud datasets requires capable processing assets, as well as the programming reflections to utilize them successfully. Moreover, users require having the capacity to increase significant bits of knowledge from such differed and quickly evolving information, running from every day exchanges to client connections and informal organization information. This paper plans to break down a few of the diverse investigation techniques and devices which can be connected to enormous information, as well as the open doors given by the utilization of enormous information investigation in different choice areas.

- **Chapter 15 (Secure Opportunistic Routing for Vehicular Adhoc Networks):** We are living in a world where the road infrastructure is something that cannot be easily improved, that is why the field of Intelligent Transportation Systems (ITS) has arisen. In this paper, an exhaustive survey of existing OR (Opportunistic Routing) protocols is done by considering various factors. More precisely, existing secure OR protocols deliberated. Future direction of research is also included, which provides a superior way to overcome some of the limitations of these existing protocols. Through this detailed survey, an outline and in-depth knowledge of existing OR protocols can be acquired.

- **Chapter 16 (Detection Approaches for Categorization of Spam and Legitimate E-Mail):** The main objective of this work is to examine and identification of the best detection approach for spam categorization. Here different types of algorithms and data mining models have been proposed, implemented and evaluated on data sets. For improvement of spam filtering technique, we analyzed the methods of feature selection and give recommendation of their use. The work finally concludes that the data mining models using combination of supervised learning algorithms provide better result rather than single data model.

- **Chapter 17 (Video Steganography Using Two-Level SWT and SVD):** Nowadays secured text data transmission plays an important role in communications. In this paper, text data is encrypted in cover video file using SWT and SVD techniques. First, the cover video is split into frames and each frame of the video acts as an image. Each character in the text data is encrypted with appropriate key value in each frame of the image using two-level SWT and SVD. The encrypted images are converted into video file which is called stego-video file. The text data can be recovered from the stego video file after converting this file into frames by applying suitable key values, two-level SWT and SVD techniques.

- **Chapter 18 (Overview of Concept Drift Detection Methodology in Data Stream):** Real-time online applications and mobile data generate huge volume of Data. There is a need to process this data into compact data structure and extract meaningful information. There are various challenges of infinite length, scan and process once, memory limitation and detection and handling of novel class. A no of approaches has been proposed in literature to overcome the issues of data stream mining. This paper summarized various issues, application techniques to process DSM to motivate researchers in order to contribute DSM processing. The paper will be a guideline for researchers to identify the research issues and select most appropriate method in order to detect and process novel class.

- **Chapter 19 (Fast Fractal Image Compression by Kicking Out Similar Domain Images):** Fractal algorithms are used to represent self–similar parts of image into mathematical transforms which can recreate original image. This research presents a fast fractal image compression technique via domain kick-out method, based on averaging of domain images to discard redundant domain images. It accelerates the encoding process by reducing the size of domain pool. Results of simulation on proposed speedup technique on three standard test images, shows that performance of proposed technique is far superior as compared to present kick out methods of fractal image compression. It has reported a speedup ratio of 31.07 in average while resulting into compression ratio and retrieved image quality comparable to Jacquin's full search method.

- **Chapter 20 (Performance Analysis of Mail Clients on Low Cost Computer With ELGamal and RSA Using SNORT):** An Intrusion Detection System (IDS) focuses on determining malicious tasks by verifying network traffic and network administrator will be informed for restricting the user or source or source ip address from accessing the network. SNORT is an open source Intrusion Detection System (IDS) and snort also acts as an Intrusion Prevention system (IPS) for monitoring and prevention of security attacks on networks. We applied encryption for text files by using cryptographic algorithms like Elgamal and RSA. This chapter tested the performance of mail clients in Low Cost, Low Power Computer RaspBery pi, and we verified that Snort is efficient for both algorithms. Within low cost, low power computer, observed that as the size of the file increases, the run time is constant for compressed data whereas in plain text, it changed significantly.

TARGET AUDIENCE

By focusing on concepts such as pattern management, conceptual modeling, logical modeling, access control, quality issues, security, clustering, fusion, knowledge retrieval, knowledge updating, pattern comparison, data filtering, this book is a comprehensive reference source for policy makers, academicians, researchers, students, technology developers, and professionals interested in the development of pattern management system for business application health care decision making. This book brings attention of researchers/professionals who are working in the area of Data management, Data mining, Data warehousing, Bigdata/Hadoop Knowledge, management, Information Retrieval, Business decision maker, Health care data manager, Big data worker.

Vivek Tiwari
International Institute of Information Technology, India

Ramjeevan Singh Thakur
Maulana Azad National Institute of Technology, India

Basant Tiwari
Hawassa University, Ethiopia

Shailendra Gupta
AISECT University, India

Acknowledgment

The editors would like to express appreciation to the numerous individuals who saw us through this book; for all those who provided support, talked things over, read, composed, offered remarks, allowed us to cite their comments and assisted in the editing, proofreading and design. Without their support, this book would not have become a reality.

I believe that the team of authors provides the perfect blend of knowledge and skills that went into composing this book. I thank each of the authors for devoting their time and effort towards this book; I believe that it will be a great asset to the community! Much obliged for everything, I look forward to writing the second edition soon! The editors wish to acknowledge the significant commitments of the reviewers regarding the improvement of quality, coherence, and content presentation of chapters. Some of the authors also served as referees; we highly appreciate their twofold undertaking.

We would like to thank to our mentors Dr. P. K. Sinha, Dr. Kamal Raj Pardasani, Dr. R.K. Pateriya, Dr. Kanak Saxena, Dr. D.K. Mishra, Dr. Shailendra Singh, Dr. D.K. Rajoriya, Dr. Jagdish Chand Bansal, Dr. Dilip Singh Sisodiya, Dr. D.P. Vidyarthi, Dr. O.P. Vyas, Dr. Pradeep Chouksey, Dr. Dharm Singh. They have been our inspiration and motivation for continuing to improve our knowledge and experience. We are likewise exceptionally appreciative of Dr. R. K. Pateriya for providing all support and faith when required.

Last and not least: I beg forgiveness of all those who have been with me over the course of the years and whose names I have failed to mention.

Vivek Tiwari
International Institute of Information Technology, India

Ramjeevan Singh Thakur
Maulana Azad National Institute of Technology, India

Basant Tiwari
Hawassa University, Ethiopia

Shailendra Gupta
AISECT University, India

Section 1
Applications and Approaches to Big Data

Chapter 1
Big Data Challenges and Solutions in the Medical Industries

Ramgopal Kashyap
Sagar Institute of Science and Technology, India

Albert Dayor Piersson
University of Cape Coast, Ghana

ABSTRACT

Big data today is being investigated to find the bits of knowledge that prompt better choices and vital business moves. The data innovations are developing to a point in which an ever-increasing number of associations are set up to pilot and embrace big data as a center part of the data administration and examination framework. It is a range of research that is blasting yet at the same time confronts many difficulties in utilizing the esteem that information brings to the table. The battle against "spam information" and information quality is a pivotal issue. Big data challenges are discussed and some solutions are proposed because the volume of made information will surpass the capacity limits and will require cautious determination.

INTRODUCTION

The appearance of advances like versatile processing, distributed computing, web of things, sensor based systems and the accessibility of web in handheld gadgets has brought about an era of extensive measure of information, both organized and unstructured, which is called "Big Data". The chance of sorting out this extensive data into important and significant data is being acknowledged by businesses, associations and organizations. However, the test with huge information is that it is hard to deal with such substantial measure of information utilizing customary techniques (Nieddu, Boatto, Pirisi, & Dessì, 2010). New apparatuses, innovations, models and systems are utilized to deal with huge information. Hadoop is an

DOI: 10.4018/978-1-5225-3870-7.ch001

open source structure used for preparing enormous information. It is a noticeable disseminated stock-piling and figure condition which is utilized for putting away and preparing of enormous information. Enormous data is a monstrous accumulation of information which is created at an exponential rate in a wide assortment of organizations and has turned out to be difficult to deal with utilizing conventional information administration instrument (Karagiannis, & Buchmann, 2016). The hypothesis of huge information depends on five V's: Volume: Large volume of information produced each second by people, associations, machines, and so forth. Velocity: Speed at which information is being created. Variety: Various configurations in which the information is accessible content, sites, tweets, video, standardized tag, databases etc. Veracity: Correctness and exactness of information. Value: Insights or data that might be produced by applying examination on enormous information. The enthusiasm of associations in huge information has ascended because of the esteem it might create for their organizations and explores (Dinov, 2016). Associations need to grow, settle on better business choices and make new items and administrations; enormous information assumes a noteworthy part in this. With a lot of information spreading over from client purchasing patterns, to twitter tweets, the information holds important data. Appropriate extraction and breaking down of this information may uncover bits of knowledge in future and help associations take gainful business choices or make significant insight (Carter, 2012).

Big Data Analytics (BDA) is the way toward applying progressed logical methods to vast shifted informational collections to accumulate bits of knowledge and find concealed examples that may help examiners, organizations and analysts in settling on speedier and better choices. Customary examination manages organized, value-based information gathered over a timeframe, in information stockrooms for performing Business Intelligence (BI). A BI expert concentrates on discovering patterns, producing reports and visual examination of information. In BDA, information researchers, prescient modelers and different investigation experts examine huge volumes of value-based, and also, information of different structures, gathered from various sorts of sources that may stay undiscovered by traditional business knowledge programs (Nieddu, Boatto, Pirisi, & Dessì, 2010). These information shapes incorporate web server logs, web click stream information, and web-based social networking content, interpersonal organization action reports, patient's human records, content from client messages, overview reactions, cell phone call detail records, and machine information caught by sensors associated with web of things. Figure 1 shows all basic V's required for Big Data and BDA can be performed on various information like, content, picture, snaps, logs and web journals to uncover bits of knowledge about behavioral examples of clients/customers, enhancing execution, taking brilliant business choices, anticipating future qualities, avoiding infections, battling wrongdoing, decreasing cheats, and moderating dangers.

Speedier, better basic leadership with the speed of Hadoop and in-memory examination, joined with the capacity to investigate new wellsprings of information, organizations can dissect data quickly and settle on choices in light of what they have realized. New items and administrations with the capacity to gage client needs and fulfillment through examination comes the ability to give clients what they need. Davenport brings up that with enormous information investigation, more organizations are making new items to address clients' issues. Today, different business and in addition open source apparatuses, such as IBM BigInsights, SAP Hana instrument, Oracle Big Data Appliance, Pivotal Big information suite, Lumify, Apache Storm, RapidMiner, etc. are accessible to perform diverse sorts of examination on Big Data.

Figure 1. Big Data's 5 V's

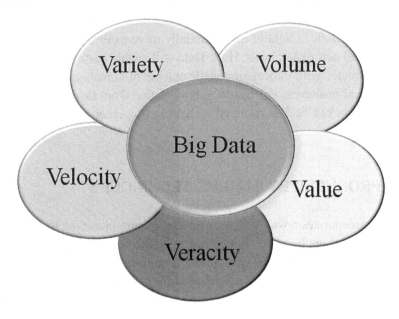

ORIGIN OF HEALTHCARE'S BIG DATA

While there have been, and existing inventive and critical machine learning applications in human services, the industry has been slower to come to and grasp the enormous information development than different ventures. Be that as it may, a snail's pace has not shielded the information from mounting, and the fundamental incentive in the information now accessible to human services suppliers and related specialist co-ops is a veritable goldmine. In this article, we give an outline of where social insurance's enormous information really originates from, and why giving hearty information investigation benefits in this segment matters. Specialists' notes, electronic restorative records, remedies and comparable data are more unmistakable, however different less solid wellsprings of data, for example, computerized information from wearable gadgets and different trackers might be ready to help change human services from a prescriptive practice into a more all-encompassing and protective way to deal with drug (Leppert, & Greiner, 2016).In 2011 alone, the U.S. medicinal services framework achieved 150 Exabyte of information. Computing rate of development, the referenced paper's creators anticipate that U.S. social insurance will soon achieve the zettabyte (1021 gigabytes) scale and, from there on, the yottabyte (1024 gigabytes). To reveal some insight into this level of mass, it (might) be useful to realize that one Exabyte of information is equivalent to one billion gigabytes (Dhar, 2014). Our psyches cannot completely get a handle on anything at that scale, however we can even now wonder about this mountain scope of data. Huge information in human services might be disorganized and disseminated, but at the same time it is a great deal more affordable to claim and work than information put away in social databases; it is likewise harder to utilize. Yet, enormous information is not estimate alone; two frequently ignored components of huge information are its capability to yield important bits of knowledge from intricate, uproarious (unstructured), longitudinal, and voluminous information, and help control us toward answers to inquiries that could not be replied earlier (Eberendu, 2016).

In that lies the brilliant probability of huge information in human services to give a more comprehensive picture of people and of populaces that is not reliant on only one or a couple of factors, yet that makes constructive connections in light of a substantially more extensive arrangement of factors, and which thus can help reveal new experiences. Huge Data will enable customary cases and methodology information to be coordinated with information made outside of human services to separate simulated boundaries between social insurance. For instance, information from market buys, online networking, and individual inclinations can be incorporated to better comprehend what impacts individual and populace health.

INFORMATION PRODUCED BY IMAGING TECHNIQUES

Therapeutic imaging incorporates a wide range of various picture obtaining techniques normally used for an assortment of clinical applications. For instance, envisioning vein structure can be performed utilizing magnetic resonance imaging (MRI), computed tomography (CT), ultrasound, and photoacoustic imaging are shown in the Figure 2. From an information measurement perspective, restorative pictures may have 2, 3, and four measurements. Positron emanation tomography (PET), CT, 3D ultrasound, and MRI are considered multidimensional therapeutic information. Current medicinal picture advancements can create high-determination pictures, for example, "four-dimensional" processed tomography (4D CT) (Chan, & Hanneman, 2015). Higher determination and measurements of these pictures produce substantial volumes of information requiring superior processing and progressed investigative strategies. For example, minuscule outputs of a human cerebrum with high determination can require 66TB of storage room. Despite the fact that the volume and assortment of therapeutic information make its investigation a major test, progresses in restorative imaging could make individualized care more viable and give quantitative data in assortment of uses, for example, sickness stratification, prescient displaying, and basic leadership frameworks. In the accompanying we allude to two restorative imaging methods and one of their related difficulties (Texter et al., 2017).

Sub atomic imaging is a noninvasive procedure of cell and subcellular occasions which has the potential for clinical analysis of ailment states, for example, malignancy. In any case, with a specific end goal to make it clinically appropriate for patients, the connection of radiology, atomic pharmaceutical, and science is essential that could entangle its computerized examination. Microwave imaging is a rising approach that could make a guide of electromagnetic wave dispersing emerging from the differentiation in the dielectric properties of various tissues (Borrill, Keskitalo, & Kisner, 2015). It has both utilitarian and physiological data encoded in the dielectric properties which can help separate and portray diverse tissues as well as pathologies. In any case, microwaves have dissipating conduct that makes recovery of data a testing errand. The incorporation of pictures from various modalities and additionally other clinical and physiological data could enhance the precision of conclusion and result expectation of malady. The part of assessing both MRI and CT images to build the precision of determination in identifying the nearness of disintegrations and osteophytes in the temporomandibular joint (TMJ) as indicated by this review concurrent assessment of all the accessible imaging methods is a neglected need (Lobo, 2017).

Progressed Multimodal Image-Guided Operating (MIGO) suite has been outlined which has angiographic X-beam framework, MRI, 3D ultrasound, and PET/CT imaging in the working room. This framework has been utilized for tumor treatment and demonstrated the change in confinement and focusing on a person's sick tissue. Other than the enormous space required for putting away every one

Figure 2. Medical Imaging Modalities

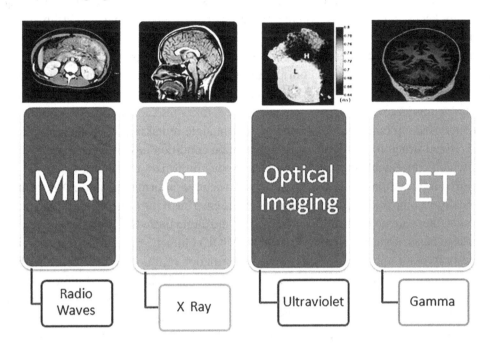

of the information and their investigation, finding the guide and conditions among various information sorts are difficulties for which there is no ideal arrangement yet (Kapur, 2016).

HOW BIG DATA DIFFERS FROM THE DATABASES CURRENTLY USED IN HEALTHCARE

The major framework contrast will demonstrate why enormous information is right now a work in advance yet still holds so much potential. The greatest contrast between huge information and social databases is that enormous information does not have the conventional table-and-section structure that social databases have. In great social databases, a construction for the information is required for instance, statistic information is housed in one table joined to different tables by a common identifier like a patient identifier (Shemberko, & Sliva, 2012). Each bit of information exists in its very much characterized format. Conversely, huge information has scarcely any structure whatsoever. Information is removed from source frameworks in its crude shape placed away in an enormous, fairly confused conveyed document framework. The Hadoop Distributed File System (HDFS) stores information over numerous information hubs in a straightforward leveled type of indexes of records. Traditionally, information is put away in 64MB pieces (documents) in the information hubs with a high level of pressure (Gemayel, 2016). By tradition, huge information is regularly not changed at all. Practically no "purifying" is done and for the most part, no business principles are connected. A few people allude to this crude information as far as the "Sushi Principle" i.e. information is best when it's crude, new, and prepared to devour. Strikingly, the Health Catalyst Late-Binding Data Warehouse takes after similar standards. Because of its unstructured nature and open source roots, huge information is a great deal more affordable to possess and work than a customary social database. A Hadoop bunch is worked from reasonable, ware equipment, and it commonly keeps running on customary circle drives in a direct connected arrangement instead of a costly stockpiling zone organize (Kim, & Hong, 2017). Most social database motors are restrictive programming and require costly permitting and support understandings. Social databases additionally require noteworthy, particular assets to configuration, direct, and keep up. Conversely, huge information, there is no need to bother with a great deal of configuration work, as such it is genuinely easy to keep up with. A considerable measure of capacity excess takes into account more bearable equipment disappointments. Hadoop bunches are intended to disentangle remaking of fizzled hubs. The absence of pre-characterized structure implies a major information condition is less expensive and less difficult to make. So what is the catch? The trouble with enormous information is that it is not unimportant to discover required information inside that gigantic, unstructured information store. An organized social database basically accompanies a guide or diagram where each bit of information exists. On the enormous information side, there are no conventional blueprints, and along these lines very little direction. With a social database, a basic, organized inquiry dialect (i.e. SQL) pulls the required information utilizing an advanced question motor upgraded for discovering information (Kim, & Hong, 2017). With enormous information, the question dialects are a great deal more entangled. An advanced information client, for example, an information researcher is expected to discover the subset of information required for applications. Making the required MapReduce calculations for questioning enormous information occasions is not for the swoon of heart. Luckily, that is changing at a genuinely quick pace with apparatuses like SparkSQL and other question devices that use traditional SQL for questioning. Enormous information inquiry motors can now change over SQL questions into MapReduce employments while others like the previously mentioned Microsoft PolyBase can join inquiries from a customary social database and Hadoop then give back a solitary outcome set (Kakkirala, & Venkateswara, 2016).

To put it plainly, enormous information is shoddy yet harder to utilize. Social databases are costly yet extremely usable. The development level of huge information innovation is low after all the enormous information travel just started a couple of short years back. Along these lines, as the tooling and security makes up for lost time with its potential, human frameworks will have the capacity to do energizing things with it. A few difficulties with enormous information presently does not seem to be tended to in the current huge information dispersions (Li, & Nath, 2014). Two barriers to the general utilization of enormous information in human services are the specialized skill required to utilize it and an absence of strong, coordinated security encompassing it. Healing facility IT specialists acquainted with SQL programming dialects and conventional social databases are not set for the lofty expectation to absorb information and different complexities encompassing huge information. According to Cybermetrics Lab, there are more than 16,500 hospitals worldwide in which most of them are using medical data modalities (Dandu, 2008) for analysis shown in Table 1.

In medicinal services, HIPAA consistence is non-debatable. Nothing is more critical than the protection and security of patient information. In any case, to be honest, there are not some great, incorporated approaches to oversee security in enormous information. Despite the fact that security is tagging along, it has been an untimely idea so far. In any case, when opening up access to a huge, various gathering of clients, security cannot be a bit of hindsight. Medicinal services associations can make a few strides today to guarantee better security of huge information (Hampton, 2013). Enormous information keeps running on open source innovation with conflicting security innovation. To stay away from huge issues, associations ought to be specific about enormous information merchants and abstain from expecting that any huge information dissemination they select will be secure. The best alternative for human services

Table 1. Medical Image Modalities and Storage Size

Value	Description	Matric(px)	Bit per px	Size
CD	Color flow Doppler	768 x 576	8	452KB
CR	Computed radiography	3520 x 4280	12	30 MB
CT	Computed tomography	512 x 512	16	536 KB
MG	Mammography	4608 x 5200	14	45.7 MB
MR	Magnetic Resonance	256 x 256	16	134 KB
NM	Nuclear Medicine	256 x 256	NA	131 KB
PET	Positron Emission Tomography – PET	128 x 128	NA	32 MB
US	Ultrasound	512 x 512	8	268 KB
MG	3D CT Scan	512 x 512	NA	850MB- 1.2 GB
MRI	3D MRI	512 x 512	NA	140-170 MB
MG	Mammograms	512 x 512	NA	120-150 MB
XA	X-Ray Angiography	512 x 512	16	40 MB

associations hoping to execute huge information is to buy an all around bolstered, business conveyance instead of beginning with a crude Apache dispersion. Another alternative is to choose a cloud-based arrangement likeAzure HDInsight to begin rapidly. A case of an organization with an all around bolstered, secure circulation is Cloudera. This organization has made a Payment Card Industry (PCI) consistent Hadoop condition supporting confirmation, approval, information security, and examining. Without a doubt other business appropriation are striving to include more refined security that will be appropriate for HIPAA consistence and other security necessities one of a kind to the human services industry.

Indeed, most associations need information researchers to control and get information out of a major information condition, information researchers are in enormous request. The uplifting news is on account of changes with the tooling, individuals with less-particular skill sets will have the capacity to effortlessly work with huge information later on. Huge information is coming to hold onto SQL as the most widely used language for questioning. What is more, when this happens, it will wind up noticeably valuable in a human framework setting. Microsoft's Polybase is a case of an inquiry apparatus that empowers clients to question both Hadoop Distributed File System frameworks and SQL social databases utilizing a developed SQL punctuation (Lee, Chung, & Lee, 2015). Different devices, for example, Impala, empower the utilization of SQL over a Hadoop database. These sorts of apparatuses will convey enormous information to a bigger gathering of clients.

BURDEN OF DISEASE DATA IN WORLD HEALTH ORGANISATION REGIONS

Regionally low and middle-income countries in the WHO South-East Asia and Western Pacific Regions had the largest environment related disease burden in 2012, with a total of 7.3 million deaths, most attributable to indoor and outdoor air pollution. Low- and middle-income countries bear the greatest environmental burden in all types of diseases and injuries, however for certain such as cardiovascular diseases and cancers, the per capita disease burden can also be relatively high in high-income countries.

More than 3.7 billion internet users,3 billion uses search engines in which health care sector is in the top 5 and 50% Doctors uses internet for study and research60% people searches about healthcare info, Medical Image Database size is increasing 35-45% per year ("DICOM Library - About DICOM most common features of study", 2017). It is estimated that Average per Hospital generating 775 TB per year which includes electronic health records, scanned data and insurance data, 75% data is unstructured including Reports, images and videos and 750 K tele health providers in the world ("An estimated 12.6 million deaths each year are attributable to unhealthy environments", 2017) as shown in Figure 3.

Looking across more than 100 disease and injury categories, this is found in the research that the vast majority of environment-related deaths are due to cardiovascular diseases, such as stroke and ischaemic heart disease, further regional statistics listed in the report include that is shown in Table 2.

Figure 3. Human Bodies as a Source for Big Data in Healthcare

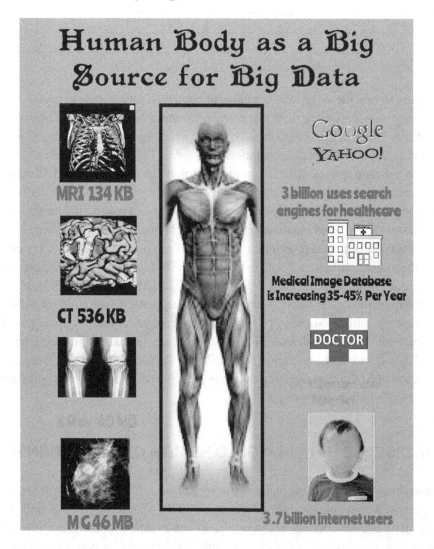

Table 2. Region wise Deaths per Year

S.N.	Region	Deaths Per Year
1	African Region	2.2 million
2	South-East Asia Region	3.8 million
3	European Region	1.4 million
4	Eastern Mediterranean Region	854,000
5	Region of the Americas	847,000
6	Western Pacific Region	3.5 million

CHALLENGES IN ANALYSIS OF MEDICAL IMAGES

Exploratory Investigation of Un-Displayed Multi Structured Information

The test with this kind of information is that it can be substantial in volume and may contain content in various dialects and organizations. It might likewise contain impressive measures of low quality information e.g. spelling blunders or contractions and out of date substance. A key necessity for fruitful content examination is to "clean" the content before examination happens. In any case, numerous organizations frequently have no instrument. Content examination goes past content investigation in that it can likewise deal with sound, video and illustrations (Knossenburg, Nogueira, & Chimenti, 2016). Advanced resource content e.g. sound and video is harder to parse and get business esteem from since the substance is not content.

COMPLEX EXAMINATION OF ORGANIZED INFORMATION

The enormous information logical workload might be on organized information taken from an information distribution center or from other information sources (e.g. operational exchange frameworks) for the particular motivation behind doing complex investigation on that information (Carter, 2012). This might be required so that power clients can mine information to create prescient models for use in consistently business operations. Medical images have become important source of huge quantities of complex and high dimension data frequently used for medical diagnosis, therapy assessment, monitoring and planning, and research (Kashyap, & Tiwari, 2017; Siuly and Zhang, 2016). Traditionally, these images are directly interpreted through visual inspection by a radiologist with the aim to improve the interpretability of depicted contents (Ritter, et al., 2011). However, this approach is cumbersome, time consuming, error prone and subject to fatigue and distraction (Gurcan, et al 2009; Sun and Reddy, 2013). Indeed, it is well-acknowledged that such a method requires a great deal of skills, knowledge and experience that may not always be readily available thus making it infeasible. A better innovative method is the use of digital technologies i.e. computer-aided diagnosis (CAD) employed in medical imaging for fast image processing, and to complement the opinion of the radiologist (Kashyap, & Gautam, 2016; Juneja, & Kashyap, 2016).

THE CAPACITY AND REPROCESSING OF FILED INFORMATION AND IMAGES

The continuous improvements in both hardware and software components of medical imaging technologies such as microarry images (Kashyap, & Gautam 2013), magnetic resonance imaging (MRI), computed tomography (CT), X-ray, molecular imaging (Waoo, Kashyap, & Jaiswal, 2010) fluoroscopy, photoacoustic imaging, positron emission tomography-computed tomography (PET-CT), single-photon emission-computed tomography (SPECT), mammography and ultrasound have witnessed a tremendous growth in modern medicine (Juneja, & Kashyap, 2016). Image segmentation is the way toward apportioning an advanced image into numerous portions sets of pixels, otherwise called superpixels. The objective of division is to disentangle or potentially change the portrayal of a picture into something that is more important and simpler to analyze. Image division is commonly used to find items and limits lines, bends, and so on. in pictures. All the more decisively, picture division is the way toward appointing a name to each pixel in a picture to such an extent that pixels with a similar mark share certain qualities.

The consequence of energy based image segmentation is an arrangement of portions that by and large cover the whole picture, or an arrangement of forms removed from the picture (Kashyap, & Gautam 2015). Each of the pixels in an area are comparative concerning some trademark or registered property, for example, shading, power, or surface. Nearby locales are altogether extraordinary as for the same characteristic. When connected to a heap of pictures, run of the mill in restorative imaging, the subsequent forms after picture division can be utilized to make 3D reproductions with the assistance of introduction calculations like Marching 3D squares. With fast improvements in engineering and computing technologies, these advances have not only not only resulted in the acquisition of high image resolution and fine-details of anatomical and functional structures of the human body, but also revolutionized advances in post processing methods and reconstruction speed. In addition, other advances revolutionized include storage and analysis systems; high resolution picture archiving and communication systems; information mining with modeling and simulation capabilities to enhance our knowledge base about the diagnosis, treatment and management of critical diseases (Kashyap, & Gautam, 2017). This method has come a long way in view of its strength not only to surmount the shortfalls associated with manual

Figure 4. Big Data and Role of Image Processing

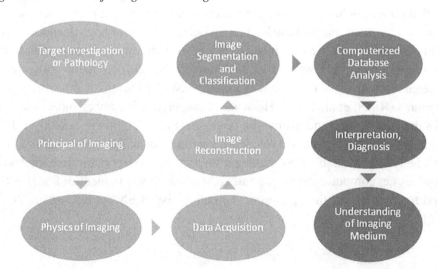

analysis, but also to improve on the analysis of the high volume of data with complexity associated with these modalities (Upadhyay, & Kashyap 2016). For this reason, CAD system is on a high demand due to the rapid growth in the number of healthcare organizations with large number of patients (Belle, et al., 2015). The demand for CAD system can be linked to its ability to provide automatic, fast, authentic, accurate, and reliable assessments and detection of various pathologies that can aid diagnosis, prognosis, and treatment processes (Siuly and Zhang, 2016). The CAD system is also capable of providing a richer set of assets, and is cost-effective and efficient (Arimura, et al., 2009).

Furthermore, CAD offers the opportunity to provide quantitative image-based assessment of medical images such as disease stratification, predictive modeling, and decision making systems (Arimura, et al., 2009; Belle, et al; 2015). This quantitative analysis of medical images is important not only from a diagnostic perspective, but also to understand the underlying reasons for a specific diagnosis being rendered (Gurcan, et al., 2009). Diseases and deaths per year are also creating healthcare data that is shown in the Table 3.

In addition, apart from being important for clinical application, quantitative characterization of imaging pathology is also important for research applications (e.g., to understand the biological mechanisms of the disease process) (Gurcan, et al., 2009). CAD also helps to reduce the subjective factor which underlies several diagnostic tasks. However one challenge with CAD is that validation of results is time consuming as there is general theory in image processing. In addition, the statistical method employed in CAD, the algorithms employed in interpretation and measurement of various nodules or tumour size is not undertaken using any robust approach (Sinha, 2016).

Although there are many available methods and frameworks developed for medical image processing (i.e. including segmentation, registration, enhancement, denoising, detection, and target location), they are not necessarily applicable for high-dimensional and complex big data applications (Sun and Reddy, 2013; Li, et al., 2014; Belle, et al., 2015). Medical image data are huge(Sun and Reddy, 2013), ranging anywhere from a few megabytes for a single study (i.e. digital x-ray studies) to hundreds of megabytes per study (e.g., thin-slice CT comprising up to 2500+ scans per study) (Siebert, 2010). This is mainly due to improvements in medical image acquisition systems with increasing pixel resolution and faster reconstruction processing (Scholl, et al., 2011). These enormous data size occurs in two different ways:

Table 3. Disease and Deaths per year in the world per year

S.N.	Diseases	Deaths Per Year
1	Stroke	2.5 million
2	Ischaemic heart disease	2.3 million
3	Unintentional injuries	1.7 million
4	Cancers	1.7 million
5	Chronic respiratory diseases	1.4 million
6	Diarrhoeal diseases	846 000
7	Respiratory infections	567 000
8	Neonatal conditions	270 000
9	Malaria	259 000
10	Intentional injuries	246 000

first, a huge amount of image data from thousands of images such as in picture archiving and communication systems (PACS) and second, a large amount of image data from a single data set (Scholl, et al., 2011). In recent times, the development of Hadoop which employs MapReduce is expected to shoulder the burden of the large data size, particularly its advantage being increased speed for processing medical images (Shvachko, et al., 2010; Sobhy, et al., 2012).

Due to their large size, medical imaging data often require large storage capacities for long-term storage which also requires high performance computing (HPC) and advanced analytical methods (Belle, et al., 2015). This problem is further compounded owing to the fact that most health organizations lack the information technology resources required for managing such an increasing volume of data (Memon, 2017). PACS are usually employed for display, archival, migration, and delivering of images to local display workstations, accomplished primarily through digital imaging and communications in medicine (DICOM) protocols in radiology departments (Dandu, 2008; Luo, et al., 2016).Thusthe introduction of PACShas contributed significantly in image-based workflow. However, the storage capacity of PACS is limited. It is evident that cost and security have become major factors underpinning the management of data storage and access (Memon, 2017). Importantly, the data storage system is the heart of the PACS system and, most often;it's most expensive component (Dandu, 2008). Some new challenges to big data like validity, venue are shown in the Figure 5.

Notably, among the potential driving forces for the increased use of cloud computing in medical imaging are raw data management and image processing and sharing demand, all of which require high-capacity data storage and computing (Memon, 2017). Another novel approach is the use of Super-PACS, a system developed by Benjamin, et al. (2010). This system can serve multiple sites and has disparate PACS, radiology information systems (RIS), reporting, and other relevant IT systems to view these sites virtually from one site and to use one virtual desktop to efficiently complete all radiology work and reporting .

Besides the huge space required for storing the images and their analysis, finding the map and dependencies among different data types are challenges for which there is no optimal solution yet (Belle, et al., 2015). However it is important to find dependencies among different type of data to improve accuracy. One promising approach is the use of a hybrid machine learning that classifies schizophrenia patients and healthy controls using functional MRI (fMRI) images and single nucleotide polymorphism (SNP)

Figure 5. New Challenges Combinations to Big Data

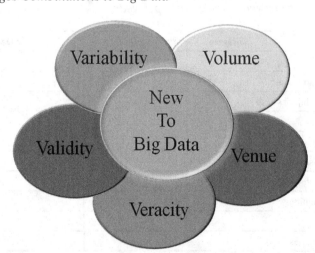

data. Using this method, Yang, et al. (2010) in their study reported an accuracy of 87% classification, which would not have been as high if they had used just fMRI images or SNP alone. Other promising methods that are currently in use include a CAD support system was developed by Chen et al. capable of assisting physicians to provide accurate treatment planning for patients suffering from traumatic brain injury (TBI); and a hybrid digital-optical correlated designed to speed up the correlation of images (Zheng, et al., 2014).

Also radiology groups face significant challenges in a data sharing infrastructure not only among themselves but also with and between multiple healthcare and research institutions (Luo, et al., 2016; Doel, et al., 2017). One important advantage of data sharing in medical imaging is for seeking for second opinion, particularly when there are doubts about establishing a definite diagnosis. This helps in cutting down much differential diagnosis that may end up increasing cost, and delayed diagnosis of patients. With increasing accessibility to the internet, and sporadic spread of web applications, it is increasingly becoming common to share medical imaging data across so many miles away, as well as providing optimal platform for relevant backup. It is therefore expected that data sharing can actually reduce the cost for patients as doctors can also have the opportunity to have access to medical imaging reports required for clinical diagnosis (Memon, 2017), and eliminate the need for travelling of patients and their escorts (Bairagi, 2016). One potentially beneficial system is GIFT-Cloud, adata sharing and collaboration platform developed to meet the needs of GIFT-Surg, an international research collaboration responsible for the development of novel imaging methods for fetal surgery (Doel, et al., 2017). Apart from this use, GIFT-Cloud also has general applicability to other areas of imaging research.

In addition, if other sources of data acquired for each patient are used during the diagnoses, prognosis, and treatment processes, then it becomes a challenge to provide a cohesive storage and developing efficient methods capable of encapsulating the broad range of Due to the difference in modality and their associated technical pearls, it is difficult integrating them if multiple datasets are involved. In comparison with the volume of research that exists on single modal medical image analysis, research initiatives on multimodal image analysis are considerably less (Belle, et al., 2015). Furthermore, when data is used at a local/institutional level, one important part of a research project is on how the developed system is evaluated and validated However, it is a challenge having annotated data or a structured method to annotate new data It even becomes more challenging when there is the need to consider the integration of large-scale data from multiple institutions.

DISCUSSION

The advanced insurgency is in progress various enterprises have officially changed their exercises or have now turned out to be broken. The main thrusts are scaling down, robotization, and now progressively the meeting of counterfeit consciousness, profound learning, and mechanical autonomy. Human services will not get away from these improvements. Truth be told, enormous information as a main impetus will play a significantly more critical part than in many businesses. In Europe, working crosswise over outskirts is the best way to ace the difficulties of this logical, mechanical, and modern transformation (Virmani, Arora, & Kulkarni, 2017). The absolute most imperative component is the workforce. Nations that are ahead in ICT capability and have a comprehension of social contrasts and a capacity and ability to cooperate have the most obvious opportunity to succeed.

The difficulties fall into two fundamental classes: monetary/arrangement and innovation. Monetary and approach issues: In an expense for-administration condition, the main way that social insurance professionals get paid is to have eye to eye experiences with patients. This makes overwhelming inclination against advancing advancements that streamline non-up close and personal connections. In any case, as we move far from that model and more towards esteem based care, where worldwide hazard based installments are made to conveyance associations (clinics, persistent focused restorative homes, responsible care associations, and so forth.), then there is more motivation to utilize new innovations that diminish pointless in-office experiences. In such a situation, eye to eye experiences are really a cost focus, not a benefit focus, and positive human results of populaces are compensated.

The medical information in reality exhibits how Big Data will change medicinal services, sooner rather than later with cost investment funds, nature of care, and care coordination.Huge information may further increase differences in human services results, making another general human concern. Keeping in mind the end goal to enhance human and sickness administration, there has been expanded excitement for tackling the utilization of enormous information in human services from mobile phones, geospatial area, and natural ongoing checking of human conditions; nonetheless, limited access to cell phones and human proficiency are sporadically appropriated by age, race, financial status, and rurality. Developing utilization of wearable sensors and associated gadgets is a new spring of huge information (Campbell, 2014) that allows consistent individual human information procurement. Protection has turned into a testing issue for the huge information period since information that are de-identifiable by Health Insurance Portability and Accountability Act (HIPAA) guidelines may end up. Associations who share information may gain as a matter of fact gathering of information on the consequences of their model of information sharing, publicizing this data and the lessons learned, and constantly refining the information sharing procedure to intensify the benefits of information sharing and lessen the dangers.

Innovation issues: The greatest specialized hindrance to accomplishing this vision is the condition of human information. Made by heritage Electronic Healthcare Records(EHR) frameworks, human information is to a great extent divided into organization focused storehouses. Now and again those storehouses are huge, yet they are still storehouses (Sweet, & Moulaison, 2013). Trading singular records between storehouses, utilizing progressively institutionalized vocabularies (code sets) and message positions (ADT messages, C-CDAs, even FHIR articles), is the place much current exertion is being coordinated. In any case, that does not tackle the issue of information discontinuity. An ever increasing number of individuals in the human data trade field are seeing that the up and coming era of human innovation is around collecting information, not just trading duplicates of individual records (the customary question reaction approach). Just by gathering the information from a wide range of sources, normalizing that information into a reliable structure, settling the information around one of a kind patient identifiers and also extraordinary supplier identifiers at exactly that point can the information turn out to be genuinely valuable. Accumulated information has two extra favorable circumstances. (1) It takes care of the interoperability issue. Frameworks and establishments never again need to fabricate information connects, and decipher how the information is organized between two exclusive frameworks; everybody rather just associates with a focal standard API "plug." If constructed right, the amassed information can be the reason for exceptionally powerful AI innovation. Such innovation is quick consider Google recommendations as-you-write in an inquiry bar, recovering proposals from billions of record choices. (2) It is additionally adequately adaptable to permit machine learning, and AI will have the capacity to work in a constant design.

These Big Data open up conceivable outcomes for better quality social insurance, and better and quicker clinical research. A key issue with Big Data is to understand the data rapidly, so by applying a Visual Analytics approach, the size of Big Data can be overpowered thus leading to a profitable resource. Intuitive representation grants everybody to see substantial, multi-source, variable-sort, and time shifting information some new challenges like vocabulary, validity and vagueness are are also creating big trouble to the healthcare and big data as shown in Figure 6.

Organizations and associations who need to put information to great use will require an exhaustive arrangement for human information gathering, streamlining and examination. Applying prescient investigation, validity, venue and vocabulary ("Top 10 Big Data Challenges – A Serious Look at 10 Big Data V's | MapR", 2017) demonstrating and gathering design based and shrewd bits of knowledge can possibly profit all "players" in the framework, including people, medicinal services professionals, general human offices, life science associations, medical coverage organizations, and restorative and pharmaceutical producers. Lessened total medicinal expenses appear to probably be one of the real advantages related with the greater part of the accompanying points of interest.

Prescription and medicinal services are experiencing significant changes entire genome sequencing and high determination imaging advancements are key drivers of this quick and essential change (Alonso, Lucas, & Hysi, 2015). Mechanical advancement consolidated with computerization and scaling down has set off a blast in information generation that will soon achieve Exabyte extents. How are we going to manage this exponential increment in information creation? The capability of "huge information" for enhancing human is huge be that as it may; in the meantime, we confront an extensive variety of difficulties to overcome desperately. Europe is extremely pleased with its social differing qualities; nonetheless, abuse of the information made accessible through advances in genomic medication, imaging, and an extensive variety of versatile human applications or associated gadgets is hampered by various verifiable, specialized, legitimate, and political hindrances. European human frameworks and databases are differing and divided. There is an absence of harmonization of information organizations, preparing, examination,

Figure 6. Validity, Vagueness and Vocabulary to Big Data

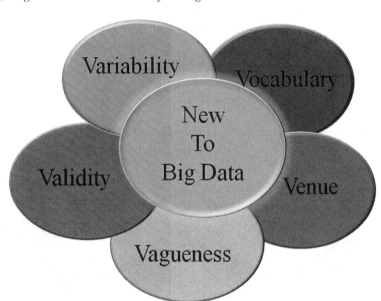

and information exchange, which prompts contrary qualities and lost open doors. Legitimate systems for information sharing are developing. Clinicians, specialists, and subjects require enhanced techniques, apparatuses, and preparing to create, break down, and question information viably.

IMPORTANCE OF BIG DATA ANALYTICS

Hadoop is a famous open source structure utilized for BDA. Many organizations like Cloudera, Hortonworks, and IBM have manufactured their enormous information arrangements on top of Hadoop. Hadoop and cloud-based examination bring noteworthy cost focal points with regards to putting away a lot of information in addition to how they can distinguish more productive methods for working together. Despite the advantages, Hadoop group are not generally the best answer for an association's information examination necessities. For instance, associations with moderately little information would not pick up colossally from a Hadoop, because regardless of the possibility that exceptional and complex information investigation is required ("Challenges with Big Data Analytics", 2015). Another disadvantage of Hadoop group is that all its mining calculations depend on parallel procedures running on discrete bunch hubs. In the event that information examination does not fit for use in a parallel handling condition, then Hadoop may not be the correct decision. The most critical hindrance in utilizing a Hadoop bunch is the expectation to absorb information related with introducing, working and supporting the group.

Advantages of big data analytics like cost effective, provides new services and helps us in taking quick decision are shown in Figure 7. Until associations have Hadoop specialists in their IT offices, it turns out to be extremely hard to play out the required information examination. Due to the flexible nature and potential benefits of Hadoop, almost every IT organization is seeking to build a Hadoop infrastructure for big data. Table 4 is showing what stakeholders wants from the big data that is described.

Figure 7. Importance of Big Data Analytics

Table 4. Big Data and some stakeholders

Stakeholder	What Patients Want From Big Data
Patients	1. Controlled access to convenient secure therapeutic data 2. Access to most ideal human results at moderate cost 3. Simple access to restorative research/clinical trials
Investigators	1. Astounding institutionalized clinical information for auxiliary utilize 2. An institutionalized innovation stage with interoperable, plausible, and united access to a wide scope of clinical information 3. Better, novel, more quick instruments of support for investigation of Big Data 4. An instrument for continuous discourse of these points including the clinical specialist group
Clinicians/ Medical insurance/ Analysts	1. Engagement crosswise over partner areas 2. Enabling patients utilizing Big Data 3. Distinguishing at-hazard populaces with Big Data choice support 4. Evaluating and furnishing suppliers with devices for accumulation, refining and perception 5. Utilizing Big Data to advance the act of medication more proficient and more agreeable 6. Showing suppliers about Big Data

SUMMARY

Preventative Healthcare and Patient Empowerment

Using human information and different factors like economics can help associations foresee missed arrangements, rebelliousness with drugs, and furthermore anticipate persistent direction after some time. The potential to yield ideal results exists crosswise over numerous situations, for instance: dissecting tolerant qualities and the cost and results of care with a specific end goal to present best-fit and financially savvy medications, which will likewise affect supplier conduct. Population-level infection profiling will enable analysts to help distinguish prescient occasions and grow more successful counteractive action activities, integrating mental human services into the customary clinical setting will help give more all encompassing administrations, and associate patients with the vital assets and support (Sakr, & Elgammal, 2016).

Improved observing of patient exercises outside the customary care setting medicine adherence administration, locally situated checking, and so on will help people assume expanded individual liability and help suppliers decide best treatment arranges. Improved persistent care coordination crosswise over human services suppliers.

Combatting Fraud and Increased Sources of Revenue

Implementing progressed expository frameworks for misrepresentation recognition and checking the exactness and consistency of cases will help limit extortion.Creating new income streams might be accessible in organizations that can give accumulated and orchestrated information persistent clinical records and claims information, for instance to outsiders who are hoping to make progresses in the field of prescription and pharmaceuticals for instance, permitting information to help pharmaceutical organizations in distinguishing patients who have picked in for cooperation in clinical trials, which thus will help drive the production of new restorative gadgets and pharmaceuticals (Ring, 2016).

Crossing Over Gaps

As we move into another period of enormous information driven human services administrations, there are two huge difficulties that face huge information investigation companies and social insurance supplier's absence of setting and obsolete information. Spearheading a major information investigation framework that depends on basic information guidelines and that furnishes clients with access to examination produced from constant information sources will be critical to making an adaptable and gainful social insurance framework.

It is hard to total and examine unstructured information, proficiently taking care of vast volumes of restorative imaging information and understanding unstructured clinical notes are difficulties. The catch, ordering and preparing of consistently gushing, fine-grained, and worldly information is a test (Cercone, F'IEEE, 2015). Information programmers have turned out to be all the more harming in enormous information. Information spillage can be exorbitant lack of foundation and strategies, models and practices that take advantage of enormous information in human services were likewise referred to as a worry.

FUTURE SCOPE

Visual information revelation devices will grow 2.5 times quicker than rest of the Business Intelligence (BI) advertises. By 2018, putting resources into this empowering influence of end client self administration will turn into a prerequisite for all ventures. Throughout the following five years spending on cloud-based Big Data and examination (BDA) arrangements will grow three times quicker than spending for on-start arrangements. Mixture on/off preface organizations will turn into a necessity. Deficiency of talented staff will hold on. In the U.S. alone there will be 181,000 profound examination parts in 2018 and five times that many positions requiring related abilities in information administration and understanding. By 2017 brought together information stage design will turn into the establishment of BDA system. The unification will happen crosswise over data administration, examination, and inquiry innovation. Development in applications joining progressed and prescient examination, including machine learning, will quicken in 2015. These applications will grow 65% speedier than applications without prescient usefulness. 70% of huge associations as of now buy outer information and 100% will do as such by 2019. In parallel more associations will start to adapt their information by offering them or offering some benefit included substance. Appropriation of innovation to ceaselessly break down floods of occasions will quicken in 2015 as it is connected to Internet of Things (IoT) examination, which is relied upon to develop at a five-year compound yearly development rate (CAGR) of 30%. Choice administration stages will extend at a CAGR of 60% through 2019 in light of the requirement for more prominent consistency in basic leadership and basic leadership process information maintenance. Rich media (video, sound, and picture) investigation will no less than triple in 2015 and develop as the key driver for BDA innovation venture.

REFERENCES

Alonso, N., Lucas, G., & Hysi, P. (2015). Big data challenges in bone research: Genome-wide association studies and next-generation sequencing. *BoneKEy Reports, 4*. doi:10.1038/bonekey.2015.2 PMID:25709812

An estimated 12.6 million deaths each year are attributable to unhealthy environments. (2017). World Health Organization. Retrieved 26 May 2017, from http://www.who.int/mediacentre/news/releases/2016/deaths-attributable-to-unhealthy-environments/en/

Arimura, H., Magome, T., Yamashita, Y., & Yamamoto, D. (2009). Computer-aided diagnosis systems for brain diseases in magnetic resonance images. *Algorithms*, *2*(3), 925–952. doi:10.3390/a2030925

Bairagi, V. K. 2016. Big Data Analytics in Telemedicine: A Role of Medical Image Compression. In Big Data Management. Cham: Springer International Publishing.

Belle, A., Thiagarajan, R., Soroushmehr, S. M. R., Navidi, F., Beard, D. A., & Najarian, K. (2015). Big Data Analytics in Healthcare. *BioMed Research International*, *2015*, 1–16. doi:10.1155/2015/370194 PMID:26229957

Benjamin, M., Aradi, Y., & Shreiber, R. (2010). From shared data to sharing workflow: Merging PACS and teleradiology. *European Journal of Radiology*, *73*(1), 3–9. doi:10.1016/j.ejrad.2009.10.014 PMID:19914789

Borrill, J., Keskitalo, R., & Kisner, T. (2015). Big Bang, Big Data, Big Iron: Fifteen Years of Cosmic Microwave Background Data Analysis at NERSC. *Computing in Science & Engineering*, *17*(3), 22–29. doi:10.1109/MCSE.2015.1

Campbell, M. (2014). Collapsing backpack charges wearable gadgets as you walk. *New Scientist*, *221*(2950), 19. doi:10.1016/S0262-4079(14)60030-0

Carter, D. (2012). Gaining additional value from secondary data resources: Using existing internal data and knowledge to create new company-centric resources. *Business Information Review*, *29*(3), 148–156. doi:10.1177/0266382112456272

Cercone, F. N. (2015). What's the big deal about big data? *Big Data And Information Analytics, 1*(1), 31-79. 10.3934/bdia.2016.1.31

Challenges with Big Data Analytics. (2015). *International Journal Of Science And Research*, *4*(12), 778–780. doi:10.21275/v4i12.nov152088

Chan, F., & Hanneman, K. (2015). Computed Tomography and Magnetic Resonance Imaging in Neonates With Congenital Cardiovascular Disease. Seminars In Ultrasound. *CT And MRI*, *36*(2), 146–160. doi:10.1053/j.sult.2015.01.006 PMID:26001944

Dandu, R. (2008). Storage media for computers in radiology. *The Indian Journal of Radiology & Imaging*, *18*(4), 287. doi:10.4103/0971-3026.43838 PMID:19774182

Dandu, R. V. (2008). Storage media for computers in radiology. *The Indian Journal of Radiology & Imaging*, *18*(4), 287–289. doi:10.4103/0971-3026.43838 PMID:19774182

Dhar, V. (2014). Why Big Data = Big Deal. *Big Data*, *2*(2), 55–56. doi:10.1089/big.2014.1522 PMID:27442294

DICOM Library - About DICOM most common features of study. (2017). Retrieved 26 May 2017, from http://www.dicomlibrary.com/dicom/study-structure/

Dinov, I. (2016). Volume and value of big healthcare data. *Journal Of Medical Statistics And Informatics*, *4*(1), 3. doi:10.7243/2053-7662-4-3 PMID:26998309

Doel, T., Shakir, D. I., Pratt, R., Aertsen, M., Moggridge, J., Bellon, E., ... Ourselin, S. (2017). GIFT-Cloud: A data sharing and collaboration platform for medical imaging research. *Computer Methods and Programs in Biomedicine*, *139*, 181–190. doi:10.1016/j.cmpb.2016.11.004 PMID:28187889

Eberendu, A. (2016). Unstructured Data: An overview of the data of Big Data. *International Journal of Computer Trends and Technology*, *38*(1), 46–50. doi:10.14445/22312803/IJCTT-V38P109

Gemayel, N. (2016). Analyzing Google File System and Hadoop Distributed File System. *Research Journal Of Information Technology*, *8*(3), 66–74. doi:10.3923/rjit.2016.66.74

Gurcan, M. N., Boucheron, L., Can, A., Madabhushi, A., Rajpoot, N., & Yener, B. (2009). Histopathological Image Analysis: A Review. *Institute of Electrical and Electronics Engineers Review Biomedical Engineering*, *2*, 147–171. PMID:20671804

Hampton, T. (2013). Human Genome Initiatives Make Strides to Better Understand Health and Disease. *Journal of the American Medical Association*, *309*(14), 1449. doi:10.1001/jama.2013.2607 PMID:23571561

Juneja, P., & Kashyap, R. (2016). Optimal Approach For CT Image Segmentation Using Improved Energy Based Method. *International Journal of Control Theory and Applications*, *9*(41), 599–608.

Juneja, P., & Kashyap, R. (2016). Energy based Methods for Medical Image Segmentation. *International Journal of Computers and Applications*, *146*(6). doi:10.5120/ijca2016910808

Kakkirala, L., & Venkateswara, K. (2016). Significant Big Data Interpretation using Map Reduce Paradigm. *International Journal of Computers and Applications*, *156*(1), 7–11. doi:10.5120/ijca2016912339

Kapur, T. (2016). MO-DE-202-03: Image-Guided Surgery and Interventions in the Advanced Multimodality Image-Guided Operating (AMIGO) Suite. *Medical Physics*, *43*(6Part30), 3699–3700. doi:10.1118/1.4957227

Karagiannis, D., & Buchmann, R. (2016). Linked Open Models: Extending Linked Open Data with conceptual model information. *Information Systems*, *56*, 174–197. doi:10.1016/j.is.2015.10.001

Kashyap, R., & Gautam, P. (2013). Microarray Image Segmentation using Improved GOGAC Method. *Science and Engineering*, *2*(4), 67–74.

Kashyap, R., & Gautam, P. (2015). Modified region based segmentation of medical images. *2015 International Conference on Communication Networks (ICCN)*, 209-216. 10.1109/ICCN.2015.41

Kashyap, R., & Gautam, P. (2016). Fast Level Set Method for Segmentation of Medical Images. In *Proceedings of the International Conference on Informatics and Analytics* (ICIA-16). ACM. 10.1145/2980258.2980302

Kashyap, R., & Gautam, P. (2017). Fast Medical Image Segmentation Using Energy-Based Method. *Pattern and Data Analysis in Healthcare Settings*, 35-60.

Kashyap, R., & Tiwari, V. (2017). Energy-based active contour method for image segmentation. *International Journal of Electronic Healthcare*, *9*(2/3), 210. doi:10.1504/IJEH.2017.083165

Kim, M., & Hong, C. (2017). Unstructured Social Media Data Mining System Based on Emotional Database and Unstructured Information Management Architecture Framework. *Advanced Science Letters*, *23*(3), 1668–1672. doi:10.1166/asl.2017.8614

Knossenburg, Y., Nogueira, R., & Chimenti, P. (2016). Contagious Content: Viral Video Ads Identification of Content Characteristics that Help Online Video Advertisements Go Viral. *Revista Brasileira De Marketing*, *15*(04), 448–458. doi:10.5585/remark.v15i4.3385

Lee, J., Chung, J., & Lee, D. (2015). Efficient Data Replication Scheme based on Hadoop Distributed File System. *International Journal of Software Engineering and Its Applications*, *9*(12), 177–186. doi:10.14257/ijseia.2015.9.12.16

Leppert, F., & Greiner, W. (2016). Big Data In Healthcare - Opportunities And Challenges. *Value in Health*, *19*(7), A463. doi:10.1016/j.jval.2016.09.677

Li, F., & Nath, S. (2014). Scalable data summarization on big data. *Distributed and Parallel Databases*, *32*(3), 313–314. doi:10.100710619-014-7145-y

Li, L., Niu, T., Cho, S., & Wang, Z. (2014). Mathematical Methods and Applications in Medical Imaging. *Computational and Mathematical Methods in Medicine*, 1-2. doi:10.1155/2014/765163 PMID:24995037

Lobo, L. (2017). Orthognatic surgery in temporomandibular joint patients: Evaluation, diagnosis, when and why to operate the temporomandibular joint. *International Journal of Oral and Maxillofacial Surgery*, *46*, 32. doi:10.1016/j.ijom.2017.02.120 PMID:27697415

Luo, J., Wu, M., Gopukumar, D., & Zhao, Y. (2016). Data Application in Biomedical Research and Health Care: A Literature Review. *Biomedical Informatics Insights*, *8*, 1–10. doi:10.4137/BII.S31559 PMID:26843812

Memon, Q. A. (2017). Authentication and Error Resilience in Images Transmitted through Open Environment. In *Medical Imaging: Concepts, Methodologies, Tools, and Applications: Concepts* (p. 1671). Medical Information Science Reference. doi:10.4018/978-1-5225-0571-6.ch069

Nieddu, M., Boatto, G., Pirisi, M., & Dessì, G. (2010). Determination of four thiophenethylamine designer drugs (2C-T-4, 2C-T-8, 2C-T-13, 2C-T-17) in human urine by capillary electrophoresis/mass spectrometry. *Rapid Communications in Mass Spectrometry*, *24*(16), 2357–2362. doi:10.1002/rcm.4656 PMID:20635321

Ring, T. (2016). Your data in their hands: Big data, mass surveillance and privacy. *Computer Fraud & Security*, *2016*(8), 5–10. doi:10.1016/S1361-3723(16)30061-6

Ritter, F., Boskamp, T., Homeyer, A., Laue, H., Schwier, M., Link, F., & Peitgen, H. O. (2011). Medical image analysis. *Institute of Electrical and Electronics Engineers Pulse*, *2*(6), 60–70. PMID:22147070

Sakr, S., & Elgammal, A. (2016). Towards a Comprehensive Data Analytics Framework for Smart Healthcare Services. *Big Data Research*, *4*, 44–58. doi:10.1016/j.bdr.2016.05.002

Scholl, I., Aach, T., Deserno, T. M., & Kuhlen, T. (2011). Challenges of medical image processing. *Computer Science Research Development*, *26*(1-2), 5–13. doi:10.100700450-010-0146-9

Seibert, J. A. (2010). *Modalities and data acquisition in Practical Imaging Informatics*. New York: Springer.

Shemberko, L., & Sliva, A. (2012). Philosophical information in the INION databases on social sciences and humanities. *Scientific and Technical Information Processing*, *39*(4), 187–198. doi:10.3103/S014768821204003X

Shvachko, K., Kuang, H., Radia, S., & Chansler, R. (2010). The Hadoop distributed file system. *Proceedings of the IEEE 26th Symposium on Mass Storage Systems and Technologies (MSST '10)*, 1–6.

Siuly, S., & Zhang, Y. (2016). Medical Big Data: Neurological Diseases Diagnosis Through Medical Data Analysis. *Data Science and Engineering*, *1*(2), 54–64. doi:10.100741019-016-0011-3

Sobhy, D., El-Sonbaty, Y., & Abou Elnasr, M. (2012). MedCloud: healthcare cloud computing system. *Proceedings of the International Conference for Internet Technology and Secured Transactions*, 161–166.

Sun, J., & Reddy, C. K. (2013). *Big Data Analytics for Healthcare*. IBM. Available at: https://www.siam.org/meetings/sdm13/sun.pdf

Sweet, L., & Moulaison, H. (2013). Electronic Health Records Data and Metadata: Challenges for Big Data in the United States. *Big Data*, *1*(4), 245–251. doi:10.1089/big.2013.0023 PMID:27447257

Texter, K., Waymach, R., Kavanagh, P., O'Brien, J., Talbot, B., Brandt, S., & Gardner, E. (2017). Identification of pyrolysis products of the new psychoactive substance 2-amino-1-(4-bromo-2,5-dimethoxyphenyl) ethanone hydrochloride (bk-2C-B) and its iodo analog bk-2C-I. *Drug Testing and Analysis*. doi:10.1002/dta.2200 PMID:28371351

Top 10 Big Data Challenges – A Serious Look at 10 Big Data V's | MapR. (2017). Retrieved 27 May 2017, from https://mapr.com/blog/top-10-big-data-challenges-serious-look-10-big-data-vs/

Upadhyay, A., & Kashyap, R. (2016). Fast Segmentation Methods for Medical Images. *International Journal of Computers and Applications*, *156*(3), 18–23. doi:10.5120/ijca2016912399

Virmani, D., Arora, P., & Kulkarni, P. (2017). *Cross domain analyzer to acquire review proficiency in big data*. ICT Express. doi:10.1016/j.icte.2017.04.004

Waoo, N., Kashyap, R., & Jaiswal, A. (2010). DNA Nano array analysis using hierarchical quality threshold clustering. In The 2nd IEEE International Conference on Information Management and Engineering (ICIME), 2010 (pp. 81-85). IEEE. doi:10.1109/ICIME.2010.5477579

Yang, H., Liu, J., Sui, J., Pearlson, G., & Calhoun, V. D. (2010). A Hybrid Machine Learning Method for Fusing fMRI and Genetic Data: Combining both Improves Classification of Schizophrenia. *Frontiers in Human Neuroscience*, *4*, 192. doi:10.3389/fnhum.2010.00192 PubMed

Zheng, T., Cao, L., He, Q., & Jin, G. (2014). Full-range in-plane rotation measurement for image recognition with hybrid digital-optical correlator. *Optical Engineering (Redondo Beach, Calif.)*, *53*(1).

KEY TERMS AND DEFINITIONS

Advanced Multimodal Image Guided Operating (AMIGO): Advanced multimodal image guided operating suite is a best-in-class medicinal and surgical research condition that houses a total exhibit of cutting edge imaging hardware and interventional surgical frameworks. Multidisciplinary groups of authorities utilize this hardware exhibit and the one of a kind plan of the suite to productively and correctly manage treatment some time recently, amid, and after surgery without the patient or restorative group regularly leaving the working room. This inventive working and imaging research suite supports coordinated effort among multidisciplinary groups of specialists, interventional radiologists, imaging physicists, researchers, biomedical designers, medical caretakers, and technologists. Tackling the advantages of cutting edge innovation and a productive three-room outline, the AMIGO groups expect to create and convey the most secure and best in class treatments in a patient-accommodating condition.

Big Data Analytics (BDA): BDA is the way toward analyzing expansive and changed informational indexes (i.e., huge information to reveal shrouded designs, obscure relationships, advertise patterns, client inclinations, and other valuable data) that can help associations settle on more-educated business choices.

Business Intelligence (BI): Business intelligence (BI) involves the arrangement of methodologies, procedures, applications, information, advancements and specialized structures which are utilized by enterprises to bolster the gathering, information investigation, introduction and spread of business data.

Computer-Aided Diagnosis (CAD): Computer aided design is an interdisciplinary innovation consolidating components of artificial intelligence and computer vision with radiological picture handling. A normal application is the location of a tumor. For example, a few healing facilities utilize CAD to bolster preventive restorative registration in mammography, the identification of polyps in the colon, and lung disease.

Digital Imaging and Communications in Medicine (DICOM): DICOM is the global standard for therapeutic pictures and related data (ISO 12052). It characterizes the configurations for medicinal pictures that can be traded with the information and quality fundamental for clinical utilize. DICOM is actualized in practically every radiology, cardiology imaging, and radiotherapy gadget (X-ray, CT, MRI, ultrasound), and progressively in gadgets in other medicinal areas, for example, ophthalmology and dentistry.

Electronic Healthcare Records (EHR): EHR is a computerized form of a patient's paper chart. EHRs are continuous, quiet focused records that make data accessible in a split second and safely to approved clients. While an EHR contains the restorative and treatment histories of patients, an EHR framework is worked to go past standard clinical information gathered in a supplier's office and can be comprehensive of a more extensive perspective of a patient's care.

Functional MRI (fMRI): Functional MRI is a useful neuroimaging strategy utilizing MRI innovation that measures cerebrum action by distinguishing changes related with blood stream. This method depends on the way that cerebral blood stream and neuronal initiation are coupled.

Hadoop Distributed File System (HDFS): The Hadoop distributed file system is the essential storage framework utilized by Hadoop applications. HDFS is a circulated document framework that gives elite access to information crosswise over Hadoop groups. Like other Hadoop-related innovations, HDFS has turned into a key instrument for overseeing pools of huge information and supporting huge information investigation applications.

Payment Card Industry (PCI): Comprises of the considerable number of associations that store, prepare, and transmit cardholder information, most for platinum cards and Visas. The security gauges are produced by the Payment Card Industry Security Standards Council which builds up the Payment Card Industry Data Security Standards utilized all through the business. Singular card brands build up consistence prerequisites that are utilized by specialist organizations and have their own consistence programs.

Picture Archiving and Communication Systems (PACS): Picture archiving and communication systems is a therapeutic imaging innovation which gives prudent capacity and helpful access to pictures from various modalities (source machine types). Electronic pictures and reports are transmitted carefully by means of PACS; this takes out the need to physically record, recover, or transport film coats. The all inclusive arrangement for PACS picture stockpiling and exchange is DICOM (Digital Imaging and Communications in Medicine).

Single Nucleotide Polymorphism (SNP): Single nucleotide polymorphism is a DNA succession variety happening when a solitary nucleotide adenine (A), thymine (T), cytosine (C), or guanine (G]) in the genome (or other shared grouping) varies between individuals from an animal types or combined chromosomes in a person.

Traumatic Brain Injury (TBI): Frequently alluded to as TBI, is regularly an intense occasion like different wounds. That is the place the comparability between traumatic mind harm and different wounds closes. One minute the individual is typical and the following minute life has suddenly changed. In most different viewpoints, a traumatic cerebrum harm is altogether different. Since our mind characterizes our identity, the results of a cerebrum harm can influence all parts of our lives, including our identity.

Temporomandibular Joint (TMJ): The temporomandibular joints (TMJ) are the two joints interfacing the jawbone to the skull. It is a two-sided synovial explanation between the transient bone of the skull above and the mandible beneath; it is from these bones that its name is inferred.

Unstructured Information (UI): Unstructured data and big data unstructured information is the inverse of organized information. Organized information for the most part lives in a social database, and therefore, it is now and again called social information. This sort of information can be effectively mapped into pre-planned fields.

Chapter 2
Investigation on Deep Learning Approach for Big Data:
Applications and Challenges

Dharmendra Singh Rajput
VIT University, India

T. Sunil Kumar Reddy
Sri Venkateswara College of Engineering and Technology, India

Dasari Naga Raju
Sri Venkateswara College of Engineering and Technology, India

ABSTRACT

In recent years, big data analytics is the major research area where the researchers are focused. Complex structures are trained at each level to simplify the data abstractions. Deep learning algorithms are one of the promising researches for automation of complex data extraction from large data sets. Deep learning mechanisms produce better results in machine learning, such as computer vision, improved classification modelling, probabilistic models of data samples, and invariant data sets. The challenges handled by the big data are fast information retrieval, semantic indexing, extracting complex patterns, and data tagging. Some investigations are concentrated on integration of deep learning approaches with big data analytics which pose some severe challenges like scalability, high dimensionality, data streaming, and distributed computing. Finally, the chapter concludes by posing some questions to develop the future work in semantic indexing, active learning, semi-supervised learning, domain adaptation modelling, data sampling, and data abstractions.

INTRODUCTION

In the recent years, machine learning concepts made major impact on different fields. The machine learning is the concept of defining the input data and generalizes the patterns for the data which are used for the future purpose. The good data representation leads to the improvement in the performance of

DOI: 10.4018/978-1-5225-3870-7.ch002

the machine learning concepts and poor representation of data causes the reduction of performance of any advanced machine learners. Therefore, the present research is concentrated on developing the data representations and exploiting concrete features from the raw data (Domingos, P.2012).

Deep learning approach is one of the feature engineering methods applied for the complex data sets to retrieve the abstract features. This type of algorithms follows the hierarchical and layered structures for representing the data, where the data is represented in low level and high level abstractions. The hierarchical structure in the deep learning approach is inspired by the data perception process of the human brain (Dalal, N, &Triggs, B.2005 and Lowe DG 1999). Deep learning algorithms are more advantages in dealing with huge volumes of unsupervised data and it follows the greedy procedure for data representations. Research studies proved that data representation using feature extractions will help in improving the machine learning outputs. For instance, invariant data representations (Goodfellow et al., 2009), probabilistic models (Salakhutdinov, R & Hinton GE, 2009) and improved classification models (Larochelle, H, et al., 2009). Deep learning made major positive impact on different machine learning approaches such as computer vision (Krizhevsky A, et al., 2012; Hinton GE,et al., 2006 and Bengio, Y., et al., 2007), speech recognition (Dahl et al., 2012; Mohamed et al., 2012; Seide et al ., 2011; Hinton et al., 2012 & Dahl et al., 2010) and NLP (Socher et al., 2011; Mikolov et al., 2011 and Bordes et al., 2012).

Big data is the recent buzz word in the data science field. It creates solution to the problems generated by large volumes of unsupervised application data with respect to the specific domain. Recent advancements in the field of data storage and computational resources have contributed lot more to the development of big data analytics (Tiwari & Thakur, in press). Major competitors like, Google, amazon, yahoo and Microsoft are managing larger proportions of data (i.e., exabytes).The users of some social media companies like Facebook, Instagram, Twitter and YouTube are posting huge volumes of data in their daily activities. Different leading companies developed their analytics platform to monitor, analyse and simulate the data for future business needs.

Data mining and data extraction are the basic operations performed on the big data for data prediction and decision making (Tiwari et al., 2010). Moreover, the data mining in big data pose many challenges which are represented in Figure 1.

This chapter deals with two major discussions, first one is how the deep learning will be beneficial for solving the problems of big data analytics and the second one is how the improvements in deep

Figure 1. Challenges of Big Data in data mining

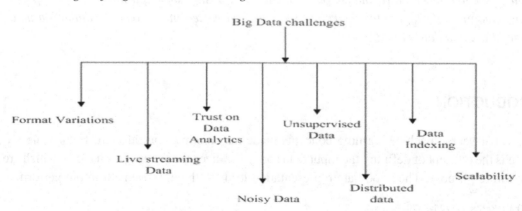

learning will affect the changes in big data analytics. To address the first discussion, the deep learning applications are explored for big data. The applications include semantic indexing, knowledge learning from huge volumes of data, data tagging and discriminative tasks. In the second discussion, this chapter focuses on different challenges faced by the deep learning models with already existing problems like live streaming of data, scalability of the data, distributed computing and high dimensionality of data in big data analytics. Finally the chapter will be concluded by identifying the areas which needs improvement in deep learning according to the big data.

Background: The Adaptation of Deep Learning

The main theme behind the deep learning approach is to automatically extract the feature of data (Bengio et al., 2013). The deep learning mechanisms use large volumes of unsupervised data to extract the abstract features. These mechanisms are basically influenced by the artificial intelligence principles such as observe the behaviour patterns, learn from the past data, making the decisions for the difficult problems. The deep learning architectures are fit to any type of environments such as local or global ways to generate the patterns without considering the neighbouring data. Deep learning is the major advancement towards the artificial intelligence. The deep learning not only provides the representation of complex tasks which are helpful in developing the AI mechanism, but also makes the AI environment to take the decisions without the help of human knowledge.

The concept of learning is built on the layered architectures. Each layer is capable of processing the input and generating the output. The motive of the layered representation is to process the data in hierarchical manner. For example, the sensor data is given as input to the first layer, it processes the sensor data and generates the output, and this output data is an input to the next layer. Applying the nonlinear transformation is the major functionality of the deep learning architectures. The number of layers in the architecture decides the complication of the transformations.

To understand the concept of deep learning approach, a human activity recognition model was given as an example. At the first layer, the data acquisition is carried using the sensor nodes. The second layer gathers the input from the data acquisition layer and identifies the activities based on the learning algorithm. The third layer identifies even more complex activities from the processed data set which is taken as input from the second layer. The final layer provides the detailed activities which are performed by the individuals. This example is provided only to understand how the deep learning algorithm identifies the abstract features from the sensed data.

The deep learning procedure contains complex procedure of learning which is also difficult to optimize such as hidden layers in the neural networks. (Hilton et al., 2006) proposed the greedy procedure for unsupervised learning in the deep learning architectures. In the proposed model, the sensor data is provided as input to the first layer. The first layer process the data and given as knowledge data to the second layer. This process is continued until the convergence criteria are met. The final layer provides the supervised data to perform the tasks.

In deep learning algorithms, there are two basic structures followed by the unsupervised learning algorithms. The first one is Deep Autoencoders (Bengio et al., 2007) and the second one is Restricted Boltzmann Machines (RBMs). Deep Autoencoders is a circuit with simple learning mechanism where it transforms the input with small value of distortion to the output. The generalized frame work for autoencoders is given in Figure 2. The $\alpha/\beta/\alpha$ encoder is derived with tuples α, β, m, X, Y, P, Q, R, δ where:

- X and Y are defined with sets
- α and β are defined with positive integers, where $0 < \beta < \alpha$.
- P represents the function form Y^β to X^α.
- Q represents the function form X^α to Y^β.
- $R = \{ r_1, r_2....r_m \}$ represents the set of m trained vectors of X^α.
- δ represents the distortion over the function X^α.

For any $p \in P$ and $q \in Q$, the input vector $r \in X^\alpha$ in the autoencoder is transformed in to output vector $p \circ q$ (r) $\in X^\alpha$. The main aim of the autoencoder $p \in P$ and $q \in Q$ is to reduce the overall distortion which is given as follows.

$$\min Z(p,q) = \min_{p.q} \sum_{t=1}^{m} \delta(p \circ q(r_t).r_t) \tag{1}$$

The second one is Deep belief network which are considered as the generalized model for the deep neural network. The deep belief network contains one visible unit and multiple hidden units that are connected to one another. The framework for deep belief network is given in Figure 3. The major module involved in developing the deep belief network is Restricted Boltzmann Machine (RBM). The restriction involved in the RBM is the units in the same layer not contain any interaction.

The typical structure of DBN is shown in figure 4, which contains number of RBMs and additional layer for tasks identification. After managing the structure of DBN, then the weights are assigned between the layers.

Before performing the action of identifying the tasks, a layered training process is initiated in RBMs. the output of one RBM layer is input of the other RBM layer. This process is continued until all RBMs are trained. This layer by layer knowledge extraction procedure is more complex when the situation of number of parameters is more. This will directly impact the time complexity of the algorithm. For simple understanding, the Bernoulli distribution is applied to the DBN, and then the probabilities of both visible and hidden layers are given as follows:

Figure 2. α/β/α encoder

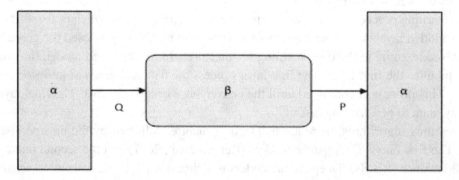

Figure 3. Semantic flow of Deep Belief Network

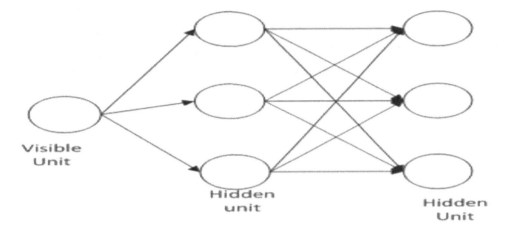

Figure 4. Typical Architecture of DBN

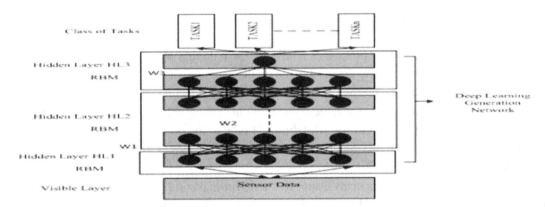

$$P(HL_j = 1 / VL; W) = \sigma(\sum_{i=1}^{N} w_{ij} VL_i + \alpha_j) \qquad (2)$$

and

$$P(VL_i = 1 / HL; W) = \sigma(\sum_{j=1}^{K} w_{ij} HL_i + \beta_i) \qquad (3)$$

Where

- VL and HL represents the visible and hidden unit with vectors of $N \times 1$ and $K \times 1$.
- W represents the weight matrix contains weights w_{ij} which are connected between the layers.
- σ represents the sigmoid function.
- α_j and β_i represents the bias variables.

- σ represents the sigmoid function.

For the case of dynamic data at the visible layer, the Bernoulli distribution is slightly changed to the distribution is referred as P(VL$_i$|HL; W) (Bengio et al., 2007). The weights w$_{ij}$ in the matrix W is calculated based on the method developed in (Hinton, G. E. 2002). For example, the weight factor w$_{ij}$ for t-th instance is calculated as follows:

$$\Delta w_{ij}(t) = x\Delta w_{ij} + \lambda(\left\langle VL_i \times HL_j \right\rangle_{data} - \left\langle VL_i \times HL_j \right\rangle_{model}) \tag{4}$$

where x represents the momentum factor, λ represents the learning rate and the distribution factors of data and model are represented with $\left\langle . \right\rangle_{data}$ and $\left\langle . \right\rangle_{model}$.

MAIN FOCUS OF THE CHAPTER

Emergence of Big Data Analytics

Big data analytics is defined as the process of analysing the data that exceeds in terms of storage, computation capacity and processing. Big data is depend on the mechanisms and tools to extract the complex features of data and analyse the patterns generated from the huge volume of data. The reason behind the development of big data is to handle the large volume of data generated, to maximize the computational capacity and to maximize the chances for availability of data to the organizations. The major motive of explaining big data analytics in this section is to present the challenges and key concepts involved in utilizing the deep learning in Big Data.

The huge volume of data creates many issues to the traditional computing environments and it needs distributed environment to support the query processing as well as scalable storage facility. Moreover, this huge volume of data plays crucial role in Big Data Analytics. Some organizations like Google, Microsoft, Twitter, Yahoo are more advantageous with Big Data Analytics (National Research Council, 2013). The major complexities of big data are given in Figure 5. First one is volume, second one is variety, third one is velocity and the final one is veracity.

The volume is the primary challenge faced by the big data due to the large volumes of raw data is generated in the users in the internet. There is a need of different mechanisms to handle the variety of data generated by the different type of persons with different type of organizations. The velocity is also major challenge in big data due to the immediate processing and analysis required. Sometime, this may leads to the data losses while accessing the data in the urgent manner. The final one veracity discusses the trust among the generated results after the analytics process is completed.

Deep Learning for Huge Volumes of Data

The Deep learning has very impressive record on different applications; however, the big data is different from other applications with the properties of distributed environment and parallel computation. Therefore, it is very typical task to apply the deep learning mechanism to the big data. The deep learning mechanisms have no certain parallel computation methods. In the recent years, due to the rapid increase

Figure 5. The 4Vs in the big data

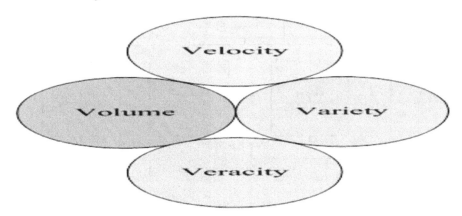

in the data volumes leads to the development of some parallel algorithms for training the layers in the deep learning (Dahl et al., 2012 and Ciresan et al., 2010).

After examining many learning algorithms, it is conclude that they are considering only the minimum number of parameters. In the deep learning algorithms, it contains number of hidden units and has the flexibility to consider the large number of parameters. Some deep learning models involve high volume of data and larger number of models. For instance, improved optimizers (Martens, J, et al., 2010), locally connected networks (Collobert et al., 2011) and parallel algorithms. (Deng et al., 2012) proposed the deep stacking network (DSN) architecture to support the parallel processing concept. This architecture consists of number of neural networks with one hidden layer. In this architecture, the stacked modules are used as input to collect the raw data and the previous module output is taken as DSN.

The utilization of the processing speed improves the layers training significantly with big data deep learning. For instance, to improve the parallel processing in deep learning is by utilizing the number of CPUs, where each CPU can handle the parallel data. (Vanhoucke et al., 2011) developed some technical stuff to address the data layout, batch computation, SS3 and SS4 implementation. This discussion will improve the performance of the deep learning in big data.

(Krizhevsky and Hinton 2009) used the Gibbs sampling where it splits the visible and hidden units in to 'n' number of samples to n machines. In order to support the parallel processing, the data transfer must be required between the machines. In the deep learning process, the visible and hidden process the data to the machines.

Some recent surveys show that the development of deep learning framework will improve the computing capacity. Consider the graphics processing units (GPU) as an example from NVIDIA. The GPUs are perfectly serves the purpose of parallel computing which contains number of transistors for parallel data processing. The architecture developed for deep learning process had major significance on data processing (CUDA C Programming Guide, 2013). Figure 6 shows the architecture for CUDA –capable CPU model. In this model, it contains four multi- processor blocks; each block contains number of streaming processors to form the building blocks (SMs). Each SM has number of stream processors (SPs). The SPs have the capability to share the memory and control logic. In this architecture, each GPU is organized with high bandwidth, global memory and high latency corresponding to the host. Both instruction level parallelism and thread level parallelism is supported by the GPU architecture. The GUP is considered as the single instruction multi thread architecture that can handle tens of thousands

Figure 6. CUDA–capable GPU architecture

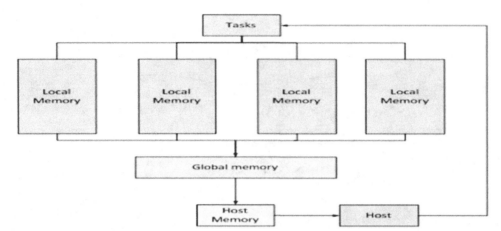

of tasks simultaneously. This type of architectures is more suited to the operations of arithmetic and it utilizes less memory for the operations.

CONTRIBUTION AND RECOMMENDATIONS

Major Challenges and Applications Involved in Deep Learning Approach for Big Data

The performance of the big data is hypothetically significant and it requires some new algorithms to resolve the many challenges. For instance, many machine learning algorithms operated for data and they completely operated in the memory. But, while discussing the topic of big data, this assumption will not be perfect. Moreover, the data considered for assumptions is very less. Therefore, an efficient algorithm is needed to learn from the big data.

After examining the recent works in the field of large scale deep learning, the research is still in initial stage. It requires major changes in the algorithms to address the challenges in big data. In (Laney, D. 2012), the authors often categorized the big data with three V's, such as Volume, variety and Velocity. The Volume refers to size of the data, variety refers to the types of data and the Velocity refers to the streaming speed of data.

Deep Learning With Respect to Volume

The deep learning considers the volume of data as a major challenge to be addressed. Big data frequently holds large data sets which consist of inputs (no. of examples), Outputs (different type of Classes) and more number of attributes. The size of the data sets leads to the increase in time complexity as well as system complexity. The huge volumes of data makes difficult to train the layers in the deep learning approach with one single processor and storage. Therefore, parallel and distributed machines are likely to be referred. In the recent years, the algorithms are proposed to address the challenges in big data. These algorithms used parallel computing by managing the cluster of GPUs or CPUs to maximize the speed of the learning process without influencing the efficiency of the deep learning algorithms. The mechanism for system parallelism, data parallelism or both was developed. For instance, the model or data in the deep learning mechanisms are divided in to blocks which can fit in to the memory. In (Coats et al., 2013), backward propagations or forward propagations (Dean et al., 2012) are utilized in parallel computing. However, the deep learning mechanisms are not completely supports parallel computing.

The recent advancements in the deep learning approach can handle large volumes of data samples and attributes. This approach has the mechanism to measure the GPUs utilization. But, the current advancement in the field of big data poses major challenge to the deep learning. Therefore, to support the deep learning mechanisms, one should develop large computational infrastructure which supports novel architectures and learning algorithms.

Other challenge related to the big data is noisy labels and in completed data. In general, machine learning mechanisms are applied to the polished data where they are noise less and highly accurate, big data is the collection of different data from different origins. Some data might be incomplete and some other doesn't contain labels.

The major advantage of deep learning algorithms is it considers the unlabelled data at the time of leaning stage. Therefore, the deep learning has the edge over the big data to treat with unlabelled data and also there is an opportunity to develop novel algorithms. Big data consists of large volumes of noisy data and unlabelled data. Here, it may be consider that dealing with large volume of unsupervised data is preferable instead of dealing with small volumes of clean and accurate data. The novel algorithms are required to the deep learning approach for handling the noisy data. Some algorithms (Wang et al., 2007; Weston et al., 2012; Sinha and Belkin, 2009) like semi supervised learning are more helpful in addressing the noisy data.

Deep Learning With Respect to Variety

The second challenge supposed to be addressed by deep learning for big data is variety. Big data is composed of different formats of data form different sources. For instance, the internet is the major source which contains multimedia contents like text files, audio files, video files, graphics, animations and still images. Data integration is the key procedure which can handle different types of data formats. The major advantage of deep learning is representation that might be supervised or unsupervised of both. Deep learning has the ability to learn for the classification, it can identify abstract or intermediate patterns from the data representation.

Deep learning is proved to be the efficient approach in data integration from sources like internet or mobile devices. For instance, (Ngiam et al., 2011) proposed the architecture for data integration in deep learning using the audio and video content. The authors explained the deep learning is generally useful in single model or multiple models with unlabelled data. In the recent survey, (Srinivas and Salakhutdinov 2012) proposed DBM which decompose the two types of data models such as text data and image data. The DBM has the ability to perform with unsupervised data: as an initial step it builds the stacked RBMs for each model.

Deep learning has the capability to handle the heterogeneous data, but some questions are remains open. For example, the data collected from different sources is a conflicting data. How the deep learning can handle conflicting data and integrate the data. The current deep learning approaches are working on bi models. (i.e two different data formats), but in the future, this bimodal is not sufficient to handle enlarged models. Moreover, there is an issue in the architectures of deep learning; it is only designed for multi models and the data integration from different formats is not possible.

Deep Learning With Respect to Velocity

The velocity of the data is also major challenge in big data. The data gathering in the big data is relative with high speed and it needs timely processing. Online learning is the mechanism which can handle the velocity of the big data. The online learning (Shalev-Shwartz, S. 2012; Littlestone et al., 1991; Freund & Schapire 1996; Blum & Burch, 2000 and Saad, D. 1998) process one instance at a time for gaining knowledge and can be used further to redefine the architecture. This online learning strategy is very useful in big data, but, the big data cannot hold entire data set in the memory.

Dynamic nature of the data poses severe challenge to the deep learning. The data need not be stationary and the data distribution is changing from time to time. In general, the high speed non-stationary data is divided in to small chunks with time labels. Therefore, the data is considered as stationary for particular period of time and measures the correlation between the data (Chien, J. T., & Hsieh, H. L. 2013; ugiyama, M., & Kawanabe, M. 2012; Elwell, R., & Polikar, R. 2009 & 2011) Deep learning has the ability to influence the velocity of big data with the help of domain adaptation and transfer learning where the training data is sampled from different sources (Bengio, Y. 2012; Schmidhuber, J. 2015; Higgins, I. 2016; Kingma et al., 2014; LeCun et al., 2015).

CONCLUSION AND FUTURE RESEARCH DIRECTIONS

Deep learning is the efficient mechanism among all the machine learning approaches. Deep learning has the ability to address the issues of learning problems and data analysis in big data. Moreover, the deep learning extracts the learning patterns form the unsupervised data. This is the major advantage to the big data, because of having large volume of unsupervised data. The deep learning has the advantage of hierarchical data extraction at different levels which helps in big data in terms of data tagging, semantic indexing, classification and prediction. This study made a contribution to explain how the big data and deep learning algorithms are useful in defining the learning process from large volumes of data. The unique characteristics of big data create problems to the deep learning approach. This discussion also provides complete understanding of how deep learning will handle the problems of big data.

REFERENCES

Bengio, Y. (2012). Deep learning of representations for unsupervised and transfer learning. *ICML Unsupervised and Transfer Learning*, 27, 17–36.

Bengio, Y. (2013). Deep learning of representations: Looking forward. In *Proceedings of the 1st International Conference on Statistical Language and Speech Processing. SLSP'13*. Springer. 10.1007/978-3-642-39593-2_1

Bengio, Y., Lamblin, P., Popovici, D., & Larochelle, H. (2007). Greedy layer-wise training of deep networks. *Advances in Neural Information Processing Systems*, 19, 153.

Blum, A., & Burch, C. (2000). On-line learning and the metrical task system problem. *Machine Learning, 39*(1), 35–58. doi:10.1023/A:1007621832648

Bordes, A., Glorot, X., Weston, J., & Bengio, Y. (2012). Joint learning of words and meaning representations for open-text semantic parsing. *International Conference on Artificial Intelligence and Statistics,* 127–135.

Chien, J. T., & Hsieh, H. L. (2013). Nonstationary source separation using sequential and variational Bayesian learning. *IEEE Transactions on Neural Networks and Learning Systems, 24*(5), 681–694. doi:10.1109/TNNLS.2013.2242090 PMID:24808420

Cireşan, D. C., Meier, U., Gambardella, L. M., & Schmidhuber, J. (2010). Deep, big, simple neural nets for handwritten digit recognition. *Neural Computation, 22*(12), 3207–3220. doi:10.1162/NECO_a_00052 PMID:20858131

Coats, A., Huval, B., Wng, T., Wu, D., & Wu, A. (2013). Deep Learning with COTS HPS systems. *Journal of Machine Learning Research, 28*(3), 1337–1345.

Collobert, R., Weston, J., Bottou, L., Karlen, M., Kavukcuoglu, K., & Kuksa, P. (2011). Natural language processing (almost) from scratch. *Journal of Machine Learning Research, 12*(Aug), 2493–2537.

CUDA C Programming Guide, PG-02829-001_v5.5. (2013). Santa Clara, CA: NVIDIA Corporation.

Dahl, G., Ranzato, M., Mohamed, A.-R., & Hinton, G. E. (2010). Phone recognition with the mean-covariance restricted boltzmann machine. In Advances in Neural Information Processing Systems. Curran Associates, Inc.

Dahl, G. E., Yu, D., Deng, L., & Acero, A. (2012). Context-dependent pre-trained deep neural networks for large-vocabulary speech recognition. *IEEE Transactions on Audio, Speech, and Language Processing, 20*(1), 30–42. doi:10.1109/TASL.2011.2134090

Dalal, N., & Triggs, B. (2005). Histograms of oriented gradients for human detection. In *Computer Vision and Pattern Recognition, 2005. CVPR 2005. IEEE Computer Society Conference On* (Vol. 1, pp. 886–893). IEEE. doi:10.1109/CVPR.2005.177

Dean, J., Corrado, G., Monga, R., Chen, K., Devin, M., Mao, M., . . . Ng, A. Y. (2012). Large scale distributed deep networks. Advances in neural information processing systems, 1223-1231.

Deng, L., Yu, D., & Platt, J. (2012). Scalable stacking and learning for building deep architectures. In *Acoustics, Speech and Signal Processing (ICASSP), 2012 IEEE International Conference on* (pp. 2133-2136). IEEE. 10.1109/ICASSP.2012.6288333

Domingos, P. (2012). A few useful things to know about machine learning. *Communications of the ACM, 55*(10), 78. doi:10.1145/2347736.2347755

Elwell, R., & Polikar, R. (2009). Incremental learning in nonstationary environments with controlled forgetting. In *Neural Networks, 2009. IJCNN 2009. International Joint Conference on* (pp. 771-778). IEEE. 10.1109/IJCNN.2009.5178779

Elwell, R., & Polikar, R. (2011). Incremental learning of concept drift in nonstationary environments. *IEEE Transactions on Neural Networks, 22*(10), 1517–1531. doi:10.1109/TNN.2011.2160459 PMID:21824845

Freund, Y., & Schapire, R. E. (1996). Game theory, on-line prediction and boosting. In *Proceedings of the ninth annual conference on Computational learning theory* (pp. 325-332). ACM. 10.1145/238061.238163

Goodfellow, I., Lee, H., Le, Q. V., Saxe, A., & Ng, A. Y. (2009). Measuring invariances in deep networks. In Advances in Neural Information Processing Systems. Curran Associates, Inc.

Higgins, I., Matthey, L., Glorot, X., Pal, A., Uria, B., Blundell, C., . . . Lerchner, A. (2016). *Early visual concept learning with unsupervised deep learning.* arXiv preprint arXiv:1606.05579

Hinton, G., Deng, L., Yu, D., Mohamed, A.-R., Jaitly, N., Senior, A., ... Kingsbury, B. (2012). Deep neural networks for acoustic modeling in speech recognition: The shared views of four research groups. *Signal Process Mag IEEE, 29*(6), 82–97. doi:10.1109/MSP.2012.2205597

Hinton, G. E. (2002). Training products of experts by minimizing contrastive divergence. *Neural Computation, 14*(8), 1771–1800. doi:10.1162/089976602760128018 PMID:12180402

Hinton, G. E., Osindero, S., & Teh, Y.-W. (2006). A fast learning algorithm for deep belief nets. *Neural Computation, 18*(7), 1527–1554. doi:10.1162/neco.2006.18.7.1527 PMID:16764513

Hinton, G. E., & Salakhutdinov, R. R. (2006). Reducing the dimensionality of data with neural networks. *Science, 313*(5786), 504-507.

Kingma, D. P., Mohamed, S., Rezende, D. J., & Welling, M. (2014). Semi-supervised learning with deep generative models. In Advances in Neural Information Processing Systems (pp. 3581-3589). Academic Press.

Krizhevsky, A., & Hinton, G. (2009). *Learning multiple layers of features from tiny images.* Academic Press.

Krizhevsky, A., Sutskever, I., & Hinton, G. (2012). Imagenet classification with deep convolutional neural networks. In Advances in Neural Information Processing Systems. Curran Associates, Inc.

Laney, D. (2012). The importance of 'big data': A definition. *Gartner. Retrieved, 21*, 2014–2018.

Larochelle, H., Bengio, Y., Louradour, J., & Lamblin, P. (2009). Exploring strategies for training deep neural networks. *Journal of Machine Learning Research, 10*, 1–40.

LeCun, Y., Bengio, Y., & Hinton, G. (2015). Deep learning. *Nature, 521*(7553), 436–444. doi:10.1038/nature14539 PMID:26017442

Littlestone, N., Long, P. M., & Warmuth, M. K. (1991). On-line learning of linear functions. In *Proceedings of the twenty-third annual ACM symposium on Theory of computing* (pp. 465-475). ACM. 10.1145/103418.103467

Lowe, D. G. (1999). Object recognition from local scale-invariant features. In *Computer Vision, 1999. The Proceedings of the Seventh IEEE International Conference On.* IEEE Computer Society. 10.1109/ICCV.1999.790410

Martens, J. (2010). Deep learning via Hessian-free optimization. In *Proceedings of the 27th International Conference on Machine Learning (ICML-10)* (pp. 735-742). Academic Press.

Mikolov, T., Deoras, A., Kombrink, S., Burget, L., & Cernock'y, J. (2011). Empirical evaluation and combination of advanced language modeling techniques. In *INTERSPEECH* (pp. 605–608). ISCA.

Mohamed, A.-R., Dahl, G. E., & Hinton, G. (2012). Acoustic modeling using deep belief networks. *Audio Speech Lang Process IEEE Trans*, *20*(1), 14–22. doi:10.1109/TASL.2011.2109382

National Research Council. (2013). *Frontiers in Massive Data Analysis*. The National Academies Press. Retrieved from http://www.nap.edu/openbook.php?record_id=18374

Ngiam, J., Khosla, A., Kim, M., Nam, J., Lee, H., & Ng, A. Y. (2011). Multimodal deep learning. In *Proceedings of the 28th international conference on machine learning (ICML-11)* (pp. 689-696). Academic Press.

Saad, D. (1998). Online algorithms and stochastic approximations. *Online Learning, 5*.

Salakhutdinov, R., & Hinton, G. E. (2009). Deep boltzmann machines. In *International Conference on, Artificial Intelligence and Statistics*. JMLR.org.

Schmidhuber, J. (2015). Deep learning in neural networks: An overview. *Neural Networks*, *61*, 85–117. doi:10.1016/j.neunet.2014.09.003 PMID:25462637

Seide, F., Li, G., & Yu, D. (2011). Conversational speech transcription using context-dependent deep neural networks. In *INTERSPEECH* (pp. 437–440). ISCA.

Shalev-Shwartz, S. (2012). Online learning and online convex optimization. *Foundations and Trends® in Machine Learning, 4*(2), 107-194.

Sinha, K., & Belkin, M. (2009). Semi-supervised learning using sparse eigen function bases. In Advances in Neural Information Processing Systems (pp. 1687-1695). Academic Press.

Socher, R., Huang, E. H., Pennin, J., Manning, C. D., & Ng, A. (2011). Dynamic pooling and unfolding recursive auto encoders for paraphrase detection. In Advances in Neural Information Processing Systems. Curran Associates, Inc.

Srivastava, N., & Salakhutdinov, R. R. (2012). Multimodal learning with deep boltzmann machines. In Advances in neural information processing systems (pp. 2222-2230). Academic Press.

Sugiyama, M., & Kawanabe, M. (2012). *Machine learning in non-stationary environments: Introduction to covariate shift adaptation*. MIT Press. doi:10.7551/mitpress/9780262017091.001.0001

Tiwari, V., Tiwari, V., Gupta, S., & Tiwari, R. (2010). Association rule mining: a graph based approach for mining frequent itemsets. *International Conference on Networking and Information Technology (ICNIT)*, 309-313. 10.1109/ICNIT.2010.5508505

Tiwari, V., & Thakur, R.S. (in press). Towards Elementary Algebra for On-Line Knowledge Processing of Pattern Cube. In *National Academy Science Letters (NASL)*. Springer.

Vanhoucke, V., Senior, A., & Mao, M. Z. (2011). Improving the speed of neural networks on CPUs. In *Proc. Deep Learning and Unsupervised Feature Learning NIPS Workshop* (*Vol. 1*, p. 4). Academic Press.

Wang, J., & Shen, X. (2007). Large margin semi-supervised learning. *Journal of Machine Learning Research*, 8(Aug), 1867–1891.

Weston, J., Ratle, F., Mobahi, H., & Collobert, R. (2012). Deep learning via semi-supervised embedding. In *Neural Networks: Tricks of the Trade* (pp. 639–655). Springer Berlin Heidelberg. doi:10.1007/978-3-642-35289-8_34

KEY TERMS AND DEFINITIONS

Big Data: Big data is a term for dataset that are huge and complex to process by traditional data processing applications.

Data Abstraction: Data abstraction is the reduction of a particular body of data to a simplified representation of the whole.

Deep Learning: It is a part of machine learning approach used for learning data representations.

Semantic Analysis (LSA): It is a technique in natural language processing, in particular distributional semantics, of analyzing relationships between a set of documents and the terms they contain by producing a set of concepts related to the documents and terms.

Supervised Learning: Supervised learning is the data mining task of inferring a function from labeled training data.

Chapter 3
An Application of Big Data Analytics in Road Transportation

Rajit Nair
Maulana Azad National Institute of Technology, India

Amit Bhagat
Maulana Azad National Institute of Technology, India

ABSTRACT

Data is being captured in all domains of society and one of the important aspects is transportation. Large amounts of data have been collected, which are detailed, fine-grained, and of greater coverage and help us to allow traffic and transportation to be tracked to an extent that was not possible in the past. Existing big data analytics for transportation is already yielding useful applications in the areas of traffic routing, congestion management, and scheduling. This is just the origin of the applications of big data that will ultimately make the transportation network able to be managed properly and in an efficient way. It has been observed that so many individuals are not following the traffic rules properly, especially where there are high populations, so to monitor theses types of traffic violators, this chapter proposes a work that is mainly based on big data analytics. In this chapter, the authors trace the vehicle and the data that has been collected by different devices and analyze it using some of the big data analysis methods.

INTRODUCTION

An important concern today in India is vehicle population which spurs due to rise in population and economic recovery creates a severe pressure on traffic management in the major urban areas of the country. According to a recent survey, the vehicle industry produced a total 23,960,940 vehicles including passenger vehicles, commercial vehicles, three wheelers, two wheelers and quadricycle in the year 2016 between the month April-March which in comparison to the vehicles produced in the year 2015 in between the same month i.e., April- March and it is almost around 23,358,047, registering an insignificant growth of 2.58 percent over the same period last year. The increase in vehicle segment will create a big

DOI: 10.4018/978-1-5225-3870-7.ch003

traffic problem for this we have to create a system which must be capable of handling the problems, so we are developing one system named it as Smart Transportation Systems (STS) which can be applied to solve or try to minimize traffic problems. STS will consider of all modes of transportation – road, rail, sea and air. The main goal of STS is to develop, evaluate, analyse and integrate new sensor, information, and communication technologies and concepts to achieve traffic efficiency, improve environmental quality, conserve time, save energy, and enhance safety and comfort for drivers, pedestrians, and other traffic groups. The technologies which are based on location information into vehicles, infrastructure, traveller information services and traffic management have proven some improvements in the efficient movement of vehicles &people in USA, Canada, Middle East, European nations, Japan and now they are doing in India also.

During the last years many countries has developed new plans and efficient way, according to their economic geography and cultural geography, to accumulate different elements interrelated to the system. In STS application we use a Traffic Management Centre (TMC) where data from different source is accumulated, studied and is added with the other operational and control idea to control the problems in transportation. Many times, some organisation divides the transportation management according to the network of traffic operation centres. Usually there is a limited spreading of information and data, so the centres can choose multiple options to reach the goals of traffic management. This freedom of interrelated functioning and managing is equally important as the multiplicity of desire and performance of collaborated system. It will also connect different elements of all modes like infrastructure, vehicles & conveyance system.

There are many similar type of STS projects have been developed in some of the Indian metropolis which are having focus on lonely distribution of placed information, advanced toll collection and controlling of the area-wise signal. Nowadays, there are very few fully developed STS applications with traffic management centres in India. So the requirements of STS are strongly needed by environmental demands and socio-economic needs. In India, there are diverse varieties of vehicles and their movement type (pedestrian, bicycle, animal drawn carts, LMV's, HMV's) large variety of vehicles (including pedestrian traffic), and poor lane discipline (partially resulting from the first two factors and partially due to cultural reasons) and a very high population density makes adoption of Western STS standards and architecture difficult. So the design of an effective STS function in India will enhance the advancement in technology, interdependency of different branches of engineering like Electronics & Communication, Information & Technology, and Transportation etc. In recent times there are many new technologies related to electronics and communication like Global Navigation Satellite System (GNSS) (Peter J.G. Teunissen and Oliver Montenbruck, 2017), Sensors (KouroshKalantar-zadeh, 2013) and Detectors (Lawrence A. Klein, Milton K. Mills, David R.P. Gibson, 2006). These devices are mainly used for maintaining the coordination between the government and research industry. We must develop a profitable detection system which will be capable of real time road-wise information storage rather than lane-wise storage system. When the system like automatic collection of data is developed, the new data can be stored and used for model development which will make possible STS applications.

STS technique will play an important role in data collection and sharing to ensure such flawless interrelationship. Through this technology we can improve the quality of general transportation that will improvise the usage and aide in transportation management. It is equally important that work force must be able to grow, run and carefully use the present and upcoming technologies for the effective layout and overall application globally. The detailed knowledge of traffic system will be important for the successful implementation of STS in India.

There must be some specific actions which must be needed to meet the challenges of STS in India, which are as follows:

- Traffic management centre should be constructed so that it can coordinate the regional and urban STS activities.
- Establishing a national STS data archive.
- Designing and implementing automated traffic data collection methodologies.
- Establishing prototype and algorithm as per STS applications.

Enhancing the influence of education societies, industries and government agencies to work on STS area. Proper working of STS can be achieved by implementing it at network level rather than in small aisle. Overall, the existing implementations show promising results and potential for the deployment of STS in India and give an initial empirical basis and data for STS deployment highlighting the data, methodological, practical and research challenges for Indian conditions.

BACKGROUND

There are many applications that have been promoted by different administrations across the world which are used to provide solution for transportation and fulfil their demands. Many of the developed countries depend on these types of applications for the congestion control and demand management, sometime also for road safety and improving the base.

This includes latest technology in communication and sensor that collect huge amount of data for the analysis purpose. These systems are developed on the geographical infrastructure of that region to match the specific region. This system consist of autonomous automobile systems, medical monitoring, process control systems, robotics systems, and automatic pilot_avionics due to the interrelation among automobile system and a distributed information gathering and dissemination infrastructure (wired and wireless networks, sensors, processors, and the accompanying software). Some of the existing applications of STS are given below:

Automated Congestion Control (ACC)

Metro cities in India like Mumbai, Bangalore, Delhi etc. are using the plan that are based on automated traffic which focused on synchronising major junction. Latest gadgets such as Multi Radar comprising Smart Cameras, Speed Check Guns and Radar sensor, medical monitoring, process control systems, Flash light generator, Tripod and Power Box were used in this plan. Predict travel time based on historical and real-time data from electronic toll collection.

Big data analytics platform is also used to predict highway travel time based on data collected from highway electronic toll collection. Various prediction models are then developed for highway travel time based on historical and real-time data to provide drivers with estimated and adjusted travel time information.

Electronic Toll Collection (ETC)

The Electronic Toll Collection (ETC) (Saijie Lu, Tiejun He and ZhaohuiGao, 2009)is one of the fast worldwide accepted method of toll collection that is highly helped by the growth of auto controlled ETC technologies. ETC technology used in Automatic Automobile Identification (AAI), Automobile Positioning System (APS). Automatic Automobile Classification (AAC) (Charles Harlow and ShiquanPeng, 2011) and Automobile Enforcement Systems (AES) (FridulvSagberg, 2000).

Latest Parking Management

The parking management system allows vehicle users to be guided by a wide range of sensors, lights, signboards and directional displays to the closest vacant space existing in the parking lot and same for identifying their car location at the time of exit. Apart from automatic online guidance at junctions, zone-wise sub-division of areas will assist easy identification.

MAIN FOCUS OF THE CHAPTER

A Traffic Management Centre (TMC) is the core area of transport management, in this system data is accumulated, studied and merged with different control and management system to control the multiple transportation networks. This is the most important point for transferring information related to transportation through media and the public and this is also the way to coordinate the responses of automobile with the agencies. The smooth functioning of the TMC and the effectiveness of STS depends mainly on the following components:

- Automated Data Acquisition system
- Fast data communication to traffic management centres
- Accurate analysis of the data at the management centres
- Reliable information to traveller/public

Data Acquisition

The fast and proper data accumulation and transfer is the most important factor for actual time observation and decision making. A well planned data acquisition, administration and communication system integrates efficient software and hardware that can accumulate authentic and strong data that can act as base component for future STS action [Figure 1]. The hardware/elements generally used are sensors, camera, GPS based automatic automobile locators and identifiers (Mashood Mukhtar, 2015). GPS based locators and identifiers and servers which can store large amounts of data for meaningful analysis. The descriptions of the elements are as follows:

Sensors

Sensors are the device which can be used for detecting and redirecting information related to traffic on highway. Previously sensors were mainly dependent on acoustic detectors, optical detectors and on

Figure 1. Data Acquisition

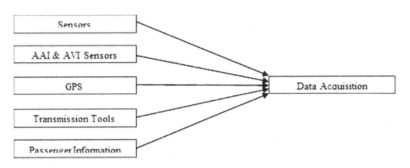

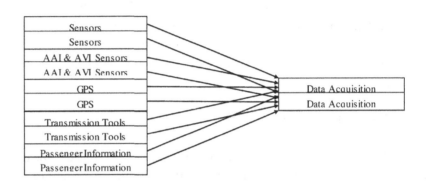

vehicle's weight induced pressure/vibration (seismic/piezoelectric sensors) on the surface of road. In today's world, a lot of advancements have been done in technology related to sensors like infrared sensor, magnetic sensor, ultrasonic sensor, radar sensor, microwave sensors, inductive loop sensors, seismic, and inertia-switch detectors and video based sensors .These sensors detect the variation in magnetic/ seismic/ optical/acoustic fields due to the movement in automobiles and compute the traffic parameters according to the movement. Most of the sensors are adjustable and positioned in the subsurface of the roadway and provide real-time traffic information on that point of the road. The volume, occupancy and speed of the vehicles are the commonly obtained traffic parameters.

A video image processor (VIP) system typically consists of one or more cameras, a microprocessor based computer for digitizing and processing the imagery, and software for interpreting the images and converting them into traffic flow data. The three main types of vehicle sensors in current practice are inductive loop sensors, magnetic sensors, and magnetometers [Figure 2].

Automatic Automobile Identifiers (AAI) and Automatic Automobile Locators (AAL)

The AAI system consists of AAI tags, AAI readers, or transponders in the vehicles, and a central processing system. AAI systems are poisoned on the roadway or skyward structured as a part of ETC (Electronic Toll Collection) booth. The antennas radiate RF signals in the desired range across different freeway lanes. When the detected vehicle enters in the range of antenna, it detect the vehicle respond the detec-

Figure 2. Types of Sensors

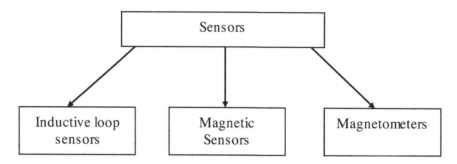

tion to the RF signal and its unique ID is assigned a time and date stamp by the reader This information is then transmitted to the central processing system, where it is processed and store. In developed countries, this unique detected vehicle ID numbers are tracked along the freeway system, and the travel time of these detected vehicles is computed as the difference between the time stamps at sequential antenna locations. This AAI system is having the capability to accumulate the information continuously with minimum human. However the information accumulation process is mainly constrained by sample size since it requires participation.

Global Positioning System (GPS)

GPS (Global Positioning System) technology became a reality through the efforts of the American military, which established a satellite-based navigation system consisting of a network of 24 satellites that were located uniformly in six orbital planes, at an altitude of approximately 20,200 km such that at least four satellites are visible at any time and from any point on the earth's surface orbiting the earth. GPS is also known as the NAVSTAR (Navigation System for Timing and Ranging). This GPS system provides information about the actual position of vehicle in fast, flexible & inexpensive way. GPS positioning is mainly based on three-dimensional positioning of manmade landmarks "stars" using trilateration related techniques. This system is used across the world in all-weather conditions to track the location of object. This technology can be accessed by any person if he has GPS receiver. Working of GPS is based on positioning and navigation, the code-phase or pseudo-ranges and carrier-phase. It provide fundamental location data in terms of latitude, longitude, elevation and UTC time. Using this information, the traffic engineer can find out all the information related to the automobiles like time, speed, distance and delay. To get authentic information related to traffic from the GPS, it is of imperative to meet the sample size requirements and follow an appropriate field procedure. The data which we get from GPS is Big Data which is useful for data analysis

Transmission Tools

In STS, the system efficiency does not only depend on the data storing and the data analysis related traffic, but it is also depends on the accurate and fast transferring of information, i.e. the information collected from the field to TMC and the data carried out by using the data and models from TMC to the public. Dedicated Short-Range Communications (DSRC) (Chen Y., Zeng Z., Zhu X., 2011) provide data transmission among the automobile and specified location of the road (for example toll plazas). Transceivers and transponders on different band like industrial, medical & scientific operated by DSRC is work on radio frequency. Wireless Communications Systems (Masao Nakagawa, Lachlan B. Michael, 1997)are dedicated to Smart Transport Systems and Road Transport. For the long and medium range continuous communication among the automobiles and the roadside using different information transferring medium like cellular and infra-red links Continuous Air interface is used.

Passenger Information

To get information related to transportation for monitoring public travel advisory system is used. Travel advisory system consist of SMS, Internet, automated messaging system, highway radio advisory unit, radio and television broadcasting and other media application. These application generates actual time data of automobiles like time of travelling, speeds, delay, area, routs etc.

Data Analysis

Data transmission, analysis and extracting information comes under data analysis. Data accumulated from the sensors and other devices are send to TMC for correction. Unpredicted data must be filtered and fine data has to be kept. Then, the additional data from different sources are combined for further analysis. This filtered and fine grained traffic data will be analysed to estimate and forecast traffic states. To generate essential information to the user, Traffic state estimation is required.

Services

The major services by big data analysis are mainly categorized into 8 services. This includes individual user services which are as follows:

- Passenger Information Services
  - ○ Passenger Information
  - ○ Passenger services and reservation
  - ○ Route Navigation
- Public Transport Management
  - ○ Transit Vehicle Tracking
  - ○ Transit Fixed-Route Operations
  - ○ Passenger and Fare Management
  - ○ Transit Maintenance
  - ○ Multi-Modal Co-ordination
  - ○ Multi-Modal Connection Protection
- Traffic Management Services
  - ○ Congestion Control
  - ○ Incident Management
  - ○ Travel Demand Management
  - ○ Environmental Conditions Management
  - ○ Operations and Maintenance

- ◦ Automated Dynamic Warning and Enforcement
- ◦ Non-Vehicular Road User Safety
- ◦ Multi-Modal Junction Safety and Control
- Electronic Payment Services
  - ◦ Electronic Payment Services
  - ◦ Commercial Vehicle Operations
  - ◦ Commercial Vehicle Electronic Clearance
  - ◦ Automated Roadside Safety Inspection
  - ◦ On-board Safety Monitoring
  - ◦ Commercial Vehicle Administrative Processes
  - ◦ Intermodal Freight Management
  - ◦ Commercial Fleet Management
- Emergency Management Services
  - ◦ Emergency Notification and Personal Security
  - ◦ Hazardous Material Planning and Incident Response
  - ◦ Disaster Response and Management
  - ◦ Emergency Vehicle Management
- Vehicle Safety and Control Systems
  - ◦ Vehicle-Based Collision Avoidance
  - ◦ Infrastructure-Based Collision Avoidance
  - ◦ Sensor-Based Driving Safety Enhancement
  - ◦ Safety Readiness
  - ◦ Pre-Collision Restraint Deployment
  - ◦ Automated Vehicle Operation
- Information Warehousing Services
  - ◦ Weather and Environmental Data Management
  - ◦ Archived Data Management

Issues

The rapidly changing economy of world has also led to spurt in the use of personal vehicles. Now a days we have fully established STS system, but it is not easy to implement this STS system. For the real implementation of such type of STS system, we need methodical approaches.

Other than the presently developed STS systems, there are many more emerging concepts, on which work has to be done like Congestion Control, Incident Management, Travel Demand Management, Environmental Conditions Management, Operations and Maintenance, Automated Dynamic Warning and Enforcement, Non-Vehicular Road User Safety, Multi-Modal Junction Safety and Control etc.

However we can say that, the present applications provide assurance for the implementation of STS and provide an experimental base and information on STS, strategically, practically and research challenges for such conditions

Required specific steps to contain or meet the challenges to STS in India are:

- Establish a nationwide STS standard for many applications and components in STS system
- Establish a nationwide STS clearing house that include designing, deployment and economical overview of STS system.
- Establish a traffic management control system which is fully functional and coordinate with the local STS working.
- Establish and deploying an automatic traffic data accumulation strategies.
- Establish a nationwide STS data library.
- Establish structure and process suited for STS deployment.
- Establish communication among education system, industries & government agencies to bring about their interest in STS area.

Problems

A data collection technique has to be improved. Well known vehicle analysis strategies like AAI and AAL are costly and require public interest. Implementations of such methods become hard due to budgetary constraint. Visual techniques are to be used to accumulate data though there is absence of homogeneity and network discipline. Although there are some extraction software which can be used to extract data from a particular types of vehicles and traffic. Those software which can take out actual time information from the visuals which are generally seen merged traffic condition is not available, creating visual is also not the right way for generating real time application. Furthermore, presently the STS information is not successfully used .Once this actual time automatic information accumulation system is developed the information taken out can be kept in library and can be used for prototype development. Some of the major challenges in this context are as follows:

- Traffic signals get failed.
- Traffic diversion during any government or public activity
- Cost on the expensive devices of monitoring system like camera, desktop or laptop, sensors and many more
- Darkness is the one of the main causes of failure analysis.

SOLUTIONS AND RECOMMENDATIONS

Big data analytics (Chun-Wei Tsai et al.,2015) is one of the latest term used in technology which is mainly used to gain insights from the available archived data which is too large and complex or which cannot be analysed with standard methods or tools. As we have already discussed, transportation industry has huge volume, velocity and collection of information, which are being generated by sensing device, information accumulation points, public accounting system, fare collection systems, vehicle location systems, resource controlling system and from the multitude of web and cellular applications. These information authorities may have existing information bins and these can be proven to be incredible resource for deep analytics for providing unprecedented insights into planning and managing multimodal transportation networks. The steps of Big Data Analytics are given in Figure 3.

Figure 3. Steps of Big Data Analysis

Big Data Analytics are used to extract the hidden information from the archive resources, as well as from the new data, to help getting informed data operational enhancement. One of the biggest problem is that, when the merged data are confined in other systems& other format for which they were not designed to work. Data from different places in any format will be accumulated and unlocked the hidden information by using Big Data Technique. Mainly the information can be structure-less data lake that's unconstrained by traditional data management architectures. This contrast sharply with the conventional approach of creating pre-defined schemas and a data warehouse that require complicated ETL (extract/transform/load) processes to convert and load data.

Next problem lies in understanding the data which has been retrieved. We blend this information from the heterogeneous information assets, and it is analysed by the graphical and statistical method for the calculation of the value of a function outside the range of known values (Tiwari V. and Thakur R.S., in press). This method allows us to shorten the information and extracted information can be easily related and readily measureable. Simulations can be created by looking back at different situations and the archived data while varying certain factors that influence the results, to gain understanding of the true impacts these factor have on outcomes. Our visualization and reporting tools present the results in a meaningful way, and in a manner that those who need to understand the results do, and to answer the original questions and informed decision making in a way that non-technical domain experts can comprehend it also.

These processes enable us to act which reveal the best choices for a multitude of derived operational and quantifiable benefits from various outcomes. Further, we implement repeatable processes that can be regularly used to measure performance and help ensure the desired outcomes are being achieved. We look forward and back to identify what other opportunities exist to reinforce this iterative improvement cycle. By the year 2020, it is estimated that more than 40 ZB of data will be generated annually. This "Big Data" is transforming every single industry. Here we will discuss about how Big Data is transforming Public Transportation. Big Data works on both the plan phase and operation phase of the transportation. We should consider the given 4 major cases in leveraging Big Data as shown in Figure 4.

Planning and Demand Modelling

With Big Data, authorities can generate more precise understanding of the customer demand on different routes. They can map customer journeys across multiple modes of transportation – trains, buses, private modes of transportation etc. They can use all this data to improve planning on the future train routes, frequency on existing train routes and size of trains. This will help reduce customer waiting time and walk time resulting in increased ridership on the trains. Authorities can also optimally plan for additional services such as retail stores on the routes through better understanding of customer journey

Figure 4. Steps in Big Data Analytics

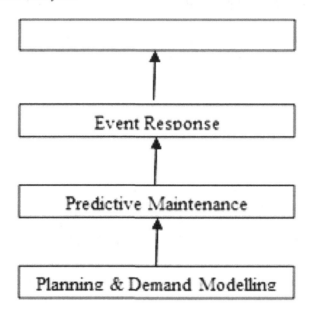

maps. E.g., open food outlets at locations where large number of commuters walk through during times of breakfast, lunch or dinner.

Predictive Maintenance

By leveraging Big Data, authorities can predict optimal maintenance requirements of the equipment – trains and tracks. With Big Data, data from the sensors installed on the equipment can be analysed at much faster rate and at more minute-level. This can be used to predict upcoming faults at the individual component levels such as brakes, a stretch of rails etc. With this, authorities can schedule maintenance of the equipment precisely at the right time – which is not too early (which is unnecessary and expensive) or not too late (which is expensive and disruptive to the service).One of our clients in the public transportation space has successfully deployed Big Data for scheduling maintenance of the equipment and the results are staggering – Mean time to failure of the equipment reduced by almost 80-90% and equipment life increased by 200%. This further improved customer safety and satisfaction enhanced equipment utilization and reduced operating costs.

Event Response

With Big Data, authorities can have an intimate understanding of customer journeys – start and end points involving trains, buses and even private modes of transportations. This helps authorities answer the following questions, and thereby, better equip them for both planned and unplanned event.

- Which customer will be impacted?
- Where should we deploy alternate means of transportation?
- How much additional capacity should be added?

- And, what is the best way to reach customers? Facebook, Twitter, Text Messages?

It is very important to have fast and optimal response especially during unplanned events and Big Data technologies today provide tools to achieve such as response.

Personalized Services

With the intimate understanding of a customer, authorities can tailor communication to each rider via preferred communication channel (Email, Text, Phone etc.). These personalized messages can include:

- Changes in the service on individual route(s) that a customer cares for.
- Looming weather-related events that might impact service.
- Upcoming events (E.g., sports games) and their impact on the service.
- Targeted advertising (E.g., food coupon for a restaurant along the route).

Instead of spam of messages that customers get these days, this level of personalization is something customers can appreciate and depend on. It improves customer satisfaction and helps increase the ridership of trains while providing authorities new revenue sources such as targeted advertising.

Technology to Be Used

The three major components which are involved in the process of capturing, processing, and evaluating streaming motions are as follows:

- **Video Camera:** It captures frames from the video stream.
- **Video Sensor:** It dynamically changes video camera settings and processes the captured frames
- **Video Detector:** It is used to determine motion in specified Regions of Interest (ROIs), and evaluates if there is any target job occurs.

In addition to above said devices there are many other subclasses that are required for performing image background subtraction, store data and run models. Some of them are as follows:

- **Mask:** Performs background subtraction on raw images, It uses powerful algorithm for performing background subtraction images, and this algorithm is implemented in OpenCV (P. Shopa, N. Sumitha, P.S.K Patra, 2014).
- **History:** A pandas Data Frame that is updated in real time to persist and access data (Karlijn Wilems, 2016).
- **Detector Assistants:** Assists the video detector in evaluating image, motion and history data. This class consists of several modules which are responsible for sampling frames from the video feed, plotting data and running models to determine the traffic status.

The technology we will use here is Python (Yoong Cheah Huei, 2014), because in today's world Python is one of the best tool used for analytics purpose, apart from there are other programming languages like R (Andreas Pfeiffer, Maria Grazia Pia, 2013), spark(Apache Spark,2017) and many more are available in market today. We will use Python 3 for coding and use the editor Jupyter Notebook (Josh Devlin, 2016) or Spyder (Spyder Project Contributors, 2017). To implement our work first we have to capture the video images of the road transportation, this can be done by the use of OpenCV's Python library. It works on the concept of frame-by-frame image processing. Through this it is possible to identify an indiscipline activity by using a video alone. This is because video is also based on motion from frame to frame. Here we have to do real time analysis, so our main focus will be on implementing a streaming road transport detection algorithm and at the same time measure its performance under real world condition. If we move down to smaller devices it will be better as compared to camera and laptop. It will be efficient if we had some experience listening to traffic using a Raspberry Pi (Romin Irani, 2016), so we bought an analyser for it and combine our video acquisition and detection/processing pipeline onto single device.

After implementing our method for a week, then only we can say how our classifier worked and the most importantly where it fails. Our classifier considers two main factors one is motion and the other one is time. Firstly we evaluate the quantity of motion in selected Region of Interest's (ROI's). This can be done at the rate of five frames per second. Now the second factor is motion over time, means a motion which occurs over a certain span of time has to be considered. We can set our threshold time at 2-3 seconds, since vehicles take about three-four seconds to pass the sensor located 20-25 feet from the roads.

FUTURE RESEARCH DIRECTIONS

The method which we discuss works well during daytime or in good lighting condition but its performance degrades when there is darkness or bad lighting because our sensors were not able to detect the vehicle after sunset or in low light condition. So future work can be done in this area where we are able to obtain promising results in bad lighting conditions also. We have been able to shorten the problem to some extent by using the NoIR model of the Pi camera, which lets lighter in during low light conditions, but the adaptive frame rate functionality on the camera didn't have sufficient dynamic range out of the box.

CONCLUSION

As we can see there is massive increase in automobile population due to rapidly increase in population which in turn instigates many problems for the traffic management system in the cities, towns and even in rural areas also. While some of the countries also get into smart transport system. The implementation of area wise & data based techniques on automobiles, framework, traffic control system and public data services provide efficient and safe movement of vehicles in USA, UK, European nations, Canada, Japan, and Middle East. STS technology is relatively a new concept in India, as the decision-makers, key planners and agencies are still in the process of understanding its potential. In India, it might be tedious to scale the working of STS to that of the existing successful STS of other nation because of geographical, cultural and practical differences among countries. We are trying to understand the existing concepts so that we can do some modification to implement in traffic conditions of India. The design of an effective STS system depends on developments given as follows:

- **Modelling of Indian Traffic:** It is very much needed that proper understanding of the traffic system must be there for the successful implementation of STS system. The existing models which are being used mainly implemented in developed countries and we have to change this system according to the traffic condition of the various countries.
- **Technology:** For STS to work in India, the successful management is very important as it is for any advancement and implementation of new technologies. The advance technologies consist of sensors, transponders, GPS and other communication devices. This advancement will maintain a coordination among academia, industries and government agencies.
- **Human Capital Development:** The intellect of human beings is important for the advancement of smooth automobile control system. As the population is increasing rapidly so new skill sets are available whose ability can be used to develop, manage and for the safely implementation of STS.
- **Supply Chain:** Proper connectivity must be there of various regions of the transportation sector for useful, adequate and secure movement of goods and services which also helps us in the conservation of natural resources and reducing environmental impacts such as the effects of carbon emissions. With the help of the applications of smart traffic control system in the country fuel efficient policies and practices will work to achieve economic and environmental benefits

To meet the challenges in establishing an effective traffic management system, the following work should be done.

- Calculating and observing the performance of current transportation management systems which is already working in many parts of the globe.
- The performance of transportation network can be improved by the use of real-time data, predictive traffic models, improved connection between individual systems, and strategies for improving safety in the environment.
- There must be near and long-term performance goals but it must be achievable.

We must always have some key initiatives and activities which advance and improve the development and use of STS in India.

REFERENCES

Chen, Y., Zeng, Z., & Zhu, X. (2011). The Analysis on the Application of DSRC in the Vehicular Networks. In M. Zhu (Ed.), *Information and Management Engineering. Communications in Computer and Information Science* (Vol. 236). Berlin: Springer. doi:10.1007/978-3-642-24097-3_25

Devlin, J. (2016). *28 Jupyter Notebook tips, tricks and shortcuts*. Retrieved on 12th October 2016 from https://www.dataquest.io/blog/jupyter-notebook-tips-tricks-shortcuts/

Harlow & Peng. (2011). Automatic vehicle classification system with range sensors. *Transportation Research Part C: Emerging Technologies*.

Huei. (2014). Benefits and introduction to python programming for freshmore students using inexpensive robots. In *IEEE International Conference on Teaching, Assessment and Learning for Engineering (TALE)*. IEEE.

Irani. (2016). *Start programming on Raspberry Pi with Python*. Retrieved on 28th October 2016 from http://opensourceforu.com/2016/10/programming-raspberry-pi-with-python/

Kalantar-Zadeh. (2013). *Sensors-An Introductory Course*. Springer.

Keisuke, U. (2005). *CALM -- Continuous Air Interface for Long and Medium range*. Retrieved on 3rd August, 2005 from https://www.ietf.org/proceedings/63/slides/nemo-4.pdf

Lu, He, & Gao. (2009). Design of electronic toll collection system based on global positioning system technique. In *Proceedings of ISECS International Colloquium on Computing, Communication, Control, and Management*. IEEE.

Mills & Gibson. (2006). Traffic Detector Handbook (3rd ed.; vol. 1). Federal Highway Administration Turner-Fairbank Highway Research Center.

Mukhtar. (2015). *GPS based Advanced Vehicle Tracking and Vehicle Control System. I.J. Intelligent Systems and Applications*.

Nakagawa, M., & Michael, L. B. (1997). Wireless Communications. In Wireless Communication Technology in Intelligent Transport Systems (pp. 491-508). Springer US.

Pfeiffer & Pia. (2013). Data analysis with R in an experimental physics environment. *Nuclear Science Symposium and Medical Imaging Conference (NSS/MIC)*.

Sagberg (2000). *Automatic enforcement technologies and systems*. Academic Press.

Spark, A. (2017). *Spark Research*. Retrieved May 2nd, 2017 fromhttps://spark.apache.org/research.html

Teunissen, P. J. G., & Montenbruck, O. (2017). *Springer Handbook of Global Navigation Satellite Systems*. Springer International Publishing. doi:10.1007/978-3-319-42928-1

The Spyder Project Contributors. (2017). *Spyder 3.1.4*. Retrieved on 24th April 2017 from https://pypi.python.org/pypi/spyder

Tiwari, V., & Thakur, R.S. (in press). Towards Elementary Algebra for On-Line Knowledge Processing of Pattern Cube. *National Academy Science Letters, 40*.

Tsai, Lai, Chao, & Vasilakos. (2015). Big data analytics: a survey. *Journal of Big Data*.

Wilems. (2016). *Pandas Tutorial: DataFrames in Python*. Retrieved October 21st, 2016 in Python from https://www.datacamp.com/community/tutorials/pandas-tutorial-dataframe-python

KEY TERMS AND DEFINITIONS

Automobiles: Automobiles are used to transport people and items from one location to another location.

Big Data Analysis: It is the process of examining large and varied data sets, mainly to uncover hidden patterns, unknown correlations, market trends, customer preferences and other useful information that can help organizations make more-informed business decisions from big data.

Detectors: The device continues to be widely used to monitor traffic flow and control signals because of their relatively low cost, maturity, aesthetics, and policy issues.

Jupyter: The Jupyter Notebook is an open-source web application that allows us to create and share documents that contain live code, equations, visualizations and explanatory text. Uses include: data cleaning and transformation, numerical simulation, statistical modelling, machine learning and much more.

Open CV: OpenCV (open source computer vision) is a library of programming functions mainly aimed at real-time computer vision.

Python: Python is a programming language that allows us to work more quickly and integrate your systems more effectively. It is mostly used for big data analysis purpose.

Raspberry Pi: The Raspberry Pi is a series of tiny single-board computers developed in the United Kingdom by the Raspberry Pi Foundation.

Sensors: A device that detects or measures a physical property and records, indicates, or otherwise responds to it.

Chapter 4
Big Data and Analytics:
Application to Healthcare Industry

Misbahul Haque
Aligarh Muslim University, India

Mohd Imran
Aligarh Muslim University, India

Mohd Vasim Ahamad
Aligarh Muslim University, India

Mohd Shoaib
Aligarh Muslim University, India

ABSTRACT

In today's world, humungous and heterogeneous data are being generated from every action of researchers, health organizations, etc. This fast, voluminous, and heterogeneous generation leads to the evolution of the term big data. Big data can be computationally analyzed to uncover hidden trends and patterns that help in finding solutions to the problems arising in various fields. Analysis of big data for manufacturing operational acquaintance at an unparalleled specificity and scale is called big data analytics. Proper utilization of analytics can assist in making effective decisions, improved care delivery, and achieving cost savings. Recognizing hidden trends and useful patterns can lead us to have a clear understanding of the valuable information that these data holds. This chapter presents a quality overview of big data and analytics with its application in the field of healthcare industries as these industries requires their stream of data to be stored and analyzed efficiently in order to improve their future perspective and customer satisfaction.

DOI: 10.4018/978-1-5225-3870-7.ch004

INTRODUCTION

Data has a historic significance of being the most vital asset for organizations and governments. In the contemporary era of wearable devices and smartphones, very hefty amount of data and information are being produced about and by the peoples, things and their relations, which are being kept as a record. These data are being stockpiled in the databases and are of humungous and heterogeneous kind and are often termed as Big Data. Big data is going to be a bigger reservoir of huge, complex, structured or unstructured data that are being generated and collected from many digital sources like network devices, wireless sensors, medical equipment, legacy systems and many other such sources. Big Data can always serve as being a good source for several industries in different sectors that aim to automatically mine strategic information in reasonable time. While we insert effort on big data, it is critical to decide whether the benefits prevail over the overheads of storage and maintenance. Several analysis tools (Gupta & Saxena, 2014) are being designed and developed to investigate large data set and to have a better understanding of the impact of massive amounts of data in business improvements. To extract more benefits researchers and experts are trying to find a way to look into the future of big data.

Big data can generally be characterized by a set of V's: volume, variety, velocity, value and veracity. Volume refers to the amount in order of petabytes or even zettabytes of data being generated in various healthcare industries and it is expected to get doubled every year. Healthcare systems are generating data at very fast pace. It includes information at the individual as well as disease/population specific levels such as medical record of a person, health information of a patient, radiology images, biometric sensor readings, 3D imaging and genomics. These data are very complex and large in volume and needs to be stored, managed and analyzed in order to extract useful information. The KMPG report (Galloro, 2008) indicates that in 2013, the healthcare data volume was about in excess of 150 Exabyte and it is increasing constantly. Variety refers to the diversity or variability of data being generated from a number of sources in the form of structured, semi-structured or unstructured data (Groves, 2013). Earlier, the organizations and enterprises were handling data that were restricted to a limited data sources and not so randomized in nature. In contrast, today's scenario has changed a lot and organizations have to deal with a more complex data that may come from unalike sources and possesses more challenge while being stored, mined and analyzed. Healthcare data like clinical data, medical records, doctor notes, paper prescriptions, MRI images and radiograph films are so complex and difficult to augment with traditional data in order to get accurate precautions for patients. Velocity may be referred as the rate with which the data has been generated by the various sources like human interaction, business processes and healthcare systems. The regular updating of healthcare data doesn't guarantee its correctness. The continuous generation of data is also accountable for being processed and analyzed. Also, the delivery of extracted and beneficial information has to be done in real time. The data moves through a number of systems of an organization varying from batch integration, then being loaded at a certain fixed interval of time to the streaming of data in real time (Sabharwal et al., 2016). Value provides the opportunity to answer questions and make decisions in emergency on the basis of insights gathered from analysis of data storage through some quality governance strategies and mechanisms that were previously considered out of reach. It also answers to the question that if the data analysis can discover a critical causative effect which may result in a remedy to a syndrome. Veracity means trustworthiness of data of different quality with meaning and applicability. To obtain proficient and effective results, high-quality data are required for analysis. Every form of information has different quality. In healthcare system, the quality of data is one of the most important aspects as the correctness of the data directly affects the life or death of patients.

Various data analytic techniques such as real time and batch data analytics can be used for analyzing big data in healthcare. Data can be transformed into actionable information by using these techniques. Relevant information extraction from big data, their analysis and representation can be done by reactive or proactive analytics of healthcare data. Heterogeneity associated issues must be addressed while going for data processing by breaking down the data domain and analyzing them as an autonomous big data analysis system by a system of systems. The newly discovered structures are then exploited in a semantically interconnected manner by making use of metadata, for combined analysis and new acquaintance establishment. In healthcare domain, the gigantic data offers an enormous ability to carry out the predictive analysis and gives the possibility to make use of an existing solution to derive solutions of new problems. We can process an enormous number of information in parallel through big data analytics and can find out the relationship between them that may resolve the problem by providing effective solution to hidden problems (Archenaa & Anita, 2015). This analytical approach can effectively be used by healthcare industries to lower their cost and prepare with the required equipment that might be needed. For example, an already occurred disease in various parts of the globe outbursts in an area, then the analytical engine can be used to predict its spread and to find out the solution and prepare the medicines for the rampant problem. Healthcare industry is still in its premature age to adopt the new possibilities offered by big data solution for effective decision making.

In this chapter, we provide an overview of big data along with an insight of big data analytics giving its architectural framework. We also discuss the need, the initiatives that have been taken in healthcare and application of big data analytics in the healthcare domain and the challenges that come in the way.

BACKGROUND

The healthcare industry may be considered as one of the largest, the most critical and fastest growing industries. Pervasive healthcare (Triantafyllidis, 2015) provides the healthcare services anytime-anywhere to individuals. Since vast amount of data is being generated in healthcare organizations related to patients' health, there comes a need of digitization for efficient storage of data and its analysis using big data analytics.

Ramesh et al. (2016) provides a detail survey of big data analytics in healthcare with the view that the prediction and analysis of data in entering into a new and innovative era with the humongous growth of big data. They have discussed the underlying problems with traditional machine learning algorithms and suggested a modification in the existing algorithms to make it more efficient for big data applications like effective decision making.

Krishnan (2016) reviewed some uses of analytics of big data in the field of healthcare and also analyzed the outcomes associated with them. The author characterizes the big data by volume, variety, velocity and veracity of huge and multifaceted data. Accessibility, security, privacy, usability, transportability, implementation costs, standardization and interoperability are some challenges that the author has discussed in this work suggesting that appropriate treatment at a reduced cost, accurate diagnosis, and improved quality in healthcare can be achieved with the application of efficient and streamlined big data analytics in healthcare.

Islam et al. (2015) provided a detailed survey of the advances that have been achieved in IoT based healthcare technologies. They have presented a review of platforms, network architecture, application and trends in IoT based healthcare solutions. Different bio markets have also been summarized by Hassanalieragh et al. (2015).

Sathiyavathi (2015) stated that the clinical workflows can be streamlined with optimized care, strengthening the doctor-patient relationship, a cut in the costs and improving the outcomes by generating a deep insight through the digitization of the health information.

Raghupathi et al. (2014) suggested that the underlying potential of big data analytics has the capability to transform the sophisticated technologies in order to gain insight into clinical and other various types of data repositories and to make decisions based on these transformations and analysis.

Kumar and Manjula (2014) said that accomplishing better results at lower costs is more important for healthcare and the implementation of Hadoop HDFS and MapReduce enable us to achieve that by uncovering the underlying information in big data sets.

Mackinsey and Company (2013) suggest that the cost in the US in clinical operations can be reduced by big data analytics and it could be up to $300 billion yearly. Around 4.2% of total GDP in India is being spent on healthcare. This large amount in healthcare necessitates the use of big data analytics in order to offer better facilities in healthcare to its citizens.

Advanced miniaturized sensors are being used to develop body sensor networks (Korzun, 2012) which are being used to examine the health conditions of patients along with wearable biosensor systems.

A distant monitoring system called BodyGuardian provides an opportunity for patients to remain at their home while being monitored for their health situation by the physicians remotely. For big data analytics in healthcare industries, usually, textual notes are taken (Kumar, 2016). The big data indexing techniques and innovative analyzing methods of the textual data would surely contribute an invaluable solution to healthcare analytics in near future.

Throughout the world today, automation is finding a place in healthcare in three stages through the computer systems and the data are managed by gathering it, sharing it and performing analytical analysis on the data (Kakria, 2015). Since data analytics is being applied to healthcare, it would be exemplified by embracing the enterprise data warehouse (EDW) which is the synonyms to the term Big Data.

To improve the quality and care, healthcare requires some reform to address system efficiencies, cost increment, poor quality and the large number of uncovered peoples under health insurance (Nambiar et al, 2013). Researchers and scientists around the globe are debating about the major reforms in healthcare. The focused reforms in healthcare are:

- To improve quality, efficiency, safety, and decreasing health discrepancies.
- To engaging Family with patients itself.
- To improve care coordination and civic health.
- To maintain the security and privacy of health information.
- To make the system transparent and efficient.
- To empower individuals.
- To bring an enhancement in clinical outcome.
- To generate more data for research on healthcare.

While healthcare industry is focusing more on improvements, Big Data Analytics simultaneously can play a major role to address the challenge that comes in mining the pertinent information in order to enable efficient and effective medical practices.

BIG DATA ANALYTICS IN HEALTHCARE

Healthcare Information Technology (HIT) has provided the possibility and capability to store huge data electronically at one place, maintain it and share the data across the globe in a matter of seconds and thus providing healthcare with remarkably growing productivity and quality of services. Rao et al. (2015) suggest that all over the globe, the medical practices are heading towards evidence centered healthcare instead of ad-hoc subjective assessment of healthcare with the intent of carrying out analysis and inferring hidden patterns and knowledge from heterogeneous records of patient's healthcare data like unstructured clinical data, outsized medical imaging data, genomic data and amorphous data from social relations and communications. Few challenging tasks are there in the storage like compilation of the hefty amount of data with more threat of the data generation with an exponential growth in speed.

Big data analytics has opened the door for improving the services and provide solutions to the problems in the healthcare area. Although data analytics has been very important part of science, big data analytics has garnered interest in recent time as it combines traditional analytics with social data analytics. New applications of big data analytics to the healthcare industry are being introduced and developed around the globe. Experts have the view that application of big data analytics can provide opportunities to discover tentative needs, forecasts, reduction of risks besides providing real-time sensing, personalized services and counter-measure in healthcare. The collective power of information from people, clinical systems, real-time devices, and historical population data makes big data a very useful tool in improving the healthcare systems.

Architectural Framework

The concept of distributed processing comes into play while processing and analyzing the healthcare data and it is done by breaking the big data into different segments and then executing across several cluster nodes. Hadoop and Map Reduce (Akhtar & Ahamad, 2017) like open source platforms are also being used encouraging the use of big data analytics in healthcare. These tools are programming models associated with some implementation used to process and generate big data sets with a parallel and distributed algorithms on a cluster (Akhtar, Ahamad & Khan, 2015).

Numerous external sources which include insurance companies, laboratories etc. and internal sources like electronic health records, clinical decision support systems etc. often produces a large volume of heterogeneous data in multiple formats. The transformation and processing of raw data can be done by either aggregating various types of data by data warehousing or by using a service-oriented architectural method combined by middleware. Thereafter, decisions are made about the distributed design, approach to the data input and analytical models. And finally, representation of healthcare data analytics applications are done in the form of queries, reports, OLAP and data mining. Figure 1 represents the entire architectural framework.

Many frameworks and methods have been designed and developed for the purpose of medical image processing. One framework called Hadoop (Shvachko et. al., 2010; Sobhy, Sonbaty & Elnasr, 2012) employs Map Reduce as a technique to analyze and transform the massive dataset. Map Reduce provides scalability across several servers in a Hadoop cluster and finds plenty of real-world applications (Dean & Ghemawat, 2008; Wang et al., 2010).

Figure 1. Architectural framework for big data analytics

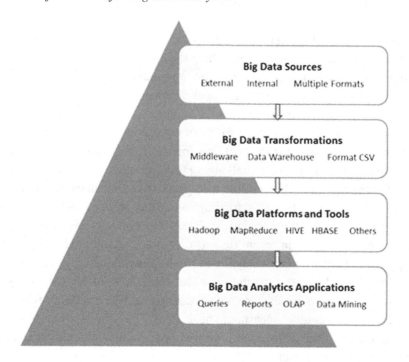

Rather than functioning well with tasks that are rigorous to input-output, Map Reduce framework is usually used to enhance the computation speed of large-scale medical image processing use-case like medical image content-based indexing and analyzing wavelets for solid texture classification besides employing machine learning mechanism to discover ideal parameters for lung texture classification, thereby reducing the execution time from about 1000h to around 10h. Critical applications which require extensive care, such as trauma assessment, need the design of a fast method so as to utilize the imaging techniques and their analysis.

Initiatives in Healthcare

Several initiatives have been taken to utilize the Big Data potential in the domain of healthcare. Some examples include:

Battling the Flu: Influenza causes millions peoples to lose their lives every year. CDC has used Big Data analytics very efficiently to combat influenza. Over 700,000 flu reports are received by the CDC every week which contains the information about the sickness, the treatment that were given and its success. This information is made available to the general public by CDC via an application *FluView* which organizes and sifts through the humongous data in order to create a crystal clear picture for doctors in real-time regarding the spreading of the disease across the country insurance (Nambiar et al, 2013). In addition of providing the location of patients precisely, it also gives details of the vaccines that are being used to combat the disease and which other medicine can aid in the recovery of the patient. Also, an application called *FluNearYou* has been developed that assist the patients to recover from the flu. It gathers data from peoples when they fall sick and a flu activity map is generated that helps users to prepare and prevent themselves from being exposed to the disease. Similarly, other applications like *Germ Tracker* and *Help, I Have the Flue* has been developed to assist peoples for their betterment.

Asthmapolis: A tracker with global positioning system (GPS) has been developed that is used to monitor inhaler usage by the patients thereby providing an opportunity for more effective treatment of asthma. A small cap which contains the GPS sensor is placed on the top of an inhaler to gather the usage information. When a patient require to use the inhaler while suffering an attack of asthma, the time and place of use is recorded by the little cap device and then this device transmits the data to a website. Center for Disease Control (CDC) then combines this information with its own available information like information about the most prominent catalyst of asthma in the air and the highest pollen count for that locality. The combination of such useful information allows a physician to create a personalized plan to identify the time period during which the risk of asthma attack could be higher so that he can alter the amount of dosage for the patient.

Diagnosis: Big Data analytics can be used to diagnose the disease, provide better treatment for them and in helping the number of patients readmitted. IBM's PureData solution for analytics in healthcare, a kind of integrated software, allows clinics and hospitals to use healthcare analytics. The software reduces the risk while delivering rapid results. Seattle's Children's Hospital is using BDA to detect commonalities between patients and make diagnosis and treatment easier and more accurate. The system gathers data from different sources throughout the hospital and analyzes the previous history of the hospital in order to decide whether there is a requirement of additional resources to achieve faster and accurate diagnosis. A computer model (Krishnan, 2016) has been developed by researchers from MGH and MIT that has the capability to distinguish between different types of lymphoma. A large set of data is collected from thousands of patients suffering from cancer and analyze it to come up with an explicit course of treatment. The technology can bring a reduction of 5 to 15% of misdiagnosed or misclassified lymphoma, and make use of the resources to diagnose other patients.

BDA for diabetes: The diabetic patients can also be benefitted by the application of Big Data analytics. A company named Common Sensing has developed a product called GoCap which has a cap to track the insulin amount that is being used on daily basis. The recorded information is then passed to either a mobile phone or a connected glucometer. Healthcare professionals then make use of this information to discover critical problems and can give required dose on correct time.

Application of BDA in Healthcare

As the expansion of healthcare data is at a very fast rate, it would not be wrong to say that data analytics can be a very powerful technique in order to gain an insight into the hidden facts and figures and to extract meaningful knowledge and discover the hidden features from the healthcare data (Andreu-Perez, 2015). A huge collection of data in healthcare has been seen in the past decade, but analysis of these data is not up to the mark due to the fact that neither the traditional techniques were that much capable nor efficiently utilized. However, the introduction of Big Data has given an opportunity to store the heterogeneous data generated from the healthcare industries and the analytics to big data introduces the benefits of gaining an insight into the ocean of healthcare data to analyze and extract hidden patterns for future usage. Application of big data analytics in an efficient manner has enabled many organizations to obtain real results and they are trying more to expand their efforts and works amalgamate more data and models. The big data analytics can be applied in healthcare in a wide-ranging area such as:

- **Early Diagnosis of Disease:** It is very much possible to identify and detect the disease in its initial stage even before the patient starts experiencing the symptoms of a particular disease by applying predictive analytics to healthcare data record available previously for the patient. It helps a physician to understand the influential health parameters for aged and disabled people by using wearable sensors, pattern detection and stream mining.
- **Public Health:** Tons of healthcare data can be converted into actionable information by applying analytics that can further be used to recognize needs, deliver required services, predict and avoid the predicament for the betterment of peoples (Jindal et al., 2017). The analysis can also help the physicians to develop more accurate medicines in order to curb a disease. Analytics can help in recognizing and tracking the pattern and outburst of a disease and take necessary action to minimize the effect of that disease.
- **Clinical Operations:** Big data analytics when applied in a better way it can lead to determine a way that is more cost-effective and clinically more relevant to diagnose the patient and provide the exact treatment.
- **Evidence-Based Medicine:** A variety of structured and unstructured data such as EMRs, genomic data, clinical data, financial and operational data are combined and then analyzed in order to find a relation in the treatment and their outcomes (Thara et al., 2016). The patients who are more prone to get affected by a disease are identified by it and the necessary care is then provided to them.
- **Fraud Analysis:** Rapid application of analysis to a lot of claims can reduce frauds, abuse and waste. In patient profile analytics, patient profiles are subjected to predictive modeling and segmentation in order to identify the individuals that would be more benefitted by the lifestyle changes. The gene sequences can be executed in a very cost-effective and efficient manner making the genomic analysis a part of consistent health care decision.
- **Research Analysis:** Analyzing the records in order to identify subsequent indications helps to find out the adverse effects before the delivery of products in the market. To improve the clinical trial design and the necessities of patients, algorithms and statistical tools can be used to match the treatments provided to a specific patient. This leads to speed up the new treatment by reducing the trial failures.

The application of potential analytics in healthcare sector has transformed it by a means of improvement in the outcomes. The healthcare sector is garnering advantages with the introduction of analytics. Appropriate analytical tools can be used to analyze the collected data and can be shared through medical information exchange, EHR and EMR. The time for decision making by the doctors can speed up based on the results obtained by applying Big Data Analytics. Identification and prediction of disease in early stages can also be improved and proper cure can be provided in lesser time. Thus, by applying different approaches such as Clinical operations and Evidence-based medicine, it is possible to eliminate the inefficiency in healthcare data.

Challenges of BDA in Healthcare

Although big data analytics has numerous advantages in healthcare domain, there are certain challenges that are associated with it. One of the most challenging tasks is to capture and store the data coming from various health organizations (Reddy & Kumar, 2016). Organizing the data after extracting them from various layers and then integrating them is also a challenging task as these organizations generate data in different formats. Therefore it is required to store these data in a common data warehouse in order to manage and access it in an efficient way.

Another serious challenge is the quality of the data. The data collected is sometimes unstructured, improper and non-standardized. Therefore, the organizations must use some techniques to transform the data into meaningful information. The analytics are always prone to errors and variations and these are not excluded from the results because of the constraints and limitations on the data quality (Bansal & Ahmad, 2016). The data generated and stored in the data warehouse must be provided with some measure of security (Mashkoor & Ahamad, 2017) so as to protect them from being altered or stolen by the frauds.

One of the critical things in healthcare is to manage and maintain the patients' data as it is kept in the form of records and are very huge in nature requiring very large space (Huang et al., 2015). These humongous data can be analyzed only by the data analytics experts. Therefore, another challenge for organizations is to hire the big data analytics experts which are very expensive because it requires peoples to have very high level of knowledge and expertise.

FUTURE RESEARCH DIRECTIONS

Although Big Data is making its way into the healthcare industry in a way that it is making the industry able to understand all the innovations that can be brought by Big Data. However, most of the platforms that are being used currently for analyzing the healthcare data are open source, so the limitations that they possess should be taken care of and the transparency and user-friendliness of the healthcare big data analytics must be ensured. Important parameters like ease of use, continuity, scalability, availability, privacy and quality assurance must be included in the platform evaluation criteria. Also the time gap between the collection of data and their processing needs to be addressed. To encourage large-scale adoption, large number of analytics models, methods and algorithms should be available. Efficiencies in healthcare sector can be improved by a greater collaboration between public and private sectors and across various industries in order to build predictive models as a result of collecting and integrating data from various sources thereby improving quality of care significantly at a reduced cost.

CONCLUSION

Today's fast growing world of humungous and heterogeneous data shows that big data is having a great impact making it an era of its own. With the growth of big data there comes a way for data analysis and prediction area to enter into a new phase. The ability to analyze humungous data in a better way paves a path for making rapid advancement in the healthcare industry in order to develop an understanding about new and better therapies and care of disease at reduced cost by bringing an enhancement in medicine and improvement in healthcare values and qualities thereby preventing the outbreaks of disease and thus saving the lives of people. The traditional machine learning algorithm has some restrictions regarding scalability and for a large data set, they might be taking too much time. Therefore, they require some modification in order to apply them for analysis of large data set. Big data analytics certainly has the capability and potential to bring a transformation in the way the sophisticated technologies were being used by the healthcare providers to analyze and extract useful and valuable information from clinical data and make the right decisions. Besides these advantages, there are certain challenges that must be taken care of so as to make use of the full potential of data analysis. These challenges include scalability, heterogeneity, provenance, and privacy, lack of structure, timeliness, visualization and error handling. Starting from collecting the data and going through various stages of analysis to the result interpretation, these challenges must be considered and transformative solutions must be provided in order to utilize the promising benefits of big data analytics in the field of healthcare industry.

REFERENCES

Akhtar, N., & Ahamad, M. V. (2017). Graph Tools for Social Network Analysis. In Graph Theoretic Approaches for Analyzing Large-Scale Social Networks. IGI Global. Doi:10.4018/978-1-5225-2814-2

Akhtar, N., Ahamad, M. V., & Khan, S. (2015). Clustering on Big Data Using Hadoop MapReduce. In *Proceedings of International Conference on Computational Intelligence and Communication Networks.*

Andreu-Perez, J., Poon, C. C. Y., Merrifield, R. D., Wong, S. T. C., & Yang, G. Z. (2015). Big Data for Health. *IEEE Journal of Biomedical and Health Informatics*, *19*(4), 1193–1208. doi:10.1109/JBHI.2015.2450362 PMID:26173222

Archenaa, J., & Anita, E. A. M. (2015). A survey of Big Data Analytics in Healthcare and Government. *Proceedings of the 2nd International Symposium on Big Data and Cloud Computing (ISBCC'15)*, 408-413. 10.1016/j.procs.2015.04.021

Bansal, P., & Ahmad, T. (2016). Methods and Techniques of Intrusion Detection: A Review. *International Conference on Smart Trends for Information Technology and Computer Communications*, 518-529.

Dean, J., & Ghemawat, S. (2008). MapReduce: Simplified data processing on large clusters. *Communications of the ACM*, *51*(1), 107–113. doi:10.1145/1327452.1327492

Galloro, V. (2008). Prime numbers. *Modern Healthcare*, *38*, 14–16.

Groves, P. (2013). The Big Data revolution in healthcare. *The McKinsey Quarterly.*

Gupta, N., & Saxena, K. (2014). Cloud Computing Techniques for Big data and Hadoop Implementation. *International Journal of Engineering Research & Technology*, *3*(4), 722–726.

Hassanalieragh, M. (2015). Health Monitoring and Management using Internet-of-Things (IoT) Sensing with Cloud-based Processing: Opportunities and Challenges. *IEEE International Conference on Services Computing*, 285-291. 10.1109/SCC.2015.47

Huang, T., Lan, L., Fang, X., An, P., Min, J., & Wang, F. (2015). Promises and Challenges in Big Data Computing in Health Science. *Big Data Research*, *2*(1), 2–11. doi:10.1016/j.bdr.2015.02.002

Islam, S. M. R., Kwak, D., Kabir, M. H., & Hossain, M. (2015). The Internet of Things for Health Care: A Comprehensive Survey. *IEEE Access: Practical Innovations, Open Solutions*, *3*, 678–708. doi:10.1109/ACCESS.2015.2437951

Jindal, A., Dua, A., Kumar, N., Vasilakos, A. V., & Rodrigues, J. J. P. C. (2017). An Efficient Fuzzy rule-based Big Data Analytics scheme for providing healthcare-as-a-service. *IEEE International Conference on Communications (ICC)*, 1-6. 10.1109/ICC.2017.7996965

Kakria, P., Tripathi, N. K., & Kitipawang, P. (2015). A Real-Time Health Monitoring System for Remote Cardiac Patients Using Smartphone and Wearable Sensors. *International Journal of Telemedicine and Applications, 2015*, 1–11. doi:10.1155/2015/373474 PMID:26788055

Korzun, D. G., Nikolavskiy, I., & Gurtov, A. (2012). *Service Intelligence support for medical sensor networks in personalized mobile health systems. Internet of things, smart spaces, and next generation networks and systems (LNCS 9247)*. Springer.

Krishnan, S. (2016). Application of Analytics to Big Data in Healthcare. *IEEE 32nd Southern Biomedical Engineering Conference*, 156-157.

Kumar, M., & Manjula, R. (2014). Big Data Analytics in Rural Health Care - A Step towards Svasth Bharat. *International Journal of Computer Science and Information Technologies, 5*(6), 7172–7178.

Kumar, P. D., Kumar, R. S., & Sujatha, K. (2016). Big data Analytics of IoT based Health Care Monitoring System. *IEEE Uttar Pradesh Section International Conference on Electrical, Computer and Electronics Engineering (UPCON)*, 55-60.

Mashkoor, A., & Ahamad, M. A. (2017). Visualization, Security and Privacy Challenges of Big Data. *International Journal of Advanced Technology in Engineering and Science, 5*(6), 394–400.

McKinsey & Company. (2013). *The Big data Revolution in Healthcare*. Center for US Health Reform Business Technology Office.

Nambiar, R., Sethi, A., Bhardwaj, R., & Vargheese, R. (2013). A Look at Challenges and Opportunities of Big Data Analytics in Healthcare. *IEEE International Conference on Big Data*, 17-22. 10.1109/BigData.2013.6691753

Raghupathi, W., & Raghupathi, V. (2014). *Big Data Analytics in Healthcare: Promise and Potential*. Health Information Science and Systems.

Ramesh, D., Suraj, P., & Saini, L. (2016). Big data Analytics in Healthcare: A Survey Approach. *IEEE International Conference on Microelectronics, Computing and Communications (MicroCom)*, 1-6. 10.1109/MicroCom.2016.7522520

Rao, S., Suma, S. N., & Sunitha, M. (2015). Security Solutions for Big Data Analytics in Healthcare. *International Conference on Advances in Computing and Communication Engineering*. 10.1109/ICACCE.2015.83

Reddy, A. R., & Kumar, P. S. (2016). Predictive Big Data Analytics in Healthcare. *Proceedings of the 2016 Second International Conference on Computational Intelligence & Communication Technology*, 623-626.

Sabharwal, S., Gupta, S., & Thirunavukkarasu, K. (2016). Insight of Big Data Analytics in Healthcare Industry. *Proceedings of International Conference on Computing, Communication and Automation (ICCCA 2016)*. 10.1109/CCAA.2016.7813696

Sathiyavathi, R. (2015). A Survey: Big Data Analytics on Healthcare System. *Contemporary Engineering Sciences*, *8*(3), 121–125. doi:10.12988/ces.2015.412255

Shvachko, K., Kuang, H., Radia, S., & Chansler, R. (2010). The Hadoop distributed file system. *Proceedings of the IEEE 26th Symposium on Mass Storage Systems and Technologies*, 1-6.

Sobhy, D., El-Sonbaty, H., & AbouElnasr, M. (2012). MedCloud: healthcare cloud computing system. *Proceedings of the International Conference for Internet Technology and Secured Transactions*, 161-166.

Thara, D. K., Premasudha, B. G., Ram, V. R., & Suma, R. (2016). Impact of Big Data in Healthcare. *Proceedings of the 2nd International Conference on Contemporary Computing and Informatics*, 729-735.

Triantafyllidis, A. K., Velardo, C., Salvi, D., Shah, S. A., Koutkias, V. G., & Tarassenko, L. (2015). A Survey of Mobile Phone Sensing, Self-reporting and Social Sharing for Pervasive Healthcare. *IEEE Journal of Biomedical and Health Informatics*. doi:10.1109/JBHI.2015.2483902 PMID:26441432

Wang, F., Ercegovac, V., & Mahmood, T. S. (2010). Large-scale multimodal mining for healthcare with MapReduce. *Proceedings of the 1st ACM International Health Informatics Symposium*, 479–483. 10.1145/1882992.1883067

KEY TERMS AND DEFINITIONS

Analytic Tools: Tools to extract, prepare, and blend the data in order to visualize and extract useful and actionable information.

Big Data: Big data can generally be characterized by a set of V's: volume, variety, velocity, value, and veracity.

Big Data Analytics: Big data in analytics comprises of tools and techniques to get insight into the huge amount of data available for useful information.

Data: Facts and statistics collected together on which operations are performed for reference or analysis.

Hadoop: Hadoop is a java based open source tool which process huge amount of data in parallel and reliable manner.

MapReduce: MapReduce is a programming model and an associated implementation for processing and generating big data sets with a parallel, distributed algorithm on a cluster.

Chapter 5
Insight Into Big Data Analytics:
Challenges, Recent Trends, and Future Prospects

Mohd Vasim Ahamad
Aligarh Muslim University, India

Misbahul Haque
Aligarh Muslim University, India

Mohd Imran
Aligarh Muslim University, India

ABSTRACT

In the present digital era, more data are generated and collected than ever before. But, this huge amount of data is of no use until it is converted into some useful information. This huge amount of data, coming from a number of sources in various data formats and having more complexity, is called big data. To convert the big data into meaningful information, the authors use different analytical approaches. Information extracted, after applying big data analytics methods over big data, can be used in business decision making, fraud detection, healthcare services, education sector, machine learning, extreme personalization, etc. This chapter presents the basics of big data and big data analytics. Big data analysts face many challenges in storing, managing, and analyzing big data. This chapter provides details of challenges in all mentioned dimensions. Furthermore, recent trends of big data analytics and future directions for big data researchers are also described.

INTRODUCTION

Big data analytics is the process of extracting hidden patterns and correlations, consumer behavior and preferences, market trends and decision making, by examining huge data sets coming from various sources such as web log files, social media, satellites and sensors, GPS data, IoT (Internet of Things) enabled devices, etc. When we click on a website, a large data is saved in the form of web log files. Which can be used in recommender services in future transactions. Facebook, Tweeter, Instagram and various other

DOI: 10.4018/978-1-5225-3870-7.ch005

social media are generating very huge data every day in terms of contents, tweets, photos etc. They must be saved for further processing. Sensor can be embedded in machines that senses the inputs from the outer world and provide it to the machine for further analysis. Hence, sensors can generate a large volume of data. There many handheld and IoT enabled devices which generated huge data. To extract meaningful pattern from big data, we need to apply application specific analytical methods. As, enormous data are coming from thousands of sources in structured, unstructured and semi-structured formats, it's a very challenging task to analyze it.

There are following challenges with respect to data storage, data management, analyzing and processing the big data, scalability, privacy and security. Huge data are coming from thousands of sources in different formats, it is a big challenge to store them in an efficient, unambiguous and scalable form. Big data is in the scale of Exabyte. Big data requires special kind of techniques to handle the data. It is not possible for the traditional tools to process the big data. To process them, we need a cluster of machines that can process the data in parallel. So, we use some big data analytics technologies such as Hadoop, Spark, Pig, Hive, etc., to manage and process the big data.

In big data analytics, we deal with huge amount of data with different format, inconsistent, noisy and incomplete data, which generates following challenges. Do all the data need to be analyzed? Do the stored data suitable for analysis? How to find interesting patterns from such a huge, multi-formed, inconsistent, incomplete, uncertain and noisy data? etc. It is much possible that the approach used for big data analytics provides good results on "small" big data but performance degrades rapidly for comparatively larger datasets. It's a challenging task to produce high quality of information from huge datasets with minimum time, resources and cost.

In recent years, large numbers of techniques and tools & technologies have been developed to analyze the big data. The techniques used for big data are clustering, classification, machine learning, neural networks, topic modelling, etc. To incorporate these techniques to analyze the big data, we have technologies such as Hadoop, Spark, Cassandra, Pig, Hive, NoSQL, HBase, MapReduce, etc. In future, advanced analytics and visualization techniques will be applied on real time business intelligence. To get high performance, in-memory datasets usage will be accelerated.

BACKGROUND

Big Data

Before the evolution of Big Data, data around the world was not so huge with limited types. Analytics methods were developed to deal with the less amount of data, some defined sources and limited types of data. Now, data is in the scale of Petabytes and Exabytes (Akhtar *et al*, 2015).

The big data is different from the traditional types of data in many dimensions. These dimensions are the foundation for defining the term Big Data. Doug Laney defined the term big data with three Vs: Volume, Velocity and Variety (Doug Laney, 2001). Some literatures also supports two other dimensions that characterizes the big data namely Variability and Value (A. Katal *et al*, 2013).

Figure 1. Five V's of Big Data

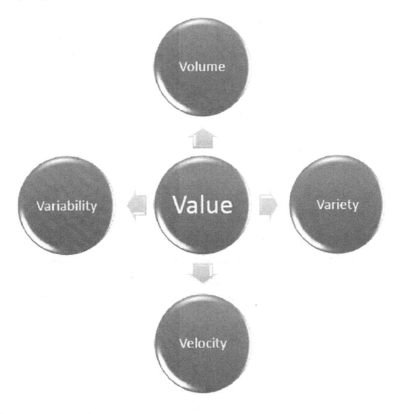

Volume

Volume characterizes the size of the data. It describes the capacity of stored as well as generating large amount of data everywhere. Nowadays, huge amount of data is generated by computers, satellites, PDAs, scientific simulators, sensors and user interaction with social media. The size of data has hugely increased than ever before and chasing the level of Exabytes and Zettabytes (N. Akhtar *et al,* 2015; Yojna Arora, Dinesh Goyal, 2016).

Variety

Variety characterizes the various sources from which data are coming. The data can be of structured, unstructured or semi-structured format. Structured data are stored in relational tables having rows and columns, where columns define the attributes of entity whose data are being stored and rows define records for each attribute. Researchers found that structured data are in very small amount, around 5-10% of all data available (Yojna Arora, Dinesh Goyal, 2016).

Most of the data available all around the world are unstructured in nature. Unstructured data can be in the form of audio, video, images, text, web log files, user search histories, scientific simulation results, satellite data, sensor data, etc. It is very difficult to store and use them effectively without any uncertainty, inconsistency and noise. Semi-structured data possesses the properties of both structured and unstructured data.

Velocity

Velocity describes the speed of data coming in from various sources and going out from the system. There are a large number of sources of data which are generating huge amount of data every moment. It can be analyzed using following statistics

- Facebook is capturing 100 TB data every day and has 40 PB of data
- Yahoo has 60 PB of data
- Twitter is generating 8 TB data per day
- EBay has 40 PB of data and capturing 50 TB data every day

Variability

Variability refers to the inconsistency in the data as well as speed with which data is coming. As most of the data is in the unstructured form, there can be inconsistency, uncertainty and noise in data being stores coming from number of sources. Before applying the big data analytics method, data need to be preprocessed to remove all anomalies, errors and noises. Variability also refers to the inconsistent velocity of data generation.

Value

Value refers to the meaningfulness of extracted data from the huge amount of variety of data coming from various resources. If analysis process doesn't provide quality results, it is of no value. This characteristics is very crucial to big data because quality results can be used in extreme personalization, target marketing, fraud detection, optimization problems, etc.

Sources of Big Data

Nowadays, very huge amount of data are generated and collected from a number of sources such as web log files, stored or archived data, social media, satellites and sensors, GPS data, IoT (Internet of Things) enabled devices, etc.

Web Data

World Wide Web is considered as one of the largest data sources. When a user visits a website, a large data is saved in the form of web log files which includes user's search pattern, personalization of web pages information, etc. This information can be used to provide better services and recommendation to the user for future visits.

Archived Data

Business entities are maintaining data centers to store the data for further analysis. These data centers stores data like customer and employee's related data, sales related data, daily transactions, and customer

Figure 2. Sources of Big Data

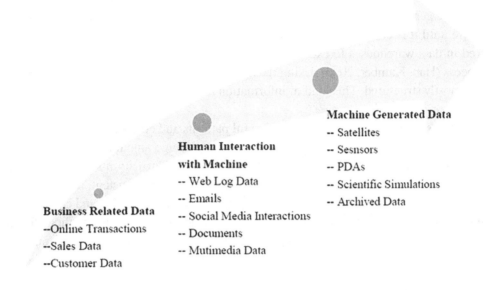

Business Related Data
--Online Transactions
--Sales Data
--Customer Data

Human Interaction with Machine
-- Web Log Data
-- Emails
-- Social Media Interactions
-- Documents
-- Mutimedia Data

Machine Generated Data
-- Satellites
-- Sesnsors
-- PDAs
-- Scientific Simulations
-- Archived Data

feedbacks. Big Data Analytics tools are used to get insight into these data which can be used in decision making in business.

Social Media

Nowadays, social media networks are heavily used interaction medium among people over the web. People are using social networks for news feeds, trending topics information, collecting opinion, connecting to a community, etc (Akhtar, Ahamad, 2017).

Social media platforms like Facebook, Tweeter, and Instagram, etc are generating very huge data every day in terms of contents, tweets, photos etc.

Sensor and Satellite Data

Sensor senses the inputs from the outside world and send it to the machine, in which it is embedded, for further analysis. Sensors embedded in scientific instruments, smart vehicles, flight simulators, etc are generating huge volume of data. Satellites are also primary source of huge amount of data. Weather forecasting systems, GPS tracking systems etc are the main example of this source.

Characteristics of Big Data

There are following characteristics of big data (Inukollu *et al,* 2014).

- Big Data integrates the structured, semi-structured and unstructured data.
- Big Data deals with speed and scalability of data coming from various data sources.
- The information extraction time and value of information is crucial.

Big Data Analytics

Nowadays, data are generated and collected more and more than ever before. But, this huge amount of data is of no use until it is converted into some useful information. Data mining techniques can be to the data stored in data warehouses to extract meaningful information using ETL (Extract, Transform and Load) process (Han, Kamber, 2000). Using these techniques, useful information are collected from data which are mostly structured. This kind of information retrieval is time taking process because ETL process is a batch oriented task.

Big data analytics is the process of extracting useful patterns and correlations from huge data coming from various sources and in various formats. Because very huge amount of data are coming from thousands of sources in structured, unstructured and semi-structured formats, it's a very challenging task to analyze it (Tiwari and Thakur, 2016). As, incoming data may be inconsistent, noisy or uncertain, it is preprocessed before applying analytics method. This makes it more complex and challenging task to get insight into the huge amount of data (Lovalekar, 2014). Traditional analytics methods forms a cluster of expensive hardware like state of the art processors to process the huge data in parallel. Big data analytics tools like HADOOP uses commodity hardware and programming models to process massive data in parallel.

To extract meaningful hidden patterns and high valued information from huge amount of structured, semi-structured and unstructured data coming from various sources, big data analytics uses advanced analytics tools and technologies. To enable such kind of analytical ability, these tools provides number of algorithms which discover meaningful hidden patterns, market trends, recommendations and correlations in the data. These big data analytics tools not only analyses the data, but also visualize and present in the form of graphs, tables, charts, statistics, etc. These results can be used in efficient decision making and optimization (Marjani *et al*, 2017).

Key Challenges of Big Data Analytics

Big data analytics deals with Exabytes, or even more, structured, semi-structured and mostly unstructured data, which may incomplete, inconsistent or noisy at times. To extract informative and business centric pattern, big data analytics tools faces following challenges:

- We have such a huge amount of data, do all these data need to be analyzed?
- We have a composition of various formats of data, Does this composite data suitable for analysis? (Tiwari and Thakur., 2015).
- We have multi-formed, inconsistent, incomplete, uncertain and noisy data, how to find interesting patterns from such kind of data?
- How to ensure that performance of big data analytics tools doesn't degrade with the increase of size of data?
- How to produce high quality decision based results from huge datasets with minimum time, resources and cost? (Tiwari andThakur., 2015).

This list of challenges in big data analytics grows rapidly, if we consider finer granularities of data and algorithms to extract hidden patterns. However, in this chapter, challenges in storing, managing and analyzing the big data are discussed.

Data Storage Challenges

Data volume is increasing day by day in huge proportion. Data are coming from social media, e-commerce portals, online transactions, handheld devices, scientific simulations, web log files, satellites and sensors, GPS data, IoT (Internet of Things) enabled devices, etc. These sources generating the multi-formed data with high velocity, say terabytes per second. It is the biggest challenge to store the data coming from various sources, in various formats into a structure suitable for analytics.

Data Management Challenges

Data management is a key challenge in big data analytics. Individuals are generating data in various formats like images, audios, videos, text documents, etc without giving much information about the data they are generating. This creates issues while collecting them into unified schema, and validating them for analytics task. It is also very challenging task to differentiate relevant and irrelevant data for analytics, as all data we collect are not relevant for a particular scenario.

Data Processing Challenges

Nowadays, variety of data are generated and collected in huge amount. But, this huge amount of data is of no use until it is converted into some useful information. Using traditional information retrieval (IR) techniques, one can get hidden patterns from data. But, this kind of information retrieval is time taking process and mostly work with structured and relatively less amount of data. It's a very challenging task to analyze very huge amount of data are coming from thousands of sources in structured, unstructured and semi-structured formats. There are many big data analytics tools like HADOOP, Spark, Pig, Hive, etc. which process massive data in parallel.

Data Security and Privacy Challenges

Before setting environment for big data analytics, one should consider the following set of security and privacy challenges (Gahi *et al*, 2016).

1. **Transparency in Data Distribution:** To analyze huge amount of data with big data analytics tools, cluster of systems are used to process the data in distributed manner. The cluster of system is a set of computers all around the world in close communication. The huge amount of data is distributed to these systems in the cluster and then processed in parallel. The main problem with this cluster structure is that the exact location of storage of part of data and its processing location is transparent and hard to know. This can result in security problems and some regulation breaches.
2. **Privacy:** The privacy of data is dependent on the fact the how the sensitive data is being used and get the special attention that it should have. Currently, big data analytics is more concerned with getting more interesting results for decision purpose rather than providing security on the data. Due to this weakness, if unauthorized user gets access of any of the system in the cluster, she can have access, exploit, destroy, and alter the data.

3. **Integrity:** Before using the analytics results from big data analytics tools, it is necessary to check the validity and the trust level of data to avoid compromised and outlier records. The validation of data is necessary because, data can be noisy, incomplete, and inconsistent. If they are not properly pre-processed before analysis, results may be inaccurate and must be validated.

4. **Secure Communication:** To analyze big data, it is divided into data chunks and stored on several computers in cluster. These data chunks are then processed in parallel on all systems and partial results of each system is communicated with others to get final results. Currently, these communications are done through ordinary public and private networks, which are vulnerable to security breach. To protect the communication among nodes of cluster, we need some secure communication protocols.

5. **Data Provenance:** Data provenance refers to the origin of data. That means, the location and time for generated data. Data are coming from number of sources, many of them may not be trustworthy (Lei Xu *et al*, 2014). If data generated from these malicious sources are taken into account, results may be faulty. It is a big challenge to detect the trustworthy and malicious sources of data.

6. **Access Control:** To protect the data from malicious data source and users, we need to deploy strong and effective access control mechanism. Only authorized users with administrative rights can participate to process the data, can be elementary access control mechanism. Applying more effective access control mechanism is still a big challenge to big data analytics.

Recent Trends of Big Data Analytics Tools

We are now in the era of Big Data. Business organizations are using big data analytics to generate decision making analytics which improves business processes (Jagadish et al, 2014). In 2017, the following trending tools and technologies are used by researchers and industries:

Hadoop

The Apache Hadoop is an open source, Java based framework developed for the distributed processing of huge amount of data in parallel with the help of clusters of computer systems. Hadoop framework is developed to scale up from single system (node) to a clusters of multiple computer systems having their own computation and storage capabilities. To provide high availability of information, it is designed to detect and handle failures automatically (N. Akhtar et al, 2015). The Apache Hadoop frameworks consists of following components:

1. **Hadoop Common:** Hadoop Common is the collection of common utilities and libraries to support its other modules.

2. **Hadoop Distributed File System (HDFS):** HDFS is the distributed file system responsible for storage, management and high throughput access of application data. HDFS splits the input dataset into manageable data chunks and stores them to different machines on Hadoop cluster. The default size of these data chunks is 64 MB for Hadoop 1.x and 128 MB for Hadoop 2.x. HDFS manages these files across number of machines on cluster and process them in distributed manner. Reliability is one of the most important feature of a distributed system. To achieve high reliability, HDFS stores data on multiple nodes by replicating them.

3.   **Hadoop YARN:** It is a sub-project of Apache Foundation which provides a framework for job scheduling and cluster management.
4.   **Hadoop MapReduce:** It is a YARN based programming model for distributed processing of large data. It is designed to write applications to process large datasets in parallel on large number of machines in a cluster. Hadoop MapReduce programming model process the data as a set of key-value pairs, and generates result in a set of key-value pairs.

Spark

The Apache Spark is an open source, fast, in-memory data processing framework designed to process read-only multi-set of data items called as resilient distributed dataset (RDD), distributed over a cluster of systems. The support for in-memory datasets makes it much faster than Hadoop. To process big data, Apache Spark needs a cluster manager and a system for distributed storage. Hadoop YARN can be used as a cluster manager and HDFS can be used for managing distributed storage. The Apache Spark consists of the Spark Core, Spark SQL, Spark SQL, Spark Streaming and MLlib (Machine Learning Library).

NoSQL

NoSQL is a database which is centered on the distributed databases. Using NoSQL, unstructured data can be stored on multiple nodes in distributed manner. This distributed architecture allows NoSQL databases to add up more system to deal with increasing data to support scalability and performance.

Pig

Pig is a high level scripting language as well as a platform to write codes that runs on Apache Hadoop. Pig enables data workers to write complex data transformations without knowing Java. Using Pig all required data manipulations can be done in Apache Hadoop. Pig can invoke codes of languages using user defined functions, also it can be embedded in codes of other programming languages. Pig processes structured, semi-structured and unstructured data, and then stores the results into the Hadoop Data File System.

Apache Hive

Apache Hive is a distributed data management software developed which runs on top of Apache Hadoop for providing data summarization, querying data, and data analysis. Apache Hive supports SQL-like queries to manage the distributed data.

Data Lake

A data lake can be defined as a method of storing data in a repository without changing its natural format. The idea behind the Data Lake is to create a single repository of all data. This data ranges from raw data coming from various sources to transformed data to be used for analytics purpose such as reporting, visualization, analytics and machine learning. The data lake creates a centralized data store by combining structured data coming from relational databases in the form of tables, semi-structured data such as CSV, log files, XML data, JSON data, and unstructured data like emails, documents, tweets, images, audio and video (Campbell Chris, 2017).

FUTURE PROSPECTS

In coming years, there will be a continued growth of analytics tools that support structured, semi-structured and unstructured forms of huge volume of data. These tools and technologies will evolve and optimize to provide much better and accurate business centric and decision based results. There are following areas where evolution and advancements will be done in coming years.

Ubiquitous Machine Learning

The importance of applying machine learning to massive amount of data is increasing day by day. It can be defined as the knowledge discovery and learning inside dynamic, distributed massive amount of data. For consumers, some sort of machine learning is already implemented in their everyday online lives, from target marketing over online shopping to extreme personalization of searched results. In future, we can expect a huge increase in the availability and capabilities of machine learning in big data analytics for end users and business organizations as well.

Big Data and the Cloud

Due to privacy issues, regulations and authorization, it's not always possible to move big data to an external data center. Sometimes, moving cost of this huge amount of data may surpass its overall benefit. To deal with such scenario, move the data to cloud. Currently, Amazon EMR, Cloudera, MapR, and Hortonworks, etc are using cloud to provide services to its users. Trends shows that, in the future, many other organizations will use cloud technologies for handling big data in multiple locations.

Big Data and the Internet of Things

The Internet of Things is a network of things (handheld/household devices). Using IoT and machine learning, analytics can be done on big data to provide healthcare services, target marketing, extreme personalization and other services through mobile applications. In future, this application can be extended to meet the requirements of business organizations and smart cities.

Big Data and the Deep Learning

Deep learning is a hierarchical approach of learning which uses multi-layer artificial neural networks to extract high-level, complex abstractions as data representations. Deep Learning is considered as the analysis and learning of huge amount of unsupervised data. This property makes deep learning a valuable approach for analyzing unlabeled and un-categorized data (Maryam M Najafabadi *et al*, 2015). As discussed earlier, most of the big data is un-categorized or unstructured, deep learning will play an evolutionary role in big data analytics.

CONCLUSION

Big data can be defined as the huge amount of data coming from various sources in various formats. Before the advent of Big Data, digital data around the world was not so big and unstructured. To gain insight to such a massive amount of data, big data analytics tools and technologies are used. Big data analytics is the process of extracting useful patterns and correlations from huge data coming from various sources and in various formats. As, enormous data are coming from thousands of sources in structured, unstructured and semi-structured formats, it's a very challenging task to analyze it.

The big data analytics challenges raise the following questions: Do all these data need to be analyzed? Does this composite data suitable for analysis? We have multi-formed, inconsistent, incomplete, uncertain and noisy data, how to find interesting patterns from such kind of data? How to ensure that performance of big data analytics tools doesn't degrade with the increase of size of data? How to produce high quality decision based results from huge datasets with minimum time, resources and cost?

To answer the above questions, business organizations are currently using big data analytics tools and technologies such as Hadoop, MapReduce, Spark, Pig, Hive, NoSQL, etc. These tools distribute the huge amount of data over distributed nodes in cluster. Each data chunk is processed in parallel on each node and finally clubbed together to provide analytics results in the form of graphs, charts, documents, etc. In future, big data analytics can be merged with cutting edge technologies like cloud computing, Internet of Things, Deep Learning, etc, to provide more accurate, secure, scalable and cost effective analytics.

REFERENCES

Akhtar, Ahamad, & Khan. (2015). Clustering on Big Data Using Hadoop MapReduce. *Proceedings of International Conference on Computational Intelligence and Communication Networks.*

Akhtar, N., & Ahamad, M. V. (2017). Graph Tools for Social Network Analysis. In Graph Theoretic Approaches for Analyzing Large-Scale Social Networks. IGI Global. Doi:10.4018/978-1-5225-2814-2.ch002

Akthar, N., Ahamad, M. V., & Khan, S. (2015). MapReduce Model of Improved K-Means Clustering Algorithm Using Hadoop MapReduce. *Proceedings of 2016 Second International Conference on Computational Intelligence & Communication Technology.*

Bansal, P., & Ahmad, T. (2016, August). Methods and Techniques of Intrusion Detection: A Review. In *International Conference on Smart Trends for Information Technology and Computer Communications* (pp. 518-529). Springer.

Campbell, C. (n.d.). *Top Five Differences between DataWarehouses and Data Lakes.* Blue-Granite.com.

Chawda & Thakur. (2016). Big Data and Advanced Analytics Tools. *2016 Symposium on Colossal Data Analysis and Networking (CDAN).*

Choudhury, T., Chhabra, A. S., Kumar, P., & Sharma, S. (2016). A Recent Trends on Big Data Analytics. *Proceedings of the SMART -2016, 5th International Conference on System Modeling & Advancement in Research Trends.*

Najafabadi, Villanustre, Khoshgoftaar, Seliya, Wald, & Muharemagic. (2015). Deep learning applications and challenges in big data analytics. *Journal of Big Data, 2015.* doi:10.118640537-014-0007-7

Gahi, Y., Guennoun, M., & Mouftah, H. T. (2016). Big Data Analytics: Security and Privacy Challenges. *Proceedings of 2016 IEEE Symposium on Computers and Communication (ISCC).*

Han, J., & Kamber, M. (2000). Data Mining: Concepts and Techniques. Morgan Kaufmann.

Inukollu, Arsi, & Ravuri. (2014). Security Issues Associated With Big Data In Cloud Computing. *International Journal of Network Security & Its Applications, 6*(3).

Jagadish, H., Gehrke, J., Labrinidis, A., Papakonstantinou, Y., Patel, J., Ramakrishnan, R., & Shahabi, C. (2014). Big data and its technical challenges. *Communications of the ACM, 57*(7), 86–94. doi:10.1145/2611567

Katal, A., Wazid, M., & Goudar, R. H. (2013). Big data: Issues, challenges, tools and Good practices. Academic Press.

Laney. (2001). 3d Data management: Controlling data volume, velocity and variety. *Appl. Delivery Strategies Meta Group, 949.*

Lovalekar, S. (2014). Big Data: An Emerging Trend In Future. *International Journal of Computer Science and Information Technologies, 5*(1), 538–541.

Marjani, Nasaruddin, Gani, Karim, Hashem, Siddiqa, & Yaqoob. (n.f.). *Big IoT Data Analytics: Architecture, Opportunities, and Open Research Challenges.* IEEE, DOI 10.1109/ACCESS.2017.2689040

Mashkoor & Ahamad. (2017). Visualization, Security and Privacy Challenges of Big Data. *International Journal of Advanced Technology in Engineering and Science, 5*(6), 394 - 400.

Mishra, A. D., & Singh, Y. B. (2016). Big Data Analytics for Security and Privacy Challenges. *Proceedings of International Conference on Computing, Communication and Automation (ICCCA2016).* 10.1109/CCAA.2016.7813688

Tiwari, V., & Thakur, R.S. (2015). P2MS- A Phase-Wise Pattern Management System for Pattern Warehouse. *Int. J. of Data Mining, Modeling and Management, 7*(4), 331-350.

Tiwari, V., & Thakur, R. S. (2016). Pattern Warehouse: Context Based Modeling and Quality Issues, National Academy of Sciences, India Section A: Physical Sciences, 85(3), 1-15.

Xu, Jiang, Wang, Yuan, & Ren. (2014). *Information Security in Big Data: Privacy and Data Mining.* IEEE. DOI 10.1109/Access.2014.2362522

Zaharia, M., Chowdhury, M., Franklin, M. J., Shenker, S., & Stoica, I. (n.d.). Spark: Cluster Computing with Working Sets (PDF). *USENIX Workshop on Hot Topics in Cloud Computing (HotCloud).*

KEY TERMS AND DEFINITIONS

Big Data Analytics: Big data analytics is the process of extracting useful patterns and correlations from huge data coming from various sources and in various formats.

Big Data: Big data is a term that is used to describe data that is high volume, high velocity, and/or high variety; requires new technologies and techniques to capture, store, and analyse it; and is used to enhance decision making, provide insight and discovery, and support and optimize processes.

Data: It is a collection of raw facts about something.

HDFS (Hadoop Distributed File System): HDFS is the distributed file system responsible for storage, management and high throughput access of application data. HDFS splits the input dataset into manageable data chunks and stores them to different machines on Hadoop cluster.

Information Retrieval: The extraction of hidden information from stored data.

Pattern: It is a summarized and information rich semantic representation of raw data.

Resilient Distributed Datasets (RDD): It is an immutable distributed collection of objects. Each dataset in RDD is divided into logical partitions, which may be computed on different nodes of the cluster.

Chapter 6
Big Data Analytics Tools and Platform in Big Data Landscape

Mohd Imran
Aligarh Muslim University, India

Mohd Vasim Ahamad
Aligarh Muslim University, India

Misbahul Haque
Aligarh Muslim University, India

Mohd Shoaib
Aligarh Muslim University, India

ABSTRACT

The term big data analytics refers to mining and analyzing of the voluminous amount of data in big data by using various tools and platforms. Some of the popular tools are Apache Hadoop, Apache Spark, HBase, Storm, Grid Gain, HPCC, Casandra, Pig, Hive, and No SQL, etc. These tools are used depending on the parameter taken for big data analysis. So, we need a comparative analysis of such analytical tools to choose best and simpler way of analysis to gain more optimal throughput and efficient mining. This chapter contributes to a comparative study of big data analytics tools based on different aspects such as their functionality, pros, and cons based on characteristics that can be used to determine the best and most efficient among them. Through the comparative study, people are capable of using such tools in a more efficient way.

INTRODUCTION

Big data technology is a revolutionary technology which is currently adapted by all scale organization varying from small private industries to large government organization. It is now agreeable among all academicians and entrepreneurs that big data is having some game changer capabilities which makes the big data analytics a great and powerful tool for market research. Now at these times, most of the business hubs as well as small organizations are coming forward to opt the big data analytics tool to

DOI: 10.4018/978-1-5225-3870-7.ch006

dig up their strategy of marketing and produce maximum output from same; despite of having their forefront challenges of investment and cost of marinating stabilization. Another benefit which business organizations are looking into consists of a well new customer experience, more reliable and efficient goal and a better look up of organization from a completely different perspective. The extensive use of this technology is in educational purpose as well as in health care organization. Research, which is augmented educational wing uses the tools of big data analytics at various level, and for numerous applications (Samiya, kashish & Alam, 2016). According to study, educational as well as healthcare sector is generating huge amount of data which make it a potential source for big data analytics but to make it happen all the data must be refined, recorded and managed. Big data analytics also have its security concern and challenges (Jayasingh et. al). The analytics tools used in big data for security must have their encrypting capabilities to protect large exploding amount of data at every level from system to forensic level. To enhance the performance, reliability, and accuracy of system, people should know the environment where the analytics tool is most suited. The Apache Hadoop is one the revolutionary platform that provides various remarkable analytics tool to manage processing and handling. Some of these are suitable for collaborative distributed computing, some are well adopted for real time streaming and likewise some are popular for their graph representing capability. Apache Hadoop consists of various tools which can be categorized as Business tools, data Science tool, Interaction tool, Sql/NoSql tool, Cognition, conversion, security, search and storage tool. Apache Spark is another add on for big data application which provides processing speed faster than Hadoop is nearly hundred times faster. It is a remarkable analytical tool, well known for its distributed computing and graph computational analytics. There are some other analytical tools are available like Hive, Pig, HBase, Cassandra, Storm, HPCC which are handy. In order to exploit feature of these tools, we have to learn a comparative analysis, by exposing them in different factors and parameters. By learning this, People are capable of using them in more simplified manner.

BACKGROUND AND MAIN FOCUS

The Big data analytics is new trending analytical standard used to fetch previously collected data which is generated by numerous applications for pattern searching that cannot be examined, processed, managed and categorized by any other existing tools or technologies (Yadav, Verma, and Kaushik, 2015).Hence new technology or tools must be adapted which can handle vast datasets generated from commodity servers which are distributed all across the globe. It is a technique of extracting useful correlated informations form massive dataset. Big data can be categorized in structured, Semi and Unstructured format. Mining of these structured, unstructured, and unrelated information collected from vast corporations, research, and healthcare organizations and make it useful by managing, structuring, controlling is main objective of big data analytics. Together, Big data analytics (BDA) is information managing tool that uncover the hidden pattern, correlated from vast big data set to make a decision control for large organization for optimized performance. The main focus is to deploy big data analytics tool in different sector of market, in order to obtain various pattern of market research.

- **Big Data in Healthcare Sector:** The health sectors are applying the big data analytics for determining the pattern of disease in various patients as well as in demographic variations. The digital image processing and communication medicine (DICOM) (D. K. Thara, B. G. Premasudha, V. R. Ram and R. Suma, 2016), HATS (HIV/ AIDS Tuberculosis and Silicosis) division are the perfect example of health sectors which uses analytics tool for premature or initial detection of disease and for prevention method (Tiwari et al., in press). According to (Groves P et. al, 2013) and (Hermon R., 2014), the utility of data analytics in health sector can be characterized in these major parts: Delivery & administration, decision support and clinical information, consumer/ behaviour market analysis and concrete analysis of gathered data from patient worldwide.

- **Big Data in Politics:** Big data analytics also emerged as one of the strongest tool in election. In prime minister election of india 2014, Big data was used to determine the flow of thought for candidate. In various district of india, various survey has been conducted, and then it is fed to big data tool to determine the strong and potential candidature of PM. Similarly US Presidential election (Plumer & Brad, 2012) was also follow the same practice and that had produced a magnificent and revolutionary change in election campaign.

- **Big Data in Social Networking:** Social Activities and Blogging also produces a large amount of data on the internet in daily basis. In today's digital era, people present their consent and opinion via social media. Twitter is the most popular platform (Arias,M., Arratia,A. and Xuriguera,R, 2014) chosen by people all around the world. Hence comes the concept of mining these opinion in order for determining likes and dislikes of people. Sometime these method is also called as sentiment analysis or opinion mining (Tan, S., Li, Y., Sun, H.,Guan∗,Z.,Yan, X., 2012). These models are generally used by product website, Stock market analysis (Bollen, J., 2010), Movie rating website as well as blog.

- **Big Data in Education Sector:** Another prime and major use of big data is in education sector. Research section of education is well growing in India. The Indian government is also empowering the research and attracting bright researchers to pursue their career in this stream by providing numerous funds for full time as well as part time. so it is also mandatory to maintain the data of all post graduate students all over India. Big data is playing a vital role in this arena. By using big data analytics, it is easy and possible to extrapolate students by filtering their research field and highlighting their achievements and ensuring that they are capable of performing satisfactory work throughout project and hence ensuring the grants are not wasted.

BIG DATA ANALYTICS TOOLS

There are numerous tools of big data analytics such as Hadoop (Bhosale & P. Gadekar, 2014), apache spark, Hbase, Storm, Grid Gain, HPCC, Casandra, Pig, Hive, and No SQL etc. It is used to improve the various factors in the development of big data and functionality of a computer system. The main concern of exploitation of these tools is to form the people virtuoso with additional analytical initiative and to urge more awareness within the areas of technologies and development. These tools are extremely most popular within the space of Business Intelligence to develop the prevailing business to larger extent and increase the economy of the company and also satisfy the business goals of the corporate. According to (Wu and Zhang, 2003; Wu, et al, 2005; Su et al, 2006) there exist a local pattern analysis model which which enhanced the knowledge mining just not in full manner but also globally.

1. **Hadoop:** Hadoop is tool based on java framework that supports the processing, managing and storage of extremely extensive dataset in an environment of distributive computing (Chawada & Thakur, 2016). It is an open source platform developed by apache software foundation as a sponsored project of apache. (Mujawar & Aishwarya Joshi, 2015). This project is designed as a storage platform which manages and processes vast datasets across hundreds to thousands of terminals operating in parallel mode. It offers a cost beneficial storage solution for all recurring data generated in voluminous amount from numerous private as well as government organization, from private business sector to healthcare and research organizations. In the Heart of Hadoop, there is MapReduce programming paradigm which offers extensive scalability. MapReduce is actually composed from the two task performed by Hadoop; first is it maps all the unrelated and structured or unstructured data (Gahi et.al.) collected from various recorded source and then reduce it with no format requirements. Hadoop consists of two main components namely HDFS and YARN.

2. **HPCC (High Performance Computing Cluster):** This is an open source solution available as an alternative to Hadoop. It is a supercomputing platform developed by LexisNexis Risk Solutions in order to enhance the capability of system. This tool is useful for both batch as well as parallel processing of applications.

Figure 1. HDOOP platform and its components

3. **Spark:** Apache spark is marvelous analytic tool for streaming, predictive and graph computational analytics. It is an open source engine packaged with advanced analytics tools which provide efficiency and advancement to application. Its processing speed is measured hundred times faster than MapReduce as it provide immediate data reuse in memory. Many research organizations uses both Hadoop and spark together although it is designed as an alternative of Hadoop. In fact both are complementary framework of big data, together they make an extremely powerful machine from batch processing using HDFS for speed analysis to streaming and in-memory distributive processing in real time.

4. **Storm:** This analytics tool is widely applicable and preferable for real time system in more reliable manner for analysis of unbounded streaming data that can be developed in any programming language. The speed of the processing is millions of tuples per second per node. The feature of this analytical tool are free, open source, fault tolerant, and real time computing system.

5. **Grid Gain:** Based on Java platform and being open source, this tools gains it popularity in commercial applications. It is also employed in many other sectors like health sector, finance, education, and retail applications. Due to its real time distributed architecture, it works fast and acts as an alternative to the MapReduce of Hadoop.

6. **HBase:** It is also an open source tool. Combined together with Hadoop, It enhances the processing speed of cluster based system accommodated with Hadoop as well as its functionality in a measurable amount. It is one of the distributed database and non-relational tool in open source environment developed after Google`s Bigtable. Its core shell is written in java funded by apache software foundation and natively integrated with Hadoop. It perform the mapping on large data and map it into number of datasets, each of which is slated into n-tuple. This is performed as a separate task for the reduction part of output and after that it merge all of them into original one.

7. **Pig:** It is one of the popular big data tool that reflects the abstraction over MapReduce of Hadoop. Based on a high level platform, it creates the program that run on apache Hadoop. The functionality of Pig tool comprises of analyzing larger datasets consisting of high level language and express them into data flow. It is one of the important key component of Hadoop ecosystem similar to hive. It was initially developed by Yahoo Company in year 2006 to provide abstraction over the complex syntax of program for MapReduce. It provide an ease in writing small program running on a high level data flow system and uses Pig latin to manipulate queries. It is multi query approach, easy to read & write, simple to understand as SQL, and equipped with nested data types like Maps, tuples that are not featured by Hadoop`s MapReduce.

8. **Hive:** In Ecosystem of Hadoop, Hive also play a vital role as analytics tool. It functionality is similar to Pig. It can be seen as a data warehouse package mounted on the top layer of Hadoop ecosystem for managing and processing huge amount of data generated. It is featured with simple interface using SQL. Hence user don't need to bother about MapReduce complex program. Hive worked to access the data set stored at Hbase. It is can be summarized as:

   a. Data Warehouse Infrastructure
   b. Definer of a Query Language popularly known as HiveQL (similar to SQL)
   c. Provides us with various tools for easy extraction, transformation and loading of data.
   d. Hive allows its users to embed customized mappers and reducers.

Table 1. Comparison table between Pig and Hive

Characteristics	Pig	Hive
Language Name	Pig Latin	HiveQL
Developed By	Yahoo	Facebook
Type of Language	Dataflow	Declarative (SQL Dialect)
Data Structures Supported	Nested and Complex	---
Relational Complete	YES	YES
Turing Complete	YES	YES
Schema Optional	YES	NO

9. **Cassandra:** Cassandra is a scalable, highly enhanced performance distributed architecture database capable of handling vast amount of structures data generated over a number of servers. Based on NoSql database, it is highly reliable and open source software by apache with no single point of failure. The main noted feature of this tool is its elasticity depending upon requirements it can support addition of multiple hardware servicing more customer at single instance. Increasing number of servers doesn't have any adverse effects on its throughput, in fact it is increased stabilizing the response time. It is flexible on distribution wherever and whenever it is needed to replicate data across distributed data centers, reflecting no point of failure over critical business transaction application, hence it is more reliable than any other tools offered by apache. Since it have NoSql database, it reflects ACID (Atomicity, Consistency, Isolation and durability) property and capable of storing huge data gathered from multiple points without affecting the reading efficiency of distributed system.
10. **Phoenix:** It is a SQL skin for HBase. Being open source software, it provides massive parallelism on handling larger relational databases. It has support over online transaction processing OLTP making it real good one. It has enhanced the performance of Hadoop`s Hbase due to its added functionality over SQL.

Comparison of Big Data Analytics Tools

The main focus on studying the different big data tools is to understand different features and functionalities provided by them so that user can easily use it depending upon need. Its study makes people who are engaged in companies, more skillful and knowledgeable about usability of these in more enhanced, simpler and more convenient way. When these tools are subjected to numerous factors and parameters, it yields their pros and cons in different environment. The importance of big data tools can be acknowledged by grouping it into 3 categories;

1. Comparison of 3 V`s (Velocity, variety, & Volume) (Shuijing, 2016)
2. Comparison of 4 C`s (Conversion, Cyber, Cognition, and Configuration
3. Basic parameters

Table 2. Comparison of Big Data Tools W.R.T Basic important Factors

Characteristics Big Data Tools	Volume	Velocity	Variety
Hadoop	250 PB	Structured, Semi and Unstructured Data	Fast Consumption, Collection and processing of Data
Storm	One million 100 bytes	Cluster of Data	High Velocity
HPCC	Petabytes	Data Centric & Query Processing	Faster than Hadoop
HBase	Petabyte	Task & Node processing	Complex processing of datasets
Grid Gain	Terabyte to Petabyte	Memory Processing	High Speed and Fast Processing

Table 3. Comparison of Big Data Analytics W.R.T 4`Cs

Characteristics Big Data Tools	Conversion	Cognition	Cyber	Configuration
Hadoop	Type Conversion, Apache Avro to Parquet format, PDI Data Type Conversion, Elastic Search	Big Data + Analysis, Saffron, Cognitive Computing, Cognitive Clouds	Cloud era, Big Yellow Elephant, Primer, MapR	Apache Hadoop 2.4.1 API, Apache Hadoop 2.7.0 API, Apache Hadoop 1.0.4 API
Storm	Batch processing and Streaming	Burgeoning Cognitive Systems, Irving WladaWsky Berger	Masergy, Beating Back Cyber Attacks, Horton Works	Apache Spark. Storm Cluster,Spout, Azura dArk Lake
HPCC	String to parse out Substring, ASCII to EBCDIC conversion, Typecasting, C++, ECL Plugins, Mainframe Binary format, ABO type Conversion	HPC, Sci Tech Daresbury, Human 00 cognition	HPC Asia, Cyber Security, White papers, Scientific Computing	Data Analytics, Tyrome, and Thor & Roxie Clusters
HBase	One text to Composite String, Stream of Binary Data, Sorting, Queries, MR Integration	Data Intensive Text processing, Apache Mahout, Cognitive Analytics, Saffron Big data	Cyber Warfare, Harnessing Big Data, Aster HBase	MATLAB using MR, Pentaho MR, Hadoop Clusters
Grid Gain	Implicit Conversion, Grid Projection type, Scalar type, Grid Cache Projection, Media Types	Rapid Cognition, Cognitive Neurodynamics, cognitive Computing	In Memory Data Fabric, Cyber Dust Leverages	Data Grid Configuration, Grid Configuration, Gridgain 6.5.0, Gridgain API

Table 4. Comparison of Big Data Analytics W.R.T Basic Performance parameters

Characteristics / Big Data Tools	Performance	Simplicity	Type of Software	Extensibility
Hadoop	Boosted	Easy	Open Source	DFS to Teradata
Storm	Accustomed Performance	Difficult	Open Source	OLA application
HPCC	High	Flexible	Open Source	Extensible to ML Platform
HBase	Efficient	Uncomplicated	Freeware	Processing of Big Data
Grid Gain	Vary	Effortless	Trail ware	Application scaling

FUTURE PERSPECTIVE AND OPPORTUNITIES

Big data is considered as a biggest transition in recent advancement of technology. It has major opportunities in various sector of society. Most of the sector has been changed due to application of analytical tools while still there are some which are untouched. We need to focus on that area, where maximum utilization of analytical tools can be possible. There are various challenges in big data which are listed below:

1. Visualization of data
2. Privacy
3. Extraction of rightful data
4. Retails and logistics
5. Data Integration and cleaning
6. Small business
7. Market evaluation
8. Web crawling (Mohd Shoaib, 2014)

CONCLUSION

In this chapter we have described about basics of big data which a tremendous and revolutionary landscape in pattern searching and data mining. We have also seen different type of data analytics tools like PIG, hive, Cassandra in Apache Hadoop ecosystem as well as their pros & cons, and features. We also have categorized the big data tool in different fields. By exposing these data analytics tools to different parameters and factors, we have represented a comparative survey where a person can easily and effectively learn that in which conditions, what tools is most suited to application. By learning these comparative analysis, people belonging to numerous sectors like healthcare, retail, finance, education and research can become capable of enhancing their performance of system in a good proportion. In brief his whole chapter describe big data both in tabulation and in well expressed and detailed manner which help people to make them more skillful and productive.

REFERENCES

Choi, T. M., Chan, H. K., & Yue, X. (2016). Recent Development in Big Data Analytics for Business Operations and Risk Management. *IEEE Transactions on Cybernetics*, 47(1), 81–92. doi:10.1109/TCYB.2015.2507599 PMID:26766385

Wu, X., Zhu, X., Wu, G. Q., & Ding, W. (2014). Data Mining with Big data. *IEEE Transactions on Knowledge and Data Engineering*, 26(1), 97–107. doi:10.1109/TKDE.2013.109

Mishra, A. D., & Singh, Y. B. (2016). Big Data Analytics for Security and Privacy Challenges. *Int. Conf. Computing, Communication, and Automation ICCCA*, 50-53 10.1109/CCAA.2016.7813688

Khan, S., Shakil, K. A., & Alam, M. (2016). Educational Intelligence: Applying Cloud based big data analytics to Indian education sector. *Int. IEEE Conf. Contemporary Computing and Informatics IC3I*, 29-34 10.1109/IC3I.2016.7917930

Jayasingh, B. B., Patra, M. R., & Mahesh, D. (2016). Security Issues and Challenges of big data analytics and visualization. *Proc. Int. IEEE Conf. Contemporary Computing and Informatics IC3I*, 204-208 10.1109/IC3I.2016.7917961

Yadav, V., Verma, M., & Kaushik, V. D. (2015, October). Big data analytics for health systems. In *Green Computing and Internet of Things (ICGCIoT), 2015 International Conference on* (pp. 253-258). IEEE. 10.1109/ICGCIoT.2015.7380468

Thara, D. K., Premasudha, B. G., Ram, V. R., & Suma, R. (2016). Impact of big data in healthcare: A survey. *2nd International Conference on Contemporary Computing and Informatics (IC3I)*, 729-735. 10.1109/IC3I.2016.7918057

Groves, P., Kayyali, B., Knot, D., & Van Kuiken, S. (2013). *The Big Data revolution in healthcare, Accelerating value and innovation.* McKinsey & Company.

Hermon & Williams. (2014). Big data in healthcare: HAT is used for SRI security research institute. Edith Cowan University.

Plumer, B. (2012, November 5). Pundit Accountability: The Official 2012 Election Prediction Thread, WONKBLOG. *The Washington Post.*

Tiwari, V., Thakur, R. S., Tiwari, B., & Choube, M. (in press). Optimization of EHR data flow towards healthcare analytics. In *International Conference on Recent Advancement in Computer and Communication (IC-RAC-2017).* Springer.

Arias, M., Arratia, A., & Xuriguera, R. (2014). Forecasting with twitter data. *ACM Trans. Intel. Syst. Technol., 5*(1).

Bollen, J., Mao, H., & Zeng, X.-J. (2010). Twitter mood predicts the stock market. *Journal of Computational Science, 2*, 8.

Wu, X., & Zhang, S. (2003). Synthesizing High-Frequency Rules from Different Data Sources. *IEEE Transactions on Knowledge and Data Engineering, 15*(2), 353–367.

Bhosale, H. S., & Gadekar, D. P. (2014). A Review Paper on Big Data and Hadoop. *International Journal of Scientific and research Publication, 4*(10).

Chawada, R. K., & Thakur, G. (2016). Big Data and Advanced Analytics Tools. *Proc. of Int. Symposium on Colossal Data Analysis and Networking CDAN*, 1-8.

Mujawar, S., & Joshi, A. (2015). Data Analytics Types, Tools and their Comparison. *IIJARCE, 4*(2), 488–491.

Gahi, Y., Guennoun, M., & Mouftah, H. T. (2016). Big Data Analytics: Security and Privacy Challenges. *Proc. Of Int. Symposium on Computer and Communication ISCC*, 952-957 10.1109/ISCC.2016.7543859

Shuijing, H. (2016). Big Data Analytics: Key Technologies and Challenges. *Proc. Int. Conf. on Robots & Intelligent Systems*, 141-145. 10.1109/ICRIS.2016.30

Shoaib, M., & Maurya, A. K. (2014, August). URL ordering based performance evaluation of Web crawler. In *Advances in Engineering and Technology Research (ICAETR), 2014 International Conference on* (pp. 1-7). IEEE. 10.1109/ICAETR.2014.7012962

KEY TERMS AND DEFINITIONS

Batch Processing: It is defined as the processing of all collected jobs/batch which are same in nature.

Data Grid: An architecture or in other word batch of services which provides a solution to individuals or bunch of users the ability to manipulate, access and transfer voluminous amount of data that is distributed geographically and intend to be used for research purposes.

Digital Image Processing and Communication Device: It is one of the standard procedures for integration of imaging devices like scanners, printers, network hardware, and servers that enables storage and communication of the medical images online.

Hadoop: Open source software that stores and analyzes massive unstructured data sets.

HATS: HATS is a HIV and AIDS testing software developed by doctor for the diagnosis of symptoms. It diagnoses and providse a quick report of patient who is tested and it can be shareable on the internet.

Hive: SQL programming framework that allows a programmer to use the MapReduce algorithm via a SQL type programming language.

MapReduce: Algorithm that is used to split massive data sets among many commodity hardware pieces in an effort to reduce computing time.

OLAP: Online analytical application processing is used in applications for analytical processing.

Opinion Mining: This is method of collecting opinions of different people on website in documented format.

Structured Query Language (SQL): Is a programming language that is specifically designed for managing data sets in a relational database management system.

Text-Processing: Refers to the discipline of mechanizing the creation or manipulation of electronic text.

Section 2
Data Mining and Computing

Chapter 7
Harnessing Collective Intelligence Through Pattern Mining in Social Computational Systems

Gaganmeet Kaur Awal
Jawaharlal Nehru University, India

K. K. Bharadwaj
Jawaharlal Nehru University, India

ABSTRACT

Due to the digital nature of the web, the social web mimics the real-world social dynamics that manifest themselves as data and can be easily mined as patterns, making the web a fertile ground for business and research-oriented analytical applications. Collective intelligence (CI) is a multifaceted field with roots in sociology, biology, and many other disciplines. Various manifestations of CI support the successful existence of large-scale social systems. This chapter gives an overview of the principles of CI and the concept of "wisdom of crowds" and highlights how to maximize the potential of big data analytics for CI. Also, various techniques and approaches have been described that leverage these CI concepts across a diverse range of ever-evolving social systems for commercial business applications like influence mining, expertise discovery, etc.

INTRODUCTION

The aim of the research, experiments, and applications of the field of artificial intelligence (AI), since long, has been to develop systems that can closely emulate human intelligence, emoting, decision-making and problem-solving abilities (Tiwari V. and Thakur R.S., 2015). Over the past few years, especially with the emergence of Web-based social networks (SNs), a paradigm shift is being witnessed in AI towards social and collective intelligence (CI). CI is a shared intelligence that emerges from the collaboration of individuals. The focus of our chapter will be to explore how to harness the power of CI exhibited

DOI: 10.4018/978-1-5225-3870-7.ch007

on online SNs for a variety of business applications. This chapter provides a structured perspective on approaches to model and analyzes CI in social computational systems.

With the emergence of Web as an all-pervasive communication medium over the last few years, especially due to the advent and deep penetration of SNs into our lives, this concept and its applications have become an active field of research. Also, this deep penetration is marked by the fact that these social networks have established another parallel world which closely mirrors and models the real world characters, their relationships, and collaborations; and factors affecting those relationships like trust, reputation, and expertise.

It provides an unparalleled opportunity to meet the goals of AI, like never before:

- **WBSNs Acting as Enablers for CI to Emerge as a New "Form Of Life":** This concept and phenomenon called CI, like many other concepts is not new and has existed in fields like sociology, communication, and behavior. Families, companies, communities, ant colonies and the research on their "collective" behavior, the human brain and its intelligence as a result of the collective behavior of the neurons, and much more such communities – all embody this phenomenon to the core.

However, the presence of the digital/social networks as a communication medium has opened many avenues to solve many intractable real-world problems through collective human and machine intelligence (ML) by enabling subject matter experts and non-experts (which, by the way, are equally important sometimes, to bring in novelty and the self-organizing nature of collectively intelligent systems fits everything into the right "perspective") from across the globe to collaborate easily and effectively and then machine intelligence (ML) supplementing it, to together generate higher levels of learning and knowledge which no single individual (howsoever elite/intelligent) or a sub-group of individuals can exhibit independently.

Wikipedia is a living example of such an intelligent "life" form that lives and breathes; and consumes and disseminates (new information), and constantly evolves and adapts. Something that has never existed before! Similarly Google's search engine is a counterpart of a researcher doing a literature review - who does research on a topic, searches and reads multiple books, papers, articles, interviews experts, finds more references and reads further and so on; and then compiles them and rank orders them to provide as an output, the latest, most relevant and popular details about the subject. These are but just two examples. Many such intelligent beings (manifestations of CI) are living and thriving (as probably overlapping entities, in some cases) across the rich information bedrock of Web.

- **To Study the Phenomena of CI and Design Effective Applications:** These SNs and their analysis enable to understand and visualize the relationships and the factors that enhance or inhibit the collaboration and sharing of information and knowledge in a (formal or informal) organization of individuals. The benefit, in this case, is that the data related to these collaborations is abundant and available in a digital form already and hence, can be utilized to study the phenomena of CI.

Researchers talk about the paradigm shift in AI towards CI. Somehow, this paradigm takes AI closer to its goal. So far, many biological metaphors (Artificial Neural Networks, Genetic Algorithms, etc.) have been used to make artificially intelligent systems to solve real-world intractable problems. On a similar note, CI has given to the AI researchers a metaphor and a method to help machines solve "intractable problems for the (supposed AI) machines" (at least so far) like human-level intelligent decision making, understanding emotions, etc. by leveraging collective human intelligence supplemented with machine intelligence through the intricate machinery of web-based networks (social or otherwise collaborative). And what results is more powerful than either; the term "collective" seems to encapsulate everything (human and artificial intelligence of a large number of participating entities) and what hence, emerges is larger than any individual or a mere sum of their individual potentials. And this again is a manifestation of the core principle behind CI, which is: "The whole is greater than the sum of its parts."

This chapter aims at providing readers an overview of the broad range (albeit not exhaustive) of applications of social computing that apply one or many of the principles of CI to achieve business, research or social objectives. In the following section, we will discuss the Web-based SNs, common approaches and various phenomena for social network analysis and will also present common notions of CI and its properties. The next section explores various manifestations of CI in social computational systems, and some examples are described in detail in the further section where analysis of SNs helps in achieving a CI goal. Finally, we conclude our chapter after summarizing research challenges and future directions.

BACKGROUND

Social Networks (SNs)

A social network (SN) is a social structure consisting of nodes which can be accounts, individuals or organizations that are connected through various social familiarities, affiliations, and relationships which range across casual acquaintance to close familial bonds.

The usage of SNs span across a huge spectrum of application areas which includes: social networking (e.g. Facebook, LinkedIn, Google+), global content sharing (e.g. YouTube, Flickr, BitTorrent), distributed creation (blogs- e.g. LiveJournal, Huffington Post), streaming/microblogging (e.g. Twitter, Tumblr), mass collaboration (Wikis-e.g. Wikipedia, Wikihow), collaborative assessment (forums, ratings, reviews- crowd-sourced opinion sites like Yelp, eBay), social bookmarking/tagging (e.g. StumbleUpon, Delicious), social news (e.g. Slashdot, Digg), e-commerce (e.g. Flipkart) and many more. These systems have become extremely popular and have changed the way, people, organizations, industries, and governments perceive, utilize, deliver and exchange information; thus making a framework for value creation. At the same time, the popularity and deep penetration of these systems offer new challenges and opportunities for research.

Since SNs are used to model the interactions and associations in web space, they can be represented as graphs where interactions correspond to edges and actors as nodes of the graph. This representation exhibits the following the phenomena of homophily, heterophily, transitivity, and bridges.

Signed Social Networks (SSNs)

Social networks with both positive and negative links are called *signed social networks* (SSNs) (Doreian & Mrvar 1996) or signed networks in short. These positive and negative links may correspond to the different relationships such as like-dislike, friends-enemies, agreement-disagreement, love-hate, trust-distrust, etc. For example, in the Epinions dataset (Massa & Avesani 2006), the signed links represents trust-distrust relations between users.

Theory of Structural Balance

The structural balance theory (Cartwright & Harary 1956; Heider 1946) and theory of status (Leskovec et al. 2010) have been proposed to explore SSNs. The most important and intensively investigated among the various theories is the structural balance theory formulated by Heider (1946), which was then formalized by Cartwright and Harary (1956). This theory asserts the phenomena that human coalitions tend to avoid tensions and conflicting relationships. It describes the way in which the relation of three users or triad can be signed and posits that the triads with an odd number of positive ("+") relations are balanced whereas those triads with an even number of positive ("+") relations are unbalanced (as shown in Figure 1).

The structural balance theory for partitioning graphs states that a signed complete digraph is balanced if and only if it can be partitioned into two subsets X and Y such that each pair of nodes within the same subset has a positive relationship while all the links between subset X and Y are negative. Davis (1967) proposed a generalized version of this theorem that a graph is k-balanced if it can be divided into k subsets of mutual friends with complete mutual antagonism between each pair of subsets. However, in real-world SSNs, complete graphs are rare, and therefore, the exact structural balance does not hold (Doreian & Mrvar 2009). It depicts the significant feature of relationships where balanced social structures affirm stability and users try to minimize tension and stress in relationships. For measuring the balance of social structure, different formulations of the social balance factor have been discussed by Zheng et al. (2015). Figure 2, 3, 4, 5 depicts the structural balance theory for partitioning graphs and real-world constraints of networks.

Figure 1. Balanced and Unbalanced Signed Triads

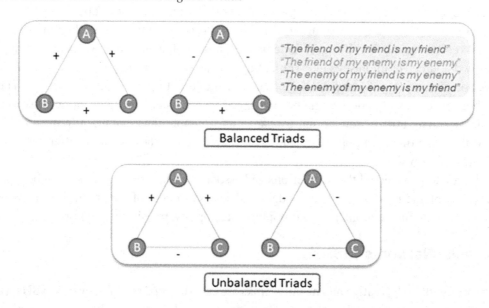

Figure 2. Example of structural balance for clustering graphs - Balanced partition into two communities with positive intra-connections (shown as blue lines) and negative inter-connections (shown as red dotted lines)

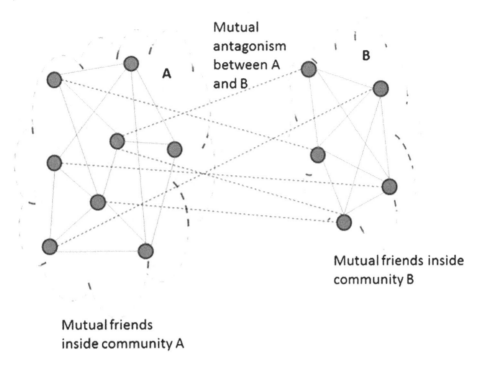

Social Computing

The research in social computing focuses on methods for harnessing the CI of groups of people by supporting social behavior in or through computational systems and also supporting computations carried out by the group so as to achieve greater insight from the interaction between users and information. Social computing refers to "*the study of social behavior and social context based on computational systems*" (Agarwal & Xu, 2011; Parameswaran & Whinston, 2007). A lot of research has been done on the social web in the past few years; however, the underlying principles of social behavior that governs the dynamics of social interaction are not fully understood. Social computing facilitates a better understanding of the behavioral modeling, pattern mining, and prediction.

Social computational systems deal with the study of complex systems of humans and computers to better understand the induced socio-technical behavior by designing systems and formulating models for enhancing knowledge creation, examining various kind of interaction, and analyzing collective actions and their manifestations as socio-political movements (Agarwal & Xu, 2011). They refer to web systems that enable users to interact, collaborate and compete with one another and produce synergies which none of them can achieve in isolation. Social network analysis serves as a perfect mechanism to facilitate and advance our understanding of such complex systems.

Figure 3. Generalized k-balanced partitioning of graph into five (k=5) communities

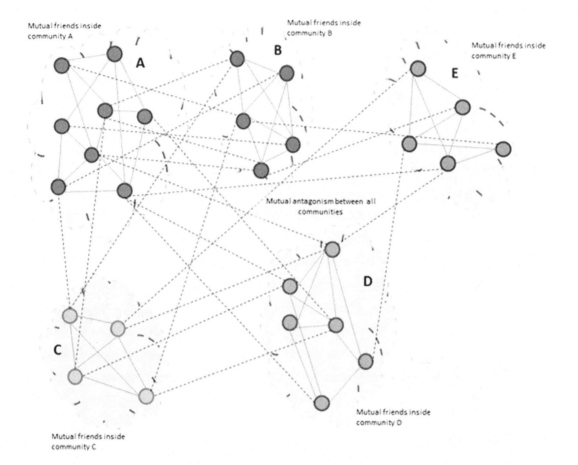

Social network analysis is the study of SNs in which the tremendous amount of *content* and *linkage* data is leveraged for analysis of relationships and behavior of individuals in the network. The linkage data mostly deals with the structure of the social network, and the interactions between the different entities and the content data comprise of text, images, tags, and other multimedia information in the network. The analysis of linkage data helps in determining the important structural patterns in the interactions between various entities or components; on the other hand, the analysis of content available on the networks can enhance the performance of overall systems by providing valuable insights from a business perspective (Bonchi et al., 2011).

Collective Intelligence (CI)

CI is a multi-disciplinary active field of research that predates the Web. It has been examined across diverse domains such as biology, sociology, economics, psychology, the theory of social choice, social network analysis, and mass behavior (Schut, 2007). The multi-disciplinary relevance and application of this domain have made CI a popular area of research of late (Awal & Bharadwaj, 2014). MIT has, in fact, setup a center for CI, and the basic objective of which is: "*How can people and computers be*

Figure 4. Exact structural balance doesn't hold because of positive links (shown as thick blue lines) between the partitioned communities

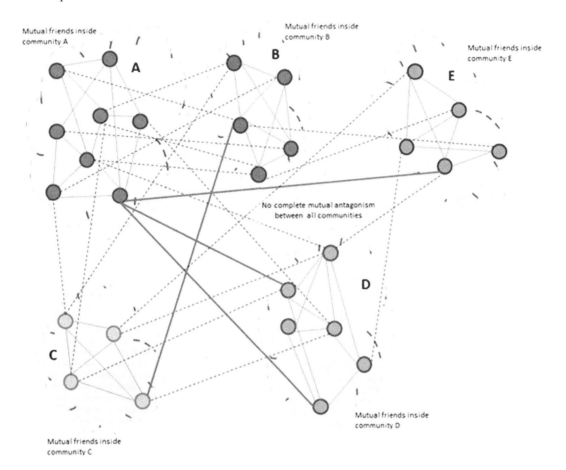

connected so that – collectively- they act more intelligently than any individuals, groups, or computers have ever done before?" The basic definition of CI is "Groups of individuals doing things collectively that seem intelligent."*

A rule-based inference system has been proposed as a computational model that formulates the measure for CI and represents the discrete nature of social structures. The elements of collectively intelligent activity in a social structure can be observed, quantified and assessed by observing: "spatial organization, displacements, actions of beings and their logical results and exchange of information" (Szuba et al., 2011). The mathematical formulation to measure CI is *"collective intelligence quotient" (CIQ)* (Szuba et al., 2011). The evaluation of the CI of social structures seems easy, however, in reality, is very complex than evaluation of IQ of an individual.

Properties of CI

The fundamental properties of CI framework that exist across various manifestations in different applications are discussed below (Schut, 2007):

Figure 5. Overlapping communities with some nodes (shown as red circles) belonging to multiple communities

- **Adaptivity:** This implies that either the individual changes its behavior if necessary or the system as a whole may be adaptive, e.g., ant colonies change behavior for food foraging.
- **Emergence:** A system exhibits emergence when there are interactions between the parts at the micro-level that dynamically give rise to coherent emergents at the macro-level.
- **Global-Local:** These are the two aggregation levels where the local level pertains to the individuals in the system, and global level represents the system as a whole. This distinction helps in positioning adaptivity and emergence in the system. When proceeding from local level to global aggregation level (i.e., emergence) then the system performance becomes more than its individual parts.
- **Interaction:** For analyzing the system behavior, one has to consider the individual behaviors as well as the interactions between them since the system thrives on how these individuals interact with each other.
- **Rules:** Rules are used as implications among inputs (observations), and outputs (actions) that describe the behavior of an individual (or whole system), e.g., representation of such rules could be if/then rules, trees or networks.

- **Redundancy:** This means the way the actual knowledge (e.g., rules) or the information exists at some different places in a system.
- **Robustness:** This means system remains persistent and tolerant to any damage or attack since the knowledge exists at multiple places in the system. So robustness of the system is the consequence of redundancy in the system.
- **Randomness:** This helps the system to show self-organized critical behavior where without an external spark such systems would be in the balance. These systems survive on the boundary of chaos where on one side there is structure and order, and on the other side, there is chaos and disorder.

Big Data Analytics and Collective Intelligence

The prodigious creation and accumulation of information generated by a plethora of sources contribute to the Big Data's enormous size and distinct characteristics (Karydis et al., 2017). Analysis of petabytes of data has numerous limitations due to noisy, ambiguous, volume, and dynamic nature of such data (Tiwari V. and Thakur R.S., 2016). The big data which render information for synergistic networks have the potential to maximize collective capabilities (Karydis et al., 2017). The synergistic networks that are also provided by big data serve as the underlying interaction web for emancipating collective intelligence.

The method of processing Big Data through distributed technologies reflects the collectivity part of CI (Karydis et al., 2017). CI along with machine learning techniques is utilized in various applications to address the need for pattern detection to cope with the data volume. The field of human-computer interaction (HCI) offers a lot of potentials to harness CI through the study of collectives' orchestration and analysis of human-to-human interactions using ICT as well as their virtual interactions. New paradigms that involve computer-supported collaborative works and computational CI methodologies are required to address big data challenges. The big data-driven CI involves research efforts in data collection and representation, knowledge discovery from big data (analyses using CI), and utilization of CI in various applications.

CI IN SOCIAL COMPUTATIONAL SYSTEMS: MAIN FOCUS

If we delve into the applications of CI in the real-world, then we will get numerous existing structures and examples that are prevalent in their stand and highly showcase the usage of CI. The framework of the amalgamated domain of social computational systems and collective intelligence which is the main focus of this chapter is shown in Figure 6. We will also discuss the concept of wisdom of crowds. Table 1 present a taxonomy of various applications based on CI, and some of them are described in detail in the next section.

Wisdom of Crowds

The *"wisdom of crowd"* represents the intelligence powered by people. It exhibits one of the key ideas of CI and is described as: "Under the right circumstances, groups are remarkably intelligent and are often smarter than the smartest people in them" (Surowiecki, 2004); and its various manifestations are:

Figure 6. Social Computational Systems and Collective Intelligence Framework

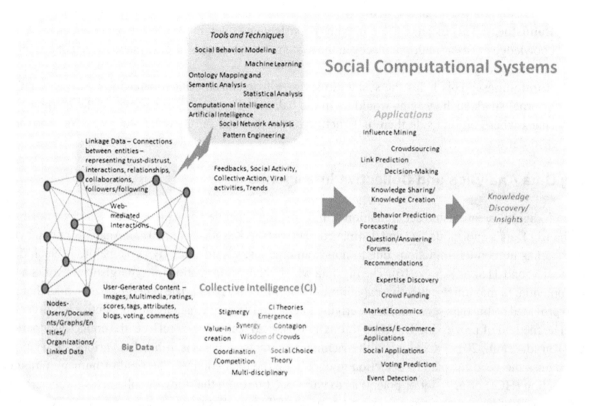

- **Crowdsourcing:** It is emerging as a general paradigm of organizing the human working and leisure activities using computerized platforms. It refers to the online/offline process of outsourcing a task /set of tasks to a distributed large set of unknown people (crowd) through an open call for solutions. The contributors submit solutions to the originator in return of monetary compensation, prizes or recognition (Yuen et al., 2011).
- **Crowdsearch:** It uses the crowd as sources for content processing and information seeking processes and information extraction directly from online humans. The *Social Search* which has gained much importance in WWW uses implicit feedback techniques to produce implicit web-rankings by reasoning over users' activities during a Web search but without recourse to explicit human intervention (Luca et al., 2009).
- **Crowdsense:** The algorithm represents *"approximating the crowd"* by estimating the crowd's majority opinion by querying only a subset of it, where we determine the subset as the most representative members of the crowd that can best represent the interest of the crowd majority (Ertekin et al., 2012).
- **Crowd Memory:** It explores how crowd algorithms are non-adaptable to the learning of the crowd in the context of human computation. It lays emphasis on realistic assumptions of crowd memory and learning over time and its implications while designing crowd algorithms for new systems (Lasecki et al., 2012).

- **Crowd-Powered Systems:** It is an interactive computing system that embeds crowd intelligence supported by users connecting and collaborating online. The hybrid systems are- Soylent (Bernstein et al., 2010) and Adrenaline (Bernstein et al., 2011). Soylent is a word processor which embeds crowd intelligence by providing aid in complex writing tasks like text shortening and proofreading. It recruits crowds in the form of paid micro-contributions. Adrenaline is a real-time crowd-powered camera that assists amateur photographers to capture the perfect moment for a photo. These hybrid systems provide a capability that neither crowd nor machine intelligence based computation can exhibit alone.
- **Crowdfunding:** It refers to an online request for different resources and financial or technical support services from the crowd often in exchange for a reward. It offers opportunities to entrepreneurs for raising funds by building ad-hoc online communities to launch new ventures (Hui et al., 2014). Different community efforts are identified in such systems to support entrepreneurship such as mentorship to novices, providing feedbacks and suggestions on campaign presentation and developing a repository of sample projects to serve as models. Kickstarter is an example of such crowdfunding platform.

SOME PROMINENT RESEARCH ISSUES AND SOLUTIONS

The data on SNs mostly comprises of user-generated information in the form of online reviews, transactional ratings, scores, and most importantly network information between users. This data is substantial in volume and leads to the problems of information and interaction overload. Leveraging the potential of CI through big data analytics can help in solving these problems by mining CI and deriving meaningful insights for businesses and enterprises to make better decisions. We will discuss a few applications in detail below:

Collective Behavior Prediction (CBP)

In the context of SNs, *user behavior* refers to a variety of social activities that users can do online like joining a group, befriending a person, rating reviews of products and services, purchasing goods, clicking on some ad, etc. (Jin et al. 2013; Tang & Liu 2010; Tang et al. 2012a). The collective behavior (CB)

Table 1. Applications of CI in social computational systems

Applications	References
(i) Decision-Making	Smartocracy (Rodriguez et al., 2007); (Watkins & Rodriguez, 2008)
(ii) Recommendations	Collaborative filtering systems (Adomavicius & Tuzhilin, 2005)
(iii) Prediction	(Malone et al., 2009), (Watkins & Jennifer, 2007)
(iv) Knowledge-Sharing/Knowledge-Creation	Communities-of-Practice (Maries & Scarlat, 2011)
(v) Expertise Discovery	SmallBlue (Lin et al., 2009)
(vi) Question and Answering forums	SSCrowd (Pedro & Hruschka, 2012)
(vii) Market Economics/Behavior	Invisible Hand (Skrzynski et al., 2011)

pertains to the phenomenon where users' behaviors tend to be influenced by the behavior of friends/ associates in a connected social network. The CBP problem deals with the prediction of the online behaviors of some users, given information on the behavior of the other users in the network and the network connectivity information.

CB reflects the behaviors of users in a networked environment, but it is not simply the aggregation of individual behavior. The behaviors of users tend to be interdependent, and this behavior correlation is guided by the concept of homophily. The users usually influence each other by participating in social forums, and this is quite subservient in developing and understanding theories of CI. Such phenomenon can be seen when users influence each other's opinions and views on products, companies, organizations, and users themselves, e.g., Epinions, Twitter, Blog Catalog, etc. are a few examples of such social platforms.

The relationships between users on the SNs are mostly heterogeneous where a user may connect to other users because they may be friends, colleagues, siblings, or may share similar interests. Unfortunately, this way of distinguishing the connections depending on the kind of affiliation is not always readily and explicitly available. So there is a necessity for developing automated algorithms and approaches that can discover and extract latent heterogeneous relationships and connections between users of the SNs. Not all associations in the network exert similar influence due to the difference in nature of an association. To discover sub-network of associations having an effect on user behavior in SNs comes into the category of "community detection" problems. Once the communities are identified, the behavior or preferences of active users can be predicted based on community preferences or CB.

The framework *SocioDim* (Tang & Liu 2009a, 2009b, 2012a) presented in Figure 7 addresses the *CBP* problem by capturing the network heterogeneity in the form of social dimensions. It leverages the predictive power of social connections to ascertain the behaviors of individuals through the following steps:

Step 1: Latent overlapping communities, also called social dimensions, are extracted from the network to capture network heterogeneity

Step 2: Discriminative learning is applied to build a classifier based on extracted dimensions.

The affiliation membership of users to different social dimensions determines one's behavior since different affiliations regulate the member behavior differently. Similar work has been proposed by Yang and Wang (2015), to study and analyze the differential effects of social influence sources (i.e., socialization agents) on attitudes and behaviors of individuals toward music piracy in the form of unauthorized downloading. Awal and Bharadwaj (2017a) extend the social dimensions based *SocioDim* framework to take the signs of the links into consideration while discovering overlapping communities for CBP in directed and signed social networks, thus capturing the multi-dimensional nature of human social life. They proposed a new metric called *"Structural Balance Index"* (SBI) which is based on the generalized theory of structural balance that determines users' degrees of affiliation towards various communities. Then the SBI measure is used to compute a refined modularity measure for SSNs called *"Structural Balance Modularity"* (SBM) as the quality indicator of the community structure of overlapping communities in the network. It adequately captures the sign, density and the overlapping nature of the links in the network, thus justifying the need for an *all-encompassing* measure.

Figure 7. Collective Behavior Prediction using SocioDim framework. The blue rectangles denote affiliations or dimensions, and the orange rectangles represent behaviors.

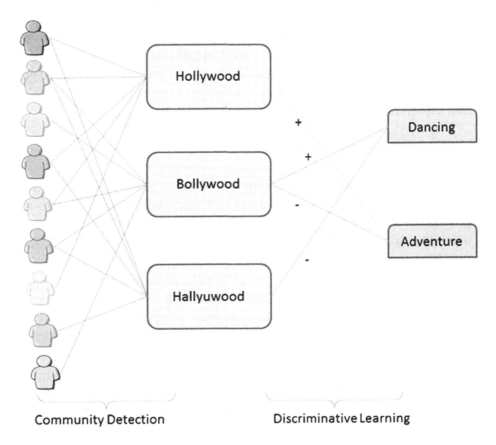

Social Influence Mining

Users on SNs get influenced by others who they think are trustworthy or with whom they have frequently interacted in the past. Social influence mining has recently gained prominence among researchers due to its applications in marketing, e.g., advertising, enterprise reputation management and personalized recommendations and viral marketing.

The computational problem of social influence maximization deals with discovering influential users from a social network so that they can activate a chain reaction of influence amongst the users in the network by word-of-mouth. The problem of discovering influential users is introduced by Domingos and Richardson (2001). They presented a model based on Markov random field that exploited the network value of customers in the context of a viral marketing application. Some of the previous studies focus on using the various network centrality measures (like degree, betweenness, closeness, and eigenvector centralities) to determine individual node's importance.

Kempe et al. (2003) presented diffusion models like Linear Threshold (LT) model and Independent Cascade (IC) model inspired from mathematical sociology. They proved influence maximization problem to be NP-hard and provided greedy approximation algorithm to maximize the influence spread of the set of users.

Most studies emphasize on the significance of each node without taking into consideration the joint influential power (*JIP*) of a set of nodes. The users are added to the group one by one as per their features and the strength of connections among them, without considering the influential power of the group as a whole. Xu et al. (2012) proposed a model that considers *JIP* of a group of users and showed that it has a considerable impact on a large number of users. Awal and Bharadwaj (2017b) proposed the MIGA model to identify a set of influencers with the maximal collective influential power which optimizes both influential power of this set of users globally as well as the actual spread of their collective influence by considering both explicit trust-distrust and interactions-based implicit information.

Expert Team Formation in Social Networks

Most fields of expertise are now too complex for any one person to master and the collective expertise of more than one expert is required, thus, necessitates the formation of a team of experts that can collaborate towards a common objective. The expertise SNs attempts to evolve productive and collective capabilities, which are sources of value creation in knowledge-based economies (Maries & Scarlat, 2011).

Lappas et al. (2009) introduced the team formation problem in the context of SNs, and after that, a lot of algorithms have been proposed recently in this field with various objectives (e.g., minimizing the coordination costs, covering all skills, etc.). The problem can be described as: "Given a particular task and a set of experts, the problem is to identify the right team of experts that can collectively perform the given task in an effective manner by covering all the required skills." Anagnostopoulos et al. (2010, 2012) addressed the formation of teams for balancing the workload offline and online for an incoming stream of tasks.

Wi et al. (2009) model the capability of a team by considering the two components of the competence of a team in SNs (e.g., co-authorship networks), that is, knowledge competence (KC) and collaboration competence (CC) (based on measures like density, degree centrality and closeness centrality). Awal and Bharadwaj (2014) attempts to maximize the collective capabilities of the team for generalized tasks and also for realistic constrained scenarios (Awal & Bharadwaj, 2016) by discovering a set of experts from an expertise-social network that can collaborate effectively to achieve a given task. The concept of CI that emerges from these collaborations attempts to maximize the potential of the team of experts, rather than only aggregating individual potentials. They proposed a quantitative measure *Collective Intelligence Index (CII)* based on two factors –the "enhanced expertise score" and the "trust-based collaboration score" (Awal & Bharadwaj 2014). They defined enhanced expertise score of an expert as "*a measure of the leverage that team members have by virtue of being connected to and having interacted with a team of experts, in addition to their respective skills.*" They introduced a hop-wise decaying and max-min path selection approach where the contribution of knowledge from the neighbors of a given expert decays with the propagation distance. The proposed model also captures the teams' dynamics by considering time-decayed trust measure to model CC, which is necessary for effective interactions among the experts. It is a synergistic alliance of experts that make the team more productive and intelligent than any of its individual members.

FUTURE RESEARCH DIRECTIONS

Since the unified multi-disciplinary field of collective intelligence and social computing is still in its infancy, there are various research challenges highlighted below that need to be investigated.

- **Data Processing and Management:** In spite of much technological advancement, processing of data with large volume, variety, and velocity remains a big obstacle. Large-scale management of ambiguous unstructured data remains inefficient and thus requires efforts to build adaptable information systems that can adequately extract, pre-process, integrate, store, transfer, analyze, and visualize such complex data.
- **Variability and Dynamicity of Social Networks:** Data-driven decision-making models usually consider static networks, however, there is a demand for efficient knowledge discovery methods so as to make important decisions and develop new network evolution models for ever-evolving networks so as to make business decisions at the right time.
- **Modeling of Human Perspective:** This paradigm still lacks proper implementation of different human socio-psychological phenomena that reflects real-life interactions between humans. Examining the dynamics of human-to-human micro-level interactions on the virtual platform and analyzing how these lead to an elaborate macro-level evolution of various phenomena paves a way to manifest CI living virtual entities. Deeper analyses of interpersonal human behavior online and how it differs from the true real-life behavior and vice versa will help in improving our understanding of these interwoven fields.
- **Channel for Value Creation:** Online social networks are the perfect medium for facilitating knowledge sharing, transfer, integration and value creation. Modeling the diffusion patterns and focussing on right environment and circumstances for comprehensions of groups and social cognitions would need further exploration. Enhancement on the vision of the global brain and collective mental map models call for attention from researchers from computer science discipline due to the presence of viable options for experimentation. How to model and quantify CI is still an open question.

In order to address these research challenges, integration of research efforts from multiple disciplines would be required.

CONCLUSION

This chapter provides a comprehensive overview of the various methods which exist for different Web-based systems that utilize social contextual information along with computational techniques to explore the tacit power of collective intelligence. The methodological perspective in the amalgamated domain of collective intelligence and social computing still suffers a lot of computational challenges due to the nature of big data. We discussed the concept of social computing and various manifestations of CI. We also focused on recent research issues in CI that are gaining traction amongst the researchers affiliated to multiple disciplines and have discussed these issues which have most relevance to social and business impact. We conclude this chapter by highlighting some future research directions.

REFERENCES

Adomavicius, G., & Tuzhilin, A. (2005). Toward the Next Generation of Recommender Systems: A Survey of the State-of-the-Art and Possible Extensions. *IEEE Transactions on Knowledge and Data Engineering, 17*(6), 734–749. doi:10.1109/TKDE.2005.99

Agarwal, N., & Xu, X. (2011). Social Computational Systems. *Journal of Computational Science, 2*(3), 189–192. doi:10.1016/j.jocs.2011.07.006

Anagnostopoulos, A., Becchetti, L., Castillo, C., Gionis, A., & Leonardi, S. (2010). Power in unity: forming teams in large-scale community systems. *Proceedings of the 19th ACM international conference on information and knowledge management, CIKM '10*, 599-608. 10.1145/1871437.1871515

Anagnostopoulos, A., Becchetti, L., Castillo, C., Gionis, A., & Leonardi, S. (2012). Online team formation in social networks. *Proceedings of the 21st international conference on world wide web, WWW '12*, 839-848. 10.1145/2187836.2187950

Awal, G. K., & Bharadwaj, K. K. (2014). Team formation in social networks based on collective intelligence - an evolutionary approach. *Applied Intelligence, 41*(2), 627–648. doi:10.100710489-014-0528-y

Awal, G. K., & Bharadwaj, K. K. (2016). Constrained Team Formation using Risk Estimation based on Reputation and Knowledge. In *Proceedings of the 1st International Conference on Advanced Computing and Intelligent Engineering (ICACIE 2016)*. Springer.

Awal, G. K., & Bharadwaj, K. K. (2017a). Leveraging collective intelligence for behavioral prediction in signed social networks through evolutionary approach. *Information Systems Frontiers*, 1–23.

Awal, G. K., & Bharadwaj, K. K. (2017b). Mining Set of Influencers in Signed Social Networks with Maximal Collective Influential Power: A Genetic Algorithm Approach. In *Proceedings of the 2nd International Conference on Information and Communication Technology for Intelligent Systems (ICTIS 2017)*. Springer.

Bernstein, M. S., Brandt, J., Miller, R. C., & Karger, D. R. (2011). Crowds in two seconds: enabling realtime crowd-powered interfaces. *Proceedings of the 24th annual ACM symposium on User interface software and technology*. 10.1145/2047196.2047201

Bernstein, M. S., Little, G., Miller, R. C., Hartmann, B., Ackerman, M. S., Karger, D. R., ... Panovich, K. (2010). Soylent: a word processor with a crowd inside. *Proceedings of the 23nd annual ACM symposium on User interface software and technology*. 10.1145/1866029.1866078

Bonchi, F., Castillo, C., Gionis, A., & Jaimes, A. (2011). Social network analysis and mining for business applications. *ACM Transactions on Intelligent Systems and Technology, 2*(3), 1–37. doi:10.1145/1961189.1961194

Cartwright, D., & Harary, F. (1956). Structural balance: A generalization of Heider's theory. *Psychological Review, 63*(5), 277–292. doi:10.1037/h0046049 PMID:13359597

Davis, J. A. (1967). Clustering and structural balance in graphs. *Human Relations, 20*(2), 181–187. doi:10.1177/001872676702000206

Domingos, P., & Richardson, M. (2001). Mining the network value of customers. *Proceedings of the seventh ACM SIGKDD International Conference on Knowledge Discovery and Data Mining*, 57-66. 10.1145/502512.502525

Doreian, P., & Mrvar, A. (1996). A partitioning approach to structural balance. *Social Networks, 18*(2), 149–168. doi:10.1016/0378-8733(95)00259-6

Doreian, P., & Mrvar, A. (2009). Partitioning signed social networks. *Social Networks, 31*(1), 1–11. doi:10.1016/j.socnet.2008.08.001

Ertekin, S., Hirsh, H., & Rudin, C. (2012). Learning to Predict the Wisdom of Crowds. *Proceedings of the Collective Intelligence (CI '12).*

Heider, F. (1946). Attitudes and cognitive organization. *The Journal of Psychology, 21*(1), 107–112. doi:10.1080/00223980.1946.9917275 PMID:21010780

Hui, J. S., Greenberg, M. D., & Gerber, E. M. (2014). Understanding the role of community in crowdfunding work. *Proceedings of the 17th ACM conference on Computer supported cooperative work & social computing.* 10.1145/2531602.2531715

Jin, L., Chen, Y., Wang, T., Hui, P., & Vasilakos, A. V. (2013). Understanding user behavior in online social networks: A survey. *IEEE Communications Magazine, 51*(9), 144–150. doi:10.1109/MCOM.2013.6588663

Karydis, I., Sioutas, S., Avlonitis, M., Mylonas, P., & Kanavos, A. (2017). A Survey on Big Data and Collective Intelligence. In T. Sellis & K. Oikonomou (Eds.), Lecture Notes in Computer Science: Vol. 10230. *Algorithmic Aspects of Cloud Computing, ALGOCLOUD 2016.* Cham: Springer. doi:10.1007/978-3-319-57045-7_11

Kempe, D., Keinberg, J., & Tardos, E. (2003). Maximizing the spread of influence through a social network. *Proceedings of the Ninth ACM SIGKDD International Conference on Knowledge Discovery and Data Mining*, 137-146. 10.1145/956750.956769

Lappas, T., Liu, K., & Terzi, E. (2009). Finding a Team of Experts in Social Networks. *Proceedings of the 15th ACM SIGKDD international conference on Knowledge discovery and data mining*, 467-476. 10.1145/1557019.1557074

Lasecki, W. S., White, S. C., Murray, K. I., & Bigham, J. P. (2012). Crowd memory: Learning in the collective. *Proceedings of the Collective Intelligence (CI'12).*

Leskovec, J., Huttenlocher, D., & Kleinberg, J. (2010). Signed networks in social media. *Proceedings of the SIGCHI Conference on Human Factors in Computing Systems, (CHI '10)*, 1361-1370.

Lin, C., Cao, N., Liu, S., Papadimitriou, S., Sun, J., & Yan, X. (2009). SmallBlue: social network analysis for expertise search and collective intelligence. *Proceedings of the 25th international conference on data engineering, ICDE '09*, 1483-1486. 10.1109/ICDE.2009.140

Luca, L., Stephen, B., & Pierpaolo, D. (2009). Information Foraging Theory as a Form of Collective Intelligence for Social Search. *Proceedings of the 1st International Conference on Computational Collective Intelligence, Semantic Web, Social Networks and Multiagent Systems (ICCCI '09)*, 63-74. 10.1007/978-3-642-04441-0_5

Malone, T. W., Laubacher, R., & Dellarocas, C. (2009). *Harnessing Crowds: Mapping the Genome of Collective Intelligence*. MIT Sloan Research Paper No. 4732-09. 10.2139/ssrn.1381502

Maries, I., & Scarlat, E. (2011). Enhancing the computational collective intelligence within communities of practice using trust and reputation models. *Transactions on Computational Collective Intelligence*, *3*, 74–95.

Massa, P., & Avesani, P. (2006). Trust-aware bootstrapping of recommender systems. *Proceedings of the ECAI Workshop on Recommender Systems*, 29-33.

MIT Center for Collective Intelligence. (n.d.). Retrieved from http://cci.mit.edu/

Parameswaran, M., & Whinston, A. B. (2007). Social Computing: An Overview. *Communications of the Association for Information Systems*, *19*(37), 762–780.

Pedro, S., & Hruschka, E. (2012). Collective intelligence as a source for machine learning self-supervision. *Proceedings of the 4th international workshop on web intelligence & communities, WI&C '12*, 5-9. 10.1145/2189736.2189744

Rodriguez, M. A., Steinbock, D. J., Watkins, J. H., Gershenson, C., Bollen, J., Grey, V., & deGraf, B. (2007). Smartocracy: Social networks for collective decision making. *Proceedings of the 40th annual Hawaii international conference on system sciences, HICSS '07*. 10.1109/HICSS.2007.484

Schut, M. (2007). *Scientific Handbook for Simulation of Collective Intelligence*. Available under Creative Commons License.

Skrzynski, P., Szuba, T., & Szydło, S. (2011). Collective intelligence approach to measuring invisible hand of the market. *Proceedings of the 3rd international conference on computational collective intelligence: technologies and applications, ICCCI'11*, *2*, 435-444. 10.1007/978-3-642-23938-0_44

Surowiecki, J. (2004). *The Wisdom of the Crowds*. London: Random House.

Szuba, T., Polanski, P., Schab, P., & Wielicki, P. (2011). On Efficiency of Collective Intelligence Phenomena. *Transactions on Computational Collective Intelligence*, *3*, 50-73.

Tang, L., & Liu, H. (2009a). Scalable learning of collective behavior based on sparse social dimensions. *Proceedings of the 18th ACM conference on Information and knowledge management (CIKM '09)*, 1107-1116. 10.1145/1645953.1646094

Tang, L., & Liu, H. (2009b). Relational learning via latent social dimensions. *Proceedings of the 15th ACM SIGKDD International Conference on Knowledge Discovery and Data Mining (KDD '09)*, 817-826. 10.1145/1557019.1557109

Tang, L., & Liu, H. (2010). Toward predicting collective behavior via social dimension extraction. *IEEE Intelligent Systems, 25*(4), 19–25. doi:10.1109/MIS.2010.36

Tang, L., Wang, X., & Liu, H. (2012a). Scalable learning of collective behavior. *IEEE Transactions on Knowledge and Data Engineering, 24*(6), 1080–1091. doi:10.1109/TKDE.2011.38

Tiwari, V., & Thakur, R.S. (2015). P2MS- A Phase-Wise Pattern Management System for Pattern Warehouse. *Int. J. of Data Mining, Modeling and Management, 7*(4), 331-350.

Tiwari, V., & Thakur, R. S. (2016). Pattern Warehouse: Context Based Modeling and Quality Issues. National Academy of Sciences, India Section A: Physical Sciences, 85(3), 1-15.

Watkins, J., & Jennifer, H. (2007). Prediction Markets as an Aggregation Mechanism for Collective Intelligence. *Proceedings of 4th UCLA Lake Arrowhead Conference Human Complex Systems*, 1-10. Retrieved from: http://escholarship.org/uc/item/8mg0p0zc

Watkins, J., & Rodriguez, M. (2008). A Survey of Web-Based Collective Decision Making Systems. In Evolution of the Web in Artificial Intelligence Environments, ser. Studies in Computational Intelligence. Springer-Verlag. doi:10.1007/978-3-540-79140-9_11

Wi, H., Oh, S., Mun, J., & Jung, M. (2009). A team formation model based on knowledge and collaboration. *Expert Systems with Applications, 36*(5), 9121–9134. doi:10.1016/j.eswa.2008.12.031

Xu, K., Guo, X., Li, J., Lau, R. Y., & Liao, S. S. (2012). Discovering target groups in social networking sites: An effective method for maximizing joint influential power. *Electronic Commerce Research and Applications, 11*(4), 318–334. doi:10.1016/j.elerap.2012.01.002

Yang, Z., & Wang, J. (2015). Differential effects of social influence sources on self-reported music piracy. *Decision Support Systems, 69*, 70–81. doi:10.1016/j.dss.2014.11.007

Yuen, M.-C., King, I., & Leung, K.-S. (2011). A Survey of Crowdsourcing Systems. *Proceedings of the 3rd IEEE International Conference on Social Computing (SocialCom-11)*, 766-773.

Zheng, X., Zeng, D., & Wang, F.-Y. (2015). Social balance in signed networks. *Information Systems Frontiers, 17*(5), 1077–1095. doi:10.100710796-014-9483-8

KEY TERMS AND DEFINITIONS

Artificial Intelligence: It refers to the development of computer systems that can simulate human intelligence through the process of learning and reasoning for solving different problems.

Collective Behavior: The users' behaviors on social networks are differentially regulated and influenced by the behaviors of other users of various affiliations.

Collective Intelligence: Leveraging the synergistic aggregation/alliance of entities to achieve intelligence of higher order that no individual entity or their simple aggregation can exhibit alone.

Influence Mining: Some users influence the views and opinions of other users in the network on different products and services according to their strength of connections with them, their popularity, and reputation.

Recommender Systems: It refers to web-based social systems that provide personalized recommendations on products and services to users based on their history and their social information (network connections, interactions, etc.).

Social Computing: It deals with the study and analysis of social behavior using contextual information on or through computational systems.

Social Network: It is a social structure consisting of nodes (representing people or other entities) with dyadic ties among them which represent familiarities, interactions, influence, or similarities between them.

Team Formation: Discovering a right set of experts for a task with varying skills requires assembling a group of experts from the social network that can collaborate with each other and can accomplish a given task.

Chapter 8

Machine Learning Models for Forecasting of Individual Stocks Price Patterns

Dilip Singh Sisodia
National Institute of Technology Raipur, India

Sagar Jadhav
National Institute of Technology Raipur, India

ABSTRACT

Stock investors always consider potential future prices before investing in any stock for making a profit. A large number of studies are found on the prediction of stock market indices. However, the focus on individual stock closing price predictions well ahead of time is limited. In this chapter, a comparative study of machine-learning-based models is used for the prediction of the closing price of a particular stock. The proposed models are designed using back propagation neural networks (BPNN), support vector regression (SVR) with SMOReg, and linear regression (LR) for the prediction of the closing price of individual stocks. A total of 37 technical indicators (features) derived from historical closing prices of stocks are considered for predicting the future price of stock in a time window of five days. The experiment is performed on stocks listed on Bombay Stock Exchange (BSS), India. The model is trained and tested using feature values extracted from the past five-year closing price of stocks of different sectors including aviation, pharma, banking, entertainment, and IT.

INTRODUCTION

Forecasting a particular stock's price has always been considered as a significant area of research and might be very useful for investors and traders. Therefore, stock traders always seem concerned about future price or trend of a particular stock. Effective and accurate individual stock price prediction model plays a significant role as aid tool for traders and investors(Tüfekci, 2016). The most popular approaches used by researchers to predict the stock prices are based on fundamental analysis and technical analysis. In fundamental analysis, fundamental attributes of companies including financial results, company's as-

DOI: 10.4018/978-1-5225-3870-7.ch008

sets, liabilities, and stock and growth forecasts are considered. However, this type of analysis is volatile in nature as newly released financial information, announcements, quarterly results, and other news can influence the fundamental outlook for a company. Therefore, technical analysis does not try to dig deep into a company's business process. It assumes that the available public information does not offer a competitive trading advantage and hence does not influence much of the stock prices. Instead, it focuses on studying a company's historical share price and on identifying patterns in the chart. The primary aim is to recognize trends in advance and to capitalize on them.

In this chapter, the technical analysis is used in which different features are calculated and analyzed to find some relation between these features and the output. These features are considered to be important indicators of stock price movement, and with these features, the model will be able to predict the closing price of the stock on next day. The software used for this research automatically calculates all the 37 features adopted from (Guo, Wang, Yang, & Miller, 2015) and (Patel, Shah, Thakkar, & Kotecha, 2015) and normalizes the data (Wang, Schäfer, & Guhr, 2015) to apply as an input to different models used for prediction. The prime objective is to build a model using back propagation neural network, support vector regression and linear regression for stock price prediction (Hung, 2016).

The rest of this chapter is organized under following sections. Section 2 of this chapter discussed the related work and literature survey of interest to this chapter and which have been used in the past for the prediction or forecasting purposes. Section 3 describes the techniques which are used in the proposed model such as BPNN, SVR, and LR. Section 4 describes the overall working of the model along with the features used and the normalization technique. Section 5 shows the results generated by the proposed model. These results have been compared using various error performance measures in tabular and graphical form. Section 6 summarizes the chapter by stating the conclusion and the scope of this chapter for future research work.

BACKGROUND

Since the advent of the stock market concept, many researchers have applied various machine learning techniques to predict the stock market indices and future stock prices. Some noteworthy contributions are k-nearest neighbor (kNN) (P. C. Chang, Fan, & Liu, 2009), neural networks (NNs) (Schierholt & Dagli, 1996), genetic algorithms (GAs)(K. Kim & Han, 2000) and (Kwon & Moon, 2007), support vector machines (SVMs) (Smola & Schölkopf, 2004), least square SVM (LS-SVM) (Ou & Wang, 2009; L. Yu, Chen, Wang, & Lai, 2009), bacterial chemotaxis Optimization (BCO) (Yudong & Lenan, 2009), rough set-based pseudo outer-product (RSPOP)(Ang & Quek, 2006), and also predict the stock price from news driven models (Gusev et al., n.d.)using sentiment analysis (Trends, Chowdhury, Routh, & Chakrabarti, 2014) and other text mining methods(Mittermayer, 2004). Hybrid techniques like independent component analysis (Lu, 2010) with neural networks, genetic complementary learning (GCL) fuzzy neural network (Tan, Quek, & Ng, 2004) and self-organizing map (SOM) with Fuzzy SVM (f-SVM) (Nguyen & Le, 2014) have also been used for prediction. In (K. Kim & Han, 2000), genetic algorithms (GA) and in (Y. M. Kim et al., 2015) nonparametric model along with artificial neural networks (ANN) have used to predict the Korean stock exchange on a daily basis. In (Afolabi & Olude, 2007) the daily stock prices have predicted by using three different approaches such as back propagation, Kohonen SOM, and a hybrid Kohonen SOM and have proved that hybrid Kohonen is better of the other two.

In (L. Q. Yu & Rong, 2010), Titan Oil's stock price have predicted with the use of back propagation neural networks (BPNN) and pattern matching. In (Wuthrich et al., 1998), the stock indices of five different countries using the news data available over the Internet have predicted. The news is collected every day, and then it is provided as an input to the proposed model which searches the news for keywords or tuples and assigns weight to every news accordingly. In (Shatnawi, 2013) the closing price of randomly selected companies from Jordanian stock exchange using k-nearest neighbor classifier (kNN) have predicted. In (Hegazy, Soliman, & Salam, 2013) the daily closing price of 13 stocks from S&P 500, USA have predicted. In (Li, Huang, Deng, & Zhu, 2014), the Hong Kong stock market has predicted by integrating the market news and stock market tick price using multiple kernel support vector regression (MVSVR). In (X. Zhang et al., 2014), the Shanghai stock exchange of China used a casual feature selection (CFS) algorithm to enhance the current prediction models in predicting the stock market. In (Guo et al., 2015) the Shanghai Stock market Index have predicted using radial basis function neural network (RBFNN) along with two-directional two-dimensional principal component analysis (PCA). The closing price of the market for the next day is predicted. The features and the historical data are stored in the form of matrix hence, the accuracy of prediction has been increased. The closing prices of Indian Stock Indices namely S&P Bombay Stock Exchange (BSE) and CNX Nifty have predicted in (Patel et al., 2015).

The reviewed literature shows that most of the articles have focused on stock indices while very few have focused on individual stocks price prediction. In this chapter, different machine learning models are used to predict the individual stock prices, and comparative analysis is performed to find the best method for more accurate prediction of the closing price of any individual stock.

DESCRIPTION OF MODELS

Back Propagation Neural Networks (BPNN)

Back propagation neural network is a supervised class of artificial neural networks (ANN) in which a large number of simple processing units known as neurons are interconnected by feed forward connections (Yoon & Swales, 1991). As compared to other machine learning techniques BPNN is superior in prediction (D. Zhang & Zhou, 2004). The learning process of BPNN is divided into two phases (L. Q. Yu & Rong, 2010). In the first phase, it performs the task of forwarding propagation of information, and in second phase backward propagation of errors is done. As shown in Figure 1, BPNN has three layers as input, hidden and output layers. By the input provided, the hidden layers calculate the output. If the desired output is not found then the weights of hidden layers are updated by backpropagation and the output is predicted again with this updated step, these steps are repeated till the desired output is found.

A precise description of the algorithm is as follows:

1. Forward Propagation
    a. **Output of the Node in Input Layer:** X_j
    b. **Output of the Node in the Hidden Layer:** $Y_i = f\left(\sum W_{ij} X_j + \theta_i\right)$ Where, W_{ij} is the connection weight between input layer and hidden layer, and θ_i is the neural threshold of hidden layer.

Figure 1. Basic Structure of BPNN

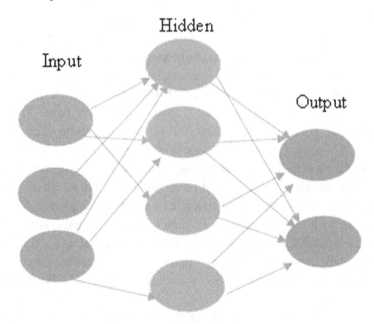

c. **Output of the Node in Output Layer:** $O_i = f\left(\sum T_{li}Y_i + \gamma_l\right)$ Where, T_{li} is the connection weight between hidden layers and the output layer, and γ_l is the neural threshold of output layer.

2. Backward propagation

Modify neural weights along the negative gradient direction of error function to enable the network convergence. The error contributed by the output unit is given by Eq.(1):

$$\partial_{li} = \left[O_i'(t) - O_i(t)\right]\left\{O_i(t)\left[1 - O_i(t)\right]\right\} \tag{1}$$

The error contributed by the hidden unit is given by Eq.(2):

$$\partial_{ij} = Y_i(t)\left[1 - Y_i(t)\right]\left(\sum \partial_i T_{li}\right) \tag{2}$$

Then modify the connection weights between output layer and hidden layer by the Eq.(3):

$$T_{li}(t+1) = T_{li}(t) + \mu \partial_{li} Y_i(t) \tag{3}$$

And modify the connection weights between the hidden layer and input layer by the Eq.(4):

$$W_{ij}(t+1) = W_{ij}(t) + \mu \partial_{ij} X_j(t) \tag{4}$$

$O_l^{'}\left(t\right)$ is the desired output, $O_l\left(t\right)$ is the actual output of the neural networks, μ is step size whose value is related to the speed of the learning rate. $T_{li}\left(t+1\right)$, $W_{ij}\left(t+1\right)$ are both correction value of the weight currently $T_{li}\left(t\right)$ and $W_{ij}\left(t\right)$ are both correction values of last learning cycle.

Support Vector Machines

Support vector machines(SVMs) are a class of algorithms characterized by the kernels usage, absence of local minima, the sparseness in the solution and capacity controls obtained by acting on the margin, or on some support vectors, etc. (Sahasrabudhe & Borse, 2013). In other words, if we have a given training data (supervised learning), the algorithm provides an output which is an optimal hyperplane which categorizes new examples. In Figure 2(a) (Yoon & Swales, 1991), it can be observed that there exist multiple hyperplanes which separate the two sets of inputs. But SVM finds the most optimal hyperplane to separate those inputs as shown in Figure 2(b).

Support Vector Regression With SMO

The SVR uses the same principles as SVM for classification, with only a few differences (Smola & Schölkopf, 2004)(Scholkopf Bernhard & Smola, 2001). In regression, a margin of tolerance, usually denoted by Epsilon, is set in approximation to the SVM, as shown in Figure 3. The main idea of the algorithm is always the same which is to minimize the error and to individualize the hyperplane which maximizes the margin by considering that part of the error is tolerated. The functions of kernel transform the data into a higher dimensional feature space which makes it possible to perform the linear separation.

As stated in (Patel et al., 2015) and (Parrella, 2007) assume that $x_i \in R_d, i = 1,2\dots\dots m$ forms a set of input vectors with corresponding response variable $y_i \in R_d, i = 1,2\dots\dots m$. SVR builds the linear regression function as shown in Eq. (5) and Eq. (6) shows Vapnik's linear -Insensitivity loss function.

$$f\left(x,w\right) = w^T x + b \tag{5}$$

Figure 2. Working of Support Vector Machines

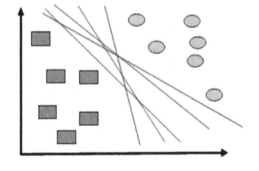

(a) SVM with multiple hyperplanes

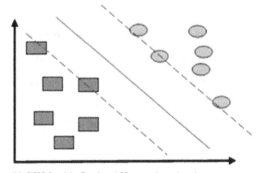

(b) SVM with Optimal Hyperplane having maximum margin from the two different sets.

Figure 3. Hyperplanes with Margin of Tolerance in SVR

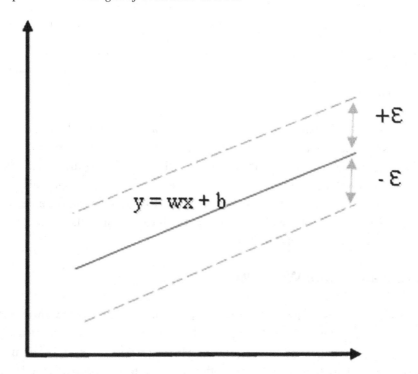

$$|y - f(x, w)| = \begin{cases} 0, if \left| y - f(x, w) \right| \leq \varepsilon \\ \left| y - f(x_i, w) \right| - \varepsilon, otherwise \end{cases} \tag{6}$$

Based on this, linear regression $f(x, w)$ is estimated by simultaneously minimizing $\|w\|^2$ and the sum of the linear e-Insensitivity losses. The constant c controls a trade-off between an approximation error and the weight vector norm ‖w‖ given by Eq.(7).

$$R = \frac{1}{2}\|w\|^2 + c\left(\sum_{i=1}^{m}\left|y - f(x_i, w)\right|\right) \tag{7}$$

Minimizing the risk R is equivalent to minimizing the risk under the constraints illustrated. Here, E_i and $\bar{E}_i$ are slack variables, one for exceeding the target value by more than ε and other for being more than ε below the target given by Eqs.(8),(9) and (10).

$$R = \frac{1}{2}\|w\|^2 + c\left(\sum_{i=1}^{m}\left|E + \bar{E}\right|\right) \tag{8}$$

$$(w^T x_i + b) - y_i \leq \varepsilon + \mathrm{E}_i \qquad (9)$$

$$y_i - (w^T x_i + b) \leq \varepsilon + \bar{E}_i \qquad (10)$$

With the following satisfying condition: E_i, $\bar{E}_i \geq 0$, i = 1,2 ......m

Recently, an iterative algorithm, called sequential minimal optimization (SMO) is proposed, for solving the problem of regression using support vector machine. SMO has a great computational speed and is easy to implement (Shevade, Keerthi, Bhattacharyya, & Murthy, 2000) (Cook, 1977). Only SMO can become inefficient due to the way it does the computation and maintains a single threshold value. SMO with SVM breaks the problem down into 2-dimensional subproblems which are solved analytically, thus, eliminating the need for a numerical optimization algorithm and matrix storage. Therefore, we have used SVM with SMO for experimentation purpose.

Linear Regression (LR)

Linear Regression is very useful when there exist many factors or features and helps in determining the impact of all these features on a single output. Linear Regression determines a kind of relationship between one dependent variable and independent variables or explanatory variables (Cook, 1977) as shown in Eq. (11).

$$Y = \beta_0 + \beta_1 X \qquad (11)$$

LR uses a linear relationship between a value X, and Y wherein Y is the output predicted using a given value X. In Figure 4 it can be observed that a linear relationship is established between X and Y

Figure 4. Linear Regression Prediction Errors

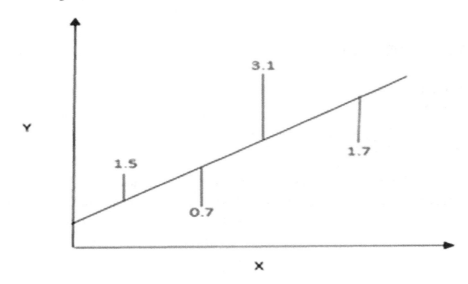

through a straight line. The red vertical lines represent the errors produced in the prediction of Y on the actual values of X.

Description of Methodology and Data

Figure 5 shows the working flow of methodology adopted in this work. Initially, a user selects the company/ stock from BSE. As soon as the company is selected, the model/software crawls on the internet and downloads the historical data for that stock. The data downloaded from the sources including Yahoo Finance and BSE India usually has some inconsistent data wherein some cell values are empty or have zero entries, or some even have historical data when the stock market was closed, i.e., on public holidays. These data may cause hindrance in the calculation of the features. Therefore, the software corrects all such inconsistencies and calculates the 51 features from the corrected data downloaded from the sources. A total 37 features are selected manually for experimentation as shown in Table 1.

Table 1 describes the mathematical formulae's used to calculate the features which have been used as an input to the model. These features have been computed from the raw data of stocks like open, close, high, low price, volume ("StockCharts: Simply the Web's Best Financial Charts," n.d.). The extracted feature values are normalized and stored in a file in CSV format. This file is provided as the input to the Models, and the output is predicted using BPNN, SVR with SMO, Linear Regression, on the basis of the 37 features values provided as the input. We have used Min-Max Normalization as it performs a linear transformation on the dataset. The experimentation has been done on the dataset in the range of [0, 1]. The conversion formula used for converting the input variables in the specified range is defined in Eq. (12).

$$z_i = \frac{x_i - \min\left(x_i\right)}{\max\left(x_i\right) - \min\left(x_i\right)} \qquad (12)$$

where, x_i = Element to be normalized ; Min(x_i) = minimum value of x_i where i=1,2……n

Max(x_i) = maximum value of x_i where i=1,2……n ; z_i = Normalized value of x_i

PERFORMANCE MEASURES

The following errors measures are calculated for testing the prediction performance of each model for every individual stock.

Mean Absolute Error (MAE)

The MAE(Eq. (13)) is the average over the verification sample of the absolute values of the differences between forecast and the corresponding observation. The MAE is a linear score which means that all the individual differences are weighted equally in the average.

Figure 5. Working of Adopted methodology

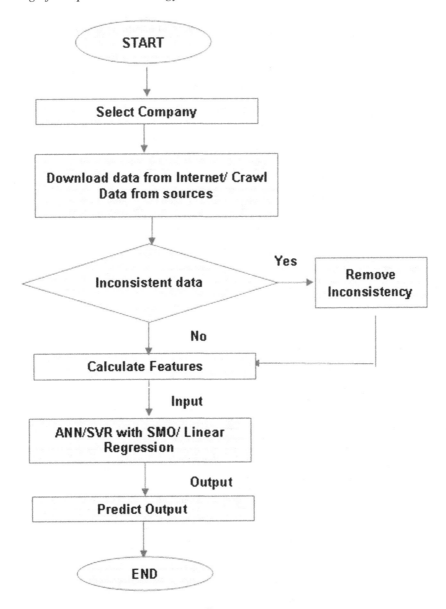

$$MAE = (\sum_{i=1}^{n} | p_i - a_i |) / n \tag{13}$$

Mean Absolute Percent Error (MAPE)

The MAPE (Eq.(14)) is the measures the size of the error in percentage terms. It is calculated as the average of the unsigned percentage error.

Table 1. Brief mathematical description of used features

Feature Name	Formula used for feature computation
Typical price	(High + Low + Close)/3
Raw Money Flow	Typical Price x Volume
Money Flow Ratio	(14-period Positive Money Flow)/(14-period Negative Money Flow)
Money Flow Index	100 - 100/(1 + Money Flow Ratio)
EMA	{Close - EMA(previous day)} x multiplier + EMA(previous day) Multiplier = (2 / (Time periods + 1)) = (2 / (10 + 1))
%K	(Current Close - Lowest Low)/(Highest High - Lowest Low) * 100
%D	3-day SMA of %K
William %R	(Highest High - Close)/(Highest High - Lowest Low) * -100
RSI	100 – (100 / (1+RS))
RS	Average Gain / Average Loss
Change	Current Close – Previous Close
Average Gain	Average of previous 14 days Gain
Average Loss	Average of previous 14 days Loss
Highest High	Maximum High Price from past 14 days
Lowest Low	Lowest Low Price from past 14 days
MACD Line	(12-day EMA - 26-day EMA)
Signal Line	9-day EMA of MACD Line
Money Flow Multiplier	[(Close - Low) - (High - Close)] /(High - Low)
Money Flow Volume	Money Flow Multiplier x Volume for the Period
ADL	Previous ADL + Current Period's Money Flow Volume
Deviation	Current 10 day SMA – Current Close price
Middle Band	20-day simple moving average (SMA)
Upper Band	20-day SMA + (20-day standard deviation of price x 2)
Lower Band	20-day SMA - (20-day standard deviation of price x 2)
Bollinger Bandwidth	((Upper Band - Lower Band) / Middle Band) * 100
Buying Pressure	Close – Minimum (Low or Prior Close).
True Range	Maximum(High or Prior Close) - Minimum(Low or Prior Close)
Average-N	(N-period BP Sum) / (N-period TR Sum)
Ultimate Oscillator	100 x [(4 x Average7)+(2 x Average14)+Average28]/(4+2+1)
Percent Drawdown	((Close - 14-period Max Close)/14-period Max Close) x 100
Squared Average (SA)	(14-perod Sum of Percent-Drawdown Squared)/14
Ulcer Index	
PPO	{(12-day EMA - 26-day EMA)/26-day EMA} x 100
Distance Moved	((H + L)/2 - (Prior H + Prior L)/2)
Box Ratio	((V/100,000,000)/(H - L))
1 period EMV	((H + L)/2 - (Prior H + Prior L)/2) / ((V/100,000,000)/(H - L))
Ease of Movement	14-Period simple moving average of 1-period EMV

$$\text{MAPE} = \frac{1}{n} * \frac{\sum_{i=1}^{n} |p_i - a_i|}{|a_i|} * 100 \tag{14}$$

Root Mean Squared Error (RMSE)

The RMSE (Eq. (15)) is the difference between forecast and corresponding observed values are each squared and then averaged over the sample. Finally, the square root of the average is taken. Since the errors are squared before they are averaged, the RMSE gives a relatively high weight to large errors.

$$\text{RMSE} = \sqrt{(\sum_{i=1}^{n} |p_i - a_i|^2)/n} \tag{15}$$

p_i is the predicted value *for i=1,2,3.........n and* a_i is the actual value. *i=1,2,3.........n*

Time Window

The time window used for this model for predicting one day ahead of time is 20 days. This model uses a sliding window protocol wherein for predicting two days ahead of time, the model initially predicts one day ahead of time and then includes this value in the time window and again predicts one day ahead of time which results in the prediction of 2 days ahead of time. This value is again included in the time window and the forecast for three days ahead of time is done. Similarly, the prediction is made for four days and five days ahead of time (Y. Kim & Sohn, 2012).

EXPERIMENT RESULTS AND DISCUSSION

The dataset of SPICEJET and PVR and other stocks as shown in Table 5 are retrieved from the official website of BSE India. The dataset are normalized for generating an optimized learning pattern, especially for back propagation neural network. The experimentation is performed on the normalized data set with the calculated features. Various tools are used for experimentation and results reporting purposes. The experimentation is carried out with the use of WEKA library (Frank, Mark A. Hall, & Witten, 2016; Hall et al., 2009) implemented in Java. The LIBSVM library(C.-C. Chang & Lin, 2011) is used for experimenting with SVR. Plotly (Plotly, 2015) tool is used for plotting of graphs. PHPExcel Library (GitHub, 2013) is used to work with the calculation of features in Excel file. This library helps to retrieve the data from the excel file and calculate the features and write it back to the excel file itself. This PHPExcel Library has been integrated with Web application developed for this project.

Extensive experiments are performed with all selected stock scripts, and three error measures are used such as MAE, MAPE, RMSE for comparison (Hassan & Nath, 2005),(Roman & Jameel, 1996). But due to space constraint we are discussing the results of two stocks in detail, i.e., PVR and SPICEJET which has a total of 414 instances for comparison. The Table 2, 3 and 4 show the error measures for forecasting of PVR and SPICEJET stocks. The error measures are calculated for BPNN, SVR with SMO and Linear Regression (LR) from 1 to 5 days ahead. MAE has been used as the main error measure for analyzing the results as MAE has a better resemblance to absolute error. It can be observed from these tables that BPNN has the least error rates for both PVR and SPICEJET which signify that BPNN gives the most optimal results and accuracy among the other two. The graphical representations of Mean Absolute Error (MAE) for PVR and SPICEJET stocks are shown in Figure 6 and Figure 7. It can be seen from these graphs that BPNN has the least error rate among SVR with SMO and Linear Regression. It can also be inferred that the error rate remains almost constant for all the three techniques as the days ahead to be forecasted are increased. This is the uniqueness of this model wherein even on increasing the number of days to be forecasted ahead, the accuracy of this model is not altered drastically.

Figure 8 shows the prediction performance of BPNN for five days ahead of time for PVR stock. The graph shows the comparison of Actual values with the predicted values. It can be seen that the predicted values by BPNN are almost equal to the actual values, and hence, this justifies the significance of this model. A similar comparison can be seen in Figure 9 which is plotted for SPICEJET stock.

Table 2. Comparison of MAE for PVR and SPICEJET stocks

Mean Absolute Error (MAE)					
Days Ahead	1 Day	2 Days	3 Days	4 Days	5 Days
PVR					
BPNN	18.8093	18.8398	18.8702	18.8918	18.8848
SVR with SMO	24.0918	24.0595	24.0313	23.9961	23.9372
LR	24.2433	24.1857	24.1311	24.0674	23.9823
SPICEJET					
BPNN	1.8089	1.8067	1.8053	1.8052	1.8059
SVR with SMO	1.9104	1.9133	1.9168	1.9213	1.9256
LR	2.0152	2.0173	2.0203	2.0244	2.0293

Table 3. Comparison of MAPE for PVR and SPICEJET stocks

Mean Absolute Percentage Error (MAPE)					
Days Ahead	1 Day	2 Days	3 Days	4 Days	5 Days
PVR					
BPNN	2.795	2.7986	2.8022	2.8038	2.7993
SVR with SMO	3.5723	3.5621	3.5528	3.5419	3.5253
LR	3.6183	3.603	3.5882	3.5714	3.5493
SPICEJET					
BPNN	8.8205	8.7938	8.7734	8.763	8.7586
SVR with SMO	8.598	8.6059	8.6184	8.6382	8.6558
LR	9.2614	9.2637	9.2721	9.2888	9.311

Table 4. Comparison of RMSE for PVR and SPICEJET stocks

Root Mean Squared Error (RMSE)					
Days Ahead	1 Day	2 Days	3 Days	4 Days	5 Days
PVR					
BPNN	23.8755	23.9029	23.9304	23.9547	23.9601
SVR with SMO	31.4274	31.412	31.4015	31.3828	31.3319
LR	30.8324	30.78	30.7323	30.6703	30.5709
SPICEJET					
BPNN	2.3898	2.389	2.3891	2.3903	2.392
SVR with SMO	3.0196	3.0231	3.0268	3.0305	3.0343
LR	2.939	2.9421	2.9454	2.949	2.9527

Figure 6. MAE plot for PVR stock

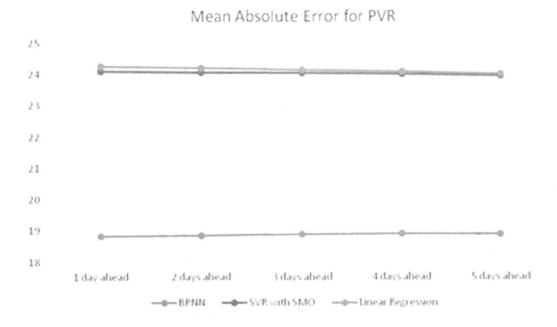

Table 5 indicates the MAE for various stocks from different sectors whose prediction was done using BPNN for one day ahead. The dataset used for these stocks has been retrieved from BSE India from 11/03/14 to 23/11/15 excluding the days when the Market was closed. Due to space constraints, the graphical representations and error measures of these stocks have been excluded from this chapter.

CONCLUSION

This chapter presented a comparative study of machine learning- models based on back propagation neural networks (BPNN), support vector regression (SVR) with SMOReg and linear regression (LR) for

Figure 7. MAE plot for SPICEJET stock

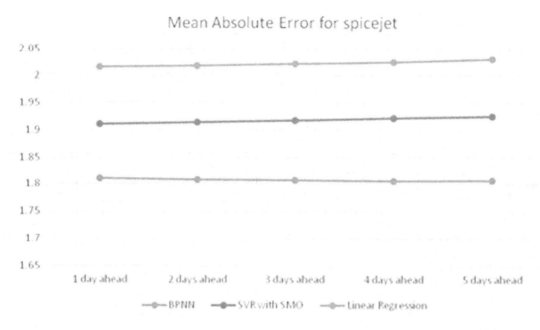

Figure 8. Actual value(red) vs. Predicted value(blue) for PVR 5 day ahead of time using BPNN

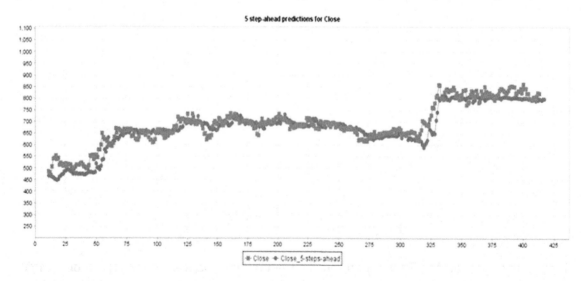

the prediction of the closing price of individual stocks. The performance of prediction model is compared using different error measures. The results suggest that BPNN produces less error rate as compared to SVR with SMO and Linear Regression. However, the dataset is concerned BPNN works better than SVR when the dataset is not high enough. If the dataset is very large, then SVR starts to dominate BPNN and gives a better accuracy of prediction. Another significant result shows that the number of days for prediction is increased; the accuracy of the model remains almost constant, which justify the uniqueness of this model. The results also suggest that the error rate for stocks with low price is much less than

Figure 9. Actual value(red) vs. Predicted value(blue) for SPICEJET 5 day ahead of time using BPNN

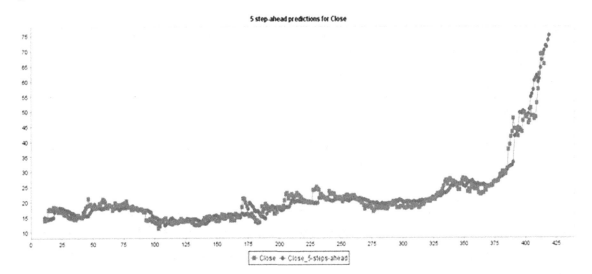

Table 5. MAE error measure for different stocks

STOCK	BPNN	SVR with SMO	LR
SBI	45.04	48.52	58.25
AJANTA PHARMA	57.31	62.35	103.67
WIPRO	32.12	44.32	48.31
INFOSYS	51.95	67.18	74.21
Glenmark	18.98	20.33	21.72
Strides Acrolab	12.85	15.21	19.85
SREI Infra	7.33	8.69	10.32
Delta Corp	34.78	39.57	45.25
Bank of India	8.22	10.28	12.27
Adani Power	11.57	15.67	17.98
Idea Cellular	5.44	8.59	11.78

stocks with high prices. So this model has a dynamic accuracy with an excellent prediction capability with small or medium price stocks. Therefore, the proposed model may be used as a prediction model by investors and traders for investing in a particular stock or for predicting the stop loss price of a particular stock of different sectors.

The results from this chapter suggest that stock prices can be predicted accurately only up to some extent. The accuracy of prediction can be improved by taking into account various other factors like the effect of Stock Exchange on a particular stock, and also, the news published about a particular company stock can be integrated into this chapter. The error measures can be kept minimum with increasing number of days, by using an empirically decided optimized time window.

REFERENCES

Afolabi, M. O., & Olude, O. (2007). predicting stock prices using a hybrid kohonen SOM. *Proceedings of the 40th Hawaii International Conference on System Sciences*, 1–8.

Ang, K. K., & Quek, C. (2006). Stock trading using RSPOP: A novel rough set-based neuro-fuzzy approach. *IEEE Transactions on Neural Networks*, *17*(5), 1301–1315. doi:10.1109/TNN.2006.875996 PMID:17001989

Chang, C.-C., & Lin, C.-J. (2011). LIBSVM : A library for support vector machines. *ACM Transactions on Intelligent Systems and Technology*, *2*(3), 1–27. doi:10.1145/1961189.1961199

Chang, P. C., Fan, C. Y., & Liu, C. H. (2009). Integrating a Piecewise Linear Representation Method and a Neural Network Model for Stock Trading Points Prediction. *IEEE Transactions on Systems, Man and Cybernetics. Part C, Applications and Reviews*, *39*(1), 80–92. doi:10.1109/TSMCC.2008.2007255

Cook, R. D. (1977). Detection of Influential Observation in Linear Regression. *Technometrics*, *19*(1), 15–18.

Frank, E., Mark, A., Hall, I., & Witten, H. (2016). The WEKA Workbench. Online Appendix for "Data Mining: Practical Machine Learning Tools and Techniques (Weka ML Tool). Morgan Kaufmann.

GitHub. (2013). *PHPEXCEL - Parsing excel files in PHP*. Retrieved November 20, 2015, from https://github.com/PHPOffice/PHPExcel

Guo, Z., Wang, H., Yang, J., & Miller, D. J. (2015). A stock market forecasting model combining two-directional two-dimensional principal component analysis and radial basis function neural network. *PLoS One*, *10*(4), 1–19. doi:10.1371/journal.pone.0122385 PMID:25849483

Gusev, M., Kroujiline, D., Govorkov, B., Sharov, S. V., Ushanov, D., & Zhilyaev, M. (n.d.). *Sell the news? A news - driven model of the stock market Sell the news? A news driven model of the stock market*. arXiv:1404.7364

Hall, M., Frank, E., Holmes, G., Pfahringer, B., Reutemann, P., & Witten, I. H. (2009). The WEKA data mining software. *ACM SIGKDD Explorations Newsletter*, *11*(1), 10. doi:10.1145/1656274.1656278

Hassan, M. R., & Nath, B. (2005). Stock market forecasting using hidden Markov model: a new approach. *Proceedings of 5th International Conference on Intelligent Systems Design and Applications (ISDA'05)*, 192–196. 10.1109/ISDA.2005.85

Hegazy, O., Soliman, O. S., & Salam, M. A. (2013). A Machine Learning Model for Stock Market. *International Journal of Computer Science and Telecommunications*, *4*(12), 17–23.

Hung, J.-C. (2016). Fuzzy support vector regression model for forecasting stock market volatility. *Journal of Intelligent & Fuzzy Systems*, *31*(3), 1987–2000. doi:10.3233/JIFS-16209

Kim, K., & Han, I. (2000). Genetic algorithms approach to feature discretization in artificial neural networks for the prediction of stock price index. *Expert Systems with Applications*, *19*(2), 125–132. doi:10.1016/S0957-4174(00)00027-0

Kim, Y., & Sohn, S. Y. (2012). Stock fraud detection using peer group analysis. *Expert Systems with Applications, 39*(10), 8986–8992. doi:10.1016/j.eswa.2012.02.025

Kim, Y. M., Han, S. K., Kim, T. Y., Oh, K. J., Luo, Z., & Kim, C. (2015). Intelligent stock market instability index: Application to the Korean stock market. *Intelligent Data Analysis, 19*(4), 879–895. doi:10.3233/IDA-150749

Kwon, Y. K., & Moon, B. R. (2007). A hybrid neurogenetic approach for stock forecasting. *IEEE Transactions on Neural Networks, 18*(3), 851–864. doi:10.1109/TNN.2007.891629 PMID:17526350

Li, X., Huang, X., Deng, X., & Zhu, S. (2014). Enhancing quantitative intra-day stock return prediction by integrating both market news and stock prices information. *Neurocomputing, 142*, 228–238. doi:10.1016/j.neucom.2014.04.043

Lu, C. J. (2010). Integrating independent component analysis-based denoising scheme with neural network for stock price prediction. *Expert Systems with Applications, 37*(10), 7056–7064. doi:10.1016/j.eswa.2010.03.012

Mittermayer, M.-a. (2004). Forecasting Intraday stock price trends with text mining techniques. *Proceedings of the 37th Annual Hawaii International Conference on System Sciences*, 1–10. 10.1109/HICSS.2004.1265201

Nguyen, D., & Le, M. (2014). A two-stage architecture for stock price forecasting by combining SOM and fuzzy-SVM. *International Journal of Computer Science and Information Security, 12*(8), 1–6.

Ou, P., & Wang, H. (2009). Prediction of Stock Market Index Movement by Ten Data Mining Techniques. *Modern Applied Science, 3*(12), 28. doi:10.5539/mas.v3n12p28

Parrella, F. (2007). *Online support vector regression* (Master's Thesis). Department of Information Science, University of Genoa, Italy.

Patel, J., Shah, S., Thakkar, P., & Kotecha, K. (2015). Predicting stock market index using fusion of machine learning techniques. *Expert Systems with Applications, 42*(4), 2162–2172. doi:10.1016/j.eswa.2014.10.031

Plotly. (2015). *Plot.ly - Online Graph Plotting Tool.* Retrieved November 20, 2015, from Plot.ly

Roman, J., & Jameel, A. (1996). Backpropagation and recurrent neural networks in financial analysis of multiple stock market returns. *System Sciences, 1996., Proceedings of the Twenty-Ninth Hawaii International Conference on, 2*, 454–460.

Sahasrabudhe, R., & Borse, P. M. (2013). Classification of Brain Encephalic Tissues From Mri Images Using Sphere Shaped Support Vector. *International Journal of Scientific & Engineering Research, 4*(7), 2343–2349.

Schierholt, K., & Dagli, C. H. (1996). Stock market prediction using different neural network classification architectures. *IEEE/IAFE Conference on Computational Intelligence for Financial Engineering*, 72–78. 10.1109/CIFER.1996.501826

Scholkopf, B., & Smola, A. J. (2001). *Learning with kernels: support vector machines, regularization, optimization, and beyond.* MIT Press. 10.1017/CBO9781107415324.004

Shatnawi, M. K. A. (2013). Stock Price Prediction Using K -Nearest Neighbor (k NN) Algorithm. *International Journal of Business Human Technology, 3*(3), 32–44.

Shevade, S. K., Keerthi, S. S., Bhattacharyya, C., & Murthy, K. R. K. (2000). Improvements to the SMO algorithm for SVM regression. *IEEE Transactions on Neural Networks, 11*(5), 1188–1193. doi:10.1109/72.870050 PMID:18249845

Smola, A., & Schölkopf, B. (2004). A tutorial on support vector regression. *Statistics and Computing, 14*(3), 199–222. doi:10.1023/B:STCO.0000035301.49549.88

StockCharts: Simply the Web's Best Financial Charts. (n.d.). Retrieved November 21, 2015, from http://stockcharts.com/

Tan, T. Z., Quek, C., & Ng, G. S. (2004). Brain-inspired Genetic Complementary Learning for Stock Market Prediction.pdf. *IEEE Congress on Evolutionary Computation*, 2653–2660.

Trends, S. P., Chowdhury, S. G., Routh, S., & Chakrabarti, S. (2014). News Analytics and Sentiment Analysis to Predict. *International Journal of Computer Science and Information Technologies, 5*(3), 3595–3604.

Tüfekci, P. (2016). Classification-based prediction models for stock price index movement. *Intelligent Data Analysis, 20*(2), 357–376. doi:10.3233/IDA-160809

Wang, S., Schäfer, R., & Guhr, T. (2015). *Price response in correlated financial markets: empirical results.* arXiv Preprint arXiv:1510.03205

Wuthrich, B., Cho, V., Leung, S., Permunetilleke, D., Sankaran, K., & Zhang, J. (1998). Daily stock market forecast from textual web data. *Proceedings of IEEE International Conference on Systems, Man, and Cybernetics (SMC'98), 3*, 1–6. 10.1109/ICSMC.1998.725072

Yoon, Y., & Swales, G. S. (1991). Predicting stock price performance: a neural network approach. *Proceedings of the Twenty-Fourth Annual Hawaii International Conference on System Sciences*, 156–162. 10.1109/HICSS.1991.184055

Yu, L., Chen, H., Wang, S., & Lai, K. K. (2009). Evolving Least Squares Support Vector Machines for Stock Market Trend Mining. *IEEE Transactions on Evolutionary Computation, 13*(1), 87–102. doi:10.1109/TEVC.2008.928176

Yu, L. Q., & Rong, F. S. (2010). Stock Market Forecasting Research Based on Neural Network and Pattern Matching. *International Conference on E-Business and E-Government*, 1940–1943. 10.1109/ICEE.2010.490

Yudong, Z., & Lenan, W. (2009). Stock market prediction of S&P 500 via combination of improved BCO approach and BP neural network. *Expert Systems with Applications, 36*(5), 8849–8854. doi:10.1016/j.eswa.2008.11.028

Zhang, D., & Zhou, L. (2004). Discovering Golden Nuggets: Data Mining in Financial Application. *IEEE Transactions on Systems, Man and Cybernetics. Part C, Applications and Reviews*, *34*(4), 513–522. doi:10.1109/TSMCC.2004.829279

Zhang, X., Hu, Y., Xie, K., Wang, S., Ngai, E. W. T., & Liu, M. (2014). A causal feature selection algorithm for stock prediction modeling. *Neurocomputing*, *142*, 48–59. doi:10.1016/j.neucom.2014.01.057

KEY TERMS AND DEFINITIONS

Closing Price: The price of particular stock at the end of trading.

Fundamental Analysis: Stock price prediction and analysis based on companies' business processes (such as financial results, company assets, liabilities, etc.).

Machine Learning Techniques: A group of methods used to learn the past trading performance of various stocks used in this chapter.

Mean Absolute Error: The average of differences between absolute values of actual stock price and predicted price of stocks.

Opening Price: The price of a stock before start of the trading on a specific day.

Stock Indices: The name of stock markets where trading of registered stocks take place such as Bombay Stock Exchange (BSE) and CNX Nifty, etc.

Technical Analysis: Stock price analysis based on company's historical share price performance and past stock buying and selling patterns.

Time Window: Advance time period used for predicting stock prices.

Chapter 9
Sentiment Analysis:
Using Artificial Neural Fuzzy Inference System

Syed Muzamil Basha
VIT University, India

Dharmendra Singh Rajput
VIT University, India

ABSTRACT

E-commerce has become a daily activity in human life. In it, the opinion and past experience related to particular product of others is playing a prominent role in selecting the product from the online market. In this chapter, the authors consider Tweets as a point of source to express users' emotions on particular subjects. This is scored with different sentiment scoring techniques. Since the patterns used in social media are relatively short, exact matches are uncommon, and taking advantage of partial matches allows one to significantly improve the accuracy of analysis on sentiments. The authors also focus on applying artificial neural fuzzy inference system (ANFIS) to train the model for better opinion mining. The scored sentiments are then classified using machine learning algorithms like support vector machine (SVM), decision tree, and naive Bayes.

INTRODUCTION

This chapter aims to make the readers understand the theoretical foundations, algorithms, methodologies for analyzing data in various domains such Retail, Finance, Risk and Healthcare. To define the core objectives of any above mentioned businesses, one should first give an attempt to understand the customer profitable attributes in order to maintain successful customer relationship. In Understanding Customers - Profiling And Segmentation, our focus is to show on how importance is understanding customer, and discussed different techniques and applications, (Basha SM et al. 2017). Among them churn prediction in the mobile Telecommunication industry is one, in which the Life Time Value (LTV) of a customer is derived using Survival Analysis, model with their limitations are discussed in detail in section Churn

DOI: 10.4018/978-1-5225-3870-7.ch009

Prediction in the Mobile Telecommunications Industries (Priss et al. 2006). The other real time application is Market Basket Analysis for a super market based on frequent item-set mining, in which data mining techniques are implemented to define new pattern by extracting associations from stores transactional data. Techniques like Apriori, K-Apriori and their detailed procedures are explained in Market Basket Analysis for a super market based on Frequent Item-set Mining. Where as in section Bankruptcy prediction for credit risk and different approaches like early Empirical Neural Network, Bayesian Network are discussed in detail, and also steps to be followed to design a model for supply chain risk propagation. In all the above application the domain and type of data varies. So, one should have good domain knowledge to perform prediction. Where as in section Text Categorization we continued our discussion on how to categorize text and the approaches to perform prediction on text data. In section Sentiment Analysis our discussion is on how to perform sentiment analysis on customers reviews and different classifier used like probabilistic, Naive Bayes, Maximum Entropy and Linear classifier like support vector machine, Neural Network, the decision tree. In addition to that other related fields where sentiment analysis is performed like Emotion detection, and prediction model for sentiment classification also discussed (Basha SM et al. 2017). With all the knowledge gained from the above sections, we identified few open problems in area of prediction which is domain specific and data centric like: Data problem, language problem. In section Open problems listed the open problems in Artificial Neural Fuzzy Inference system applied to the field of sentiment analysis on Text data. In section Artificial Neuro-fuzzy inference system (ANFIS) is a fuzzy system. In which, membership function parameters have been adjusted using Neuro-adaptive learning methods similar to those used in training neural networks, and also listed out steps to create, train, and test Sugeno-type fuzzy systems using the Neuro-Fuzzy Designer (Basha SM et al. 2017).

BACKGROUND AND MAIN FOCUS

Forensic In any industry, the first step to finding and creating profitable customers is determining what drives profitability and more successful customer relationship management. Predicting the customer attributes and behaviors, which drives companies in to profit, this information can be used to direct their Marketing efforts as well. In this context (Scridon et al. 2008) have discussed several techniques and applications for understanding customers. Defining the objective is as critical as the objective can be elaborated by evaluating the terms of profiling and segmentation. Profiling is defined as an act of making use of data to describe as group of people. It is performed on complete database or different parts of it. The different parts are termed as segments, which are mutually exclusive in nature. Segmentation is the process of splitting a database into different distinct segments. The basic approaches for segmentation are: First, Market driven approach, which allow managers to make use of user characteristics that they determine to be important drivers of their business. On the other hand, data-driven approach. Which make use of cluster analysis in order to find homogeneous groups from complete database. If the company makes an attempt to understand the customer behavior, it will find different levels of customers with their associated profit to company using the existing database. This is the advantage of both segmentation and profiling.

RFM: Recency Frequency Monetary

In Segmentation the customers are segmented in to different segments based on their buying behavior, through which the efficiency of marketing efforts with existing customers can be improved. The three different segments are termed as follows, (Scridon, M. A. et al. 2008). Recency: This value indicates the number of months since the last purchase made and more likely to make another purchase than someone who did not recently make a purchase. Frequency: This value indicates the number of purchases within a specific time frame, which relates to future purchases. Monetary: This value indicates the total currency amount within a specific time frame, the significance of the value can be improved, when these metric is used in combination with other segments (Basha SM et al. 2017).

RFM Analysis

The relevant variables to be identified in the database to discover the effects of these RFM measures are: Final purchase (FP) - Months since final purchase, Total purchases (TP) - Total Number of purchases made in the last specified time period. Total Amount (TA) - Total monetary amount of purchases made in the specified time period (Basha SM et al. 2017).

Penetration Analysis

It is an effective method for comparing the distribution of the customer base to the general population. The methodology commence with a frequency distribution of demographic variables like: age and income of a person, (Cambria et al. (2010), Cambria et al. (2012)).

Understanding Cluster Analysis

Cluster analysis is a statistical techniques that partition data into cluster based on similarity of characteristics (Scridon, M. A. 2008). It uses Euclidean distance in formation of cluster observations together that are related in several characteristics, while attempting to split observations that are dissimilar in same characteristics.

Clustering algorithm are designed for large data sets where small scale statistic are not applicable. It commence by randomly conveying cluster centers. Each observation is dispensed to the nearest center. The value of cluster center is then initialized to the mean in each cluster. The procedure is repeated until the change in the center happens to be sufficiently small, (Basha SM et al. 2017).

Churn Prediction in the Mobile Telecommunications Industry (MTI)

The MTI Changed from a rapidly growing market, into a state of saturation and fierce competition, Focus shifted from building a large customer base into keeping customers 'in house', Acquiring new customers is more expensive than retaining existing customers. (Alberts et al. 2006) stated that the loss of a customer is "churn". Churn prevention can be done in two steps:

1. Acquiring more loyal customers initially.
2. Identifying customers most likely to churn.

Predictive Churn Modeling

It is applied in the field of Applied in the field of, Banking, Mobile telecommunication, Life insurances and Etcetera. The Common models are: Neural networks, Decision trees, Support vector machines. OPERATIONAL CHURN: It is to indicate when a customer has permanently stopped using service of a company as early as possible. It require a labeled dataset for training purposes, Based on number of successive months with zero usage, (Basha SM et al. 2017). The definition on OPERATIONAL CHURN consists of two parameters, a and b, where a is fixed value and b is the maximum number of successive months with zero usage, *(a+b)* is used as a threshold. Customers with b greater than (or) equal to 5 left out, considered as outliers (Mohammad, S. et al. 2014).

SURVIVAL ANALYSIS

Survival analysis is a collection of statistical methods which model time-to-event data, the time until the event occurs is of interest, In our discussion the event is churn (Priss et al. 2006).

$$s(t) = \Pr(T > t) = 1 - F(t) = \int_t^\infty f(x)dx \qquad (1)$$

Figure 1. Survival Analysis

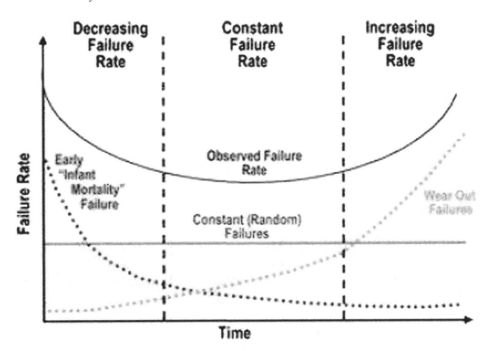

whereas $T = $ *event time*, $f(t) = $ *density function*, $F(t) = $ *cum. Density function*. The survival at time t is the probability that a subject will survive to that point in time. Probability that event occurs in current interval, given that event has not already occurred.

Hazard Model

The hazard (rate) at time t describes the frequency of the occurrence of the event in events per time period (Cambria et al. (2010), Cambria et al. (2012)).

$$\lambda(t) = \frac{\lim_{\delta t \to 0} \Pr(t, T, t + \delta t \mid T > t)}{\delta t} = \frac{f(t)}{1 - F(t)} \tag{2}$$

COX Model

$$\lambda_i(t) = \lambda_0(t) e^{X_i \beta} \tag{3}$$

where $\lambda(t)$ is Hazard for individual i at time t, $\lambda_0(t)$ is Baseline hazard: the 'average' hazard curve, and $e^{X_i \beta}$ is the influence of the variables X_i on the baseline hazard. The drawback of Cox model is hazard at time t only dependent on baseline hazard, not on variables. If we want to include time-dependent covariates variables that vary over time, like: the number of SMS messages per month. That is possible using Extended Cox model (Cambria et al. (2010), Cambria et al. (2012)).

$$\lambda_i(t) = \lambda_0(t) \exp \left[\sum_{i=1}^{p_1} X_i \beta + \sum_{i=1}^{p_2} X_j(t) \beta \right] \tag{4}$$

Now we can compute the hazard for time t, but in fact we want to forecast. In fact, to find the outdated data, Lagging of variables is required:

$$\lambda_i(t) = \lambda_0(t) \exp \left[\sum_{i=1}^{p_1} X_i \beta + \sum_{i=1}^{p_2} X_j(t - L_j) \beta \right] \tag{5}$$

Principal Component Analysis (PCA)

Transform variables into new ones. It reduces the dimensionality of the dataset while retaining as much as possible of the variation present in the dataset (Quinlan et al. 1986).

Principal Component Regression

It Use principal components as variables in model, Reduces collinearity, which causes inaccurate estimations of the regression coefficients, also reduces dimensionality and used as Safe choice, because principal components with largest variances are not necessarily the best predictors (Priss et al. 2006). Survival models not designed to be predictive models. Then using Scoring method we decide if a customer is churned (or) not. A threshold applied on the hazard in turn used to indicate churn.

Decision Tree

An iterative process of splitting the data up into partitions, (Quinlan et al. 1986). Drawback is over fitting: noise present in the dataset, As a result predictive power is lost. Solution to avoid this problem is either, pre-pruning or post-pruning. In post-pruning n-fold cross-validation is performed, where the training set is split into n subsets, each of the n subsets is left out in turn, train on the other subsets and Test on the one left out. With Oversampling the proportion of the outcomes is altered in the training set that increases the proportion of the less frequent outcome (churn). Proportion changed to 1/3churn and 2/3 non-churn.

Modeling Customer Lifetime Value (LTV)

Customer LTV is a straightforward measure that produce customer profitability and level of churn risk management at individual customer. LTV of an individual customer can help organizations to develop customer loyalty and treatment strategies to exploit customer value. For newly attained customers, LTV can help organizations in develop strategies to grow the exact customers. The key factor to estimate customer LTV is the customer survival curve. In this section, survival analysis is applied to estimate customer survival curve, therefore customer LTV is calculated. Whereas (Lu and Park 2003) has calculated customer LTV through estimating customer survival curve using survival analysis techniques. Our discussion is to develop customer loyalty and treatment strategies of maximize customer value.

Steps to Develop the Concept of Customer LTV

The evaluation of customer LTV differ from one organization to the other. For example, consider, in telecommunications industry, customer monthly margin (MM) and customer survival curve (CSC) are the two major components of customer LTV. The customer LTV is the net present value of customers evaluated profit over a specified time period (Quinlan et al. 1986).

$$LTV = MN \times \sum_{i=1}^{T} \frac{p^i}{(1 + r\,/\,12)^{i-1}} \qquad (6)$$

where *MM* is the monthly margin for newly attained customer. It can be estimated through a set of regression models. *T* is the total number of months considered to evaluate the customer LTV. *r* is the discount rate, p^i is the series of customer survival probabilities (customer survival curve) from month 1 through Month *T*, where $p^1 = 1$:p^i is estimated through customer survival model.

Figure 2. Decision Tree

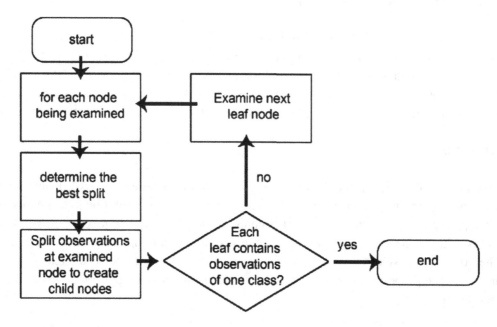

Estimation of Customer LTV

This process contains the following five major steps.

1. **Investigative Data Analysis:** It is to prepare the data for the survival analysis. The uni-variate frequency analysis is used to identify value distributions, missing values and outliers.
2. **Feature Reduction:** All the categorical features with a chi-square value or t statistics significant at 0:05 or less were kept. Further PROC PHREG is used to further reduce the number of variables.
3. **Model Estimation:** The customer survival function and hazard function were estimated, before applying survival analysis procedures on the final data set. The purpose of estimating customer survival function and customer hazard function is to gain knowledge of customer survival/churn hazard characteristics.
4. **Model Validation:** In validation data set each customer being scored for predicted survival probabilities for different specified time periods.
5. **Estimation of Customer LTV:** With the model successfully estimating customer survival curve, customer LTV can be estimated for each individual customer.

Market Basket Analysis for a Supermarket

The main challenge for any organization is to making investigation in customer data collection is to extract relevant important information from their existing huge customer databases and product feature databases to gain competitive advantage. In retail industry, retailer must understand the needs of customers and should get adapted to them. Market basket analyses gives retailer good enough information about related sales on group of goods. It makes sense that these groups are placed next to each other in a retail center. So that customers can access them quickly and to lead them through the center in a logical manner. It determine the placement of goods, designing sales promotions for different segments of customers to improve customer satisfaction and hence the profit of the supermarket. (Loraine Charlet and Kumar 2012) has addressed the issue for supermarket using frequent item-set mining, which make use of the efficient K-Apriori algorithm to generate association rules.

These rules are derived from the frequent item-sets using support and confidence as threshold levels. The sets of items which have minimum support are known as Frequent Item-set. The support of an item-set is termed as the proportion of transactions in the data set which contain the item-set. Confidence is termed as the measure of certainty associated with each discovered pattern. Frequent hidden item-set extraction is done using Apriori, FP-Growth Algorithm.

Apriori algorithm is a level-wise, breadth-first algorithm which counts transactions, using prior knowledge of frequent item-set properties. In which n-item-sets are used to explore (n+1) item-sets. To improve the efficiency of the level-wise generation of frequent item-sets Apriori property is used here. Apriori property persevere that all non-empty subsets of a frequent item-set must also be frequent. This is made possible because of the anti-monotone property of support measure - the support for an item-set in no way beats the value of support for its subsets.

K-Apriori is the most influential algorithm for efficient association rule discovery, in which it uses the abovementioned Apriori property. This algorithm performance is good when sparse datasets are considered. The K-Apriori algorithm mines a set of frequent item-sets from the data, and then pulls out the rules with the highest information content for different groups of customers by dividing the customers in different clusters. Procedure of the K-Apriori algorithm is as follows (Charlet and Kumar 2012).

1. Binary data is transformed into real domain using linear Wiener transformation on a vector basis.
2. The Wiener transformed data is partitioned using the multi-pass K-means algorithm.
3. Then the Apriori procedure is executed for the K clusters in which the sets of items which are greater than minimum support are found iteratively.
4. Using these frequent item-sets based on confidence, Association rules are derived.
5. The items in the clusters are very similar, so that multiple and high informative frequent item-sets are effectively generated. Procedure to understand the transformation of binary data vector X_i of size 1*q in to vector data Y_i of size 1*q is as follows:
   a. Calculate the mean m for the input vector Xi around each element.
   b. Calculate the variance pi^2 around each element for the vector.
   c. Perform wiener transformation for each element in the vector using equation Y based on its neighborhood

$$Y(n_1, n_2) = \mu + \frac{\sigma^2 - \lambda^2}{\sigma^2}(X(n_1, n_2) - \mu) \tag{7}$$

where λ^2 is the average of all the local estimated variances.

Evaluation of Credit Risk

The prediction of corporate bankruptcies is an important and widely studied topic since it can have significant impact on bank lending decisions and profitability. (Atiya et al. 2001) has proposed novel indicators for the NN system that provides a noteworthy improvement in accuracy prediction (Chen et al. (2000), Chen et al. (2011)).

Early Empirical Approaches

Beaver was the first researchers to make a study on prediction of bankruptcy using financial statement data based on studying one financial ratio at a time and on developing a cutoff threshold for each ratio. Altman and Ohlson are essentially linear models that classify between healthy/bankrupt firms using financial ratios as inputs and used the classical multivariate discriminant analysis technique (MDA). Which is based on applying the Bayes classification procedure, assuming that the two classes have Gaussian distributions with equal covariance matrices. The covariance matrix and the class means are estimated from the training set. (Domingos et al. 1997) established the logistic regression approach (LR) to the bankruptcy prediction problem with a linear model using a sigmoid function:

$$f(x) = \frac{1}{1 + e^{-x}} \tag{8}$$

Neural-Network (NN) approach

Bankruptcy prediction using Neural Network was started in 1990. There are a number of motivations to understand, why a non-linear approach is better to a linear approach? It can be squabbled that there are saturation effects in the relationships between the financial ratios and the prediction of default. The reason is that highly leveraged firms have a harder time borrowing money to finance their deficits. Currently, several of the major commercial loan default prediction products are based on NNs. Altman's financial ratios are inputs to the NN, and applied their method, as well as MDA as a comparison, to a number of bankrupt and solvent US firms, where the data used for the bankrupt firms are from the last financial statement before declaring bankruptcy.

Bayesian Network Approach

The Basic idea on which Bayesian theory is framed, that we embrace beliefs in certain events given our prior knowledge on them. If other events transpire, however, we have a tendency to modify our original beliefs of the related events. If we assume that x represents all of our prior knowledge, then we can form available theory on probabilities that account for new information which becomes available to us. Bayesian networks leverage Bayesian theory on probabilities by exploiting independent conditional probabilities. Of even more importance to Bayesian networks is the concept of probabilistic inference and learning. Inference refers to the fact that we have prior beliefs of the world around us structured in the form of a Bayesian network. Whenever, we assume that a particular event in our network has taken place, we must bring up to date all of our beliefs that are dependent on the event which implicit to take place; this leads to a posterior belief. Learning on the other hand involves permanently updating our belief network once we have actually observed an event happen. Bayesian networks correspond to the joint probability distribution function of all the variables in the network as a product of the smaller conditional probability distributions of each variable by developing the expansion rule (Domingos et al. 1997):

$$p(X \mid \xi) = \sum_{i-1}^{n} p(X \mid Y = y_i, \xi) p(y = y_i \mid \xi) \tag{9}$$

The notion of conditional independence must be formally defined since the theory of Bayesian networks relies on it. If we assume that we only have our background knowledge x, we can usually as certain whether two events would be independent or dependent. Suppose we have two events, E1 and E2 about which we know little of their dependence to each other. Now suppose for the moment that we observed a third event, E3, with which we can now conclude the first two events as independent. This concept is known as conditional independence, more formally:

$$p(E_1, E_2 \mid E_3, \xi) = p(E_1 \mid E_3, \xi) p(E_2 \mid E_3, \xi) \tag{10}$$

While this method is common with in Bayesian network models, its form is difficult to update if we wish to learn new information. A solution to this is to assume that the probability of an events X_i belongs to X a random variable q. We would then have $P(X_i) = E[deta]$. Typically deta is assumed to have as its prior distribution the beta distribution $beta(a_1; a_2)$. When given the new information x, we must change our distribution to incorporate the new data. To determine the posterior distribution of deta, Bayes theorem and the likelihood function of binomial sampling are used to find that $Beta(a_1 + n_1; a_2 + n_2)$, where n_1, n_2 are the number of observations for each outcome. By representing the distribution this way, learning becomes relatively easy. Thus we have our updated belief of X_i as:

$$p(Xi \mid \xi) = E(\phi \mid \xi) = \frac{a_1 + n_1}{a_1 + n_1 + a_2 + n_2} \tag{11}$$

We must note that we took advantage of the implicit assumption that X_i had no parents. The author (Garvey et al. 2015) has designed model for supply chain risk propagation with the building following Hypothesis.

Creation of Hypothesis

- **H1:** The complete structure of the supply network is known in prior.
- **H2:** All risks measured are representation as a binary random variable.
- **H3:** All possible risks to a supply network independent of any location in the network have been accounted for.
- **H4:** Given a set of risks, the underlying relationships among the risks are resolute in a procedural and objective manner that results in an acyclic directed graph.

- **H5:** Given a set of risks, the procedure for influential the causal structure of the risks must be based on the structure of the supply network.
- **H6:** The data for all risks and conditional probability tables' distributions can be resolute in full.
- **H7:** The consequential network allows for obedient probabilistic inference
- **H8:** The consequential Bayesian network constructed using the risks inherent in a supply network using the procedure given below is the best fit network to the data.
- **H9:** All risks that are dependent on business decisions are static and have only a single distribution.

Text Categorization

Text categorization (Ruiz and Srinivasan et al. 1999) and (Sebastiani et al. 2002) defined as the task of assigning a Boolean value to each pair $(d_j; c_i)$ to D_C, where D is a domain of documents and $C = c_1, ..., c_p$ C_j is a set of predefined categories. A value of T assigned to $(d_j; c_i)$ indicates a decision to file d_j under c_i while a value of F indicates a decision not to file d_j under c_i. More formally, the task is to approximate the unknown target function beta: $D*C$ tends to T_iF (that describes how documents ought to be classified) (Della Pietra et al. 1997) by means of a function alpha: $D*C$ tends to T_iF called the classifier (aka rule, or hypothesis, or model) such that a and b as much as possible Keshtkar et al. (2013)".

SENTIMENT ANALYSIS (SA) OF CUSTOMERS REVIEWS VIA APPLICATION OF TEXT MINING

The Internet is a rich source of reviews and commenter's about almost anything. More and more people see information posted in review sites as a trustful information source and use it for decision making, (Balahur et al. 2012). Also, the organizations have realized the importance of opinions found on the Internet and increasingly use this data to retrieve customers' opinion and insights through data mining techniques. This type of data is especially appealing to organizations because of its availability, volume, and diversity. Also, this kind of data can be obtained faster and analyzed almost real time in such a way providing almost immediate feedback. (IVASCENKO 2016) has make use of airline customer reviews retrieved from two review websites Trip-Advisor and Sky-Trax has examined through application of topic modeling and sentiment analysis, also investigated sentiment polarity, retrieve factors that influence customer satisfaction in air transport sector, and analyze the strength and weaknesses of three airlines, namely British Airways, Turkish Airlines, and Lufthansa, Terms frequency inverse document frequency (tf-idf) and Mutual Information (MI) (Lu and Lin et al. 2010) and Maximum Entropy (Nigam, K., Lafferty et al. 1999) are three term weighting methods used in his research. It is essential to understand the common difference between sentiment and opinion; According to Cambridge Dictionaries Online, sentiment is "thought, opinion, or idea based on a feeling about a situation, or a way of thinking about something". Whereas a term opinion is defined as "the ideas that a person or a group of people have about something or someone, which are based mainly on their feelings and beliefs, or a single idea. Thus, the task of SA or Opinion Mining (OM) (Kontopoulos et al. 2013) is to extract people's expressed sentiment, opinion, mood, feeling (Neviarouskaya et al. (2007), Neviarouskaya et al. (2009) and Neviarouskaya et al. (2010)), emotion (Plutchik et al. 1980) and subjectivity in text towards an entity by employing Natural Language Processing (NLP) and text mining techniques (Chakrabarti et al. 2003).

An entity in SA can be anything people express their opinion about, for example, product, service, topic, issue, person, organization, or event. OM task is to extract and analyze people's opinion about an entity while SA identifies the sentiment stated in a text and analyzes it afterward. In this chapter, such a distinction is not used, and SA denotes both tasks. SA is essentially a text classification problem. Traditional text classification mainly classifies documents of different topics; that is why topic-related words are the key features. Depending on the research field and the domain of analysis, sentiment classification can be binary, multiclass, regression/ranking (Mohammad et al. 2011). The task of binary classification is to classify text as either positive or negative, in other words, polarity. Multiclass classification task with three classes introduces the third group – neutral which contains documents that do not express neither positive nor negative opinion about a particular entity; or mixed or ambivalent group containing documents which represent a positive and negative aspects of the same entity. The ranking is also a multiclass classification problem, and it tends to determine the degree of positivity or negativity. For example, both positive and negative groups can be divided into the two subgroups – very positive, positive, and negative and very negative (Larkey et al. 1998).

There are three main classification levels:

1. **Document-Level:** A term document in text mining represents a different type and different length of the text. The document can be as long as a novel or as short as a review or post in a micro-blog. So document-level classification problem deals with the task of classifying an opinion expressed in a whole document. This level of analysis assumes that each document expresses views on a single entity. Therefore, is not applicable to documents which evaluate or compare multiple entities (Lewis et al. (1994), Lewis et al.(1998)).

2. **Sentence-Level:** We should determine the polarity within each sentence. It can be considered analogous document-level classification because the sentence can be perceived as a short document. In Sentence-level classification problem contains one additional text preprocessing step, that is breaking the text into separate sentences (Li and Tsai et al. (1998), Li and Tsai et al. (2011), Li and Tsai et al. (2013)).

3. **Aspect Level (Xianghua and Guo et al. 2012):** This is the Most granular level at which SA is conducted. Not only it determines polarity but also discovers what people like or dislike about a particular entity. Thus, the aim of this level of analysis is to discover sentiments on entities and/or their aspects, (Mudinas et al. 2012). In this chapter, we addresses the binary document-level polarity classification problem, dealing with classifying documents into two sentiment groups - positive and negative. Before SA can be performed it is necessary to extract features. Which features are more appropriate for analysis depends on the data, task, and method in use. Some examples of commonly used features are provided below:

   a. **Terms Presence of Frequency:** These features are individual words or unigrams or word groups as bi-grams, tri-gram, generally speaking, n-grams, where n stands for a number of related words in a group. Features are also an n-gram frequency count. It either gives the words binary weighting (zero if the word appears or one otherwise) or uses term frequency weights to determine the relative importance of the feature. Part of speech (POS): Every word in a sentence has its role, which is called syntactic role or POS. In English, there are eight POS: the verb, the noun, the pronoun, the adjective, the adverb, the prepositions, the conjunctions and the interjections (Fangand Zhan, 2015). It is considered that the adjectives, adverbs, verbs are POS that contribute the most in SC, but nouns are important in the tasks of aspect based SA. The advantage of POS features it that irrelevant word groups can be filtered out. Sentiment Words and phrases: "Sentiment words are words in a language that are used to express positive and negative sentiment". In SC, sentiment words that indicate positive or negative opinions are more important than others. The most specific sentiment word groups are adjectives and adverbs, but nouns and verbs can also contain a sentiment. Negation: Negation word in the sentence changes the opinion orientation. For example, word good has a positive meaning, while not good implies a negative sense. A typical way of dealing with negation is reversing its polarity, i.e. change a score of words sentiment from positive to negative. It seems to work for positive words like good and great. However, a negation of a negative word does not change its meaning to a positive, rather, less negative, for instance, terrible and not terrible. This issue can be addressed by using two different dictionaries with predefined scores – one for affective terms but another for negated terms. Negation is more important in the case of lexicon-based SA. Intensifiers: words like very, really and extremely make adjectives stronger. This feature is especially important in the cases with more than three (positive, negative, neutral) classification groups when the strength of the positive or negative sentiment is under investigation. The approaches to derive SA is broadly classified in to two categories, namely Machine Learning Approach and Lexicon-based Approach. The advantage of the lexicon-based approach is that is it applicable to a wide variety of domains and also languages because it is only matter of a dictionary. However, this method also possess some limitations:

i.   Lexicon is costly to build.
ii. It is restricted to constant prior sentiment values of terms regardless of context.
iii. Full dependence on the presence of words that explicitly reflect sentiment.
iv. Tends to achieve less accuracy in results.

Whereas the main advantage of machine learning classifiers is good classification results with accuracies reported in the range of 80-87%. However, there are two main limitations of this approach:

1. It is difficult to obtain training data.
2. As classifier is trained on a domain specific data it is domain dependent, and it tends to produce unsatisfactory results when applied to data from other domain.

Researchers have tried to overcome the first limitation by employing different metadata or features as labels. For review data, the star, dot or numeric ranking are used. Sentiment polarity categorization is performed on Amazon.com customer reviews. The positive group was formed from the reviews with the ranking of four and five stars, but the negative group included reviews with a star ranking one, two and three. However, for social media data emoticons and hash-tags are widely used as document labeling elements. As machine-learning approach achieves more accurate classification performance results and has fewer disadvantages, this method was discussed in this chapter. Machine learning approach consists of algorithms that learn underlying patterns from training data, meaning that classes are pre-coded beforehand for each instance. Further, the task of the trained classifier is to classify unlabeled data and achieve the highest performance measures. This approach can further be divided into supervised and unsupervised learning methods. The supervised methods make use of a vast number of labeled training documents. The unsupervised methods are used when it is difficult to obtain labeled training documents.

The most popular supervised sentiment classifiers are Support Vector Machine (SVM) (Joachims et al. 1998), Naive Bayes, Maximum Entropy, Neural Networks, and Bayesian Networks. (Li and Li 2013) proposed the Numeric Opinion Summarization Framework, which summarizes text opinions into traceable numeric scores. The framework incorporates four modules – Trendy Topic Detection module, Subjectivity Analysis module, Sentiment Classification module, Credibility Assessment Module. The authors applied this model to Twitter data for three brands – Google, Microsoft, and Sony; and three products - iPhone, iPad, Mac Book. The training data set was created by employing emoticons, But SVM was used to perform SC. (Ye et al. 2009) compared three sentiment classifier methods, namely, Naïve Bayes, SVM, and Dynamic Language Model classifier. The authors collected tourists' reviews about the seven most popular travel destinations in the US and Europe from the travel column of Yahoo.com. Research results show that with increasing training dataset size, the classification accuracy also increases. All three methods can reach the accuracy of more than 80%, but SVM demonstrated the best results –maximum 86%. (MartíN-Valdivia et al. 2013) addressed the task of sentiment polarity detection in Spanish corpus of movie reviews with a parallel corpus translated into English. They have applied meta-classifier which is a combination of supervised and unsupervised approaches and tested four different feature weighting methods in conjunction with three different pre-processing steps. The highest accuracy was obtained when the term-frequency – inverse document frequency (tm-idf) weighting was used without applying neither stop word removal nor stemming– reaching an accuracy of 87.69%. However, authors concluded that the accuracy difference between the second best model is not so significant - 87.66% and preferred a model with removed stop words as it reduces features and classification process is more efficient. (Moraes et al. 2013) aimed to perform a document-level SC on four review data sets by employing and comparing the performance of two classifiers - SVM and not so commonly used Artificial Neural Networks (ANN) within a context of SA. Also, they test the performance of classifiers with a different number of terms. In conclusion, ANN outperformed SVM or showed comparable results. Regarding the number of terms used, the best results were reached with 1000 terms.

(Jakopovi´c and Preradovi´c 2013) used Croatia Airlines as an object of SA during the period of reconstruction of the airline. The main objective of the study was to determine the customers' opinion towards airline during the time of change. Authors employed an SA tool called SentiStrengh and analyzed data retrieved from Twitter and Face book page. (Yee Liau and Pei Tan 2014) tended to investigate customers' opinions towards low-cost airlines in Malaysia. The authors used lexicon-based approach by employing (Hu and Liu 2004) English dictionary as well as creating their own for Mali language to classify Twitter data in positive, negative and neutral groups. In addition to sentiment polarity detection, they also used a cluster analysis to identify the topics discussed with in each polarity group. Also (Adeborna and Siau 2014) used lexicon-based approach by employing (Hu and Liu 2004) English dictionary to perform SA on Twitter data by classifying documents in three traditional groups – positive, negative, and neutral. Moreover, they sought to learn the most representative topics in each sentiment group and assessed Airline Quality Rating based on customers' sentiment towards airline rather than traditional customer survey data. (Simone Guercini et al. 2014) made a study to investigate how information from Twitter can be used to identify critical elements in airline customer experiences and how to use identified elements to enhance service performance. Also in this study authors used lexicon-based SA. However (Wan and Gao 2015) applied a supervised machine learning approach in their research. The aim of this study was to compare the performance of different commonly used SC methods, namely Naive Bayes, SVM, Bayesian Network, C4.5 Decision Tree and Random Forest algorithms and develop an ensemble approach. The algorithms were tested on the Twitter data set which contained tweets about airline services of most

Figure 3. Sentiment Analysis Techniques

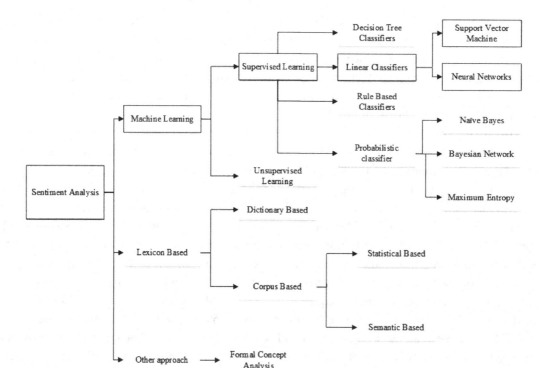

airline service brands in North America. (Pang et al. 2002) performed experiments on three standard algorithms: Naive Bayes classification, maximum entropy classification, and support vector machines.

Probabilistic Classifiers

Probabilistic classifiers use mixture models for classification. The mixture model assumes that each class is a component of the mixture. Each mixture component is a generative model that provides the probability of sampling a particular term for that component. These kinds of classifiers are also called generative classifiers (Tsytsarau and Palpanas et al. 2012). Three of the most famous probabilistic classifiers are discussed in the next subsections.

Naive Bayes Classification

In which, text classification is to assign to a given document d the class $c = $ argmaxc $P(c|d)$ by first observing that by Bayes' rule that lead to design Naïve Bayes Classifier.

$$p(c \mid d) = \frac{p(c) \times p(d \mid c)}{p(d)} \qquad (12)$$

where P(d) plays no role in selecting class C. To estimate the term $P(d|c)$.

$$P_{NB}(c \mid d) = \frac{p(c)\left(\prod_{i=1}^{m} p(f_1 \mid c)^{n_i(d)}\right)}{p(d)} \tag{13}$$

Our training method consists of relative-frequency estimation of *P(c)* and *P(d|c)*, using add-one smoothing. Despite its simplicity and the fact that its conditional independence assumption clearly does not hold in real-world situations.

How-To-Do: Sentiment Analysis With Core NLP

Simply once we parse data, in our case ten example of ten sample news articles, once we have that information, basically we are going to do is per document, predicting polarity of input text, sentence, So sentence level polarity detection or sentiment analysis is specified and coded into loop. Second loop is the sentence splitting, so you put each sentence, you're going to predict polarity from zero to four, so it's a five scale sentiment analysis. The Core NLP, (Berger et al. 1996) explain, what we do is in pipeline, you call tokenize pipe, sentence split pipe, parse, tree pipe. And then sentiment pipe, so in order for it to do sentiment analysis with Core NLP, we need to call parse tree pipe beforehand. The sentence, that's been the frustrating part, and the sentiment of that sentence is one. Remember, the scale is zero to four. One is mild negative and "we're just not driving in any runs", Collins said. This is also one. The Stanford Core NLP assigns a one score to this sentence. If you recall, the sentiment analysis of Stanford Core NLP. The left one is positive, the right one is negative. So in order to predict the sentiment score by Stanford Core NLP, at first parse tree, and then tree level which means a sentence level prediction is possible. It takes time, some sentence is hard to parse. If it's a long or if it's not well written sentence, then parsing tree takes time. Sometimes it throws an exception, so depending on the level of difficulties of your sentence, the way it's written, it takes time, more time or less time.

How-To-Do: Sentiment Analysis With LINGPIPE

Using a sentiment dataset in order to train a logistic regression model and use the trained model to classify sentiment. One should first train the classifier using answer sets. Which means some data needs to be pre-identified as negative data. And the other data sets we need to have positive data if it's a binary classifier. So negative data which means if it's movie review data then each movie review, we need to identify whether it's a negative or positive. If it's a positive movie review than we place it under a certain folder. If it's a negative review we place that in a certain folder. This is manually classified by experts. If they assign a positive score to this review that means whatever tokens, whatever features in there are leaning toward the positive expressions of movie reviews. We are going to read them all and then basically use them to train the model. And then you pass that to a classifier, dynamic LM classifier. And then you train the classifier based on the correct pre-identified answer sets. Later serialized your classifier into the sentiment model. And then close out the file. Then basically for each sentence you predict the polarity of the sentence based upon that trained classifier, logistic regression classifier. And then predict the polarity of the particular sentence. In the real world scenario, we expect you are facing a much bigger size of dataset. That means it takes more times, sometimes you run into keep size memory error or you run into several other problems. So, what you need to do is you're probably going to simply increase the memory size, keep memory size. Or you're probably going to reduce the feature space, in terms of document metrics by removing stammers, remove some words that less frequently occur, minimum occurrence of term is two or five. Or commonly, very commonly occurring terms, you just simply eliminate all of them. By doing that, keep very meaningful and important terms. Importance here means discriminative value is high for that particular term. Which means it takes much less time. LingPipe's logistic regression based sentence classifier predicts this is a positive, and so on and so forth. Compared to this, Stanford CoreNLP depends on the size of data. Stanford Core NLP performs better. Simply because the training data of this logistic regression model is based on the very handful size of the training dataset. If you have more data, more high quality data, then it performs better. The performance is significantly improved (Cambria and Havasi et al. 2012).

How-To-Do: Sentiment Analysis With SENTI Word NET

We will discuss about dictionary-based sentiment classifier based on dictionary call Senti Word Net. We're going to use the same data set that we used for Stanford Core NLP and LingPipe logistic regression classifier, which is New York Times data set. Senti Word Net-based approach is unsupervised learning, which means there is no need for training data, and training phase. What it do is simply Parse our data, it happens over here, reading and parsing. And then if the match, if given token or word has matched entry in Senti Word Net, then it gives a score to that particular word, either negative, either positive. So, let's look at the logic of how scoring works based on Senti Word Net by going in to get Sentiment WordNet (Ye and Zhang et al. 2009), so let's select Open the. And simply, if this means high enough, which, the very big size of the word, and then either you, if you create a Senti Word Net model, it's basically you serialize the model. It's not the classifier, you simply, this Senti Word Net 3.0 version of Senti Word Net and to serialize it. Because this Senti Word Net has a huge number of sentiment tokens in there, so probably what we want to do is we want to have effective or efficient searching algorithm, a data structure, like a tire data structure, and so that it has a fast lookup. And this file basically suit the needs. If you have a serialized model, then you simply instantiate Senti Word Net object. If not, then encrypt them. So let's go Senti Word Net object. What you do there is, the first constructor is based on the assumption that you have a serialized model. Second constructor is, it's just a Senti Word Net dictionary, and take that input and then you serialize them. Here it called initialize Dictionary. The initialize Dictionary just simply does dictionary lookup based on Hash Map. So Java has, the map container has built-in data structure, so it relies on this Hash Map. As we explained before, you can use tire data structure. Tire data structure, in fact, performs better in terms of speed. But since this size of Senti Word Net, Hash Map handles properly. But all it does is, initialize Dictionary means, we simply take Senti Word Net input, and then parse this Word Net synset based on Senti Word Net structure. And then for each information there, like whether the term has positive value or negative value or objective value, depending on the value of a query of a given term, then you simply assign that information to the particular comment and store them in this Hash Map. Lets understand what's happening inside this initialize Dictionary. so given this, after we have constructed, get Sentiment function takes a sentence and then for each sentence, the sentence has preprocessed information by Stanford Core NLP. It has the lemma term, it has POS tag for each term. Then here it has several if-else-if statements. If POS tag is adjective or noun or verb, then Senti Word Net has its own POS tagging, and you simply match with the Senti Word Net POS tag with sample coordinate p. And then if that is matched and lemma form is matched with the entry of Senti Word Net along with its POS tag, then it simply gets that information and its score assigned to the particular entry and appended to a sentiment score. As each sentence have aggregated sentiment score. Which means, if the sentence has several sentiment words, the sentiment word has negative, positive or objective. Then based on the sum of each sentiment word per given sentence, then this is a total sentiment score per each sentence. Let's stop here. So some makes sense, some doesn't make sense. So what we can say here is Senti Word Net-based approach, some cases is it achieves really high performance in terms of accuracy. In many cases it performs really poor because the tokenized terms from test data set, many of them are not match entries in Senti Word Net because this is a jargon, and this is a new word, or lemmatized form is not correct. There are many possible reasons. Because of that, Senti Word Net, or any dictionary-based sentiment classification, performs poorer in large-scale experiments or real-world application settings.

Artificial Neuro-Fuzzy Inference System (ANFIS)

In Artificial neuro-fuzzy inference system using a given input/output data set, the toolbox function anfis constructs a fuzzy inference system (FIS) whose membership function parameters are tuned (adjusted) using either a back propagation algorithm alone or in combination with a least squares type of method. This adjustment allows your fuzzy systems to learn from the data they are modeling, (Basha SM et al. 2017). When to Use Neuro-Adaptive Learning, the basic structure of Mamdani fuzzy inference system is a model that maps input characteristics to input membership functions, input membership functions to rules, rules to a set of output characteristics, output characteristics to output membership functions, and the output membership functions to a single-valued output or a decision associated with the output. Such a system uses fixed membership functions that are chosen arbitrarily and a rule structure that is essentially predetermined by the user's interpretation of the characteristics of the variables in the model. ANFIS and the Neuro-Fuzzy Designer apply fuzzy inference techniques to data modeling. As you have seen from the other fuzzy inference GUIs, the shape of the membership functions depends on parameters, and changing these parameters change the shape of the membership function. Instead of just looking at the data to choose the membership function parameters, you choose membership function parameters automatically using these Fuzzy Logic Toolbox applications. Suppose you want to apply fuzzy inference to a system for which you already have a collection of input/output data that you would like to use for modeling, model-following, or some similar scenario. You do not necessarily have a predetermined model structure based on characteristics of variables in your system. In some modeling situations, you cannot discern what the membership functions should look like simply from looking at data. Rather than choosing the parameters associated with a given membership function arbitrarily, these parameters could be chosen so as to tailor the membership functions to the input/output data in order to account for these types of variations in the data values. In such cases, you can use the Fuzzy Logic Toolbox neuro-adaptive learning techniques incorporated in the anfis command (Wang et al. 2014).

Model validation is the process by which the input vectors from input/output data sets on which the FIS was not trained, are presented to the trained FIS model, to see how well the FIS model predicts the corresponding data set output values. One problem with model validation for models constructed using adaptive techniques is selecting a data set that is both representative of the data the trained model is intended to emulate, yet sufficiently distinct from the training data set so as not to render the validation process trivial. If you have collected a large amount of data, hopefully this data contains all the necessary representative features, so the process of selecting a data set for checking or testing purposes is made easier. However, if you expect to be presenting noisy measurements to your model, it is possible the training data set does not include all of the representative features you want to model. The testing data set allows you check the generalization capability of the resulting fuzzy inference system. The idea behind using a checking data set for model validation is that after a certain point in the training, the model begins over fitting the training data set.

FUTURE RESEARCH DIRECTIONS

In future, we would like to focus on applications of sentiment analysis for each domain specified in this chapter, the techniques and methods used to extract sentiments labels from the labeled reviews to be illustrated with implementation as finding out the depth in sentiment and its intensity is the emerging trend towards effective decision making in production team. This chapter focus on extracting hidden pattern in text, available in the form of tweets, collected from twitter. The implementation details of the techniques discussed in this chapters on Big Data Frameworks like Hadoop and Spark to be carried out in Future. We found that, there is a huge scope of opportunity available within the domain of Sentiment analysis. Finally, suggested to apply fuzzy logic on top of machine learning classification algorithms.

CONCLUSION

We would like to conclude that readers of this chapter can understand the theoretical foundations, algorithms, methodologies for analyzing data in various domains such Retail, Finance, Risk and Healthcare. And importance of understanding customer, different techniques and applications. Therefore in all the above mentioned application the domain and type of data varies. so, how one can get good domain knowledge to perform prediction can be understood. In addition to that how to perform sentiment analysis on customers reviews and different classifier used like probabilistic, Naive Bayes, Maximum Entropy and Linear classifier like support vector machine, Neural Network, the decision tree are explained in detail. Addressed few open problems in Artificial Neural Fuzzy Inference system applied to the field of sentiment analysis on Text data. And also listed out steps to create, train, and test Sugeno-type fuzzy systems using the Artificial Neuro-Fuzzy Inference system tool available in MATLAB.

REFERENCES

Adeborna, E., & Siau, K. (2014). *An Approach to Sentiment Analysis-the Case of Airline Quality Rating*. PACIS.

Alberts, L. J. S. M., Peeters, I. R. L. M., Braekers, R., & Meijer, C. (2006). *Churn Prediction in the Mobile Telecommunications Industry* (Doctoral dissertation). Department of General Sciences-Maastricht University, Maastricht, The Netherlands.

Atiya, A. F. (2001). Bankruptcy prediction for credit risk using neural networks: A survey and new results. *IEEE Transactions on Neural Networks*, *12*(4), 929–935. doi:10.1109/72.935101 PMID:18249923

Balahur, A., Hermida, J. M., & Montoyo, A. (2012). Detecting implicit expressions of emotion in text: A comparative analysis. *Decision Support Systems*, *53*(4), 742–753. doi:10.1016/j.dss.2012.05.024

Basha, S. M., Rajput, D. S., & Vandana, V. (2018). Impact of Gradient Ascent and Boosting Algorithm in Classification. *International Journal of Intelligent Engineering and Systems, 11*(1), 41-49.

Basha, S. M., Zhenning, Y., Rajput, D. S., Caytiles, R. D., & Iyengar, N. (2017). Comparative Study on Performance Analysis of Time Series Predictive Models. *International Journal of Grid and Distributed Computing, 10*(8), 37–48. doi:10.14257/ijgdc.2017.10.8.04

Basha, S. M., Zhenning, Y., Rajput, D. S., Iyengar, N., & Caytiles, R. D. (2017). Weighted Fuzzy Rule Based Sentiment Prediction Analysis on Tweets. *International Journal of Grid and Distributed Computing, 10*(6), 41–54. doi:10.14257/ijgdc.2017.10.6.04

Basha, S. M., Zhenning, Y., Rajput, D. S., Iyengar, N., & Caytiles, R. D. (2017). Domain Specific Predictive Analytics: A Case Study With R. *International Journal of Multimedia and Ubiquitous Engineering, 12*(6), 13-22.

Basha, S. M. H., Balaji, D. S., Caytiles, R. D., & Iyengar, N. (2017). A Soft Computing Approach to Provide Recommendation on PIMA Diabetes. *International Journal of Advanced Science and Technology, 106*(1), 19–32. doi:10.14257/ijast.2017.106.03

Berger, A. L., Pietra, V. J. D., & Pietra, S. A. D. (1996). A maximum entropy approach to natural language processing. *Computational Linguistics, 22*(1), 39–71.

Cambria, E., Benson, T., Eckl, C., & Hussain, A. (2012). Sentic PROMs: Application of sentic computing to the development of a novel unified framework for measuring health-care quality. *Expert Systems with Applications, 39*(12), 10533–10543. doi:10.1016/j.eswa.2012.02.120

Cambria, E., Havasi, C., & Hussain, A. (2012, May). SenticNet 2: A Semantic and Affective Resource for Opinion Mining and Sentiment Analysis. In FLAIRS conference (pp. 202-207). Academic Press.

Cambria, E., Hussain, A., Havasi, C., Eckl, C., & Munro, J. (2010). Towards crowd validation of the UK national health service. *WebSci10*, 1-5.

Chakrabarti, S., Roy, S., & Soundalgekar, M. V. (2003). Fast and accurate text classification via multiple linear discriminant projections. *The VLDB Journal—The International Journal on Very Large Data Bases, 12*(2), 170-185.

Chen, C. C., & Tseng, Y. D. (2011). Quality evaluation of product reviews using an information quality framework. *Decision Support Systems, 50*(4), 755–768. doi:10.1016/j.dss.2010.08.023

Chen, S. F., & Rosenfeld, R. (2000). A survey of smoothing techniques for ME models. *IEEE Transactions on Speech and Audio Processing, 8*(1), 37–50. doi:10.1109/89.817452

Della Pietra, S., Della Pietra, V., & Lafferty, J. (1997). Inducing features of random fields. *IEEE Transactions on Pattern Analysis and Machine Intelligence, 19*(4), 380–393. doi:10.1109/34.588021

Domingos, P., & Pazzani, M. (1997). On the optimality of the simple Bayesian classifier under zero-one loss. *Machine Learning, 29*(2-3), 103–130. doi:10.1023/A:1007413511361

Garvey, M. D., Carnovale, S., & Yeniyurt, S. (2015). An analytical framework for supply network risk propagation: A Bayesian network approach. *European Journal of Operational Research, 243*(2), 618–627. doi:10.1016/j.ejor.2014.10.034

Hu, M., & Liu, B. (2004, August). Mining and summarizing customer reviews. In *Proceedings of the tenth ACM SIGKDD international conference on Knowledge discovery and data mining* (pp. 168-177). ACM.

Hu, Y., & Li, W. (2011). Document sentiment classification by exploring description model of topical terms. *Computer Speech & Language, 25*(2), 386–403. doi:10.1016/j.csl.2010.07.004

Ivascenko, A. (2016). *Topic and Sentiment Analysis of Customers Reviews via Application of Text Mining*. Academic Press.

Jakopović, H., & Preradović, N. M. (2013, January). Evaluation in public relations–sentiment and social media analysis of Croatia Airlines. *7th European Computing Conference (ECC'13)*.

Joachims, T. (1998, April). Text categorization with support vector machines: Learning with many relevant features. In *European conference on machine learning* (pp. 137-142). Springer Berlin Heidelberg. 10.1007/BFb0026683

Keshtkar, F., & Inkpen, D. (2013). A bootstrapping method for extracting paraphrases of emotion expressions from texts. *Computational Intelligence, 29*(3), 417–435. doi:10.1111/j.1467-8640.2012.00458.x

Kontopoulos, E., Berberidis, C., Dergiades, T., & Bassiliades, N. (2013). Ontology-based sentiment analysis of twitter posts. *Expert Systems with Applications, 40*(10), 4065–4074. doi:10.1016/j.eswa.2013.01.001

Larkey, L. S. (1998, August). Automatic essay grading using text categorization techniques. In *Proceedings of the 21st annual international ACM SIGIR conference on Research and development in information retrieval* (pp. 90-95). ACM. 10.1145/290941.290965

Lewis, D. D. (1998, April). Naive (Bayes) at forty: The independence assumption in information retrieval. In *European conference on machine learning* (pp. 4-15). Springer Berlin Heidelberg. 10.1007/BFb0026666

Lewis, D. D., & Ringuette, M. (1994, April). A comparison of two learning algorithms for text categorization. *Third annual symposium on document analysis and information retrieval, 33*, 81-93.

Li, S. T., & Tsai, F. C. (2011, June). Noise control in document classification based on fuzzy formal concept analysis. In *Fuzzy Systems (FUZZ), 2011 IEEE International Conference on* (pp. 2583-2588). IEEE. 10.1109/FUZZY.2011.6007449

Li, Y. H., & Jain, A. K. (1998). Classification of text documents. *The Computer Journal, 41*(8), 537–546. doi:10.1093/comjnl/41.8.537

Li, Y. M., & Li, T. Y. (2013). Deriving market intelligence from microblogs. *Decision Support Systems, 55*(1), 206–217. doi:10.1016/j.dss.2013.01.023

Loraine Charlet, A., & Kumar, A. (2012). *Market Basket Analysis for a Supermarket based on Frequent Itemset Mining*. Academic Press.

Lu, C. Y., Lin, S. H., Liu, J. C., Cruz-Lara, S., & Hong, J. S. (2010). Automatic event-level textual emotion sensing using mutual action histogram between entities. *Expert Systems with Applications*, *37*(2), 1643–1653. doi:10.1016/j.eswa.2009.06.099

Lu, J., & Park, O. (2003). Modeling customer lifetime value using survival analysis—an application in the telecommunications industry. *Data Mining Techniques*, 120-128.

Martín-Valdivia, M.-T., Martínez-Cámara, E., Perea-Ortega, J.-M., & Ureña-López, L. A. (2013). Sentiment polarity detection in Spanish reviews combining supervised and unsupervised approaches. *Expert Systems with Applications*, *40*(10), 3934–3942. doi:10.1016/j.eswa.2012.12.084

Mohammad, S. (2011, June). From once upon a time to happily ever after: Tracking emotions in novels and fairy tales. In *Proceedings of the 5th ACL-HLT Workshop on Language Technology for Cultural Heritage, Social Sciences, and Humanities* (pp. 105-114). Association for Computational Linguistics.

Moraes, R., Valiati, J. F., & Neto, W. P. G. (2013). Document-level sentiment classification: An empirical comparison between SVM and ANN. *Expert Systems with Applications*, *40*(2), 621–633. doi:10.1016/j.eswa.2012.07.059

Mudinas, A., Zhang, D., & Levene, M. (2012, August). Combining lexicon and learning based approaches for concept-level sentiment analysis. In *Proceedings of the First International Workshop on Issues of Sentiment Discovery and Opinion Mining* (p. 5). ACM. 10.1145/2346676.2346681

Neviarouskaya, A., Prendinger, H., & Ishizuka, M. (2007, July). Recognition of affect conveyed by text messaging in online communication. In *International Conference on Online Communities and Social Computing* (pp. 141-150). Springer Berlin Heidelberg. 10.1007/978-3-540-73257-0_16

Neviarouskaya, A., Prendinger, H., & Ishizuka, M. (2009, July). Emoheart: Automation of expressive communication of emotions in second life. In *International Conference on Online Communities and Social Computing* (pp. 584-592). Springer Berlin Heidelberg. 10.1007/978-3-642-02774-1_63

Neviarouskaya, A., Prendinger, H., & Ishizuka, M. (2010, August). Recognition of affect, judgment, and appreciation in text. In *Proceedings of the 23rd international conference on computational linguistics* (pp. 806-814). Association for Computational Linguistics.

Nigam, K., Lafferty, J., & McCallum, A. (1999, August). Using maximum entropy for text classification. In IJCAI-99 workshop on machine learning for information filtering (Vol. 1, pp. 61-67). Academic Press.

Pang, B., Lee, L., & Vaithyanathan, S. (2002, July). Thumbs up?: sentiment classification using machine learning techniques. In *Proceedings of the ACL-02 conference on Empirical methods in natural language processing-Volume 10* (pp. 79-86). Association for Computational Linguistics. 10.3115/1118693.1118704

Plutchik, R. (1980). A general psychoevolutionary theory of emotion. *Theories of Emotion, 1*(3-31), 4.

Priss, U. (2006). Formal concept analysis in information science. *Arist*, *40*(1), 521–543.

Quinlan, J. R. (1986). Induction of decision trees. *Machine Learning*, *1*(1), 81–106. doi:10.1007/BF00116251

Ruiz, M. E., & Srinivasan, P. (1999, August). Hierarchical neural networks for text categorization (poster abstract). In *Proceedings of the 22nd annual international ACM SIGIR conference on Research and development in information retrieval* (pp. 281-282). ACM. 10.1145/312624.312700

Scridon, M. A. (2008). Understanding customers-profiling and segmentation. *Management & Marketing-Craiova*, (1), 175-184.

Sebastiani, F. (2002). Machine learning in automated text categorization. *ACM Computing Surveys*, *34*(1), 1–47. doi:10.1145/505282.505283

Tsytsarau, M., & Palpanas, T. (2012). Survey on mining subjective data on the web. *Data Mining and Knowledge Discovery*, *24*(3), 478–514. doi:10.100710618-011-0238-6

Wan, Y., & Gao, Q. (2015, November). An ensemble sentiment classification system of Twitter data for airline services analysis. In *Data Mining Workshop (ICDMW), 2015 IEEE International Conference on* (pp. 1318-1325). IEEE. 10.1109/ICDMW.2015.7

Xianghua, F., Guo, L., Yanyan, G., & Zhiqiang, W. (2013). Multi-aspect sentiment analysis for Chinese online social reviews based on topic modeling and HowNet lexicon. *Knowledge-Based Systems*, *37*, 186–195. doi:10.1016/j.knosys.2012.08.003

Ye, Q., Zhang, Z., & Law, R. (2009). Sentiment classification of online reviews to travel destinations by supervised machine learning approaches. *Expert Systems with Applications*, *36*(3), 6527–6535. doi:10.1016/j.eswa.2008.07.035

Yee Liau, B., & Pei Tan, P. (2014). Gaining customer knowledge in low cost airlines through text mining. *Industrial Management & Data Systems*, *114*(9), 1344–1359. doi:10.1108/IMDS-07-2014-0225

KEY TERMS AND DEFINITIONS

Artificial Neuro-Fuzzy Inference System (ANFIS): In ANFIS using a given input/output data set, the toolbox function ANFIS constructs a fuzzy inference system (FIS) whose membership function parameters are tuned using either a back-propagation algorithm alone or in combination with a least squares type of method.

Decision Tree (DT): An iterative process of splitting the data up into partitions.

Life Time Value (LTV): Is a straightforward measure that produce customer profitability and level of churn risk management at individual customer.

Natural Language Processing (NLP): An approach to analysis the text information.

Sentiment Analysis (SA): It is to measure the opinion of a user about, product, service, topic, issue, person, organization, or event.

Survival Analysis (SA): It is a collection of statistical methods which model time-to-event data, the time until the event occurs is of interest.

Chapter 10

A Relative Performance of Dissimilarity Measures for Matching Relational Web Access Patterns Between User Sessions

Dilip Singh Sisodia
National Institute of Technology Raipur, India

ABSTRACT

Customized web services are offered to users by grouping them according to their access patterns. Clustering techniques are very useful in grouping users and analyzing web access patterns. Clustering can be an object clustering performed on feature vectors or relational clustering performed on relational data. The relational clustering is preferred over object clustering for web users' sessions because of high dimensionality and sparsity of web users' data. However, relational clustering of web users depends on underlying dissimilarity measures used. Therefore, correct dissimilarity measure for matching relational web access patterns between user sessions is very important. In this chapter, the various dissimilarity measures used in relational clustering of web users' data are discussed. The concept of an augmented user session is also discussed to derive different augmented session dissimilarity measures. The discussed session dissimilarity measures are used with relational fuzzy clustering algorithms. The comparative performance binary session similarity and augmented session similarity measures are evaluated using intra-cluster and inter-cluster distance-based cluster quality ratio. The results suggested the augmented session dissimilarity measures in general, and intuitive augmented session (dis)similarity measure, in particular, performed better than the other measures.

DOI: 10.4018/978-1-5225-3870-7.ch010

INTRODUCTION

The access data genrated by Web applications are growing with phenomenal rate, and this web usage data is used to gain extra knowledge about the users' navigation patterns. The knowledge extrated from the accesses patterns of users may be utilized to serve the needs of the user in a better way. The access patterns of Web users are stored in the server logs and logs are partitioned into user sessions for analysis.

The user sessions are represented as a feature vector of accesed page URLs. The number of accessed page URLs represented the dimension and assigned binary values such as zero and one. Where one and zero denotes the accessing and not accessing respectively of web page (URL) in an individual session (Nasraoui, Hichem, Krishnapuram, & Joshi, 2000).

Let's consider n number of web pages in any website then Eq. (1) may be used to represent the ith user session as n - dimensional binary vector space of web pages.

$$S_j^i = \begin{cases} 1, if\ the\ user\ accessed\ the\ j^{th}\ web\ page\ in\ i^{th}\ session \\ 0, \qquad Otherwise, \qquad\qquad\qquad j = 1,2,3\ldots n \end{cases} \tag{1}$$

The similarity measures are defined between any two user sessions using binary feature vector representation of Eq. (1) and incorporating accessed URLs along with their For better understanding and clear distinction conventional web user session similarity measures are renamed as binary session similarity (BSS), binary URL syntactic similarity (BUSS) and combined binary session similarity (CBSS) (Sisodia, Verma, & Vyas, 2016d). A simple binary session similarity measure between web user sessions S_i^k and S_i^ℓ is given by Eq. (2). In this similarity measure individual accessing web page URLs in any user session are completely ignore the syntactic structure of URL and assumed totally independent.

$$BSS_{(S_i^k, S_i^\ell)} = \frac{\sum_{i=1}^n S_i^k \times S_i^\ell}{\sqrt{\sum_{i=1}^n S_i^{k^2}} \sqrt{\sum_{i=1}^n S_i^{l^2}}} \tag{2}$$

The main limitations of BSS measure are that it completely ignores the syntactic structure of accessing URLs. In literature (Nasraoui et al., 2000) an alternative URL based syntactic similarity measure is also reported to overcome the limitations of BSS which is renamed as BUSS. The BUSS measure employed the syntactic similarity between any pair of URLs given by Eq. (3).

$$USS_{\left(S_{p_i}^k, S_{p_j}^l\right)} = Min\left(1, \frac{\left|LoP\left(P_{(k,i)}\right) \cap LoP\left(P_{(l,j)}\right)\right|}{Max\left(1, Max\left(LoP\left(P_{(k,i)}\right), LoP\left(P_{(l,j)}\right)\right) - 1\right)}\right) \tag{3}$$

where $LoP\left(\mathcal{P}_{(k,i)}\right)$ is length of URL (or number of edges) of path traversed from root node to respective node of $\mathcal{P}_i$ in user session $\mathcal{S}^k_{p_i}$. The Eq. (3) used to incorporate the syntactic similarities of URLs between two binary sessions $\left(\mathcal{S}^k_{p_i}, \mathcal{S}^\ell_{p_j}\right)$ and computed by Eq. (4).

$$BUSS_{\left(\mathcal{S}^k_{p_i}, \mathcal{S}^\ell_{p_j}\right)} = \frac{\sum_{i=1}^{n}\sum_{j=1}^{n}\mathcal{S}^k_{p_i} \times \mathcal{S}^\ell_{p_j} \times USS_{\left(\mathcal{S}^k_{p_i}, \mathcal{S}^\ell_{p_j}\right)}}{\sum_{i=1}^{n}\mathcal{S}^k_{p_i} \times \sum_{j=1}^{n}\mathcal{S}^\ell_{p_j}} \tag{4}$$

The combined similarity measure between two sessions that takes advantage of similarity measures as defined in Eq. (2) and (4) and given in Eq. (5).

$$CBSS_{\left(\mathcal{S}^k_{p_i}, \mathcal{S}^\ell_{p_j}\right)} = Max\left\{BSS_{(S^k_i, S^\ell_j)}, BUSS_{\left(\mathcal{S}^k_{p_i}, \mathcal{S}^\ell_{p_j}\right)}\right\} \tag{5}$$

The session similarity measures as discussed in Eq. (2), (4) and (5) give only binary consideration (accessed or not accessed) to accessing pages in any web user session. The binary consideration is not sufficient to categorize user access patterns. However, the web user's habits, interest, and expectations should also be considered by measuring the relevance of pages in every session because all of the URLs visited in a session are not equally important to the user. At the same time, one cannot ignore the syntactic structure of the accessing page URL and hierarchical position of this URL in website organization. By considering the above-stated facts, the discussed intuitive augmented session dissimilarity measure is used to capture the resemblance between two user sessions.

METHODOLOGY

In this section, we are going to present a detailed description of the methodology adopted for this work. The proposed methodology is described in following subsections.

Pre-Processing of Web Server Logs

The weblogs keep a record of metadata of all documents accessed explicitly or implicitly by clients in the form of standard fields. The exact sequence and number of the field are varying from one log format to others. However essential information including address and the login name of the remote host, name of the user, request time, method, and full path of the server, used protocol, status code, access data size, and agents used to access the information are present in every format. However, all recorded entries are not useful always and increase the size of weblogs. Mostly these are implicit requests made for embedding objects within web pages, requests made by automated software agents(Sisodia, Verma, & Vyas, 2015b), unsuccessful requests of users, and requests with access methods other than GET, etc. First, we remove these entries from log files using various heuristics reported in literature. Second, user sessions are created from cleaned logs. The sessions are a unit of interaction between a web user and a web server. In this chapter most popular timeout based session identification heuristics (Cooley, Mobashar, & Srivastava, 1999) are used. A session is created when a new IP address is found in the weblog entries, and subsequently, a request from the same IP address is added to the session as long as the elapsed time between two consecutive requests does not exceed a predefined threshold value, set for 30 minutes in our work. Otherwise, the current session closes, and a new session starts. A web user's historical access pattern may have more than one session because he or she may visit a website from time to time and spend an arbitrary amount of time between consecutive visits (Sisodia, Verma, & Vyas, 2015a).

Augmented Web User Sessions

In simple binary web user sessions representation, only presence or absence of any visited page URL is considered. However, a web user may find some page URLs more relevant than others based on their interest, and expectations. Therefore, the notion of augmented web user sessions may be used to approximate the relevance of any page for the individual web user (Sisodia, 2017). In subsequent sub-section computation of relevance of page URL in any web user session is discussed.

User Sessions Representation in Vector Space

It is assumed that; there are m users' sessions are identified from the web server log $S_i = \left\{ S_1, S_2, ... S_m \right\}$. These m users' sessions accessing n number of different pages URL's $P_i = \left\{ P_1, P_2, ... P_n \right\}$ on a given website in some time interval. We represent each user session S_i by following equation $S_i = \left\{ S_i^1, S_i^2, ... S_i^n \right\}$, $\forall i = 1, 2, ..., n$. where each S_k^i represents a harmonic mean of the number of visits to the page P_h within the session S_i, and the duration of the page (in seconds) P_k in session S_i, which is represented by Eq. (6) and Eq. (7)(Sisodia, Verma, & Vyas, 2016a).

$$S_k^i \rightarrow \begin{cases} Page\, frequency \\ Page\, duration\ (in\ \sec onds) \\ Page\, size\ (in\, bytes) \end{cases} \qquad (6)$$

$$\mathcal{R}\left[m, n\right] = \begin{pmatrix} S_1^1 & S_1^2 & \cdots & S_1^n \\ S_2^1 & S_2^2 & \cdots & S_2^n \\ \vdots & \vdots & \ddots & \vdots \\ S_m^1 & S_m^2 & \cdots & S_m^n \end{pmatrix} \qquad (7)$$

Deriving the Page Relevance Based Augmented Session

Web users' interests for any page are computed by implicit measures (Chan, 1999),(Xiao & Zhang, 2001). The page duration and number of frequent visits to the page(frequency) are considered most popular implicit measures for finding the user interest on particular page (Liu & Keselj, 2007). The following metrics are used to compute the relevance of a page in any user session. Further, this relevance is used to measure the web user concern for a web page.

Duration of Page $\left(DoP \right)$

Duration of page or Page stay time defined as the time spent on a page by web user, and it is the difference between the exact time of the request for page $\mathcal{P}_i$ and the time of the request for the next webpage in the session from the access log file. A Higher value of page stay time implies more concern of the user to any page. However, sometimes the small size of a web page may lead to a swift transition to another page. Therefore, the time spent on the page is normalized by the page size. The Eq. (8) is used to compute the duration of a web page ($\mathcal{P}_i$) in user session ($\mathcal{S}_k$).

$$\left(DoP \right)_{\mathcal{P}_i} = \frac{\dfrac{\sum \text{Time Spent on} \left(\mathcal{P}_i \right)}{\text{Size of}(\mathcal{P}_i)}}{\text{Max}\left(\forall_{j \in \mathcal{S}_k} \dfrac{\sum \text{Time Spent on}(\mathcal{P}_{j)}}{\text{Size of} \left(\mathcal{P}_j \right)} \right)} \tag{8}$$

where $0 \leq \left(DoP \right)_{\mathcal{P}_i} \leq 1$

However, in the case of last access page, it is not feasible to compute the difference of requests time. Therefore, the average duration of the relevant session may be considered.

Table 1. Example of the duration of pages in respective accessing user sessions

Web Pages User sessions	P_1	P_2	P_n
S_1	$\left(DoP \right)_{11}$	$\left(DoP \right)_{12}$	$\left(DoP \right)_{1n}$
S_2	$\left(DoP \right)_{21}$	$\left(DoP \right)_{22}$	$\left(DoP \right)_{2n}$
S_m	$\left(DoP \right)_{m1}$	$\left(DoP \right)_{m2}$	$\left(DoP \right)_{mn}$

Frequency of Page $\left(FoP\right)$

Frequency is the number of times the web page P_i has been visited in the session. The high values of this number point towards more interest of a user for any page. The frequency of a page is divided by the accumulated frequency in the session: The Eq. (9) is used to compute the frequency of the web page (P_i) in user session (S_k).

$$\left(FoP\right)_{P_i} = \frac{\sum \# \text{ of visits to}\left(P_i\right))}{\text{Max}\left(\forall_{j \in S_k} \sum \# \text{ of visits to}\left(P_j\right)\right)} \tag{9}$$

where $0 \leq \left(FoP\right)_{P_i} \leq 1$

These two metrics can be combined to measure the relevance of a web page to a user. We can compute the harmonic mean of $\left(DoP\right)_{P_i}$ and $\left(FoP\right)_{P_i}$ for estimating user concern in a page because it will moderate the impact of large and small outliers (Vakali, Pokorný, & Dalamagas, 2004) web user sessions. After applying Eq. (8) and (9) on pre-processed log intermediate results are generated as shown in Table 3.

Relevance of the Page $\left(RoP\right)$

From Table 3 the page relevance is computed by the harmonic mean of DoP and FoP. because this harmonic mean will moderate the impact of large and small outliers (Joydeep, Strehl, Ghosh, Mooney, & Strehl, 2000). Eq. (10) is used to compute the relevance of a web page (P_i) in user session (S_k).

$$\left(RoP\right)_{P_i} = \frac{2 \times \left(DoP\right)_{P_i} \times \left(FoP\right)_{P_i}}{\left(DoP\right)_{P_i} + \left(FoP\right)_{P_i}} \tag{10}$$

where $0 \leq \left(RoP\right)_{P_i} \leq 1$

Table 2. Example of frequency of pages in respective accessing user sessions

Web Pages User sessions	P_1	P_2	P_n
S_1	$\left(FoP\right)_{11}$	$\left(FoP\right)_{12}$	$\left(FoP\right)_{1n}$
S_2	$\left(FoP\right)_{21}$	$\left(FoP\right)_{22}$	$\left(FoP\right)_{2n}$
S_m	$\left(FoP\right)_{m1}$	$\left(FoP\right)_{m2}$	$\left(FoP\right)_{mn}$

Table 3. Web user sessions with frequency, duration, and size of accessing pages

Session ID	Host Name	Actual list of pages accessed during session	No. Of Pages accessed during session	Frequency of each page	Duration on each page	Size of each page
1	IP_1	P_{11}	N_1	f_{11}	d_{11}	s_{11}
		P_{12}		f_{12}	d_{12}	s_{12}
		.		.	.	.
		P_{1n}		f_{1n}	d_{1n}	s_{1n}
2	IP_2	P_{21}	N_2	f_{21}	d_{21}	s_{21}
		P_{22}		f_{22}	d_{22}	s_{22}
		.		.	.	.
		P_{2n}		F_{2n}	d_{2n}	s_{2n}
i	IP_i	P_{i1}	N_i	f_{i1}	d_{i1}	s_{i1}
		.		.	.	.
		P_{in}		f_{in}	d_{in}	s_{in}

The equation (10) shows that user interests for a particular web page in any session are considered more when both of access duration and access frequency are high.

Augmented Web User Sessions

The page relevance matrix ($\mathcal{RM}_{m \times n}$) is computed using equations (9) to (10). This relevance matrix will define the relevance of each page in every session. If the page has high relevance means the user has more concern in this page. This relevance matrix is given by Eq. (11).

$$\mathcal{RM}_{m \times n} = \begin{pmatrix} \left(RoP\right)_{11} & \left(RoP\right)_{12} & \cdots & \left(RoP\right)_{1n} \\ \left(RoP\right)_{21} & \left(RoP\right)_{22} & \cdots & \left(RoP\right)_{12} \\ \vdots & \vdots & \ddots & \vdots \\ \left(RoP\right)_{m1} & \left(RoP\right)_{m2} & \cdots & \left(RoP\right)_{mn} \end{pmatrix} \tag{11}$$

By incorporating page relevance in to user access behavior matrix, simple web user sessions converted to augmented web user sessions. The augmented web session is represented as follows $\mathcal{AS}_a = \{(\mathcal{P}1, \left(RoP\right)_{\mathcal{P}1}, \left(\mathcal{P}2, \left(RoP\right)_{\mathcal{P}2}\right) \dots \left(Pn, \left(RoP\right)_{pn}\right)\}$. Where, Pi, and $\left(RoP\right)_{pi}$ are the visiting page, and its relevance respectively.

Augmented Web User Session Based Dissimilarity Measures

In this section, the concept of an augmented web user sessions is used to derive different augmented session dissimilarity measures. It is believed that augmented session dissimilarity measures are more realistic and represent session dissimilarities based on the web user's habits, interest, and expectations as compared to simple binary session dissimilarity measures.

Page Relevance-Based Augmented Session Similarity

Here relevance of pages accessed in user sessions is incorporated in simple cosine similarity measure Eq. (12). This augmented session similarity measure may represent more meaningful web user session similarity as compared to simple user session based cosine measure (Nasraoui et al., 2000).

$$
ASS_{(AS_a, AS_b)} = \frac{\sum_{i=1}^{n} AS_a(RoP)_i \times AS_b(RoP)_j}{\sqrt{\sum_{i=1}^{n} AS_a(RoP)_i^2} \sqrt{\sum_{j=1}^{n} AS_b(RoP)_j^2}}
\tag{12}
$$

This augmented session similarity measure is more realistic and represents session similarities based on the web user's habits, interest, and expectations as compared to simple binary session similarity based cosine measure.

A URL Syntactic Similarity between i^{th} and j^{th} Page URL

In (Nasraoui et al., 2000) authors defined an alternative URL based syntactic similarity measure to compute the syntactic similarity between any pair of URLs given by Eq. (13).

$$
USS_{\left(us_a^{p_i}, us_b^{p_j}\right)} = Min\left(1, \frac{\left|LoP\left(\mathcal{P}_{(a,i)}\right) \cap LoP\left(\mathcal{P}_{(b,j)}\right)\right|}{Max\left(1, Max\left(LoP\left(\mathcal{P}_{(a,i)}\right), LoP\left(\mathcal{P}_{(b,j)}\right)\right) - 1\right)}\right)
\tag{13}
$$

where $LoP\left(\mathcal{P}_{(a,i)}\right)$ is length of URL (or number of edges) of path traversed from root node to respective node of $\mathcal{P}_i$ in user session US_a. By applying this syntactic similarity of URL's, the similarity between two augmented web user sessions $\left(AS_a^{p_i}, AS_b^{p_j}\right)$ is computed by Eq. (2.14).

$$
AUSS_{\left(AS_a^{p_i}, AS_b^{p_j}\right)} = \frac{\sum_{i=1}^{n} \sum_{j=1}^{n} AS_a(RoP)_i \times AS_b(RoP)_j \times USS_{\left(us_a^{p_i}, us_b^{p_j}\right)}}{\sum_{i=1}^{n} AS_a(RoP)_i \times \sum_{j=1}^{n} AS_b(RoP)_j}
\tag{14}
$$

Intuitive Augmented Session Dissimilarity Measure

Intuitive augmented session dissimilarity utilizes the properties of two measures and considers the maximum optimistic aggregation of these measures to give remarkable similarities between web user sessions. Intuitive augmented session similarity computed using Eq. (15).

$$\mathcal{IASS}_{(AS_a, AS_b)} = Max \left\{ ASS_{(AS_a, AS_b)}, AUSS_{\left(AS_a^{p_i}, AS_b^{p_j} \right)} \right\}$$ (15)

As a requirement of relational clustering, this Intuitive augmented session similarity is converted to the dissimilarity/distance measure. The intuitive augmented session dissimilarity is computed using Eq. (16).

$$\mathcal{D}^2_{(AS_a, AS_b)} = \left(1 - \mathcal{IASS}_{(AS_a, AS_b)} \right)^2$$ (16)

where $0 < \mathcal{D}^2_{(AS_a, AS_b)} \leq 1$, for AS_a, $AS_b = 1, 2.....m$. This dissimilarity (distance) measure satisfies the following necessary conditions of a metric (Huang, 2008).

1. The distance between any two sessions must be nonnegative.
2. The distance between two sessions must be zero if and only if the two sessions are identical.
3. The Distance must be symmetric, that is, the distance from AS_a to AS_b is the same as the distance from AS_a to AS_b.

The pseudo-code for the above-described process is presented as algorithm 1. This algorithm is used to generate the essential dissimilarity matrices between web user sessions from the raw web server log file. The entire process of intuitive augmented session dissimilarity matrix generation is shown in Figure 1. The next section will describe the relational fuzzy clustering of web user sessions using the augmented session dissimilarity measures presented in this section.

Augmented Session Dissimilarity Based Relational Fuzzy Clustering

Given a set of augmented user sessions $\mathcal{AS}_i = \left\{ \mathcal{AS}_1, \mathcal{AS}_2, ... \mathcal{AS}_m \right\}$ $for\ i = 1, 2, ... m$. Where, each session is represented by vector of n dimensions $\mathcal{S}_i = \left\{ \mathcal{AS}_i^1, \mathcal{AS}_i^2, ... \mathcal{AS}_i^n \right\}$, $\forall i = 1, 2, ..., n$.

First, in subsequent subsection relational fuzzy c-means (RFCM) clustering algorithm is elucidated in the context of clustering web user session using different session dissimilarity measures.

Table 4. Pseudo code for computation of page relevance based augmented session dissimilarity matrix (Algorithm 1) (Sisodia, Verma, & Vyas, 2016b)

Input:{web server log file: $\mathcal{L}$ of n records where $\mathcal{L} \leftarrow \left\{r_1, r_2 \ldots r_n\right\}$, where n $\ggg 1$,

$\forall \varepsilon r_i \left\langle \text{ip,time,method,url,protocol,size,status,agent,referrer} \right\rangle$

$USS_{\left(us_a^{p_i}, us_b^{p_j}\right)}$ — URL based Syntactic Similarity matrix }

Output: { $\mathcal{D}_{m \times m}$ | augmented session dissimilarity matrix}

1: Pre-processing of web server access log

a. Removing of extraneous information- $\mathcal{L} \leftarrow \left\{r_1, r_2 \ldots r_n\right\}$ is a cleaned web log file

b. Identification of web users $\mathcal{U}_i = \left\{\mathcal{U}_1, \mathcal{U}_2, \ldots \mathcal{U}_n\right\}$ $for\, i = 1, 2, \ldots n.$

c. Identification of web user sessions $\mathcal{S} = \left\{\mathcal{S}_1, \mathcal{S}_2, \ldots \mathcal{S}_m\right\}$ $for\, i = 1, 2, \ldots m$. Where $m \geq n$

2: Vector representation of web user sessions: $\mathcal{S}_i = \left\{\mathcal{S}_i^1, \mathcal{S}_i^2, \ldots \mathcal{S}_i^n\right\}, \forall i = 1, 2, \ldots, n.$ Where, $\mathcal{S}_k^i$ *represents a harmonic*

mean of the number of visits to the page $\mathcal{P}_k$ *within the session* $\mathcal{S}_i$*, and the duration of the page (in seconds)* $\mathcal{P}_k$ *in session* $\mathcal{S}_i$

3: Computation of relevance of any web page in user sessions for each pair of ($\mathcal{S}_k, \mathcal{P}_i$) session $\mathcal{S}_k$ and page

P_i $where$ $i = 1, 2, \ldots n$ and $k = 1, 2, \ldots m.$

a. The duration of a web page (P_i) in user session ($\mathcal{S}_k$) is computed using Eq. (8).

b. The Frequency of web page ($\mathcal{P}_i$) in user session ($\mathcal{S}_k$) is computed using Eq. (9).

c. The relevance of web page ($\mathcal{P}_i$) in user session ($\mathcal{S}_k$) is computed using Eq. (10).
    4: The page relevance based augmented session similarity matrix is computed using Eq. (12)
    5: The page relevance and URL syntactic similarity based augmented session similarity matrix are computed using Eq. (14).
    6: The Intuitive augmented session similarity is computed by using Eq. (15)

7: The page relevance based Intuitive augmented session dissimilarity matrix $\mathcal{D}_{m \times m} = \mathcal{D}_{\left(AS_a, AS_b\right)}^2$ is calculated using Eq.(16)

Relational Fuzzy C-Mean Clustering

In this section, a relational fuzzy c-means (RFCM) clustering algorithm (R.J. Hathaway, J.W. Davenport, 1989) is presented for grouping pairwise dissimilarity values in an augmented session dissimilarity matrix D. The RFCM is dual to the fuzzy c-means (FCM) (Bezdek, James C., Robert Ehrlich, 1984) object data algorithm when D is a Euclidean matrix. Let $d_{\mathcal{R}, ik}$ is the relational distance between cluster prototype and augmented session $\mathcal{AS}_h$ and $\mathcal{V}_\mathcal{R} \leftarrow \left\{v_{\mathcal{R},1}, v_{\mathcal{R},2}, \ldots v_{\mathcal{R},c}\right\}$ represent a set of relational cluster centres in $\mathcal{D}$.

The objective function of relational fuzzy c-means algorithm seeks to c representative sessions as relational cluster centers (known as centroid), such that the total distance of other sessions to their closest centroid is minimized. The objective function of relational fuzzy c-means (RFCM) is defined as Eq. (17) and membership function is given by Eq. (18).

$$\mathcal{F}_{\mathcal{R}FCM} = \sum_{j=1}^{c} \frac{\sum_{i=1}^{n}\sum_{k=1}^{n}\mu_{ij}^{f}\mu_{kj}^{f}d_{\mathcal{R},ik}}{2\sum_{i=1}^{n}\mu_{ij}^{f}} \qquad (17)$$

$$\mu_{ik} = \frac{\left(d_{\mathcal{R},ik}\right)^{-\frac{1}{(f-1)}}}{\sum_{j=1}^{c}\left(d_{\mathcal{R},ik}\right)^{-\frac{1}{(f-1)}}} \qquad (18)$$

Figure 1. Process of intuitive augmented dissimilarity matrix generation

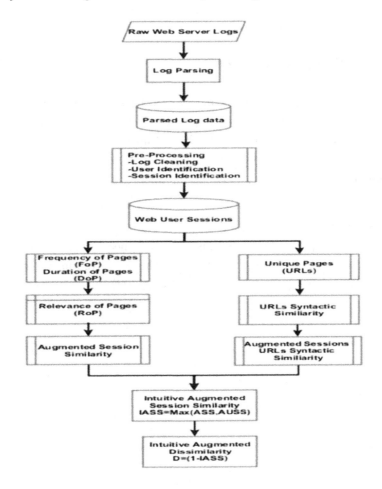

Where, $f \in [1, \infty]$ is a fuzzification coefficient and The Euclidean distance $d_{\mathcal{R},ik}$ is the relational distance between cluster prototype and augmented session $\mathcal{AS}_k$ and this distance is calculated based on memberships in $\mathcal{U}$ and dissimilarities in $\mathcal{D}$ using Eq.(19) and the relational cluster centres are updated by using Eq.(20).

$$d_{\mathcal{R},ik} = \left(D v_{\mathcal{R},i}^{t-1} \right)_k - \frac{1}{2} \left(v_{\mathcal{R},i}^{t-1} \right)^T D v_{\mathcal{R},i}^{t-1} \quad \text{for } 1 \leq i \leq c \text{ and } 1 \leq k \leq n \tag{19}$$

$$v_{\mathcal{R},i}^t = \frac{\left(\mu_{i1}^{\ f}, \ \mu_{i2}^{\ f}, \dots \ \mu_{in}^{\ f} \right)}{\sum_{i=1}^{n} \mu_{ik}^{\ f}} \quad \text{for } 1 \leq i \leq c \tag{20}$$

The Pseudo code for augmented session dissimilarity based fuzzy relational c-means (RFCM) clustering is presented as Algorithm 2 (R.J. Hathaway, J.W. Davenport, 1989)(Sisodia, Verma, & Vyas, 2016c). Which summarizes the steps involved in fuzzy relational c-means clustering to discover web user clusters from page relevance based relational matrix of augmented web user sessions.

In next section relational fuzzy c-medoids clustering is explained in details to cluster the web user sessions by using session dissimilarity measures.

Relational Fuzzy C-Medoids Clustering

In this section, the concept of fuzzy relational c-medoids(R. Krishnapuram, Joshi, & Liyu Yi, 1999) is reproduced in the present context to used with augmented session similarity measures. In a previous study (Raghu Krishnapuram, Joshi, Nasraoui, & Yi, 2001) fuzzy relational c-medoids (FCMdd) clustering has been used for web user session clustering using simple binary session similarity measure. Let $d\left(\mathcal{AS}_i, \mathcal{AS}_j \right)$ represent the dissimilarity between augmented session $\mathcal{AS}_i$ and session $\mathcal{AS}_j$. Let $\mathcal{V} \leftarrow \{v_1, v_2, \dots v_c\}$, $v_i \in \mathcal{D}$ represent a subset of augmented dissimilarity matrix $\mathcal{D}$ with cardinality c. Let $\mathcal{D}^c$ represents the set of all c-subsets $\mathcal{V}$ *of* $\mathcal{D}$ of the objective function of relational fuzzy c-medoids algorithm seek to c representative sessions (known as medoids), such that the total dissimilarity of other sessions to their closest medoid is minimized. The objective function of fuzzy c-medoids is defined as Eq. (21) and membership functions is given by Eq. (22)

$$\mathcal{F}_{FCMdd} = \sum_{j=1}^{c} \left(\sum_{i=1}^{n} \mu_{ij}^f \ d\left(\mathcal{AS}_i, v_j \right) \right) \tag{21}$$

Table 5. Pseudo code for augmented session dissimilarity based fuzzy relational c-means (RFCM) algorithm (Algorithm 2)

Input: { $\mathcal{D}_{m \times m}$ |Augmented session dissimilarity matrix, c | Number of clusters $f > 1$ | fuzzifier, t_{max} |maximum no of iterations, ε| step }

Output:{ $\mathcal{V}_{\mathcal{R}} \leftarrow \{v_{\mathcal{R},1}, v_{\mathcal{R},2}, \cdots v_{\mathcal{R},c}\}$ | set of relational cluster centres, $\mathcal{U}$ |Fuzzy membership matrix}

1: Initialize step=ε, $t = 1$; and randomly chose c rows of $\mathcal{D}$ as initial centres.

2: While $\left(t \leq t_{max} \text{ and step} \geq \mu \right)$

3: Compute Euclidean distance ($d_{\mathcal{R},ik}$)between augmented sessions $\mathcal{AS}_k$ and centroid of clusters using Eq.(19)

4: For $k \leftarrow 1, 2, \ldots n \quad do$

5: If $d_{\mathcal{R},ik} \neq 0 \qquad \forall i$

6: calculate membership function matrix $\left(\mathcal{U}\right)$ using Eq.(18)

    7: Else

8: Set $\mu_{ik} > 0 \, for \, d_{\mathcal{R},ik} = 0, \quad \mu_{ik} \in \left[0, 1\right]$ and $\sum_{j=1}^{c} \mu_{jk} = 1$

    9: End If
    10: End For

11: Update the value of relational cluster centers($v_{\mathcal{R},i}^{t}$) using Eq.(20)

12: $step \leftarrow \max_{\substack{1 \leq i \leq c \\ 1 \leq k \leq n}} \left\{ \left\| \mathcal{V}_{\mathcal{R}}^{t} - \mathcal{V}_{\mathcal{R}}^{(t-1)} \right\| \right\}$

13: $t \leftarrow t + 1$;
    14: End While

$$\mu_{ij} = \frac{\left(d\left(\mathcal{S}_i, v_j\right)\right)^{-\frac{1}{(f-1)}}}{\sum_{j=1}^{c} \left(d\left(\mathcal{S}_i, v_j\right)\right)^{-\frac{1}{(f-1)}}} \qquad (22)$$

where, $d\left(\mathcal{AS}_i, v_j\right)$ is the dissimilarity between augmented session $\mathcal{AS}_i$ and medoid of cluster $\mathcal{AS}_j$ and $f \in \left[1, \infty\right]$ is fuzzification coefficient.

The Pseudo code for augmented session dissimilarity based fuzzy c-medoids clustering is shown in Algorithm 3(R. Krishnapuram et al., 1999) (Sisodia et al., 2016d). Algorithm 3 summarized the steps involved in augmented dissimilarity based Relational Fuzzy c-medoids clustering to discover web user clusters from page relevance based relational matrix of augmented web user sessions.

After detail description of web user session clustering, next section will explain the performance measures used to evaluate the quality of generated clusters.

Table 6. Pseudo code for augmented session dissimilarity based fuzzy c-medoids clustering algorithm (Algorithm 3)

Input: { $\mathcal{D}_{m \times m}$ |Augmented session dissimilarity matrix, c |Number of clusters,

t_{max} |maximum no of iterations}

Output: { $\mathcal{V} \leftarrow \{v_1, v_2, \dots v_c\}$, | set of real session medoids,

$\mathcal{U}$ |Fuzzy membership matrix}

1: Fix the number of medoids $c > 1$ and select first medoids randomly;

2: set $\mathcal{V} \leftarrow \{v_1\}$; $t \leftarrow 1$;

3: for $t \leftarrow 2, \dots, c$

4: $q \leftarrow \underset{1 \leq i \leq n; S_i \notin \mathcal{V}}{\mathrm{argmax}} \underset{1 \leq \varphi \leq |\mathcal{V}|}{\min} d\left(v_j, \mathcal{AS}_i\right)$; $\mathcal{V}_t \leftarrow \mathcal{S}_q$;

5: $\mathcal{V} \leftarrow \mathcal{V} \cup \{\mathcal{V}_t\}$;

6: $t \leftarrow t + 1$;

   7: End for

8: set $t \leftarrow 0$;

9: chose set of initial medoids: $\mathcal{V} \leftarrow \{v_1, v_2, \dots v_c\}$ from $\mathcal{D}^c$

10: While $\left\{\left(t \leq t_{max}\right) \text{ or } \mathcal{V}_{old} \leftarrow \mathcal{V}\right\}$

   Compute memberships $\frac{1}{4ij}$ that minimizes $\mathcal{F}_{FCMdd}$:

11: For $j \leftarrow 1, 2, \dots c \;\; do$

12: For $i \leftarrow 1, 2, \dots n$

   13: The membership function is calculate using Eq.(22)

   14: End for

   15: End for

16: Store the current medoid: $\mathcal{V}_{old} \leftarrow \mathcal{V}$;

   Compute the new medoids v_i that minimize $\mathcal{F}_{FCMdd}$:

17: For $\;\; j \leftarrow 1, 2, \dots c \;\; do$

18: $q \leftarrow \underset{1 \leq k \leq n; S_i \neq v_i}{\mathrm{argmin}} \sum_{i=1}^{n} \mu_{ij}{}^{f} d\left(\mathcal{AS}_j, \mathcal{AS}_i\right)$; $v_j \leftarrow \mathcal{AS}_q$;

   19: End for

20: $t \leftarrow t + 1$

   21: End While

PERFORMANCE EVALUATION MEASURES

The performance of various dissimilarity measures discussed in this chapter is evaluated using an unsupervised evaluation method. The method is based on intra-cluster and inter-cluster distance measures (Halkidi, Batistakis, & Vazirgiannis, 2001),(Halkidi, Batistakis, & Vazirgiannis, 2002). The average distance between all pair of sessions in any of the ith cluster is known as Intra-cluster distance. The Intra-cluster distance represents compactness of a cluster and the small value of intra cluster distance is desirable for good quality of clusters.

The separation between clusters is measured by inter-cluster distance and calculated as an average of the distance between sessions from i^{th} cluster and sessions from j^{th} cluster. The high value of inter-cluster distance is expected for good partition (Brun et al., 2007). The Eq. (23) and Eq. (24) are used to calculate the intra-cluster and inter-cluster distance respectively. The ratio of average intra cluster and average inter-cluster distance is also used to assess the quality of clusters and given by Eq. (25).

$$\mathcal{D}_{intra} = \frac{\sum_{S_{k \in c_i}} \sum_{S_{\ell \in c_i, \ell \neq k}} d_{k\ell}^2 \left(\mathcal{AS}_k, \mathcal{AS}_\ell \right)}{\left| c_i \right| \left(\left| c_j \right| - 1 \right)} \tag{23}$$

$$\mathcal{D}_{inter} = \frac{\sum_{S_{k \in c_i}} \sum_{S_{\ell \in c_j, \ell \neq k,}} d_{k\ell}^2 \left(\mathcal{AS}_k, \mathcal{AS}_\ell \right)}{\left| c_i \right| \left| c_j \right|} \tag{24}$$

$$\text{Cluster Quality Ratio} \left(c \right) = \frac{\text{Avg. Intra Cluster Distance}}{\text{Avg. Inter Cluster Distance}} \tag{25}$$

where, $d_{k\ell}^2 \left(\mathcal{AS}_k, \mathcal{AS}_\ell \right)$ is the distance between two sessions in any cluster c_i and $\left| c_i \right|$ is the number of sessions in cluster. the

Till now we have discussed the prerequisite theoretical background of this study, in next section, experimental design and results are presented.

EXPERIMENTAL RESULTS AND DISCUSSIONS

In this section, the performance evaluation of simple binary session dissimilarity measures(BS, BUSS and CBSS) and augmented session dissimilarity measures(ASS, AUSS, and IASS) are presented by applying it on open-access NASA web server log data(NASA_SeverLog, 1995). The used dissimilarity measures and relational fuzzy clustering algorithms are implemented using MATLAB (R2012a) package(MATLAB(2012a), n.d.). All experiments were performed on an HPZ420 workstation with an Intel(R) Xeon(R) CPU E51620 0 @ 3.60 GHz, and 4 GB RAM, running under the MS Windows-7 operating system(64-bit). The different numbers of web user sessions are randomly selected from a pre-processed NASA access log dataset.

Data Set Description

The data set used for experimentation (NASA_access_log_Aug95) contains all HTTP requests made on the NASA Kennedy Space Centre's web server in Florida for one month's period from 00:00:00 August 1, 1995, through 23:59:59 August 31, 1995. The uncompressed content of the dataset is 167.8 MB and contains 1,569,898 records with timestamps having a 1-second resolution.

Pre-Processing and Dissimilarity Matrix Generation

After cleaning of irrelevant entries(image, icons, sound files, etc.) from the original log file, it has been reduced to 525981 entries results are shown in the figure. However, we did not find any entries for automated software (web robots, spiders, crawlers, indexers, etc.) probably due to old log files. In this log data, a total number of 75060 unique hosts'/IP are requesting 4030 individual pages.

The sessions are identified by setting 30 minutes threshold time, as it is widely accepted to capture the user notion in most of the weblog dataset, and a total of 139,086 sessions are identified. To alleviate processing overhead, randomly selected user sessions of size 1000, 2000 and 3000 are considered from an enormous number of sessions for further processing.

The default root / and mini sessions of size 1 are filtered out from the total generated sessions as they did not contribute any significant information for user session clustering. From pre-processed sample logs frequency of page (FoP), duration of the page (DoP) and consequently relevance of page (RoP) matrix is computed. The page relevance matrix is harmonic mean of the frequency of page (FoP) and duration of the page (DoP) and gives equal importance to both matrices. Different similarity/dissimilarity matrices are computed by using the notion of binary sessions(BSS, BUSS, and IBSS)as given in(Nasraoui et al.,

Figure 2. Web Server Log Cleaning Results

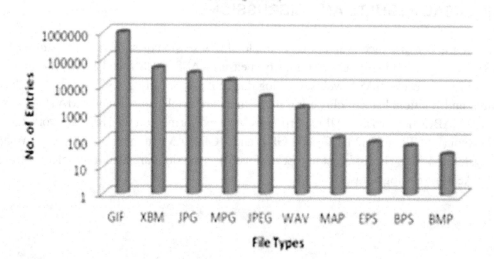

2000) and augmented sessions(ASS, AUSS, and IASS) using Algorithm 1.The summary of computed results is presented in Table 7.

Performance Evaluations

Extensive experiments have been performed to evaluate the quantitative performance of different session dissimilarity (binary and augmented) measures. For performance evaluation relational fuzzy c-means (RFCM) and relational fuzzy c-medoids (RFCMdd), clustering approaches are used. Multiple runs of RFCM and RFCMdd clustering algorithms were performed over six dissimilarity matrices. The default parameter setting as given in Table 8 was used consistently during execution of RFCM and RFCMdd.

Three binary session dissimilarity measures (BSS, BUSS, and CBSS) and three augmented sessions dissimilarity measures (ASS, AUSS, and IASS) are used to generate the dissimilarity matrices of size (665×665, 1341×1341 and 2048×2048) respectively for each measure.

For varying number of clusters (c=6, 8, 10), average intra cluster (compactness), average inter-cluster (separation) distance is computed for each dissimilarity measure. The low value of average Intra cluster distance represents good partition while a high value of average inter-cluster distance indicates the better cluster quality. It is very difficult to judge the cluster quality through any single measure. Therefore, cluster quality ratio (CQR) is also computed to consider both compactness and separation for dissimilarity measure evaluation. The low value of cluster quality ratio (CQR) will represent the better quality of generated clusters. Total 216 numbers of experiments have been performed [6(dissimilarity measure) × 3(different size of dissimilarity matrices) × 2(clustering algorithms) × 3(number of clusters) × 3(evaluation parameters)] to evaluate the performance of web user session dissimilarity measures. The performance evaluation results of different dissimilarity measures are presented in Table 9, 10 and 11.

Table 7. Summary of Results

Parameters	Values		
Number of initial sessions	1000	2000	3000
Number of valid sessions	665	1341	2048
Size of FoP/DoP/RoP matrices	665×419	1341×589	2048×731
Number of unique URLs in sessions	419	589	731
Size of URL syntactic similarity matrices	419×419	589×589	731×731
Size of (BSS, BUSS, and CBSS) /(ASS,AUSS, and IASS)/ ($D_{m \times m}$) matrices	665×665	1341×1341	2048×2048

Table 8. The default values of parameters used in RFCM and RFCMdd clustering algorithms

Parameters	Symbols	Choose Values
Step size	ε	0.0001
maximum number of iterations	t_{max}	1000
Fuzzifier	f	1.5 to 2

Table 9. Performance evaluation of different dissimilarity measures (size of matrices $\mathcal{D}_{m\times m} = 665\times665$) with RFCM and RFCMdd clustering algorithms

Number of Clusters	Session Dissimilarity Measures	Average Intra Cluster Distance		Average Inter Cluster Distance		Cluster Quality Ratio(CQR)	
		RFCM	RFCMdd	RFCM	RFCMdd	RFCM	RFCMdd
C=6	BSS	0.349	0.323	0.921	0.892	0.379	0.362
	BUSS	0.374	0.229	0.851	0.667	0.439	0.343
	CBSS	0.347	0.227	0.756	0.705	0.459	0.322
	ASS	0.308	0.331	0.805	0.902	0.383	0.367
	AUSS	0.303	0.254	0.803	0.691	0.378	0.367
	IASS	0.231	0.217	0.730	0.761	**0.316**	**0.285**
C=8	BSS	0.222	0.273	0.895	0.871	0.247	0.314
	BUSS	0.206	0.215	0.804	0.768	0.257	**0.280**
	CBSS	0.184	0.199	0.735	0.650	0.250	0.306
	ASS	0.365	0.315	0.893	0.918	0.409	0.343
	AUSS	0.217	0.201	0.748	0.665	0.289	0.302
	IASS	0.178	0.220	0.780	0.739	**0.228**	0.297
C=10	BSS	0.232	0.280	0.895	0.859	0.260	0.326
	BUSS	0.194	0.197	0.809	0.708	0.239	0.278
	CBSS	0.178	0.194	0.749	0.663	0.237	0.292
	ASS	0.333	0.233	0.845	0.760	0.394	0.306
	AUSS	0.237	0.192	0.668	0.680	0.355	0.282
	IASS	0.163	0.191	0.727	0.734	**0.224**	**0.260**

In first experiment dissimilarity metrics of size $\mathcal{D}_{m\times m} = 665\times665$) is generated using abovementioned measures. The RFCM and RFCMdd are used to produce different number of clusters (c=6, 8, 10).The experiment results are presented in Table 9. It has been observed from presented results that for six number of clusters IASS measure produce the optimum value of CQR. For eight numbers of clusters IASS measure using RFCM and BUSS measure with RFCMdd produce the optimum value of CQR. Similarly for ten numbers of clusters IASS measure produce the optimum value of CQR using both clustering algorithms.

In second experiment dissimilarity metrics of size $\mathcal{D}_{m\times m} = 1341\times1341$) is generated for all dissimilarity measures. By using same clustering algorithms six, eight and ten number of clusters is generated and experiment results are presented in Table 10. The presented results show that for six numbers of clusters AUSS measure with RFCM and IASS measure with RFCMdd produce the optimum value of CQR. For eight numbers of clusters IASS measure using both clustering algorithms produce the optimum value of CQR. Similarly for ten numbers of clusters AUSS measure with RFCM and BUSS measure with RFCMdd give the minimum value of CQR.

Table 10. Performance evaluation of different dissimilarity measures (size of matrices $\mathcal{D}_{m \times m}$ = 1341×1341) with RFCM and RFCMdd clustering algorithms

Number of Clusters	Session Dissimilarity Measures	Avg. Intra Cluster Distance		Average Inter Cluster Distance		Cluster Quality Ratio(CQR)	
		RFCM	RFCMdd	RFCM	RFCMdd	RFCM	RFCMdd
C=6	BSS	0.286	0.293	0.846	0.838	0.339	0.350
	BUSS	0.293	0.226	0.812	0.642	0.361	0.353
	CBSS	0.243	0.206	0.654	0.592	0.372	0.348
	ASS	0.362	0.339	0.937	0.928	0.386	0.365
	AUSS	0.277	0.190	0.791	0.654	**0.298**	0.291
	IASS	0.268	0.197	0.815	0.687	0.329	**0.286**
C=8	BSS	0.266	0.278	0.907	0.816	0.293	0.341
	BUSS	0.213	0.170	0.837	0.644	0.255	0.264
	CBSS	0.178	0.194	0.751	0.691	0.237	0.281
	ASS	0.261	0.313	0.848	0.903	0.308	0.346
	AUSS	0.203	0.203	0.774	0.634	0.262	0.320
	IASS	0.184	0.188	0.808	0.743	**0.227**	**0.253**
C=10	BSS	0.243	0.289	0.910	0.904	0.267	0.320
	BUSS	0.197	0.185	0.835	0.774	0.236	**0.239**
	CBSS	0.180	0.187	0.715	0.680	0.252	0.275
	ASS	0.230	0.300	0.808	0.911	0.284	0.329
	AUSS	0.157	0.193	0.763	0.681	**0.206**	0.284
	IASS	0.171	0.188	0.795	0.711	0.215	0.264

In third experiment dissimilarity metrics of size $\mathcal{D}_{m \times m}$ = 2048 × 2048) is generated for all dissimilarity measures. By using same clustering algorithms six, eight and ten number of clusters is generated and experiment results are presented in Table 11. The presented results show that for six and eight numbers of clusters IASS measure using both clustering algorithms produce the optimum value of CQR while for ten numbers of clusters IASS measure with RFCM and AUSS measure with RFCMdd give the best value of CQR.

The above-discussed experimental results suggested that augmented session dissimilarity measures in general and intuitive augmented user sessions dissimilarity measure, in particular, performs superior to other measures. This conclusion may be generalized because with different size of matrices (665×665, 1341×1341 and 2048×2048) and different algorithms(RFCM and RFCMdd) are used to perform the experiments.

Table 11. Performance evaluation of different dissimilarity measures (size of matrices $\mathcal{D}_{m \times m} = 2048 \times 2048$) with RFCM and RFCMdd clustering algorithms

Number of Clusters	Session Dissimilarity Measures	Avg. Intra Cluster Distance		Average Inter Cluster Distance		Cluster Quality Ratio(CQR)	
		RFCM	RFCMdd	RFCM	RFCMdd	RFCM	RFCMdd
C=6	BSS	0.310	0.292	0.822	0.886	0.377	0.329
	BUSS	0.270	0.286	0.735	0.796	0.367	0.360
	CBSS	0.271	0.233	0.675	0.777	0.402	0.300
	ASS	0.268	0.321	0.772	0.916	0.347	0.350
	AUSS	0.231	0.201	0.677	0.656	0.341	0.306
	IASS	0.219	0.244	0.779	0.826	**0.281**	**0.295**
C=8	BSS	0.198	0.280	0.844	0.903	0.235	0.310
	BUSS	0.216	0.230	0.785	0.815	0.276	0.283
	CBSS	0.219	0.203	0.746	0.766	0.294	0.265
	ASS	0.298	0.314	0.827	0.926	0.361	0.339
	AUSS	0.261	0.227	0.735	0.739	0.355	0.307
	IASS	0.194	0.184	0.829	0.655	**0.234**	**0.281**
C=10	BSS	0.246	0.299	0.767	0.890	0.321	0.336
	BUSS	0.190	0.204	0.833	0.783	0.228	0.261
	CBSS	0.175	0.213	0.778	0.819	0.225	0.260
	ASS	0.291	0.291	0.849	0.929	0.343	0.313
	AUSS	0.179	0.167	0.826	0.743	0.217	**0.225**
	IASS	0.147	0.181	0.786	0.683	**0.187**	0.264

Performance Comparison

To visualize the comparative performance of different session dissimilarity measures graphs have been plotted. These graphs are plotted between cluster quality ratio and a varying number of clusters with different clustering algorithms and for different size of dissimilarity matrices. Figure 3(A) to (C) are used to show the comparative performance of different dissimilarity measures (BSS, BUSS, CBSS, ASS, AUSS, and IASS) with different size of dissimilarity matrices(665×665, 1341×1341 and 2048×2048) using relational fuzzy c-means clustering(RFCM) clustering algorithm. Similarly, Figure 3(D) to (F) is used to show the comparative performance using relational fuzzy c-medoids clustering (RFCMdd) with the dissimilarity above measures and different size of dissimilarity matrices.

It has been observed from the plotted graphs that clusters formed with intuitive augmented user sessions dissimilarity measure are consistently producing good results as compared to other dissimilarity measures.

Figure 3. Performance Evaluation of Various Dissimilarity Measures for different size of matrices with RFCM and RFCMdd clustering algorithms

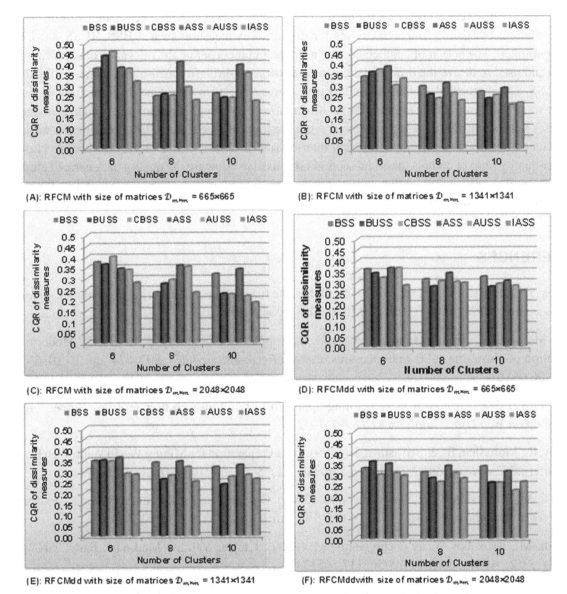

*For a more accurate representation see the electronic version.

FUTURE RESEARCH DIRECTIONS

In this study, only a small size log was considered to avoid pre-processing overhead. However, in the future study may be extended to a large number of user sessions. The same hypothesis can be tested with other clustering algorithms with different web log data to generalize the results. This approach can be more refined and leads to the development of new relational clustering algorithms.

CONCLUSION

In this chapter, different user session similarity for matching relational web access patterns is discussed. The limitations of existing simple binary session dissimilarity measures such as BSS, BUSS, and CBSS are highlighted. The notion of augmented web user session incorporate the relevance of accessing web URLs and used to derive the different augmented session dissimilarity measures such as ASS, AUSS, and IASS. The augmented session dissimilarity measures are used to overcome the limitations of simple binary session dissimilarity measures. The relational fuzzy clustering algorithms are used to generate the web user session clusters by using mention session dissimilarity measures. The clustering performance is evaluated by computing average intra and inter-cluster distances with a varying number of clusters. Cluster quality ratio of compactness and separation is used to compare the quality of generated clusters. Experimental results suggested that augmented session dissimilarity measures in general and intuitive augmented user sessions dissimilarity measure, in particular, performs superior to other measures.

REFERENCES

Bezdek, J. C., Ehrlich, R., & Full, W. (1984). FCM: The fuzzy c-means clustering algorithm. *Computers & Geosciences*, *10*(2), 191–203. doi:10.1016/0098-3004(84)90020-7

Brun, M., Sima, C., Hua, J., Lowey, J., Carroll, B., Suh, E., & Dougherty, E. R. (2007). Model-based evaluation of clustering validation measures. *Pattern Recognition*, *40*(3), 807–824. doi:10.1016/j.patcog.2006.06.026

Chan, P. K. (1999). A non-invasive learning approach to building web user profiles. *Proceedings of Workshop on Web Usage Analysis(KDD-99)*, 7–12.

Cooley, R., Mobashar, B., & Srivastava, J. (1999). Data Preparation for Mining World Wide Web Browsing Patterns. *Knowledge and Information Systems*, *1*(1), 5–32. doi:10.1007/BF03325089

Halkidi, M., Batistakis, Y., & Vazirgiannis, M. (2001). On clustering validation techniques. *Journal of Intelligent Information Systems*, *17*(2–3), 107–145. doi:10.1023/A:1012801612483

Halkidi, M., Batistakis, Y., & Vazirgiannis, M. (2002). Cluster Validity Methods : Part I. *SIGMOD Record*, *31*(2), 40–45. doi:10.1145/565117.565124

Hathaway, R. J., Davenport, J. W., & Bezdek, J. C. (1989). Relational duals of the c-means clustering algorithms. *Pattern Recognition*, *22*(2), 205–212. doi:10.1016/0031-3203(89)90066-6

Huang, A. (2008). Similarity measures for text document clustering. *Proceedings of the sixth New Zealand computer science research student conference (NZCSRSC2008)*, 49–56.

Joydeep, A. S., Strehl, E., Ghosh, J., Mooney, R., & Strehl, A. (2000). The impact of Similarity Measures on Webpage Clustering. In *Workshop on Artificial Intelligence for Web Search* (pp. 58–64). AAAI.

Krishnapuram, R., Joshi, A., Nasraoui, O., & Yi, L. (2001). Low-complexity fuzzy relational clustering algorithms for Web mining. *IEEE Transactions on Fuzzy Systems*, *9*(4), 595–607. doi:10.1109/91.940971

Krishnapuram, R., Joshi, A., & Yi, L. (1999). A fuzzy relative of the k-medoids algorithm with application to web document and snippet clustering. In *IEEE International Fuzzy Systems. Conference Proceedings(FUZZ-IEEE'99)* (Vol. 3, pp. 1281–1286). IEEE. 10.1109/FUZZY.1999.790086

Liu, H., & Keselj, V. (2007). Combined mining of Web server logs and web contents for classifying user navigation patterns and predicting users' future requests. *Data & Knowledge Engineering*, *61*(2), 304–330. doi:10.1016/j.datak.2006.06.001

MATLAB. (2012a). *Software package*. Retrieved from http://www.mathworks.com

NASA_SeverLog. (1995). *NASA Kennedy space center's www server log data*. Retrieved from http://ita.ee.lbl.gov/html/contrib/NASA-HTTP.html

Nasraoui, O., Hichem, F., Krishnapuram, R., & Joshi, A. (2000). Extracting web user profiles using relational competitive fuzzy clustering. *International Journal of Artificial Intelligence Tools*, *9*(4), 509–526. doi:10.1142/S021821300000032X

Sisodia, D. S. (2017). Augmented Session Similarity-Based Framework for Measuring Web User Concern from Web Server Logs. *International Journal on Advanced Science Engineering and Information Technology*, *7*(3), 1007–1013. doi:10.18517/ijaseit.7.3.1563

Sisodia, D. S., Verma, S., & Vyas, O. (2016a). A Discounted Fuzzy Relational Clustering of Web Users ' Using Intuitive Augmented Sessions Dissimilarity Metric. *IEEE Access: Practical Innovations, Open Solutions*, *4*(1), 2883–2993.

Sisodia, D. S., Verma, S., & Vyas, O. P. (2015a). A Comparative Analysis of Browsing Behavior of Human Visitors and Automatic Software Agents. *American Journal of Systems and Software*, *3*(2), 31–35. doi:10.12691/ajss-3-2-1

Sisodia, D. S., Verma, S., & Vyas, O. P. (2015b). Agglomerative Approach for Identification and Elimination of Web Robots from Web Server Logs to Extract Knowledge about Actual Visitors. *Journal of Data Analysis and Information Processing*, *3*(2), 1–10. doi:10.4236/jdaip.2015.31001

Sisodia, D. S., Verma, S., & Vyas, O. P. (2016b). Augmented Intuitive Dissimilarity Metric for Clustering Of Web User Sessions. *Journal of Information Science*, *43*(4), 480–491. doi:10.1177/0165551516648259

Sisodia, D. S., Verma, S., & Vyas, O. P. (2016c). Performance Evaluation of an Augmented Session Dissimilarity Matrix of Web User Sessions Using Relational Fuzzy C-means clustering. *International Journal of Applied Engineering and Research*, *11*(9), 6497–6503.

Sisodia, D. S., Verma, S., & Vyas, O. P. (2016d). Quantitative Evaluation of Web User Session Dissimilarity measures using medoids based Relational Fuzzy clustering. *Indian Journal of Science and Technology*, *9*(28), 1–9. doi:10.17485/ijst/2016/v9i28/89455

Vakali, A., Pokorný, J., & Dalamagas, T. (2004). An overview of web data clustering practices. In *Current Trends in Database WebKdd* (pp. 597–606). Springer Berlin Heidelberg. doi:10.1007/978-3-540-30192-9_59

Xiao, J., & Zhang, Y. (2001). Clustering of web users using session-based similarity measures. *International Conference on Computer Networks and Mobile Computing*, 223–228. 10.1109/ICCNMC.2001.962600

KEY TERMS AND DEFINITIONS

Augmented Sessions: Considered web user's habits, interest, and expectations for accessed page URLs by measuring the relevance of pages in every session because all of the URLs visited in a session are not equally important to the user.

Augmented Sessions Similarity: Similarity between two augmented sessions using the notion of augmented sessions.

Binary Sessions: The accessed page URLs considered as either accessed or not accessed and represented binary values such as zero and one.

Binary Sessions Similarity: Session similarity between two user sessions considering binary sessions.

Duration of Page: Time spent on a page by web user, and it is the difference between the exact time of the request for previous page and the time of the request for the next webpage in the session from the access log file.

Frequency of Page: The number of times any web page is visited in the session.

Sessions: Session is as a set of web resources requested in a particular time during a website visit.

Chapter 11
Wavelet Transform Algorithms

Arvind Kumar Kourav
BITS Bhopal, India

Shilpi Sharma
BIT, India

Vimal Tiwari
BIT, India

ABSTRACT

Digital image processing has an enormous impact on technical and industrial applications. Uncompressed images need large storage capacity and communication bandwidth. Digital images have become a significant source of information in the current world of communication systems. This chapter explores the phenomenon of digital images and basic techniques of digital image processing in detail. With the creation of multimedia, the requirements for the storage of a larger amount of high quality pictures and data analysis are increasing.

INTRODUCTION

Digital image processing is vital field of engineering and technology, in current era every field are based on the applications of digital image processing, in digital image processing, digital depictions of images commonly require a large number of bits. In various applications, it is significant to study procedures for signifying an image, or the information contained in the image, with fewer bits. By eliminating redundant or unnecessary information, image compression is the activity that addresses this aim. Image processing techniques have been applied in several areas of image and video processing such as communication, video conferencing etc. In the digital image and video compression it is required to reduce bit rate requirement and improves speed of transmission. Image compression techniques are mainly in two groups is lossless and lossy (C. Villegas Q. & J. Climent, 2008). In image de-noising it is required to recover the original image at the output, In both analysis main objective is to improve quality of image in term of PSNR by block transform methods, and compare result for better PSNR.

DOI: 10.4018/978-1-5225-3870-7.ch011

$$w(a,b) = \frac{1}{\sqrt{a}} \int\limits_{-\infty}^{\infty} f(t)\psi\left(\frac{t-b}{a}\right) dt \tag{1}$$

where 'a' is the dilation factor, 'b' is the translation factor and ψ(t) is the mother wavelet. $1/\sqrt{a}$ is an energy normalization term that makes wavelets of different scale has the same amount of energy. In this wavelet based algorithms are used for the comparative analysis of image compression, representation of wavelet base algorithms are shown in Figure 1

BACKGROUND AND MAIN FOCUS

In this a series of image compression methods of block transform analysis is discuss. Wavelet transforms algorithms also produce the better result in the field of signal processing and image processing in the last decade, these field analyzed different types of application such as s time-frequency analysis, data and image compression, image segmentation, feature analysis, pattern recognition, image de-noising, echo cancellation etc. All these developments of wavelet transform developed during the past decade (Deepti G. & Shital M., 2003). The theory of wavelets transform is based on the quantum and function analysis in unifying and wavelet analysis is executed by a prototype function called a wavelet function. Wavelets analysis is functions defined in a finite interval and set the having average tends to zero.

Wavelet Transform

Wavelet transform representation is defined by an f(t) in arbitrary form depend on a superposition of a set of such wavelets or base functions (Devi P. & Mini M., 2012), this wavelet analysis defined by

Figure 1. Wavelet Transform Algorithms

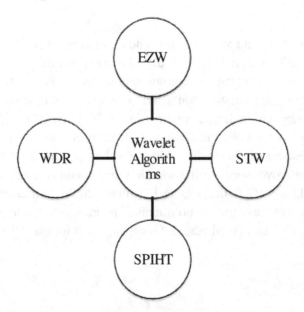

the basic functions or baby wavelets, baby wavelet is based on the mother wavelet, this function follow scaling and shifting property of transform, from the Fast Fourier Transform algorithms and short length finite impulse response analysis implementation of wavelet transform can be developed, Assumption to developed wavelet to reduce the computational complexity of computation, development of wavelet transform overcome the limitation of the short time Fourier transforms. Basic process of Wavelet transform is similar to short time Fourier transform analysis, but key differences are as follows.

1. Fourier transforms are not based on windowed sequence, so the negative frequencies are not measure in this.
2. Most significant characteristic of wavelet transform is to width of the window are not fixed and changed during the transform is computed for every single spectral component. In digital image processing, processing of image is a big challenge to analyses. For the Image quality a number of parameter which use to estimate according the application where it is used. There are different methods for the measuring of image quality these methods are digital image compression, Image reconstruction, Image enhancement etc. This work produce a concept for the improvement of image quality in the field of digital image compression (Nilima D. M. & Wani V. P., 2012).

Basic reasons for the Improvement of compressed image quality are.

1. The importance of inaccuracies in the dense image axes on inflexibly on their position in the unique image.
2. Realistic eminence of errors be contingent on their position in the original image, e.g., errors on relevant edges, or on the face of a description will move appreciation more than errors in the training.
3. Compressed image may be actual representation of the image which are used and convey the same "high level" material as the original. Intended for creating effective image compression structure, it is essential eliminate the whole dismissals vital in image Processing. Coding method and internal pixel redundancies analyses are successfully subjugated the benefit of coding in many compression classifications.

Types of Wavelet Transform

Basically two types of wavelet transform are discussed in this section, these transform are continuous wavelet transform and discrete wavelet transform.

Continuous Wavelet Transform

To overcome the limitation and resolution problem of short time Fourier transforms continuous wavelet transform was established. Continuous wavelet transform is defined according to the relationship as.

$$CWT_x\Psi\left(\tau,s\right) = \Psi_x\Psi\left(\tau,s\right)$$

$$= 1 / \sqrt{s} \int x(t) \Psi * \left(t - \tau \,/\, s \right) dt \tag{2}$$

Calculations:

1. Select the input signal.
2. Select the mother wavelet in this the analysis of compression is based on the value of s for the increase and decrease.
3. Initially select time = 0.
4. Wavelet transform is developed with the signal and linked at all eras for value of 1/sqrt{s}.
5. Set s =1 and moved to the right by τ repeat above process till the completion of the signal.

For frequency band analysis sample function is defined as.

$$\Psi t = 2 sinc 2t - sinc t = \left\{ sin 2\pi t - sin \pi t \right\} \,/\, \pi t$$

With the (normalized) sinc function
The subspace of degree 'a' or frequency band [1/a, 2/a] is ended by the functions.

$$\Psi_{a,b}(t) = 1 / \sqrt{a} \; \Psi \left((t - b) / a \right) \tag{3}$$

$$WT_{\Psi} \left\{ X \right\}(a,b) = \left(x, \; \Psi_{a,b} \right) \tag{4}$$

With wavelet coefficients

$$WT_{\Psi} \left\{ X \right\}(a,b) = \left(x, \; \Psi_{a,b} \right)$$

$$= \int x(t) \Psi_{a,b}(t) dt \tag{5}$$

Discrete Wavelet Transform

It is basically difficult to estimate a signal using all wavelet coefficients, so any one singularity which is acceptable to take a discrete subset of the better half plane to be able to re-form a signal from the consistent wavelet coefficients will be taken as concern. The comparative discrete subclass of the half plane contains of all the facts (a^m, na^m b) by (m, n) in 'Z'. The equivalent baby wavelets are currently specified as.

$$\Psi_{m,n}\left(t\right) \ = a^{-m/2}\Psi\left(a^{-m}t - nb\right) \tag{6}$$

An essential system for the renewal of first signal 'x' of a determinate energy by the formulary:

$$X(\text{t}) = \sum\sum\left(x, \ \Psi_{m,n}\right)\cdot \Psi_{m,n}\left(t\right) \ where \ m, n\epsilon z$$

WAVELET TRANSFORM ALGORITHMS

Wavelet transform algorithms EZW, SPIHT, WDR and STW are proposed, it is based on bit plan encoding (Farnoosh N. & Mohammad A., 2012).

Embedded Zero Tree Wavelet (EZW)

The EZW is principal wavelet transform based algorithm for image compression, this algorithms is developed from the research of Shapiro. In this algorithm a encoder and decoder is used for the analysis of image, in EZW encoder an image is converted into a bit stream to increase the accuracy of compress image. There are two important phenomenon's on which EZW encoder is based.

1. In the analysis of natural image first process is low pass filtering and have a low pass spectrum, this image is based on sub band analysis, energy in sub band decrease as the scale decrease. This shows that the encoding process is very usual to compress wavelet transformed image.
2. Large wavelet coefficients study is more important than small wavelet coefficients. Both these analysis are suitable by coding the wavelet coefficients in decreasing order, in several permits. EZW encoder only restructures wavelet coefficients in a way, that they can be compressed very well.

Features of EZW:

*   This method gives better performance than the other method.
*   This uses zero tree concept
*   Tree coding with single character
*   Produce better result lacking pre-stored tables codebooks, training.

Demerits of EZW:

*   Position of Transmitted coefficient position is not clear
*   Not have a real compression
*   Encoder based arithmetic analysis

Set Partitioning in Hierarchical Trees (SPIHT)

This is image compression algorithm; working principal of this algorithm is based on wavelet transform. In primary analysis at the input stage, first image are converted into wavelet sub band and transmitted this according to the wavelet coefficient. At the output stage (receiver side) reverse process are applied to get original image by inverse transformation, compress image are based on the value of PSNR, SPIHT algorithms improve the PSNR value of image. In the EZW algorithm only stable image are proceed for the transmission and based on the vector quantization and wavelet quantization, not require any training sequence. SPIHT are better from other algorithms by following characteristics.

- Produce better PSNR
- Improve the speed of process and computation
- A fully progressive bit -stream
- Can be used for lossless compression

Demerits of SPIHT:

- Indirectly locates position of significant coefficient
- Memory required for large process is more.
- Based on the variety of natural images

Wavelet Difference Reduction (WDR)

From the discussion of SPIHT algorithms, it is clear that this method is used for the analysis of image for the position of significant coefficient; due to this draw back SPIHT algorithms are not suitable to implement procedures which depend on the site of significant transform values.
Features of WDR:

- Uses ROI concept
- Better perceptual image quality than SPIHT
- No searching through quad trees as in SPIHT
- Less complex then SPIHT
- Better preservation of edges than SPIHT

Demerits of WDR:

- PSNR is not higher than SPIHT.

Spatial-Orientation Tree Wavelet (STW)

Basic principal of STW algorithm similar to SPIHT algorithm, main difference in both analysis is process of computation and carefulness and complexity, it is simple to explain SPIHT using the concepts underlying STW. From the STW, we can analyze SPIHT compresses images. STW algorithm consider

Figure 2. Image p1, CR=10.1592, BPP=2.4382

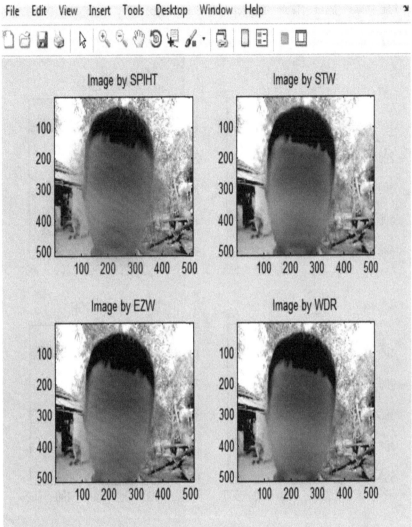

the analysis of state transition model for the encoding from one threshold to the next, from the use of state transition model bit requirement of transmitted image are reduced.

Implementation of Algorithm's

This section produces the implementation of wavelet algorithms.

Embedded Zero Tree Wavelet (EZW)

Implement step for EZW algorithm include following step for encoding and decoding

Figure 3. Image p4, CR=5.2292, BPP=1.2550

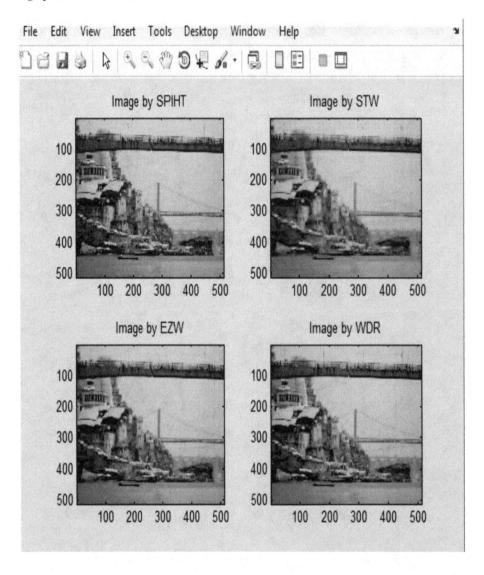

1. Choose initial value of threshold, for the initial value of time $T = T_0$, the transform values satisfy $|w(m)| < T_0$ and at smallest one transform value satisfies $|w(m)| >= T_0/2$
2. Updating the threshold, let

$$T_k = T_{k-1/2}$$

3. For Significance analysis first scans insignificant values. Experiment for the significance of w (m) we follows

Uncertainty $|w(m)j| >= T_k$, then the output w(m) Set $w_Q(m) = T_k$ otherwise if $|w(m)| < T_k$ then $w_Q(m)$ retain its initial value of 0.

Figure 4. Image p9, CR= 7.5490, BPP= 1.8118

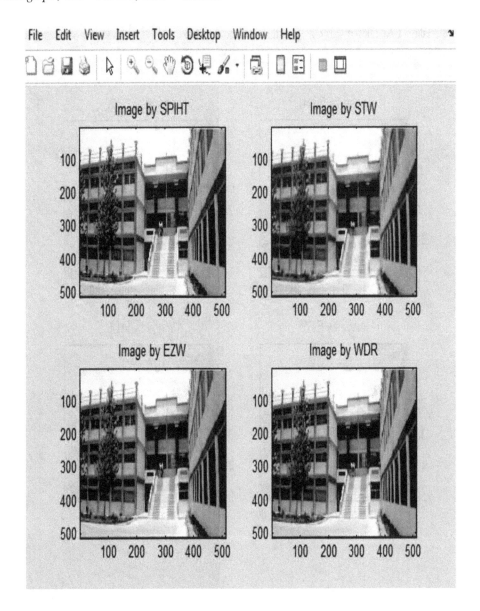

4. In enrichment study find upper value of threshold for weighty coefficient if threshold values Tj, for j < k (if k = 1 null stage). For each significant value w(m), do the consequent: If

|w(m)| $\in$ (w_Q(m),w_Q(m) + T_k), Then output bit 0

Else if

|w(m)| $\in$ (w_Q(m) + Tk,w_Q(m) + 2T_k), Then the output bit 1, Change value of w_Q(m) by w_Q(m) + Tk

Figure 5. Image p11, CR= 10.2210, BPP= 2.4530

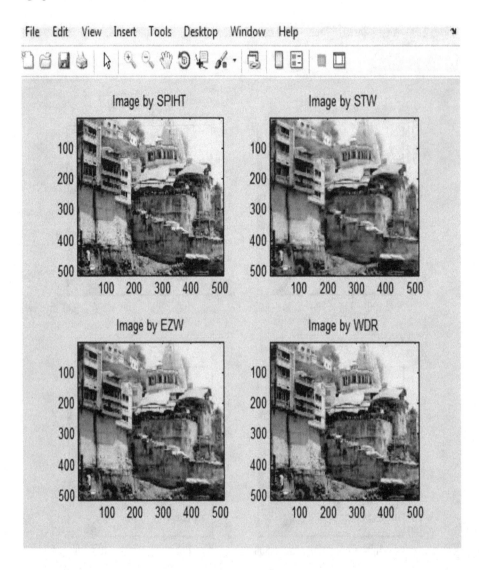

5.   Repeat above steps 2 to 4.

STW Algorithm

Step 1 (Reset). Select preliminary threshold, $T = T_0$, so transform values satisfy $|w(m)| < T0$ and minimum one satisfies $|w(m)|\_ T_0=2$. Give all keys for the L_{th} level, wherever L is the integer of levels in the wavelet transform, to the main list. Set the alteration list of keys equal to the unfilled set.

Step 2 Take $T_k = T_k-1/2$.

Step 3 (Significance pass). Test over insignificant standards by baseline algorithm scan command. Experiment all value w(m) as:

If

Figure 6. CR graph for WDR, STW, EZW and SPIHT

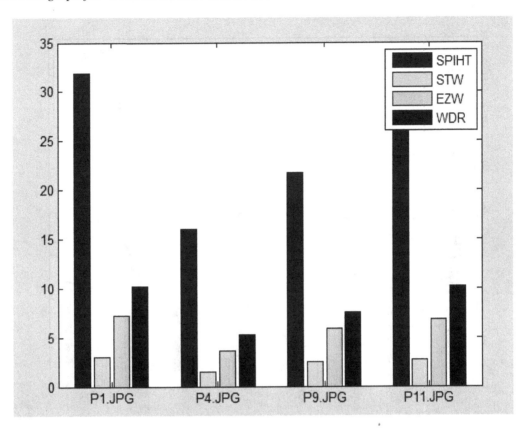

$|w(m)| >= T_k$

Then, output sign

Set $w_Q(m)$ is equal to T_k

Otherwise if $|w(m)| < T_k$ then

Take wQ(m) recall for main significance of 0.

Step 4 (Modification pass). Test over weighty values initiate with upper threshold values Tj, for j < k (if k = 1 avoid this). For every main significance w(m), ensure the subsequent: If

If

$|w(m)| \in [w_Q(m), w_Q(m) + T_k)$

Then

Output bit 0

Otherwise if

$|w(m)| \in [wQ(m) + T_k, w_Q(m) + 2T_k)$

Then

Output bit 1

Interchange $w_Q(m)$ by $w_Q(m) + Tk$.

Step 5 (Loop). Repeat steps 2 to 4.

Figure 7. BPP graph for WDR, STW, EZW and SPIHT

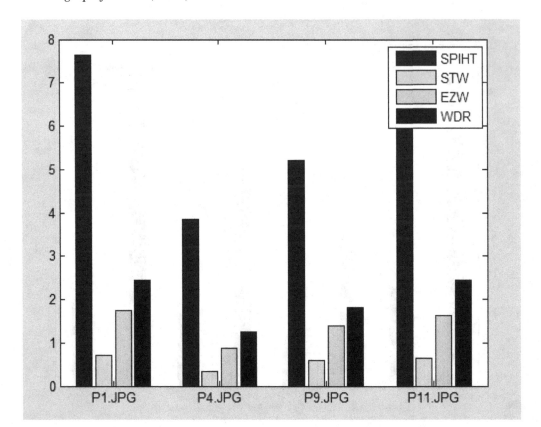

WDR Algorithm

Major drawback of SPIHT is that it only traces the position of significant coefficients. This makes it difficult to attain procedures, such as segment select of compressed data, which depend on the exact position of key transform. On the basis of region choice, this also predictable a region of interest (ROI), selecting a helping of a compressed image which requires better resolution. WDR methods not create higher PSNR values than SPIHT (Sunill M. & Neelesh G., 2002).

SPIHT ALGORITHM

This algorithm is based on the set partitioning operation of single and multiple element sub sets for the analysis of significant and insignificant pixels, convert insignificant pixels to significant pixels from each and every insignificant set.

Encoding Process

- In the encoding process first satisfy wavelet transform $|w(m)| < T0$.
- Set threshold by k type integer $Tzk = Tzk-1/2$.

Figure 8. MSE graph for WDR, STW, EZW and SPIHT

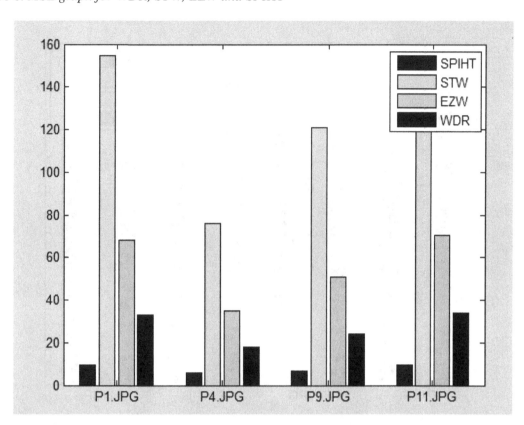

- If LIS and LIP is list of insignificant sets and list of insignificant pixels then LSP is list of significant pixels

  X(m) = {Descending keys of the index m}

  Y(m) = {Child keys of the index m}

  Then Grandchildren of m is Z(m) = X(m) − Y(m)

  In all m in LIP, Output $S_k[m]$

  If $S_k[m] = 1$ then m tends to end of LSP

  Output sign of w(m); set $w_Q(m)$ = Tzk

  Stay until end of LIP

  On behalf of every m in LIS do: If m is of kind D then and there

  Output $S_k[X(m)]$

  If $S_k[X(m)] = 1, n \in Y(m)$ do: Output Sk[n],If Sk[Y(m)] = 1 then, Add Y(m) to LIS, all type D

    Eliminate m from LIS Continue until end of LIS

  If

  |w(m)| $\in$[wQ(m),wQ(m) + Tzk]

  Then Output bit 0

  Else if

  |w(m)| $\in$[wQ(m) + Tzk,wQ(m) + 2Tz$_k$]

  Replace $w_Q(m)$ by $w_Q(m)$ + Tzk .

Figure 9. PSNR graph for WDR, STW, EZW and SPIHT

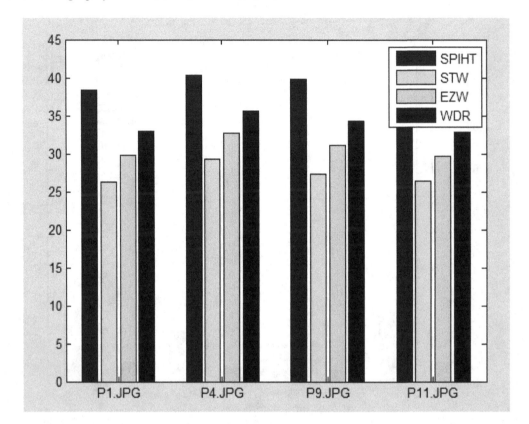

Repeat

Practical Implementation of Algorithms

This practical approach of wavelet transform algorithms is based on the Matlab software simulation and coding analysis, for the better result analysis all image are tested. Result analysis is produce for after the practical analysis of wavelet transform algorithms on the different parameter the analysis of image quality.

CONCLUSION

These works try to develop a Wavelet transform based algorithms for the image analysis, comparative result of EZW, WDR, SPIHT and STW are produced all the algorithms are implemented by the MAT-LAB Software using wavelet tool box. This result is comparing the parameter of compressed image for the value of PSNR, MSE, CR and BPP for the better quality of compressed image

REFERENCES

Alani, D., Averbuch, A., & Dekel, S. (2007). Image coding with geometric wavelets. *IEEE Transactions on Image Processing, 16*(1), 69–77. doi:10.1109/TIP.2006.887727 PMID:17283766

Chang, C.-L., & Girod, B. (2007). Direction-Adaptive Discrete Wavelet Transform for Image Compression. *IEEE Transactions on Image Processing, 16*(5), 1289–1302. doi:10.1109/TIP.2007.894242 PMID:17491460

Chopra, G. (2011). *An Improved Image Compression Algorithm Using Binary Space Partition Scheme and Geometric Wavelets. IEEE Transactions on Image.*

Gao, Y., & Leung, M. K. H. (2002). Face recognition using line edge map. *IEEE Transactions on Pattern Analysis and Machine Intelligence, 24*(6), 764–779. doi:10.1109/TPAMI.2002.1008383

Gomathi, E., & Baskaran, K. (2012). Face Recognition Fusion Algorithm Based on Wavelet. *European Journal of Scientific Research, 74*(3), 450-455.

Gupta, D., & Mutha, S. (2003). *Image Compression Using Wavelet Packet. IEEE.*

Hui, K.-C., & Siu, W. C. (2007). Extended analysis of motion compensated frame difference for block-based motion prediction error. *IEEE Transactions on Image Processing, 16*(5), 1232–1245. doi:10.1109/TIP.2007.894263 PMID:17491455

Malviya & Gupta. (2002). An Improved Image Compression Algorithm Based on Daubechies- Wavelets with Arithmetic Coding. *JIEA, 3*(6), 46-50.

Maske & Patil. (2012). Comparison of Image Compression using Wavelet for Curvelet Transform & Transmission over Wireless Channel. *International Journal of Scientific and Research Publications, 5*(2).

Negahban & Shafieian. (2012). Various Novel Wavelet Based Image Compression Algorithms Using a Neural Network as a Predictor. *J. Basic. Appl. Sci. Res., 3*(6), 280-287.

Psa & MG. (2012). *Compression of computed radiographic images using linear prediction on wavelet coefficients*. ICACC.

Reichel, J., Menegaz, G., Nadenau, M. J., & Kunt, M. (2001). Integer Wavelet Transform for Embedded Lossy to Lossless Image Compression. *IEEE Transactions on Image Processing, 10*(3), 383–392. doi:10.1109/83.908504 PMID:18249628

Villegas-Quezada, C., & Climent, J. (2008). Holistic face recognition using multivariate approximation, genetic algorithms and adaboost classifier: Preliminary results. *World Academy of Science, Engineering and Technology, 44*, 802–806.

Zhou, M., & Wei, H. (2006). Face verification using gabor wavelets and AdaBoost. *Proceedings of the 18th International Conference on Pattern Recognition (ICPR '06), 1*, 404–407. 10.1109/ICPR.2006.536

KEY TERMS AND DEFINITIONS

Bits Per Pixel (BPP): It denotes number of bits per pixel.

Digital Image Processing (DIP): It is the processing techniques of digital images.

Matrix Laboratory (MATLAB): It is a tool used for matrix and mathematical analysis in the fields of engineering and technology.

Peak Signal to Noise Ratio (PSNR): It is the ratio between maximum powers of signal to noise.

Chapter 12
Web Access Patterns of Actual Human Visitors and Web Robots:
A Correlated Examination

Dilip Singh Sisodia
National Institute of Technology Raipur, India

ABSTRACT

Web robots are autonomous software agents used for crawling websites in a mechanized way for non-malicious and malicious reasons. With the popularity of Web 2.0 services, web robots are also proliferating and growing in sophistication. The web servers are flooded with access requests from web robots. The web access requests are recorded in the form of web server logs, which contains significant knowledge about web access patterns of visitors. The presence of web robot access requests in log repositories distorts the actual access patterns of human visitors. The human visitors' actual web access patterns are potentially useful for enhancement of services for more satisfaction or optimization of server resources. In this chapter, the correlative access patterns of human visitors and web robots are discussed using the web server access logs of a portal.

INTRODUCTION

Web robots are automated programs mainly designed to traverse websites over the internet. Web robots are used for a variety of functions including searching, indexing, hacking, scraping, spamming and spying, etc. (Gaffan, 2012). With the advent of web 2.0 services, web robots are playing a key role in everything that we do online and shaping our web experience. It is believed that first web robots were introduced in 1993 and since their origin, they are escalating with the unprecedented rate. Web robots are very simple to create as well as offer a great job by circumventing the collection of information (Tan & Kumar, 2002). Depending on their core functionality Web robots are also known as following (Derek Doran & Gokhale, 2011):

DOI: 10.4018/978-1-5225-3870-7.ch012

1. **Indexers (or Search Engine Crawlers):** This seeks to harvest as much web content as possible on a regular basis, to build and maintain large search indexes.
2. **Analyzers (or Shopping Bots):** It is used to crawl the web to compare prices and products sold by different e-Commerce sites.
3. **Experimenters (Focused Crawlers):** This seeks and acquires web pages belonging to pre-specified thematic areas.
4. **Harvesters (Email Harvesters):** This is used to collect email addresses on behalf of email marketing companies or spammers.
5. **Verifiers (Site-Specific Crawlers):** It is used to perform various website maintenance chores, such as mirroring web sites or discovering their broken links.
6. **RSS Crawlers:** It is used to retrieve information from RSS feeds on a web site or a blog.
7. **Scrapers:** It is used to create copies of websites for malicious purposes automatically.

The normal perception is that the major chunk of web server resources is used to handle human visitor's generated traffic for any web portal. This perception is changed if we observed the recent reports (Gaffan, 2012) which state that major portion of web traffic is generated through automatic software agents. Most website owners simply rely on web analytics tools("Google Analytics," 2013) to track who's visiting their site.However, these tools don't show you 51% of your site's traffic including some seriously shady non-human visitors such as web robots.

RELATED WORK

The various studies thoroughly studied web access pattern induced by human visitors. Arlitt and Williamson proposed a series of metrics to describe the aggregate web traffic (Arlitt & Williamson, 1996). Crovella and Bestavros discussed the self-similarity of Web access pattern (Crovella & Bestavros, 1997). Almeida et al. proposed a hierarchical approach for workload characterization of the request generated by robots at the different timescale. Characterization was done at the session, function and request levels (Almeida et al., 2001). Yu et al. classified a particular web site's visitors into different groups according to their purchase habits (Yu, Ou, Zhang, & Zhang, 2005). Li et al. performed cluster based analysis to classify a large number of sessions into several coherent classes that efficiently describe web server workloads (Li, Goševa-Popstojanova, & Ross, 2007). The inclusive study of human visitors induced web traffic leads to design for various solutions such as effective and efficient website design (Spiliopoulou, 2000), optimal cache replacement policies (Shyu, Haruechaiyasak, & Chen, 2006) (Almeida et al., 2001) according to the variations in human navigation patterns (White & Drucker, 2007) (Lin, Quan, & Wu, 2008). Dikaiakos et al. statistically investigated the various properties of crawler-induced HTTP traffic. This study includes the distribution of HTTP requests and reply-codes, the type and size of resources sought and retrieved, the distribution of crawler requests across a Website, the frequency, and pattern of crawler re-visits, and the temporal characteristics of crawler activity (Dikaiakos, Stassopoulou, & Papageorgiou, 2005). Lee et al. carried out an empirical study on a very large data to classify various robots by their access pattern (Lee, Cha, Lee, & Lee, 2009). Huntington et al. studied robots pattern in scholarly information environment (Huntington, Nicholas, & Jamali, 2008). Jacob et al. presented the inherent access pattern of crawlers on online social network sites (OSNS) (Jacob, Kirda, Kruegel, & Vigna, 2012). Doran et al. performed a comparative analysis between web robot sessions and humans on the types of resources requested by Web robots using recent Weblogs from an academic Web server. The author did a rigorous study of the distribution of response sizes and response codes, the types of resources requested, and popularity of resources for requests from Web robots (D Doran, Morillo, & Gokhale, 2013). However, most of the contributions above were done either before the emergence of web 2.0 based services or focused on web robots or human visitors in the independent/isolated way. The author did not find any significant contributions except (D Doran et al., 2013) which compare and differentiate between the web access pattern of web robots and human visitors. However, in (D Doran et al., 2013) authors compared only resource request patterns of both type of visitors and ignores the other aspects of web access pattern of web robots and human visitors.

In this chapter, a correlated examination of web access patterns of actual human visitors and web robots are performed

METHODOLOGY

In this section, a brief description of the adopted methodology to carry out the current work has been explained through process flowchart of Figure 1.

Data Set Description

To perform an experimental analysis, a real time access log of a Web portal providing global assistance for a visa, insurance, and other related services to worldwide visitors in the USA. This web server access log was recorded in the extended log file (ELF) and had stored the detailed information of each request made from user's web browsers to the web server in chronological order(D. Sisodia & Verma, 2012). An example of classic web server log entries is given in Figure 1 and brief description in Table 1.

Session Identification

As discussed in the previous chapter, any user can visit the particular website many times during a specific period. Session identification aims at dividing the multi visiting user sessions into single ones. However, due to inherent constraints of the HTTP protocol (i.e., HTTP is stateless and connectionless protocol), these records are incomplete. One cannot assign distinctively all the requests contained in web server logs to the entity that has performed them. Therefore, discovering the user sessions from web server logs is a multifaceted and tricky task. The log analyzer used in the present work uses session-duration heuristic in conjunction with same user agent where total session duration may not exceed a threshold θ and describe by the same user agent string. Given t0, the timestamp for the first request in a constructed session S, the request with a timestamp t is assigned to S, if $t - t0 \leq \theta$. This heuristics varies from 25.5

Figure 1. Example of typical web log entry

```
11.111.11.111      -      -     [15/Dec/2013:00:01:02      -0800]     "GET/forum/member.php?45067-Carla-
Zenis&tab=activitystream&type=all HTTP/1.1" 200 10463 "http://www.google.com/bot.html" "Mozilla/5.0
(compatible; Googlebot/2.1)"
```

Figure 2. Methodology for comparison of Web Robots vs. Humans

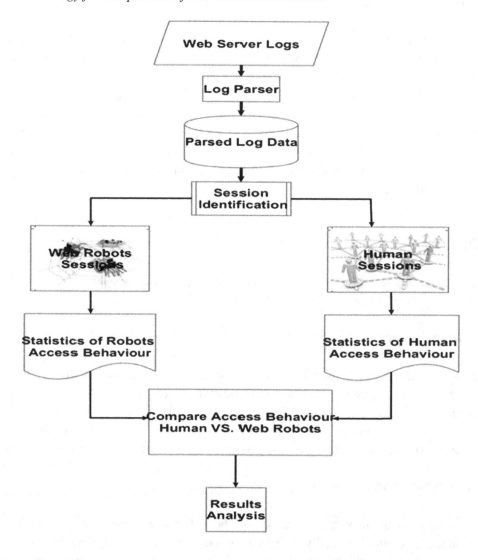

minutes to 24 hours while 30 minutes is the most used default timeout for session duration(Spiliopoulou, Mobasher, Berendt, & Nakagawa, 2003),(D. S. Sisodia, Verma, & Vyas, 2015).

Definition 1 - (Session Identification): For two records, r_1 and r_2, to be located consecutively in the same session, the following properties must be satisfied: (i) both records r_1 and r_2 have the same IP and user agent. (ii) Record r_1 has a link with record r_2 (iii) the records have visiting times within a predefined time window τ_1 (threshold1) (iv) A predefined maximum session time is not exceeded τ_2 (threshold 2).

Let

$\mathcal{S}_{set}$ is the set of real sessions constituting a *cleaned web log file*

$\mathcal{L}$ *of n records where,* $\mathcal{L} \leftarrow \{r_1, r_2 \dots r_n\}$. An arbitrary order may be imposed over the elements of $\mathcal{S}_{set}$ to refer the ith real session $\mathcal{S}_i \in \mathcal{S}_{set}$. If the following properties are hold:

Table 1. Brief description of web log entry headers

Log Entry Headers	Description of Headers
11.111.11.111	Remote host address
-	Remote log name
-	Username
15/Dec/2013:00:01:02	Timestamp
-800	Time zone of the request
GET	Request method
/forum/member.php?45067-Carla-Zenis&tab=activitystream&type=all	Path on the server
HTTP/1.1	Protocol version
200	Service status code
10463	Size of the returned data
http://www.google.com/bot.html	*Referrer
Mozilla/5.0 (compatible; Googlebot/2.1)	*User agent
*These fields only appear in the extended log file (ELF).	

1. $\forall \mathcal{S}_i \in \mathcal{S}_{set}$, $\forall i = 2, \dots n.$ $r_{i+1}.time > r_i.time$

2. All requests in $\mathcal{L}^c$ and only these appear in the sessions of $\mathcal{S}_{set}$: $\bigcup_{\mathcal{S}_i \in \mathcal{S}_{set}} \left(\bigcup_{i=1}^{i=n} \mathcal{S}_i \right) = \mathcal{L}^c$

3. Each request in $\mathcal{L}^c$ belongs to exactly one session of $\mathcal{S}_{set}$: $\forall \mathcal{S}_i \in \mathcal{S}_{set}$, $\forall i = 2, \dots n.$ $\nexists i' = i$ $\mathcal{S}_i = \mathcal{S}_{i'}$

The above properties ensure that $\mathcal{S}_{set}$. partitions $\mathcal{L}^c$ in an order-preserving way.

Human and Web Robot Sessions Identification

Human visitor's sessions are identified by using time oriented heuristics. Web robot sessions are extracted by using multi fold approaches in the first step we applied well-known heuristics proposed in (Tan & Kumar, 2002). However, this has left some robot sessions without identification. Therefore, in second step our log analyzer uses the database of IP addresses and user agent fields of well-known bots (WRD, 2014),(UAD, 2014). If the web server log session's IP addresses or user agent is matched with IP or user agent of well-known crawlers, then the session is labeled as web robot sessions, and it effectively obtains a sizable sample of requests from web robots to infer significant trends. This information is summarized in Table 2

Statistical Information

This log has parsed and pre-processed with the help of customized program which is based on an open source tool (AWStats, n.d.). An assortment of statistical log information has been extracted from a given log like some requests, request duration, the number of users, page hits, domains and countries of host visitors used operating system, using the browser, robots activity, HTTP errors and much more.

Figure 3. Pseudo code for user session identification algorithm

```
Pseudo code for web user session identification algorithm
Input: cleaned web log file: L^c of n records where L^c ← {r_1, r_2 ... r_n} ,where n >>> 1
       ∀∃ r_i < ip, time, method, url, protocol, size, status, agent, referrer >
       τ1: User defined upper bound for page stay time
       τ2: User defined upper bound for session duration time
Output: S_set ← { S_1, S_2 ... S_n}
1:   Initialization: S_0 ← {φ} ;  Session_set ← {φ}
2:   for i = 1,2, ... n, read (r_i) from L^c
3:     for j = i + 1 mod n.
4:       if ((r_i.ip = r_j.ip ) ∧(r_i.agent = r_j.agent) ∧(r_i.ref = r_j.ref) ∧
     (r_j.time − r_i.time) ≤ τ1) ;
5:       then S_i ← {r_i ∪ r_j}; Add record to the session;
6:       else go to step 3; search new record for the session;
7:       end of if
8:         while (( r_last.time − r_first.time) ≤ τ2) do
9:                S_set ← ∪ { S_i}; goto step 2 ; create new session
10:      end of while
11:    end of for
12:  end of for
13:  Update session set:  S_set ← { S_1, S_2 ... S_n}
```

Table 2. Web server access log of 20 day's duration (from 09-12-13 to 28-12-13)

Parameters	Total Traffic		Human-induced traffic		Web robots induced traffic	
	Before Pre-processing	After Pre-processing	Before Pre-processing	After Pre-processing	Before Pre-processing	After Pre-processing
# of requests	14022101	4432393	13427825	3942093	594276	490300
#Avg.req/day	701105	221619	671391	197104	29713	24515
# of users	213864	182337	210694	179814	3170	2636
# of sessions	471974	319554	447317	303826	24657	15728

EXPERIMENTAL RESULTS AND DISCUSSION

In this section, different experiments have been performed to draw the comparison between access pattern of human visitors and web robots. As shown in Table 2, very large number of requests, users and sessions are generated for the web server logs. To capture the microscopic view and avoid processing overhead for this analysis the sample of this log has been used to demonstrate the comparative pattern.

Comparison of Resource Acquisition Patterns

In this experiment, the comparison of resource acquisition patterns between human and web robots have been drawn to a different type of resources. The percentage of requests, percentage of visitors and percentage of bandwidth consumed by human and web robots for each specific type of resources are computed. The comparative statistics of results are summarized in Table 3. The comparative performance of resource acquisition patterns of human and web robots have been plotted in Figure 4 to Figure 6 for a percentage of requests, the percentage of visitors and percentage of bandwidth respectively.

The most striking observation to emerge from the data comparison (Figure 4) was that robots exhibited their aggression to only access web resources (*.html, *.php, *.htm etc.) and an engrossed number of requests, visitors and consumed more bandwidth as compared to human visitors. While Human visitors show uniform access pattern for all type of resources and receive less number of requests and visitors and consumed less bandwidth for web resources but the aggregate value (including all type resources) is quite high as compared to robots. Interestingly, there were also differences in the ratios of the web to image resources accessed by humans and robots. This value is very large for robots than humans. It is reasonable to expect humans to request many web resources as they browse from page to page to retrieve information and download files. But, this percentage may be low because humans' liking may be twisted towards embedded resources (*.jpg, *.png,*.gif, etc.) with web pages.

Table 3. Requests generated from different visitors and bandwidth consumed for different types of resources by web robots and human sessions

Resource Type	Resource Class	H-Requests	R-Requests	H-Visitors	R-Visitors	H-Bandwidth	R-Bandwidth
.html	Pages	26.74	38.98	14.08	42.88	25.98	30.11
.php	Pages	8.42	58.33	12.07	26.96	10.8	67.59
.txt	pages	6.07	0.72	15.99	10.19	6.46	0.01
.htm	Pages	0.04	0.46	0.24	2.84	0.02	0.21
.js	Pages	0.02	0.19	0.11	2.05	0	0.15
.jpg	Images	27.34	0.49	14.78	4.89	27.29	1.19
.png	Images	21.76	0.23	12.65	2.36	24.84	0.16
.gif	Images	3.34	0.1	10.21	1	0.33	0.01
.ico	Images	1.32	0	9.16	0.05	0.22	0
.com	Images	0	0.1	0.01	1.05	0.01	0.14
.css	Others	4.87	0.1	10.3	1.26	3.8	0.05
.swf	Others	0.06	0.04	0.29	0.47	0.16	0.03
.doc	Others	0.01	0.02	0.07	0.32	0.01	0.03
.pdf	Others	0	0.01	0.01	0.11	0.07	0.09

Figure 4. Web Robots vs. Humans-Percentage of requests generated for different types of resources

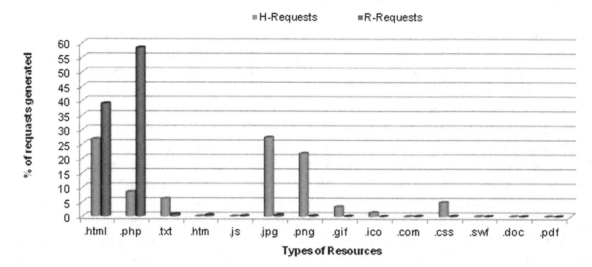

Figure 5. Web Robots vs. Humans-Percentage of visitors visited for different types of resources

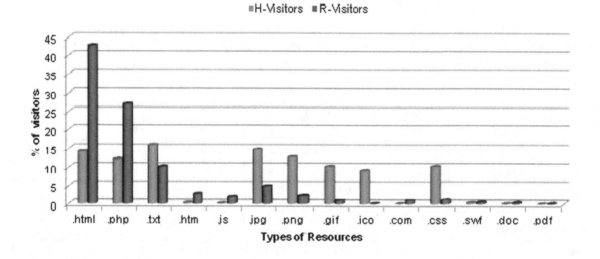

Comparison of General Web Access Patterns

In this experiment, the hourly distributions of requests, visitors, and bandwidth consumed by robots and humans have been investigated. Table 4 is used to show the statistical information of the hourly distribution of requests generated from different visitors and bandwidth consumed by web robots and human sessions. The comparative access pattern of hourly activity of human visitors and web robots has been shown in Figures 7 to Figure 9.

It is evident from the experiment results (Figure 7 to Figure 9) that the human visitors exhibit a consistent access tendency throughout the day, but robots initially (red spikes) generates a vast amount of traffic to request a large number of resources and consumed a significant amount of band width.

Figure 6. Web Robots vs. Humans-Percentage of bandwidth consumed for different types of resources

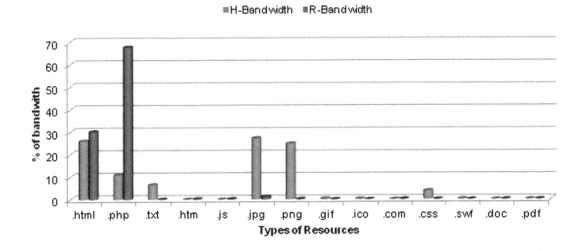

Table 4. Hourly distribution of requests generated from different visitors and bandwidth consumed by web robots and human sessions

Hour	H-Requests	R-Requests	H-Visitors	R-Visitors	H-Bandwidth	R-Bandwidth
0	2.89	3.29	2.72	3.14	3.02	3.17
1	2.69	3.76	2.64	3.24	2.65	3.59
2	2.61	3.07	2.47	4.81	2.74	2.98
3	2.81	3.04	2.66	7.54	2.79	3.14
4	2.91	3.43	2.9	5.36	3.13	3.44
5	3.44	3.9	3.61	3.69	3.67	3.81
6	4.21	4.46	4.5	4.35	4.37	4.52
7	4.71	6.15	4.75	3.14	4.58	6.08
8	4.74	5.92	4.78	3.14	4.56	8.92
9	5.13	6.06	4.41	4	4.95	6.61
10	4.56	4.72	4.16	3.19	4.59	4.12
11	3.7	5.2	3.9	3.89	3.79	4.86
12	3.83	4.57	3.66	3.74	4.02	4.36
13	3.44	6.08	3.5	4.7	3.51	5.3
14	3.31	4.07	3.73	4.4	3.18	3.68
15	3.7	3.87	4.19	3.84	3.56	3.68
16	3.71	3.73	4	3.39	3.81	3.29
17	4.62	3.37	4.56	3.95	4.49	3.07
18	5.27	3.39	5.1	4.6	4.99	3.38
19	5.48	4.16	5.45	4.15	5.35	4.24
20	5.75	3.54	6.1	4	5.8	3.46
21	5.69	3.29	5.25	4.65	5.64	3.44
22	5.91	3.07	5.61	4.3	6.04	2.92
23	4.88	3.84	5.35	4.81	4.78	3.95

Figure 7. Web Robots vs. Humans-Percentage of hourly generated requests

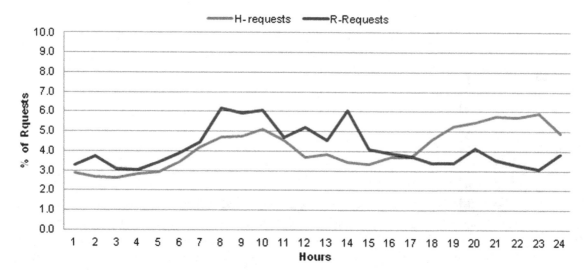

Figure 8. Web Robots vs. Humans-Percentage of hourly visitors

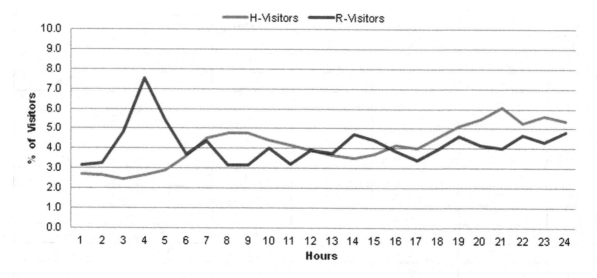

Comparison of Popular Web Resources

In this experiment, the comparison has been drawn between human and robot session's access pattern on for most popular resources. Table 5 shows the percentage of popular webpages accessed by web robots and human sessions. Figure 10 used to drawn comparisons between percentages of requests generated for popular URLs by web robots and human sessions.

It has been observed from the presented graph (Figure 10) that robots and humans access popular web resources are localized in different localities, but human visitors are monotonous and restricted to few web resources while robots perform an exhaustive search for a multiplicity of resources.

Figure 9. Web Robots vs. Humans-Percentage of hourly consumed bandwidth

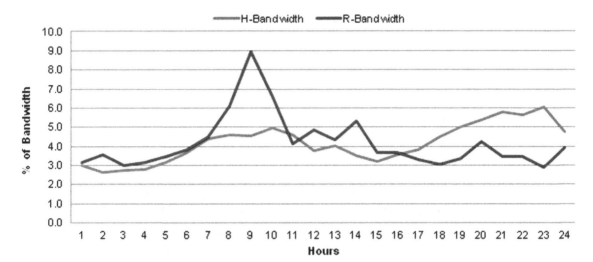

Table 5. Popular web pages accessed by web robots and human sessions

Pages	H	R	Pages	H	R
/	1.03	0.64	/forum/register.php	0.45	0.02
/aboutp2u/privacy.htm	0.04	0.01	/forum/search.php	0.02	1.67
/ads/www/delivery/ai.php	11.75	0.03	/forum/showthread.php	1.72	15.68
/ads/www/delivery/ajs.php	36.81	0.09	/forum/forumdisplay.php	0.27	11.25
/blog/	0.04	0.01	/forum/tags.php	0.01	0.66
/forum/	0.11	0.05	/insurance/	0.05	0.03
/forum/attachment.php	0.01	0.03	/insurance/compare/	0.02	0.03
/forum/cron.php	0.47	0.07	/insurance/health-insurance-for-h1-visa.html	0.01	0.02
/forum/css.php	3.33	11.03	/insurance/health-insurance-for-h4-visa.html	0.01	0.02
/forum/forum.php	0.12	0.22	/insurance/visitor-insurance.htm	0.01	0.02
/forum/index.php	0.05	0.03	/insurance/visitors-insurance-type.htm	0.01	0.02
/forum/loading.html	1.06	0.02	/loading.html	4.77	0.03
/forum/member.php	0.17	35.91	/robots.txt	0.06	0.97
/forum/newreply.php	0.07	0.05	/travel/	0.13	0.02

Comparison of Top Entry Pages

In this experiment, the comparison of accessing top entry pages by humans and web robots have been made. The entry page is the first one a user sees when coming to the site; its quality determines whether the user will visit further pages. This analysis is very important for customer-oriented services. The summary of experimental results is shown in Table 6, and comparative percentage of requests generated for top entry pages are plotted in Figure 11. The experimental results suggest that entry pages of web robots

Figure 10. Web Robots vs. Humans-Percentage of requests generated for popular URLs

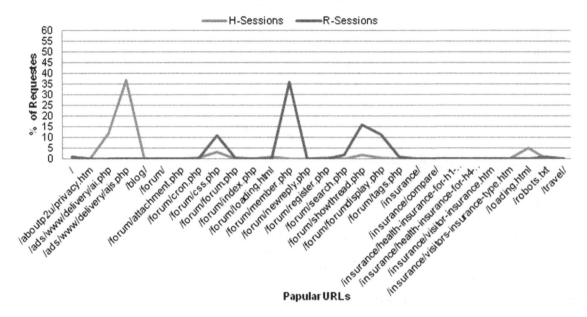

and human sessions are localized in different localities and quantum of the percentage of exit pages for human sessions are much more than the web robot sessions.

Comparison of Top Exit Pages

In this experiment, comparative studies of top exit pages accessed by web robots and human sessions have been performed. The exit page is one at which the user abandoned the site; if it is desirable that the user does not leave the site at this page, then page redesign is necessary. Table 7 shows the percentage of top exit pages accessed by web robots and human sessions and Figure 12 shows the comparison between top exit pages accessed by web robots and human sessions. It has been observed from the graph (Figure 12) that most of the human sessions (around 40%) leave the web portal on a single URL and rest of the time it exhibits the uniform exit path. Web robots sessions follow the zigzag exit path. The entry and exit path of robots and human sessions are just opposite to each other.

In following experiments, the demographic origins of robots and human visitors have been investigated in details. The three fold demographic analysis of origin web robots and human sessions was done by country, global city and the Indian city of origin.

Country-Wise Comparison

In this experiment, web robots and humans sessions generated from different countries are compared. The statistics of experimental results are shown in Table 8, and comparative plot of their origination is displayed in Figure 13. It is observed from the experimental results (Figure 13) that largest share of web robots and human visitors sessions are credited to the USA and followed by India. China is the only country who had made a significant contribution to web robots sessions but the very small share

Table 6. Top entry pages accessed by web robots and human sessions

Entry Pages	H-Hits	R-Hits
/	6.95	13
/ads/www/delivery/ai.php	1.16	0.22
/ads/www/delivery/ajs.php	**58.28**	1.35
/ads/www/delivery/lg.php	2.35	1.35
/forum/css.php	0.32	0.78
/forum/forumdisplay.php	0.29	0.56
/forum/member.php	1.93	3.59
/forum/showthread.php	16.79	**22.42**
/loading.html	6.28	0.67
/robots.txt	0.67	20.63

Figure 11. Web Robots vs. Humans-Percentage of requests generated for top entry pages

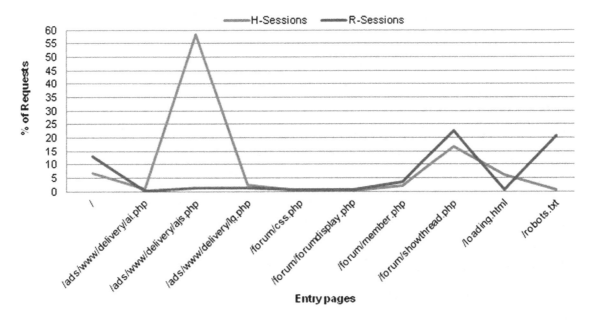

of human visitors. Probable reason might be less popularity of English language (in which web portal is designed) or unavailability Chinese version of the web portal.

In this experiment, web robots and humans sessions generated from different cities across the world are compared. The statistics of experimental results are shown in Table 9, and comparative plot of their origination is displayed in Figure 14. The experimental results suggest that the majority of web robot sessions are generated from world cities including Beijing, Mountain View, Chicago, and Singapore, etc. At the same time, human sessions are originated from all over the world except China. However, the majority of human visitor's share is contributed from Indian cities including Hyderabad, Bangalore,

Table 7. Top exit pages accessed by web robots and human sessions

Exit pages	H	R
/loading.html	**40.74**	0.67
/ads/www/delivery/lg.php	23.1	1.01
/	4.14	13.34
/ads/www/delivery/ajs.php	3.84	1.46
/forum/showthread.php	2.71	**23.99**
/forum/member.php	0.68	4.6
/forum/register.php	2.25	0.11
/forum/forumdisplay.php	0.53	1.35
/robots.txt	0.51	15.13
/forum/css.php	0.31	0.9
/forum/search.php	0.03	0.45

Figure 12. Web Robots vs. Humans-Percentage of requests generated for top exit pages

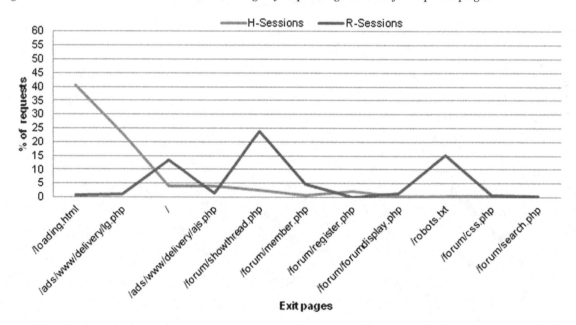

Mumbai, etc. where technology-based companies are flourishing, USA cities including San Francisco, Loss Angeles, Chicago, etc., Singapore and Dubai.

In this experiment, web robots and humans sessions generated from different Indian cities are compared. The statistics of experimental results are shown in Table 10, and comparative plot of their origination is displayed in Figure 15. The experimental results suggest that in India both robots and human sessions are generated from almost same cities, but the quantum of human sessions is much more than robot sessions.

Table 8. Sessions generated from different countries by web robots and humans

Countries	H-Sessions	R-Sessions
Canada	1.92	1.98
China	0.51	15.94
Germany	0.53	1.13
India	25.60	10.52
Other	9.88	9.92
Pakistan	1.09	0.82
Philippines	1.83	0.78
Singapore	0.76	3.29
United Kingdom	2.40	3.12
United States	50.16	46.67

Figure 13. Web Robots vs. Humans-Percentage of sessions generated from different countries

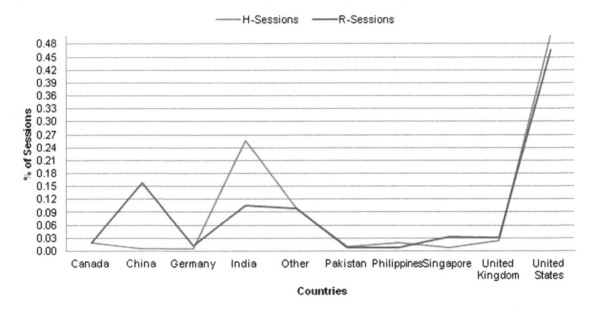

Comparison of Access Paths

In this experiment, the number of different access path, the maximum frequency of any path and the maximum length of the path followed by web robots and human sessions are investigated. Table 11 shows the summary of different statistics regarding access path by web robots and human sessions and Figure16 shows the comparative plot of access path parameters followed by web robots and human sessions. The experimental results show that human visitor sessions followed diverse paths as compared to robots. However, the web robots sessions used very long paths and generated a high frequency for these paths because they are mechanized to do the same job repeatedly.

Table 9. Sessions generated from different global cities by web robots and humans

City	Human	Robot	City	Human	Robot
Ahmadabad	0.44	0.23	Jersey City	0.48	0.25
Arlington	0.18	0.26	Karachi	0.28	0.29
Atlanta	0.68	0.44	London	0.96	0.55
Austin	0.51	0.28	Los Angeles	1.49	1.13
Bangalore	3.18	1.21	Miami	0.34	0.25
Beijing	0.20	7.16	Mountain View	0.25	3.72
Boston	1.01	0.68	Mumbai	3.54	1.47
Charlotte	0.45	0.29	New Delhi	2.40	1.00
Chennai	1.39	0.53	New York City	1.38	1.29
Chetput	0.44	0.18	Newark	0.63	0.84
Chicago	1.25	1.94	Philadelphia	0.29	0.26
Cincinnati	0.16	0.24	Phoenix	0.78	0.43
Columbus	0.51	0.35	Pune	0.83	0.28
Dallas	1.23	1.10	Saint Louis	0.21	0.51
Delhi	1.78	0.70	San Antonio	0.30	0.41
Dhaka	0.54	0.23	San Diego	0.61	0.25
Dubai	1.05	0.26	San Francisco	2.04	1.23
Fairfax	0.21	0.16	San Jose	0.60	0.30
Farmington	0.18	0.61	Santa Clara	0.23	0.19
Fremont	0.40	0.19	Seattle	1.11	1.01
Hong Kong	0.38	0.30	Singapore	0.76	3.17
Houston	1.14	0.75	Slough	0.16	1.27
Hyderabad	4.25	1.55	Sunnyvale	0.23	0.19
Islamabad	0.39	0.33	Tokyo	0.23	0.34
Jacksonville	0.16	0.23	Toronto	0.39	0.36
			Washington	0.51	0.84

Comparison of Response Codes

This experiment investigates the responses received by web robots and human visitor's sessions. The statistics of experimental results are shown in Table 12, and comparative plot of their origination is displayed in Figure 17. The experimental results suggest that most of the time request made by Human visitors are served successfully. However, the request generated by Web robots received error codes. The probable reason for getting frequent erroneous responses from servers is that the web robots are automated software and follow the broken links on webpages or try to access unavailable resources.

Figure 14. Web Robots vs. Humans-Percentage of sessions generated from different global cities

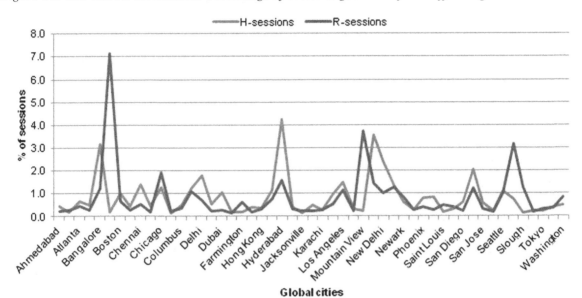

Table 10. Sessions generated from different Indian cities by web robots and humans

City	H-Sessions	R-Sessions	City	H-Sessions	R-Sessions
Ahmadabad	0.44	0.23	Kukatpalli	0.16	0.05
Ariyalur	0.06	0.09	Ludhiana	0.14	0.08
Aurangabad	0.11	0.09	Mangalore	0.04	0.04
Bangalore	3.18	1.21	Mohali	0.04	0.04
Chandigarh	0.11	0.06	Moradabad	0.01	0.03
Chennai	1.39	0.53	Mumbai	3.54	1.47
Chetput	0.44	0.18	Mysore	0.03	0.08
Cochin	0.20	0.09	Nellore	0.11	0.06
Coimbatore	0.24	0.14	New Delhi	2.40	1.00
Darbhanga	0.04	0.09	Noida	0.28	0.10
Delhi	1.78	0.70	Powai	0.35	0.09
Gurgaon	0.24	0.10	Pune	0.83	0.28
Hisar	0.03	0.04	Sarkhej	0.13	0.06
Hyderabad	4.25	1.55	Serilingampalle	0.08	0.03
Indore	0.05	0.04	Surat	0.11	0.06
Jaipur	0.10	0.05	Thiruvananthapuram	0.14	0.04
Jalandhar	0.09	0.05	Trichur	0.03	0.03
Jammu	0.09	0.06	Vellore	0.04	0.04
Kakinada	0.04	0.03	Vijayawada	0.19	0.04
Kanpur	0.04	0.05	Vishakhapatnam	0.04	0.05
Kolkata	0.41	0.08	Washim	0.08	0.08

Figure 15. Web Robots vs. Humans-Percentage of sessions generated from different Indian cities

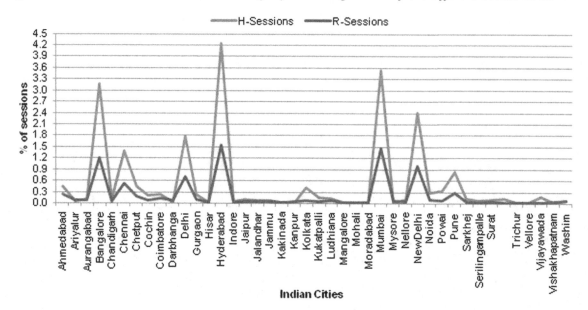

Figure 16. Web Robots vs. Humans-Number of sessions accessed a different number of paths, path lengths, and maximum frequency

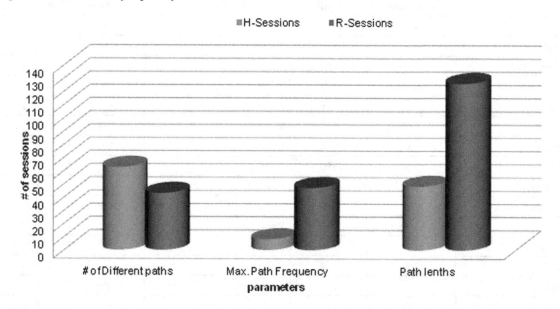

Comparison of Operating Systems

In this experiment, investigations of operating systems used by web robots and humans sessions have been performed. Various operating systems (OS) are used by human visitors and web robots. However, humans visitors are preferred graphical user interface (GUI) based desktop OS systems and web robots used server based OS along with GUI based desktop OS.

Table 11. Different number of paths, path lengths and maximum frequency generated by web robots and humans

Parameters	H-Sessions	R-Sessions
# of Different paths	6254	4309
Max. Path Frequency	810	4710
Path lengths	4830	12610

Figure 17. Web Robots vs. Humans-Number of entries and generated status code

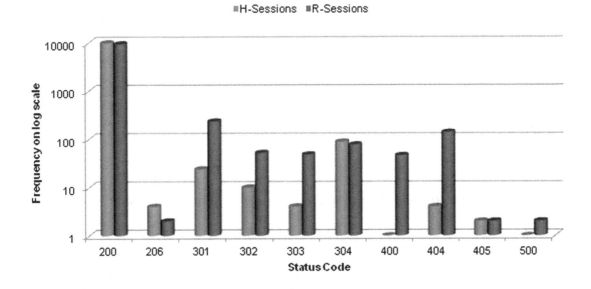

Table 12. Number of status codes generated by web robots and humans

Status Code	H-Sessions	R-Sessions
200(OK)	98.62	93.97
206(Partial Content)	0.04	0.02
301(Moved Permanently)	0.24	2.35
302(Found (Temporary Redirect))	0.1	0.52
303(See Other)	0.04	0.48
304(Not Modified (Cached))	0.88	0.77
400(Bad Request)	0.01	0.46
404(Not Found)	0.04	1.39
405(Method Not Allowed)	0.02	0.02
500(Internal Server Error)	0.001	0.02

Table 13. Number of sessions generated from different operating systems

Operating Systems	H-Sessions	R-Sessions
Android	7.52	11.6
iPhone	8.23	8.73
Linux	0.86	4.6
Macintosh	16.55	23.95
Windows 2000	0.01	0.05
Windows 2003 Server	0.17	0.31
Windows 7	13.8	9.29
Windows 7 64-bit	31.64	19.16
Windows 8	0.93	0.52
Windows 8 64-bit	5.94	2.96
Windows NT 4.0	3.63	2.25
Windows Vista	2.07	1.78
Windows Vista 64-bit	0.6	0.29
Windows XP or SP3	7.92	9.23
Windows XP SP2	0.11	5.17

Figure 18. Web Robots vs. Humans-Number of sessions generated from different operating systems

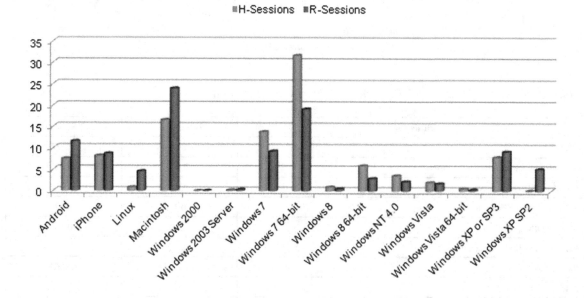

FUTURE RESEARCH DIRECTIONS

The most obvious finding to emerge from this chapter is that web robots traffic may cause the performance bottleneck of web server because it drains a significant portion of the server resources if it remains unnoticed. In future the findings of the currently discussed work may used to develop new techniques for identification of web robots and minimize their impact on server resources. This knowledge is useful for enhancement of services for more satisfaction of genuine visitors or optimization of server resources. Some more logs from numerous domains will also be analyzed to confirm further our findings.

CONCLUSION

The objective of this chapter is to discuss the correlative access patterns of human visitors and Web robots. This study was conducted on web server logs obtained from the web portal engaged in providing visa, insurance, and travel related services to global visitors to the USA. Based on experimental results it can be concluded that Web robots are interested only in accessing web pages while Human visitors showed their uniform access pattern for all type of resources. Human visitor's access patterns are consistent throughout the day, but web robots initially request a large number of resources and consumed a significant amount of band width. Human visitor sessions followed diverse paths as compared to robots. Most of the time requests made by Human visitors are served successfully, however; request generated by Web robots received error codes. Entry pages of web robots and human sessions are localized in different localities. The human visitors leave the web portal on a single URL and rest of the time it exhibits the uniform exit path while Web robots sessions follow the zigzag exit path. Human visitors followed diverse paths as compared to web robots. Human sessions are originated from all over the world while web robots are localized particular cities. Humans visitors used graphical user interface (GUI) based desktop OS systems while web robots preferred server based OS along with other systems.

REFERENCES

Almeida, V., Menasce, D., Riedi, R., Peligrinelli, F., Fonseca, R., & Meira, W. (2001). Analyzing Web robots and their impact on caching. *Proc. Sixth Workshop on Web Caching and Content Distribution*, 20–22.

Arlitt, M. F., & Williamson, C. L. (1996). Web server workload characterization. *Performance Evaluation Review*, *24*(1), 126–137. doi:10.1145/233008.233034

AWStats. (n.d.). *A free logfile analyzer for advanced statistics (GNU GPL)*. Retrieved January 1, 2014, from http://awstats.sourceforge.net/

Crovella, M. E., & Bestavros, A. (1997). Self-similarity in World Wide Web traffic: Evidence and possible\ncauses. *IEEE/ACM Transactions on Networking*, *5*(6), 835–846. doi:10.1109/90.650143

Dikaiakos, M., Stassopoulou, A., & Papageorgiou, L. (2005). An investigation of web crawler behavior: Characterization and metrics. *Computer Communications, 28*(8), 880–897. doi:10.1016/j.comcom.2005.01.003

Doran, D., & Gokhale, S. S. S. (2011). Web robot detection techniques: Overview and limitations. *Data Mining and Knowledge Discovery, 22*(1–2), 183–210. doi:10.100710618-010-0180-z

Doran, D., Morillo, K., & Gokhale, S. S. (2013). A comparison of Web robot and human requests. In *Advances in Social Networks Analysis and Mining (ASONAM), 2013 IEEE/ACM International Conference on* (pp. 1374–1380). IEEE. 10.1145/2492517.2500239

Gaffan, M. (2012). *BOTS & DDOS*. Retrieved from https://www.incapsula.com/blog/what-google-doesnt-show-you-31-of-website-traffic-can-harm-your-business.html

Google Analytics. (2013). Retrieved March 1, 2013, from https://analytics.google.com/

Huntington, P., Nicholas, D., & Jamali, H. R. (2008). Web robot detection in the scholarly information environment. *Journal of Information Science, 34*(5), 726–741. doi:10.1177/0165551507087237

Jacob, G., Kirda, E., Kruegel, C., & Vigna, G. (2012). PubCrawl: Protecting Users and Businesses from CRAWLers. *21st USENIX Security Symposium (USENIX Security 12)*, 507–522.

Lee, J., Cha, S., Lee, D., & Lee, H. (2009). Classification of web robots: An empirical study based on over one billion requests. *Computers & Security, 28*(8), 795–802. doi:10.1016/j.cose.2009.05.004

Li, F., Goševa-Popstojanova, K., & Ross, A. (2007). Discovering Web workload characteristics through cluster analysis. In *Proceedings - 6th IEEE International Symposium on Network Computing and Applications, NCA 2007* (pp. 61–68). IEEE. 10.1109/NCA.2007.15

Lin, X., Quan, L., & Wu, H. (2008). An automatic scheme to categorize user sessions in modern HTTP traffic. *GLOBECOM - IEEE Global Telecommunications Conference*, 1485–1490. 10.1109/GLOCOM.2008.ECP.290

Shyu, M. L., Haruechaiyasak, C., & Chen, S. C. (2006). Mining user access patterns with traversal constraint for predicting web page requests. *Knowledge and Information Systems, 10*(4), 515–528. doi:10.100710115-006-0004-z

Sisodia, D., & Verma, S. (2012). Web Usage Pattern Analysis Through Web Logs: A Review. *IEEE 9th International Joint Conference on Computer Science and Software Engineering (JCSSE 2012)*, 49–53. 10.1109/JCSSE.2012.6261924

Sisodia, D. S., Verma, S., & Vyas, O. P. (2015). Agglomerative Approach for Identification and Elimination of Web Robots from Web Server Logs to Extract Knowledge about Actual Visitors. *Journal of Data Analysis and Information Processing, 3*(2), 1–10. doi:10.4236/jdaip.2015.31001

Spiliopoulou, M. (2000). Web usage mining for Website evaluation. *Communications of the ACM, 43*(8), 127–134. doi:10.1145/345124.345167

Spiliopoulou, M., Mobasher, B., Berendt, B., & Nakagawa, M. (2003). A Framework for the Evaluation of Session Reconstruction Heuristics in Web-Usage Analysis. *INFORMS Journal on Computing, 15*(2), 171–190. doi:10.1287/ijoc.15.2.171.14445

Tan, P. N., & Kumar, V. (2002). Discovery of web robot sessions based on their navigational patterns. *Data Mining and Knowledge Discovery, 6*(1), 9–35. doi:10.1023/A:1013228602957

UAD. (2014). *User Agents Database*. Retrieved February 20, 2014, from http://www.user-agents.org/index.shtml

White, R. W., & Drucker, S. M. (2007). Investigating behavioral variability in web search. In *Proceedings of the 16th international conference on World Wide Web (WWW '07)* (pp. 21–30). Academic Press. 10.1145/1242572.1242576

WRD. (2014). *Web Robots Database*. Retrieved February 20, 2014, from http://www.robotstxt.org/db.html

Yu, J. X., Ou, Y., Zhang, C., & Zhang, S. (2005). Identifying interesting visitors through weblog classification. *IEEE Intelligent Systems, 20*(3), 55–60. doi:10.1109/MIS.2005.47

KEY TERMS AND DEFINITIONS

Access Paths: Sequence of URLs traversed to retrieve particular resources.

Access Patterns: Repeated web user access behavior over a period of time.

Popular Web Resources: Web resources frequently accessed by users through any version of the HTTP protocol (for Example, HTTP 1.1 or HTTP-NG).

Response Codes: Unique code generated by web servers in response to any HTTP request.

Sessions: Session is a set of web resources requested in a particular time during a website visit.

Visitors: A person or software who requests services from the web server.

Web Robots: Mechanized software programs designed to traverse and retrieve web resources for malicious and non-malicious reasons.

Chapter 13
Web Usage Mining:
Concept and Applications at a Glance

Vinod Kumar
Maulana Azad National Institute of Technology, India

R. S. Thakur
Maulana Azad National Institute of Technology, India

ABSTRACT

Websites have become the major source of information, and analysis for web usage has become the most important way of investigating a user's behaviour and obtaining information for website owners to use to make any strategic decisions. This chapter sheds light on the concept of web usage mining, techniques, and its application in various domains.

INTRODUCTION

World Wide Web has become the most popular platform for people. More than millions of users are interacting daily with the websites and visiting large numbers of websites, leaving behind a variety of information. Due to its various attractive and beneficial services web is getting more popular day by day. Now, No one is untouched with magic of World Wide Web service of internet technology. Website proves to be a popular means for information circulation among to the world. Today, almost every organization provides services and significant information to the targeted person through their websites. Such as resource sharing, online shopping using e-commerce, online banking, e-learning, e-banking, online news broadcast, online rail ticket reservation, hotel's room booking and many more. Due to cloud computing and other supporting services, the World Wide Web is getting ubiquitous and a usual instrument for day to day life's activities of common man. Because of unprecedented and exponential growth in popularity of web, there have been great efforts by the researchers in development of techniques to deal with the web data. Initially, the data mining techniques were being used to retrieve, search and organize the information over the web. There was no distinct term for the area of web. It was Etzioni (Etzioni, 1996) who first coined the term web mining in his paper. Since, then this area of research is studied under this term "Web mining" (Zdravko, M. & Daniel, T.L., 2007) defined web mining as the application of data

DOI: 10.4018/978-1-5225-3870-7.ch013

mining techniques to discover the patterns in web content, structure and usage. Further, the web mining has been categorized into three major parts-Web content mining, web structure mining, and web usage mining. Figure 1 shows the taxonomy of web mining.

Web Content Mining (WCM)

As the name implies, it is the process of extraction of information from web document, Text, audio, video, structured records such as- list, tables. Web content mining (Adeniyi, D.A. & Wei, Z. Yangquan, Y., 2016) involves techniques for Summarization, Classification, and Clustering of information on over the World Wide Web. It also collects interesting patterns about user's needs and customer behaviour. It targets knowledge discovery in which it collects information from text documents, multimedia documents such as images and video which are embedded or linked in a web. Web content mining mines unstructured, semi-structured, structured, and multimedia data. These are the tools used to extract essential information that one needs- Screen scraper, Automation anywhere, Web content extractor, Web info, and extractor.

Web Structure Mining (WSM)

Web structure mining is also called link mining. Based on the topology of the hyperlink, web structure mining (Adeniyi, D.A. & Wei, Z. Yangquan, Y., 2016) will categorize the web page and generates the information. Such as similarity and relationship between different Website .It is a tool to extract patterns from hyperlinks in the web. It also generates structural summary about website and webpage by analyzing the link. Firstly, Hits and Page rank algorithm is the popular web structure mining algorithm where Hits algorithm ranks the web pages by processing in-links and out-links of the web pages. In this algorithm, the web page is named as authority if the web page is pointed by many hyperlinks and web pages is named as hub if the webpage point to various hyperlinks. Secondly, Page rank Algorithm, It is the most commonly used algorithm for ranking various pages. Working of PageRank Algorithm depends upon the link structure of the web pages. PageRank algorithm considers a back link in deciding the rank score.

Web Usage Mining (WUM)

Web Usage Mining (Mobasher, B., 2005) is defined as the application of data mining techniques to discover the useful pattern from web log data to know the user's behaviour as result of activities performed on the web. It is explained in detail in the subsequent section.

BACKGROUND

It has always been the point of interest to know about the visitors who are visiting the website of any organization or individual person. In the field of e-commerce it is inevitable to know the users behaviour and sentiments about a product or services provided by any company or organization. There have been tremendous efforts towards the development of the tools and techniques for discovery of the useful pattern and other significant information about the user's activity performed over the World Wide Web. Web usage mining which comes under the category of web mining is the area mining which deals with

Figure 1. Classification of Web Mining

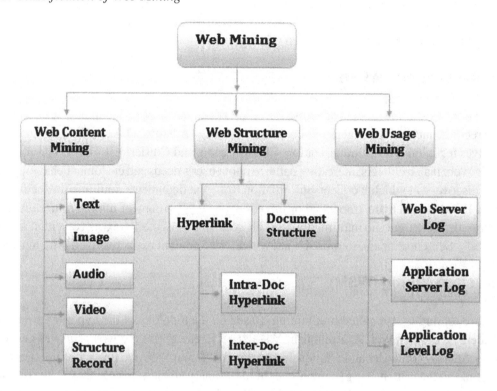

the web log data to extract the fruitful information. In the upcoming section of this chapter detailed discussion about web usage mining is done.

Web Log Data

Web usage mining process requires the web data to process it and present the result from it. There are three sources from which the log data is extracted and database of log is created. A log file to be found in three different places namely- Web Servers, Web proxy Servers and Client browsers.

A web log (Cooley R., Mobasher B., & Srivastava J., 2000) is a file where the web server writes the information each moment a user requests a website from that particular server. The given Table 1 shows the ten lines of web log data for sample format. This web log sample is hits made by visitors to the NASA Kennedy Space Centre, World Wide Web server kept in Florida City (Web Log Data, 1995).

1. **Web Server Log:** This belongs to the first type of source of the log. A server log (Cooley R., Mobasher B., & Srivastava J., 2000) is a log file/s automatically generated and maintained by a web server of actions performed by it. A typical example is a web server log which maintains a history of page requests. The W3C is responsible for maintaining a standard format for web server log files, but other commercial and proprietary formats also exist. Generally, the most recent entry is appended to end of the log file.
2. **Web Proxy Server Log:** A Proxy server is said to be an intermediate server that exist between the client and the Web server. It is the second kind of source where the log file/s can be found.

Table 1. Typical sample of web log data

S.N.	Web Log Data
1	ottgate2.bnr.ca - - [01/Jul/1995:00:18:37 -0400] "GET /shuttle/technology/images/et-lox_1-small.gif HTTP/1.0" 200 36098
2	ppp24.swcp.com - - [01/Jul/1995:00:18:39 -0400] "GET /shuttle/countdown/count.gif HTTP/1.0" 200 40310
3	ppp24.swcp.com - - [01/Jul/1995:00:18:39 -0400] "GET /images/KSC-logosmall.gif HTTP/1.0" 200 1204
4	ppp24.swcp.com - - [01/Jul/1995:00:18:39 -0400] "GET /images/NASA-logosmall.gif HTTP/1.0" 200 786
5	cu-dialup-1005.cit.cornell.edu - - [01/Jul/1995:00:18:39 -0400] "GET /pub/winvn/readme.txt HTTP/1.0" 404 -
6	whlane.cts.com - - [01/Jul/1995:00:18:41 -0400] "GET /images/NASA-logosmall.gif HTTP/1.0" 200 786
7	whlane.cts.com - - [01/Jul/1995:00:18:41 -0400] "GET /images/KSC-logosmall.gif HTTP/1.0" 200 1204
8	burger.letters.com - - [01/Jul/1995:00:18:43 -0400] "GET /shuttle/countdown/liftoff.html HTTP/1.0" 304 0
9	h-shining.norfolk.infi.net - - [01/Jul/1995:00:18:42 -0400] "GET /images/KSC-logosmall.gif HTTP/1.0" 200 1204
10	ix-tam1-26.ix.netcom.com - - [01/Jul/1995:00:18:43 -0400] "GET /shuttle/missions/sts-68/images/ksc-upclose.gif HTTP/1.0" 200 86984

Consequently, if the Web server gets a request of the client through the proxy server then the entries to the log file will be the information of the proxy server (Cooley R., Mobasher B., & Srivastava J., 2000) and not of the original user. These web proxy servers keep a separate log file for collecting the information about the visitor.

3. **Client Browser's Log:** This kind of log files can be made to reside in the client's browser (Cooley R., Mobasher B., & Srivastava J., 2000) window itself. The entries to the log file are done only by the Web server. Figure 2 shows the location of the log file where it exists in the World Wide Web and network system.

Figure 2. Web Log Data Sources

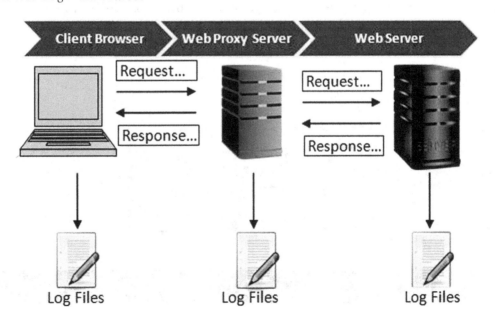

Web Usage Mining

The web mining (Mobasher, B. 2005) is described as the process of identifying useful patterns by ana-lyzing the web log data which is left behind by the visitors while surfing the web. It helps in knowing the user's behaviour over the web. Broadly, the process of Web usage mining is categorized into three sub processes. 1. Data pre-processing, 2. Pattern discovery tools, 3. Pattern analysis, Figure 3 depicts the basic steps involved in the WUM process.

After web data collection, Data pre-processing (Michal, M., Kapusta, J., Švec, P., & Hlinku, Tr. A., 2012) is the first step in the process of web usage mining. So what is data pre-processing? It filters or cleans web log files, it eliminates outliers and irrelevant items from web log data. Filtering the irrelevant data is important for web traffic analysis. For Example, the embedded graphics can be filtered out form web log files whose suffix is usually in the form of .gif, .jpeg, .png. The next step is to integrate data from all sources to form a visitor's profile data. Figure 4 presents the detailed steps involved in WUM process.

Pattern Discovery

Pattern discovery (Adeniyi, D.A. Wei, Z. Yangquan, Y., 2016, Tiwari V. & Thakur RS, 2016) imple-ments techniques from data mining, psychology information theory on web data collected from web data sources. There are several web mining methods and algorithms that are applied to discover the pattern from the web database. Few pattern discovery techniques are discussed here-

Path Analysis

In pattern discovery, path analysis plays a very significant role in web usage mining. Path analysis takes the help graph theory, in this; the customer clicks on web pages are represented by graphics model. So, graph models are used for path analysis. Let's have an example for better understanding- suppose we have performed a path analysis on an e-commerce website and by analyzing the path we find that 70 percentages of customer visits only first 4 web pages of the website, so, it is better for web webmaster to design those pages and retain the customer.

Figure 3. Basic steps in web usage mining

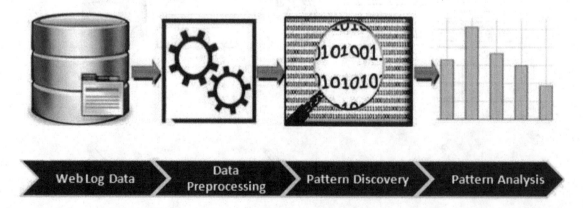

Grouping

User's gets conclusion by grouping the information together based on some characteristics. For example-

1. Grouping the location visits of customer.
2. Grouping the keywords used by customer.
3. Grouping the browser techniques together.
4. Grouping maximum links clicked by the customers.

This productive information is used by the e commerce gems like- eBay, Amazon, flipcart, shopclues, *homeshop18, jabong* and so on. Thus they improve and expand their business in the world.

Filtering

The next technique is filtering -based on the customer's request filters the information. It answers the question like- How many clicks a particular link received for this week. How many visitors visited the site from particular domain? How many visitors from a particular browser visited a site?

Statistical Analysis

Statistical analysis is an important pattern discovery technique which uses the statistical method on the numerical part of data existing in the web log data. This analysis gives the analysis result in numerical form which helps the needy in more accurate decision making about their business prospects. Using the data of session file one can perform many kinds of statistical analysis on variables such as page views, viewing time length of navigational path, average view time of page and so on.

Association Rule

Association rule is used to find the relation among the web pages of the websites in the world wide web. Association rule may relieve a relation between users who visited the page containing the electronic products to those who access a page about the sporting equipment (Tiwari V. et al., 2010).

Clustering

Clustering is a technique to group together a set of items having similar characteristics.

- **Example:** Persons who applied for credit card was in group between 25 and 30 with annual income of dollar Rs, 2 Lakhs.

Sequential Pattern

Sequential patterns is to find inter transaction patterns such that the presence of set of items is followed by another items based on time stamp order transaction setup web log files can record the set of transactions in time sequence.

- **Example:** 50 percentages of clients who bought computers also placed orders on ups after 15 days up.

Sequential patterns in web pages gives the trace path of the web page visited by the visitors which surfing the website. Let's take the web pages of a website abc.com which has WebPages- Home, product, services, contact, payment, support, feedback, contact. Here there exist various sequences among the web pages. One possible web page sequence may be Home ->Product-> Payment, services-> support> feedback and so on.

Classification

Classification is the technique that required into predefined classes. Example- 50 percentage of users who placed order lives in northern part of America. 60 percentages of users who placed order used the internet explorer web browser.

Pattern Analysis Tools

Pattern analysis is the concluding phase in web usage mining which is aimed at visualizing interesting rules, pattern or statistics obtained from the result of pattern discovery. This transforms the information into the knowledge. Pattern analysis provides the main crux of the analysis of web log. Webmasters are extremely interested in questions like how are people using the websites? Which pages are being accessed most frequently? This answers the questions of structure and hyperlinks as well as the content of the page. The end product of such analysis might be - Frequency of visits per document, most recent visits per document, how frequently each hyperlink is clicked? Who is visiting which document from which location? Which is the most recent use of each hyperlink? And many more answers of similar questions. Pattern analysis tools take the help of the visualization techniques, online analytical processing (OLAP), Data and knowledge querying, Usability analysis.

Web Log Analyzers

Web log analyzer is a unified software tool which helps to analyze web site's user's behaviour and provide the complete website usage statistics in many ways and easy step. Web analytics software helps to know exactly where website's visitors come from and how they move through the website i.e. their location and the access path in the website. Some general statistics (Goel N. & Jha C.K., 2013) provided by these automated software tools of web usage mining are- Hits summary, visits summary, technical summary, search engines summary, page views summary, referral summary, error report summary, etc. Table -1 presents summarized information about popular web log analyzer (Kumar, V. & Thakur R. S., 2017) software tools.

Figure 4. Process of web usage mining

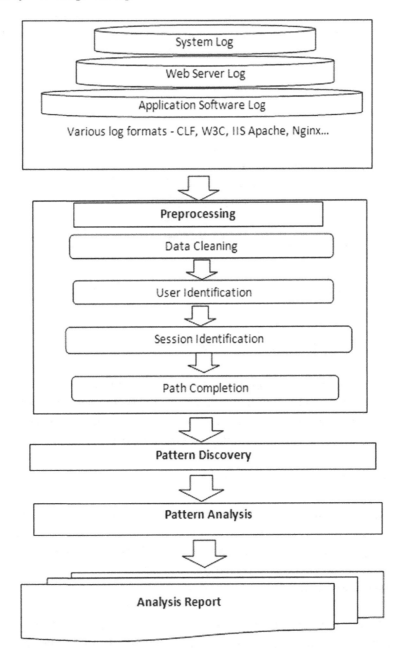

ISSUES AND CHALLENGES IN WEB USAGE MINING

As the Web usage mining is interesting in web world of digital space, at the same time it also encompasses the many issues and challenges in performing mining task. Some of the challenging and issues are discussed here briefly.

Table 2. Some popular weblog analyzers

SN	Name	Vendor	Current version	License	Source URL
1	Google Analytics	Google Inc.	Single	Free	http://www.google.com/analytics
2	Open Web Analytics	Open web analytics	1.5.7	GNU-GPL	http://www.openwebanalytics.com
3	Deep Log analyzer	Deep Software Inc.	7.0	Proprietary	http://www.deep-oftware.com/
4	Visitors	Salvatore Sanfilippo	0.7	GNU-GPL	http://www.hping.org/visitors/
5	Webalizer	Webalizer	2.23 - 08	GNU-GPL	http://www.webalizer.org/
6	Piwik	Piwik Inc.	2.16.5	GNU-GPL	http://www.piwik.org/
7	Web Log Expert	Alentum Software	9.3	Proprietary	http://www.weblogexpert.com/
8	Web log Storming	Dataland Software	3.2	Proprietary	http://www.weblogstorming.com
9	Nihuo Log Analyzer	Nihuo Software Inc	4.19	Proprietary	http://www.loganalyzer.net
10	GoAccess	MIT Licensed	1.0	Open Source	https://goaccess.io/

Data Collection and Integration

The web data exists over the different web servers sometimes distributed geographically in the network. All These servers create their own log files to record the users activities performed on the website. These separately stored log data on various data sources are required to be extracted from the web servers. The import and integration of desired data into single unified repository is a very challenging task.

Unstructured and Heterogeneity of Data

Unstructured data represents almost every kind of data being produced through the interaction of web. Usually, the log file created by the web server is in text format which contains textual and numerical values. That's why; Digging into the unstructured data is cumbersome and costly.

Storage and Processing Issues

Millions of users interact on the web every second and they leave the trace of navigation behind them which is stored somewhere in the web server. Thus, every moment the log data is getting bigger in size. The storage available is not enough for storing the large amount of data which is being produced by almost everything: Social Media websites are themselves a big contributor. If somehow, it is managed to store the log data, the processing of the large enormous size of data is quite difficult with the tradition machines. Sophisticated networks, high performance of processing and storage devices are required to deal with this all.

Quality of Data

Collection of huge amount of data and its storage comes at a cost. More web data if used for decision making or for predictive analysis (Kavita, et. al. 2016) in business will certainly lead to better outcome. This further guide to various questions like how it can be confirmed that which data is relevant, how much data would be sufficient for decision making and whether the stored data is correct or not to draw final result from it etc.

Data Pre-Processing

Data mining field has given techniques to pre-process the data. The same pre-processing techniques (Michal, M., Kapusta, J., Švec, P., & Hlinku, Tr. A., 2012) are also used to perform the pre-processing task. Since, the log files exist in the textual form in text file or similar to this file. Because of its textual form, the processing of log file is quite difficult to present in the desired form to perform the web usage mining process. As the cleaning, reduction of high dimensional data to low dimensional data, filtering, sampling, fitting of data etc. leads to loss of relevant data from the web log data.

Privacy Issues

As the use of World Wide Web by people increased in the world, and the web has become an essential part of the human life. In Parallel, the privacy issues have also grieved to a great extent in the internet world. The issue of privacy (Kavita, Mahani P. & Ruhil., 2016) revolves around the fact that the majority of the users wish to safeguard stringent anonymity over the Web. They don't want that someone monitor their visit and track their navigation on web. On the other hand, administrators of the e-commerce websites have their own business need to know about the user. That's why the privacy of visitor over the internet has become a very serious issue in current scenario. Many solutions have developed and adopted to tackle this severe problem but still there is no clear and appropriate solution for this. One solution is given to make the user data anonymous before handing over to the analyst by the administrator to protect the privacy of the user. The users should also be made alert of the privacy policies by clearly mentioning in website to the visitors, so that they can take an informed decision on the subject of revealing their personal information.

APPLICATION OF WEB USAGE MINING

In today's digital world, where every business is e-commercialized, business is reaching to the customers via web and customer is reaching to their requirements through this same channel. In this scenario, the web usage mining plays its vital role and it has many important applications (Srivastava, T. Desikan, P., Kumar V., 2005) in the web world. Some the important application of web usage mining is discussed briefly herein.

Web Personalization

Website Personalization (Mobasher, B., 2005) is the process of composing tailored experiences for users to a website more willingly than providing a solo, wide experience; website personalization allows companies to present visitors with unique experiences tailored to their needs and desires. Web personalization makes efforts in one to one attentiveness and transforms it into digital world. This aids in providing the focused offers to customers based on the browsing activities. Tour and travel websites can serve users with promotions. News and other media websites can float up specific videos to targeted audience based on where they live and what they want. Travel sites can present visitors with promotions on the basis of the current season.

Improves System Performance

For a website, the user satisfaction always remains the main focus for the web site, administrators. Service quality and performance (Mobasher, B., 2005) network throughput, database, load on web data traffic over the website are very crucial to the visitors' satisfaction. Web usage mining gives the technical information for improving the system (web server, network, storage, and database) where the websites are hosted for accessing.

User Behaviour Analysis

Web usage mining helps in exploring user's behaviour (Kumar, V. Thakur & R. S. 2016) as a result of activity performed on the web from Web Log Data. Using automated analyzer software tool like- Deep Log Analyzer, Web log expert quick analysis is done.

Recommendation System

The fast expansion of e-commerce has caused product overload where customers on the Web are no longer able to efficiently select the products they are displayed to. To get rid of the problem from selection of appropriate product economically, web usage mining provides several recommendation systems (Cho, Y. H. Kim, J. K., 2004) to the customers. Collaborative filtering is one the most doing well recommendation system in this regard. It does rating of the database by tracking the customers' shopping behaviour to give better recommendations

Prediction

Web usage mining is widely used in the prediction of the way things will happen in the future often but not always based on experience or knowledge obtained from the web log data. Some of the framework has been developed that predicts the user's next requests (Géry, M. Haddad, & Hatem, 2003) based on their behaviour discovered from Web Logs data. That is why, the web searching system are getting more and more intelligent day by day.

Website Design Improvement

Web usage mining provides recommendations to website administrator to improve the design of their website. It is widely used in the e-commerce web world. Data mining techniques such as clustering, association rule and subgroup discovery techniques are applied to bring out the facts from target website. The results obtained in this way are shown to the webmaster team for interesting conclusions to improve the design of the website. The paper (Carmona, C.J & et al., 2012) presents the methodology used in an e-commerce website of extra virgin olive oil sale called www.OrOliveSur.com.this presents the complete analysis of web usage mining in the website OrOliveSur.com. More insights can be obtained herein.

The web usage mining is playing a crucial role in the web world of this digital era. There are many applications of WUM. The major leading websites, Google, Yahoo, and Social Networking sites, etc. uses web usage mining for advertisements, web page optimization, web search, vertical search etc.

CONCLUSION

This chapter has contributed to make the audience aware of the web usage mining basic concepts, tools and techniques which are being used in the current web world to get the promising advantage from the World Wide Web. Here, the effort has also been made to find out the issues and challenges which web mining is still facing. The importance and utility of web usage mining has also been shown by presenting its application in various domains. Now, in short, the final goal of web mining is to improve the system performance, enhance the security of system, to facilitate in website design modification for better presentation to visitors, and also providing the support for the marketing design by analysing the user's behaviour.

FUTURE RESEARCH DIRECTIONS

In this chapter, it is examined in the available techniques of web usage mining, reprocessing of web log data is quite challenging to do it without loss of relevant information. It needs to be improved; privacy is a big issue that is needed to be solved effectively. The exiting recommendation systems for web are not so good to give accurate recommendation.

REFERENCES

Adeniyi, D.A. Wei, Z. Yangquan, Y. (2016). An automated web usage data mining and recommendation system using K-nearest Neighbour (KNN) classification method. *Applied Computing and Informatics, 12*, 90-108.

Carmona, C. J., Ramírez-Gallego, S., Torres, F., Bernal, E., Jesus, M.J., & García, S. (2012). Web usage mining to improve the design of an e-commerce website: OrOliveSur.com. *Expert Systems with Applications, 39*(12), 11243-11249.

Cho, Y. H., & Kim, J. K. (2004). Application of web usage mining and product taxonomy to collaborative recommendations in e-commerce. *Expert Systems with Applications, 26*(2), 233-246.

Cooley, R., Mobasher, B., & Srivastava, J. (2000). Web Usage Mining: Discovery and Applications of Usage Patterns from Web Data. *ACM SIGKDD, 1*(2), 12–23. doi:10.1145/846183.846188

Etzioni, O. (1996). The World Wide Web: Quagmire or gold mine. *Communications of the ACM, 39*(11), 65–68. doi:10.1145/240455.240473

Géry, M. Haddad, Hatem. (2003). Evaluation of web usage mining approaches for user's next request prediction. In *Proceedings of the 5th ACM international workshop on Web information and data management (WIDM '03)*. ACM. 10.1145/956699.956716

Goel, N., & Jha, C. K. (2013). Analyzing users behaviour from web access logs using automated log analyzer tool. *International Journal of Computers and Applications, 62*(2).

Habin, L., & Vlado, K. (2007). Combining mining of web server logs and web content for classifying users' navigation pattern and predicting users future request. *J. Data Knowledge Eng, 61*(2), 304–330. doi:10.1016/j.datak.2006.06.001

Kavita, M. P., & Ruhil, N. (2016). Web data mining: A perspective of research issues and Challenges, *IEEE, International Conference on Computing for Sustainable Global Development (INDIACom)*, 3235-3238.

Kumar, V., & Thakur, R. S. (2016). Exploring behaviour of visitor's activity at granular level from web log data using deep log analyzer. *International Journal of System and Software Engineering, 4*(1), 16–26.

Kumar, V., & Thakur, R. S. (2017). A brief investigation on web usage mining tools (WUM). *Saudi J. Eng. Technol, 2*(1), 1-11.

Liu, B. (2006). *Web data mining: Exploring hyperlinks, contents, and usage data (datacentric systems and applications)*. Springer-Verlag.

Michal, M., Kapusta, J., Švec, P., & Hlinku, Tr. A. (2012). Data preprocessing evaluation for web logs mining: Reconstruction of activities of a web visitor. *J. Proc. Comput. Sci., 1*, 2273–2280.

Mobasher, B. (2005). *Web usage mining and personalization*. CRC Press, LLC.

Srivastava, T., Desikan, P., & Kumar, V. (2005). Web mining – concepts, applications and research directions. In W. Chu & T. Young Lin (Eds.), *Foundations and Advances in Data Mining. Studies in Fuzziness and Soft Computing* (Vol. 180). Berlin: Springer. doi:10.1007/11362197_10

Tiwari, V., & Thakur, R. S. (2016). Pattern Warehouse: Context Based Modeling and Quality Issues. *Proceedings of the National Academy of Sciences, India Section A: Physical Sciences, 86*(3), 417-431.

Tiwari, V., Tiwari, V., Gupta, S., & Tiwari, R. (2010, June). Association rule mining: A graph based approach for mining frequent itemsets. In *Networking and Information Technology (ICNIT), 2010 International Conference on* (pp. 309-313). IEEE. 10.1109/ICNIT.2010.5508505

Web Log Data. (1995). Retrieved from http://ita.ee.lbl.gov/html/contrib/NASA-HTTP.html

Zdravko, M., & Daniel, T. L. (2007). *Data mining the Web, Uncovering patterns in Web content, structure, and usage*. John Wiley & sons Inc.

KEY TERMS AND DEFINITIONS

Web Content Mining: It is the process of extraction of information from web document, video, audio, text, structured records such as lists and tables.

Web Log Analyzer: It is a software tool that quickly extracts summarized statistics of information from web log data as an automated system.

Web Log Data: It is the data generated automatically by the web server as a result of interaction with the website by the visitors.

Web Mining: It is the application of data mining techniques to discover the patterns in web content, structure, and usage.

Web Structure Mining: It is the process to extract patterns from hyperlinks in the web. It is also called link mining.

Web Usage Mining: It is defined as the application of data mining techniques to extract the patterns of information from web log data.

Chapter 14
Management and Monitoring Patterns and Future Scope

Ramgopal Kashyap
Sagar Institute of Science and Technology, India

Pratima Gautam
AISECT University, India

Vivek Tiwari
International Institute of Information Technology, India

ABSTRACT

Extricating information from expansive, heterogeneous, and loud datasets requires capable processing assets, as well as the programming reflections to utilize them successfully. The deliberations that have risen in the most recent decade mix thoughts from parallel databases, dispersed frameworks, and programming dialects to make another class of adaptable information investigation stages that shape the establishment of information science. In this chapter, the scene of important frameworks, the standards on which they depend, their tradeoffs, and how to assess their utility against prerequisites are given.

INTRODUCTION

The human brain process a large number of images, development, sound and other exclusive data from numerous sources. The cerebrum is astoundingly productive and successful in its ability to endorse and coordinate a game-plan and shrouds any figuring power accessible today. Cell phones now record and offer images, sounds and recordings at an extraordinarily expanding rate, constraining our brains to handle more. Innovation is making up for lost time to the cerebrum (Kune, Konugurthi, Agarwal, Chillarige & Buyya, 2016). Google's image acknowledgment in "Self-educated Software" is attempting to imitate the cerebrum's ability to learn through involvement. In parallel, prescriptive investigation is getting to be noticeably much more wise and proficient than prescient examination. Like the mind, prescriptive investigation learns and adjusts as it forms images, recordings, sounds, content and numbers to endorse a strategy (Gilge, 2016).

DOI: 10.4018/978-1-5225-3870-7.ch014

Google is dealing with mimicking the human cerebrum's capacity to process, assess and pick a game-plan utilizing enormous neural systems. The image and video examination science has scaled with progresses in machine vision, multi-lingual discourse acknowledgment and principles based choice motors. Extraordinary premium exists in prescriptive examination driven by constant surges of rich image and video content. Purchasers with cell phones drive a blast of area followed image and video information. Bringing down expenses has democratized cloud-based elite registering. Image investigation is viewed as a potential answer for social, political, monetary and industry issues (Bhatti, 2015). On the utilization side, versatile utilization of video is developing significantly. Data transmission is no longer a worry. Prescriptive examination is ready to convey significant video to watchers past Netflix' calculation for DVDs to lease in light of review interests.

IMAGE ANALYTICS: TECHNOLOGY PROCESS

Image examination is the programmed algorithmic extraction and legitimate investigation of data found in image information utilizing advanced image handling systems. The utilization of standardized tags and QR codes are straightforward cases, however intriguing illustrations are as intricate as facial acknowledgment and position and development examination. Today, images and image recordings make up around 80 percent of all corporate and open unstructured enormous information. As development of unstructured information increments, investigative frameworks must absorb and decipher images and recordings and additionally they translate organized information, for example, content and numbers (Dunigan, King & Morse, 2011). An image is an arrangement of signs detected by the human eye and prepared by the visual cortex in the mind making a distinctive affair of a scene that is in a split second connected with ideas and questions beforehand saw and recorded in one's memory. Images are either a raster image or a vector image. Basically, raster images are a grouping of pixels with attentive numerical esteems for shading; vector images are an arrangement of shading explained polygons. To perform investigation on images or recordings, the geometric encoding must be changed into develops delineating physical components, articles and development spoken to by the image or video. These builds can then be sensibly broke down by a computer. The way toward changing enormous information counting image information into more elevated amount builds that can be dissected is sorted out in dynamic strides that each increases the value of the first data in an esteem chain. Prescriptive examination use the rise of enormous information and computational and logical advances in the fields of insights, arithmetic, operations look into, business principles and machine learning.

Prescriptive examination is basically this chain of changes whereby organized and unstructured huge information is handled through middle of the road portrayals to make an arrangement of remedies recommended future activities (Eberendu, 2016). These activities are basically changes over a future time span to factors that impact measurements important to a venture, government or another establishment. These factors impact target measurements over a predetermined time span. The structure of the connection between a metric and the factors that impact it is a called a prescient model. A prescient model speaks to identified examples, time arrangement and connections among sets of factors and measurements. Prescient models of key measurements can extend future time arrangement of measurements from anticipated impacting factors. The initial phase in the prescriptive examination handle changes the underlying unstructured and organized information sources into scientifically arranged information. In spite of the fact that there are parallels with standard information warehousing/ETL, this progression is not quite the same as that approach in that it battles with the complexities of pre-preparing of unstructured information, and organized information including databases, account content documents, images, recordings and sound.

RESISTANCE AND SECURITY DRIVING DEMAND

The need to break down information and proactively recommend activities is unavoidable in almost every dynamic development industry, government and institutional division. This has made a vacuum, or request, for prescriptive examination frameworks. Protection and security, and social insurance, are especially great cases of enterprises that are driving interest for such frameworks. The resistance business has pushed the envelope for image handling, and it is reflected in the capacity that is being acquired by government (Tsetoura, 2013). "Guard organizations are the biggest spenders on a for every office premise at the government level for electronic information stockpiling." The Army, Navy and Air Force, alongside the Department of Defense, represent 58.4 percent of all elected spending for capacity. The expansion of caught information important to safeguard and security originates from four clear sources.

1. Predator automatons gathering insight by means of video and image surveillance at diminished hazard as they search out unfriendly situations.
2. Input reconnaissance cameras progressively predominant out in the open spots, overseen by elected, state and nearby governments.
3. Stationary business and institutional reconnaissance mounted out in the open spots of business, the working environment, healing centers and schools.
4. Consumer-made image and video shared on YouTube, Facebook, Twitter, web journals and other online web-based social networking sharing/distributing destinations.

While the request drives multiplication, it likewise introduces a contention amongst security and protection. Individuals esteem reconnaissance as an asset when a kid is taken or a friend or family member disappears. Then again, individuals consider it to be an attack of protection amid ordinary exercises. Moreover, individuals esteem sharing their own photographs with family and companions, yet they are worried that their images and recordings might be secretly prepared and broke down to recognize criminal action (Lafuente, 2015). Where is the moral line of "excessively" drawn? Also, do more youthful eras have a similar protection misfortune point of view? Significant urban communities around the globe, from London to Las Vegas, have cameras introduced so thickly that it's almost difficult to move about the city without being recorded. Staying aware of the establishment measurements is practically outlandish. The accessibility of simple to-convey, shopper introduced cameras is universal. This rate of appropriation for security video catch makes an exact appraisal of how much video is being recorded troublesome we simply know it is BIG.

Is this observation combined with the capability of video/image investigation making a difference? Observation and image investigation gives give information that can enable authorities to seek after criminal movement and seek after equity, but ex post facto. How does cost drive the interest for video and image examination? Individuals expect the country's resistance and security push to be practical. This implies the nation will move to a littler however more instructed battling power and in the meantime increment the utilization of remote detecting, perception and checking apparatuses. Basically, this implies more images and video catch or reconnaissance all over the place. Human services a Perfect Domain Parametric reaction mapping lung images. The multifaceted nature of social insurance makes it an ideal area to investigate the potential for prescriptive examination and imaging. Medicinal services has been a pioneer in catching rich imaging data and assembled databases to build up an assortment of measurable therapeutic standards. The subsequent stage is to utilize this image investigation to give ongoing understanding to human services suppliers amid finding and treatment. The advances in medicinal science come quick, and doctors have a troublesome time staying aware of new methodology, medications and pharmacology while they administer to patients. Advanced medical decision support systems (MDDS) interface gigantic learning bases to different clinical databases (Bhandari, Deaves & Hassanein, 2009). These thus are connected to a patient's information. These mind boggling frameworks have fluctuating schemata, near image banks and teach vocabularies even nearby dialects. Image investigation lessens changing subjective elucidation and human mistake, in this manner quickening the procedure of treatment and recuperation. With an image investigation framework that can precisely prepare and recommend activity, it's conceivable to imagine ongoing patient checking frameworks with rules-based examination and parental figure warning.

The expanding part of algorithmic conclusion and treatment makes the ideal chance to incorporate images with prescriptive examination. Coordinating image investigation with such innovation in a prescriptive examination framework holds potential to settle on speedier and more educated choices, streamline costs and comprehensively enhance the quality and financial aspects of social insurance (Zhang, 2016). The human mind all the while forms a huge number of images, development, sound and other recondite data from numerous sources. The mind is uncommonly proficient and successful in its ability to endorse and coordinate a game plan and obscurations any registering power accessible today. Cell phones now record and offer images, sounds and recordings at an unfathomably expanding rate, constraining our brains to handle more. Innovation is making up for lost time to the mind. Google's image acknowledgment in "Self-trained Software" is attempting to duplicate the mind's ability to learn through involvement. In parallel, prescriptive examination is getting to be plainly much more savvy and competent than prescient investigation. Like the cerebrum, prescriptive examination learns and adjusts as it forms images, recordings, sounds, content and numbers to recommend a game-plan.

DIFFICULTIES WITH BIG DATA

1. **Anonymisation and Re-Recognizable Proof:** No dataset can be splendidly anonymsed by drawing a progression of relationships between various datasets, one can get data that could possibly add to recognizing at least one information subjects a supposed "induction assault".
2. **Appropriate to be Overlooked:** While the law stipulates that clients have the privilege to ask for data about themselves to be erased or redressed, this does not really apply to the data surmised because of enormous information investigation.
3. **Client Separation:** User profiling can prompt segregation not just as indicated by the individual information given by clients e.g., age, sex, ethnic foundation additionally as indicated by the data deduced from huge information examination e.g., wellbeing condition, social foundation, and so on. The main building blocks of big data and machine learning communication contain people, data, process and things that are shown in the figure 1.

Figure 1. Building Blocks of Big Data and Machine Learning Communication (D'Orazio, Choo & Yang, 2017)

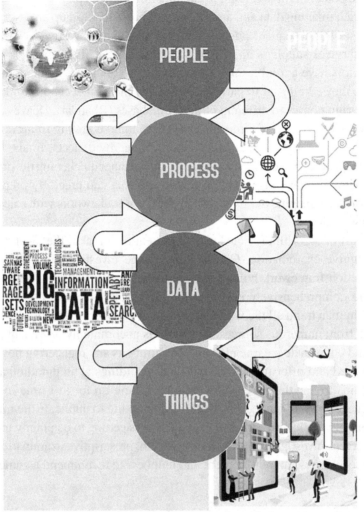

4. **Example Coordinating:** Big information examination and example coordinating systems now and again delivers result that could be mixed up for reality. Clients are profiled into particular classifications on the premise of their past and current practices, paying little heed to whether they have really demonstrated or affirmed to have a place into one of these classifications.
5. **Client Profiling:** Although client profiles are gotten from their previous practices, prescriptive examination additionally constitutes a driver for future conduct, making a circle that will at last fortify the profile which has been doled out to every client, and along these lines transforming a forecast into reality.

A meaning of image examination is a change from images and recordings to diagnostically readied information. With the end goal of this prologue to image examination, we characterize aimage as the rendering of a still scene and a video as the rendering of a scene containing a still or panning foundation fragment and moving forefront portions. Note that by suggestion, a video is additionally a succession of images likewise called a grouping of casings (Waoo, N., Kashyap, R., & Jaiswal, A., 2010). All the more particularly, the goal of image examination is to bring an unstructured version of reality as images and recordings into a machine analyzable portrayal of an arrangement of factors. A variable is spoken to by a progression of qualities identified with an element for example, deals, Ram's feelings, client notion, and so on. Each such esteem is time stamped, making it conceivable to regard a variable as a period arrangement. In software engineering or building, the discovery of items, confronts, development et cetera in images has many names including image preparing or Computer vision. Particular changes are utilized for image examination. These image examination framework in changing images and recordings to logically set up a dataset an arrangement of time arrangement, one for each factor (Juneja, P., & Kashyap, R., 2016).

At this level, image investigation keeps on being an arrangement of changes on image input that include esteem and make a rich arrangement of time arrangement as logically arranged information yield. The primary change steps sections images into organized components and sets them up for include extraction i.e., the distinguishing proof of low-level elements in the image. The second change step is the identification of connections between these components, factors and time. The third change step is the extraction of factors with time-stamped values.

DIVISION AND FEATURE EXTRACTION

Images and recordings are divided utilizing calculations and computerized handling systems known as image division. Sections are spatially important districts of image or video scenes that have a typical arrangement of elements (Kashyap, R., & Gautam, P.2013). These can be shading disseminations, force levels, surface, moving and stationary parts of a video scene and other criteria. There are various distributed image division calculations, each with a particular reason and profound specialized application. These procedures procedure a dim scale or shading variant of a image to recognize edges, limits, districts, development and numerous other essential criteria. Prevalent image division calculations include:

- Boundary, edge and bend discovery
- Brightness angles
- Texture angles
- Color angles
- Contour maps
- Multi-scale angle greatness
- Second minute grids
- Segmentation actuated by scale invariance
- Video scene sections

Highlight extraction is next all the while to aid the recognition of more elevated amount attributes, low-level elements are separated and put away with each example (Upadhyay, A., & Kashyap, R., 2016). Immense research in this area has finished in numerous calculations in the accompanying classes:

- **Color Histograms:** Decide 3D shading histograms as "shading fingerprints" of images.
- **Edges and Lines:** Distinguish edges by dissecting force slope around each pixel.
- **Corners:** Distinguish corners utilizing differential geometry administrators.
- **Shapes (Curves, Circles, Lines, Polygons):** Take after edges to recognize shapes.
- **Textures:** Distinguish regular surface locales.
- **Scale and Relative Change Invariant Elements:** Recognize highlights with scale and relative change techniques.
- **Movement Components of Video:** Distinguish development vectors and fields from video successions related with moving portions.
- **Image Include Total for Video:** Consolidate groupings of basic components crosswise over image sub-succession or video.

CONNECTIONS AMONG FACTORS, ELEMENTS AND TIME

To distinguish connections between factors, components and time, a computerized reasoning sub-teach known as Machine Learning is joined with Applied Statistics to make the relationship "knowledge" that is the center of the image investigation handle (Kashyap, R., & Gautam, P., 2017). The connections among factors, components and time in image examination are spoken to as a prescient model. Before a prescient model can be made, an arrangement of occurrences is separated from all the given images as well as all the given recordings being broke down.

A case is:

- An image one of all the given images.
- A section at least one fragments of an image.
- A sub-set of all the given images.
- A video one of all the given recordings.
- Clip from a video.

That is nuclear as for the granularity of the separate image examination space. This definition and settings characterizing the limits of occasions frame the contribution to the calculation that concentrates all examples from every given image as well as recordings. From a prescient displaying perspective, three sub-sets of all extricated cases are of intrigue:

- Training occasions
- Test occasions
- Predicted occasions

A machine learning or measurable displaying calculation prepares a prescient model in light of the arrangement of clarified preparing examples. Demonstrating calculations depend on known methods including neural systems, adaptable vector machines, work learning, Bayesian systems, relapse and some more. Test occurrences are utilized to ascertain the precision of a prescient model made by a demonstrating calculation. The preparation procedure is frequently rehashed with various arrangements of preparing and test occurrences and additionally calculation parameters until the exactness of the prescient model is at an adequate level. After the prescient model has been prepared, it is utilized to group anticipated examples in a procedure portrayed in more detail underneath.

CLARIFIED TRAINING

The reason for the clarified preparing occasions is to set up a relationship among low-level image/video highlights separated from cases, variable substances, factors esteems and time. A human or programmed/algorithmic chief can play out the errand of comment of preparing cases. The boss includes the name of a variable to the rundown of factors contained in the comment of the occasion if the substance speaking to the variable is coordinated decidedly on the case(Kashyap, R., & Gautam, P., 2015). Such a positive match of an element speaking to a variable on an occasion happens when an example of low-level elements additionally called an element vector that describes the particular element likewise called an element coordinating example are coordinated utilizing an element vector examination work to an arrangement of components separated from the occurrence allude to include extraction above. For instance, if the element related with the variable "Emotion_of_Ram" is Ram, at that point a client can physically explain all preparation cases containing Ram's face with the substance "Dwindle." As another case, a comment calculation can likewise coordinate an element coordinating example containing various low-level components, for example, the state of a human face describing Ram's face and a shading histogram containing extensive canisters of red skin shading since Ram's appearance is red on all preparation cases to naturally clarify the preparation cases that contain Ram's face. In a next explanation step, the estimations of factors recorded in the comment of each preparation example are recognized in the particular case utilizing an approach like that of substance coordinating depicted previously. For instance, the administrator can give all preparation examples commented on with the variable "Emotion_of_Ram" that contain a cheerful outward appearance the clear cut variable esteem "Glad" or "Irate" on account of a furious face. Such esteem can likewise be naturally identified by a calculation in view of an example of low-level components related with the estimation of a variable called an esteem coordinating example (Juneja, P., & Kashyap, R.,2016). For instance, an esteem coordinating example may depict a specific number of onlookers wearing the shading orange in an image of a football stadium in view of various components, for example,

- A shading histogram with expansive canister of orange shading.
- A polygon that describes the upper portion of the human body.
- A disparity characterizing the edge.

At last, preparing examples are time stamped for time arrangement examination purposes. We comment on preparing examples related with a specific time an incentive with the string or numerical portrayal of the separate time esteem (Kashyap, R., & Tiwari, V.,2017). For instance, expecting we are utilizing yearly quarters for the time granularity, at that point we can explain preparing occurrences containing snow and winter scenes as "Q1", occasions containing spring blooms and blossoms as Q2, cases containing a considerable measure of summer green and blue skies as "Q3," and cases containing red, dark colored and orange fall foliage as "Q4"and so on. A period comment calculation utilizes a period coordinating quality example related with each discrete time esteem or time esteem range to comment on the preparation cases consequently. The image examination framework now sees how to investigate a given arrangement of information images and additionally recordings in view of the prescient models made in the earlier stride. The last stride of the image examination handle is to make the scientifically arranged information. This last yield is made by utilizing these prescient models to anticipate a period arrangement of variable esteems for each factor from the staying set of occasions called anticipated occurrences.

IMPACT OF OPTALYSYS IN BIG DATA

Optalysys is creating optical elite figuring equipment for huge information handling, which works at more elevated amounts than what can be accomplished with customary gadgets at a small amount of the cost and vitality utilization (Kashyap, R., & Gautam, P.,2016). Optalysys innovation utilizes light, as opposed to power, to perform processor-concentrated numerical capacities, (for example, Fourier Transforms) in parallel at amazingly high speeds and resolutions. Optalysys innovation can be utilized to perform design coordinating, contrasting info information with reference pictures and distinguishing likenesses or irregularities.

- **Genome Analysis:** In genomics, design coordinating against a grouping of nucleotides or amino acids is basic to the get together, comment and examination of complex genomes. This handles illnesses in people, for example, disease and in crops that give worldwide nourishment security. The general population sequencing databases that contain this information are multiplying in measure at regular intervals or less. Broad quests of these DNA databases is winding up noticeably excessively costly and requires get to, making it impossible to expansive High Performance Computing (HPC) assets that expend huge measures of vitality for power and cooling. ("Pattern Matching - Optalysys", 2017) How Optalysys innovation can offer assistance: Optalysys innovation will play out this broad database seeks at speeds that are extents speedier than conventional silicon HPC frameworks and at a small amount of the vitality utilization and cost. This not just makes this innovation more available and moderate for existing HPC clients additionally grows the compass to new clients where the cost is as of now restrictive e.g. it could in the long run prompt a framework in each GP surgery for early conclusion and safeguard measures.
- **X-Ray Scanner:** X-ray scanners are normally used to profile inside structures of the body in high detail. As of now an example of the pictures is broke down by eye for variations from the norm after a lot of time has been spent checking a little zone of the body. How Optalysys innovation can offer assistance: In conjunction with the manual examination, Optalysys innovation could break down the greater part of the information gathered by the scanners instead of only a specimen to distinguish potential ranges that may have been disregarded. This could prompt quicker, more exhaustive examining. Optalysys innovation will give 'Enormous Data' examination abilities, managing huge scale assignments that can't right now be made do with existing electrical handling.
- **Square Kilometer Array:** The Square Kilometer Array is a worldwide science venture to fabricate the world's biggest radio telescope. By 2024 it will be gathering and handling information proportional to 100 times today's worldwide web activity. How Optalysys innovation can offer assistance: Optalysys innovation can possibly handle information at requests of extent speedier than today's (and even future) electrical supercomputers. For a venture with this measure of information, this will be major to its prosperity. What's more, Optalsys innovation will essentially

Figure 2. Role of Optalysys in Managing Pattern Matching

diminish handling costs as the vitality utilization is a small amount of electrical supercomputer necessities.

- **Alan Turing Project:** The Alan Turing venture was declared by the UK government in March 2014 to take a gander at better approaches for gathering, arranging and breaking down 'Huge Data'. It underpins the UK government's go for the UK to be a world pioneer in the examination and use of 'Enormous Data'. The venture is supported by £42 million more than 5 years and gatherings can offer for the financing to setup the organization. How Optalysys innovation can offer assistance: Correspondingly to the Square Kilometer Array illustration, Optalysys innovation can possibly handle information at requests of greatness quicker than todays and future electrical supercomputer abilities. Optalysys innovation will altogether diminish handling costs as the vitality utilization is a small amount of electrical supercomputer necessities.

THE ROAD AHEAD

Big data can be put away, procured, prepared, and dissected from multiple points of view. Each huge information source has diverse qualities, including the recurrence, volume, speed, sort, and veracity of the information. At the point when huge information is prepared and put away, extra measurements become possibly the most important factor, for example, administration, security, and strategies. Picking a design and building a fitting enormous information arrangement is testing since such a large number of elements must be considered. This "Enormous information design and examples" arrangement introduces an organized and example based way to deal with improve the undertaking of characterizing a general huge information engineering. Since it is essential to survey whether a business situation is a major information issue, we incorporate pointers to help figure out which business issues are great possibility for enormous information arrangements. On the off chance that you've invested any energy researching huge information arrangements, you know it's no straightforward undertaking. This arrangement makes you through the real strides required in finding the huge information arrangement that addresses your issues.

We start by taking a gander at sorts of information portrayed by the expression "Big Data." To disentangle the multifaceted nature of enormous information sorts, we arrange huge information as per different parameters and give a consistent design to the layers and abnormal state parts required in any huge information arrangement (Shmueli, 2017). Next, we propose a structure for grouping enormous information business issues by characterizing nuclear and composite characterization designs. These examples help decide the proper arrangement example to apply. We incorporate specimen business issues from different ventures. Lastly, for each segment and example, we introduce the items that offer the significant capacity in this arrangement cover the accompanying points:

- Defining a legitimate design of the layers and segments of a major information arrangement
- Understanding nuclear examples for enormous information arrangements
- Understanding composite examples to use for huge information arrangements
- Choosing an answer design for a major information arrangement
- Determining the reasonability of a business issue for a major information arrangement
- Selecting the correct items to execute a major information arrangement

Ordering business issues as indicated by enormous information sort, business issues can be ordered into sorts of huge information issues. Not far off, we'll utilize this sort to decide the suitable arrangement design (nuclear or composite) and the fitting huge information arrangement. However, the initial step is to outline business issue to its huge information sort. The accompanying table records basic business issues and doles out a major information sort to each.

- **Big Data Business Issues by Sort Utilities (Predict Control Consumption):** With machine produced datautility organizations have taken off savvy meters to gauge the utilization of water, gas, and power at customary interims of one hour or less. These keen meters produce tremendous volumes of interim information that should be investigated. Utilities additionally run huge, costly, and confounded frameworks to produce control (Sizov, 2016). Every network incorporates modern sensors that screen voltage, current, recurrence, and other essential working qualities. To increase working effectiveness, the organization must screen the information conveyed by the sensor. A major information arrangement can dissect control era (supply) and power utilization (request) information utilizing brilliant meters.
- **Broadcast Communications:** Customer agitate analytics web and social information, exchange data Telecommunications administrators need to assemble point by point client agitate models that incorporate web-based social networking and exchange information, for example, CDRs, to stay aware of the opposition. The estimation of the beat models relies on upon the nature of client qualities (client ace information, for example, date of birth, sex, area, and pay) and the social

Figure 3. Role of Pattern Matching in Big Data Analysis

conduct of clients (Shin, Yen, Tseng & Liu, 2011). Broadcast communications suppliers who execute a prescient examination technique can oversee and foresee agitate by dissecting the calling examples of endorsers.

- **Showcasing:** Sentiment analysis on web and social data, marketing divisions utilize Twitter bolsters to lead notion investigation to figure out what clients are saying in regards to the organization and its items or administrations, particularly after another item or discharge is propelled. Client supposition must be incorporated with client profile information to infer important outcomes. Client input may change as indicated by client socioeconomics (Shirin Matwankar & Dr. Shubhash K. Shinde, 2015).
- **Client Benefit:** Call monitoring Human generated, IT divisions are swinging to enormous information answers for break down application logs to pick up knowledge that can enhance framework execution. Log records from different application sellers are in various arrangements; they should be institutionalized before IT divisions can utilize them (Jing, Zhu & Li, 2014).
- **Retail:** Personalized informing in light of facial acknowledgment and social media Web and social information Biometrics , retailers can utilize facial acknowledgment innovation in mix with

a photograph from web-based social networking to make customized offers to clients in view of purchasing conduct and area. This capacity could tremendously affect retailers? Reliability programs, however it has genuine protection consequences. Retailers would need to make the fitting protection divulgences before actualizing these applications.

- **Retail and Promoting:** Mobile information and area based targeting Machine-produced information exchange data Retailers can target clients with particular advancements and coupons based area information. Arrangements are regularly intended to recognize a client's area upon passage to a store or through GPS. Area information joined with client inclination information from interpersonal organizations empower retailers to target on the web and in-store promoting efforts in light of purchasing history. Warnings are conveyed through versatile applications, SMS, and email.

- **Healthcare Fraud Detection:** Machine-produced information, exchange information Human-generated Fraud administration predicts the probability that a given exchange or client account is encountering extortion. Arrangements break down exchanges continuously and create proposals for quick activity, which is basic to ceasing outsider misrepresentation, first-party extortion, and consider abuse of record benefits (Bajaj, 2012).Arrangements are ordinarily intended to distinguish and avert bunch extortion and hazard sorts over different enterprises, including:
  - Credit and charge installment card extortion
  - Deposit account extortion
  - Technical extortion
  - Bad obligation
  - Healthcare extortion
  - Medicaid and Medicare extortion
  - Property and setback protection extortion
  - Worker pay extortion
  - Insurance extortion
  - Telecommunications extortion

Arranging big data issues by sort makes it less difficult to see the qualities of every sort of information. These qualities can enable us to see how the information is obtained, how it is handled into the fitting arrangement, and how every now and again new information ends up noticeably accessible. Information from various sources has diverse qualities; for instance, online networking information can have video, pictures, and unstructured content, for example, blog entries, coming in ceaselessly (Kshetri, 2014). According to the survey information as indicated by these basic attributes, canvassed in detail in the following segment:

- The configuration of the substance.
- The kind of information: exchange information, recorded information.
- The recurrence at which the information will be made accessible.
- The purpose: how the information should be handled specially appointed question on the information.
- Whether the handling must occur continuously, close constant, or in clump mode utilizing enormous information sort to characterize huge information qualities. It's useful to take a gander at the qualities of the enormous information along specific lines for instance, how the information is gathered, broke down, and handled.

LIMIT CHOICES FOR INVESTIGATION ON BIG DATA

- **Investigative RDBMS:** Analytical RDBMS stages are social DBMS systems that conventionally continue running all alone exceptional hardware especially redesigned for logical get ready.
- **Hadoop Game Plans:** The Hadoop stack enables bunch intelligent applications to use a large number of PC centers to prepare petabytes of data set away in a scattered record system.
- **NoSQL DBMS:** In extension to Hadoop HDFS, HBase, and Hive, there are other NoSQL DBMSs decisions available as a logical data store. They fuse key regard stores; chronicle DBMSs, columnar DBMSs, outline databases and XML DBMSs. Some NoSQL databases are not away for immense data examination. Others are away for examination of tremendous data or, then again for specific sorts of inspects.

NEW GENERATION OF DIGITAL HEALTH ADVISORS

Once a data store has been worked from an extensive variety of sources EHR data, payer data, contraption and IoT data, understanding audit responses, customer human data and has been consolidated into an incorporated data structure, at that point AI can yield vital bits of learning. AI, taking all things into account, is about illustration affirmation, differentiating a particular case of data around a given individual with equivalent (not by any stretch of the imagination undefined) outlines found elsewhere, and making farsighted proposals in perspective of what happened in those diverse conditions (Kowser, 2016). This is especially what clinicians do when working out "clinical judgment" perceiving an illustration, considering restorative issues, drugs, labs qualities, individual and family history, and standing out it from similar cases from the clinician's inclusion.

Another time of "Human Coaches", Tele-Carers or Digital Health Advisors can be set up to make these AI-decided recommendations important. They ought to be anything besides hard to use, customer orientated individuals who can connect with the amassed data store and the AI examination engines that sit on top of that. They can draw in clients/patients, and diminish the demand stack on clinicians. Will they supplant clinicians? No, clearly not. Regardless, they will help channel the demand to the people who truly ought to be seen, while drawing in patients with continuous, reliable and redid heading for the more regular things in regular day to day existence. So what impedes digital health advisors approach needs to bolster self-personalities and empower strong practices, rather than stimulating in office master visits? Furthermore, in the meantime, human data needs to wind up recognizably upgraded with a particular true objective to draw in AI and drive the improvement of new applications and related advances. It will be a while before we arrive, yet we can see the route to that new time of therapeutic administrations development. Hadoop can be used as noteworthy data structure versatility, and adjustment to non-basic disappointment for the occupation waiting is finished. (Big Data, RDBMS and HADOOP - A Comparative Study", 2016).In any case, gigantic data is not in any manner like data associating: with data interfacing the emphasis is on singular security issues, however tremendous data examination is focused on the framework (Xiang, Wang, Pickering & Zhang, 2016).

In this new condition, therapeutic administrations accomplices have more important inspirations to accumulate and exchange information. Indeed, even with fundamental repayment changes, human services supplier affiliations have money related and managerial consistence addresses that require being conviction based and not just "gut feel": "How are the specialists performing in association with costs

Figure 4. Challenge of Perfect Pattern Matching with Increasing Data

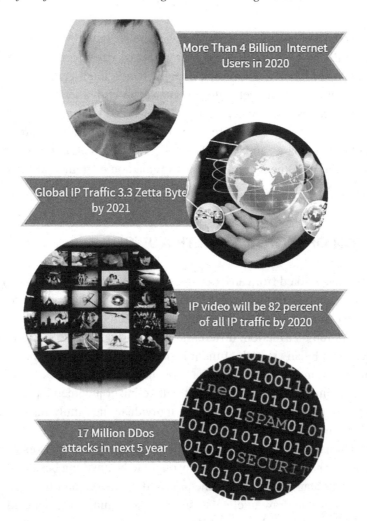

and quality?" "What number of patients is re-conceded following 30 days of discharge?" "What are the wage consequences of different reimbursement models?" "In what capacity may we perceive patients in the midst of a stay?'' "Who is high risk for readmission?" "By what method may we propel our execution under another reimbursement strategy?" "By what means may we best treat sub-masses of patients who are at high peril for readmission?" To answer these requests, you require a solid data foundation that can: (1) question the data; (2) watch reasonable action; and (3) drive execution. This foundation normally experiences 4 periods of execution; Part 1: Data Collection (Characterized by the augmented gathering of EMRs) Part 2: Data Sharing (Characterized by the expanded gathering of HIEs) Part 3: Data Analysis (Characterized by the gathering of data appropriation focuses) Part 4: Data analytics (Characterized by the choice of bleeding edge showing and deciding strategies).

Colossal data has ended up being fundamental to every affiliation except then its criticalness is being undermined. The US restorative administrations system is rapidly grasping electronic human records, which will altogether fabricate the measure of clinical data that are available electronically. In the meantime, fast advances have been made in clinical examination, i.e. methodology for separating broad measures of data and assembling new bits of learning from that examination. This examination and examination of data to understand it is called gigantic data. Immense data is not just about extending advantages and cutting, its usage in restorative administrations has been past this with the capacity to envision plagues, cure sicknesses, upgrade individual fulfillment and keep up a vital separation from preventable passing's. Therapeutic science is forming and considering the necessities now of masses with a negligible drawn out future as well as rather a presence with various new diseases jumping up, the models and strategies for treatment is also advancing. One such noteworthy change is the use of immense data, to expect and treat contaminations and besides find a cure.

Focus extensive datasets of patient components, aftereffects of drugs and their cost would help be able to recognize the most clinically reasonable and savvy pharmaceuticals to apply. Separating colossal datasets of patient characteristics, consequences of prescriptions and their cost would help is able to recognize the most clinically convincing and cost-capable solutions to apply. The four V's (velocity, veracity, volume, and value) are frequently used to speak to different characteristics of tremendous data. Steady illness, a developing masses, and new and changing client wants are moving the way social protection is gotten, gained, and acquired ("The Four V's of Big Data", 2017). Electronic long range informal communication and compact developments has upgraded access to mind and therapeutic administrations movement in new ways.

Social protection structures in numerous countries are changing portion models from a charge for-organization approach to manage comes about based or capable approach, extending the prerequisite for more correct data and data taking after, and making documentation necessities more particular. Absence of a comprehensive point of view of clinical and operational systems required for exposure of areas where progression was essential and operation in light of misty or fragmented cost or care estimations have really tormented social protection affiliations. Distinctive endeavors have driven the course in changing over how data and examination are used and the social protection industry is finally begun to take after their lead. Both sorted out and unstructured data from clinical, operational, and cash related structures; spouting data from looking at and identifying devices over the scope of care movement by and large; and data from outside a relationship, for instance, electronic long range informal communication and general human records are huge data sources. A load of present and future up and coming data sources is the best way to deal with recognize likely options for therapeutic administrations affiliations.

The way cardiovascular and stroke look into is coordinated and clinical care passed on is impacted by Big data. Gigantic data has phenomenal assurance for changing this examination and how clinical care is passed on. "Gigantic Data," which connotes huge and multifaceted datasets including, for example, biomedicine, genomic, clinical, and normal data and basically novel methodologies for data stockpiling, association, joining, examination, and portrayal. Uncomplicated cardiovascular research datasets are multidimensional in character with a wide extent of clinical and biomarker comes about; for example, electrocardiogram, contractile limit, nuclear imaging, channel works out, genomics, and proteomics, metabolomics, and phenotype depictions (Fotland & Kvale, 2015). Regardless, this sort of data is collected and uncovered in calculate data outlines; they are moreover unevenly spread. In this manner, the datasets are extensively scattered and separated, making learning extraction troublesome whether by singular labs or made legitimate attempts by methods for joint effort. The growing move to electronic data stages for the organization of human information is making an unfamiliar resource with the capacity to change social protection.

DISCUSSION

Colossal data have been described as broad datasets from a combination of sources and data sorts for instance, numeric, content based and imaging data that can't be administered or arranged using standard programming gadgets inside a sensible time. Basically, it suggests datasets of a satisfactory volume, variety, and speed with a specific end goal to allow disclosure of new bits of learning or new sorts of noteworthy worth that couldn't be found in more diminutive datasets. Visual analytics reinforces Big Data by giving instinctive portrayals that empower people to investigate these datasets. Visual analytics has been described as "the craft of logical deduction empowered by natural visual interfaces." Visual analytics is something past portrayal of the data; it is an approach that unites recognition, human segments and data examination. Huge Data are all the more proficient when joined with visual analytics, as the consolidated information that Big Data gives can be seen more quickly. This extends utility of Big Data for fundamental authority frames that ought to be put aside a couple of minutes continuously. Regardless of the way that there is the perfect open door for quiet reflection after clinical decisions are made, quality contemplations given through right clinical decisions are affected by information continuously. Both of these rising fields will broaden current exchange on Big Data in human, which have portrayed the likelihood to make new clinical learning by looking at unstructured

substance based data, assisting with getting the hang of disseminating by using data driven decision support instruments, translating redid tranquilize e.g. genomics into clinical practice, and passing on information direct to patients. Both Big Data and visual analytics with 10 v's value, venue, volume, variety, veracity, vocabulary, validity, vagueness, variability and velocity are playing important role in the growth of big data ("Top 10 Big Data Challenges – A Serious Look at 10 Big Data V's | MapR", 2017) can contribute basically to upgrading the way of social protection as shown in the figure 5. A key statute in quality change is to gage the technique where change is searched for, which can routinely be a singular measure, for instance, time for a patient to get a specific treatment. Regardless, every data point contains a ton of supporting information i.e. a wide dataset, which can include: understanding measurement information; tolerant co-morbidities; time of day that the treatment happened; the specific conclusions; content based specialist observes; the physician and restorative administrations specialists that were incorporated into the care; the cures that the patient was taking; imaging data et cetera. This supporting information can speak to a degree of the variability in the measure that is being pushed ahead. Through instinctive portrayal of the measure, a quality change master or inspector can explore the factors related with this change and get a more significant appreciation of possible causality. For example, patients with no less than two co-morbidities may have delays in treatment on account of extended conditions anticipated that would ensure a true blue assurance, or patients that land for treatment in the midst of off hours may have delays in treatment in light of openness of particular specialists. By applying Big Data and visual analytics analyze, diverse individuals can examine this wide dataset to understand components influencing nature of care. Generally, these requests would take be able to into thought: 1) the progression of better QI systems; 2) utilization of more noteworthy structure redesigns by taking out the secret in the model for Improvement's course of action do-consider six sigma's portray measure-separate upgrade control get ready) and 3) the ability to outline viable changes finishing solidly controlled enormity in restorative administrations despite assortment in patients and care settings. Enormous data and visual

Figure 5. Big Data V's

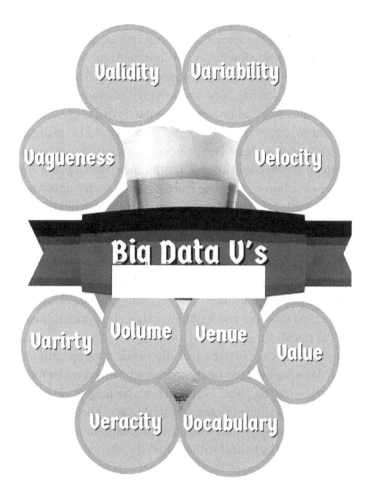

analytics can in a general sense add to clinical research by using de-perceived human data and down to business clinical trials. Randomized Controlled Trials (RCTs) give the strangest measure of evidence while executing clinical research into clinical practice. Regardless, the cost of running RCTs is as often as possible prohibitive, and new, more serious responses for standard RCTs are being discussed, which consolidate randomized registry trials and practical RCTs. By using a randomized registry approach, an all the more even disapproved, generalizable and sharp approach to manage clinical research can be endeavored. The randomized registry trial as a spine offers the likelihood to quickly choose patients, test mediations, and make a translation of triumphs into clinical best practice for extreme stroke mind. Novel programming game plans can energize consent and randomization into clinical trials by working with examiners to better appreciate the time objectives, moral concerns, and security issues. Plus, the electronic portrayals of the data would guarantee be able to fitting anonymization required by the trial traditions. Visual analytics would give be able to the ability to continuously connect with the data and reliably offer ways to deal with move between essential audits and patient specific information as required by the pros.

CONCLUSION

Various tremendous data science methodologies and procedures, for instance, data mining, machine learning counts, crowd sourcing clarification stages, appropriated registering establishment, and Bayesian framework computations are later in the basic cardiovascular society. These approaches are practicable in the domain of major cardiovascular science. New data mining and examination practices would moreover enable researchers to ask for qualities and proteins associated with CVD and stroke. Various qualities and in addition proteins that together cause CVD and stroke could be recognized using a structures approach. With propels, for instance, these could support new prognostic markers and, theoretically, healing targets. Joined with an appropriated system, for instance, Hadoop, the Apache Mahout structure passes on a valuable course of action of machine learning libraries for applying showing assignments, for instance, gathering and bundling disregarding the way that there is liberal need to discover impelled zone i.e. use of these computations. Hadoop is a run of the mill open source layout execution, and is at this moment being utilized as another option to store and process incredibly broad datasets on item gear. Dodging hospitalization is an important estimation for diminishing patient dreariness, upgrading calm outcomes, and reducing therapeutic administrations costs. There is a prerequisite for advancing work to utilize tremendous data structure for arranged risk figuring instruments, sketching out considerably more minds boggling farsighted showing and highlight extraction systems, and dragging out proposed answers to expected clinical threats.

Most telemedicine organizations are offered recently inside a recuperating office, between middle and a specific specialist's office, or between under-resourced focuses and a metropolitan center, which don't have adequate wide organization zone. Furthermore, the length of the organizations is when in doubt, constrained by the openness of experienced cardiologists. There are numerous great conditions to taking an assurance law methodology to testing tremendous data perception: the laws are standard based, which gives them the versatility to deal with the making challenges of data planning and judicious examination. Assurance law, a prominent framework for occupants and governments gives them a point of convergence through which to survey the odds of enormous data perception and the authentic liveli-hoods of that data for consistence. There is a need to pass on the most ideal approach to get the more broad societal obscenities of fearless and general tremendous data surveillance and shape that into the oversight appear. In addition, there may be underhanded disciplines or bothers related to immense data that is not the circumstance with data associations i.e. being in a perceptive order versus coordinated as a specific individual. There is a need to push toward the academic group and experts in the human rights field. This exchange must contain what sorts of government-held data we are set up to control for enormous data, and what sorts we are definitely not.

FUTURE SCOPE

There is enormous potential in design acknowledgment. For instance, another activity was as of late propelled by AstraZeneca to screen around two million genome arrangements to acquire information that will control the revelation and advancement of medications. As a component of this new activity, AstraZeneca has built up a few coordinated efforts, incorporating with Human Longevity, a US sequenc-ing master. Human Longevity expects to arrangement and examines the examples utilizing a scope of strategies, including design acknowledgment and machine-learning (1). At the flip side of the range, an article distributed in the UK's Guardian, (2) refers to the 'Shady with a Chance of Pain' ponder (3), a vast scale consider in light of Smartphone information that investigated a relationship between's manifestations of agony and the climate. This will at that point turn into a 'Native Science' activity, wherein both the general population and members are urged to wind up design spotters and "analysts," with the goal that speculations and affiliations can be hailed up to researchers, who will then do formal investigations in light of the recommendations. The essential part measurements and analysts play, with their capacity to devour a lot of information, intellectual PCs have favorable position over individuals with regards to handling huge information. Be that as it may, these PCs are less compelling regarding their judgment or capacity to comprehend the ramifications of any choices made. In 2014, Google made the news for all the wrong reasons when its drive Google Flu Trends, "a perfect case for the energy of huge information investigation" (4) was blamed for "huge information hubris." as it were, the assumption that enormous information examination is better than regular gathering and investigation. The American Statistical Association at that point discharged a strategy articulation (5) in October 2015, supporting the vital part of factual science in enormous information investigation.

REFERENCES

Bajaj, K. (2012). Promoting Data Protection Standards through Contracts: The Case of the Data Security Council of India. *The Review of Policy Research, 29*(1), 131–139. doi:10.1111/j.1541-1338.2011.00541.x

Bhandari, G., Deaves, R., & Hassanein, K. (2009). Corrigendum to Debiasing investors with decision support systems: An experimental investigation. *Decision Support Systems, 47*(1), 74. doi:10.1016/j.dss.2009.01.002

Bhatti, B. (2015). Social Media and Image Management: An Analysis of Facebook Usage in Celebrity Public Relations. *Media Watch, 6*(3), 339. doi:10.15655/mw/2015/v6i3/77896

Big Data, RDBMS, and HADOOP - A Comparative Study. (2016). *International Journal of Science and Research, 5*(3), 1455-1458. 10.21275/v5i3.nov162167

D'Orazio, C., Choo, K., & Yang, L. (2017). Data Exfiltration From Internet of Things Devices: iOS Devices as Case Studies. *IEEE Internet Of Things Journal, 4*(2), 524–535. doi:10.1109/JIOT.2016.2569094

Dunigan, B., King, T., & Morse, B. (2011). A preliminary examination of the effect of massage on state body image. *Body Image, 8*(4), 411–414. doi:10.1016/j.bodyim.2011.06.004 PMID:21764398

Eberendu, A. (2016). Unstructured Data: An overview of the data of Big Data. *International Journal of Computer Trends and Technology, 38*(1), 46–50. doi:10.14445/22312803/IJCTT-V38P109

Fotland, M., & Kvale, L. (2015). The data explosion – A huge challenge and a gigantic opportunity. *Septentrio Conference Series*, (5). 10.7557/5.3662

Gilge, C. (2016). Google Street View and the Image as Experience. *Geohumanities, 2*(2), 469–484. doi:10.1080/2373566X.2016.1217741

Jing, C., Zhu, Y., & Li, M. (2014). Customer satisfaction-aware scheduling for utility maximization on geo-distributed data centers. *Concurrency and Computation, 27*(5), 1334–1354. doi:10.1002/cpe.3318

Juneja, P., & Kashyap, R. (2016). Optimal Approach For CT Image Segmentation Using Improved Energy Based Method. *International Journal of Control Theory and Applications*, *9*(41), 599–608.

Juneja, P., & Kashyap, R. (2016). Energy based Methods for Medical Image Segmentation. *International Journal of Computers and Applications*, *146*(6).

Kashyap, R., & Gautam, P. (2013). Microarray Image Segmentation using Improved GOGAC Method. *Science and Engineering*, *2*(4), 67–74.

Kashyap, R., & Gautam, P. (2015, November). Modified region based segmentation of medical images. In *Communication Networks (ICCN), 2015 International Conference on* (pp. 209-216). IEEE. 10.1109/ICCN.2015.41

Kashyap, R., & Gautam, P. (2016, August). Fast Level Set Method for Segmentation of Medical Images. In *Proceedings of the International Conference on Informatics and Analytics* (p. 20). ACM. 10.1145/2980258.2980302

Kashyap, R., & Gautam, P. (2017). Fast Medical Image Segmentation Using Energy-Based Method. *Pattern and Data Analysis in Healthcare Settings*, 35-60.

Kashyap, R., & Tiwari, V. (2017). Energy-based active contour method for image segmentation. *International Journal of Electronic Healthcare*, *9*(2-3), 210–225. doi:10.1504/IJEH.2017.083165

Kowser, S. (2016). *Digital Remembrance Based User Validation for Internet of Things. International Journal Of Engineering And Computer Science*. doi:10.18535/ijecs/v5i5.16

Kshetri, N. (2014). The emerging role of Big Data in key development issues: Opportunities, challenges, and concerns. *Big Data & Society*, *1*(2), 205395171456422. doi:10.1177/2053951714564227

Kune, R., Konugurthi, P., Agarwal, A., Chillarige, R., & Buyya, R. (2016). XHAMI - extended HDFS and MapReduce interface for Big Data image processing applications in cloud computing environments. *Software, Practice & Experience*, *47*(3), 455–472. doi:10.1002pe.2425

Lafuente, G. (2015). The big data security challenge. *Network Security*, *2015*(1), 12–14. doi:10.1016/S1353-4858(15)70009-7

Matwankar & Shinde. (2015). Sentiment Analysis for Big Data using Data Mining Algorithms. *International Journal of Engine Research*, *4*(9). doi:10.17577/ijertv4is090801

Pattern Matching - Optalysys. (2017). *Optalysys*. Retrieved 7 June 2017, from http://www.optalysys.com/applications/pattern-matching/

Shin, H., Yen, M., Tseng, C., & Liu, H. (2011). Fast data access and energy-efficient protocol for wireless data broadcast. *Wireless Communications and Mobile Computing*, *12*(16), 1429–1441. doi:10.1002/wcm.1076

Shmueli, G. (2017). Research Dilemmas with Behavioral Big Data. *Big Data*, *5*(2), 98–119. doi:10.1089/big.2016.0043 PMID:28632441

Sizov, I. (2016). Big data – big data in business. *Economy Business, Computer Science*, (3): 8–23. doi:10.19075/2500-2074-2016-3-8-23

The Four V's of Big Data. (2017). *IBM Big Data & Analytics Hub*. Retrieved 10 June 2017, from http://www.ibmbigdatahub.com/infographic/four-vs-big-data

Top 10 Big Data Challenges – A Serious Look at 10 Big Data V's | MapR. (2017). Retrieved 26 June 2017, from https://mapr.com/blog/top-10-big-data-challenges-serious-look-10-big-data-vs/

Tsetoura, A. (2013). Property Protection as a Limit to Deteriorating Social Security Protection. *European Journal of Social Security*, *15*(1), 55–78. doi:10.1177/138826271301500105

Upadhyay, A., & Kashyap, R. (2016). Fast Segmentation Methods for Medical Images. *International Journal of Computers and Applications*, *156*(3), 18–23. doi:10.5120/ijca2016912399

Waoo, N., Kashyap, R., & Jaiswal, A. (2010, April). DNA Nano array analysis using hierarchical quality threshold clustering. In *The 2nd IEEE International Conference on Information Management and Engineering (ICIME), 2010* (pp. 81-85). IEEE.10.1109/ICIME.2010.5477579

Xiang, W., Wang, G., Pickering, M., & Zhang, Y. (2016). Big video data for light-field-based 3D telemedicine. *IEEE Network*, *30*(3), 30–38. doi:10.1109/MNET.2016.7474341

Zhang, J. (2016). High-performance data processing for image and data fusion. *International Journal of Image and Data Fusion*, *7*(1), 1–2. doi:10.1080/19479832.2016.1122697

KEY TERMS AND DEFINITIONS

Client Profiling: Customer profiling is an approach to make a picture of your clients to enable you to settle on plan choices concerning your administration. Your clients are separated into gatherings of clients having comparable objectives and attributes and each gathering is given a delegate with a photograph, a name, and a portrayal.

Clinical Database: A clinical quality database is a registry containing chose quantifiable markers. In light of the individual patient's infection time frame, the pointers can help evaluate some portion of or the general nature of the endeavors by the human services framework and the ensuing outcomes. The gathered information are utilized to screen the nature of treatment with a specific end goal to frequently assess any alternatives for enhancing the quality level.

Image Examination: Image investigation is the capacity of PCs to perceive properties inside a picture. Do you utilize Google Photos or Apple's Photos application on your cell phone? They both utilize some fundamental picture investigation components to perceive confronts and order them in your photographs so you can take a gander at all of your photographs of a specific individual.

Optalysys: Optalysys innovation utilizes light, instead of power, to perform processor concentrated numerical capacities (for example, Fourier Transforms) in parallel at inconceivably high-velocities and resolutions. It can possibly give multi-exascale levels of preparing, controlled from a standard main supply. The mission is to convey an answer that requires a few requests of extent less power than conventional high-performance computing (HPC) structures.

QR Code: QR code is the trademark for a sort of grid standardized tag (or two-dimensional scanner tag) first intended for the car business in Japan. A scanner tag is a machine-comprehensible optical mark that contains data about the thing to which it is connected.

Section 3
Data–Oriented Security and Networking

Chapter 15
Secure Opportunistic Routing for Vehicular Adhoc Networks

Harsha Vasudev
Birla Institute of Technology and Science, India

Debasis Das
Birla Institute of Technology and Science, India

ABSTRACT

More study is needed to make VANETs more relevant. Opportunistic routing (OR) is a new model that has been proposed for wireless networks. OR has emerged from the research communities because of its ability to increase the performance of wireless networks. It benefits from the broadcast characteristic of wireless mediums to improve network performance. The basic function of OR is its ability to overhear the transmitted packet and to coordinate among relaying nodes. In this chapter, an exhaustive survey of existing OR protocols is done by considering various factors. More precisely, existing secure OR protocols are deliberated. Future directions of research are also included, which provide a superior way to overcome some of the limitations of these existing protocols. Through this detailed survey, an outline and in-depth knowledge of existing OR protocols can be acquired.

INTRODUCTION

With the growing importance of useful, harmless, and high-efficient transportation, Vehicular Adhoc Networks (VANETs) have turned into acute technology in smart transportation systems. In recent years VANETs has been observed as one of the key enabling technologies to provide a wide variety of services, such as road safety, enhanced traffic and travel efficiency, convenience and comfort for travellers and drivers. VANETs technology has emerged as an important research area over the last few years. It is an active research area right now and evolving type of network aimed at improving safe driving, traffic optimization, and some other services through either Vehicle to Vehicle communication (V2V) or Vehicle to Infrastructure communication (V2I). They are created by applying the principles of Mobile ad hoc networks (MANETs), the spontaneous creation of a wireless network for data exchange to the domain of vehicles. These networks have no fixed infrastructure, dynamic in nature and instead rely on the vehicles

DOI: 10.4018/978-1-5225-3870-7.ch015

themselves to provide network functionality. Being ad-hoc in nature, VANETs is a type of networks that is created from the concept of establishing a network of cars for a specific need or situation. In straight road or highway road, it is a sparse network. Depends upon time the network may become dense. But in intersection or junction road, it is always be dense network. Figure 1 shows a highway road and Figure 2 shows a 4-way intersection road.

Modern advances in hardware, software, and communication technologies are allowing the design and implementation of a whole range of dissimilar types of networks that are being organised in various environments. One such network that has received a lot of interest in the recent years is the VANETs. VANETs has become an active area of research, standardization, and development because it has incredible potential to improve vehicle and road safety, traffic effectiveness, and convenience as well as comfort to both drivers and passengers. Recent research efforts have placed a strong emphasis on novel VANETs design architecture and implementations. A lot of research work have done in the area of VANETs, which focused on specific areas including routing, broadcasting, Quality of Service (QoS), security etc. In this paper, a comprehensive survey considering all these factors is done. Figure 3 shows an example of VANETs communication. In the figure, the first vehicle, which is ahead informs the following vehicle that there is a problem in the road and should take alternate path. This security information passed between all following vehicles through VANETs communication system. It is also possible that, the source vehicle (means vehicle which is ahead) will pass the message to all the following vehicles if all the vehicles are within DSRC with the source vehicle.

In Intelligent Transportation System (ITS), every vehicle acts as sender, receiver and router to broadcast the information inside the vehicular network, and the information can be used to ensure safe, free flow traffic. V2V is a multi-hop multicast / broadcast communication used to transmit traffic related information over multiple hops to a group of receiver vehicles. ITS is mostly concerned with the road ahead and not on the road behind. ITS mainly use two types of message advancing methods. Naive Broadcasting and Intelligent Broadcasting. In Naive broadcasting, periodic broadcasting of messages at regular intervals occurs. If the message originates from behind then the vehicle ignores the message, but if the message originates from a vehicle ahead then the receiving vehicle send its own broadcast message to the vehicles behind it. The main limitation is that, it increases network overhead, because a

Figure 1. Highway Road

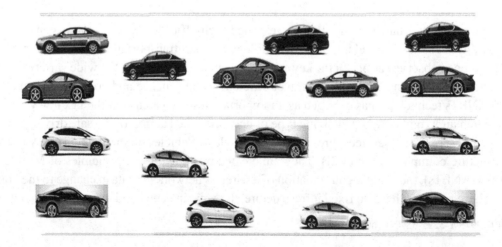

Figure 2. Four Way Intersection

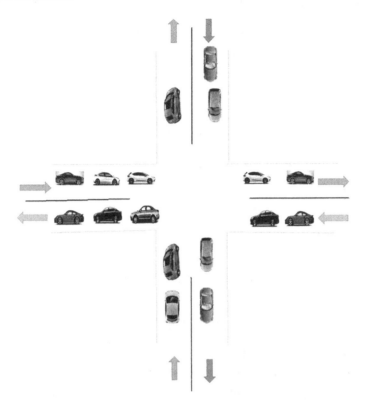

Figure 3. VANETs communication example

large number of broadcast messages are generated. Intelligent broadcasting overcomes the limitation of Naive broadcasting, by using acknowledgements. So it bounds the number of message broadcasts. If the event detecting vehicle receives the same message from behind it, it assumes that at least one vehicle in the back has received it and will be responsible for further transmitting the message.

DISTINGUISHED FEATURES OF VANETS

VANETs can be distinguished from other ad-hoc networks by the following features:

- **Extremely Dynamic Topology:** The topology of VANET is always changing due to high speed movement of vehicles.
- **Mobility:** The movement of vehicles are constrained by highways, street roads or intersection roads which can't be changed. With the map of current geographic location and speed of vehicle, the position of vehicle in the future can be easily determined.
- **Hard Delay Constraints:** Emergency Safety Messages (ESM) should reach other vehicles as soon as possible, there should not be slightest delay or network interruption.
- **Sufficient Energy and Storage:** Vehicles have sufficient energy and computing power for storage and processing.
- **Altered Communication Atmospheres:** Includes simple highway traffic scenarios and complex city traffic scenarios.

BACKGROUND

The major motivation behind the development of VANETs is to build a Smart city, where every vehicle can communicate with neighbour vehicles within a short range, called DSRC (Dedicated Short Range Communication). DSRC is developed by USA and is a short to medium range communications service that is used for V2I and V2V communication. In October 1999, United states Federal Communications Commission (FCC) had allocated 750 MHz of spectrum i.e from 8.5 GHz to 9.25 GHz to be used by DSRC. DSRC spectrum has 7 channels with each channel 100 MHz wide. Out of 7 channels, six channels are used for service purpose and remaining one for control purpose. VANETs communication using DSRC is showed in Figure 4. In August 2008, the European Telecommunications Standards Institute (ETSI) allocated 30 MHz of spectrum in the 5.9 GHz band for ITS. By 2003, it was used in Europe and Japan in electronic toll collection. DSRC systems in Europe, Japan and U.S. are not compatible and include some very significant variations (5.8 GHz, 5.9 GHz or even infrared, different baud rates, and different protocols. Dedicated short-range communications are one-way or two-way short-range to medium-range wireless communication channels. They are mainly considered for automotive use and a corresponding set of protocols and standards.

Opportunistic Routing (OR) is a new promising paradigm that has been proposed for wireless networks. OR has gained a lot of attention from the research communities for its ability to increase the performance of wireless networks. It benefits from the broadcast characteristic of wireless mediums to improve network performance. The basic function of OR is its ability to overhear the transmitted packet and to coordinate among relaying nodes. In OR, a candidate set is a potential group of nodes that is selected as the next-hop forwarders. Hence, each node in OR can use different potential paths to send packets toward the destination. Any of the candidates of a node that have received the transmitted packet may forward it. The decision of choosing the next forwarder is made by coordination between candidates that have successfully received the transmitted packet. In OR, by using a dynamic relay node to forward the packet, the transmission reliability and network throughput can be increased. By using OR, each packet is allowed to dynamically build the route toward the destination, this is done according to the condition of the wireless links at the moment when the packet is being transmitted. In OR, the nodes do not select an identical next hop before the transmission starts. OR selects a set of nodes as potential candidates. The candidates that have received the transmitted packet coordinate among each other to decide which of them must forward the packet and which must discard it. This process is usually called candidate

Figure 4. VANETs communication using DSRC

coordination. In other words, a sender broadcasts the data packet first, and one of its candidates that has received the packet will continue the forwarding process, therefore the chance of delivering the packet to the destination is increased. Another benefit of OR is its ability to have backup links in the case of transmission failures in one of the wireless links. This is more useful when it combines weak links in a virtual link. The delivery probability of the virtual link is stronger than that of each link, hence this reduces failure probability.

Figure 5, shows how OR communication done in VANETs. It is a highway road where the source vehicle sends some message to destination vehicle. Here, source vehicle sends the message to all vehicles which are under DSRC. After that candidate coordination happens and any one vehicle (which is near to destination vehicle) will pass the message to destination vehicle. An Opportunistic Routing approach is a method where there is no predefined rule for choosing the next node to destination. Different types of Opportunistic Routing protocol exits. Two examples of VANET Opportunistic Routing is presented in the paper, Opportunistic Vehicular Routing (Baker.,Starke. Hill-Jarrett. and McNair, 2017). They are Delay Tolerant geo-inspired routing and real time video stream multicast. In Least Cost OR (Ferriere., Grossglauser. and Vetterli, 2007), concept, a set of candidate next-hops at each node for a given destination is assigned such that the expected cost of forwarding a packet to the destination is minimized.

Figure 5. OR in VANETs

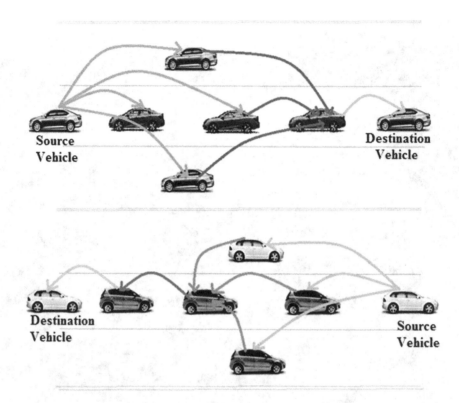

In simple OR (Biswas and Morris, 2005) and EXOR (Biswas and Morris, 2005), broadcasting nature of wireless medium is used. EXOR is an integrated routing and MAC protocol that increases the throughput of large unicast transfers in multi-hop wireless networks. Both the papers have its own advantages and disadvantages. Some OR related protocols depends mainly focus on the different features such as topology, geographic position etc. Examples are, POR (Position Based OR) (Yang, Zhong C.K, Yeo S, Lee B.S and Boleng.J,2009), GOSR (Geographical Opportunistic Source Routing for VANETs) (Zhongyi., Tong, Wei. and Xiaoming., 2009), QoS Swarm Bee (Quality of service Multipath Routing Protocol) (Bitam., Mellouk and 2011, and EMOR (Enhanced Mobility based Opportunistic Routing Protocol) (Tahooni., Darehshoorzadeh. and Boukerche., 2014).

There exists so many works related with security. Some of them are, A Novel Packet Salvaging Model to Improve the Security of Opportunistic Routing Protocols (Salehi. and Boukerche., 2017). In Vivo Evaluation of the Secure Opportunistic Schemes Middleware using a Delay Tolerant Social Network (Baker., Starke., Hill-Jarrett., McNair. J, 2017),Secure Opportunistic Vehicle-to-Vehicle Communication (Mihaita., Dobre., Pop., Mavromoustakis, and Mastorakis., 2017). VANETs have emerged recently as one of the most attractive topics for researchers and automotive industries due to their tremendous potential to improve traffic safety, efficiency and other added services. Since it is an emerging field so many researches are going on. An overview and challenges of VANETs is discussed in the paper, Vehicular Ad-Hoc Networks (VANETs) - An Overview and Challenges (Rehman., Khan., Zia and Zheng., 2013). They are concluding that the research challenges in VANETs are not limited to the areas such as Quality of service (QoS), Network Security, Co-operative Communication etc. A flexible VANET testbed architecture that is tailored for VANETs application needs is introduced in the paper, A flexible testbed architecture for VANET (Ahmed., Pierre., Quintero., 2017). The implementation of this architecture is tested using standard VANET applications to evaluate its feasibility for vehicular applications. They are concluding that, proposed testbed meets VANET requirements. Architectures, challenges and future directions of Vehicular cloud networks is presented in the paper, Vehicular cloud networks: Challenges, architectures, and future directions (Mekkia, Jabrib., Rachedic and Jemaaa., 2016), an overview of the motivation of Vehicular Clouds and design challenges are discussed.

CHALLENGES

1. **Bandwidth Restrictions:** One of the key issues in the VANETs is the absence of a central co-ordinator that controls the communications between vehicles. The central coordinator has the responsibility of managing the bandwidth and contention operation. There is a high probability that channel congestion can occur, owing to the limited range of bandwidth frequency.
2. **Connectivity:** The high mobility and quick changes of topology, leads to frequent fragmentation in networks.
3. **Signal Failing:** In between two communicating vehicles, one of the main challenge is the objects that may come and act as obstacles that can affect the efficiency of VANETs. These obstacles can be other vehicles or buildings distributed along roads especially in the cities.
4. **Lesser Effective Diameter:** Due to small effective network diameter of VANETs, it leads to a weak connectivity in the communication between vehicles. Therefore, maintaining the whole world-wide topology of the network is impracticable for a vehicle. The restricted effective diameter results in problems when applying existing routing algorithms to VANETs.
5. **Security and Privacy:** Maintaining a realistic balance between the security and privacy is one of the key challenge in VANETs. Trust (Coppola., Moristo.MandTorino., 2016), is the major concen for ensuring the security.

DETAILS OF OPPORTUNISTIC ROUTING PROTOCOLS

OR has attained a lot of attention from the research communities for its ability to increase the performance of wireless networks. In the paper, Opportunistic Routing in MultiHop Wireless Networks (Biswas and Morris, 2005), an Extremely Opportunistic Routing (ExOR), a new unicast routing technique for multi-hop wireless networks is mentioned. ExOR forwards each packet through a sequence of nodes, deferring the choice of each node in the sequence until after the previous node has transmitted the packet. ExOR then determines which node, of all the nodes that successfully received that transmission, is the node closest to the destination. That closest node transmits the packet. EXOR routing approach is presented in the paper, ExOR: Opportunistic Multi-Hop Routing for Wireless Networks (Biswas and Morris, 2005). EXOR is an integrated routing and MAC protocol that increases the throughput of large unicast transfers in multi-hop wireless networks. ExOR takes each hop of a packets route after the transmission for that hop, so that the choice can reveal which intermediate nodes really received the transmission. ExOR design face have several challenges. The agreement protocol must have low overhead, but must also be robust enough that it hardly forwards a packet zero times or more than once.

The main advantages are,

1. In EXOR, each transmission may have more distinct chances of being received and forwarded.
2. It takes advantage of transmissions that reach unexpectedly far, or fall unexpectedly short.
3. ExOR will work better with interference localized at each receiver than with global interference.
4. ExOR is likely to increase total network capacity as well as individual connection throughput. It transmits each packet fewer times than traditional routing, which should cause less interference for other users of the network and of the same spectrum.

The limitations are

1. This technique does not say what to do with the received frames which contains bit errors.
2. Not mentioned about the protocols that can deal with multiple transmit bit rates.

GOSR, Geographical Opportunistic Source Routing for VANETs is introduced in the paper (Zhongyi. Tong, Wei. and Xiaoming, 2009),. It is a simple but powerful routing algorithm combining GSR (Geographical Source Routing) and opportunistic routing. The authors are concluded that GOSR can achieve a reduction of hop count. A new quality of service multipath routing protocol adapted for VANETs is presented in the paper, Quality of Service (QoS) Swarm Bee Routing Protocol for Vehicular Ad Hoc Networks (Bitam. and Mellouk, 2011). It is based on ideas of the autonomic bee communication. It is based on biological paradigm of communication between bees in the food source searching behaviour. The advantage is that, the End-to-end delay is less compared with AODV (On-Demand Distance Vector routing and DSDV (Destination Sequence Distance Vector).The normalized overhead load is greater than that of, AODV and DSDV, is the major limitation of this concept. In the paper, EMOR-Enhanced Mobility-based Opportunistic Routing OR protocol (Tahooni., Darehshoorzadeh. and Boukerche, 2014), a new metric proposed which considers the geographical position of the candidates, the link delivery probability to reach them, the number of the neighbouring nodes of the candidate, and the predicted position of nodes using the motion vector of the nodes.

A packet salvaging model, is presented in the paper, A Novel Packet Salvaging Model to Improve the Security of Opportunistic Routing Protocols (Salehi. and Boukerche., 2017). This model empowers OR protocols to defend against malicious nodes by saving a proportion of dropped or manipulated packets. The proposed approach is modelled using Discrete-Time-Markov-Chain (DTMC), and is applicable in wireless mesh networks. Vehicular communications are a part of any such ITS, and represent a particular set of networks in which the vehicles and roadsides are considered to be the peers of the networks between which messages are exchanged, in order to form a safer and smarter way to drive. In the paper, Secure Opportunistic Vehicle-to-Vehicle Communication (Mihaita., Dobre., Pop., Mavromoustakis. and Mastorakis,2017), a solution is presented to create a security mechanism in the context of ITS. The solution is a heterogeneous solution in which both symmetrical and asymmetrical encryption are used.

Ghaleb et al. (Ghaleb, Razzaque. and Isnin., 2013) presented a mobility pattern based misbehaviour detection approach in VANETs. The researchers developed a Location Anonymous Message based approach. The simulation results shows that it has the potential to improve security and maintain privacy in VANETs. SMSS: Symmetric-Masquerade Security Scheme for VANETs (Zhu., Wang and Lim,2011), is a novel security scheme, named Symmetric-Masquerade Security Scheme (SMSS), which can achieve the security requirements while keeping a low system overhead. SMSS focussed on V2V communications. Symmetric encryption is used to ensure the consistency of the messages, the local pseudonyms are furnished to protect the privacy, and the pre-shared keys are introduced to ensure the authentication. This paper makes a detailed description of the novel scheme, then analyses its performance in comparison with that of the PKI security scheme.

An Identity-Based batch Verification (IBV) (Tzeng., Horng.,, Wang., Huang. and Khan,, 2017)scheme has been recently proposed to make VANETs more secure and efficient for practical use. IBV scheme has some security risks. It is an improved scheme that can satisfy the security and privacy desired by vehicles. The proposed IBV scheme provides the provable security in the random oracle model. It needs only a small constant number of pairing and point multiplication computations, independent of the number of messages. In terms of computation delay and transmission overhead, performance evaluation is done. Routing and security analysis is the main content of the paper, Routing and security analysis in Vehicular Ad-hoc Networks (VANETs) (Deepak, Kumar. and Rshi., 2016). Different types of routing techniques and some security measures are presented.

A comparison among different OR protocols is presented in Table 1. Communication paradigm means, whether it is unicast or broadcast. Forwarding strategy says whether packet forwarding or multihop etc. The different forwarding strategy included are greedy forwarding, datamuling, packet forwarding etc. The different types of scenarios are real city traces, grid city traces, road traces, urban and rural road traces etc. From this table, it is evident that, most of all protocols are broadcast in nature, mainly used for packet forwarding, the architecture used is V2V, and most of all are used in real city, and are variable bit rate. The drawback field is mainly included to know which performs well and which is to be modified so that it will work perfectly. Table 1 shows details of routing protocols.

MAIN FOCUS

Life became rapid in current scenario and vehicles play a dynamic role in this never ending race. Smart vehicles furnished with latest tools are becoming a part of ITS and point of attraction among drivers. Securing VANETs along with suitable protection of the privacy of drivers is a very challenging task. Driver's character can be reflected in the mobility patterns of the vehicles (rational driving). Security plays a vital role in the system design with the development of VANETs. Because of the unreliable communications in VANETs, security protocols need more considerations, such as privacy, authentication, confidentiality and consistency of messages.

OBJECTIVES OF THE FUTURE DIRECTION OF RESEARCH

VANETs become a promising field of research once the world is advancing towards the vision of ITS. Dramatic increase in the number of vehicles equipped with computing technologies and wireless communication strategies created new application scenarios that were not feasible before. Highly dynamic and portioned network topology due to the constant and rapid movement of vehicles makes VANETs more specific. Currently, some clustering algorithms are widely used as the control schemes to make VANET topology less dynamic for Medium Access Control (MAC), routing and security protocols. For the implementation of safe protocols, it is necessary to define the objectives that the security mecha-

Table 1. Various routing protocols

PROTOCOL FOR SECURE WIRELESS ROUTING	Communication Paradigm	Forwarding Strategy	Archi tecture	Scenario	Application	Drawbacks
OR(Opportunistic Routing) [2003]	Unicast	Multihop Forwarding	V2V	Real City	Constant Traffic	Analytical model isn't included.
EXOR (Extremely Opportunistic Routing) [2005]	Unicast	Multihop Forwarding	V2V	Real City	Variable Traffic	Don't mentioned about the protocols that can deal with multiple transmit bit rates.
POR (Position based opportunistic routing) [2009]	Multicast	Packet Forwarding	V2V	Real City	variable traffic	Doesn't include a defensive mechanism against malicious nodes.
GOSR: Geographical Opportunistic Source Routing for VANETs [2009]	Broadcast	Packet forwarding	V2V,V2I	Real City	variable traffic	Didn't evaluate the protocol under different mobility models.
EMOR Enhanced Mobility-based Opportunistic Routing protocol. [2014]	Broadcast	Packet forwarding	V2V	Real City	variable traffic	Some modifications need to be done in MAC layer to increase the efficiency.
A Novel Packet Salvaging Model to Improve the Security of Opportunistic Routing Protocols. [2017]	Broadcast	Packet Forwarding	V2V	Real City	variable traffic	Quality of Service (QoS) aspects in routing isn't considered.
In Vivo Evaluation of the Secure Opportunistic Schemes Middleware using a Delay Tolerant Social Network. [2017]	Broadcast	Packet Forwarding	V2V	Real City	variable traffic	Sometimes, node mobility tends to become stationary.
Secure Opportunistic Vehicle-to-Vehicle Communication. [2017]	Broadcast	Packet Forwarding	V2V	Real City	variable traffic	It cannot grant anonymity, and that the infrastructure can restore any paths of the participating vehicles.

nisms to be incorporated. The classic security requirements that must be observed are authentication, confidentiality, integrity, non-repudiation, and availability.

The main objective is to propose a scheme, which is responsible for increasing the reliability of routing in VANETs. Such type of routing protocol for multi-hop wireless networks will be less effective if some vehicular nodes in the wireless multihop environment act as a selfish or a malicious node at highway/ interaction. Our objectives are,

1.   To build an open and flexible application strategy for Smart Connected Vehicles (Coppola, Moristo. and Torino., 2016), and ITS, that powers emerging and future sensor, wireless communications, Internet of things, Grid computing and cloud computing technologies.

2. To make large-scale smart traffic management applications on the Smart Connected Vehicles (Coppola., Moristo. and Torino., 2016), and ITS platform using IOV (Internet of Vehicles) (Contreras,. Zeadally and. Ibanez, 2017), that will increase safety and efficiency in the publicly-operated ITS.

3. To construct and develop fresh applications that influence the smart city platform and that can be offered by the private sector for connected vehicle environments.

4. **Less Accidents and Less Pollution:** Drivers are getting more additional information such as, the nearest vehicle status, correct route between places and the deviations in advance, environmental conditions, such as weather, fog etc, so the chances of accidents are less. The waiting time of each vehicle is less, because each vehicle can know the upcoming traffic, traffic jams and accidents, vehicles can move in a better road without delay, so fuel consumption is less and therefore no pollution.

PROPOSED DIRECTION OF RESEARCH

1. **Authentication:** Authentication is the crucial part of VANETs communication. However, authentication may reveal a user's personal information such as identity or location, and therefore, the privacy of honest user must be protected. Authentication is very essential for ensuring security. Authentication problem is critical in VANETs because if the vehicles failed to prove their authenticity (i.e., malicious) then they will not be allowed in the further communication process. The On-Board Unit (OBU) have proper mechanisms for checking the authenticity of both vehicle and driver. Below some authentication mechanisms are provided.

Existing Solutions: These are some existing mechanisms:

1. **Driver Ownership:** A driver owns some unique identity (i.e., identity card, driving license etc.).
2. **User Knowledge:** A user knows some unique things (i.e., passwords, human responses through secret questions etc.).
3. **Biometrics Solutions:** These include the signature, thumb expression, face and voice.

So many researches are going on to ensure proper authentication, because it is the primary requirement of VANETs. So VANETs communication needs perfect authentication and it is a major criterion. If a fraud vehicle starts communication, with the other vehicles within DSRC, then it may lead to serious situations like accidents. An efficient method for authentication called, CRL (Certificate Revocation Lists) is the main concept of the paper, An Efficient CRL Authentication Scheme for Vehicular Communications (Vinothini. and Subha., 2015). This concept works based on the cryptography concepts, signatures, certificates and trusted authority. A comprehensive survey of all authentication schemes is deliberated in the paper, A survey on authentication schemes of VANETs (Anita. and Jenefa., 2016). In this paper, the authenticity is verified through Cryptographic Techniques, Digital Signatures and Message Verification Techniques. A taxonomy of authentication schemes, advantages, and disadvantages are discussed here.

In the paper, A comparison on VANET authentication schemes: Public Key vs. Symmetric Key (Ibrahim and Hamdy., 2015), different VANETs authentication schemes discussed. More precisely, a comparison is done between Public key Schemes and Symmetric Key Schemes in supporting security for VANETs. VANET Authentication using Signatures and TESLA++ (VAST) (Studer.A, Bai.F, Bellur.B andPerrig.A, 2009), combines the advantages of ECDSA (Elliptic Curve Digital Signature Algorithm) signatures and TESLA++ (Timed Efficient Stream Loss-Tolerant Authentication). ECDSA signatures provide fast authentication and non-repudiation, but are computationally expensive. TESLA++ prevents memory and computation-based denial of service attacks. For conditional privacy preservation, researchers developed an efficient and practical pseudonymous authentication protocol (Raiput., Abbas. and Oh.,2013), which proposes a hierarchy of pseudonyms based on the time period of their usage. The idea of primary pseudonyms is mentioned with relatively longer time periods that are used to communicate with semi-trusted authorities and secondary pseudonyms with a smaller life time that are used to communicate with other vehicles.

Group based authentication scheme is the primary concern of the paper, Security Enhancement in a group based authentication for VANET (Waghmode., Gonsalves., and Ambawade., 2016). Here, one time authentication scheme for a group and then V2V communication is done using group symmetric key. Researchers concluding that the scheme satisfies security and privacy requirements such as authentication, non-repudiation and conditional traceability. In VANET, remote network authentication servers can't authenticate the identity of vehicles without the aid of home domain authentication servers if the vehicles are in non-local regions. It results longer communication delay. To address this problem, an Anonymous Authentication scheme Based on Cloud Storage (AABCS) (Chen., Shi., Yu. and Fei., 2016), for cross-regional vehicles in VANETs proposed. This secure cloud storage technology is used to construct a public Traffic Cloud (TFC) as a storage media to avoid the problem of a single point failure. In MAVANET: Message Authentication in VANET using social networks (Paranjothi., Khan., Nijim. and Challoo., 2016), social networks are used to create an active topology from all possible users in sender's profile, who are active at a particular point of time. Message authentication attained by providing profile of user and Quick Response Code (QR code) technique. Researchers concluding that the proposed architecture is used from the car dashboard.

PROPOSED SCHEME

1. **Digital Licence Plates (DLPs) or Electronic Licence Plates:** Each vehicle manufacturer should provide a Digital Number Plate mechanism for identification. This is the most powerful key for unique identification of a vehicle.
2. **Driving Licence:** This is a mandatory document that a driver should have.
3. A face recognition system is maintained to verify the driver's identity. This mechanism is added for high security, in the cases where the vehicle is legitimate and driver is a fraud. When the driver is fraud, with correct licence, fails in the face detection system.
4. **Trust Value:** Trust plays a vital role in secure communication and Routing. Each vehicle should maintain a trust value. The possible values are 0 and 1. Trust value can be calculated using the above authentication techniques. By using these parameters such as Digital Licence Plate (DLP), Driving Licence and Face recognition system, trust value can be easily calculated. For example, if a vehicle have correct DLP, Driving Licence and Face recognition check then the trust value will

be 1 and it is treated as a trusted vehicle. If a vehicle fails to prove any one of the parameters, then trust value will be 0, and the vehicle is treated as malicious. When a vehicle identified as malicious, then it will not allow to participate in the further secure communication process.

In order to protect VANETs from malicious actions, each vehicle must be able to evaluate, decide and react locally on the information received from other vehicles. In the paper, Trust On the Security of Wireless Vehicular Ad-hoc Networking (Rawat., Yan., Bista and Weigle., 2014), probabilistic and deterministic approaches deliberated for VANET security. The probabilistic approach determines the trust level of the peer vehicles based on received information. The trust level is used to determine legitimacy of the message, which is used to decide whether the message would be considered for further transmission over the VANET or dropped. The deterministic approach measures the trust level of the received message by using distances calculated using Received Signal Strength (RSS) and the vehicle's geolocation. A trust-based framework for message propagation and evaluation in VANETs, is discussed in (Zhang., Chen.C and Cohen.,2010),. In the framework, peers share information regarding road condition or safety and others provide opinions about whether the information can be trusted. It collects and propagates peers opinions in an efficient, secure and scalable way by dynamically controlling information dissemination.

5. **Secure Routing:** In VANETs, highly challenging task is to transport information from one vehicle to another or all vehicles within DSRC. More than simply routing, secure routing is the key challenge in VANETs. For secure routing, first task is to find the shortest route between source and destination vehicle.
    a. **Select Shortest Route:** Using OR mechanisms, vehicle coordination and actual forwarder (vehicle head) selection is done. Not only other vehicle status, but also environmental conditions also checked (i.e., weather conditions, traffic jams, fog, road conditions etc.). Multihop forwarding is the major characteristic of VANETS. Whenever there is large number of vehicles within DSRC, then the information passed between the intermediate vehicles and at last the destined vehicle, through this secure routing method. OR always find shortest path between source and destination vehicles.

A new Position Based Secure Routing Protocol (PBSRP) (Bhoi. and Khilar.,2013), is introduced which is a hybrid of Most Forward within Radius (MFR) and Border Node based Most Forward within Radius (B-MFR) routing protocols. A security module is added in this protocol by using station to station key agreement protocol to prevent the system from various attacks.

6. **Malicious Vehicle Detection:** Whenever a vehicle enters in DSRC, trust value is calculated based on the parameter values (i.e., Digital Licence Plate (DLP), Driving Licence and Face recognition system). If the calculated value is 0, then it is malicious and suddenly the actual forwarder vehicle broadcasts the information, that is, unique number of the vehicle to all vehicles within DSRC, and the vehicle is not allowed to participate in the further routing process. Before sending sensitive information to each vehicle, the actual forwarder gets the knowledge of trustworthiness of each vehicle. Through this way the malicious vehicle is detected and ensures that the message passes only through trusted vehicles.

In VANETs communication, identifying malicious vehicle is the difficult task. In the paper, Review To Detect and Isolate Malicious Vehicle in VANET (Kateshiya. J.P andSingh. A.P, 2015), a routing protocol and different security attacks in VANETs is discussed. Some techniques put forwarded to isolate and prevent possible attacks on VANETs. A comprehensive survey of VANETs security challenges is deliberated in the paper, VANET security challenges and solutions: A survey (Hasrounya., Samhatb., Bassilc. and Laouitia, 2017). Diverse type of security challenges are measured from different perspectives and possible solutions also mentioned. iParking (Yang., Ju, Hsieh., Lin., Tsai. and Chang., 2017), is a real time parking space monitoring and guiding system. Availability of parking spaces is recognized through image analysis, where the images come from the event recorders embedded in cars on the roads. When parking request is received, the system searches for a nearest parking space, and then directly navigates the requesting driver to the available parking space. The system is expected to benefit all drivers and the government, and to improve safety and traffic on the roads. A survey on security attacks is deliberated in, Security Attacks and Solutions in Vehicular Ad Hoc Networks: A Survey (Hoa. and Cavalli., 2014),. Different types of attacks such as, Sybil attack, Timing attack, Global Positioning System (GPS) Spoofing, Hidden vehicle and Tunnel attack, Illusion attack Denial of Service (DoS) and Distributed Denial of Service (DDos), Black Hole attack, Grey Hole attack, Wormhole attack, Man in the Middle Attack (MiMA) are presented.

PROPOSED SOLUTION

In the proposed scheme, different techniques for secure communication in VANETs is presented. It includes Digital Licence Plates (DLPs) or Electronic Licence Plates, trust value calculation, techniques for secure routing and malicious vehicle detection. In this section we are intended to give a clear idea about all these methods.

1. **Trust Value Analysis:** In algorithm 1, a Trust based calculation is done. Whenever a vehicle wants to be a part of VANETs communication process, its DLP, Licence of driver are checked. These are the mandatory steps. If a vehicle fails in the DLP checking phase then the vehicle won't be participated in the further communication process. If DLP, driving licence and face recognition check is perfect then it will return value 1 and allowed in the further communication process. If it fails to prove either DLP or licence then that vehicle won't allowed to participate. The face recognition check is optional, not mandatory. If the values of DLP and licence are correct and fails in the face recognition check then also that vehicle will be allowed to participate in the VANETs communication process.

Algorithm 1: Trust Value Analysis

Let 'n' be the total number of vehicles within a communication range.

```
    for i=0 to n do
       If vehicle have correct DLP,Driving Licence and Face recognition check
then
              TRUSTVALUE = 1; Vehicles allowed to participate in the
```

```
further
                    communication process.
        else
                    TRUSTVALUE = 0;Vehicles aren't allowed to participate
in the
                    further communication
process.
End
```

REPLACE (Hu., Lu, Zhang. and Shao, 2017) is a reliable trust-based platoon service recommendation scheme, to help the user vehicles avoid choosing badly behaved platoon head vehicles. Specifically, at the core of REPLACE, a reputation system is designed for the platoon head vehicles by collecting and modelling their user vehicle's feedback. ART (Attack-Resistant Trust management scheme) (Li. and Song., 2016)is proposed to detect and cope with malicious attacks and also evaluate the trustworthiness of both data and mobile nodes in VANETs. Specially, data trust is evaluated based on the data sensed and collected from multiple vehicles; node trust is assessed in two dimensions, i.e., functional trust and recommendation trust. The proposed trust management theme is applicable to a wide range of VANET applications to improve traffic safety, mobility, and environmental protection with enhanced trustworthiness.

2. **Secure Opportunistic Routing in VANETs**: Algorithm 2, focus on 4 major areas such as performance matrix calculation, priority assignment, candidate coordination and candidate selection. The route selection done by considering all these facts. In performance matrix calculation, PDR, PLR, ETX values are used. Priority assignment implies finding the shortest distance vehicle from destination. OR approaches suggest each vehicle to employ a subset of neighbour vehicles to act as potential next-hop forwarders. This subset of vehicles is called candidate set. The candidate set is selected and prioritized. Vehicles in the candidate set will be responsible to cooperate with each other following a candidate coordination method. Finally, one of the selected vehicles which has received a copy of the packet will act as the actual next-hop forwarder and will be in charge of progressing the data packet one hop closer to the destination. Shortest path is calculated so that the packet delivery ratio will be high.

Algorithm 2: Secure Opportunistic Routing

Let 'n' be the total number of vehicles.

```
for i=0 to n do Candidate Coordination phase.
  if Candidate Coordination phase. then
        Throuh any Candidate Coordination algorithm coordination done.
  end
  if Finding Candidateset then
        Through Coordination, a set of vehicles which are under one
           communication region obtains.
  end
```

```
    if Shortest path calculation. then
                Increases the packet delivery ratio.
    end
    if Selection Process then
                One vehicle will select as actual forwarder to destination .
    end
end
```

3. **Malicious Node Detection in VANETs:** Malicious vehicle detection can be done through the existing concept Markov Chains (Salehi, Darehshoorzadeh. and Boukerche, 2015),. Here, an extended concept, called DTMC - Discrete-Time Markov Chains is used for detecting malicious vehicles. A DTMC with two absorbing states can be imagined as an OR protocol with either delivering the packet to its destination (Success state) or dropping the packet (Fail state) after a certain number, say K, of retransmissions. In order to model OR paradigm using DTMC, a perfect coordination between candidates and defined the tuple of (ID,RTX) to represent a state where ID is the vehicle's identifier and RTX shows the number of retransmissions of a packet occurred in that vehicle. In this paper, the proposed model in two absorbing states are used to show the delivery of a packet to its destination (Success state) or failure of it after K retransmissions (Fail state).The proposed Markov model is valid for any number of candidates and retransmissions, including any kind of topology and candidate selection algorithm. Algorithm 3 explains the malicious vehicle detection procedure. In the paper, Isolating Malicious Vehicles and Avoiding Collision between Vehicles in VANET (Praba. and Ranichitra., 2013), traffic control is achieved by sustaining the distance between the vehicles and the malicious vehicles The existing Ad hoc On Demand Distance Vector (AODV) protocol has been suitably modified to achieve better road safety measures.

Algorithm 3: Malicious Node Detection

Discrete-Time Markov Chain (DTMC), is used to detect malicious vehicles. A DTMC with two absorbing states can be imagined as an OR protocol

   if delivering the packet to its destination, after a certain number **then**

```
                SUCCESS STATE Means Vehicle isnt malicious, Say K, of
                retransmissions.
else
        FAIL STATE Means Dropping the packet after a certain number, say
        K of retransmissions)
```

Generally, the Detection of Malicious Node (DMN) is based on the following basic concepts -

•   A vehicle is considered to indicate an unusual behaviour if it drops or duplicate the packets received to it so as to build congestion in the road, misguide other vehicles or destroy crucial messages for their selfish motives.

- An honest vehicle forwards the messages received to it correctly to other vehicles in the communication range or creates right messages for transmission.
- A vehicle will be tagged as a malicious vehicle, if the vehicle repeats unusual behaviour that is mentioned above.

FUTURE DIRECTION OF RESEARCH

VANETs is a growing interest and research area over recent years for it offers enhanced safety and non-safety applications for transportation. It is a developing technology that is yet unclear to many security issues. Security and routing concerns that are unique to VANETs present great challenges. In this paper, we proposed a scheme basically to solve the black hole (finding malicious vehicle) attack. Black-hole and gray hole are the well-known routing attacks through which malicious nodes try to downgrade the communication performance. In this paper, we focus on recent proposals, which are really meant to improve VANETs security and routing in systematic and proper way.

The Information-Centric Networking (ICN) has turned out to be a promising paradigm for different network scenarios, including VANETs to tackle the massive content distribution in today's Internet. Several preliminary investigations have been performed on a widely known ICN instance, i.e., the Named-Data Networking (NDN) (Signorello., Palattella. and Grieco, 2016),. NDN architecture presents a new set of security vulnerabilities. Interest flooding attacks, cache poisoning attacks and privacy violation attacks by means of content names represent concrete NDN threats. Here, security challenges in future NDN-Enabled VANETs is presented. (CoMoSeF Dasuha. and Mantoro, 2016), is a Car to Car communication, using Co-operative mobility services of future, where sensor Controller Area Network (CAN) bus installed in every vehicle and the sensor functions as communication between vehicles. The sensors connected to a mobile device when there is a vehicle which may experience a collision with him.

CONCLUSION

Every year, the number of traffic accidents in the world may increase as the number of vehicles. These were caused by improper use of vehicles such as the location unawareness, not obeying traffic signs or a lack of tolerance. The biggest cause of the accident was due to human negligence. Since a common person spends a large amount of time inside vehicles, VANETs security should be a major concern in the upcoming life. This paper gives an extensive overview of existing OR protocols. All protocols compared from different perspectives. More than that, Future direction in the research field of VANETs also mentioned. We focused on three algorithms, for increasing security. These algorithms enable VANETs to efficiently implement a system for trusting vehicles and protect it from any malicious vehicles. If we are able to successfully implement security in VANETs, then the situation where drivers would be warned of a potential crash by the vehicle they are driving and communication between vehicles, can be done in the nearest future and other future possibilities are just around the corner.

REFERENCES

Ahmed, H., Pierre, S., & Quintero, A. (2017, April 20). A flexible testbed architecture for VANET. *Vehicular Communications.*

Anita, E. A. M., & Jenefa, J. (2016), A survey on authentication schemes in VANETs, *International Conference on Information Communication and Embedded Systems,* 1-7. 10.1109/ICICES.2016.7518946

Baker, C. E., Starke, A., Hill-Jarrett, T. G., & McNair, J. (2017). In Vivo Evaluation of the Secure Opportunistic Schemes Middleware using a Delay Tolerant Social Network. *IEEE 37th International Conference on Distributed Computing Systems (ICDCS),* 2537-2542.

Bhoi, S. K., & Khilar, P. M. (2013). A Secure Routing Protocol for Vehicular Ad Hoc Network to Provide ITS Services. *International conference on Communication and Signal Processing.* 10.1109/iccsp.2013.6577240

Biswas, S., & Morris, R. (2005). ExOR: Opportunistic Multi-Hop Routing for Wireless Networks. *Proceedings of the conference on Applications, technologies, architectures, and protocols for computer communications,* 133-144. 10.1145/1080091.1080108

Biswas, S., & Morris, S. (2005). Opportunistic Routing in MultiHop Wireless Networks, *Proceedings of the conference on Applications, technologies, architectures, and protocols for computer communications,* 133-144.

Bitam, S., & Mellouk, A. (2011). QoS Swarm Bee Routing Protocol for Vehicular Ad Hoc Networks. *IEEE International Conference on Communications (ICC).* 10.1109/icc.2011.5963424

Chen, C., Shi, F. Yu. H., & Fei, N. (2016). Anonymous authentication based on cloud storage for cross-regional vehicles in VANET. *IEEE International Conference on Ubiquitous Wireless Broadband,* 1-8. 10.1109/ICUWB.2016.7790425

Contreras, S. Z., & Ibanez, J. A. G. (2017). *Internet of Vehicles: Architecture, Protocols and Security. IEEE Internet of Things Journal.*

Coppola, R., Moristo, M., & Torino, P. D. (2016). Connected Car: Technologies, Issues, Future Trends. *ACM Computing Surveys,* 46.

Dasuha, L. C., & Mantoro, T. (2016). CoMoSeF- Car to car communication in VANET using Co-operative Mobility Services of the Future. *5th International Conference on Multimedia Computing and Systems.* 10.1109/ICMCS.2016.7905637

Deepak, K. R., & Rshi, R. (2016). Routing and security analysis in vehicular ad-hoc networks (VANETs). *IEEE International Conference on Power Electronics, Intelligent Control and Energy Systems.* 10.1109/ICPEICES.2016.7853606

Ferriere, H. D., Grossglauser, M., & Vetterli, M. (2007). *Least-Cost Opportunistic Routing.* EPFL Technical Report LCAV-REPORT.

Ghaleb, F. A., Razzaque, F. A., & Isnin, I. F. (2013). Security and privacy enhancement in VANETs using mobility pattern. *Fifth International Conference on Ubiquitous and Future Networks (ICUFN)*. 10.1109/ICUFN.2013.6614808

Hasrounya, H., Samhatb, A. E., Bassilc, C., & Laouitia, A. (2017). VANet security challenges and solutions: *A survey. Vehicular Communications, 7*, 7–20. doi:10.1016/j.vehcom.2017.01.002

Hoa, V., & Cavalli, A. (2014). Security Attacks And Solutions In Vehicular Ad Hoc Networks: A Survey. *International Journal on AdHoc Networking Systems*.

Hu, H., Lu, R., Zhang, Z., & Shao, J. (2017). REPLACE: A Reliable Trust-Based Platoon Service Recommendation Scheme in VANET. *IEEE Transactions on Vehicular Technology, 66*(2), 1786–1797. doi:10.1109/TVT.2016.2565001

Ibrahim, S., & Hamdy, M. (2015). A comparison on VANET authentication schemes: Public Key vs. Symmetric Key. *Tenth International Conference on Computer Engineering and Systems*. 10.1109/IC-CES.2015.7393072

Kateshiya, J.P., & Singh, A.P. (2015). Review To Detect and Isolate Malicious Vehicle in VANET. *International Journal of Innovative Research in Science, Engineering and Technology*.

Lee, K. C., & Gerla, M. (2010). Opportunistic Vehicular Routing, invited paper. *IEEE European Wireless Conference*, 873-880.

Lee, K. C., & Gerla, M. (2010). Opportunistic Vehicular Routing. *European Wireless Conference*, 873-880.

Li, W., & Song, H. (2016). ART: An Attack-Resistant Trust Management Scheme for Securing Vehicular Ad Hoc Networks. *IEEE Transactions on Intelligent Transportation Systems, 17*(April), 960–969. doi:10.1109/TITS.2015.2494017

Mekkia, T., Jabrib, I., Rachedic, A., & Jemaaa, M. (2016, November 28). Vehicular cloud networks: Challenges, architectures, and future directions. *Vehicular Communications*.

Mihaita, A. E., Dobre, C., Pop, F., Mavromoustakis, C. X., & Mastorakis, G. (2017). *Secure Opportunistic Vehicle-to-Vehicle Communication, Advances in Mobile Cloud Computing and Big Data in the 5G Era. In Studies in Big Data* (Vol. 22). Springer.

Movahedi, Z., Langar, R., & Pujolle, G. (2010). A Comprehensive Overview of Vehicular Ad hoc Network Evaluation Alternatives. *8th Asia-Pacific Symposium on Information and Telecommunication Technologies*.

Paranjothi, A., Khan, M. S., Nijim, M., & Challoo, R. (2016). MAvanet: Message authentication in VANET using social networks. *IEEE Annual Ubiquitous Computing, Electronics and Mobile Communication Conference*.

Paul, B., Ibrahim, M., & Bikas, M. A. N. (2011). VANET Routing Protocols: Pros and Cons. *International Journal of Computers and Applications, 20*, 28–34. doi:10.5120/2413-3224

Praba, V. L., & Ranichitra, A. (2013). Isolating malicious vehicles and avoiding collision between vehicles in VANET. *International Conference on Communication and Signal Processing*, 811 – 815. 10.1109/iccsp.2013.6577169

Raiput, U., Abbas, F., & Oh, H. (2013). A Hierarchical Privacy Preserving Pseudonymous Authentication Protocol for VANE. *IEEE Access: Practical Innovations, Open Solutions*, 7770–7784.

Rawat, D. B., Yan, G., Bista, B., & Weigle, M. C. (2014). Trust On the Security of Wireless Vehicular Ad-hoc Networking. *Ad-Hoc & Sensor Wireless Networks*, 1–23.

Rehman, S., Khan, M.A., Zia, T.A., & Zheng, L. (2013). Vehicular Ad-Hoc Networks (VANETs) - An Overview and Challenges. *Journal of Wireless Networking and Communications*, 29-38.

Salehi, M., & Boukerche, A. (2017, July). A Novel Packet Salvaging Model to Improve the Security of Opportunistic Routing Protocols. *Computer Networks*, *122*(20), 163–178. doi:10.1016/j.comnet.2017.04.019

Salehi, M., Darehshoorzadeh, A., & Boukerche, A. (2015). On the Effect of Black-hole Attack on Opportunistic Routing Protocols. *Proceedings of the 12th ACM Symposium on Performance Evaluation of Wireless Ad Hoc, Sensor, and Ubiquitous Networks*, 93-100. 10.1145/2810379.2810386

Signorello, S., Palattella, M. R., & Grieco, L. A. (2016). *Security Challenges in Future NDN-Enabled VANETs, IEEE Trustcom, BigDataSE*. ISPA.

Studer, A., Bai, F., Bellur, B., & Perrig, A. (2009). Flexible, extensible, and efficient VANET authentication. *Journal of Communications and Networks (Seoul)*, *11*(6), 574–588. doi:10.1109/JCN.2009.6388411

Tahooni, A., Darehshoorzadeh, A., & Boukerche, A. (2014). Mobility-based Opportunistic Routing for Mobile Ad-Hoc Networks. *Proceedings of the 11th ACM symposium on Performance evaluation of wireless ad hoc, sensor,and ubiquitous networks*, 9-16. 10.1145/2653481.2653485

Tzeng, S. F., Horng, S. J., Li, T., Wang, X., Huang, P. H., & Khan, M. K. (2017). Enhancing Security and Privacy for Identity-Based Batch Verification Scheme in VANETs. *IEEE Transactions on Vehicular Technology*, *66*(4), 3235–3248. doi:10.1109/TVT.2015.2406877

Vinothini, S., & Subha, T. (2015). An Efficient Crl Authentication Scheme For Vehicular Communications. *International Conference on Computing and Communications Technologies*, 282 – 285. 10.1109/ICCCT2.2015.7292761

Waghmode, R., Gonsalves, R., & Ambawade, D. (2016). Security enhancement in group based authentication for VANET. *IEEE International Conference on Recent Trends in Electronics, Information and Communication Technology*. 10.1109/RTEICT.2016.7808069

Yang, C.F., Ju, Y.H., Hsieh, C.Y., Lin, C.Y., Tsai, M.H., & Chang, H.L. (2017). iParking – a real-time parking space monitoring and guiding system. *Vehicular Communications*.

Yang, Z. C. K., Yeo, S., Lee, B.S., & Boleng, J. (2009). Position based Opportunistic Routing for Robust Data Delivery in MANETs. *Proceedings of the 28th IEEE conference on Global telecommunications*, 1325-1330. 10.1109/GLOCOM.2009.5425351

Zhang, J., Chen, C., & Cohen, R. (2010). *A Scalable and Effective Trust-Based Framework for Vehicular Ad-Hoc Networks*. Advances in Trust Management.

Zhongyi, L., Tong, Z., Wei, Y., & Xiaoming, L. (2009). *GOSR: Geographical Opportunistic Source Routing for VANETs. In Mobile Computing and Communications Review* (pp. 48–51). ACM SIGMOBILE.

Zhu, L., Wang, X., & Lim, A. O. (2011). SMSS: Symmetric-Masquerade Security Scheme for VANETs. *10th International Symposium on Autonomous Decentralized Systems (ISADS).*

KEY TERMS AND DEFINITIONS

Intelligent Transportation System (ITS): Advanced application that provides innovative services related to different modes of transport and traffic management.

Malicious Vehicle Detection: Faulty vehicles forwards wrong information to others; identifying these vehicles is a major issue.

Opportunistic Routing: New promising paradigm that has been proposed for wireless networks, which increases the performance of wireless networks.

Trust Factor: All vehicles in the DSRC must have a valid trust factor for participating in the further communication process.

Vehicular Adhoc Networks (VANETs): The spontaneous creation of a wireless network for data exchange to the domain of vehicles.

Chapter 16
Detection Approaches for Categorization of Spam and Legitimate E-Mail

Rachnana Dubey
LNCT, India

Jay Prakash Maurya
LNCT, India

R. S. Thakur
Maulana Azad National Institute of Technology, India

ABSTRACT

The internet has become very popular, and the concept of electronic mail has made it easy and cheap to communicate with many people. But, many undesired mails are also received by users and the higher percentage of these e-mails is termed spam. The goal of spam classification is to distinguish between spam and legitimate e-mail messages. But, with the popularization of the internet, it is challenging to develop spam filters that can effectively eliminate the increasing volumes of unwanted e-mails automatically before they enter a user's mailbox. The main objective of this chapter is to examine and identify the best detection approach for spam categorization. Different types of algorithms and data mining models are proposed, implemented, and evaluated on data sets. For improvement of spam filtering technique, the authors analyze the methods of feature selection and give recommendations of their use. The chapter concludes that the data mining models using a combination of supervised learning algorithms provide better results than single data models.

INTRODUCTION

E-mail is the most powerful medium of today communication. But E-mail spam is one the major problem for internet user. Every user is facing this problem on his day to day communication. Along with the growth of E-mail communication, spam's are also continuously growing day by day. Spamming is of

DOI: 10.4018/978-1-5225-3870-7.ch016

Figure 1. Flow Chart to find out spam

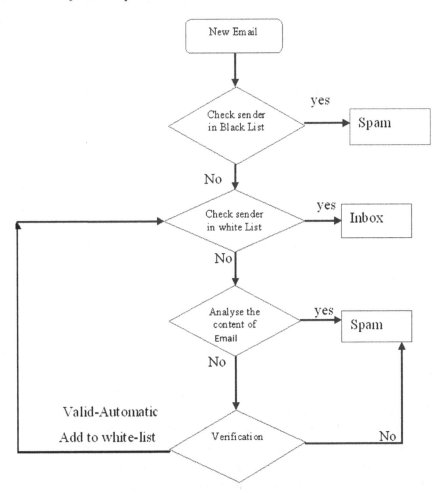

electronic communication systems to send unsought bulk messages or to push merchandise or services, that area unit nearly universally unwanted. Many problems arise due to spam mail; one of the major problem is many companies faces big financial loss (AnirudhRama, 2006). Another problem is that user needs to spend time on checking and deleting spam from their inbox. In addition, due to spam E-mails may contain malicious software (i.e. phishing software), illegal advertising, such as image schemes and attractive information, it has become a serious security issue on internet. The one of the best solution for solving spam issue is data mining with machine learning algorithm (Nema et al., 2016). Data mining as the approach for finding the spam type (spam or legitimate) text patterns from large amount of data through machine learning (Yadav et al., 2016), discover the similar pattern which are adopted by smart spammers as Shown in Figure 1.

Five algorithms have been used for spam and legitimate categorization. The algorithms results are based on supervised learning algorithms (Naïve Bayes, Random Forest, Random tree, Bagging and Boosting). Moreover, Support Vector Machine can be used for spam categorization. Support vector machine is the supervised learning algorithm. SVM works on linear separable in different feature levels.

In this proposed work, machine learning algorithm is evaluated using WEKA, Rapid Minor and SVM tool for finding accuracy, efficiency of classifiers and various types of errors. We have analyzed the most effective categorization methodology on bench mark dataset. This comprises 9324 records and 500 instances (70% for Training and 30% for Testing) to make the model. We described approaches and learning models for eliminate bulky commercial mails, malicious code, fraud E-mails. The main aim is to finding the unwanted keyword, which are mostly using for spam (Battista, 2011).

SVM Based Classification

More formally, a support vector machine constructs a hyperplane or set of hyperplanes in a high or infinite dimensional space, which can be used for classification, regression or other tasks. Intuitively, a good separation is achieved by the hyperplane that has the largest distance to the nearest training data points of any class (so-called functional margin), since in general the larger the margin the lower the generalization error of the classifier (Nema et al., 2016). SVM has verified to be one in all the foremost economical kernel strategies. The success of SVM is principally because of its high generalization ability. Unlike several learning algorithms, SVM results in good performances while not the necessity to include previous info (Anil. K Jain, 1999). Moreover, the employment of positive definite kernel within the SVM will be taken as associate embedding of the input space into a high dimensional feature space wherever the classification is applied, without using the feature space. Hence, the matter of selecting design for a neural network application is replaced by the matter of selecting an appropriate kernel for a Support Vector Machine.

Classifying data is a common task in machine learning problems. Suppose some data points are given and each belong to one of two classes, the goal is to decide in which class a new data point will resides. In support vector machines, a data point is arranged as a P-dimensional vector (p numbers). The user want to know whether user can separate such points with a ($p - 1$) dimensional hyperplane (linear classifier). There are many hyperplanes that might classify the data. One affordable alternative because the best hyperplane that represents the most important separation, or margin, between two classes. therefore user chooses the hyperplane so the space from it to the closest information on both sides is maximized. If such a hyperplane exists, it is known as the maximum-margin hyperplane and the linear classifier it defines is known as a maximum margin classifier. Support Vector Machine has shown power in Binary Classifier and has Good Theoretical Foundation and Well Mastered learning algorithm. It shows Good Results in static data classification. The only disadvantage is that takes more time and memory consuming when size of data is enormous. SVM can be used to solve Linearly Separable as well as Non Linear Separable Problems.

Linear Separable Problems

While Classify, if points can be separated using Linear Decision Boundary then it is Linear Separable Problem as Shown in Figure 2. The Main aim is to find the appropriate Decision Boundary. There may be many decision boundaries for some classification problem but we have to choose the best one. The decision boundary (Michael, 2006) should be as far away from the data of both classes as possible. We should maximize *m (margin)*.

- Let $\{x_1, ..., x_n\}$ be our data set and let y_i Î$\{1,-1\}$ be the class label of x_i .
    - The decision boundary should classify all points correctly.
    - $_{o\ Yi} (w^T x_i + b) \geq 1, \forall_i$
- Constrain for optimization of decision boundary

Minimize ½ ||w||²

Subjecting to $Y_i (w^T x_i + b) \geq 1, \forall_i$

This Optimization can be done using Lagrange's Dual Problem (M.Soranamageswari 2011).

Non-Linearly Separable Problems

The Problem that cannot be classified linearly is Non Linear Separable Problems as Shown in Figure 3. Here we allow error £$_i$ if error is in between 0<= £$_i$ <= 1, it is properly classified but if £$_i$ > 1 it is misclassified. Thus we should minimize error. So we minimize$\sum$ £$_i$, £$_i$ can be computed by

$w^T x_i + b \geq 1 - $ £$_{i,}$ $Y_i = 1$

$w^T x_i + b \leq -1 + $ £$_{i,}$ $Y_i = -1$

£$_i \geq 0$

Thus the Optimization Problem Becomes Minimize ½ ||w||² + C $\sum_{i=1}^{n}$ £$_i$, Subject to $Y_i (w^T x_i + b) \geq$ 1- £$_i$ £$_i \geq 0$. To Obtain Non Linear Decision Boundary, input space should be transform to feature space.

The key idea is to transform x$_i$ to a higher dimensional space called feature space to make it easier. Input space: the space the point x$_i$ is located Feature space: the space of f (x$_i$) after transformation. Transformation is needed as linear operation in the feature space is equivalent to non-linear operation in input space and classification can become easier with a proper transformation (Mark Johnson, 2012) as Shown in Figure 4. In the XOR problem. E.g - adding a new feature of x$_1$x$_2$ make the problem linearly separable.

Kernel Methods

Kernel methods are a class of algorithms for pattern analysis, whose best known element is the support vector machine (SVM). The general task of pattern analysis is to find and study general types of relations (for example clusters, rankings, principal components, correlations, classifications) in general types of data (such as sequences, text documents, sets of points, vectors, images, etc.) (Cormack, 2007).

Figure 2. Linear Separable Problems

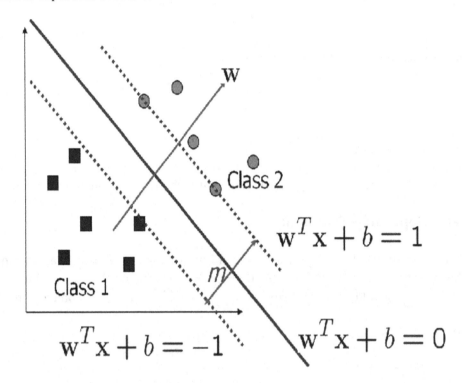

Figure 3. Non-Linear Separable Problems

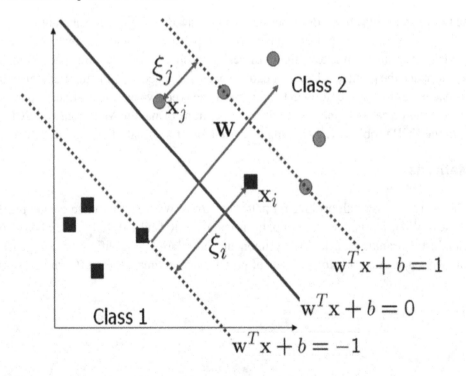

Figure 4. Mapping from input space to feature space

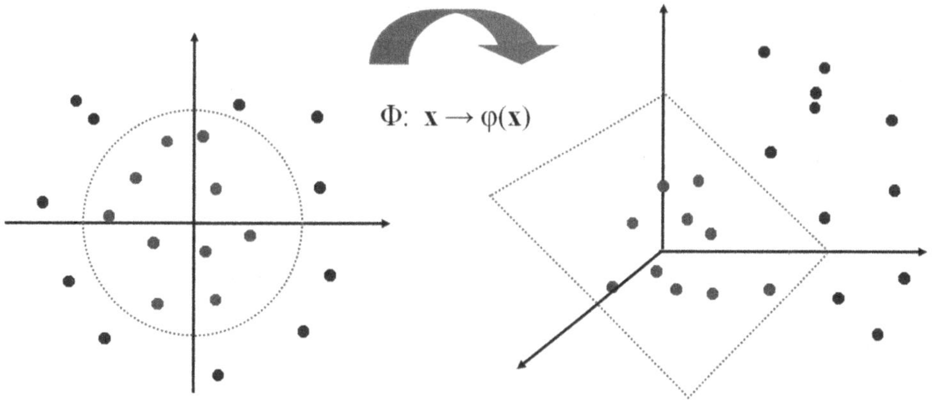

Table 1. Kernels types

kernel types
There are following types of kernel function is selected through this parameter: dot, radial, polynomial, neural, anova, epachnenikov, gaussian combination, multiquadric
Dot: It is defined by k(x,y)=x*y i.e. Dot kernel is inner product of x and y.
Radial: It is defined by exp (-g ‖x-y‖^2) where g is the gamma, radial kernel is specified by the kernel gamma parameter. The adjustable parameter gamma plays a major role in the performance of the kernel, and should be carefully tuned to the problem at hand.

BACKGROUND

Various Datasets for Spam Filtering

There has been vital effort to come up with public benchmark datasets for anti-spam filtering. one in all the most issues is a way to defend the privacy of the users whose ham messages area unit enclosed within the datasets. the primary approach is to use ham messages collected from freely accessible newsgroups, or mailing lists with public archives.

1. Author [Zhong, 2011] conduct a comprehensive study to handle this scaling issue by proposing a series of acceleration techniques that speed up theorem filters supported approximate classifications. The core approximation technique uses hash-based search and loss coding. Search approximation relies on the popular Bloom filter arrangement with AN extension to support price retrieval. Loss coding is employed to more compress the info structure. Whereas these approximation ways introduce further errors to a strict theorem approach, we have a tendency to show however the errors will be each reduced and biased toward a false negative classification. [Zhong, 2011] demonstrate a 6×speedup over 2 well-known spam filters (bogo filter and qsf) whereas achieving a regular false positive rate and similar false negative rate to the first filters. The proposed extended Bloom filter demonstrates the tradeoffs between the accuracy and the speed. In different from the traditional Bloom filter, this extension is applicable for data retrieval. Although the nature of approximations

prevents this scheme from being applied to the applications that require precise data retrieval. Zhenyu Zhong are currently exploring the feasibility to apply the scheme to other statistical-based applications, such as risk management, and reputation-based filtering.

2. Author [Sharma, 2011] gives experimental results in the WEKA environment by using four algorithms namely ID3, J48, Simple CART and Alternating Decision Tree on the spam email dataset are compared with terms of classification accuracy. According to him simulation results the J48 classifier outperforms the ID3, CART and AD-Tree in terms of classification accuracy. It is clear from the simulation results that the highest classification accuracy performance is for the J48 classifier for the spam email datasets containing 58 attributes with each 4601.

Enron Dataset

In Enron investigation, the non-public files of roughly one hundred fifty Enron staff were created in public obtainable. These files have an outsized variety of non-public E-mail messages that are accustomed produce E-mail classification benchmarks. Throughout the development of the latter benchmark, many spam filters were utilized to weed spam out of the Enron message assortment. Author [Basavaraju and Prabhakar, 2010] discussed a novel method of spam mail detection using text based clustering approach. In this work discussed the efficient clustering algorithm using the k-means and BIRCH, Mr. Prabhakar proposed technique includes the distance between all the attributes of E-mails. They used the ling spam corpus dataset in c language for finding the result. They presented the combination of BIRCH and KNN is gives best for large data scanning.

SPAM FILTERING TRADITIONAL TECHNIQUES

The Filtering software checks how well different approaches work correctly in identifying as spam or desirable messages as legitimate (David, 2002).

Hiding Contact Information

Some email users add only selected person in their contact list for avoiding spam emails. For these people, an e-mail address is something to be revealed only to selected, trusted parties. As extra precautions should be there that an e-mail address can be chosen to avoid easily guessed names and dictionary words, and addresses can be disguised when posting to public areas. All have seen e-mail addresses cutely encoded in forms like "<babyROM@SP<.gnosis.cso>" or "energyd@tablet.pk | rx Pzon N-to-MA-N". For hiding the contact information several email users use temporary email-id and also used third party id. The real "confidantes only" address is kept protected. It is found that a category of e-mail users gains sufficient protection from these basic precautions.

Author [Thuy and T.T. Nguyen, 2008] discussed IP traffic classification techniques that do not rely on 'well known' TCP or UDP port number, or interpreting the contents of packet payload. New work is emerging the use of statistical traffic characteristics to assist in the identification and classification process. This paper looks at emerging research into the application of Machine Learning (ML) techniques to IP traffic classification - an inter-disciplinary blend of IP networking and data mining techniques. We provide context and motivation for the application of ML techniques to IP traffic classification, and review 18 significant works that cover the dominant period from 2004 to early 2007. These works are categorized and reviewed according to their choice of ML strategies and primary contributions to the literature. We also discuss a number of key requirements for the employment of ML-based traffic classifiers in operational IP networks, and qualitatively critique the extent to which the reviewed works meet these requirements. Open issues and challenges in the field are also discussed. Index Terms—Traffic classification, Internet Protocol, Machine Learning, Real Time, Payload inspection, Flow clustering, Statistical traffic properties.

Basic Structured Text Filters

This filter has the potential to type incoming E-mail supported straightforward strings found in specific header fields, the header normally, and/or within the body. Its capability is incredibly straightforward and doesn't even embody regular expression matching. Most E-mail shoppers have this lot of filtering capability. Several of those straightforward filters properly catch concerning eightieth of the spam messages received. Sadly, they even have a comparatively high false positive rate that it's required to manually examine a number of the spam folders from time to time.

- Author [wonk, 2009] discussed how to extract attribute-value pairs from web pages. It consists of two phases: candidate generation, in which syntactically likely attribute-value pairs are annotated; and candidate filtering, in which semantically improbable annotations are removed. Yuk describes three types of candidate generators and two types of candidate filters, all of which are designed to be massively parallelizable. Our methods can handle 1 billion web pages in less than 6 hours with 1,000 machines. The best generator and filter combination achieves 70% F-measure compared to a hand-annotated corpus.
- Author [Clark, 2007] present structured text retrieval by means of affordances offers a proposal for some research on the retrieval of structured text, such as extensible mark-up language (XML). They believe that capturing the way in which a reader perceives the meaning of documents, especially genres of text, may have implications for information retrieval. Previous research on 'shallow' features of structured text has shown that categorization by form is possible. Gibson's theory of 'affordances' and genre offer the reader the meaning and purpose through structure of a text, before the reader has even begun to read it, and should therefore provide a good basis for the 'deep' skimming and categorization of texts. We believe that Gibson's 'affordances' will aid the user to locate, examine and utilize shallow or deep features of genres and retrieve relevant output. Our proposal puts forward two hypotheses, with a list of research questions to test them, and culminates in experiments involving the studies of human categorization behavior when viewing the structures of E-mails and web documents. Finally, we will examine the effectiveness of adding structural layout cues to a Yahoo discussion forum (currently only a bag-of-words), which is rich in structure, but only searchable through a Boolean search engine.

White List or Verification Filters

This filter is totally work on fair list, means in our inbox only enter selected candidate list, those are available in mail list. Several tools are based on white list filter like TDMA. This tool is open source.

Sender programs read all contacts of a user and let mail from those contacts trough directly. A white list directly connected to mail server.

PPROBLEM DOMAIN

Spam has a problem that it tends to swamp desirable E-mail; a few years ago we occasionally received an random irrelevant message, one or two every day. Every day of this month, we received many times more spam than we did legitimate correspondences. On an average, we probably get 10 spams for every appropriate e-mail. In some ways we are unusual -as a public writer, we maintain a widely published e-mail address; moreover, we both welcome and receive frequent correspondence from strangers related to my published writing and to my software libraries. Unfortunately, a letter from a stranger - with who-knows-which e-mail application, OS, native natural language, and so on, is not immediately obvious in its purpose; and spammers try to slip their messages underneath such ambiguities. Our seconds are valuable to me, especially when we are claimed many times during every hour of a day. All mail server is not control spam mail, so that we are exploring some more work on spam data analysis, and give some accurate point for controlling them.

SOLUTIONS AND RECOMMENDATIONS

As it is known that email is one of the fastest ways of communication medium. Millions of people used email facility in their day to day life. But with the growth of email communication the spam is also grew. An antispam filter is similar to an anti-virus which scans files to check for virus signatures (Basavaraju, 2010).

In order to block the spam mail companies, business user and email service providers have used keyword 'detection' and block the frequent keywords. Researchers have proposed many statistical frameworks for spam filtering which can quickly and efficiently block unwanted messages in your email inbox, but most of the filtering methods are not 100% accurate. The maximum filters work on 75-80% per day. Our goal is classification of spam and ham mails by various detection approaches. Spammer ideas are very strong as compared to normal human, as they always attack on human brain, because every spammer wants the user money." Legitimate companies send emails through their company website for example help@microsoft.com. Every mail @ and .com are very common patterns. So, most of the company send their advertisement, commercial message through content based. In content based mail real information is hidden, only body of the message is visible. Spammer companies never send direct mails. They don't care about time and cost of normal users. They collect the email addresses from chat room social networking side and various data mart. Today's world maximum spammer used the bagging of mails, means one advertisement mails are connected with each several advertisements. Spam mails are classified in broadly two categories' (Chih-Hung,2009). The first class is spam with attachment and therefore the second class is spam while not attachment. Spam with attachment is classified into four varieties like image file (.gif), text message (use PDF), stand out and nothing file attachment. each user waste their time in deleting the spam mails. One of best approach to reduce the spam mails is classification and categorization of spam and legitimate mail. Currently, machine learning for spam classification is an important research issue at present. Support Vector Machines (SVMs) are a new learning method and achieve substantial improvements over the currently preferred methods, and behave robustly whilst tackling a variety of different learning tasks. Due to its high dimensional input, fewer irrelevant features and high accuracy, the SVMs are more important to researchers for categorizing spam. This thesis explores and identifies the use of different learning algorithms for classifying spam and legitimate messages from e-mail. A comparative analysis among the filtering techniques has also been presented in this thesis. We have used SVM, WEKA and Rapid Minor for analysis the spam and ham mails. Normal E-mail filters work on black list and white list based (Qin,2009).

When any new mail entered to the mail server, then mail server is automatically review the all-white list. Second blacklist are collection of known spammer addresses, when the mail server finds a match in blacklist category, then message is automatically bounced. Means blacklist is like a wrong address. The aim of all antispam filters is produce the good and useful mail. In this thesis we have generated the model for providing the best solution for deletion of the spam and we have introduced a comparative analysis of various detection approach. Our classification approach is shows the best result according voting criteria. The major task of machine learning is to identify the spam word and labels the legitimate mails. Machine learning techniques are very effective and are also adaptive Based on the following: -

- Text classification methods: TFIDF, Naive Bays, N-gram, SVM, Boosting, etc. (Xiaosong, 2006).
- Phenomenally accurate.
- Learns new spammer tactics automatically.
- Adapt to changing spam.

We follow the two steps fist learning of the bench mark data set and second categorize the dataset in two categories. We introduce the naive bayes, random tree, random forest, bagging, boosting for classification. The boosting and bagging both algorithms train the classifier on different subsets of the overall dataset. Bagging combines the result of classifiers trained on sub sampling of the dataset. In random tree several decision trees are generate. The basic objective of this thesis is to provide email Classification based on vector space model. Spam categorization are categorizing by binary data.

PROPOSED WORK

We follow two steps learning of the bench mark data set and second categorize the dataset in two categories [Shown in Figure 5]. We introduce the naive bayes, random tree, random forest, bagging, boosting for classification. The boosting and bagging both algorithms train the classifier on different subsets of the overall dataset. Bagging combines the result of classifiers trained on sub sampling of the dataset. In random tree several decision trees are generate. The basic objective of this thesis is to provide email classification based on vector space model. Spam categorization are categorizing by binary data. [Shown in Figure 6], shows the brief structure of selection and categorization steps.

EMAIL CATEGORIZATION

There are mainly two steps involved in data classification

Figure 5. Selection and categorization steps

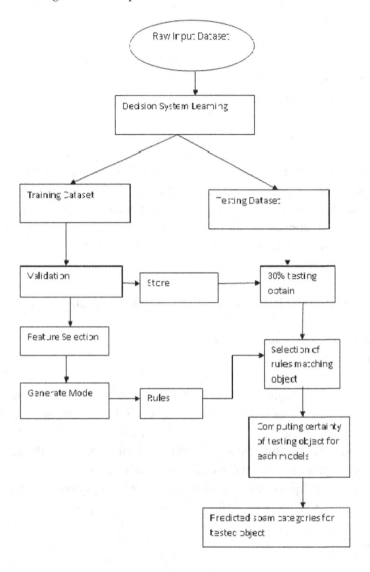

- **Learning:** Training data are analyzed by a classification algorithm. The learned model or classifier is represented in the form of classification rules.
- **Classification:** Test data are used to estimate the accuracy of the classification rules. If the accuracy is considered acceptable, the rules can be applied to the classification of new data tuples. The classifier for spam and legitimate classification as Shown in Figure 7 .

Classification is the best approach for identification and cauterization of spam and legitimate mail. In this thesis we used the WEKA, Rapid Minor and SVM for finding the best classifier .Spam filtering is control by variety of ways like Rule Based(Apply handmade rule for removal and identification of spam, Domain filters(Keep maintain the track or path only valid users),Blacklisting (work or apply on database server),White list (Mailer read the all contact list and then mail to specific authorized user), Hiding address(hiding original email from the spammers by receiving all emails at temporary id, which

Figure 6. Classifier for spam and legitimate classification

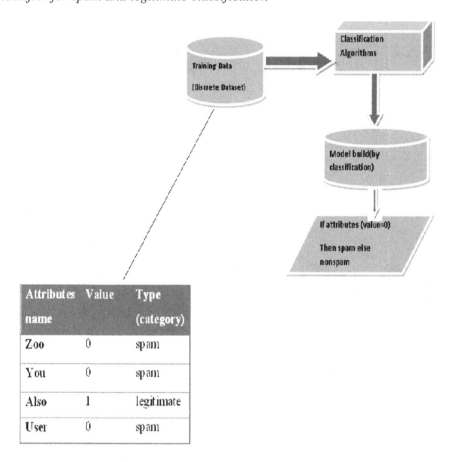

Attributes name	Value	Type (category)
Zoo	0	spam
You	0	spam
Also	1	legitimate
User	0	spam

is then forwarded to the original email id),Scanning the header massage by self(Because main header massage show the actual useful or unwanted mails).Spam is a bulk messages, unsolicited email and commercial mail. The aim of spam categorization is to distinguish between spam and legitimate email message. WEKA is the best tool for machine learning algorithm. This thesis is comparative analysis of the different spam detection by machine learning using WEKA, Rapid Minor. WEKA tools solve large amounts of problem such as classification, clustering, association rule, neural network. It is open source tools implemented in Java platform. WEKA has capacity to convert CSV file to flat file. We used classification method for measure the accuracy of algorithm. It can be run on Windows, Linux and Mac. It consists of collection of machine learning algorithms for implementing data mining tasks. GUI based tool mainly used for preprocessing tools, evaluation methods and has an environment for comparing learning techniques. Many classification methods have been developed with the aid of learning algorithms such as Bayesian, Decision Tree, Random Forest, K-nearest neighbor, Support Vector Machine (SVM), Bagging and boosting. All these classifiers are basically learning methods and adopt sets of rules. Bayesian classifiers are derived from Bayesian Decision Theory (Means probability of words which are spam or not). This is the simplest and most widely used classification method due to its changing capabilities of keywords and associated probabilities according to the classification decisions and performance. The training data consist of pairs of input objects (typically vectors), and desired outputs. The output of the

Figure 7. Proposed Model for Classification

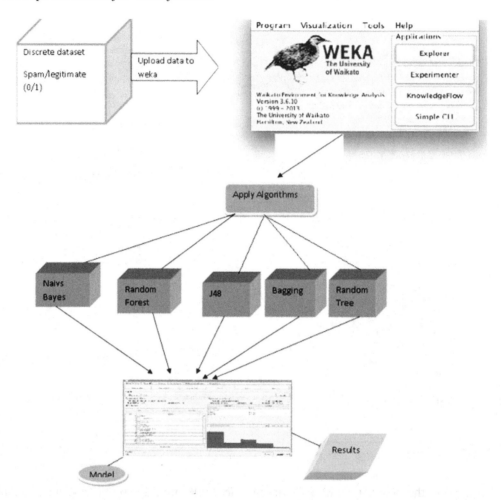

function can be a continuous value (called regression), or can predict a class label of the input object (called classification).

PREPROCESSING OF DATA

Dataset Preparation

The 3 datasets were subjected to the subsequent pre-processing steps. First, messages sent by the owner of the mailbox has been removed (by checking if the address of the owner appeared within the 'to:', 'Cc:', or 'Bcc:' fields), since it's believed that e-mail users square measure progressively adopting higher ways that to stay copies of outgoing messages. Second, as a simplification, all HTML tags are removed and therefore the headers of the messages, keeping solely their subjects and bodies.

Dataset is an important aspect when formulating a spam classification is the data used for evaluating its accuracy. This is a benchmark dataset namely, spam Assassin, publicly free available online. Ling

Spam, Enron-Spam, and Usenet are other benchmark dataset are also freely available online. Table 2, shows different benchmark datasets with total number of instances and number of attributes.

Algorithm Followed

1. Following are the steps to be performed on the above pre-processed datasets.
2. Convert the random mails (Both Training and Testing modules) into .csv (comma separated values) format.
3. Compute most frequent words in training module (both legitimate and spam).
4. We took the top 5000 most frequent words from both spam and legitimate mails mixed them to form around 7000 most frequent words.
5. Assign a unique integer value for each word.
6. Converting the original .csv format (both training and testing) into ARFF format.
7. Create a model by applying SVM, RapidMiner and WEKA for training dataset file and find out recall and precession values.
8. Applying SVM, RapidMiner and WEKA to test module using SVM generated model, RapidMiner and WEKA train and check the recall and precession.
9. The above algorithm is repeated by changing the kernel function and different types of algorithms for dataset.

Implementation Work With Five Algorithms

In this proposed work, we have analyzed a comparative study of accuracy of different supervised learning algorithms using different data mining tools for spam classification. We have also analyzed simulation errors of different supervised algorithms using different data mining tools. We have also analyzed accuracy of different kernel functions of Support Vector Machine using in Rapid Miner tool. So using this analysis, we can apply particular data mining tool including supervised algorithms for predict the more spam filtering.

In this proposed work, we are searching a best classifier which could find out spam mail means which could differentiate between spam and legitimate mails. Moreover, we are searching the best data mining simulation tool which could efficiently categorize the spam and non-spam mails. So, in this work, first we have used WEKA simulation. We have only performed our benchmark dataset with supervised learning algorithms either with WEKA or Rapid Miner simulations. So, we have tried to know the best simulation tool as well as best supervised algorithm for spam and legitimate mails. We have found out that WEKA is outperformer simulation tool for spam and legitimate mails. Moreover, we have also found that Random forest is the best classifier for spam and legitimate mails.

Table 2. Train and Test Dataset

Name	Instance	Attributes	Work
Usenet	9375	475	Analysis
Enron	7455	301	Analysis
Spam Assian	9321	501	Result

In this proposed work, we have also tried to find out the performance of Support Vector Machine for our data set. One thing we have noticed when we applied Support Vector Machine. Support Vector Machine takes lot of time to find out the accuracy. The main reason to take SVM was want to find out the comparative study of all simulation models. In this proposed work, we have also tried to know various types of errors that could be possible using different simulations, different supervised learning algorithms, reduced feature sets, all feature sets and different ratio of dataset. Moreover, we have also tried to know improved accuracy that could be possible using different simulations, different supervised learning algorithms, reduced feature sets, all feature sets and different ratio of dataset.

We have also tried to find out, which algorithm out of five algorithms namely Naive Bays, Random Forest, Random Tree, Bagging and Boosting is going to performed best in term of accuracy.

EXPERIMENTAL RESULT

Experiment Design

Spam Assian Dataset is used by varying simulation models. 70% data is used as a training set and rest 30% is used as testing set. To conduct experiments Support Vector Machine is employed that contains three basic Kernel Functions Dot, Radial and Polynomial. Moreover Rapid Miner and WEKA simulation models are also used with supervised algorithms. We have also found out the various errors. We compare the classification accuracy results of the four decision tree algorithms- Navies Bays, Random Tree, Random Forest and Bagging. The simulations were trained and tested using spam email dataset consisting of 9321 instances, each instance consist of 501 attributes. The UCI dataset has been changed consequently. All simulations were performed with the help of WEKA, Rapid Miner and SVM that consists of assortment of in style learning schemes that may be used for sensible data processing. We tend to list below the steps taken to attain desired results:-

Performance Measure

Accuracy and time is performance parameter in our dataset to build model, and comparing the classifiers. The classifier is trained to classify e-mails as legitimate and spam. An accuracy of 95% may make the classifier accurate, but what if only 5-6% of the training samples are actually "spam"? Clearly an accuracy of 84% may not be acceptable –the classifiers can correctly labeling only the legitimate samples. Instead we would like to access how well the classifier can recognize "spam" samples. The recall and specificity measures can be used, respectively for this purpose. In addition, we may use precision to access the percentage of samples labelled as "spam" that actually are "spam". The evaluation measures which are used in approach for testing process in our research work could be defined as follows:

- **True Positive (TP):** The no. of spam documents correctly classified as spam.
- **True Negative (TN):** The no. of non-spam documents correctly classified as non-spam.
- **False Positive (FP):** The no. of spam classified as non-spam.
- **False-Negative (FN):** The no. of non-spam document classified as spam.
- **Precision:** The ratio of true positive to true and false positives. This determines how many identified objects in a class were correct.

- ○ Precision (P) = TP / (TP+FP)
- **Recall:** The ratio of true positives to the number of true positive and false negatives. This determines how many objects in a class are misclassified as something else.
    - ○ Recall (R) = TP / (TP+FN)
- **Accuracy:** The defined as the sum of all True positives and True Negative to the total number of test instances. This measures the overall accuracy of the classifier.
    - ○ Accuracy = (TP+TN) / (TP+ TN+FP+FN)

The results of experiment are shown in no of factors like Mean Absolute Errors as shown in Figure 8, Relative Absolute Errors as shown in Figure 9, Root Relative Squared Errors as shown in Figure 10, Accuracy of SVM for different kernels as shown in Figure 11, Accuracies of different Machine tool [Shown in Figure 12], Accuracies-wise comparison of simulator as shown in Figure 13.

Confusion Matrix

One of the methods to judge the performance of a classifiers using confusion matrix the quantity of correctly classified instances is sum of diagonals within the matrix; all others are incorrectly classified. The following terminology is used when referring to the counts tabulated in the confusion matrix.

Figure 8. Mean Absolute Errors

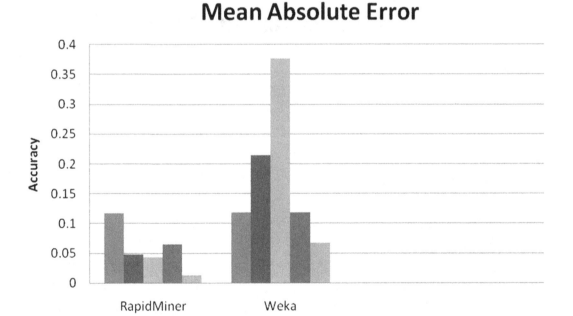

Figure 9. Relative Absolute Errors

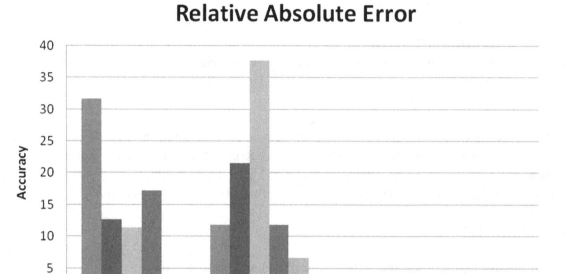

Figure 10. Root Relative Squared Errors

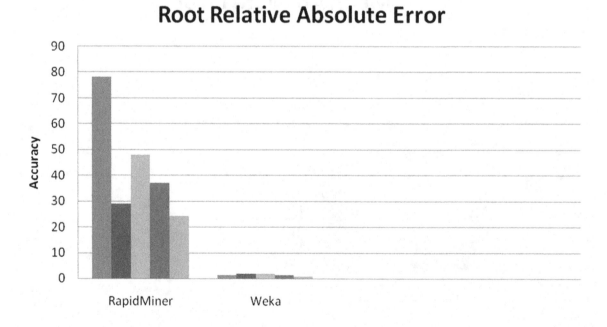

Figure 11. Accuracy of SVM for different kernels

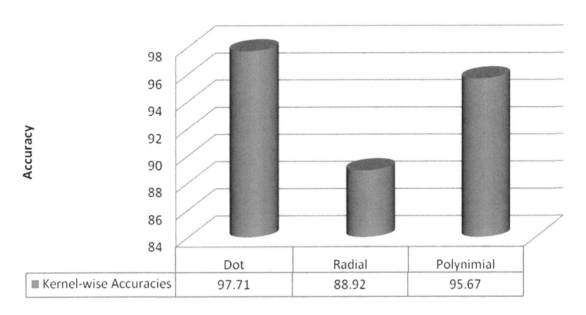

Kernel-wise Accuracies

	Dot	Radial	Polynimial
▣ Kernel-wise Accuracies	97.71	88.92	95.67

Figure 12. Accuracies of different Machine tool

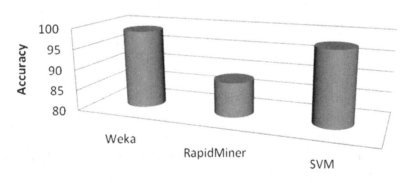

Comparative Accuracies

	Weka	RapidMiner	SVM
▣ Comparative Accuracies	98.82	88.24	97.71

FUTURE RESEARCH DIRECTION

In future, more classifiers can be used to evaluate the performance. Parallel Algorithms may be developed to reduce simulation error in classification, increase the accuracy and search best classifier for

Figure 13. Accuracies-wise comparison of simulator

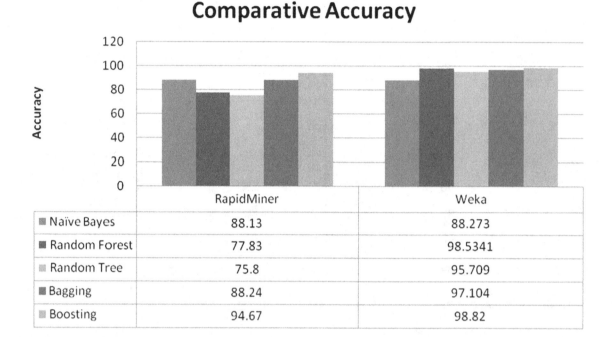

Comparative Accuracy

	RapidMiner	Weka
▪ Naïve Bayes	88.13	88.273
▪ Random Forest	77.83	98.5341
▪ Random Tree	75.8	95.709
▪ Bagging	88.24	97.104
▪ Boosting	94.67	98.82

Table 3. A Confusion Matrix

Predicted Class Actual Class	Spam	Legitimate
Spam	TP	FN
Legitimate	FP	TN

spam categorization. The performance can also be measured on dataset using unsupervised algorithms. Because, unsupervised algorithms do work on clusters.

We can also evaluate the other tools like Tanagra, and Mat Lab. We can also apply the neural network concept for spam categorization. We can also evaluate the results by modifying some parameters of different algorithms on different data mining tools.

- Feature selection Algorithms can be used to reduce redundancy of dataset.
- Common words which are same in legitimate and spam differing by some threshold can be eliminated.
- Parallel Algorithm may be developed to reduce time required in classification.

Other variants of Support Vector Machine can also be explored

Limitation

- The pre-processing selects the attributes based on the frequency and hence there is a possibility for information gain of few attributes is zero which is a drawback as it increases the time required for classification.
- As there is no Benchmark Dataset available in discrete form, so the results obtained cannot be compared with the previous research work.

CONCLUSION

The E-mail makes it possible to communicate with many people in an easy way. But, many spam are received by users without their desire. As time goes on, a higher percentage of the e-mails are treated as spam. For efficiently solve the above problems, the work is going on; many authors have worked with different classification methods, as seen in Literature Review.

The Classifiers like Decision Tree have large memory requirement. The features for spam filtering are more than 500, and may vary from 500 to large number. In order to evaluate these attributes, SVM has proved as good classifier because of its sparse data format and acceptability on Recall and Precision Value. SVM is also regarded as an important example of "kernel methods", one of the key areas in machine learning. Using SVM Classifier, evaluation of spam filtering over Spam Assian dataset has been done and it is found that the Classification results obtained by combining kernel functions is much better than the results obtained through individual kernel function.

In this thesis, spam categorization by five machine learning algorithm is evaluated using three data mining tools over benchmark dataset. The results are comparing in terms of Mean Absolute Error, Mean Squared Error, Relative Absolute Error, Root Relative Squared Error and accuracy and time taken to build model. This thesis shows best data mining tool for spam categorization. This thesis recommends WEKA tool for spam filtering. WEKA outperforms the other data mining tools approaches. This thesis shows the Rapid Miner is best tool for Root Relative Squared Error. Boosting runs efficiently on large data bases. This thesis shows the Boosting is best classifier for overall accuracy. It is an effective method for estimating missing data and maintains accuracy when a large proportion of the data are missing. In case of Support Vector machine, the Dot kernel gives best accuracy over polynomial and radial kernel.

REFERENCES

Basavaraju. (2010). A Novel Method of Spam Mail Detection using Text Based Clustering Approach. *International Journal of Computer Applications*, 5(4).

Biggio, B., & Corona, I. (2011). Bagging Classifiers for Fighting Poisoning Attacks in these types of Adversarial Classification Tasks. *International Workshop on Multiple Classifier Systems*, 6713, 350.

Carpen-Amarie. (2011). Bringing Introspection Into Blobseer: Towards A Self–Adaptive Distributed Data Management System Computer Science. International Journal of Applied Mathematics and Computer Science, 21(2), 229-242.

Chandran, Dagon, & Feamste. (2006). DNS-based Blacklists keep up with Bots. *CEAS 2006*.

Clark, M. (2007). *Structured text retrieval by means of affordances and genre*. Presented in School of Computing the Robert Gordon University BCS IRSG Symposium: Future Directions in Information Access (FDIA 2007).

Cormack, G. V. (2007, April). Email Spam Filtering: A Systematic Review, Published in. *Journal Foundations and Trends in Information Retrieval, 1*(4), 335–455. doi:10.1561/1500000006

Hovold, J. (2005, July). *Naive Bayes Spam Filtering Using Word-Position-Based Attributes*. CEAS.

Jain, P.W., & Mao. (1999). Statistical Pattern Reorganization: A Review. *IEEE Transactions on Pattern Analysis and Machine Intelligence, 22*(1), 4-37.

Johnson, M. (2012). Using Rejuvenation in order to improve the Particle Filtering for especially Bayesian Word Segmentation. *Proceedings of the 50th Annual Meeting of the Association for Computational Linguistics*, 85–89.

Karpagam Shanmuga Priya, D., Kavitha, B., Naveen Kumar, R., & Banuroopa, K. (2010). Improvising BayesNet Classifier Using Feature Reduction Method for Spam Classification. *IJCST, 1*(2).

Koprinska, I., Poon, J., Clark, J., & Chan, J. (2007). Learning to classify e-mail. *Information Sciences, 177*(10), 2167–2187. doi:10.1016/j.ins.2006.12.005

Lang. (2002). *Implementation of Navie Bayesian classifier in java*. Kaiserslautern university of applied sciences dept.

Li, F. (2006). An empirical study of clustering behavior of spammers and Group based Anti-spam strategie. *CEAS, 2006*, 21–28.

Mertz, D. (2002). *Spam Filtering Techniques: Comparing a Half-Dozen Approaches to Eliminating Unwanted Email*. Availableat: http://gnosis.cx/publish/progrflamming/filtering-spam.html

Nagamalai, D, & Lee. (2006). A Novel Mechanism to defend DOS attacks caused by spam. *International Journal of Smart Home*, 83-96.

Nema, A., Tiwari, B., & Tiwari, V. (2016, March). Improving Accuracy for Intrusion Detection through Layered Approach Using Support Vector Machine with Feature Reduction. In *Proceedings of the ACM Symposium on Women in Research 2016* (pp. 26-31). ACM. 10.1145/2909067.2909100

Pu & Webb. (2006). Observed trends in spam construction techniques: A case study of spam evolution. *CEAS 2006*, 104-112.

Qin, Xia, Prabhakar, & Tu. (2009). A Rule-Based Classification Algorithm for Uncertain Data. *IEEE International Conference on Data Engineering,* 1633 - 1640.

Sharma, A. K. (2011). A Comparative Study of Classification Algorithms for Spam Email Data Analysis. IJCSE, 3(5).

Soranamageswari, M., & Meena, C. (2011). A Novel Approach towards Image Spam Classification. *International Journal of Computer Theory and Engineering, 3*(1).

Wu. (2009). Behavior-based spam detection using a hybrid method of rule-based techniques and neural networks. Expert Systems with Applications, 36(3), 4321–4330.

Bruckner, M., Haider, P., & Scheffer, T. (2006). Highly Scalable Discriminative Spam Filtering. *Proceedings of 15th Text Retrieval Conference (TREC).*

Fang, F. F., & Qu, L. B. (2011, April). Applying Bayesian trigram filter model in spam identification and its disposal. In *Electric Information and Control Engineering (ICEICE), 2011 International Conference on* (pp. 3024-3027). IEEE.

Kishore Kumar, R. (2012). A Comparative Study of the algorithms related to the Classification for Spam Email Data Analysis. IMECS.

Lou & Hwang. (2006). *Adaptive Content Poisoning To Prevent Illegal File Distribution in P2P Networks Fellow.* IEEE.

Metsis, V., Androutsopoulos, I., & Paliouras, G. (2006). Spam Filtering with Naive Bayes – Which Naive Bayes? *CEAS 2006 Third Conference on Email and Anti Spam.*

Nguyen, T. T. T., & Armitage, G. (2008). A Survey of Techniques for Internet Traffic Classification using Machine Learning. *IEEE Communications Surveys and Tutorials, 10*(4), 2008. doi:10.1109/SURV.2008.080406

Wah, Y., & Wong, D. W. (2009). Scalable Attribute-Value Extraction from Semi-Structured Text, *ICDM Workshop on Large-scale Data Mining: Theory and Applications.*

Yadav, S., Tiwari, V., & Tiwari, B. (2016, March). Privacy Preserving Data Mining With Abridge Time Using Vertical Partition Decision Tree. In *Proceedings of the ACM Symposium on Women in Research 2016* (pp. 158-164). ACM. 10.1145/2909067.2909097

Zhong, Z. (2011). Speed Up Statistical Spam Filter by Approximation. *IEEE Transaction on Computers, 60*(1), 120 – 134.

Zhou, X. C., Shen, H. B., Huang, Z. Y., & Li, G. J. (2012). Largemargin classification for combating disguise attacks on spam filters. *Journal of Zhejiang University-Science C, 13*(3), 187–195. doi:10.1631/jzus.C1100259

KEY TERMS AND DEFINITIONS

Categorization: Is a process where the objects are understood, recognized, and differentiated.

Legitimate: According to law.

Mean Absolute Error: The mean absolute error (MAE) is a quantity used to measure how close predictions are to the eventual outcomes.

Mean Squared Error: The difference between the estimator and what is estimated.

Relative Absolute Error: The absolute error is the magnitude of the difference between the exact value and the approximation.

Optimization: Optimization is the process of adjusting a trading system in an attempt to make it more effective.

Chapter 17
Video Steganography Using Two-Level SWT and SVD

Lingamallu Naga Srinivasu
Kallam Haranadha Reddy Institute of Technology, India

Kolakaluri Srinivasa Rao
Kallam Haranadha Reddy Institute of Technology, India

ABSTRACT

Secured text data transmission plays an important role in communications. Discrete wavelet transform (DWT) is a time variant transform. The drawback of DWT can be overcome by stationary wavelet transform (SWT). SWT is designed to achieve the translation invariance. This chapter presents a novel secured text data transmission through video steganography using two-level stationary wavelet transform (SWT) and singular value decomposition (SVD). SVD of an image can be factored into its three components. In this chapter, text data is encrypted in cover video file using SWT and SVD techniques. First, the cover video is split into frames and each frame of the video acts as an image. Each character in the text data is encrypted with appropriate key value in each frame of the image using two-level SWT and SVD. The encrypted images are converted into video files that are called stego-video files. The text data can be recovered from the stego-video files after converting these files into frames by applying suitable key values, two-level SWT and SVD techniques.

INTRODUCTION

Video steganography changes the digital data in the video in a manner that only the sending person and the corresponding receiving person can recognize the message. The below equation gives a description of steganographic process

$$cover\_video + text\ data + stego\_key = stego\_video \qquad (1)$$

DOI: 10.4018/978-1-5225-3870-7.ch017

where cover_video is a video file which is used to embed the text data with stego_key values. The output is stego_video. The appearance of stego_video is same as the cover_video. The embedded text data doesn't make the distortion in cover video. (Shivani Khosla, & Paramjeet Kaur, 2014)

Any video file format can be used as a cover video in steganography. But that video file has high degree quality and redundancy. If the redundant bits of the video can be changed then there is no change detected in the video. Video files are suitable for to embed the confidential information. The categories of steganography are shown in Figure 1.

The text staganography method was to conceal a confidential message in every nth letter of every word of a text message (Shivani Khosla, & Paramjeet Kaur, 2014). Digital video contains a set of images(frames). These frames are passed sequentially based on the video standards that constitute a video. In video steganography, each letter in text message is embedded in every frame of the video. This process is very difficult to identify the hidden message in stego video.

Now a days secured data transmission plays an important role in data communication. Secured data main aim is to protect the data from the demolition forces and data hackers. In order to protect the data on public channels, secured data transmission is needed. There are so many secured techniques are available to transmit the data from source to destination like digital watermarking, audio steganography, video steganography, etc,.

Video stegnography is a promising technique to achieve the secured data transmission from source to destination. Steganography is a greek word, it means "covered writing" or "concealed writing". Video steganography changes the digital data in the video in a manner that only the sending person and the corresponding receiving person can recognize the message. Steganalysis means that discern the concealed message. The main aim of steganalysis is to meet if an algorithm can determine whether a given video contains confidential information. The confidential information can be hidden into video in a manner that cannot be detectable.

Video steganography is nothing but to hide the text data into video. In video steganography, text data act as a secret message and video act as a cover to the secret message. In this paper, text data is encrypted in cover video file using SWT and SVD techniques. SWT is one of the wavelet transformation techniques. It converts the spatial domain into frequency domain. SWT also provides the edge enhancement to an image. SVD of an image can be factored into its three components.

Figure 1. Categories of Steganography

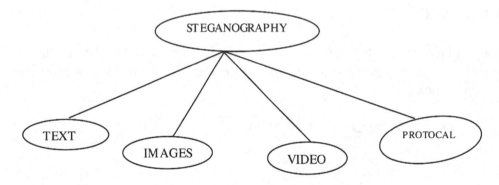

In audio steganography, the text data is encrypted in audio signal. This type of encryption makes the distortion in encrypted audio signal. The audibility in audio steganography is very less. The performance characteristics of original audio signal may be differing in encrypted audio signal.

Digital watermarking is also one of the secured transmission techniques. Digital watermarking techniques develop the robustness and invisibility (Shivani Khosla, & Paramjeet Kaur, 2014). In digital watermarking, the secret data is hiding into cover image. This encryption changes the quality of the original image. The encrypted image appearance is may be differ to appearance of original image. Digital watermarking is used to recognize the authorized person and to track the illegal copies.

Video steganography achieves the encryption effectively. In video steganography, the appearance of original video is same as the encrypted video. Video steganography can be achieved by so many techniques. In this paper, video steganography is achieved by using SWT (stationary wavelet transform) and SVD (singular value decomposition).

There is difference in video steganography and digital watermarking in respect of purpose, and encryption/decryption methods. The main difference is that the goal of digital watermarking is that the copy right protection is provided by the host signal with the embedded data. The aim of steganography is to transmit the implanted message. In steganography the secret message cannot detect by third person. In watermarking, the third person cannot replace the confidential information.

BACKGROUND

Steganography is nothing but to conceal the secret information in another one for security purpose. The origin of steganogaraphy is 450 BC. But the concept of steganography was formulated from the 15th century. The name of the steganography was created by two greek words which are 'stegano' and 'grafia'. The meaning of stegano is secret and grafia is writing. Although this word is exists in greek but it was not used in any literature. But this word has come to use after a publication on trilogy by Johannes Trithemius in 1606.

1. **Early Steganography:** In days of old, the secret information was concealed in various ways like tattooed on the head of slave, concealed on pills capped with paraffin, wrote on the tummy of dogs, etc,. In the time of 484-425 BC, Herodotus used steganography concept to transfer the information his master . He shaved the head of the slave and the information to conceal was tattooed on his head and capped with growing hair (Swetha V, Prajith V, & Kshema V, 2015). Whenever the slave reached the destination, the head was shaved to recover the concealed message. In earliest of greece paraffin capped pills are used to transfer the concealed information. In this procedure, tablet-shaped wood is used. The secret message was scrapped on the pill of wood and then covered with paraffin. Once this tablet reached the destination and then paraffin was removed on the tablet to recover the message. At that time, another technique was also used to conceal the information in women earring or eagle legs.

2. **Linguistic Steganography:** It is one of the oldest steganography techniques. Aeneas Tactician develops the linguistic techniques and leads to linguistic steganogarphy. It can be treated as text steganography (Swetha V, Prajith V, & Kshema V, 2015). Aeneas Tactician achieves the steganography by marking the letters with small dos or holes. Francis Bacon proposed another linguistic steganogarphy, in which secret letters are concealed in binary form using italic format. Brewster

proposed a photographic technique in 1857. In this technique the secret letters size are reduced to dirt-sized. This stegano message can be read at only high levels of magnification. This technique is used during the period of world war-1 by the germans.

3. **Modern Steganography:** The steganography technologies are changing rapidly. It plays an important role while transferring the secret information through the internet. Various multimedia files like 2D-image, audio signal and video are used as a cover files to conceal the secret information. The usage of technologies increases day by day for the data transfer through the internet (Swetha V, Prajith V, & Kshema V, 2015). So it is very important to provide the secured data transmission otherwise data will be hacked by the hackers. The solution of this problem is to use the modern steganography. In modern steganography, the concealed secret information can't be identified by the hacker and looks like an ordinary multimedia file. The hidden capacity of secret information depends upon the size of the cover multimedia file. The steganography can be classified as follows based on the cover file.

    a. **Image Steganography:** In Image steganography the cover medium is image. If the secret information was concealed in the image, it is called image steganography. In this technique, the information is concealed in image by using the pixel values and secret key. The vessel or container is another name of the cover image. The resultant image of after concealment of information in the container image is called stego image. The secret information can be recovered from the stego-image by using the secret key used in the encryption procedure.

    b. **Network Steganography:** In network steganography the cover medium is network protocols. If the secret information was concealed in the network protocols it is called network steganography (Shivani Khosla, & Paramjeet Kaur, 2014). In network steganography, TCP,UDP,ICMP are used as a network protocols. The protocol steganography is the another name of the network steganography.

    c. **Video Steganography:** In video steganograph the cover medium is video. If the secret information was concealed in the video is called video steganography. In this technique, any kind of files is concealed in the video by using the pixel values and secret key. Video is nothing but a combination of successive frames .The resultant video of the concealed information in the cover video is called stego-video. The video formats are used in video steganography are .MP4, MPEG, .AVI, .3GP, etc,.

    d. **Audio Steganography:** Voice signal is used as a cover file in audio steganography. If the secret information was concealed in the popular audio it is called audio steganography. The formats of the audio steganography are .WAV, MIDI, etc,.

4. **Dwt Based Data Hiding Using Video Steganography:** This is one of the methods to achieve the video steganography by using DWT (S.Kamesh, K.Durga Devi, & S.N.V.P.Raviteja, 2017). This method contains two domains such as encryption and decryption. Encryption operation is performed at the transmitter side and another one at the receiver side. The algorithm of video steganography usig DWT at transmitter side is as follows.

    a. Select the cover video and the cover video format may be any one of the formats like .MP4, MPEG, .AVI, .3GP.

    b. Convert the cover video into number of frames. Each frame act as an image.

    c. Apply the DWT to all frames, and then four sub-band images are generated.

    d. Select any one sub band and conceal the secret information in predefined chosen location.

    e. This procedure is repeated until the end of last frame.

f.   All stego-frames are reconstructed into video is called stego-video.
     The algorithm of video steganography usig DWT at receiver side is as follows.

g.   The stego-video is converted into number of frames

h.   Apply the DWT to all frames, and then four sub-band images are generated.

i.   Select the appropriate sub band and collect the secret information from predefined chosen location.

j.   This procedure is repeated until the end of the last frame.

k.   Finally, the secret information was obtained.

In this technique, there are some drawbacks. Here DWT is time variant transform and also performs the down sampling. In this method, single level DWT is applied. Hence there may be a chance to recover the information by the hacker. The stego-video is not same as the cover video. These drawbacks can be overcome by proposed method

STATIONARY WAVELET TRANSFORM (SWT)

Discrete Wavelet Transform (DWT) is a time variant transform. The drawback of DWT can be overcome by Stationary Wavelet Transform (SWT) (Mirajkar Pradnya P, & Sachin D. Ruikar, 2013). SWT is designed to achieve the translation invariance. This can be achieved by eliminating the DWT downsamplers and DWT upsamplers besides upsampling the coefficients of filter by a factor of 2(j-1). In SWT, filters are applied at each level. In this, filters are applied first to the rows and then filters are applied to columns.

Decimation process is not performed in SWT. If SWT is applied to one particular image then four sub band images are produced. One for approximation and remaining three are detailed images. The names of the three detailed images are horizontal, vertical and diagonal. These four images are having half of the resolution of the previous one. The sizes of the four sub band images are same. The resultant images of the SWT algorithm are represented in the levels of parallel piped mechanism as shown in Figure 2.

Figure 2. Block diagram of SWT

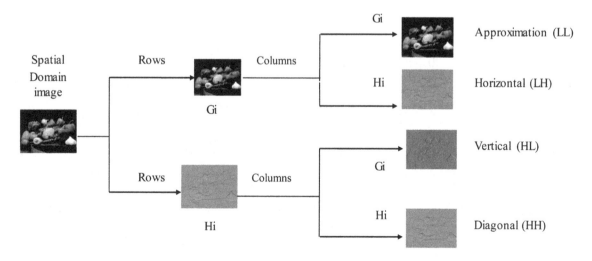

Gi and Hi in Figure 2 represents the low pass and high pass filters. The results of approximation and detail coefficients after SWT to an image are shown in Figure 2. DWT and SWT are similar processes, but SWT only suppresses the down sampling. The block diagram of SWT decomposition is shown in Figure 2. In the above SWT decomposition, decimation operation is not performed at any level. Decimation process is applied to DWT decomposition and upsampling is applied to inverse DWT decomposition.

Singular Value Decomposition

Singular Value Decomposition of a matrix D is given as $D = S*V*C^T$ where V is diagonal matrix whose size is m×n and its diagonal values are singular and CT is the complex conjugate of the transpose of C for which the size is n×n (Qiuping Wang, Junwen Ma, Xiaofeng Wang, & Fengqun Zhao 2017). S and C are unitary matrices and these contained singular vectors as columns. The size of Matrix S is m×m. The SVD of a matrix D can be factored into three components for which the product $D = S*V*C^T$. The concept of SVD is widely used for many purposes. Data matrix D is used to find the low rank matrix which is an approximate of D. We can generate matrix B of rank K which is closely an approximation of D by performing SVD of D. SVD is applicable for all matrices such as square, rectangular, diagonal etc.,. In SVD, the columns of C and the columns of S are called right singular vectors and left singular vectors respectively. These vectors form an orthogonal set. If the matrix D is square matrix and invertible the inverse of $D = S* V *C^T$. The calculation of SVD of a particular matrix D can be explained as below.

$$D = \begin{matrix} 2 & 4 & 8 \\ 8 & 9 & 4 \\ 7 & 5 & 5 \end{matrix} \qquad (1)$$

The components of SVD for the above matrix D are given as

$$S = \begin{matrix} -0.4432 & 0.8692 & -0.2192 \\ -0.7019 & -0.4886 & -0.5183 \\ -0.5576 & -0.0758 & 0.8267 \end{matrix} \qquad (2)$$

$$V = \begin{matrix} 17.6110 & 0 & 0 \\ 0 & 5.5074 & 0 \\ 0 & 0 & 1.8765 \end{matrix} \qquad (3)$$

$$C =$$

$$
\begin{array}{ccc}
-0.5908 & -0.4904 & 0.6407 \\
-0.6177 & -0.2359 & -0.7502 \\
-0.5190 & 0.8390 & 0.1635
\end{array}
\tag{4}
$$

Proposed Method

This paper contains two modules. First one is transmitter module and second one is receiver module. The block diagram of transmitter and receiver module is shown Figure 3 and Figure 4 respectively. Transmitter module is used to encrypt the secret data or text data into cover video to generate the stego-video. The generated stego-video is transmitted into receiver. Receiver module is used to decrypt the stego video with appropriate key values to generate the secret data or text data.

In transmitter module, a cover video is taken, the length of which decides the number of characters of the text message to be encrypted. This cover video may exist in any format like .AVI, .MP4, .3GP,etc,. This cover video is converted into frames. The length of the frames is equal to the length of the video. Each frame of the video can act as an image.

Now single level SWT is applied to the frame of the video then obtained four sub-band images namely approximation (LL1), horizontal (LH1), vertical (HL1) and diagonal (HH1). SWT performs the translation invariance to each frame of the video. This can be achieved by eliminating the DWT downsamplers and DWT upsamplers besides upsampling the coefficients of filter by a factor of $2^{(j-1)}$. In SWT, filters are applied at each level. In this, filters are applied first to the rows and then to columns of frame of the video which results four sub band images namely approximation (LL1), horizontal (LH1), vertical (HL1) and diagonal (HH1).

Select the any one of the sub-band, apply SVD and second level SWT. After applying the second level SWT then another four sub-bands are obtained namely approximation (LL2), horizontal (LH2), vertical (HL2) and diagonal (HH2). Select any one of the sub-band among the eight sub-bands and then apply the SVD.

The sub-band image contains rows and columns appearing as a matrix. Singular Value Decomposition of a frame D is given as $D = S*V*C^T$ where V is diagonal matrix (frame) whose size is m×n and its diagonal values are singular and C^T is the complex conjugate of the transpose of C for which the size is n×n. S and C are unitary matrices (frames) and these contained singular vectors as columns. The size of Matrix (frame) S is m×m. Data matrix (frame) D is used to find the low rank matrix which is an approximate of D.

After applying the SVD, each character of text data is converted into a value and it is added with a specific key value. This key value can be generated randomly. This value is placed in any one location in the selected sub-band image. After placing the character of the text message in the image then apply 2-level inverse SWT. The inverse SWT is nothing but a reverse process of SWT. This process is repeated until the end of characters of the message.

Due to the above process obtain the text encrypted images. These encrypted images are converted into video format. The look of this video is same as the original video but this video has secret message which is called Stego-video. This stego-video can be generated in any video format like .AVI, .MP4, .3GP, etc,.

In receiver module, the stego-video is converted into frames. This stego-video may exist in any format like.AVI, .MP4, .3GP,etc,. Each frame of which can act as an image. Now first level SWT is applied to a frame of this video then obtained four sub-band images namely approximation (LL1), horizontal (LH1), vertical (HL1) and diagonal (HH1).

Select the appropriate sub-band, apply SVD and second level SWT. After applying the second level SWT then another four sub-bands are obtained namely approximation (LL2), horizontal (LH2), vertical (HL2) and diagonal (HH2). Select the appropriate sub-band among the eight sub-bands and then apply the SVD.

After applying the SVD, pick up the value from the appropriate position. This value is subtracted by the known key value and then converted into character. The same procedure is repeated until the end of the images. Due to the above process obtain the secret message from the stego-video.

Results

The transmitter of GUI window is shown in Figure 5. The cover videos is selected by clicking the VIDEO SELECTION push button then open the new window and browse the one suitable video among the several videos. The secret message can be given by clicking the INPUT TEXT push button then new window is opened and entered the text in that window on the GUI window.. The number of frames and characters are displayed in the indicated static boxes shown in Figure 5. The Encryption can be done by clicking the ENCRYPTION push button. The selected cover video and encrypted video can be played by clicking the PLAY button. The applied secret message can be separately shown in notepad file with the name of ENCRYPTED is shown in Figure 6.

Figure 3. Block diagram of transmitter module

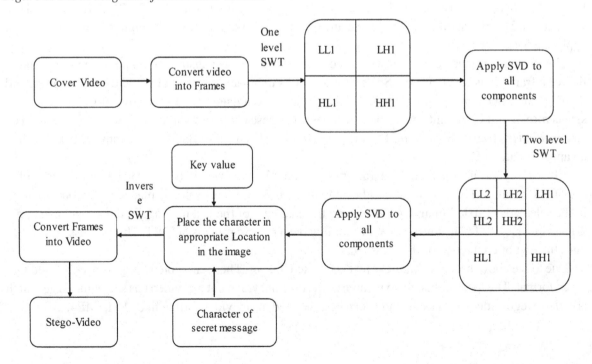

Figure 4. Block diagram of receiver Module

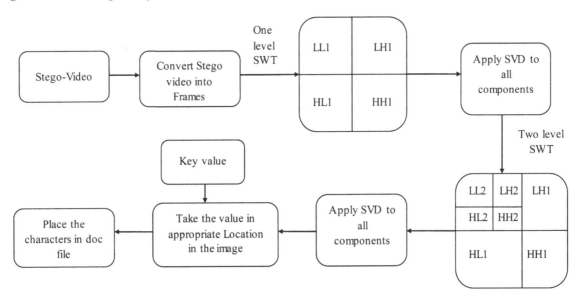

Figure 5. Transmitter Module

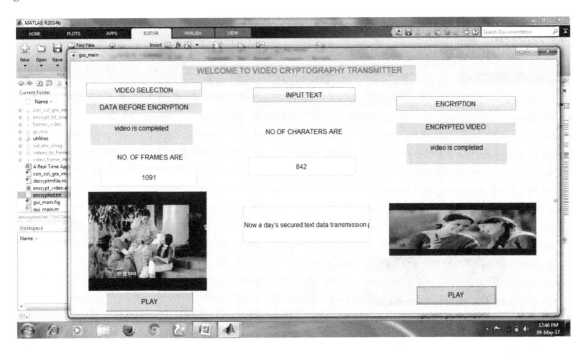

The receiver of GUI window is shown in Figure 7. The stego video is applied by clicking the VIDEO SELECTION push button then new window is opened and select the stego video on the GUI window. The stego video can be played by clicking the play button on the GUI window. DECRYPTION button is pressed to retrieve the original message. This decrypted message is separately shown in notepad file with the name of DECRYPTED is shown in Figure 8.

Figure 6. Notepad file for encryption

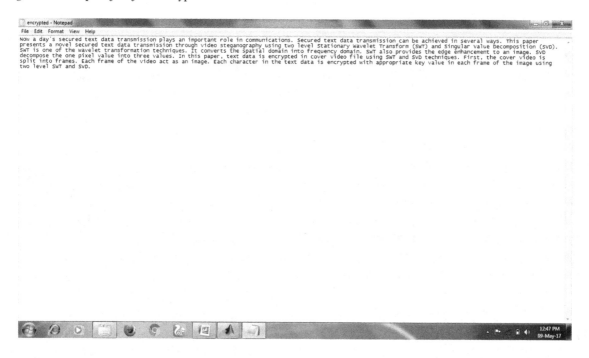

Figure 7. Receiver Module

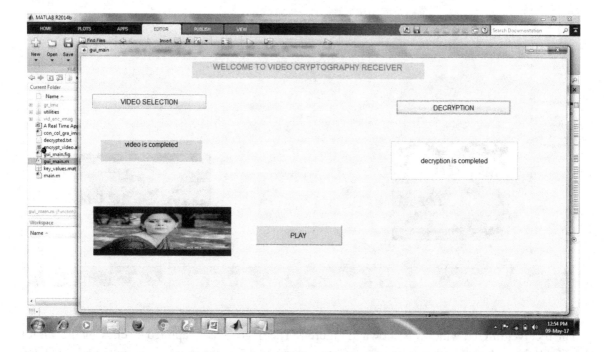

Figure 8. Decrypted notepad file

CONCLUSION

In this paper, It is effectively designed the encryption and decryption procedure by using the video. A stego-video is developed by using SWT and SVD algorithms which keeps a stego video looking alike the cover video. The message before encryption and after decryption is separately shown in notepad files. This proposed method is more secure method for data communication and it is checked by taking the message and hiding it in a video and the results of the experiment are obtained successfully. The future work is using a different algorithm other than SWT and SVD. It can also use two videos as an input and hiding the secret message in both input videos. The other quality features can be checked to verify the quality of the algorithm.

REFERENCES

Abdulaziz, N. K., & Pang, K. K. (2000). Robust data hiding for images. *Proceedings of IEEE International Conference on Communication Technology, WCC-ICCT*, 2, 380-383.

Chincholkar, A. A., & Urkude, D. A. (2012). Design and Implementation of Image Steganography. *Journal of Signal and Image Processing, 3*(3), 111–113.

Hwang, R. J., Shih, K. T., & Kao, C. H. (2001). Lossy compression tolerant steganography, *Proceedings of the 1st International Conference on The Human Society and the Internet-Internet Related Socio-Economic Issues, Lecture Notes In Computer Science*, 2105, 427-435. 10.1007/3-540-47749-7_34

Kamesh, S., Durga Devi, K., & Raviteja, S. N. V. P. (2017). Dwt Based Data Hiding Using Video Steganography. *International Journal of Engineering Sciences & Research Technology,* 361-367.

Kaur, Kaur, & Singh. (2011). Steganographic approach for hiding image in dct domain. *International Journal of Advances in Engineering and Technology*, 1(3).

Khosla & Kaur. (2014). Secure Data Hiding Technique Using Video Steganography and Watermarking. *International Journal of Computer Applications, 95.*

Kumar & Pooja. (2010). Steganography A Data Hiding Technique. *International Journal of Computer Applications*, 9(7).

Mirajkar Pradnya, & Ruikar. (2013). Image Fusion Based On Stationary Wavelet Transform. *International Journal of Advanced Engineering Research and Studies*, 99-101.

Mstafa, R. J., Elleithy, K. M., & Abdelfattah, E. (2017). A Robust and Secure Video Steganography Method in DWT-DCT Domains Based on Multiple Object Tracking and ECC. *IEEE Access: Practical Innovations, Open Solutions, 5,* 5354–5365.

Nosrati, Karimi, & Hariri. (2012). Video Steganography A Survey on Recent Approaches. *World Applied Programming*, 2(3).

Sadasiva Rao, K. S., & Damodaram, A. (2017). A steganographic technique for transferring source image file without stego file with high level of robustness. *International Conference on Inventive Systems and Control (ICISC),* 1-4.

Sadek, Khalifa, & Mostafa. (2015). *Video steganography: a comprehensive review.* Springer Science+Business Media. DOI 10.1007/s11042-014-1952-z

Singh. (2014). Video Steganography Text Hiding In Video By LSB Substitution. *International Journal of Engineering Research and Applications*, 4, 105-108.

Swetha, V., Prajith, V., & Kshema, V. (2015). Data Hiding Using Video Steganography-A Survey. *International Journal of Computer Science & Engineering Technology*, 5, 206–213.

Wang, Q., Ma, J., Wang, X., & Zhao, F. (2017). Image watermarking algorithm based on grey relational analysis and singular value decomposition in wavelet domain. *Proceedings of 2017 International Conference on Grey Systems and Intelligent Services (GSIS)*, 94-98. 10.1109/GSIS.2017.8077676

KEY TERMS AND DEFINITIONS

Cover Video: The video in which information is concealed.

Digital Watermarking: The secret image concealed in cover image is called digital watermarking.

Discrete Wavelet Transform: Discrete wavelet transform (DWT) is a time variant transform that is used to find the wavelet coefficients.

Singular Value Decomposition: It is used to find the factorization of the matrix or image.

Spatial Domain: The pixel representation of the image is called spatial domain. In spatial domain, the operations are directly applied to pixel values.

Stego Video: The appearing video after the steganography.

SWT Sub-Bands: The sub-bands generated after applying the SWT.

Chapter 18
Overview of Concept Drifts Detection Methodology in Data Stream

Shabina Sayed
Jodhpur National University, India

Shoeb Ahemd Ansari
Shri Jagadish Prasad Jabnormal Tibrewala University, India

Rakesh Poonia
Bikaner Government College of Engineering, India

ABSTRACT

Real-time online applications and mobile data generate huge volume of data. There is a need to process this data into compact data structures and extract meaningful information. A number of approaches have been proposed in literature to overcome the issues of data stream mining. This chapter summarizes various issues and application techniques. The chapter is a guideline for research to identify the research issues and select the most appropriate method in order to detect and process novel class.

INTRODUCTION

Consistently, enormous volumes of tactile, value-based, and web information are ceaselessly created as streams, which should be examined online as they arrive. The volumes of naturally produced information are continually expanding. As indicated by (Gantz and Reinsel, 2012) more than 2.8ZB of information were made and prepared in 2012, with an anticipated increment of 15 times by 2020. The different issues (Mark G et. al, 1999) in handling information stream are recorded in Table 1. The incredible development in the creation of computerized information comes about because of our encompassing condition being furnished with an ever-increasing number of sensors. Individuals conveying advanced mobile phones deliver information, database exchanges are being checked and put away, surges of information are removed from virtual conditions as logs or client produced. A noteworthy piece of such informa-

DOI: 10.4018/978-1-5225-3870-7.ch018

tion is unpredictable, which implies it should be dissected progressively as it arrives. The appropriation creating the things of an information stream can change after some time. These changes, depending on the research area, are referred to as temporal evolution, covariate shift, nonstationary or concept drift (Bifet et.al, 2009). The principle qualities of the information stream display infer the accompanying limitations (Bifet, 2009):

- It is difficult to store all the information from the information stream. Just little outlines of information streams can be processed and put away, and whatever is left of the data is discarded.
- The incoming speed of information stream tuple compels every specific component to be handled essentially in real time and afterward disposed of.
- The dispersion producing the things can change after some time. Along these lines, information from the past may wind up plainly insignificant or even unsafe for the current summary.

CONCEPT DRIFT

A normal for information stream is consistent stream of information. Information measure is to a great degree expansive and possibly unending. It's impractical to store all information. Be that as it may, significant issues identified with information stream mining are Boundless length, novel class advancement, and novel class float. Boundless length implies information stream have a vast length so require limitless length storage and training time. Concept evolution (John F et. al, 2008) implies creating novel class and Concept drift implies information changes after some time. The most prominent case to introduce the issue of concept drift is that of distinguishing and sifting through spam email. The refinement amongst undesirable and honest to goodness messages is user specific and advances with time. Novel class does not exist on the off chance that we expect no of classes are settled. Be that as it may, sometime information stream characterization issue happen like intrusion detection, content grouping, and fault detection. So this presumption is not substantial for real streaming environment, at the point when new classes might be develop whenever. Most existing information stream characterization procedure disregards this critical part of stream information, which is the landing of a Novel Class. Concept evolution takes care of the issue of endless length and novel class. As concept drift is thought to be erratic, occasional regularity is typically not considered as a novel class issue. As a special case, if regularity is not known with assurance, it may be viewed as a concept drift issue. The center supposition, when managing the concept drift issue, is vulnerability about what's to come. We expect that the wellspring of the objective occasion is not known with sureness. It can be accepted, evaluated, or anticipated, yet there is no assurance (˘Zliobait, 2010). (Mark G, 1999) displayed three routes in which concept drift may happen: A normal for information stream is nonstop stream of information. Information estimate is amazingly substantial and conceivably limitless. It's impractical to store all information. Be that as it may, significant issues identified with information stream mining are: Unending length, concept evolution, and concept drift. Unending length implies information stream have a vast length so require interminable length stockpiling and training time. Concept evolution (John F. et. al, 2008) implies creating novel class and drift may occur:

- Prior probabilities of classes, $P(c_1),..., P(c_k)$ may change over time,
- Class-conditional probability distributions, $P(X|c_i)$, $i = 1,..., k$ might change,

Table 1.Classification of data stream mining challenges

Research	Issues	Challenges Approaches
Memory management	Fluctuated and irregular data Arrival rate over time	Summarizing techniques
Data pre-processing	Quality of mining results and automation of pre-processing technique	Light-weight pre-processing
Compact data structure	Limited memory size and large volume of data stream	Incremental maintaining of data structure, novel indexing, storage and querying techniques
Resource-aware	Limited resources like storage and computation capabilities	AOG
Visualization of results	Problems in data analysis and quick decision making by user	Still is a research issue.

- Posterior probabilities $P(c_i|X)$, $i = 1,...., k$ might change.

It is important that the conveyances $P(X \mid ci)$ may change such that the class participation is not influenced (e.g. symmetric development to opposite direction). This is one reason why this kind of changed is frequently known as virtual drift and change in $P(c_i \mid X)$ is referred as real drift. Figure 1 shows six fundamental sorts of changes that may happen in a solitary variable along time. The main plot (Sudden) indicates unexpected changes that immediately and irreversibly change the variables class membership. Genuine cases of such changes incorporate season change in deals. The following two plots (Incremental and Gradual) show changes that happen gradually after some time. Incremental float happens when factors gradually change their values after some time, and progressive drift happens when the change includes the class appropriation of factors. A few specialists don't recognize these two sorts of drift and utilize the terms gradual and incremental as equivalent words. An ordinary case of incremental drift is value development because of expansion, while continuous changes are exemplified by gradually changing meanings of spam or client fascinating news encourages. The left-base plot (Recurring) speaks to changes that are just brief and are returned after some time. This kind of progress is viewed by a few analysts as local drift. It happens when a few information producing sources are required to switch after some time and return at irregular time interims. This drift is not unquestionably intermittent, it is not clear when the source may return, that is the difference from the seasonality concept used in statistics (ˇZliobait ́, 2010). The fifth plot (Blip) speaks to an "uncommon occasion", which could be viewed as an anomaly in a static conveyance. In spilling information, identified blips ought to be disregarded as the change they speak to is arbitrary. Cases of blips incorporate irregularities in landfill gas discharge, fake card exchanges, and system interruption. The last plot in Figure 1 speaks to irregular changes, which ought to be shifted through. Noise should not be considered as concept drift as it is an inconsequential variance that is not associated with any adjustment in the source dispersion.

Speed of progress is by all account not the only normal for drifts. The seriousness of a drift likewise assumes an imperative part. In the writing (Minku and Yao, 2009) the seriousness is defined as follows. Assume cases of context C_i and cases of the accompanying context C_{i+1} are from some info space S. Cases from context, C_i and C_{i+1}, can show up during the drift. The seriousness of drift is defined as the rate of S that has its class label changed after the drift is finished, that is when just the cases of C_{i+1} are emitted.

Figure 1. Types of changes in streaming data, apart from noise and blip, all the presented changes are treated as concept drift and require model adaptation

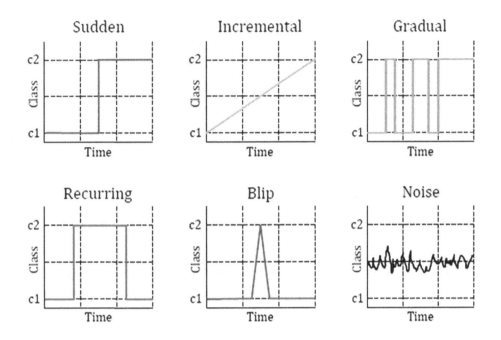

NOVEL CLASS DETECTION

In all genuine circumstances, the concept we are attempting to model may change throughout adapting, particularly when information are investigated over longer timeframes. This is an essential issue when gaining from information streams because of their dynamic nature. The adjustments in the hidden factors or setting instigate changes in the objective idea which is known as concept drift. Diverse systems are considered. Methods have their calculations which are assessed broadly in an assortment of settings including artificial and real data. To the best of our insight, there is no other universally useful algorithm for incremental realizing which can perform explicit change identification and perform adaptation. Decision tree, neural system, regression are couple of algorithm that can perform online and in real time. They watch every illustration just once at the speed of entry and maintain at any-time a ready-to-use model.

APPLICATIONS

Table 2 provide some of the main data stream application domains in which concept drift plays an important role. It lists the various application of data stream in various sectors.

Table 2. Data mining application in various sectors

Monitoring system	DSS	Agriculture	Retail industry	Healthcare	AI
Network security	Finance	Climate influence on crops	Market basket analysis	Insurance fraud detection	Navigation system
Transportation	Biomedical application	Crop yield estimation	Cross marketing	CRM	Smart home and virtual reality
Industrial monitoring	Telecommunication	Pest control damage	Sequence pattern discovery	Better and more affordable health service.	Biological data and DNA analysis
Newsfeed	Recommendation system	Mushroom grading	Sales analysis and forecast	Identification of effective treatment	Spam filtering

BACKGROUND AND MAIN FOCUS

Single Classifier

Traditional classifier consists of single classifier. They used to process streaming data. They have ability of online learning and forgetting mechanism. These classifiers have ability to process data but they cannot adapt according to the concept drift. These classifiers are based on neural network, Naive Bayes, nearest neighbor, and decision rule. The analytical framework of single classifier is as shown in Table 3.Windowing technique deal with time changing data. It uses sliding window. This method considers most learners to be adapted to data stream. Based on the concept of hoeffding bound (Domingo and Hulton, 2000) proposed a new classifier called as very fast decision rule (VFDR).This algorithm induces a decision tree from data stream incrementally, without the need for storing example after they have been used to update the tree. It can be used for any type of distribution. A disadvantage of this method is, it is more conservative than a distribution depended bound. Thus it requires more example than really necessary.

VFDT was design for static data steam and provide no forgetting mechanism. (Hulten, 2001) in his paper" Mining time changing data stream" proposed a new method called CVFDT. It uses fixed size window to determine which nodes are aging and may need updating. Outdated examples are forgotten by updating node statistic and necessary model changes are performed on subtree rather than whole classifier. EWMA or ADWIN method gives better performance than CVFDT. The only problem with these methods is they require more time to process a single example.

Table 3. Analytical framework of single classifier

Type	Classifier	Author	Year	Description
Weighted Window-based	FISH FAMILY ADWIN	Zliobate Albert Bifet	2010,2006 2007	Suitable for dynamic data Suitable when sudden drift
Drift detector	DDM EDM	Gama et.al Baena andGarcia	2004 2006	Uses binomial distribution Uses distance error rate
Hoeffding tree	VFDT CVFDT	Domingoand Holting Hulten	2000 2001	Incremental decision tree Forgetting mechanism

ENSEMBLE CLASSIFIER

Ensemble algorithm is sets of single classifier whose decision is aggregated by voting rule. Their combine Decision to classify an example is more accurate than that of single classier. Studies shows that to boost their decision it is necessary that classifier should be differ each other by the data they have been trained on, the attribute they use or base learner they are created from. The analytical framework for ensemble classifier is as shown in Table 4 ensemble training is a costly process. It requires at least k time more accuracy than training of single classifier. In addition to this member selection and weighted assignment is a lengthy process. In a massive data stream single classifier works well but when accuracy is required ensemble is the best solution.

Streaming ensemble algorithm (SEA) is proposed by (Street and Kim, 2001).It changes its structure according to the drift. If any ensemble classifier is weaker, then it is dropped and new classifier takes its place. They assign weight to each classifier according to their accuracy and additionally diversify the candidate classifier weight. According to (Bifet, 2009) SEA perform best when no more than 25 classifier were used, base classifier are un pruned and simple majority voting is used.

AWE proposed by (Wang et.al, 2003). They train a new classifier C on each incoming data chunk and uses that chunk to evaluate all existing ensemble member to select best classifier. AWE works well on data stream with recurring concept as well as different type of drift. Its performance depends on the data chunk size.

HOT proposed by (Kirkby, 2007) provides a compact structure that works like a set of weighted classifier. Just like regular hoeffding tree, they are built in incremental fashion. HOT is accurate but time and memory expensive. Traditional ensemble methods are fast but less accurate. ASHT bagging proposed by (Bifet, 2006 and 2007). It diversifies ensemble member by using chunks of different size. ASHT bagging provides a forgetting mechanism. It is more accurate than HOT but it is also time and memory expensive.

CONCLUSION

As indicated by above area there is a need to design ensemble classifier with weighted member. The member can be include or expel effectively. They ought to dependably be refreshed. There ought not to be any farthest point on their base classifier estimate. They ought not to utilize any windows based technique. They should refresh classifiers just on the off chance that they are sufficiently exact as per current dispersion. Numerous choice undertakings can be figured as stream mining issues and in this

Table 4. Analytical framework of single classifier

Type	Classifier	Author	Year	Description
Streaming ensemble	SEA	Street andKim	2001	Works well up to 25 components
Adaptive ensemble	AWE	Wang et.al	2003	Performance depend on data chunk size
Incremental ensemble	HOT	R.Kirby	2007	Time andmemory expensive
	ASHT bagging	Albert Bifet et.al	2009	Forgetting mechanism

way, numerous new algorithms for information streams have been proposed. Decision rules are a standout amongst the most interpretable and flexible models for predictive information mining. By the by, just a couple of algorithm have been proposed in the literature to learn rule models for time changing and rapid stream of information. As there are a few applications which introduce inherent incremental conditions and permit heavier memory and time necessities. Incremental learning is as yet a critical range of study. However, besides the fact that incremental learning approaches present the problems explained above, online approaches can be used to solve both online and incremental problems.

REFERENCES

Bifet, Holmes, Fahringer, Kirkby, & Gavald. (2009). A New ensemble method for evolving data streams. KDD, 139–148.

Bifet, A., & Gavald, R. (2006). A. Kalman filters and adaptive windows for learning in data streams. *Discovery Science, 4625,* 29–40.

Bifet, A., & Gavald, R. (2007). *A Learning from time-changing data with adaptive windowing. SDM.* SIAM.

Bifet, A., Holmes, G., Pfahringer, B., & Gavald, R. (2009). A Improving adaptive bagging methods for evolving data streams. *ACML, 5828,* 23–37.

Bifet. (2009). *Adaptive learning and mining for data streams and frequent patterns* (Ph.D. thesis). Universitat Polit'ecnica de Catalunya.

Domingos, P., & Hulten, G. (2000). Mining high-speed data streams. *KDD: Proceedings / International Conference on Knowledge Discovery & Data Mining. International Conference on Knowledge Discovery & Data Mining,* 71–80.

Gama, J., Medas, P., Castillo, G., & Rodrigues, P. (2004). Learning with drift detection. *SBIA Brazilian Symposium on Artificial Intelligence,* 286–295.

Gantz, J., & Reinsel, D. (2012). *The digital universe in 2020: Big data, bigger digital shadows, and biggest growth in the Far East.* Academic Press.

Gantz, J. F., Reinsel, D., Chute, C., Schlichting, W., Minton, S., Toncheva, A., & Manfrediz, A. (2008). *The expanding digital universe: An updated forecast of worldwide information growth through 2011. Technical report.* IDC Information and Data.

Garc'ia, Campovila, Fidalgo, Bifet, Gavald'a, & Morales-Bueno. (2006). Early drift detection method. *Fourth International Workshop on Knowledge Discovery from Data Streams.*

Hulten, G., Spencer, L., & Domingos, P. (2001). Mining time-changing data streams. *KDD: Proceedings / International Conference on Knowledge Discovery & Data Mining. International Conference on Knowledge Discovery & Data Mining,* 97–106.

Kelly, M. G., Hand, D. J., & Adams, N. M. (1999). The impact of changing populations on classifier performance. *KDD: Proceedings / International Conference on Knowledge Discovery & Data Mining. International Conference on Knowledge Discovery & Data Mining*, 367–371. doi:10.1145/312129.312285

Kholghi & Keyvanpour. (2011). An analytical framework for Data stream mining techniques Based on challenges and Requirements. *IJEST*, *3*, 2507-2513.

Kirkby, R. (2007). *Improving Hoeffding Trees* (Ph.D thesis). Department of Computer Science, University of Waikato.

Minku, L. L., & Yao, X. (2012). DDD: A New Ensemble Approach for Dealing With Concept Drift. *IEEE Transactions on Knowledge and Data Engineering*, *24*(4), 619–633. doi:10.1109/TKDE.2011.58

Roberts. (2000). Control chart tests based on geometric moving averages. *Technometrics*, *42*(1), 97–101.

Street & Kim. (2001). A streaming ensemble algorithm(SEA) for large-scale classification. *KDD*, 377–382.

Wang, H., Fan, W., Philip, S. Yu., & Han, J. (2003). Mining concept-drifting data streams using ensemble classifiers. *KDD: Proceedings / International Conference on Knowledge Discovery & Data Mining. International Conference on Knowledge Discovery & Data Mining*, 226–235.

Zliobaite. (2010). *Adaptive training set formation* (Ph.D thesis). Vilnius University.

KEY TERMS AND DEFINITIONS

Concept Drift: It is defined as change in the underlying class of the data due to change in the behavior.

Data Stream: It is continuous, real-time huge volume of data generated continuously from various online applications.

DSM: Is an abbreviation used for data stream mining.

Ensemble Classifier: It consists of more than one classifier for data classification.

Novel Class: It is defined as a newly discovered class that was previously unknown.

Single Classifier: It consists of only one classifier of any time for classifying the data.

Chapter 19
Fast Fractal Image Compression by Kicking Out Similar Domain Images

Shilpi Sharma
Birla Institute of Technology and Science, India

Arvind Kumar Kourav
Birla Institute of Technology and Science, India

Vimal Tiwari
Birla Institute of Technology and Science, India

ABSTRACT

Fractal algorithms are used to represent similar parts of images into mathematical transforms that can recreate the original image. This chapter presents a fast fractal image compression technique via domain kick-out method, based on averaging of domain images to discard redundant domain images. It accelerates the encoding process by reducing the size of the domain pool. Results of a simulation on the proposed speedup technique on three standard test images shows that performance of the proposed technique is far superior to the present kick out methods of fractal image compression. It has reported a speedup ratio of 31.07 in average while resulting into compression ratio and retrieved image quality comparable to Jacquin's full search method.

INTRODUCTION

Fractal Image compression is an innovative technique in the field of image compression. This technique is based on the existence of self-symmetry in the image. It is a lossy image compression method and achieves high levels of compression. The method is best suited for photographs of natural scenes. This technique has grabbed much consideration in recent years because of various advantages like, very high compression ratio, high decompression speed, high bit-rate and resolution independence. Fractal theories are totally different from the others, its phenomenon is based on fractals rather than pixels. Fractal im-

DOI: 10.4018/978-1-5225-3870-7.ch019

age compression is also called as fractal image encoding because compressed image is represented by contractive transforms and mathematical functions required for reconstruction of original image. These transforms are composed of the union of a number of affine mappings on the entire image, known as iterated function system (IFS). The usual approach of fractal image compression is based on the college theorem, which provides distance between the image to be encoded and the fixed point of a transform, in terms of the distance between the transformed image and the image itself. This distance is known as college error and it should be as small as possible.

BACKGROUND AND MAIN FOCUS

Fractal encoding is a mathematical process which is used to encode bitmaps containing a real-world image as a set of mathematical data. This mathematical data describes the fractal properties of any image. Fractal encoding utilizes the fact that all natural, and most artificial, objects contain redundant information in the form of similar, repeating patterns (Benoit Mandelbrot,1982) first observed and described the occurrence of repeating patterns in many different structures; he called these repeating patterns as *fractals*. The theory of iterated function systems was introduced by (Hutchinson,1981). This theory is used to model the collections of contractive transformations in a metric space as dynamical systems(M. Barnsley,1988). His idea was to use the Contractive Mapping Fixed-Point Theorem to show the existence and uniqueness of fractal sets that arise as fixed points of such systems.

M. F. Barnsley observed that many fractals that can be very compactly specified by iterated function systems have a "natural" appearance. Barnsley with S. Demko gave the idea of using iterated function systems (IFS's) to encode images in year(M. Barnsley,1988). This was the seed of the inverse problem of fractal approximation; Barnsley and Demko were the first to suggest that IFS could be used to approximate natural objects. A moderate quality picture on a pixel-by-pixel basis might require more than 500,000 bytes (or characters) of data to store and communicate. But Barnsley's thought if we find IFS whose attractor is the picture;as fairly complicated IFS consumes only a few thousand characters to represent the image. In this way, it occupies far less space to record the IFS than the original picture. Hence representation of image in the form of IFS can also be regarded as Image Compression. A doctoral student of Barnsley's, A.E. Jacquin gave first publication on Fractal image compression with partitioned IFS (PIFS) in 1990 .Jacquin used a block classification scheme(B. Ramamurthy and A. Gersho, 1986,Nasser M. Nasrabadi, and Robert A. King,1988) for his encoding scheme, he partitioned the input image in sub-images called as 'Range blocks' and PIFS are applied on sub-images, rather than the entire image. Each range image is regarded as individual image. This scheme is used worldwide in practical implementation. He purposed the first automatic algorithm in software, in 1992.

FRACTAL IMAGE COMPRESSION

The fractal image encoding is a combination of five sections. Whole process is shown in Figure 1. In any Fractal compression system the first decision is to choose the type of image partitioning scheme for the range blocks formation. A wide variety of partitions have been investigated. Fixed size square blocks are the simplest possible partition (Y. Fisher,1994). Adaptive schemes like Quad-tree partitions(Ruhl, H. Hartenstein and D. Saupe,1997) and Horizontal-Vertical (HV) partitions (Y. Fisher,1994). It uses vari-

Figure 1. Block Diagram of fractal image encoding process

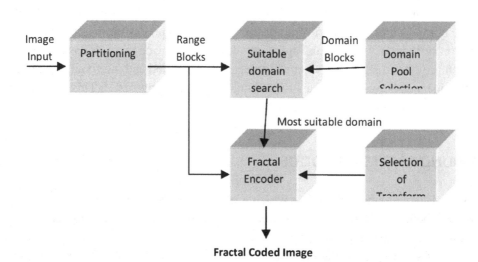

able size of partitions depending on complexity of region. Two innovative techniques are also proposed, Polygonal blocks of different shapes (B. Wohlberg and G.D. Jager,1999,Tanimoto, H. Ohyama and T. Kimoto,1996,F. Davoine, J. Svensson, and J.-M. Chassery,1995) and Irregular partitions. With further advancement a new partition scheme based on Delaunay Triangulation have proposed (F. Davoine, M. Antonini, J.M. Chassery and M. Barlaud,1996), this partition provides a reduced number of blocks as compared to square partitions and, thus minimizes the number of mappings at a rate 0.25 to 0.5 depending on the nature of image.

Domain pool selection is the second level of decision making in fractal image compression. This choice depends on the type of partition scheme used. Since domain blocks must be transformed to cover range blocks. The domain pool in fractal encoding is similar to the codebook in vector quantization (VQ) (B. Ramamurthy &A. Gersho,1986), referred as virtual codebook or domain codebook (A.E Jaquin,1993). Global domain pool was the first and simplest type of domain pool (E.W Jacobs, Y Fisher, & R. D. Boss,1992). In it a fixed domain block is used for all range blocks of image, or for particular class of range blocks in the image. Latter it is observed that the results are much better when spatial distance between range block and respective domain block is less. This requirement restricts the region of domain pool about the range block. The domain pool is generated by following a spiral search path outward from spatial position of range block (J. M. Beaumont,1990). Another way used to generate domain pool is masking of range block. The mask is centred at range block; it is dense near the centre and becomes shallower progressively as we move towards edges. This is known as local domain pool. A more advance type of domain pool is the synthetic codebook (R. Hamzaoui, M. Muller & D. Saupe,1996), here the domain pool is extracted from low resolution image approximation rather then images itself. Sometimes a combination of domain block mapping and fixed VQ-codebook is used; it is called as hybrid codebook and provides much better results.

Selection of the set of transform is the most crucial part of a fractal-encoding scheme. These transforms are applied on domain blocks to form range blocks and determines the convergence properties of decoding. The partition scheme used and the type of domain pool used restrict the choice of transforms. Since domain blocks are mapped into range blocks using these transforms. All the transform used for this purpose should be contractive in nature. Each of transform can skew, stretch, rotate, scale and translate any domain image.

The general form of transformations suggested by Jacquin is given as sum of elementary block transformations (A.E Jaquin,1992).

These transforms do not modify pixel values; they simply shuffle pixels within a range block in a deterministic way. They are also called as isometries. The generally used operators are orthogonal reflection about desired axis and Rotation about centre of block, through some required degree. These transform also perform some gray scale operations like, gray level scaling, Translation and absorption of gray scale. Above explained scheme is universally accepted for fractal transformation. Affine transforms other than isometries have also been considered, and generalized square isometries constructed by conformal mapping from a square to a disk gives improved the performance over the conventional square isometries.

An affine mapping scheme is as well applicable on nonrectangular partitions. These affine transforms require that the vertices of transformed domain blocks should match to the vertices of the range blocks. Another approach is wavelet-Based-Fractal-Transform (WBFT); it links the theory of multi-resolution analysis (MRA) with iterated-function-system (IFS) . It provides a local time frequency analysis on the image as well as an iterative construction of the same image using IFS and fixed-point theory. Transform (1) could be extended by using multiple fixed blocks i.e. fixed blocks with constant gradient in the horizontal and vertical directions respectively. Further extensions are possible by including blocks with quadratic form and also by adding cubic blocks. Second order transform provides best results in a rate distortion sense. Another transformation used in fractal encoding is Discrete-Cosine-Transform (DCT) (Wang X., & Li F.,2009). DCT basis vector is superior then polynomial transform, since they form an efficient basis for image blocks due to existence of mutual orthogonality.

In suitable domain search the most compatible domain block for every range block is searched. Each domain block is transformed by every transform in the IFS and compared with the range block to be encoded. For each comparison the college error is calculated and stored. The domain block and transform corresponding to the least college error are considered as best candidate for the selected range block. This process is repeated for all range blocks. In this way the suitable candidate (suitable domain block) for every range block is searched. This domain block is used as temporary image in encoding phase for respective range block. This phase of fractal image compression consumes huge time because of its high computational expenses.

The range block along with its suitable domain block is given to fractal encoder. In encoding process suitable domain block is mapped to form range block. This mapping is done with the affine transforms. Affine transforms involved in system should be contractive in nature and follow fixed point theorem to ensure the convergence of process. These mathematical transforms are separated and the mapping is repeated for all the range blocks one by one. Union of affine mapping transforms for every range block is formed; this union is the fractal coded image or simply fractal code for image.

In decoding part the fractal codes are applied on any initial image in an iterative loop. Attractor (fix point) of this transformation is the decoded image corresponding to the fractal codes. Decoding of fractal image compression is very simple and fast and can be done on any scale. Quality of retrieved image is independent of the size of decoded image.

PROBLEM FORMULATION

Lots of research is done to search a more efficient partitioning technique to result optimal coverage in least possible number of range images. A wide variety of fast suitable domain search has also been proposed. Domain reduction techniques have performed quite well. Among them kick out based techniques results are of very good quality but there speed is limited. In this research an innovative domain reduction technique based on similarity is proposed. Further the effective numbers of range blocks are reduced by similarity search among them based on feature extraction. As a whole reduction in number of blocks in suitable domain search will lead towards a faster system. Reduction in effective number of range blocks will also provide rise in compression ratio.

METHODOLOGY USED

The number of range-domain comparisons in full-search method comes as $R \times D$. In this proposed speedup method redundant domains is discarded to make a fast fractal image compression system, the process consists of following stages.

- Choosing the image to be compressed (I).
- Size of the image is (S x S).
- Partitioning the image into smaller non-overlapping sub-images of size (r x r) called as range blocks (R_i).
- This process results R range images.
- Partitioning the same image into over-lapping sub-images of size $d \ x \ d: d = 2r$, called as domain blocks (D_j).
- This process results D domain images.
- Now applying the **domain kick-out condition**
- For it first an average domain image is formed by the following process.

AVERAGE DOMAIN IMAGE FORMATION

In the proposed method average domain image ($\overline{A_D}$) is formed.

$$\overline{A_D} = \sum_{j=1}^{D} (\frac{D_j}{D})$$

(1)

where ($\overline{A_D}$) is the average domain image, D_j's is domain images and D is the number of domain images formed after partitioning. It has the same size as that of domain images and gray-level at every pixel is equal to the average of gray-level of corresponding point on all domain images.

$$a_{(xy)} = \frac{1}{D} \sum_{j=1}^{D} D_{j(xy)} \tag{2}$$

where x= 1,2,3….,d , y = 1,2,3…,d

The entire domain images (D_j) are compared with the average domain image ($\overline{A_D}$). The distance between the average domain image ($\overline{A_D}$) and j^{th} domain image is given as

$$d_{rms}(\overline{A_D}, D_j) = [\sum_{\alpha=1}^{d} \sum_{\beta=1}^{d} \{\overline{A_D}(\alpha, \beta) - D_j(\alpha, \beta)\}^2]^{1/2} \tag{3}$$

Here α and β gives the pixel position on the respective image. The distance between Average domain image ($\overline{A_D}$) and j^{th} domain blocks is represented as $\Psi_{\overline{A_D}}(j)$, where

$$\Psi_{\overline{A_D}}(j) = d_{rms}(\overline{A_D}, d(j)) \tag{4}$$

For { j=1 to D}
Then for all the D domain images $\Psi_{\overline{A_D}}(j)$ is calculated and stored, which is given by $\theta(j)$

$$\theta(j) = unique\{\Psi_{\overline{A_D}}(j)\forall j\} \tag{5}$$

So we get all the different (unique) domain images. In this way unique domain images are seek out from the complete domain pool set and the redundant domain blocks are kicked out resulting smaller domain set D_X containing X unique domain blocks.

In the proposed domain kick out method for all the range images R_i suitable domain image is selected from the effective domain blocks D_x instead of the entire domain set. This reduces the SDS time to a large effect. Rest of the processes [transform selection, encoding and decoding] remains the same as the conventional method or base-line [Jacquin's method] which is given in following sections.

SUITABLE DOMAIN SEARCH METHOD

The distance between the ith range image and g[th] domain image is given as

$$d_{rms}(R_i, D_g) = [\sum_{\alpha=1}^{r} \sum_{\beta=1}^{r} \{R_i(\alpha, \beta) - D_j(\alpha, \beta)\}^2]^{1/2} \tag{6}$$

Here α and β gives the pixel position on the respective image. The distance between i^{th} range block and g^{th} domain blocks is represented as $\psi_i(g)$, where

$$\psi_i\,(g) = d_{rms}\,(r\,(i),\,d(g)) \tag{7}$$

For {i = 1 to R and g=1 to X}

Then for any i^{th} range image suitable domain image is searched by finding minimum of $\psi_i(g)$, which is given by $\varphi(i)$.

$$\varphi(i) = \min\left\{\psi_i(g)\forall\ u\right\} \tag{8}$$

If $\varphi(i) = \psi_i(g)$ then we can say that g^{th} domain image shows maximum compatibility with i^{th} range image. In this way suitable domain images for every range image is searched from the reduced domain pool.

At the end of this process we get suitable domain block for all the range blocks from X domain images instead of the entire D domain images. Now transform selection is mentioned in the next section.

TRANSFORMATION SELECTION

In this step of fractal image compression, we choose a set of transforms which are used to form range block by applying them on compatible domain images. Affine transforms are used for this purpose. Since we are using fixed size square partitioning, it is must that transformed image should also be of same shape.

If μ is the image to be transformed, then the eight canonical isometries of a square block are:

1. Identity $(\boldsymbol{i_0})$ $i_0\left(\mu_{i,j}\right) = \mu_{i,j}$
2. Orthogonal reflection about mid-vertical axis $j = 2r - 1/2$ of block $(\boldsymbol{i_1})$ $i_1\left(\mu_{i,j}\right) = \mu_{i,2r-1-j}$
3. Orthogonal reflection about mid-horizontal axis $i = 2r - 1/2$ of block $(\boldsymbol{i_2})$ $i_2\left(\mu_{i,j}\right) = \mu_{2r-1-i,j}$
4. Orthogonal reflection about first diagonal $(i=j)$ of block $(\boldsymbol{i_3})$ $i_3\left(\mu_{i,j}\right) = \mu_{j,i}$
5. Orthogonal reflection about second diagonal $(I + j = 2r - 1)$ of block $(\boldsymbol{i_4})$ $i_4\left(\mu_{i,j}\right) = \mu_{2r-1-j,2r-1-i}$
6. Rotation around centre of block, through $+90^o(\boldsymbol{i_5})$ $i_5\left(\mu_{i,j}\right) = \mu_{j,2r-1-i}$
7. Rotation around centre of block, through $+180^o(\boldsymbol{i_6})$ $i_6\left(\mu_{i,j}\right) = \mu_{2r-1-i,2r-1-j}$
8. Rotation around centre of block, through $-90^o(\boldsymbol{i_7})$ $i_7\left(\mu_{i,j}\right) = \mu_{2r-1-i,j}$

Jacquin have used all the eight isometries in their transformations which are also used in the proposed methods.

FRACTAL ENCODING

This is the final stage of fractal image compression of any image. Here, firstly the range images are formed by applying appropriate transform on their suitable domain images.

A range image R_i is taken with its suitable domain image D_j first need to resize D_j to the size of R_i. The re-sizing of domain image is done by replacing four adjacent pixels from its average value. Then D_j is transformed by set of selected transforms and gives the transformed image $i_k(D_j) \ \forall \ k$. The RMS difference between range image and transformed domain images is computed as

$$d_{rms}(R_i, i_k(D_j)) = \left[\sum_{\alpha=1}^{r} \sum_{\beta=1}^{r} \left\{ R_{i(\alpha,\beta)} - i_k(D_j)_{(\alpha,\beta)} \right\}^2 \right]^{\frac{1}{2}} \tag{9}$$

where $k = 1, 2, \ldots, 8$ *for Jacquin's & proposed method*

Minimum value of computed differences is searched i.e. $\min\{d(R_i, i_k(D_j))\}$. For this minimum difference pair R_i and $i_k(D_j)$, further we need to calculate the contrast control parameter s_i and brightness control parameter o_i. The value of *s* and *o* is based on the distribution of pixel intensities in range image and transformed domain image. Let both of these images contain *n* number of pixels with intensities, $a_1, a_2, \ldots, a_n$ for range image R_i and $b_1, b_2, \ldots, b_n$ for $i_k(D_j)$. Contrast and brightness adjustments are done to have least square distance of affinely transformed a_i values from the b_i values. The optimum value of R_i occurs when the partial derivatives with respect to *s* and *o* are zero, which occurs when the following expressions are satisfied.

$$s = \frac{\left[n\sum_{x=1}^{n} a_x b_x - \sum_{x=1}^{n} a_x \sum_{x=1}^{n} b_x \right]}{\left[n\sum_{x=1}^{n} a_x^2 - \left(\sum_{x=1}^{n} a_x \right)^2 \right]} \tag{10}$$

and

$$o = \frac{1}{n} \left[\sum_{x=1}^{n} b_i - s\sum_{x=1}^{n} a_i \right] \tag{11}$$

The index of suitable domain image, transform i_k for which $d(R_i, i_k(D_j))$ is minimum along with s_i and o_i are stored as an entity w_i. This ensemble of information i.e. w_i is the fractal code for range image R_i. The affine transform for every range image is formed by following the above explained procedure and a union of these affine transforms for all the range images along with index of respective SDB is the Whole Fractal Code (W) for any image.

$$W(.) = \bigcup_{i=1}^{R} w_i(.) \qquad\qquad (12)$$

The W for the given input image would contain the following information:

- Index of suitable domain image.
- Six parameter values of appropriate affine transform.
- Contrast control parameter s.
- Brightness control parameter o.

In this way we can see that the relevant information of whole image is conveyed through few parameter values instead of a large amount of pixel data. This information is sufficient for the reconstruction of image at decoder.

IMPLEMENTATION AND RESULTS

The proposed speedup method is implemented using MATLAB™ version 6.12 on 'Intel *i3*' processor with 4-GB RAM and results are presented and compared with base method. Coding simulations have been tested on three standard, 8-bit/pixel greyscale bitmap natural images, shown in Figure 2.

In pre-processing, the image to be encoded is partitioned in fixed size non-overlapping rectangular parts to form range blocks. This is done to increase the amount of self-symmetry. All the images in three sizes 256×256, 512×512 and 1024×1024 have been used. The performance is investigated for four sizes of range blocks i.e. 32×32, 16×16, 8×8 and 4×4. The performance of proposed method is compared with full search method [6]. The comparison is based on three evaluation parameters; PSNR, Speedup ratio and compression ratio. Following are the results obtained when all the three proposed methods are applied along with the Conventional method:

Figure 2. Natural greyscale bmp images of 8bits/pixel: (a) Lena (standard), (b) Pepper (standard), (c) Baboon (standard)

 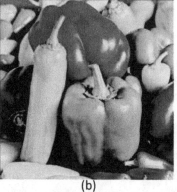 

(a) (b) (c)

Table 1. Results of conventional method for Lena Image

Size of Image	Range partition size	No. of range images	No. of domain images	SDS time (sec)	Encoding time (sec)	Compression time (sec)	C_R	PSNR (dB)
256 x 256	32 x 32	64	49	1.07	2.91	3.98	145.6356	17.427
256 x 256	16 x 16	256	225	7.37	10.27	17.64	36.5307	20.032
256 x 256	8 x 8	1024	961	91.85	36.6	128.45	9.1403	22.154
256 x 256	4 x 4	4096	3969	1510.14	148.96	1659.1	2.2856	27.901
512 x 512	32 x 32	256	225	18.95	10.25	29.2	146.1226	19.606
512 x 512	16 x 16	1024	961	128.75	38.09	166.84	36.5612	22.354
512 x 512	8 x 8	4096	3969	1549.17	146.65	1695.82	9.1422	24.613
512 x 512	4 x 4	16384	16129	24636.6	640.39	25276.9658	2.2857	28.989
1024 x 1024	32 x 32	1024	961	321.67	40.86	362.53	146.2449	22.145
1024 x 1024	16 x 16	4096	3969	2156.72	151.89	2308.61	36.5689	26.292
1024 x 1024	8 x 8	16384	16129	29849.5	677.56	30527.0585	9.1427	31.132
1024 x 1024	4 x 4	65536	65025	490570	3388.42	493958.439	2.2857	33.125

Table 2.Number Of Domains Remaining For Varying Image Size Along With Varying Range Partition Size(Results Obtained For Three Images)

Image			Lenna	Baboon	Pepper
Size of image	Range partition size	Domains	Effective domain	Effective domain	Effective domain
256 x 256	32 x 32	49	28	25	24
256 x 256	16 x 16	225	61	55	60
256 x 256	8 x 8	961	85	76	90
256 x 256	4 x 4	3969	91	90	106
512 x 512	32 x 32	225	66	56	61
512 x 512	16 x 16	961	84	77	89
512 x 512	8 x 8	3844	90	89	107
512 x 512	4 x 4	16129	100	108	112
1024 x 1024	32 x 32	961	85	75	90
1024 x 1024	16 x 16	3969	91	90	106
1024 x 1024	8 x 8	16129	100	110	113
1024 x 1024	4 x 4	65025	106	121	120

Table 3. Results of Domain Kick Out Method Applied on Lena Image

Size of image	Range partition size	Domain kick out time (sec)	SDS time (sec)	Encoding time (sec)	Compression time (sec)	C_R	PSNR (dB)	Speed up ratio
256 x 256	32 x 32	0.04	0.61	2.87	3.52	145.636	17.216	1.13068
256 x 256	16 x 16	0.04	2.14	9.99	12.17	36.5307	19.7127	1.44947
256 x 256	8 x 8	0.06	8.94	38.23	47.23	9.1403	21.8513	2.71967
256 x 256	4 x 4	0.05	33.95	149.52	183.52	2.2856	26.74	9.04043
512 x 512	32 x 32	0.04	5.64	10.79	16.47	146.123	19.2216	1.77292
512 x 512	16 x 16	0.04	11.59	38.6	50.23	36.561	21.5944	3.32152
512 x 512	8 x 8	0.08	35.55	149.76	185.39	9.1422	24.1973	9.14731
512 x 512	4 x 4	0.14	148.47	597.66	746.27	2.2857	28.0246	33.8711
1024 x 1024	32 x 32	0.07	28.87	41.75	70.69	146.245	21.2789	5.12844
1024 x 1024	16 x 16	0.09	50.02	158.3	208.41	36.5689	25.2728	11.0772
1024 x 1024	8 x 8	0.16	155.59	599.33	755.08	9.1427	29.6497	40.4289
1024 x 1024	4 x 4	0.48	626.34	3388.42	4015.24	2.2857	32.8705	123.020

Table 4. Results of Domain Kick Out Method Applied on Baboon Image

Size of image	Range partition size	Domain kick out time (sec)	SDS time (sec)	Encoding time (sec)	Compression time (sec)	C_R	PSNR (dB)	Speed up ratio
256 x 256	32 x 32	0.03	0.55	2.79	3.37	145.64	15.45	1.1839
256 x 256	16 x 16	0.03	1.97	10.1	12.1	36.531	16.789	1.452
256 x 256	8 x 8	0.03	7.71	39.84	47.58	9.1403	17.7203	2.730
256 x 256	4 x 4	0.05	34.59	152.75	187.39	2.2856	18.6912	8.868
512 x 512	32 x 32	0.04	4.93	10.92	15.89	146.12	16.6523	1.882
512 x 512	16 x 16	0.04	10.75	39.12	49.91	36.561	17.5616	3.319
512 x 512	8 x 8	0.06	35.32	152.85	188.23	9.1422	18.5377	8.941
512 x 512	4 x 4	0.13	160.51	602.25	762.89	2.2857	19.8572	33.135
1024 x 1024	32 x 32	0.07	25.62	41.31	67.00	146.24	17.9414	5.207
1024 x 1024	16 x 16	0.08	49.77	150.91	200.76	36.568	18.8832	11.274
1024 x 1024	8 x 8	0.16	173.35	598.95	772.46	9.1427	20.4826	39.501
1024 x 1024	4 x 4	0.51	726.62	3322.427	4049.557	2.857	26.519	122.11

Table 5. Results of Domain Kick Out Method Applied on Pepper Image

Size of image	Range partition size	Domain kick out time (sec)	SDS time (sec)	Encoding time (sec)	Compression time (sec)	C_R	PSNR (dB)	Speed up ratio
256 x 256	32 x 32	0.04	0.53	2.87	3.44	145.636	15.913	1.163
256 x 256	16 x 16	0.03	2.1	9.96	12.09	36.531	18.815	1.433
256 x 256	8 x 8	0.04	10.96	48.19	59.19	9.140	21.648	2.175
256 x 256	4 x 4	0.07	48.94	183.46	232.47	2.286	25.978	7.120
512 x 512	32 x 32	0.04	6.51	13.11	19.66	146.123	18.712	1.479
512 x 512	16 x 16	0.05	14.5	48.99	63.54	36.561	21.781	2.633
512 x 512	8 x 8	0.08	53.34	188.73	242.15	9.1422	25.4	7.025
512 x 512	4 x 4	0.19	208.32	756.92	965.43	2.286	30.734	26.219
1024 x 1024	32 x 32	0.1	38.25	52.07	90.42	146.245	21.564	4.0185
1024 x 1024	16 x 16	0.1	71.82	177.78	249.7	36.569	25.627	9.291
1024 x 1024	8 x 8	0.2	204.63	722.85	927.68	9.143	30.077	32.954
1024 x 1024	4 x 4	0.6	963.69	3218.15	4182.44	2.286	36.513	118.11

FUTURE RESEARCH DIRECTIONS

The combination of other fast fractal methods along with kick-out conditions can decrease the computation time. In future we can apply kick-out condition on range images along with domain images so that encoding time reduces further and fractal image compression scheme can be useful for more applications.

CONCLUSION

Fractal image compression is a revolutionary technique with sublime advantages. It is based on the concept of self-similarity in fractals. But it is not widely used due to the excessive time consumption in suitable domain search which consist of huge number of image comparisons on pixel basis. A lot of efforts have been made to reduce the time requirement of Suitable Domain Search till date. It may be trim down either by reducing the amount of computations involved or by diminishing the complexity of computations. In this thesis, work is done to reduce the amount of computations.

In this work a new speed-up technique has been proposed to reduce the size of domain pool by kicking out redundant domain images and results notable reduction in time consumption. This method reported a speedup ratio nearly 120 with approximate reduction up to 1.5 dB while maintaining the compression ratio comparable to conventional method.

REFERENCES

Barnsley, M. (1988). *Fractals Everywhere*. New York: Academic.

Beaumont, J. M. (1990). Advances in block based fractal coding of still pictures. IEEE Colloq.: The Application of Fractal Techniques in Image Processing, 3.1–3.6.

Davoine, F., Antonini, M., Chassery, J. M., & Barlaud, M. (1996). Fractal image compression based on Delaunay triangulation and vector quantization. *IEEE Transactions on Image Processing, 5*(2), 338–346. doi:10.1109/83.480769 PMID:18285117

Davoine, F., Svensson, J., & Chassery, J.-M. (1995). A mixed triangular and quadrilateral partition for fractal image coding. *IEEE Int. Conf. Image Processing, 3*, 284–287. 10.1109/ICIP.1995.537633

Farhadi, G. (2003). An enhanced fractal image compression based on Quadtree partition. *ISPA03 Proc. on Image and Signal Processing and Analysis.*

Fisher, Y. (1992). Fractal Image Compression. *SIGGRAPH'92 Course Notes.*

Fisher, Y. (1994). *Fractal Image Compression: Theory and Application.* New York: Springer-Verlag.

Fisher, Y., Jacobs, E. W., & Boss, R. D. (1992). *Fractal image compression using iterated transforms. In Image and Text Compression* (pp. 35–61). Boston, MA: Kluwer.

Hamzaoui, R., Muller, M., & Saupe, D. (1996). VQ-enhanced fractal image compression. *IEEE Int. Conf.Image Processing, 1*, 153–156. 10.1109/ICIP.1996.559456

He, Wang, Wu, Hintz, & Hur. (2006). Fractal Image Compression on Spiral Architecture. *IEEE International Conference on Computer graphics, Image visualization,* 76-83.

Hurtgen, B., & Stiller, C. (1993), Fast hierarchical codebook search for fractal coding of still images, *Proc. EOS/SPIE Visual Communications PACS Medical Applications '93, Berlin, Germany.* 10.1117/12.160484

Hutchinson, J. E. (1981). Fractals and self-similarity. *Indiana University Mathematics Journal, 3*(5), 713–747. doi:10.1512/iumj.1981.30.30055

Jacobs, E. W., Fisher, Y., & Boss, R. D. (1992). Image compression: A study of iterated transform method. *Signal Processing, 29*(3), 251–263. doi:10.1016/0165-1684(92)90085-B

Jacquin, A. E. (1990). A novel fractal block-coding technique for digital Images. *ICASSP International Conference on Acoustics, Speech, and Signal Processing.* 10.1109/ICASSP.1990.116007

Jaquin, A. E. (1992). Image coding based on a fractal theory of iterated contractive image transformation. *IEEE Transactions on Image Processing, 1*(1).

Jaquin, A. E. (1993). Fractal image coding: A review. Proceeding of tile IEEE, 81(10).

Mandelbrot, B. (1982). *The Fractal Geometry of Nature.* San Francisco: W. H. Freeman and Co.

Nasrabadi, N. M., & King, R. A. (1988). Image coding using vector quantization: A Review. *IEEE Transactions on Communications, 36*(8), 957–971. doi:10.1109/26.3776

Ramamurthy, B., & Gersho, A. (1986). Classified vector quantization of images. *IEEE Transactions on Communications, COM-34*(11), 1105–1115. doi:10.1109/TCOM.1986.1096468

Ruhl, H. H., & Saupe, D. (1997). Adaptive partitioning for fractal image compression. *IEEE Int. Conf. Image Processing, 2,* 310–313. 10.1109/ICIP.1997.638753

Saupe. (1995). Accelerating Fractal Image Compression by Multi-Dimensional Nearest Neighbor Search. *Proceedings DCC'95 Data Compression Conference.*

Saupe, D., & Ruhl, M. (1996). Evolutionary fractal image compression. *IEEE Int. Conf. Image Processing, 1,* 129–132. 10.1109/ICIP.1996.559449

Tanimoto, H. O., & Kimoto, T. (1996). A new fractal image coding scheme employing blocks of variable shapes. *IEEE Int. Conf. Image Processing, 1,* 137–140. 10.1109/ICIP.1996.559452

Wein, C. J., & Blake, I. F. (1996). On the performance of fractal compression with clustering. *IEEE Transactions on Image Processing, 5*(3), 522–526. doi:10.1109/83.491325 PMID:18285137

Weistead, S. (2005). Fractal and Wavelet Image Compression Technique. PHI.

Wohlberg, B., & Jager, G. D. (1999). A review of fractal image coding literature. *IEEE Transactions on Image Processing, 8*(12), 1716–1729. doi:10.1109/83.806618 PMID:18267449

Xing-yuan, W., Fan-ping, L., & Shu-guo, W. (2009, November). Fractal image compression based on spatial correlation and hybrid genetic algorithm. *Journal of Visual Communication and Image Representation, 20*(8), 505–510. doi:10.1016/j.jvcir.2009.07.002

KEY TERMS AND DEFINITIONS

Discrete Cosine Transform (DCT): The discrete cosine transform (DCT) helps separate the image into parts (or spectral sub-bands) of differing importance (with respect to the image's visual quality). The DCT is similar to the discrete Fourier transform: it transforms a signal or image from the spatial domain to the frequency domain.

Iterated Function System (IFS): Iterated function systems are a method of constructing fractals; the resulting fractals are often self-similar. IFS fractals are more related to set theory than fractal geometry.

Multi-Resolution Analysis (MRA): A multiresolution analysis (MRA) or multiscale approximation (MSA) is the design method of most of the practically relevant discrete wavelet transforms (DWT) and the justification for the algorithm of the fast wavelet transform (FWT).

Wavelet-Based Fractal Transform (WBFT): Wavelet-based fractal transform (WBFT) links the theory of multiresolution analysis (MBA) with iterated function systems (IFS).

Chapter 20
Performance Analysis of Mail Clients on Low Cost Computer With ELGamal and RSA Using SNORT

Sreerama Murthy Kattamuri
Sreenidhi Institute of Science and Technology, India

Vijayalakshmi Kakulapati
Sreenidhi Institute of Science and Technology, India

Pallam Setty S.
Andhra University, India

ABSTRACT

An intrusion detection system (IDS) focuses on determining malicious tasks by verifying network traffic and informing the network administrator for restricting the user or source or source IP address from accessing the network. SNORT is an open source intrusion detection system (IDS) and SNORT also acts as an intrusion prevention system (IPS) for monitoring and prevention of security attacks on networks. The authors applied encryption for text files by using cryptographic algorithms like Elgamal and RSA. This chapter tested the performance of mail clients in low cost, low power computer Raspberry Pi, and verified that SNORT is efficient for both algorithms. Within low cost, low power computer, they observed that as the size of the file increases, the run time is constant for compressed data; whereas in plain text, it changed significantly.

DOI: 10.4018/978-1-5225-3870-7.ch020

INTRODUCTION

Intrusion Detection System(IDS)

An *Intrusion Detection System* (Mrdovic and Zajko, 2005) is a software tool or mechanism that watches network tasks for abnormal activities or policy violations and generates reports to a management station. Intrusion Detection and Prevention Systems (IDPS)(Albin and Neil, 2012) majorly dealt with finding probable occurrences, storing data and covering number of attempts.

Freeware Intrusion Detection Systems

- Prelude Hybrid DS
- AIDE
- Suricata
- Bro NIDS(Mohd Nazri Ismail andMohd Taha Ismail, 2009)
- Samhain
- Snort(Hussein Alnabulsi, Md Rafiqul Islam and Quazi Mamun, 2014)
- ACARM
- OSSEC HIDS (Sang-Jun Han and Sung-Bae Cho, 2003)

Nids

Network Intrusion Detection Systems (Hornig C, 1984, Mrdovic and Zajko, 2005 and Yogesh Suryawanshi and Kakde, 2013) placed within the network to watch traffic to and from all devices over the network. Preferably, one would watch all inbound and outbound traffic, which create a bottleneck that would harm the general fastness of the network.

Hids

Host Intrusion Detection Systems (Cleary, Donnelly and Graham 2000) works on individual devices or hosts over the network. A HIDS (Maziero1 and Jamhour, 2007) watches both inbound and outbound packets from device and will intimate the administrator or user of malignant task.

Snort is a freeware NIDS (Tan and Sherwood, 2005) system, and can provide real-time traffic investigation and can log packets on IP networks.

RASPBERRY PI

All Raspberry Pi (Naik and Harode, 2016) models emphasize a Broadcom framework on a chip (SoC), which includes an ARM (Kumaresan and Manivannan M, 2010) perfect focal preparing unit (CPU) and an on-chip representation handling unit (GPU, a VideoCore IV). CPU rums anywhere from 700 MHz to 1.2 GHz for the Pi 3, on board memory broaden from 256 MB to 1 GB RAM. Secure Digital (SD) cards are use to accumulate the working framework and program memory in either the SDHC or MicroSDHC sizes. Most sheets have in the proximity of first and fourth USB openings, HDMI and composite video yield, and a 3.5 mm telephone jack for sound. Bring down level yield is provided by several GPIO pins which boosts basic principles like I²C. The B-models have an 8P8C Ethernet port and the Pi 3 and Pi Zero W have on board Wi-Fi 802.11n (Vrushali, Deore and Umale, 2012) and Bluetooth.

Snort is a packet investigation tool. In the Snort, we focused on sniffer mode (S. Ansari, Rajeev S.G. and Chandrasekhar H.S, 2003 and Ryan Spangler, 2003). Snort will read the network data and print them to the screen. Snort is considered as an advanced Network Intrusion Detection System when compared to other industrial machines. In this chapter evaluated the performance of several mail clients by using Snort. In the simulation study, we select three mail clients (Gmail, Yahoo, Hotmail).By varying the text sizes from 50 kb to 2mb, hotmail has shown high performance (Dabir and Matrawy, 2007) where its runtime is less when compared to others.

Later, in this chapter verify Snort to the encrypted text where we applied RSA and ELGamal (Ateniese, Benson and Hohenberger, 2009). From simulation results, this chapter describes that there is negligible difference in the case of for compression data from Snort.

SNORT OVERVIEW

Snort

Snort is a freeware Network Intrusion Detection System (NIDS) (Mrdovic and Zajko, 2005 and Bai and Hidetsune Kobayashi., 2003) and Network Intrusion Prevention System (Lin Tan and Timothy Sherwood, 2005) and created by Martin Roesch in 1998. Snort's freeware network-based intrusion detection system (NIDS) (Janakiraman, Waldvogel, Zhang and Indra, 2003), with Snort, real-time traffic analysis

Figure 1. Raspberry Pi

and packet-logging can be performed. With Snort, one can do content searching, content matching, and protocol analysis. We can use Snort for detecting attacks. We can configure Snort in 3 ways: sniffer mode, packet logger mode, and network intrusion detection. In sniffer mode, the program will examine network information and display them on the console, whereas in packet logger mode, the program will record information to a storage device. In intrusion detection mode, the program will examine network traffic and verifies against a rule set given by the user.

Snort Modes

Snort can run in three different modes:

Sniffer Mode

Sniffer mode simply examines the packets from the network and displays them in an uninterrupted stream on the console.

Options

```
$ sudo snort  -v
    Display TCP/IP header onto the screen (also for UDP/ICMP).
$sudo snort -vd
Display application data along with TCP/IP header data.
$ Sudo  ./snort -vde
 Prints the data link layer contents as well.
```

Packet Logger Mode

Packet logger mode records the packet information to the storage device.

Figure 2. Snort model

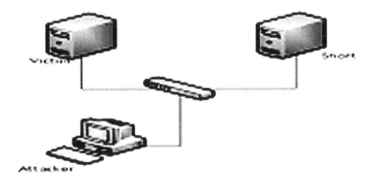

Options

```
$ sudo snort -dev -l ./log
 Stores the packet information to the directory mentioned.
 $ Sudo ./snort -l ./log -b
Displays binary log, and we can read binary file back by using -r switch.
```

MAIL CLIENTS

An email reader, email client, or mail user agent (MUA), is a software program used for administering and accessing user's email.

A 'Mail Client' can refer to any machine capable of managing the user's email mailbox, and it can be a mail user agent, a relay server, or a simple terminal where user types in. Apart from above, a mail client can even provide services such as composition, reception functions, and message management, and it can even be called as webmail.

Commonly used web-based mail clients: Gmail, Yahoo! Mail, mail.com, Lycos mail, and Hotmail

Gmail

Gmail is a freely available, advertising-supported email service provided by Google. Users can use Gmail as secure webmail via IMAP4 or POP3 protocols. Gmail released its invitation-only beta version on April 1, 2004 and available to the general public on February 7, 2007. Gmail has upgraded its beta status on July 7, 2009, along with the Google Apps suite.

Yahoo

Yahoo! Inc. is an American multinational internet corporation, and its headquarters in Sunnyvale, California. Yahoo is popular for web portal, Yahoo! Search, and related services, including Yahoo! News, Yahoo! Directory, Yahoo! Mail, Yahoo! Groups, Yahoo! Answers, Yahoo! Finance, advertising, fantasy sports, video sharing, online mapping, and its social media website. Yahoo is one of the most commonly used website in the United States.

Products and Services

- Storing personal information and tracking usage.
- Advertising
- Content
- Mobile services
- Communication

Hotmail

Hotmail also known as *Outlook.com, MSN Hotmail,* and *Windows Live Hotmail,* is a freeware web-based email service controlled by Microsoft. Hotmail was reported as one of the first web-based email services. Our outlook.com was initially launched by Sabeer Bhatia and Jack Smith as "HoTMaiL" in July 1996, and later HoTMaiL was taken over by Microsoft in 1997, and it was renamed to "MSN Hotmail", the latest version was released in 2011. MSN Hotmail again renamed to Outlook.com in February 2013 as part of the rebranding of the Windows Live suite of products.

ENCRYPTION

In cryptography, encryption is the process of encoding messages or information. With the help of encryption, only authorized persons can read the messages, but not eavesdroppers or hackers. In encryption methodology, an encryption algorithm is used to encrypt the plain text, and it transfers the plain text into an unreadable cipher text (ibid.). An encryption key plays a major role, which specifies the message encoding format (Sanai, 2001). Any malignant user cannot determine anything about the original message by observing the cipher text. The receiver or the authorized party will have a decryption key and they use a decryption algorithm to convert into original message whereas the malignant users do not have the decryption key. It uses key-generation algorithms to generate keys.

There are 2 kinds of encryption (Canetti and and Hohenberger, 2007) methodologies: Symmetric-key and public-key encryption. In symmetric-key schemes, the encryption and decryption keys are the same, where both sender and receiver will decide a secret key before their communication. In public-key schemes, the sender and receiver uses two different keys, i.e., encryption key and decryption key. The encryption key can be used by anyone for encrypting messages, whereas the decryption key can be accessed by the receiver only, and receiver can read the encrypted messages. Public-key encryption is the popular encryption methodology to be used rather symmetric key, which was used historically.

ElGamal

ElGamal (Gamal, 1985) is called as an asymmetric key encryption algorithm, used for public-key cryptography and is based on the Diffie–Hellman key exchange.

Elgamal encryption (Trabelsi, Rahmani, Kaouech and Frikha, 2004) holds three parts:

- Key generator.
- Encryption algorithm.
- Decryption algorithm.

Efficiency

ElGamal encryption is probabilistic, i.e. a single plain text can be encrypted to numerous cipher texts that this encryption can produce a 2:1 growth in size from plain text to cipher text. ElGamal encryption (Bresson Catalano and Pointcheval, 2003) need two exponentiations; whereas decryption needs only one exponentiation and these exponentiations are free of the message size and can be calculated beforehand if required.

RSA

Public-key cryptography and it is based on the apparent complexity of factoring big integers, the factoring problem. RSA stands for Ron Rivest, Adi Shamir and Leonard Adleman, who explained the algorithm in 1977. An RSA user generates and produces the multiplication of 2 big prime numbers, besides an auxiliary value, which is used as the public key (Rahmani, Kaouech and Frikha, 2004).

Secrecy should be maintained for the prime factors. Anybody can use the public key to encrypt a message, but with currently published methods, if the public key is large enough. RSA encryption breaking is like an open question as factoring as the RSA problem.

The RSA algorithm involves three steps:

- Key generation.
- Encryption.
- Decryption.

EXPERIMENTAL RESULTS

Snort With ElGamal Technique

The experiment has been carried out to examine the data produced by snort while sending plain text files and encrypted text files of different sizes varying from 50 Kb to 2 MB (50KB, 100KB, 500KB, 1MB, and 2MB) in all 3 mail clients.

Primarily, the plain text files are sent and the data produced by snort is compared to the encrypted files data.

Figure 3. Key generation of RSA algorithm

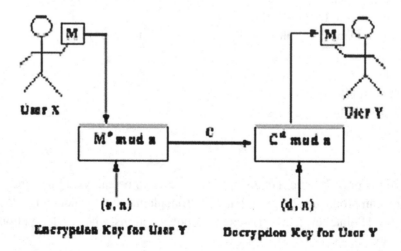

Applying ElGamal Technique in Gmail With Snort

Below is the analysis of data produced by snort when files are sent through Gmail. The first row represents plain text data packets captured by Snort whereas the second row represents encrypted text data of the same plain text by using ElGamal.

Total Packets: ElGamal-Gmail

Total packets are the total number of packets received by the snort from the network.

In Figure 4, the total packets received by Snort is higher for plain text whereas it is similar for all packet sizes in the encrypted text, and it increases the runtime and memory is also occupied more in plain text case.

Analyzed Packets

Analyzed packets are the number of packets analyzed by Snort during runtime. Snort analyzes only some of the packets from the packets received from Ethernet, and some will be buffered for processing

Following is the representation of analyzed packets in plain text to encrypted text of files of various sizes in Gmail. As the analyzed packets increases, the performance of the encrypted algorithm also increases.

Figure 5 shows a consistency in the total number of analyzed packets in encrypted text from plain text.

Table 1. Total packets ElGamal-Gmail

Size	50kb	100kb	500kb	1mb	2mb
Plain text	225	295	776	1866	2612
Encrypted	119	113	114	222	252

Figure 4. Total packets ElGamal-Gmail

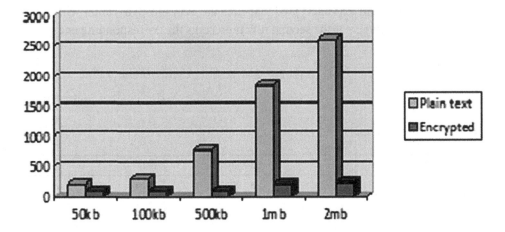

Table 2. Analyzed packets ElGamal-Gmail

Size	50kb	100kb	500kb	1mb	2mb
Plain text	225	295	776	1866	2612
Encrypted	119	113	114	222	252

Figure 5. Analyzed Packets ElGamal-Gmail

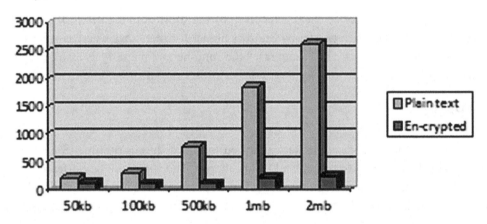

Run Time

The total amount of time taken by Snort for analyzing the packets received from the Ethernet is called *"Run Time"*. Applying encryption is beneficial if the run time of sending of plain text is higher than the runtime of encrypted text, then we can assume encrypting the text saves the processing time and memory. Below is the comparison of run time of sending plain text files and encrypted files.

Figure 6 shows the run time for encrypted text is less than the runtime taken by plain text when running Snort.

Applying ElGamal in Yahoo With Snort

Below is the analysis when plain text/encrypted text files are sent through Yahoo with Snort. The first row represents plain text data whereas the second row represents the corresponding encrypted text using Yahoo encryption technique.

Table 3. RunTime ElGamal-Gmail

Size	50kb	100kb	500kb	1mb	2mb
Plain text	24.238	25.167	35.827	56.544	65.231
Encrypted	22.92	21.326	25.323	32.11	23.511

Figure 6. Run Time ElGamal-Gmail

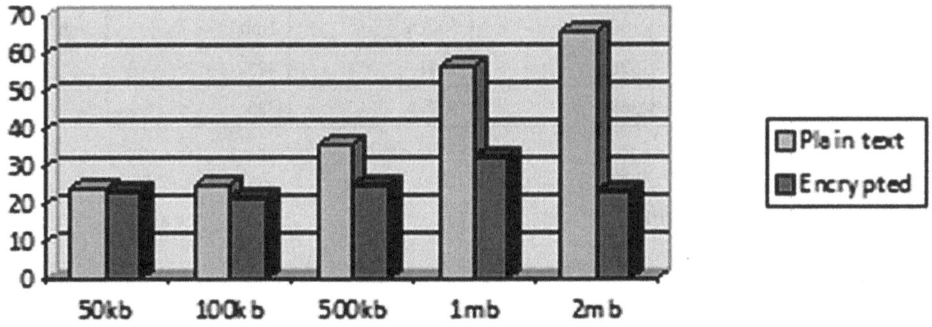

Total Packets ElG-Yahoo

Total Packets: Total packets are the total number of packets received by Snort from the Ethernet.

In Figure 7 the total packets of encrypted text files have considerably reduced by using ElGamal technique, which saves a lot time of processing.

Analyzed Packets

Table 5 shows the comparison of analyzed packets in plain text and encrypted text of files of various sizes in Yahoo.

Table 4. Total packets ElGamal-Yahoo

Size	50kb	100kb	500kb	1mb	2mb
Plain text	400	598	1041	2263	3241
Encrypted	324	368	584	244	314

Figure 7. Total Packets ElG-Yahoo

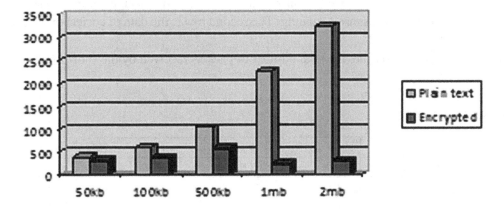

Table 5. Analyzed Packets ElG-Yahoo

Size	50kb	100kb	500kb	1mb	2mb
Plain text	397	598	1041	2257	3223
Encrypted	319	368	569	235	307

Figure 8. Analyzed Packets ElG-Yahoo

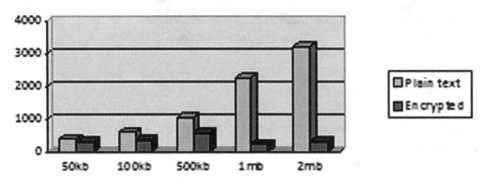

In Figure 8, the number of analyzed packets by Snort is significantly reduced due to the less number of total packets.

Run Time

The total amount of time taken by Snort for analyzing the packets received from the Ethernet. Applying encryption is beneficial if the run time of sending of plain text is higher than the runtime of encrypted text, then we can assume encrypting the text saves the processing time and memory.

Below is the comparison of run time for plain text to encrypted text.

In Figure 9 the run time taken by encrypted text is more than plain text for 100 KB size, which indicates that if we are using file size of 100 kb then sending the plain text saves memory and time.

Applying ElGamal Technique in Hotmail With Snort

Table 7 is the analysis of data produced by snort when files are sent through Hotmail. The first row is the data of plain text sent when snort is running. The second row is the data of corresponding encrypted text using Elgamal.

Total Packets: Total packets are the total number of packets received by the snort from the Ethernet

Table 6. Run Time ElG-Yahoo

Size	50kb	100kb	500kb	1mb	2mb
Plain text	29.568	31.95	42.153	56.66	71.356
Encrypted	34.74	28.376	20.233	20.668	19.25

In Figure 10 the total number of packets produced by Snort remained consistent irrespective of file sizes when compared to plain texts.

Analyzed Packets

Following is the table of comparison of analyzed packets in plain text and encrypted text of files of various sizes in Hotmail.

In Figure 11, Snort analyzed more number of packets for plain text when compared to encrypted text.

Figure 9. Run Time ElG-Yahoo

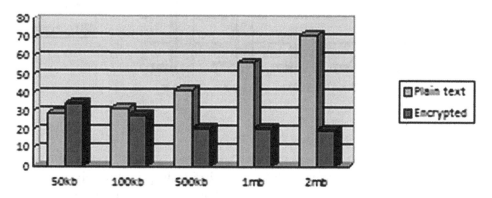

Table 7. Total packets Elg-Hotmail

Size	50kb	100kb	500kb	1mb	2mb
Plain text	190	258	807	1788	2821
Encrypted	102	81	75	160	81

Figure 10. Total packets Elg-Hotmail

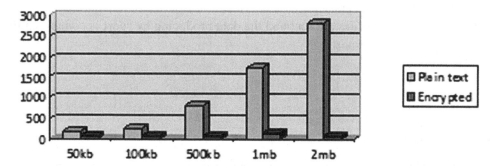

Table 8. Analyzed Packets-Elg-Hotmail

Size	50kb	100kb	500kb	1mb	2mb
Plain text	190	258	796	1788	2475
Encrypted	102	81	75	149	81

Figure 11. Analyzed Packets-Elg-Hotmail

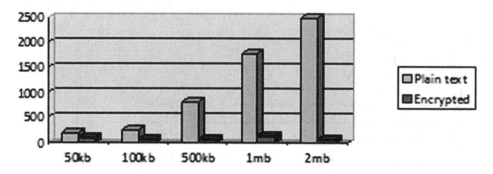

Run Time

Run time is the total amount of time taken by Snort for analyzing the packets received from the Ethernet. Applying encryption is beneficial if the run time of sending of plain text is higher than the runtime of encrypted text, then we can assume encrypting the text saves the processing time and memory.

Table 9 shows the comparison of run time during sending plain text files and encrypted files.

In Figure 12 run time taken by Snort through hotmail is higher for plain text when compared to encrypted text.

Snort With RSA Technique

An experiment has been carried out to analyze the data produced by snort during sending plain text files and encrypted text files of different sizes from 50 KB to 2 MB (50kb, 100kb, 500kb, 1mb, and 2mb) in GMail, Yahoo, and Hotmail mail clients.

Primarily, the un-encrypted files are sent and the data producing by snort is comparing to the data of encrypted files producing by snort.

Table 9. Run Time-Elg-Hotmail

Size	50kb	100kb	500kb	1mb	2mb
Plain text	28.483	22.822	31.156	55.52	60.925
Encrypted	17.35	15.52	14.55	16.47	18.798

Figure 12. Run Time-Elg-Hotmail

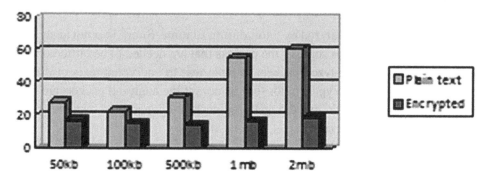

Applying RSA Technique in Gmail With Snort

Table 10 is an analysis of data produced by snort when files are sent through Gmail. The first row represents plain text whereas the second row represents corresponding encrypted text using RSA algorithm.

Total Packets

Total packets are the total number of packets received by the snort from the Ethernet.

In Figure 13 the total number of packets analyzed by snort using RSA algorithm is consistent when the compared to number of packets in plain text.

Table 10. Total packets-RSA-Gmail

Size	50kb	100kb	500kb	1mb	2mb
Plain text	225	295	776	1870	2835
Encrypted	166	155	149	188	144

Figure 13. Total packets-RSA-Gmail

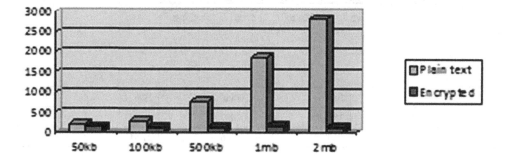

Analyzed Packets

Analyzed packets are the packets analyzed by Snort during runtime. Snort does not analyze all the packets received by the Ethernet; it drops some of the packets that are needed to be buffered for processing.

Below is the comparison of analyzed packets of plain text to encrypted texts of different sizes in Gmail. The performance of the encrypted algorithm is more if the analyzed packets are more.

From Figure 14, we can conclude that the analyzed packets in encrypted text file are less than the packets that are analyzed in plain text.

Run Time

Run time is the total amount of time taken by Snort for analyzing the packets received from the Ethernet. Applying encryption is beneficial if the run time of sending of plain text is higher than the runtime of encrypted text, then we can assume encrypting the text saves the processing time and memory.

Below is the comparison of run time between plain text to encrypted text.

Figure 15 represents that the total run time taken for encrypted text is less when compared to plain text by Snort.

Table 11. Analyzed packets-RSA-Gmail

Size	50kb	100kb	500kb	1mb	2mb
Plain text	225	295	776	1866	2612
Encrypted	119	113	114	222	252

Figure 14. Analyzed packets-RSA-Gmail

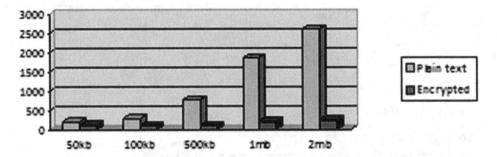

Table 12. Run Time -RSA-Gmail

Size	50kb	100kb	500kb	1mb	2mb
Plain text	24.238	25.167	35.827	56.544	65.231
Encrypted	21.11	24.1	24.276	31.619	26.29

Figure 15. Run Time -RSA-Gmail

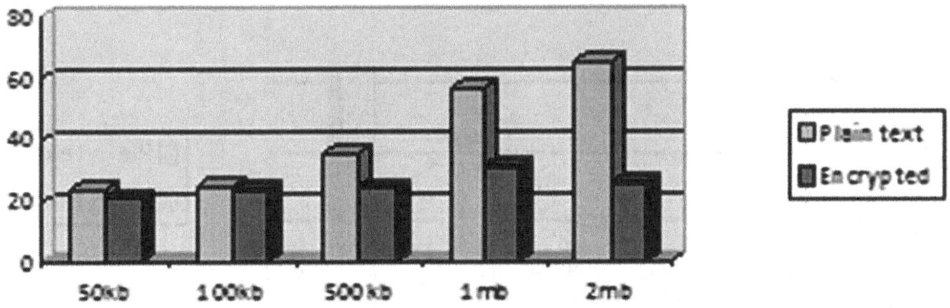

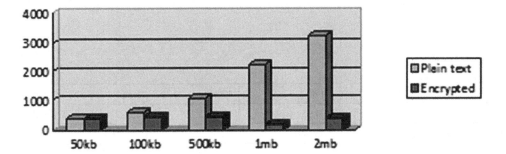

Applying RSA in Yahoo With Snort

Table 13 shows the analysis of data produced by snort when files are sent through yahoo. The first row is the data of plain text sent when snort is running. The second row is the data of corresponding encrypted text using RSA encryption technique.

Total Packets

Total packets are the total number of packets received by the snort from the Ethernet. Figure 16 represents the total number of packets for encrypted text is less than the plain text by Snort.

Analyzed Packets

Table 14 compares the analyzed packets in plain text and encrypted text of files of various sizes in Yahoo.

Table 13. Total packets-RSA-Yahoo

Size	50kb	100kb	500kb	1mb	2mb
Plain text	400	598	1041	2263	3241
Encrypted	372	451	445	168	368

Figure 16. Total packets-RSA-Yahoo

Figure 17. Analyzed Packets -RSA-Yahoo

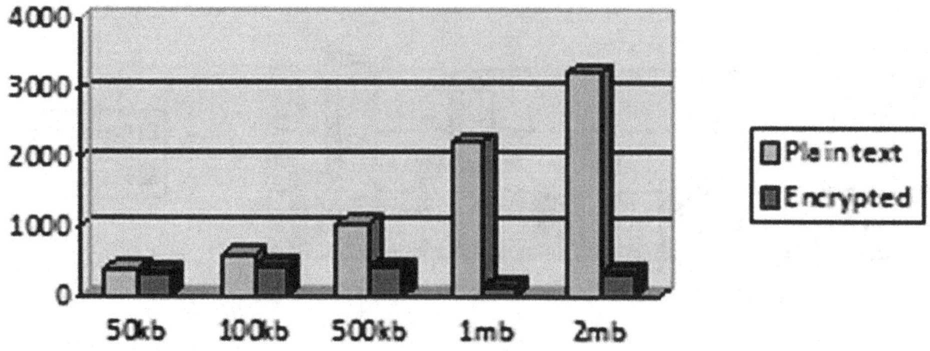

Table 14. Analyzed Packets -RSA-Yahoo

Size	50kb	100kb	500kb	1mb	2mb
Plain text	397	598	1041	2257	3223
Encrypted	364	449	421	154	361

In Figure 17 the number of analyzed packets by Snort remained same in both plain text and encrypted text for 50 kb file size, but for other file sizes the number variation is higher.

Run Time

Run time is the total amount of time taken for analyzing the packets received from the Ethernet by Snort. Applying encryption is beneficial if the run time of sending of plain text is higher than the runtime of encrypted text, then we can assume encrypting the text saves the processing time and memory.

Below is the comparison of run time from plain text to encrypted text.

Applying RSA Technique in Hotmail With Snort

Table 16 shows the analysis of data produced by snort when files are sent through Hotmail. The first row represents the plain text whereas the second row represents the corresponding encrypted text using RSA by Snort.

Table 15. Run Time-RSA-Yahoo

Size	50kb	100kb	500kb	1mb	2mb
Plain text	29.568	31.95	42.153	56.66	71.356
Encrypted	25.93	25.726	22.8	29.987	24.57

Figure 18. Run Time-RSA-Yahoo

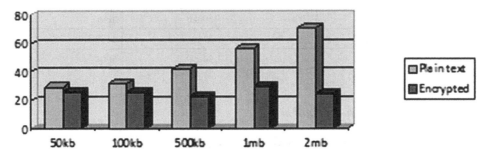

Total Packets

Total packets are the total number of packets received by the snort from the Ethernet.

Figure 19 shows the number of packets received for encrypted text remained consistent irrespective of the file size by Snort.

Analyzed Packets

Below is the comparison of analyzed packets in the plain text to encrypted text of files of different sizes in Hotmail.

Figure 20 represents the number of packets analyzed for the encrypted text remained consistent, irrespective of different sizes whereas it varied significantly for plain text by Snort.

Table 16. Total packets-RSA-Hotmail

Size	50kb	100kb	500kb	1mb	2mb
Plain text	190	258	807	1788	2821
Encrypted	132	115	94	169	144

Figure 19. Total packets-RSA-Hotmail

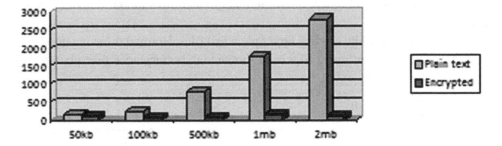

Table 17. Analyzed Packets -RSA-Hotmail

Size	50kb	100kb	500kb	1mb	2mb
Plain text	190	258	796	1788	2475
Encrypted	132	115	94	160	144

Figure 20. Analyzed Packets -RSA-Hotmail

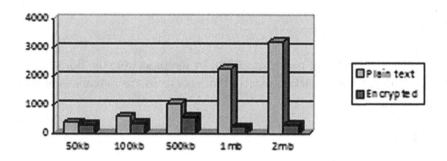

Run Time

Run time is the total amount of time taken by Snort for analyzing the packets received from the Ethernet. Applying encryption is beneficial if the run time of sending of plain text is higher than the runtime of encrypted text, then we can assume encrypting the text saves the processing time and memory.

Table 18 shows the comparison of run time from plain text files to encrypted text files.

Figure 21 represents the run time taken for encrypted text is less when compared to the plain text by Snort.

ANALYSIS OF PERFORMANCE

Based on the simulation results:

This chapter found that hotmail is best for sending larger text and yahoo should be less preferred for the same purpose.

This chapter observed that while sending larger plain text files, Hotmail is having good performance.

This chapter observed that encrypted files have shown high performance than plain text files.

Table 18. Run Time -RSA-Hotmail

Size	50kb	100kb	500kb	1mb	2mb
Plain text	28.483	22.822	31.156	55.52	60.925
Encrypted	19.923	18.357	18.77	22.932	20.343

Figure 21. Run Time -RSA-Hotmail

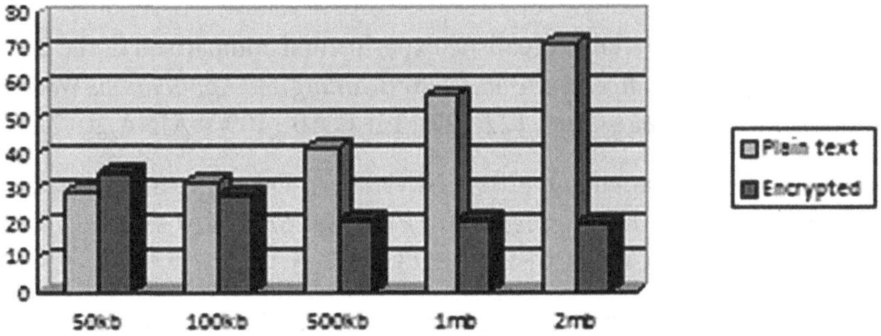

This has been proved with both RSA and ElGamal techniques. From simulation scenarios observed that as the size of the file increase, the runtime is constant for compressed data.

This chapter observed that while sending larger files hotmail is having performance. Compression ratio is higher for Hotmail mail client when digital signature encryption algorithm is used.

When ElGamal algorithm is used Yahoo has lower Compression Ratio when compared to Hotmail and Gmail.

When RSA is used Compression Ratio is higher for Hotmail mail client. Finding the compression ratio, in the conclusion of the chapter represents mail client and crypto-algorithm that is to be used for varying text sizes.

CONCLUSION

In this chapter, implement a low cost low power computer called RaspBerry Pi to analyze the performance of different mail clients like Gmail, Yahoo mail, and hotmail using Snort, a free intrusion detection tool. We verified the performance of all mail clients by sending different files varying different sizes from 50 KB to 2 MB. This chapter describes the analysis in Raspberry Pi, and there also, we could observe that hot mail has shown significant performance when compared to other mail client while sending larger files.

Then, in this chapter applied cryptography by using algorithms like Elgamal and RSA to the plain text files and were sent through the same three mail clients in Raspberry Pi. From simulation scenarios, found that in Raspberry Pi also, the encrypted files have shown significant performance over plain text files. It is proved with Elgamal and RSA techniques as well.

FUTURE ENHANCEMENT

In this chapter experimented with RSA and Elgamal algorithms in the low cost low power computer. There is even scope to extend these experiments with other encryption algorithms as well. There is even scope to extend these experiments with other encryption algorithms like RSA and Digital signatures as well. There is still scope to find out the best suitable mail clients for transferring of data based on the size. And also in further work intended to verify the performance of intrusion detection over wireless protocols such as Bluetooth and wifi. Then check for alternative to snort.

REFERENCES

Albin, E., & Rowe, N. C. (2012, March). A realistic experimental comparison of the Suricata and Snort intrusion-detection systems. In *Advanced Information Networking and Applications Workshops (WAINA), 2012 26th International Conference on* (pp. 122-127). IEEE. 10.1109/WAINA.2012.29

Alnabulsi, H., Islam, M. R., & Mamun, Q. (2014, November). Detecting SQL injection attacks using SNORT IDS. In *Computer Science and Engineering (APWC on CSE), 2014 Asia-Pacific World Congress on* (pp. 1-7). IEEE. 10.1109/APWCCSE.2014.7053873

Ansari, Rajeev, & Chandrasekhar. (2002). Packet Sniffing: A brief Introduction. *IEEE Potentials, 21*(5), 17 – 19.

Ateniese, G., Benson, K., & Hohenberger, S. (2009, April). *Key-Private Proxy Re-encryption* (Vol. 5473). CT-RSA.

Bai, Y., & Kobayashi, H. (2003). Intrusion Detection Systems: technology and Development. *17th International Conference of Advanced Information Networking and Applications.*

Bresson, E., Catalano, D., & Pointcheval, D. (2003, November). *A simple public-key cryptosystem with a double trapdoor decryption mechanism and its applications* (Vol. 2894). Asiacrypt. doi:10.1007/978-3-540-40061-5_3

Canetti & Hohenberger. (2007). Chosen-ciphertext secures proxy re-encryption. *ACM Conference on Computer and Communications Security*, 185–194.

Cleary, J., Donnelly, S., & Graham, I. (2000). Design Principles for Accurate Passive Measurement, *Proc. PAM 2000 Passive and Active Measurement Workshop.*

Deore & Umale. (2012). Wireless Monitoring of the Green House System Using Embedded Controllers. *IJSER, 3*(2).

El Gamal, T. (1985). A public key cryptosystem and a signature scheme based on discrete logarithms. *IEEE Transactions on Information Theory, 31*(4), 469–472. doi:10.1109/TIT.1985.1057074

Han, S.-J., & Cho, S.-B. (2003). Combining Multiple Host-Based Detectors Using Decision Tree. *Australian Joint Artificial Intelligence Conference.* 10.1007/978-3-540-24581-0_18

Hornig, C. (1984). *A standard for the transmission of IP datagrams over ethernet networks*. RFC 894.

Ismail, M. N., & Ismail, M. T. (2009). Framework of Intrusion Detection System via Snort Application on Campus Network Environment. *International Conference on Future Computer and Communication*, 33(1), 456-459. 10.1109/ICFCC.2009.10

Janakiraman, Waldvogel, Zhang, & Indra. (2003). A peer-to-peer approach to network intrusion detection and prevention. *Enabling Technologies: Infrastructure for Collaborative Enterprises.*

Kumaresan, N., & Manivannan, M. (2010). Embedded web server and GPRS Based Advanced Industrial Automation using Linux RTOS. *International Journal of Engineering Science and Technology, 2*(11), 6074–6081.

Laureano, Maziero, & Jamhour. (2007). Protecting Host-Based Intrusion Detectors through Virtual Machines. *The International Journal of Computer and Telecommunications Networking.*

Matrawy. (2007). Bottleneck Analysis of Traffic Monitoring Using Wireshark. *4th International Conference on Innovations in Information Technology, 2007,* 18-20. 10.1109/IIT.2007.4430446

Mrdovic, S., & Zajko, E. (2005). Secured Intrusion Detection System Infrastructure. University of Sarajevo/Faculty of Electrical Engineering.

Naik, P., & Harode, U. (2016). Raspberry Pi and Iot Based Industrial Automation. *International Journal of Industrial Electronics and Electrical Engineering, 4*(10).

Patinge, Suryawanshi, & Kakde. (2013). *Design of ARM Based Data Acquisition and Control Using GSM and TCP/IP Network.* IEEE.

Sanai, D. (2002). *Detection of Promiscuous Nodes Using ARP Packets.* Retrieved from http://www.securityfriday.com

Spangler, R. (2003). *Packet sniffer detection with antisniff. University of Wisconsin* Whitewater, Department of Computer and Network Administration.

Tan & Sherwood. (2005). A High Throughput String Matching Architecture for Intrusion Detection and Prevention. *Proceedings of the 32nd Annual International Symposium on Computer Architecture.*

Trabelsi, Z., Rahmani, H., Kaouech, K., & Frikha, M. (2004). Malicious Sniffing System Detection Platform. In *Proceedings of the 2004 International Symposium on Applications and the Internet.* IEEE Computer Society. 10.1109/SAINT.2004.1266117

KEY TERMS AND DEFINITIONS

HIDS (Host-Based Detection System): This system aims at examining network flows for detecting and preventing malicious attacks.

IDS (Intrusion Detection System): A system that is designed to identify malicious activities and report to administrators for taking necessary security measures.

IPS (Introduction Prevention System): Aims at examining network flows for detecting and preventing malicious attacks.

NIDS (Network Intrusion Detection System): Similar to network intrusion prevention.

Raspberry Pi: A model B single board computer with wireless and Bluetooth connectivity.

RSA: RSA provides industry-wide security solutions for superior threat detection and cyber incident reaction, discovery, and access management.

SNORT: Similar to intrusion detection and prevention systems.

Compilation of References

Abdulaziz, N. K., & Pang, K. K. (2000). Robust data hiding for images. *Proceedings of IEEE International Conference on Communication Technology, WCC-ICCT, 2*, 380-383.

Adeborna, E., & Siau, K. (2014). *An Approach to Sentiment Analysis-the Case of Airline Quality Rating*. PACIS.

Adeniyi, D.A. Wei, Z. Yangquan, Y. (2016). An automated web usage data mining and recommendation system using K-nearest Neighbour (KNN) classification method. *Applied Computing and Informatics, 12*, 90-108.

Adomavicius, G., & Tuzhilin, A. (2005). Toward the Next Generation of Recommender Systems: A Survey of the State-of-the-Art and Possible Extensions. *IEEE Transactions on Knowledge and Data Engineering, 17*(6), 734–749. doi:10.1109/TKDE.2005.99

Afolabi, M. O., & Olude, O. (2007). predicting stock prices using a hybrid kohonen SOM. *Proceedings of the 40th Hawaii International Conference on System Sciences*, 1–8.

Agarwal, N., & Xu, X. (2011). Social Computational Systems. *Journal of Computational Science, 2*(3), 189–192. doi:10.1016/j.jocs.2011.07.006

Ahmed, H., Pierre, S., & Quintero, A. (2017, April 20). A flexible testbed architecture for VANET. *Vehicular Communications*.

Akhtar, Ahamad, & Khan. (2015). Clustering on Big Data Using Hadoop MapReduce. *Proceedings of International Conference on Computational Intelligence and Communication Networks*.

Akhtar, N., & Ahamad, M. V. (2017). Graph Tools for Social Network Analysis. In Graph Theoretic Approaches for Analyzing Large-Scale Social Networks. IGI Global. Doi:10.4018/978-1-5225-2814-2

Akhtar, N., & Ahamad, M. V. (2017). Graph Tools for Social Network Analysis. In Graph Theoretic Approaches for Analyzing Large-Scale Social Networks. IGI Global. Doi:10.4018/978-1-5225-2814-2.ch002

Akhtar, N., Ahamad, M. V., & Khan, S. (2015). Clustering on Big Data Using Hadoop MapReduce. In *Proceedings of International Conference on Computational Intelligence and Communication Networks*.

Akthar, N., Ahamad, M. V., & Khan, S. (2015). MapReduce Model of Improved K-Means Clustering Algorithm Using Hadoop MapReduce. *Proceedings of 2016 Second International Conference on Computational Intelligence & Communication Technology*.

Alani, D., Averbuch, A., & Dekel, S. (2007). Image coding with geometric wavelets. *IEEE Transactions on Image Processing, 16*(1), 69–77. doi:10.1109/TIP.2006.887727 PMID:17283766

Alberts, L. J. S. M., Peeters, I. R. L. M., Braekers, R., & Meijer, C. (2006). *Churn Prediction in the Mobile Telecommunications Industry* (Doctoral dissertation). Department of General Sciences-Maastricht University, Maastricht, The Netherlands.

Albin, E., & Rowe, N. C. (2012, March). A realistic experimental comparison of the Suricata and Snort intrusion-detection systems. In *Advanced Information Networking and Applications Workshops (WAINA), 2012 26th International Conference on* (pp. 122-127). IEEE. 10.1109/WAINA.2012.29

Almeida, V., Menasce, D., Riedi, R., Peligrinelli, F., Fonseca, R., & Meira, W. (2001). Analyzing Web robots and their impact on caching. *Proc. Sixth Workshop on Web Caching and Content Distribution*, 20–22.

Alnabulsi, H., Islam, M. R., & Mamun, Q. (2014, November). Detecting SQL injection attacks using SNORT IDS. In *Computer Science and Engineering (APWC on CSE), 2014 Asia-Pacific World Congress on* (pp. 1-7). IEEE. 10.1109/APWCCSE.2014.7053873

Alonso, N., Lucas, G., & Hysi, P. (2015). Big data challenges in bone research: Genome-wide association studies and next-generation sequencing. *BoneKEy Reports*, *4*. doi:10.1038/bonekey.2015.2 PMID:25709812

An estimated 12.6 million deaths each year are attributable to unhealthy environments. (2017). World Health Organization. Retrieved 26 May 2017, from http://www.who.int/mediacentre/news/releases/2016/deaths-attributable-to-unhealthy-environments/en/

Anagnostopoulos, A., Becchetti, L., Castillo, C., Gionis, A., & Leonardi, S. (2010). Power in unity: forming teams in large-scale community systems. *Proceedings of the 19th ACM international conference on information and knowledge management, CIKM '10*, 599-608. 10.1145/1871437.1871515

Anagnostopoulos, A., Becchetti, L., Castillo, C., Gionis, A., & Leonardi, S. (2012). Online team formation in social networks. *Proceedings of the 21st international conference on world wide web, WWW '12*, 839-848. 10.1145/2187836.2187950

Andreu-Perez, J., Poon, C. C. Y., Merrifield, R. D., Wong, S. T. C., & Yang, G. Z. (2015). Big Data for Health. *IEEE Journal of Biomedical and Health Informatics*, *19*(4), 1193–1208. doi:10.1109/JBHI.2015.2450362 PMID:26173222

Ang, K. K., & Quek, C. (2006). Stock trading using RSPOP: A novel rough set-based neuro-fuzzy approach. *IEEE Transactions on Neural Networks*, *17*(5), 1301–1315. doi:10.1109/TNN.2006.875996 PMID:17001989

Anita, E. A. M., & Jenefa, J. (2016), A survey on authentication schemes in VANETs, *International Conference on Information Communication and Embedded Systems*, 1-7. 10.1109/ICICES.2016.7518946

Ansari, Rajeev, & Chandrasekhar. (2002). Packet Sniffing: A brief Introduction. *IEEE Potentials, 21*(5), 17 – 19.

Archenaa, J., & Anita, E. A. M. (2015). A survey of Big Data Analytics in Healthcare and Government. *Proceedings of the 2nd International Symposium on Big Data and Cloud Computing (ISBCC'15)*, 408-413. 10.1016/j.procs.2015.04.021

Arias, M., Arratia, A., & Xuriguera, R. (2014). Forecasting with twitter data. *ACM Trans. Intel. Syst. Technol., 5*(1).

Arimura, H., Magome, T., Yamashita, Y., & Yamamoto, D. (2009). Computer-aided diagnosis systems for brain diseases in magnetic resonance images. *Algorithms*, *2*(3), 925–952. doi:10.3390/a2030925

Arlitt, M. F., & Williamson, C. L. (1996). Web server workload characterization. *Performance Evaluation Review*, *24*(1), 126–137. doi:10.1145/233008.233034

Ateniese, G., Benson, K., & Hohenberger, S. (2009, April). *Key-Private Proxy Re-encryption* (Vol. 5473). CT-RSA.

Atiya, A. F. (2001). Bankruptcy prediction for credit risk using neural networks: A survey and new results. *IEEE Transactions on Neural Networks*, *12*(4), 929–935. doi:10.1109/72.935101 PMID:18249923

Awal, G. K., & Bharadwaj, K. K. (2014). Team formation in social networks based on collective intelligence - an evolutionary approach. *Applied Intelligence, 41*(2), 627–648. doi:10.100710489-014-0528-y

Awal, G. K., & Bharadwaj, K. K. (2016). Constrained Team Formation using Risk Estimation based on Reputation and Knowledge. In *Proceedings of the 1st International Conference on Advanced Computing and Intelligent Engineering (ICACIE 2016)*. Springer.

Awal, G. K., & Bharadwaj, K. K. (2017a). Leveraging collective intelligence for behavioral prediction in signed social networks through evolutionary approach. *Information Systems Frontiers*, 1–23.

Awal, G. K., & Bharadwaj, K. K. (2017b). Mining Set of Influencers in Signed Social Networks with Maximal Collective Influential Power: A Genetic Algorithm Approach. In *Proceedings of the 2nd International Conference on Information and Communication Technology for Intelligent Systems (ICTIS 2017)*. Springer.

AWStats. (n.d.). *A free logfile analyzer for advanced statistics (GNU GPL)*. Retrieved January 1, 2014, from http://awstats.sourceforge.net/

Bairagi, V. K. 2016. Big Data Analytics in Telemedicine: A Role of Medical Image Compression. In Big Data Management. Cham: Springer International Publishing.

Bai, Y., & Kobayashi, H. (2003). Intrusion Detection Systems: technology and Development. *17th International Conference of Advanced Information Networking and Applications*.

Bajaj, K. (2012). Promoting Data Protection Standards through Contracts: The Case of the Data Security Council of India. *The Review of Policy Research, 29*(1), 131–139. doi:10.1111/j.1541-1338.2011.00541.x

Baker, C. E., Starke, A., Hill-Jarrett, T. G., & McNair, J. (2017). In Vivo Evaluation of the Secure Opportunistic Schemes Middleware using a Delay Tolerant Social Network. *IEEE 37th International Conference on Distributed Computing Systems (ICDCS)*, 2537-2542.

Balahur, A., Hermida, J. M., & Montoyo, A. (2012). Detecting implicit expressions of emotion in text: A comparative analysis. *Decision Support Systems, 53*(4), 742–753. doi:10.1016/j.dss.2012.05.024

Bansal, P., & Ahmad, T. (2016). Methods and Techniques of Intrusion Detection: A Review. *International Conference on Smart Trends for Information Technology and Computer Communications*, 518-529.

Barnsley, M. (1988). *Fractals Everywhere*. New York: Academic.

Basavaraju. (2010). A Novel Method of Spam Mail Detection using Text Based Clustering Approach. *International Journal of Computer Applications, 5*(4).

Basha, S. M., Rajput, D. S., & Vandana, V. (2018). Impact of Gradient Ascent and Boosting Algorithm in Classification. *International Journal of Intelligent Engineering and Systems, 11*(1), 41-49.

Basha, S. M., Zhenning, Y., Rajput, D. S., Iyengar, N., & Caytiles, R. D. (2017). Domain Specific Predictive Analytics: A Case Study With R. *International Journal of Multimedia and Ubiquitous Engineering, 12*(6), 13-22.

Basha, S. M. H., Balaji, D. S., Caytiles, R. D., & Iyengar, N. (2017). A Soft Computing Approach to Provide Recommendation on PIMA Diabetes. *International Journal of Advanced Science and Technology, 106*(1), 19–32. doi:10.14257/ijast.2017.106.03

Basha, S. M., Zhenning, Y., Rajput, D. S., Caytiles, R. D., & Iyengar, N. (2017). Comparative Study on Performance Analysis of Time Series Predictive Models. *International Journal of Grid and Distributed Computing, 10*(8), 37–48. doi:10.14257/ijgdc.2017.10.8.04

Basha, S. M., Zhenning, Y., Rajput, D. S., Iyengar, N., & Caytiles, R. D. (2017). Weighted Fuzzy Rule Based Sentiment Prediction Analysis on Tweets. *International Journal of Grid and Distributed Computing*, *10*(6), 41–54. doi:10.14257/ijgdc.2017.10.6.04

Beaumont, J. M. (1990). Advances in block based fractal coding of still pictures. IEEE Colloq.: The Application of Fractal Techniques in Image Processing, 3.1–3.6.

Belle, A., Thiagarajan, R., Soroushmehr, S. M. R., Navidi, F., Beard, D. A., & Najarian, K. (2015). Big Data Analytics in Healthcare. *BioMed Research International*, *2015*, 1–16. doi:10.1155/2015/370194 PMID:26229957

Bengio, Y. (2012). Deep learning of representations for unsupervised and transfer learning. *ICML Unsupervised and Transfer Learning*, *27*, 17–36.

Bengio, Y. (2013). Deep learning of representations: Looking forward. In *Proceedings of the 1st International Conference on Statistical Language and Speech Processing. SLSP'13*. Springer. 10.1007/978-3-642-39593-2_1

Bengio, Y., Lamblin, P., Popovici, D., & Larochelle, H. (2007). Greedy layer-wise training of deep networks. *Advances in Neural Information Processing Systems*, *19*, 153.

Benjamin, M., Aradi, Y., & Shreiber, R. (2010). From shared data to sharing workflow: Merging PACS and teleradiology. *European Journal of Radiology*, *73*(1), 3–9. doi:10.1016/j.ejrad.2009.10.014 PMID:19914789

Berger, A. L., Pietra, V. J. D., & Pietra, S. A. D. (1996). A maximum entropy approach to natural language processing. *Computational Linguistics*, *22*(1), 39–71.

Bernstein, M. S., Brandt, J., Miller, R. C., & Karger, D. R. (2011). Crowds in two seconds: enabling realtime crowd-powered interfaces. *Proceedings of the 24th annual ACM symposium on User interface software and technology*. 10.1145/2047196.2047201

Bernstein, M. S., Little, G., Miller, R. C., Hartmann, B., Ackerman, M. S., Karger, D. R., ... Panovich, K. (2010). Soylent: a word processor with a crowd inside. *Proceedings of the 23nd annual ACM symposium on User interface software and technology.* 10.1145/1866029.1866078

Bezdek, J. C., Ehrlich, R., & Full, W. (1984). FCM: The fuzzy c-means clustering algorithm. *Computers & Geosciences*, *10*(2), 191–203. doi:10.1016/0098-3004(84)90020-7

Bhandari, G., Deaves, R., & Hassanein, K. (2009). Corrigendum to Debiasing investors with decision support systems: An experimental investigation. *Decision Support Systems*, *47*(1), 74. doi:10.1016/j.dss.2009.01.002

Bhatti, B. (2015). Social Media and Image Management: An Analysis of Facebook Usage in Celebrity Public Relations. *Media Watch*, *6*(3), 339. doi:10.15655/mw/2015/v6i3/77896

Bhoi, S. K., & Khilar, P. M. (2013). A Secure Routing Protocol for Vehicular Ad Hoc Network to Provide ITS Services. *International conference on Communication and Signal Processing*. 10.1109/iccsp.2013.6577240

Bhosale, H. S., & Gadekar, D. P. (2014). A Review Paper on Big Data and Hadoop. *International Journal of Scientific and research Publication*, *4*(10).

Bifet, Holmes, Fahringer, Kirkby, & Gavald. (2009). A New ensemble method for evolving data streams. KDD, 139–148.

Bifet. (2009). *Adaptive learning and mining for data streams and frequent patterns* (Ph.D. thesis). Universitat Polit'ecnica de Catalunya.

Bifet, A., & Gavald, R. (2006). A. Kalman filters and adaptive windows for learning in data streams. *Discovery Science*, *4625*, 29–40.

Bifet, A., & Gavald, R. (2007). *A Learning from time-changing data with adaptive windowing. SDM.* SIAM.

Bifet, A., Holmes, G., Pfahringer, B., & Gavald, R. (2009). A Improving adaptive bagging methods for evolving data streams. *ACML, 5828*, 23–37.

Big Data, RDBMS, and HADOOP - A Comparative Study. (2016). *International Journal of Science and Research, 5*(3), 1455-1458. 10.21275/v5i3.nov162167

Biggio, B., & Corona, I. (2011). Bagging Classifiers for Fighting Poisoning Attacks in these types of Adversarial Classification Tasks. *International Workshop on Multiple Classifier Systems, 6713*, 350.

Biswas, S., & Morris, S. (2005). Opportunistic Routing in MultiHop Wireless Networks, *Proceedings of the conference on Applications, technologies, architectures, and protocols for computer communications*, 133-144.

Biswas, S., & Morris, R. (2005). ExOR: Opportunistic Multi-Hop Routing for Wireless Networks. *Proceedings of the conference on Applications, technologies, architectures, and protocols for computer communications*, 133-144. 10.1145/1080091.1080108

Bitam, S., & Mellouk, A. (2011). QoS Swarm Bee Routing Protocol for Vehicular Ad Hoc Networks. *IEEE International Conference on Communications (ICC).* 10.1109/icc.2011.5963424

Blum, A., & Burch, C. (2000). On-line learning and the metrical task system problem. *Machine Learning, 39*(1), 35–58. doi:10.1023/A:1007621832648

Bollen, J., Mao, H., & Zeng, X.-J. (2010). Twitter mood predicts the stock market. *Journal of Computational Science, 2, 8.*

Bonchi, F., Castillo, C., Gionis, A., & Jaimes, A. (2011). Social network analysis and mining for business applications. *ACM Transactions on Intelligent Systems and Technology, 2*(3), 1–37. doi:10.1145/1961189.1961194

Bordes, A., Glorot, X., Weston, J., & Bengio, Y. (2012). Joint learning of words and meaning representations for open-text semantic parsing. *International Conference on Artificial Intelligence and Statistics*, 127–135.

Borrill, J., Keskitalo, R., & Kisner, T. (2015). Big Bang, Big Data, Big Iron: Fifteen Years of Cosmic Microwave Background Data Analysis at NERSC. *Computing in Science & Engineering, 17*(3), 22–29. doi:10.1109/MCSE.2015.1

Bresson, E., Catalano, D., & Pointcheval, D. (2003, November). *A simple public-key cryptosystem with a double trapdoor decryption mechanism and its applications* (Vol. 2894). Asiacrypt. doi:10.1007/978-3-540-40061-5_3

Bruckner, M., Haider, P., & Scheffer, T. (2006). Highly Scalable Discriminative Spam Filtering. *Proceedings of 15th Text Retrieval Conference (TREC).*

Brun, M., Sima, C., Hua, J., Lowey, J., Carroll, B., Suh, E., & Dougherty, E. R. (2007). Model-based evaluation of clustering validation measures. *Pattern Recognition, 40*(3), 807–824. doi:10.1016/j.patcog.2006.06.026

Cambria, E., Havasi, C., & Hussain, A. (2012, May). SenticNet 2: A Semantic and Affective Resource for Opinion Mining and Sentiment Analysis. In FLAIRS conference (pp. 202-207). Academic Press.

Cambria, E., Hussain, A., Havasi, C., Eckl, C., & Munro, J. (2010). Towards crowd validation of the UK national health service. *WebSci10*, 1-5.

Cambria, E., Benson, T., Eckl, C., & Hussain, A. (2012). Sentic PROMs: Application of sentic computing to the development of a novel unified framework for measuring health-care quality. *Expert Systems with Applications, 39*(12), 10533–10543. doi:10.1016/j.eswa.2012.02.120

Campbell, C. (n.d.). *Top Five Differences between DataWarehouses and Data Lakes.* Blue-Granite.com.

Campbell, M. (2014). Collapsing backpack charges wearable gadgets as you walk. *New Scientist, 221*(2950), 19. doi:10.1016/S0262-4079(14)60030-0

Canetti & Hohenberger. (2007). Chosen-ciphertext secures proxy re-encryption. *ACM Conference on Computer and Communications Security*, 185–194.

Carmona, C. J., Ramírez-Gallego, S., Torres, F., Bernal, E., Jesus, M.J., & García, S. (2012). Web usage mining to improve the design of an e-commerce website: OrOliveSur.com. *Expert Systems with Applications, 39*(12), 11243-11249.

Carpen-Amarie. (2011). Bringing Introspection Into Blobseer: Towards A Self–Adaptive Distributed Data Management System Computer Science. International Journal of Applied Mathematics and Computer Science, 21(2), 229-242.

Carter, D. (2012). Gaining additional value from secondary data resources: Using existing internal data and knowledge to create new company-centric resources. *Business Information Review, 29*(3), 148–156. doi:10.1177/0266382112456272

Cartwright, D., & Harary, F. (1956). Structural balance: A generalization of Heider's theory. *Psychological Review, 63*(5), 277–292. doi:10.1037/h0046049 PMID:13359597

Cercone, F. N. (2015). What's the big deal about big data? *Big Data And Information Analytics, 1*(1), 31-79. 10.3934/bdia.2016.1.31

Chakrabarti, S., Roy, S., & Soundalgekar, M. V. (2003). Fast and accurate text classification via multiple linear discriminant projections. *The VLDB Journal—The International Journal on Very Large Data Bases, 12*(2), 170-185.

Challenges with Big Data Analytics. (2015). *International Journal Of Science And Research, 4*(12), 778–780. doi:10.21275/v4i12.nov152088

Chan, P. K. (1999). A non-invasive learning approach to building web user profiles. *Proceedings of Workshop on Web Usage Analysis(KDD-99)*, 7–12.

Chandran, Dagon, & Feamste. (2006). DNS-based Blacklists keep up with Bots. *CEAS 2006*.

Chan, F., & Hanneman, K. (2015). Computed Tomography and Magnetic Resonance Imaging in Neonates With Congenital Cardiovascular Disease. Seminars In Ultrasound. *CT And MRI, 36*(2), 146–160. doi:10.1053/j.sult.2015.01.006 PMID:26001944

Chang, C.-C., & Lin, C.-J. (2011). LIBSVM : A library for support vector machines. *ACM Transactions on Intelligent Systems and Technology, 2*(3), 1–27. doi:10.1145/1961189.1961199

Chang, C.-L., & Girod, B. (2007). Direction-Adaptive Discrete Wavelet Transform for Image Compression. *IEEE Transactions on Image Processing, 16*(5), 1289–1302. doi:10.1109/TIP.2007.894242 PMID:17491460

Chang, P. C., Fan, C. Y., & Liu, C. H. (2009). Integrating a Piecewise Linear Representation Method and a Neural Network Model for Stock Trading Points Prediction. *IEEE Transactions on Systems, Man and Cybernetics. Part C, Applications and Reviews, 39*(1), 80–92. doi:10.1109/TSMCC.2008.2007255

Chawada, R. K., & Thakur, G. (2016). Big Data and Advanced Analytics Tools. *Proc. of Int. Symposium on Colossal Data Analysis and Networking CDAN*, 1-8.

Chawda & Thakur. (2016). Big Data and Advanced Analytics Tools. *2016 Symposium on Colossal Data Analysis and Networking (CDAN)*.

Chen, C. C., & Tseng, Y. D. (2011). Quality evaluation of product reviews using an information quality framework. *Decision Support Systems, 50*(4), 755–768. doi:10.1016/j.dss.2010.08.023

Chen, C., Shi, F. Yu. H., & Fei, N. (2016). Anonymous authentication based on cloud storage for cross-regional vehicles in VANET. *IEEE International Conference on Ubiquitous Wireless Broadband*, 1-8. 10.1109/ICUWB.2016.7790425

Chen, S. F., & Rosenfeld, R. (2000). A survey of smoothing techniques for ME models. *IEEE Transactions on Speech and Audio Processing*, *8*(1), 37–50. doi:10.1109/89.817452

Chen, Y., Zeng, Z., & Zhu, X. (2011). The Analysis on the Application of DSRC in the Vehicular Networks. In M. Zhu (Ed.), *Information and Management Engineering. Communications in Computer and Information Science* (Vol. 236). Berlin: Springer. doi:10.1007/978-3-642-24097-3_25

Chien, J. T., & Hsieh, H. L. (2013). Nonstationary source separation using sequential and variational Bayesian learning. *IEEE Transactions on Neural Networks and Learning Systems*, *24*(5), 681–694. doi:10.1109/TNNLS.2013.2242090 PMID:24808420

Chincholkar, A. A., & Urkude, D. A. (2012). Design and Implementation of Image Steganography. *Journal of Signal and Image Processing, 3*(3), 111–113.

Cho, Y. H., & Kim, J. K. (2004). Application of web usage mining and product taxonomy to collaborative recommendations in e-commerce. *Expert Systems with Applications*, *26*(2), 233-246.

Choi, T. M., Chan, H. K., & Yue, X. (2016). Recent Development in Big Data Analytics for Business Operations and Risk Management. *IEEE Transactions on Cybernetics*, *47*(1), 81–92. doi:10.1109/TCYB.2015.2507599 PMID:26766385

Chopra, G. (2011). *An Improved Image Compression Algorithm Using Binary Space Partition Scheme and Geometric Wavelets. IEEE Transactions on Image.*

Choudhury, T., Chhabra, A. S., Kumar, P., & Sharma, S. (2016). A Recent Trends on Big Data Analytics. *Proceedings of the SMART -2016, 5th International Conference on System Modeling & Advancement in Research Trends.*

Cireşan, D. C., Meier, U., Gambardella, L. M., & Schmidhuber, J. (2010). Deep, big, simple neural nets for handwritten digit recognition. *Neural Computation*, *22*(12), 3207–3220. doi:10.1162/NECO_a_00052 PMID:20858131

Clark, M. (2007). *Structured text retrieval by means of affordances and genre.* Presented in School of Computing the Robert Gordon University BCS IRSG Symposium: Future Directions in Information Access (FDIA 2007).

Cleary, J., Donnelly, S., & Graham, I. (2000). Design Principles for Accurate Passive Measurement, *Proc. PAM 2000 Passive and Active Measurement Workshop.*

Coats, A., Huval, B., Wng, T., Wu, D., & Wu, A. (2013). Deep Learning with COTS HPS systems. *Journal of Machine Learning Research*, *28*(3), 1337–1345.

Collobert, R., Weston, J., Bottou, L., Karlen, M., Kavukcuoglu, K., & Kuksa, P. (2011). Natural language processing (almost) from scratch. *Journal of Machine Learning Research*, *12*(Aug), 2493–2537.

Contreras, S. Z., & Ibanez, J. A. G. (2017). *Internet of Vehicles: Architecture, Protocols and Security. IEEE Internet of Things Journal.*

Cook, R. D. (1977). Detection of Influential Observation in Linear Regression. *Technometrics*, *19*(1), 15–18.

Cooley, R., Mobashar, B., & Srivastava, J. (1999). Data Preparation for Mining World Wide Web Browsing Patterns. *Knowledge and Information Systems*, *1*(1), 5–32. doi:10.1007/BF03325089

Cooley, R., Mobasher, B., & Srivastava, J. (2000). Web Usage Mining: Discovery and Applications of Usage Patterns from Web Data. *ACM SIGKDD*, *1*(2), 12–23. doi:10.1145/846183.846188

Coppola, R., Moristo, M., & Torino, P. D. (2016). Connected Car: Technologies, Issues, Future Trends. *ACM Computing Surveys*, 46.

Cormack, G. V. (2007, April). Email Spam Filtering: A Systematic Review, Published in. *Journal Foundations and Trends in Information Retrieval*, *1*(4), 335–455. doi:10.1561/1500000006

Crovella, M. E., & Bestavros, A. (1997). Self-similarity in World Wide Web traffic: Evidence and possible\ncauses. *IEEE/ACM Transactions on Networking*, *5*(6), 835–846. doi:10.1109/90.650143

CUDA C Programming Guide, PG-02829-001_v5.5. (2013). Santa Clara, CA: NVIDIA Corporation.

D'Orazio, C., Choo, K., & Yang, L. (2017). Data Exfiltration From Internet of Things Devices: iOS Devices as Case Studies. *IEEE Internet Of Things Journal*, *4*(2), 524–535. doi:10.1109/JIOT.2016.2569094

Dahl, G., Ranzato, M., Mohamed, A.-R., & Hinton, G. E. (2010). Phone recognition with the mean-covariance restricted boltzmann machine. In Advances in Neural Information Processing Systems. Curran Associates, Inc.

Dahl, G. E., Yu, D., Deng, L., & Acero, A. (2012). Context-dependent pre-trained deep neural networks for large-vocabulary speech recognition. *IEEE Transactions on Audio, Speech, and Language Processing*, *20*(1), 30–42. doi:10.1109/TASL.2011.2134090

Dalal, N., & Triggs, B. (2005). Histograms of oriented gradients for human detection. In *Computer Vision and Pattern Recognition, 2005. CVPR 2005. IEEE Computer Society Conference On* (Vol. 1, pp. 886–893). IEEE. doi:10.1109/CVPR.2005.177

Dandu, R. (2008). Storage media for computers in radiology. *The Indian Journal of Radiology & Imaging*, *18*(4), 287. doi:10.4103/0971-3026.43838 PMID:19774182

Dasuha, L. C., & Mantoro, T. (2016). CoMoSeF- Car to car communication in VANET using Co-operative Mobility Services of the Future. *5th International Conference on Multimedia Computing and Systems*. 10.1109/ICMCS.2016.7905637

Davis, J. A. (1967). Clustering and structural balance in graphs. *Human Relations*, *20*(2), 181–187. doi:10.1177/001872676702000206

Davoine, F., Antonini, M., Chassery, J. M., & Barlaud, M. (1996). Fractal image compression based on Delaunay triangulation and vector quantization. *IEEE Transactions on Image Processing*, *5*(2), 338–346. doi:10.1109/83.480769 PMID:18285117

Davoine, F., Svensson, J., & Chassery, J.-M. (1995). A mixed triangular and quadrilateral partition for fractal image coding. *IEEE Int. Conf. Image Processing, 3*, 284–287. 10.1109/ICIP.1995.537633

Dean, J., Corrado, G., Monga, R., Chen, K., Devin, M., Mao, M., . . . Ng, A. Y. (2012). Large scale distributed deep networks. Advances in neural information processing systems, 1223-1231.

Dean, J., & Ghemawat, S. (2008). MapReduce: Simplified data processing on large clusters. *Communications of the ACM*, *51*(1), 107–113. doi:10.1145/1327452.1327492

Deepak, K. R., & Rshi, R. (2016). Routing and security analysis in vehicular ad-hoc networks (VANETs). *IEEE International Conference on Power Electronics, Intelligent Control and Energy Systems*. 10.1109/ICPEICES.2016.7853606

Della Pietra, S., Della Pietra, V., & Lafferty, J. (1997). Inducing features of random fields. *IEEE Transactions on Pattern Analysis and Machine Intelligence*, *19*(4), 380–393. doi:10.1109/34.588021

Deng, L., Yu, D., & Platt, J. (2012). Scalable stacking and learning for building deep architectures. In *Acoustics, Speech and Signal Processing (ICASSP), 2012 IEEE International Conference on* (pp. 2133-2136). IEEE. 10.1109/ICASSP.2012.6288333

Deore & Umale. (2012). Wireless Monitoring of the Green House System Using Embedded Controllers. *IJSER, 3*(2).

Devlin, J. (2016). *28 Jupyter Notebook tips, tricks and shortcuts*. Retrieved on 12th October 2016 from https://www.dataquest.io/blog/jupyter-notebook-tips-tricks-shortcuts/

Dhar, V. (2014). Why Big Data = Big Deal. *Big Data, 2*(2), 55–56. doi:10.1089/big.2014.1522 PMID:27442294

DICOM Library - About DICOM most common features of study. (2017). Retrieved 26 May 2017, from http://www.dicomlibrary.com/dicom/study-structure/

Dikaiakos, M., Stassopoulou, A., & Papageorgiou, L. (2005). An investigation of web crawler behavior: Characterization and metrics. *Computer Communications, 28*(8), 880–897. doi:10.1016/j.comcom.2005.01.003

Dinov, I. (2016). Volume and value of big healthcare data. *Journal Of Medical Statistics And Informatics, 4*(1), 3. doi:10.7243/2053-7662-4-3 PMID:26998309

Doel, T., Shakir, D. I., Pratt, R., Aertsen, M., Moggridge, J., Bellon, E., ... Ourselin, S. (2017). GIFT-Cloud: A data sharing and collaboration platform for medical imaging research. *Computer Methods and Programs in Biomedicine, 139*, 181–190. doi:10.1016/j.cmpb.2016.11.004 PMID:28187889

Domingos, P. (2012). A few useful things to know about machine learning. *Communications of the ACM, 55*(10), 78. doi:10.1145/2347736.2347755

Domingos, P., & Hulten, G. (2000). Mining high-speed data streams. *KDD: Proceedings / International Conference on Knowledge Discovery & Data Mining. International Conference on Knowledge Discovery & Data Mining*, 71–80.

Domingos, P., & Pazzani, M. (1997). On the optimality of the simple Bayesian classifier under zero-one loss. *Machine Learning, 29*(2-3), 103–130. doi:10.1023/A:1007413511361

Domingos, P., & Richardson, M. (2001). Mining the network value of customers. *Proceedings of the seventh ACM SIGKDD International Conference on Knowledge Discovery and Data Mining*, 57-66. 10.1145/502512.502525

Doran, D., Morillo, K., & Gokhale, S. S. (2013). A comparison of Web robot and human requests. In *Advances in Social Networks Analysis and Mining (ASONAM), 2013 IEEE/ACM International Conference on* (pp. 1374–1380). IEEE. 10.1145/2492517.2500239

Doran, D., & Gokhale, S. S. S. (2011). Web robot detection techniques: Overview and limitations. *Data Mining and Knowledge Discovery, 22*(1–2), 183–210. doi:10.100710618-010-0180-z

Doreian, P., & Mrvar, A. (1996). A partitioning approach to structural balance. *Social Networks, 18*(2), 149–168. doi:10.1016/0378-8733(95)00259-6

Doreian, P., & Mrvar, A. (2009). Partitioning signed social networks. *Social Networks, 31*(1), 1–11. doi:10.1016/j.socnet.2008.08.001

Dunigan, B., King, T., & Morse, B. (2011). A preliminary examination of the effect of massage on state body image. *Body Image, 8*(4), 411–414. doi:10.1016/j.bodyim.2011.06.004 PMID:21764398

Eberendu, A. (2016). Unstructured Data: An overview of the data of Big Data. *International Journal of Computer Trends and Technology, 38*(1), 46–50. doi:10.14445/22312803/IJCTT-V38P109

El Gamal, T. (1985). A public key cryptosystem and a signature scheme based on discrete logarithms. *IEEE Transactions on Information Theory*, *31*(4), 469–472. doi:10.1109/TIT.1985.1057074

Elwell, R., & Polikar, R. (2009). Incremental learning in nonstationary environments with controlled forgetting. In *Neural Networks, 2009. IJCNN 2009. International Joint Conference on* (pp. 771-778). IEEE. 10.1109/IJCNN.2009.5178779

Elwell, R., & Polikar, R. (2011). Incremental learning of concept drift in nonstationary environments. *IEEE Transactions on Neural Networks*, *22*(10), 1517–1531. doi:10.1109/TNN.2011.2160459 PMID:21824845

Ertekin, S., Hirsh, H., & Rudin, C. (2012). Learning to Predict the Wisdom of Crowds. *Proceedings of the Collective Intelligence (CI '12)*.

Etzioni, O. (1996). The World Wide Web: Quagmire or gold mine. *Communications of the ACM*, *39*(11), 65–68. doi:10.1145/240455.240473

Fang, F. F., & Qu, L. B. (2011, April). Applying Bayesian trigram filter model in spam identification and its disposal. In *Electric Information and Control Engineering (ICEICE), 2011 International Conference on* (pp. 3024-3027). IEEE.

Farhadi, G. (2003). An enhanced fractal image compression based on Quadtree partition. *ISPA03 Proc. on Image and Signal Processing and Analysis*.

Ferriere, H. D., Grossglauser, M., & Vetterli, M. (2007). *Least-Cost Opportunistic Routing*. EPFL Technical Report LCAV-REPORT.

Fisher, Y. (1992). Fractal Image Compression. *SIGGRAPH'92 Course Notes*.

Fisher, Y. (1994). *Fractal Image Compression: Theory and Application*. New York: Springer-Verlag.

Fisher, Y., Jacobs, E. W., & Boss, R. D. (1992). *Fractal image compression using iterated transforms. In Image and Text Compression* (pp. 35–61). Boston, MA: Kluwer.

Fotland, M., & Kvale, L. (2015). The data explosion – A huge challenge and a gigantic opportunity. *Septentrio Conference Series*, (5). 10.7557/5.3662

Frank, E., Mark, A., Hall, I., & Witten, H. (2016). The WEKA Workbench. Online Appendix for "Data Mining: Practical Machine Learning Tools and Techniques (Weka ML Tool). Morgan Kaufmann.

Freund, Y., & Schapire, R. E. (1996). Game theory, on-line prediction and boosting. In *Proceedings of the ninth annual conference on Computational learning theory* (pp. 325-332). ACM. 10.1145/238061.238163

Gaffan, M. (2012). *BOTS & DDOS*. Retrieved from https://www.incapsula.com/blog/what-google-doesnt-show-you-31-of-website-traffic-can-harm-your-business.html

Gahi, Y., Guennoun, M., & Mouftah, H. T. (2016). Big Data Analytics: Security and Privacy Challenges. *Proceedings of 2016 IEEE Symposium on Computers and Communication (ISCC)*.

Gahi, Y., Guennoun, M., & Mouftah, H. T. (2016). Big Data Analytics: Security and Privacy Challenges. *Proc. Of Int. Symposium on Computer and Communication ISCC*, 952-957 10.1109/ISCC.2016.7543859

Galloro, V. (2008). Prime numbers. *Modern Healthcare*, *38*, 14–16.

Gama, J., Medas, P., Castillo, G., & Rodrigues, P. (2004). Learning with drift detection. *SBIA Brazilian Symposium on Artificial Intelligence*, 286–295.

Gantz, J. F., Reinsel, D., Chute, C., Schlichting, W., Minton, S., Toncheva, A., & Manfrediz, A. (2008). *The expanding digital universe: An updated forecast of worldwide information growth through 2011. Technical report*. IDC Information and Data.

Gantz, J., & Reinsel, D. (2012). *The digital universe in 2020: Big data, bigger digital shadows, and biggest growth in the Far East*. Academic Press.

Gao, Y., & Leung, M. K. H. (2002). Face recognition using line edge map. *IEEE Transactions on Pattern Analysis and Machine Intelligence, 24*(6), 764–779. doi:10.1109/TPAMI.2002.1008383

Garc'ia, Campovila, Fidalgo, Bifet, Gavald'a, & Morales-Bueno. (2006). Early drift detection method. *Fourth International Workshop on Knowledge Discovery from Data Streams*.

Garvey, M. D., Carnovale, S., & Yeniyurt, S. (2015). An analytical framework for supply network risk propagation: A Bayesian network approach. *European Journal of Operational Research, 243*(2), 618–627. doi:10.1016/j.ejor.2014.10.034

Gemayel, N. (2016). Analyzing Google File System and Hadoop Distributed File System. *Research Journal Of Information Technology, 8*(3), 66–74. doi:10.3923/rjit.2016.66.74

Géry, M. Haddad, Hatem. (2003). Evaluation of web usage mining approaches for user's next request prediction. In *Proceedings of the 5th ACM international workshop on Web information and data management (WIDM '03)*. ACM. 10.1145/956699.956716

Ghaleb, F. A., Razzaque, F. A., & Isnin, I. F. (2013). Security and privacy enhancement in VANETs using mobility pattern. *Fifth International Conference on Ubiquitous and Future Networks (ICUFN)*. 10.1109/ICUFN.2013.6614808

Gilge, C. (2016). Google Street View and the Image as Experience. *Geohumanities, 2*(2), 469–484. doi:10.1080/2373566X.2016.1217741

GitHub. (2013). *PHPEXCEL - Parsing excel files in PHP*. Retrieved November 20, 2015, from https://github.com/PHPOffice/PHPExcel

Goel, N., & Jha, C. K. (2013). Analyzing users behaviour from web access logs using automated log analyzer tool. *International Journal of Computers and Applications, 62*(2).

Gomathi, E., & Baskaran, K. (2012). Face Recognition Fusion Algorithm Based on Wavelet. *European Journal of Scientific Research, 74*(3), 450-455.

Goodfellow, I., Lee, H., Le, Q. V., Saxe, A., & Ng, A. Y. (2009). Measuring invariances in deep networks. In Advances in Neural Information Processing Systems. Curran Associates, Inc.

Google Analytics. (2013). Retrieved March 1, 2013, from https://analytics.google.com/

Groves, P. (2013). The Big Data revolution in healthcare. *The McKinsey Quarterly*.

Groves, P., Kayyali, B., Knot, D., & Van Kuiken, S. (2013). *The Big Data revolution in healthcare, Accelerating value and innovation*. McKinsey & Company.

Guo, Z., Wang, H., Yang, J., & Miller, D. J. (2015). A stock market forecasting model combining two-directional two-dimensional principal component analysis and radial basis function neural network. *PLoS One, 10*(4), 1–19. doi:10.1371/journal.pone.0122385 PMID:25849483

Gupta, D., & Mutha, S. (2003). *Image Compression Using Wavelet Packet. IEEE*.

Gupta, N., & Saxena, K. (2014). Cloud Computing Techniques for Big data and Hadoop Implementation. *International Journal of Engineering Research & Technology*, *3*(4), 722–726.

Gurcan, M. N., Boucheron, L., Can, A., Madabhushi, A., Rajpoot, N., & Yener, B. (2009). Histopathological Image Analysis: A Review. *Institute of Electrical and Electronics Engineers Review Biomedical Engineering*, *2*, 147–171. PMID:20671804

Gusev, M., Kroujiline, D., Govorkov, B., Sharov, S. V., Ushanov, D., & Zhilyaev, M. (n.d.). *Sell the news? A news - driven model of the stock market Sell the news? A news driven model of the stock market.* arXiv:1404.7364

Halkidi, M., Batistakis, Y., & Vazirgiannis, M. (2001). On clustering validation techniques. *Journal of Intelligent Information Systems*, *17*(2–3), 107–145. doi:10.1023/A:1012801612483

Halkidi, M., Batistakis, Y., & Vazirgiannis, M. (2002). Cluster Validity Methods : Part I. *SIGMOD Record*, *31*(2), 40–45. doi:10.1145/565117.565124

Hall, M., Frank, E., Holmes, G., Pfahringer, B., Reutemann, P., & Witten, I. H. (2009). The WEKA data mining software. *ACM SIGKDD Explorations Newsletter*, *11*(1), 10. doi:10.1145/1656274.1656278

Hampton, T. (2013). Human Genome Initiatives Make Strides to Better Understand Health and Disease. *Journal of the American Medical Association*, *309*(14), 1449. doi:10.1001/jama.2013.2607 PMID:23571561

Hamzaoui, R., Muller, M., & Saupe, D. (1996). VQ-enhanced fractal image compression. *IEEE Int. Conf.Image Processing*, *1*, 153–156. 10.1109/ICIP.1996.559456

Han, J., & Kamber, M. (2000). Data Mining: Concepts and Techniques. Morgan Kaufmann.

Han, S.-J., & Cho, S.-B. (2003). Combining Multiple Host-Based Detectors Using Decision Tree. *Australian Joint Artificial Intelligence Conference*. 10.1007/978-3-540-24581-0_18

Harlow & Peng. (2011). Automatic vehicle classification system with range sensors. *Transportation Research Part C: Emerging Technologies*.

Hasrounya, H., Samhatb, A. E., Bassilc, C., & Laouitia, A. (2017). VANet security challenges and solutions: *A survey*. *Vehicular Communications*, *7*, 7–20. doi:10.1016/j.vehcom.2017.01.002

Hassanalieragh, M. (2015). Health Monitoring and Management using Internet-of-Things (IoT) Sensing with Cloud-based Processing: Opportunities and Challenges. *IEEE International Conference on Services Computing*, 285-291. 10.1109/SCC.2015.47

Hassan, M. R., & Nath, B. (2005). Stock market forecasting using hidden Markov model: a new approach. *Proceedings of 5th International Conference on Intelligent Systems Design and Applications (ISDA'05)*, 192–196. 10.1109/ISDA.2005.85

Hathaway, R. J., Davenport, J. W., & Bezdek, J. C. (1989). Relational duals of the c-means clustering algorithms. *Pattern Recognition*, *22*(2), 205–212. doi:10.1016/0031-3203(89)90066-6

He, Wang, Wu, Hintz, & Hur. (2006). Fractal Image Compression on Spiral Architecture. *IEEE International Conference on Computer graphics, Image visualization*, 76-83.

Hegazy, O., Soliman, O. S., & Salam, M. A. (2013). A Machine Learning Model for Stock Market. *International Journal of Computer Science and Telecommunications*, *4*(12), 17–23.

Heider, F. (1946). Attitudes and cognitive organization. *The Journal of Psychology*, *21*(1), 107–112. doi:10.1080/00223980.1946.9917275 PMID:21010780

Hermon & Williams. (2014). Big data in healthcare: HAT is used for SRI security research institute. Edith Cowan University.

Higgins, I., Matthey, L., Glorot, X., Pal, A., Uria, B., Blundell, C., ... Lerchner, A. (2016). *Early visual concept learning with unsupervised deep learning.* arXiv preprint arXiv:1606.05579

Hinton, G. E., & Salakhutdinov, R. R. (2006). Reducing the dimensionality of data with neural networks. *Science, 313*(5786), 504-507.

Hinton, G. E. (2002). Training products of experts by minimizing contrastive divergence. *Neural Computation, 14*(8), 1771–1800. doi:10.1162/089976602760128018 PMID:12180402

Hinton, G. E., Osindero, S., & Teh, Y.-W. (2006). A fast learning algorithm for deep belief nets. *Neural Computation, 18*(7), 1527–1554. doi:10.1162/neco.2006.18.7.1527 PMID:16764513

Hinton, G., Deng, L., Yu, D., Mohamed, A.-R., Jaitly, N., Senior, A., ... Kingsbury, B. (2012). Deep neural networks for acoustic modeling in speech recognition: The shared views of four research groups. *Signal Process Mag IEEE, 29*(6), 82–97. doi:10.1109/MSP.2012.2205597

Hoa, V., & Cavalli, A. (2014). Security Attacks And Solutions In Vehicular Ad Hoc Networks: A Survey. *International Journal on AdHoc Networking Systems.*

Hornig, C. (1984). *A standard for the transmission of IP datagrams over ethernet networks.* RFC 894.

Hovold, J. (2005, July). *Naive Bayes Spam Filtering Using Word-Position-Based Attributes.* CEAS.

Huang, A. (2008). Similarity measures for text document clustering. *Proceedings of the sixth New Zealand computer science research student conference (NZCSRSC2008)*, 49–56.

Huang, T., Lan, L., Fang, X., An, P., Min, J., & Wang, F. (2015). Promises and Challenges in Big Data Computing in Health Science. *Big Data Research, 2*(1), 2–11. doi:10.1016/j.bdr.2015.02.002

Huei. (2014). Benefits and introduction to python programming for freshmore students using inexpensive robots. In *IEEE International Conference on Teaching, Assessment and Learning for Engineering (TALE)*. IEEE.

Hu, H., Lu, R., Zhang, Z., & Shao, J. (2017). REPLACE: A Reliable Trust-Based Platoon Service Recommendation Scheme in VANET. *IEEE Transactions on Vehicular Technology, 66*(2), 1786–1797. doi:10.1109/TVT.2016.2565001

Hui, J. S., Greenberg, M. D., & Gerber, E. M. (2014). Understanding the role of community in crowdfunding work. *Proceedings of the 17th ACM conference on Computer supported cooperative work & social computing.* 10.1145/2531602.2531715

Hui, K.-C., & Siu, W. C. (2007). Extended analysis of motion compensated frame difference for block-based motion prediction error. *IEEE Transactions on Image Processing, 16*(5), 1232–1245. doi:10.1109/TIP.2007.894263 PMID:17491455

Hulten, G., Spencer, L., & Domingos, P. (2001). Mining time-changing data streams. *KDD: Proceedings / International Conference on Knowledge Discovery & Data Mining. International Conference on Knowledge Discovery & Data Mining*, 97–106.

Hu, M., & Liu, B. (2004, August). Mining and summarizing customer reviews. In *Proceedings of the tenth ACM SIGKDD international conference on Knowledge discovery and data mining* (pp. 168-177). ACM.

Hung, J.-C. (2016). Fuzzy support vector regression model for forecasting stock market volatility. *Journal of Intelligent & Fuzzy Systems, 31*(3), 1987–2000. doi:10.3233/JIFS-16209

Huntington, P., Nicholas, D., & Jamali, H. R. (2008). Web robot detection in the scholarly information environment. *Journal of Information Science, 34*(5), 726–741. doi:10.1177/0165551507087237

Hurtgen, B., & Stiller, C. (1993), Fast hierarchical codebook search for fractal coding of still images, *Proc. EOS/SPIE Visual Communications PACS Medical Applications '93, Berlin, Germany.* 10.1117/12.160484

Hutchinson, J. E. (1981). Fractals and self-similarity. *Indiana University Mathematics Journal, 3*(5), 713–747. doi:10.1512/iumj.1981.30.30055

Hu, Y., & Li, W. (2011). Document sentiment classification by exploring description model of topical terms. *Computer Speech & Language, 25*(2), 386–403. doi:10.1016/j.csl.2010.07.004

Hwang, R. J., Shih, K. T., & Kao, C. H. (2001). Lossy compression tolerant steganography, *Proceedings of the 1st International Conference on The Human Society and the Internet-Internet Related Socio-Economic Issues, Lecture Notes In Computer Science, 2105*, 427-435. 10.1007/3-540-47749-7_34

Ibrahim, S., & Hamdy, M. (2015). A comparison on VANET authentication schemes: Public Key vs. Symmetric Key. *Tenth International Conference on Computer Engineering and Systems.* 10.1109/ICCES.2015.7393072

Inukollu, Arsi, & Ravuri. (2014). Security Issues Associated With Big Data In Cloud Computing. *International Journal of Network Security & Its Applications, 6*(3).

Irani. (2016). *Start programming on Raspberry Pi with Python.* Retrieved on 28th October 2016 from http://opensource-foru.com/2016/10/programming-raspberry-pi-with-python/

Islam, S. M. R., Kwak, D., Kabir, M. H., & Hossain, M. (2015). The Internet of Things for Health Care: A Comprehensive Survey. *IEEE Access: Practical Innovations, Open Solutions, 3*, 678–708. doi:10.1109/ACCESS.2015.2437951

Ismail, M. N., & Ismail, M. T. (2009). Framework of Intrusion Detection System via Snort Application on Campus Network Environment. *International Conference on Future Computer and Communication, 33*(1), 456-459. 10.1109/ICFCC.2009.10

Ivascenko, A. (2016). *Topic and Sentiment Analysis of Customers Reviews via Application of Text Mining.* Academic Press.

Jacob, G., Kirda, E., Kruegel, C., & Vigna, G. (2012). PubCrawl: Protecting Users and Businesses from CRAWLers. *21st USENIX Security Symposium (USENIX Security 12)*, 507–522.

Jacobs, E. W., Fisher, Y., & Boss, R. D. (1992). Image compression: A study of iterated transform method. *Signal Processing, 29*(3), 251–263. doi:10.1016/0165-1684(92)90085-B

Jacquin, A. E. (1990). A novel fractal block-coding technique for digital Images. *ICASSP International Conference on Acoustics, Speech, and Signal Processing.* 10.1109/ICASSP.1990.116007

Jagadish, H., Gehrke, J., Labrinidis, A., Papakonstantinou, Y., Patel, J., Ramakrishnan, R., & Shahabi, C. (2014). Big data and its technical challenges. *Communications of the ACM, 57*(7), 86–94. doi:10.1145/2611567

Jain, P.W., & Mao. (1999). Statistical Pattern Reorganization: A Review. *IEEE Transactions on Pattern Analysis and Machine Intelligence, 22*(1), 4-37.

Jakopović, H., & Preradović, N. M. (2013, January). Evaluation in public relations–sentiment and social media analysis of Croatia Airlines. *7th European Computing Conference (ECC'13).*

Janakiraman, Waldvogel, Zhang, & Indra. (2003). A peer-to-peer approach to network intrusion detection and prevention. *Enabling Technologies: Infrastructure for Collaborative Enterprises.*

Jaquin, A. E. (1993). Fractal image coding: A review. Proceeding of tile IEEE, 81(10).

Jaquin, A. E. (1992). Image coding based on a fractal theory of iterated contractive image transformation. *IEEE Transactions on Image Processing*, *1*(1).

Jayasingh, B. B., Patra, M. R., & Mahesh, D. (2016). Security Issues and Challenges of big data analytics and visualization. *Proc. Int. IEEE Conf. Contemporary Computing and Informatics IC3I*, 204-208 10.1109/IC3I.2016.7917961

Jindal, A., Dua, A., Kumar, N., Vasilakos, A. V., & Rodrigues, J. J. P. C. (2017). An Efficient Fuzzy rule-based Big Data Analytics scheme for providing healthcare-as-a-service. *IEEE International Conference on Communications (ICC)*, 1-6. 10.1109/ICC.2017.7996965

Jing, C., Zhu, Y., & Li, M. (2014). Customer satisfaction-aware scheduling for utility maximization on geo-distributed data centers. *Concurrency and Computation*, *27*(5), 1334–1354. doi:10.1002/cpe.3318

Jin, L., Chen, Y., Wang, T., Hui, P., & Vasilakos, A. V. (2013). Understanding user behavior in online social networks: A survey. *IEEE Communications Magazine*, *51*(9), 144–150. doi:10.1109/MCOM.2013.6588663

Joachims, T. (1998, April). Text categorization with support vector machines: Learning with many relevant features. In *European conference on machine learning* (pp. 137-142). Springer Berlin Heidelberg. 10.1007/BFb0026683

Johnson, M. (2012). Using Rejuvenation in order to improve the Particle Filtering for especially Bayesian Word Segmentation. *Proceedings of the 50th Annual Meeting of the Association for Computational Linguistics*, 85–89.

Joydeep, A. S., Strehl, E., Ghosh, J., Mooney, R., & Strehl, A. (2000). The impact of Similarity Measures on Webpage Clustering. In *Workshop on Artificial Intelligence for Web Search* (pp. 58–64). AAAI.

Juneja, P., & Kashyap, R. (2016). Energy based Methods for Medical Image Segmentation. *International Journal of Computers and Applications*, *146*(6). doi:10.5120/ijca2016910808

Juneja, P., & Kashyap, R. (2016). Optimal Approach For CT Image Segmentation Using Improved Energy Based Method. *International Journal of Control Theory and Applications*, *9*(41), 599–608.

Kakkirala, L., & Venkateswara, K. (2016). Significant Big Data Interpretation using Map Reduce Paradigm. *International Journal of Computers and Applications*, *156*(1), 7–11. doi:10.5120/ijca2016912339

Kakria, P., Tripathi, N. K., & Kitipawang, P. (2015). A Real-Time Health Monitoring System for Remote Cardiac Patients Using Smartphone and Wearable Sensors. *International Journal of Telemedicine and Applications*, *2015*, 1–11. doi:10.1155/2015/373474 PMID:26788055

Kalantar-Zadeh. (2013). *Sensors-An Introductory Course*. Springer.

Kamesh, S., Durga Devi, K., & Raviteja, S. N. V. P. (2017). Dwt Based Data Hiding Using Video Steganography. *International Journal of Engineering Sciences & Research Technology*, 361-367.

Kapur, T. (2016). MO-DE-202-03: Image-Guided Surgery and Interventions in the Advanced Multimodality Image-Guided Operating (AMIGO) Suite. *Medical Physics*, *43*(6Part30), 3699–3700. doi:10.1118/1.4957227

Karagiannis, D., & Buchmann, R. (2016). Linked Open Models: Extending Linked Open Data with conceptual model information. *Information Systems*, *56*, 174–197. doi:10.1016/j.is.2015.10.001

Karpagam Shanmuga Priya, D., Kavitha, B., Naveen Kumar, R., & Banuroopa, K. (2010). Improvising BayesNet Classifier Using Feature Reduction Method for Spam Classification. *IJCST*, *1*(2).

Karydis, I., Sioutas, S., Avlonitis, M., Mylonas, P., & Kanavos, A. (2017). A Survey on Big Data and Collective Intelligence. In T. Sellis & K. Oikonomou (Eds.), Lecture Notes in Computer Science: Vol. 10230. *Algorithmic Aspects of Cloud Computing, ALGOCLOUD 2016*. Cham: Springer. doi:10.1007/978-3-319-57045-7_11

Kashyap, R., & Gautam, P. (2016). Fast Level Set Method for Segmentation of Medical Images. In *Proceedings of the International Conference on Informatics and Analytics* (ICIA-16). ACM. 10.1145/2980258.2980302

Kashyap, R., & Gautam, P. (2017). Fast Medical Image Segmentation Using Energy-Based Method. *Pattern and Data Analysis in Healthcare Settings*, 35-60.

Kashyap, R., & Gautam, P. (2013). Microarray Image Segmentation using Improved GOGAC Method. *Science and Engineering*, 2(4), 67–74.

Kashyap, R., & Gautam, P. (2015). Modified region based segmentation of medical images. *2015 International Conference on Communication Networks (ICCN)*, 209-216. 10.1109/ICCN.2015.41

Kashyap, R., & Tiwari, V. (2017). Energy-based active contour method for image segmentation. *International Journal of Electronic Healthcare*, 9(2/3), 210. doi:10.1504/IJEH.2017.083165

Katal, A., Wazid, M., & Goudar, R. H. (2013). Big data: Issues, challenges, tools and Good practices. Academic Press.

Kateshiya, J.P., & Singh, A.P. (2015). Review To Detect and Isolate Malicious Vehicle in VANET. *International Journal of Innovative Research in Science, Engineering and Technology*.

Kaur, Kaur, & Singh. (2011). Steganographic approach for hiding image in dct domain. *International Journal of Advances in Engineering and Technology*, 1(3).

Kavita, M. P., & Ruhil, N. (2016). Web data mining: A perspective of research issues and Challenges, *IEEE, International Conference on Computing for Sustainable Global Development (INDIACom)*, 3235-3238.

Keisuke, U. (2005). *CALM -- Continuous Air Interface for Long and Medium range*. Retrieved on 3rd August, 2005 from https://www.ietf.org/proceedings/63/slides/nemo-4.pdf

Kelly, M. G., Hand, D. J., & Adams, N. M. (1999). The impact of changing populations on classifier performance. *KDD: Proceedings / International Conference on Knowledge Discovery & Data Mining. International Conference on Knowledge Discovery & Data Mining*, 367–371. doi:10.1145/312129.312285

Kempe, D., Keinberg, J., & Tardos, E. (2003). Maximizing the spread of influence through a social network. *Proceedings of the Ninth ACM SIGKDD International Conference on Knowledge Discovery and Data Mining*, 137-146. 10.1145/956750.956769

Keshtkar, F., & Inkpen, D. (2013). A bootstrapping method for extracting paraphrases of emotion expressions from texts. *Computational Intelligence*, 29(3), 417–435. doi:10.1111/j.1467-8640.2012.00458.x

Khan, S., Shakil, K. A., & Alam, M. (2016). Educational Intelligence: Applying Cloud based big data analytics to Indian education sector. *Int. IEEE Conf. Contemporary Computing and Informatics IC3I*, 29-34 10.1109/IC3I.2016.7917930

Kholghi & Keyvanpour. (2011). An analytical framework for Data stream mining techniques Based on challenges and Requirements. *IJEST*, 3, 2507-2513.

Khosla & Kaur. (2014). Secure Data Hiding Technique Using Video Steganography and Watermarking. *International Journal of Computer Applications, 95*.

Kim, K., & Han, I. (2000). Genetic algorithms approach to feature discretization in artificial neural networks for the prediction of stock price index. *Expert Systems with Applications*, 19(2), 125–132. doi:10.1016/S0957-4174(00)00027-0

Kim, M., & Hong, C. (2017). Unstructured Social Media Data Mining System Based on Emotional Database and Unstructured Information Management Architecture Framework. *Advanced Science Letters*, 23(3), 1668–1672. doi:10.1166/asl.2017.8614

Kim, Y. M., Han, S. K., Kim, T. Y., Oh, K. J., Luo, Z., & Kim, C. (2015). Intelligent stock market instability index: Application to the Korean stock market. *Intelligent Data Analysis*, *19*(4), 879–895. doi:10.3233/IDA-150749

Kim, Y., & Sohn, S. Y. (2012). Stock fraud detection using peer group analysis. *Expert Systems with Applications*, *39*(10), 8986–8992. doi:10.1016/j.eswa.2012.02.025

Kingma, D. P., Mohamed, S., Rezende, D. J., & Welling, M. (2014). Semi-supervised learning with deep generative models. In Advances in Neural Information Processing Systems (pp. 3581-3589). Academic Press.

Kirkby, R. (2007). *Improving Hoeffding Trees* (Ph.D thesis). Department of Computer Science, University of Waikato.

Kishore Kumar, R. (2012). A Comparative Study of the algorithms related to the Classification for Spam Email Data Analysis. IMECS.

Knossenburg, Y., Nogueira, R., & Chimenti, P. (2016). Contagious Content: Viral Video Ads Identification of Content Characteristics that Help Online Video Advertisements Go Viral. *Revista Brasileira De Marketing*, *15*(04), 448–458. doi:10.5585/remark.v15i4.3385

Kontopoulos, E., Berberidis, C., Dergiades, T., & Bassiliades, N. (2013). Ontology-based sentiment analysis of twitter posts. *Expert Systems with Applications*, *40*(10), 4065–4074. doi:10.1016/j.eswa.2013.01.001

Koprinska, I., Poon, J., Clark, J., & Chan, J. (2007). Learning to classify e-mail. *Information Sciences*, *177*(10), 2167–2187. doi:10.1016/j.ins.2006.12.005

Korzun, D. G., Nikolavskiy, I., & Gurtov, A. (2012). *Service Intelligence support for medical sensor networks in personalized mobile health systems. Internet of things, smart spaces, and next generation networks and systems (LNCS 9247)*. Springer.

Kowser, S. (2016). *Digital Remembrance Based User Validation for Internet of Things. International Journal Of Engineering And Computer Science*. doi:10.18535/ijecs/v5i5.16

Krishnan, S. (2016). Application of Analytics to Big Data in Healthcare. *IEEE 32nd Southern Biomedical Engineering Conference,* 156-157.

Krishnapuram, R., Joshi, A., Nasraoui, O., & Yi, L. (2001). Low-complexity fuzzy relational clustering algorithms for Web mining. *IEEE Transactions on Fuzzy Systems*, *9*(4), 595–607. doi:10.1109/91.940971

Krishnapuram, R., Joshi, A., & Yi, L. (1999). A fuzzy relative of the k-medoids algorithm with application to web document and snippet clustering. In *IEEE International Fuzzy Systems. Conference Proceedings(FUZZ-IEEE'99)* (Vol. 3, pp. 1281–1286). IEEE. 10.1109/FUZZY.1999.790086

Krizhevsky, A., & Hinton, G. (2009). *Learning multiple layers of features from tiny images*. Academic Press.

Krizhevsky, A., Sutskever, I., & Hinton, G. (2012). Imagenet classification with deep convolutional neural networks. In Advances in Neural Information Processing Systems. Curran Associates, Inc.

Kshetri, N. (2014). The emerging role of Big Data in key development issues: Opportunities, challenges, and concerns. *Big Data & Society*, *1*(2), 205395171456422. doi:10.1177/2053951714564227

Kumar & Pooja. (2010). Steganography A Data Hiding Technique. *International Journal of Computer Applications*, *9*(7).

Kumar, V., & Thakur, R. S. (2017). A brief investigation on web usage mining tools (WUM). *Saudi J. Eng. Technol*, *2*(1), 1-11.

Kumaresan, N., & Manivannan, M. (2010). Embedded web server and GPRS Based Advanced Industrial Automation using Linux RTOS. *International Journal of Engineering Science and Technology, 2*(11), 6074–6081.

Kumar, M., & Manjula, R. (2014). Big Data Analytics in Rural Health Care - A Step towards Svasth Bharat. *International Journal of Computer Science and Information Technologies, 5*(6), 7172–7178.

Kumar, P. D., Kumar, R. S., & Sujatha, K. (2016). Big data Analytics of IoT based Health Care Monitoring System. *IEEE Uttar Pradesh Section International Conference on Electrical, Computer and Electronics Engineering (UPCON),* 55-60.

Kumar, V., & Thakur, R. S. (2016). Exploring behaviour of visitor's activity at granular level from web log data using deep log analyzer. *International Journal of System and Software Engineering, 4*(1), 16–26.

Kune, R., Konugurthi, P., Agarwal, A., Chillarige, R., & Buyya, R. (2016). XHAMI - extended HDFS and MapReduce interface for Big Data image processing applications in cloud computing environments. *Software, Practice & Experience, 47*(3), 455–472. doi:10.1002pe.2425

Kwon, Y. K., & Moon, B. R. (2007). A hybrid neurogenetic approach for stock forecasting. *IEEE Transactions on Neural Networks, 18*(3), 851–864. doi:10.1109/TNN.2007.891629 PMID:17526350

Lafuente, G. (2015). The big data security challenge. *Network Security, 2015*(1), 12–14. doi:10.1016/S1353-4858(15)70009-7

Laney. (2001). 3d Data management: Controlling data volume, velocity and variety. *Appl. Delivery Strategies Meta Group, 949.*

Laney, D. (2012). The importance of 'big data': A definition. *Gartner. Retrieved, 21,* 2014–2018.

Lang. (2002). *Implementation of Navie Bayesian classifier in java.* Kaiserslautern university of applied sciences dept.

Lappas, T., Liu, K., & Terzi, E. (2009). Finding a Team of Experts in Social Networks. *Proceedings of the 15th ACM SIGKDD international conference on Knowledge discovery and data mining,* 467-476. 10.1145/1557019.1557074

Larkey, L. S. (1998, August). Automatic essay grading using text categorization techniques. In *Proceedings of the 21st annual international ACM SIGIR conference on Research and development in information retrieval* (pp. 90-95). ACM. 10.1145/290941.290965

Larochelle, H., Bengio, Y., Louradour, J., & Lamblin, P. (2009). Exploring strategies for training deep neural networks. *Journal of Machine Learning Research, 10,* 1–40.

Lasecki, W. S., White, S. C., Murray, K. I., & Bigham, J. P. (2012). Crowd memory: Learning in the collective. *Proceedings of the Collective Intelligence (CI'12).*

Laureano, Maziero, & Jamhour. (2007). Protecting Host-Based Intrusion Detectors through Virtual Machines. *The International Journal of Computer and Telecommunications Networking.*

LeCun, Y., Bengio, Y., & Hinton, G. (2015). Deep learning. *Nature, 521*(7553), 436–444. doi:10.1038/nature14539 PMID:26017442

Lee, J., Cha, S., Lee, D., & Lee, H. (2009). Classification of web robots: An empirical study based on over one billion requests. *Computers & Security, 28*(8), 795–802. doi:10.1016/j.cose.2009.05.004

Lee, J., Chung, J., & Lee, D. (2015). Efficient Data Replication Scheme based on Hadoop Distributed File System. *International Journal of Software Engineering and Its Applications, 9*(12), 177–186. doi:10.14257/ijseia.2015.9.12.16

Lee, K. C., & Gerla, M. (2010). Opportunistic Vehicular Routing, invited paper. *IEEE European Wireless Conference*, 873-880.

Lee, K. C., & Gerla, M. (2010). Opportunistic Vehicular Routing. *European Wireless Conference*, 873-880.

Leppert, F., & Greiner, W. (2016). Big Data In Healthcare - Opportunities And Challenges. *Value in Health*, *19*(7), A463. doi:10.1016/j.jval.2016.09.677

Leskovec, J., Huttenlocher, D., & Kleinberg, J. (2010). Signed networks in social media. *Proceedings of the SIGCHI Conference on Human Factors in Computing Systems, (CHI '10)*, 1361-1370.

Lewis, D. D. (1998, April). Naive (Bayes) at forty: The independence assumption in information retrieval. In *European conference on machine learning* (pp. 4-15). Springer Berlin Heidelberg. 10.1007/BFb0026666

Lewis, D. D., & Ringuette, M. (1994, April). A comparison of two learning algorithms for text categorization. *Third annual symposium on document analysis and information retrieval*, *33*, 81-93.

Li, F., Goševa-Popstojanova, K., & Ross, A. (2007). Discovering Web workload characteristics through cluster analysis. In *Proceedings - 6th IEEE International Symposium on Network Computing and Applications, NCA 2007* (pp. 61–68). IEEE. 10.1109/NCA.2007.15

Li, S. T., & Tsai, F. C. (2011, June). Noise control in document classification based on fuzzy formal concept analysis. In *Fuzzy Systems (FUZZ), 2011 IEEE International Conference on* (pp. 2583-2588). IEEE. 10.1109/FUZZY.2011.6007449

Li, F. (2006). An empirical study of clustering behavior of spammers and Group based Anti-spam strategie. *CEAS*, *2006*, 21–28.

Li, F., & Nath, S. (2014). Scalable data summarization on big data. *Distributed and Parallel Databases*, *32*(3), 313–314. doi:10.100710619-014-7145-y

Li, L., Niu, T., Cho, S., & Wang, Z. (2014). Mathematical Methods and Applications in Medical Imaging. *Computational and Mathematical Methods in Medicine*, 1-2. doi:10.1155/2014/765163 PMID:24995037

Lin, C., Cao, N., Liu, S., Papadimitriou, S., Sun, J., & Yan, X. (2009). SmallBlue: social network analysis for expertise search and collective intelligence. *Proceedings of the 25th international conference on data engineering, ICDE '09*, 1483-1486. 10.1109/ICDE.2009.140

Lin, X., Quan, L., & Wu, H. (2008). An automatic scheme to categorize user sessions in modern HTTP traffic. *GLOBECOM - IEEE Global Telecommunications Conference*, 1485–1490. 10.1109/GLOCOM.2008.ECP.290

Littlestone, N., Long, P. M., & Warmuth, M. K. (1991). On-line learning of linear functions. In *Proceedings of the twenty-third annual ACM symposium on Theory of computing* (pp. 465-475). ACM. 10.1145/103418.103467

Liu, B. (2006). *Web data mining: Exploring hyperlinks, contents, and usage data (datacentric systems and applications)*. Springer-Verlag.

Liu, H., & Keselj, V. (2007). Combined mining of Web server logs and web contents for classifying user navigation patterns and predicting users' future requests. *Data & Knowledge Engineering*, *61*(2), 304–330. doi:10.1016/j.datak.2006.06.001

Li, W., & Song, H. (2016). ART: An Attack-Resistant Trust Management Scheme for Securing Vehicular Ad Hoc Networks. *IEEE Transactions on Intelligent Transportation Systems*, *17*(April), 960–969. doi:10.1109/TITS.2015.2494017

Li, X., Huang, X., Deng, X., & Zhu, S. (2014). Enhancing quantitative intra-day stock return prediction by integrating both market news and stock prices information. *Neurocomputing*, *142*, 228–238. doi:10.1016/j.neucom.2014.04.043

Li, Y. H., & Jain, A. K. (1998). Classification of text documents. *The Computer Journal, 41*(8), 537–546. doi:10.1093/comjnl/41.8.537

Li, Y. M., & Li, T. Y. (2013). Deriving market intelligence from microblogs. *Decision Support Systems, 55*(1), 206–217. doi:10.1016/j.dss.2013.01.023

Lobo, L. (2017). Orthognatic surgery in temporomandibular joint patients: Evaluation, diagnosis, when and why to operate the temporomandibular joint. *International Journal of Oral and Maxillofacial Surgery, 46*, 32. doi:10.1016/j.ijom.2017.02.120 PMID:27697415

Loraine Charlet, A., & Kumar, A. (2012). *Market Basket Analysis for a Supermarket based on Frequent Itemset Mining.* Academic Press.

Lou & Hwang. (2006). *Adaptive Content Poisoning To Prevent Illegal File Distribution in P2P Networks Fellow.* IEEE.

Lovalekar, S. (2014). Big Data: An Emerging Trend In Future. *International Journal of Computer Science and Information Technologies, 5*(1), 538–541.

Lowe, D. G. (1999). Object recognition from local scale-invariant features. In *Computer Vision, 1999. The Proceedings of the Seventh IEEE International Conference On.* IEEE Computer Society. 10.1109/ICCV.1999.790410

Lu, He, & Gao. (2009). Design of electronic toll collection system based on global positioning system technique. In *Proceedings of ISECS International Colloquium on Computing, Communication, Control, and Management.* IEEE.

Lu, J., & Park, O. (2003). Modeling customer lifetime value using survival analysis—an application in the telecommunications industry. *Data Mining Techniques*, 120-128.

Lu, C. J. (2010). Integrating independent component analysis-based denoising scheme with neural network for stock price prediction. *Expert Systems with Applications, 37*(10), 7056–7064. doi:10.1016/j.eswa.2010.03.012

Lu, C. Y., Lin, S. H., Liu, J. C., Cruz-Lara, S., & Hong, J. S. (2010). Automatic event-level textual emotion sensing using mutual action histogram between entities. *Expert Systems with Applications, 37*(2), 1643–1653. doi:10.1016/j.eswa.2009.06.099

Luca, L., Stephen, B., & Pierpaolo, D. (2009). Information Foraging Theory as a Form of Collective Intelligence for Social Search. *Proceedings of the 1st International Conference on Computational Collective Intelligence, Semantic Web, Social Networks and Multiagent Systems (ICCCI '09)*, 63-74. 10.1007/978-3-642-04441-0_5

Luo, J., Wu, M., Gopukumar, D., & Zhao, Y. (2016). Data Application in Biomedical Research and Health Care: A Literature Review. *Biomedical Informatics Insights, 8*, 1–10. doi:10.4137/BII.S31559 PMID:26843812

Malone, T. W., Laubacher, R., & Dellarocas, C. (2009). *Harnessing Crowds: Mapping the Genome of Collective Intelligence.* MIT Sloan Research Paper No. 4732-09. 10.2139/ssrn.1381502

Malviya & Gupta. (2002). An Improved Image Compression Algorithm Based on Daubechies- Wavelets with Arithmetic Coding. *JIEA, 3*(6), 46-50.

Mandelbrot, B. (1982). *The Fractal Geometry of Nature.* San Francisco: W. H. Freeman and Co.

Maries, I., & Scarlat, E. (2011). Enhancing the computational collective intelligence within communities of practice using trust and reputation models. *Transactions on Computational Collective Intelligence, 3*, 74–95.

Marjani, Nasaruddin, Gani, Karim, Hashem, Siddiqa, & Yaqoob. (n.f.). *Big IoT Data Analytics: Architecture, Opportunities, and Open Research Challenges.* IEEE, DOI 10.1109/ACCESS.2017.2689040

Martens, J. (2010). Deep learning via Hessian-free optimization. In *Proceedings of the 27th International Conference on Machine Learning (ICML-10)* (pp. 735-742). Academic Press.

Martín-Valdivia, M.-T., Martínez-Cámara, E., Perea-Ortega, J.-M., & Ureña-López, L. A. (2013). Sentiment polarity detection in Spanish reviews combining supervised and unsupervised approaches. *Expert Systems with Applications, 40*(10), 3934–3942. doi:10.1016/j.eswa.2012.12.084

Mashkoor & Ahamad. (2017). Visualization, Security and Privacy Challenges of Big Data. *International Journal of Advanced Technology in Engineering and Science, 5*(6), 394 - 400.

Mashkoor, A., & Ahamad, M. A. (2017). Visualization, Security and Privacy Challenges of Big Data. *International Journal of Advanced Technology in Engineering and Science, 5*(6), 394–400.

Maske & Patil. (2012). Comparison of Image Compression using Wavelet for Curvelet Transform & Transmission over Wireless Channel. *International Journal of Scientific and Research Publications, 5*(2).

Massa, P., & Avesani, P. (2006). Trust-aware bootstrapping of recommender systems. *Proceedings of the ECAI Workshop on Recommender Systems*, 29-33.

MATLAB. (2012a). *Software package*. Retrieved from http://www.mathworks.com

Matrawy. (2007). Bottleneck Analysis of Traffic Monitoring Using Wireshark. *4th International Conference on Innovations in Information Technology, 2007*, 18-20. 10.1109/IIT.2007.4430446

Matwankar & Shinde. (2015). Sentiment Analysis for Big Data using Data Mining Algorithms. *International Journal of Engine Research, 4*(9). doi:10.17577/ijertv4is090801

McKinsey & Company. (2013). *The Big data Revolution in Healthcare*. Center for US Health Reform Business Technology Office.

Mekkia, T., Jabrib, I., Rachedic, A., & Jemaaa, M. (2016, November 28). Vehicular cloud networks: Challenges, architectures, and future directions. *Vehicular Communications*.

Memon, Q. A. (2017). Authentication and Error Resilience in Images Transmitted through Open Environment. In *Medical Imaging: Concepts, Methodologies, Tools, and Applications: Concepts* (p. 1671). Medical Information Science Reference. doi:10.4018/978-1-5225-0571-6.ch069

Mertz, D. (2002). *Spam Filtering Techniques: Comparing a Half-Dozen Approaches to Eliminating Unwanted Email*. Availableat: http://gnosis.cx/publish/progrflamming/filtering-spam.html

Metsis, V., Androutsopoulos, I., & Paliouras, G. (2006). Spam Filtering with Naive Bayes – Which Naive Bayes? *CEAS 2006 Third Conference on Email and Anti Spam*.

Michal, M., Kapusta, J., Švec, P., & Hlinku, Tr. A. (2012). Data preprocessing evaluation for web logs mining: Reconstruction of activities of a web visitor. *J. Proc. Comput. Sci., 1*, 2273–2280.

Mihaita, A. E., Dobre, C., Pop, F., Mavromoustakis, C. X., & Mastorakis, G. (2017). *Secure Opportunistic Vehicle-to-Vehicle Communication, Advances in Mobile Cloud Computing and Big Data in the 5G Era. In Studies in Big Data* (Vol. 22). Springer.

Mikolov, T., Deoras, A., Kombrink, S., Burget, L., & Cernock'y, J. (2011). Empirical evaluation and combination of advanced language modeling techniques. In *INTERSPEECH* (pp. 605–608). ISCA.

Mills & Gibson. (2006). Traffic Detector Handbook (3rd ed.; vol. 1). Federal Highway Administration Turner-Fairbank Highway Research Center.

Minku, L. L., & Yao, X. (2012). DDD: A New Ensemble Approach for Dealing With Concept Drift. *IEEE Transactions on Knowledge and Data Engineering*, *24*(4), 619–633. doi:10.1109/TKDE.2011.58

Mirajkar Pradnya, & Ruikar. (2013). Image Fusion Based On Stationary Wavelet Transform. *International Journal of Advanced Engineering Research and Studies*, 99-101.

Mishra, A. D., & Singh, Y. B. (2016). Big Data Analytics for Security and Privacy Challenges. *Proceedings of International Conference on Computing, Communication and Automation (ICCCA2016)*. 10.1109/CCAA.2016.7813688

MIT Center for Collective Intelligence. (n.d.). Retrieved from http://cci.mit.edu/

Mittermayer, M.-a. (2004). Forecasting Intraday stock price trends with text mining techniques. *Proceedings of the 37th Annual Hawaii International Conference on System Sciences*, 1–10. 10.1109/HICSS.2004.1265201

Mobasher, B. (2005). *Web usage mining and personalization*. CRC Press, LLC.

Mohamed, A.-R., Dahl, G. E., & Hinton, G. (2012). Acoustic modeling using deep belief networks. *Audio Speech Lang Process IEEE Trans*, *20*(1), 14–22. doi:10.1109/TASL.2011.2109382

Mohammad, S. (2011, June). From once upon a time to happily ever after: Tracking emotions in novels and fairy tales. In *Proceedings of the 5th ACL-HLT Workshop on Language Technology for Cultural Heritage, Social Sciences, and Humanities* (pp. 105-114). Association for Computational Linguistics.

Moraes, R., Valiati, J. F., & Neto, W. P. G. (2013). Document-level sentiment classification: An empirical comparison between SVM and ANN. *Expert Systems with Applications*, *40*(2), 621–633. doi:10.1016/j.eswa.2012.07.059

Movahedi, Z., Langar, R., & Pujolle, G. (2010). A Comprehensive Overview of Vehicular Ad hoc Network Evaluation Alternatives. *8th Asia-Pacific Symposium on Information and Telecommunication Technologies*.

Mrdovic, S., & Zajko, E. (2005). Secured Intrusion Detection System Infrastructure. University of Sarajevo/Faculty of Electrical Engineering.

Mstafa, R. J., Elleithy, K. M., & Abdelfattah, E. (2017). A Robust and Secure Video Steganography Method in DWT-DCT Domains Based on Multiple Object Tracking and ECC. *IEEE Access: Practical Innovations, Open Solutions*, *5*, 5354–5365.

Mudinas, A., Zhang, D., & Levene, M. (2012, August). Combining lexicon and learning based approaches for concept-level sentiment analysis. In *Proceedings of the First International Workshop on Issues of Sentiment Discovery and Opinion Mining* (p. 5). ACM. 10.1145/2346676.2346681

Mujawar, S., & Joshi, A. (2015). Data Analytics Types, Tools and their Comparison. *IJARCE*, *4*(2), 488–491.

Mukhtar. (2015). *GPS based Advanced Vehicle Tracking and Vehicle Control System. I.J. Intelligent Systems and Applications*.

Nagamalai, D, & Lee. (2006). A Novel Mechanism to defend DOS attacks caused by spam. *International Journal of Smart Home*, 83-96.

Naik, P., & Harode, U. (2016). Raspberry Pi and Iot Based Industrial Automation. *International Journal of Industrial Electronics and Electrical Engineering*, *4*(10).

Najafabadi, Villanustre, Khoshgoftaar, Seliya, Wald, & Muharemagic. (2015). Deep learning applications and challenges in big data analytics. *Journal of Big Data*, *2015*. doi:10.118640537-014-0007-7

Nakagawa, M., & Michael, L. B. (1997). Wireless Communications. In Wireless Communication Technology in Intelligent Transport Systems (pp. 491-508). Springer US.

Nambiar, R., Sethi, A., Bhardwaj, R., & Vargheese, R. (2013). A Look at Challenges and Opportunities of Big Data Analytics in Healthcare. *IEEE International Conference on Big Data*, 17-22. 10.1109/BigData.2013.6691753

NASA_SeverLog. (1995). *NASA Kennedy space center's www server log data.* Retrieved from http://ita.ee.lbl.gov/html/contrib/NASA-HTTP.html

Nasrabadi, N. M., & King, R. A. (1988). Image coding using vector quantization: A Review. *IEEE Transactions on Communications, 36*(8), 957–971. doi:10.1109/26.3776

Nasraoui, O., Hichem, F., Krishnapuram, R., & Joshi, A. (2000). Extracting web user profiles using relational competitive fuzzy clustering. *International Journal of Artificial Intelligence Tools, 9*(4), 509–526. doi:10.1142/S021821300000032X

National Research Council. (2013). *Frontiers in Massive Data Analysis.* The National Academies Press. Retrieved from http://www.nap.edu/openbook.php?record_id=18374

Negahban & Shafieian. (2012). Various Novel Wavelet Based Image Compression Algorithms Using a Neural Network as a Predictor. *J. Basic. Appl. Sci. Res., 3*(6), 280-287.

Nema, A., Tiwari, B., & Tiwari, V. (2016, March). Improving Accuracy for Intrusion Detection through Layered Approach Using Support Vector Machine with Feature Reduction. In *Proceedings of the ACM Symposium on Women in Research 2016* (pp. 26-31). ACM. 10.1145/2909067.2909100

Neviarouskaya, A., Prendinger, H., & Ishizuka, M. (2007, July). Recognition of affect conveyed by text messaging in online communication. In *International Conference on Online Communities and Social Computing* (pp. 141-150). Springer Berlin Heidelberg. 10.1007/978-3-540-73257-0_16

Neviarouskaya, A., Prendinger, H., & Ishizuka, M. (2009, July). Emoheart: Automation of expressive communication of emotions in second life. In *International Conference on Online Communities and Social Computing* (pp. 584-592). Springer Berlin Heidelberg. 10.1007/978-3-642-02774-1_63

Neviarouskaya, A., Prendinger, H., & Ishizuka, M. (2010, August). Recognition of affect, judgment, and appreciation in text. In *Proceedings of the 23rd international conference on computational linguistics* (pp. 806-814). Association for Computational Linguistics.

Ngiam, J., Khosla, A., Kim, M., Nam, J., Lee, H., & Ng, A. Y. (2011). Multimodal deep learning. In *Proceedings of the 28th international conference on machine learning (ICML-11)* (pp. 689-696). Academic Press.

Nguyen, D., & Le, M. (2014). A two-stage architecture for stock price forecasting by combining SOM and fuzzy-SVM. *International Journal of Computer Science and Information Security, 12*(8), 1–6.

Nguyen, T. T. T., & Armitage, G. (2008). A Survey of Techniques for Internet Traffic Classification using Machine Learning. *IEEE Communications Surveys and Tutorials, 10*(4), 2008. doi:10.1109/SURV.2008.080406

Nieddu, M., Boatto, G., Pirisi, M., & Dessì, G. (2010). Determination of four thiophenethylamine designer drugs (2C-T-4, 2C-T-8, 2C-T-13, 2C-T-17) in human urine by capillary electrophoresis/mass spectrometry. *Rapid Communications in Mass Spectrometry, 24*(16), 2357–2362. doi:10.1002/rcm.4656 PMID:20635321

Nigam, K., Lafferty, J., & McCallum, A. (1999, August). Using maximum entropy for text classification. In IJCAI-99 workshop on machine learning for information filtering (Vol. 1, pp. 61-67). Academic Press.

Nosrati, Karimi, & Hariri. (2012). Video Steganography A Survey on Recent Approaches. *World Applied Programming*, *2*(3).

Ou, P., & Wang, H. (2009). Prediction of Stock Market Index Movement by Ten Data Mining Techniques. *Modern Applied Science*, *3*(12), 28. doi:10.5539/mas.v3n12p28

Pang, B., Lee, L., & Vaithyanathan, S. (2002, July). Thumbs up?: sentiment classification using machine learning techniques. In *Proceedings of the ACL-02 conference on Empirical methods in natural language processing-Volume 10* (pp. 79-86). Association for Computational Linguistics. 10.3115/1118693.1118704

Parameswaran, M., & Whinston, A. B. (2007). Social Computing: An Overview. *Communications of the Association for Information Systems*, *19*(37), 762–780.

Paranjothi, A., Khan, M. S., Nijim, M., & Challoo, R. (2016). MAvanet: Message authentication in VANET using social networks. *IEEE Annual Ubiquitous Computing, Electronics and Mobile Communication Conference*.

Parrella, F. (2007). *Online support vector regression* (Master's Thesis). Department of Information Science, University of Genoa, Italy.

Patel, J., Shah, S., Thakkar, P., & Kotecha, K. (2015). Predicting stock market index using fusion of machine learning techniques. *Expert Systems with Applications*, *42*(4), 2162–2172. doi:10.1016/j.eswa.2014.10.031

Patinge, Suryawanshi, & Kakde. (2013). *Design of ARM Based Data Acquisition and Control Using GSM and TCP/IP Network*. IEEE.

Pattern Matching - Optalysys. (2017). *Optalysys*. Retrieved 7 June 2017, from http://www.optalysys.com/applications/pattern-matching/

Paul, B., Ibrahim, M., & Bikas, M. A. N. (2011). VANET Routing Protocols: Pros and Cons. *International Journal of Computers and Applications*, *20*, 28–34. doi:10.5120/2413-3224

Pedro, S., & Hruschka, E. (2012). Collective intelligence as a source for machine learning self-supervision. *Proceedings of the 4th international workshop on web intelligence & communities, WI&C '12*, 5-9. 10.1145/2189736.2189744

Pfeiffer & Pia. (2013). Data analysis with R in an experimental physics environment. *Nuclear Science Symposium and Medical Imaging Conference (NSS/MIC)*.

Plotly. (2015). *Plot.ly - Online Graph Plotting Tool*. Retrieved November 20, 2015, from Plot.ly

Plumer, B. (2012, November 5). Pundit Accountability: The Official 2012 Election Prediction Thread, WONKBLOG. *The Washington Post*.

Plutchik, R. (1980). A general psychoevolutionary theory of emotion. *Theories of Emotion, 1*(3-31), 4.

Praba, V. L., & Ranichitra, A. (2013). Isolating malicious vehicles and avoiding collision between vehicles in VANET. *International Conference on Communication and Signal Processing*, 811 – 815. 10.1109/iccsp.2013.6577169

Priss, U. (2006). Formal concept analysis in information science. *Arist*, *40*(1), 521–543.

Psa & MG. (2012). *Compression of computed radiographic images using linear prediction on wavelet coefficients*. ICACC.

Pu & Webb. (2006). Observed trends in spam construction techniques: A case study of spam evolution. *CEAS 2006*, 104-112.

Qin, Xia, Prabhakar, & Tu. (2009). A Rule-Based Classification Algorithm for Uncertain Data. *IEEE International Conference on Data Engineering*, 1633 - 1640.

Quinlan, J. R. (1986). Induction of decision trees. *Machine Learning*, *1*(1), 81–106. doi:10.1007/BF00116251

Raghupathi, W., & Raghupathi, V. (2014). *Big Data Analytics in Healthcare: Promise and Potential*. Health Information Science and Systems.

Raiput, U., Abbas, F., & Oh, H. (2013). A Hierarchical Privacy Preserving Pseudonymous Authentication Protocol for VANE. *IEEE Access: Practical Innovations, Open Solutions*, 7770–7784.

Ramamurthy, B., & Gersho, A. (1986). Classified vector quantization of images. *IEEE Transactions on Communications*, *COM-34*(11), 1105–1115. doi:10.1109/TCOM.1986.1096468

Ramesh, D., Suraj, P., & Saini, L. (2016). Big data Analytics in Healthcare: A Survey Approach. *IEEE International Conference on Microelectronics, Computing and Communications (MicroCom)*, 1-6. 10.1109/MicroCom.2016.7522520

Rao, S., Suma, S. N., & Sunitha, M. (2015). Security Solutions for Big Data Analytics in Healthcare. *International Conference on Advances in Computing and Communication Engineering*. 10.1109/ICACCE.2015.83

Rawat, D. B., Yan, G., Bista, B., & Weigle, M. C. (2014). Trust On the Security of Wireless Vehicular Ad-hoc Networking. *Ad-Hoc & Sensor Wireless Networks*, 1–23.

Reddy, A. R., & Kumar, P. S. (2016). Predictive Big Data Analytics in Healthcare. *Proceedings of the 2016 Second International Conference on Computational Intelligence & Communication Technology*, 623-626.

Rehman, S., Khan, M.A., Zia, T.A., & Zheng, L. (2013). Vehicular Ad-Hoc Networks (VANETs) - An Overview and Challenges. *Journal of Wireless Networking and Communications*, 29-38.

Reichel, J., Menegaz, G., Nadenau, M. J., & Kunt, M. (2001). Integer Wavelet Transform for Embedded Lossy to Lossless Image Compression. *IEEE Transactions on Image Processing*, *10*(3), 383–392. doi:10.1109/83.908504 PMID:18249628

Ring, T. (2016). Your data in their hands: Big data, mass surveillance and privacy. *Computer Fraud & Security*, *2016*(8), 5–10. doi:10.1016/S1361-3723(16)30061-6

Ritter, F., Boskamp, T., Homeyer, A., Laue, H., Schwier, M., Link, F., & Peitgen, H. O. (2011). Medical image analysis. *Institute of Electrical and Electronics Engineers Pulse*, *2*(6), 60–70. PMID:22147070

Roberts. (2000). Control chart tests based on geometric moving averages. *Technometrics*, *42*(1), 97–101.

Rodriguez, M. A., Steinbock, D. J., Watkins, J. H., Gershenson, C., Bollen, J., Grey, V., & deGraf, B. (2007). Smartocracy: Social networks for collective decision making. *Proceedings of the 40th annual Hawaii international conference on system sciences, HICSS '07*. 10.1109/HICSS.2007.484

Roman, J., & Jameel, A. (1996). Backpropagation and recurrent neural networks in financial analysis of multiple stock market returns. *System Sciences, 1996., Proceedings of the Twenty-Ninth Hawaii International Conference on*, *2*, 454–460.

Ruhl, H. H., & Saupe, D. (1997). Adaptive partitioning for fractal image compression. *IEEE Int. Conf. Image Processing*, *2*, 310–313. 10.1109/ICIP.1997.638753

Ruiz, M. E., & Srinivasan, P. (1999, August). Hierarchical neural networks for text categorization (poster abstract). In *Proceedings of the 22nd annual international ACM SIGIR conference on Research and development in information retrieval* (pp. 281-282). ACM. 10.1145/312624.312700

Saad, D. (1998). Online algorithms and stochastic approximations. *Online Learning, 5*.

Sabharwal, S., Gupta, S., & Thirunavukkarasu, K. (2016). Insight of Big Data Analytics in Healthcare Industry. *Proceedings of International Conference on Computing, Communication and Automation (ICCCA 2016)*. 10.1109/CCAA.2016.7813696

Sadasiva Rao, K. S., & Damodaram, A. (2017). A steganographic technique for transferring source image file without stego file with high level of robustness. *International Conference on Inventive Systems and Control (ICISC)*, 1-4.

Sadek, Khalifa, & Mostafa. (2015). *Video steganography: a comprehensive review.* Springer Science+Business Media. DOI 10.1007/s11042-014-1952-z

Sagberg (2000). *Automatic enforcement technologies and systems.* Academic Press.

Sahasrabudhe, R., & Borse, P. M. (2013). Classification of Brain Encephalic Tissues From Mri Images Using Sphere Shaped Support Vector. *International Journal of Scientific & Engineering Research*, *4*(7), 2343–2349.

Sakr, S., & Elgammal, A. (2016). Towards a Comprehensive Data Analytics Framework for Smart Healthcare Services. *Big Data Research*, *4*, 44–58. doi:10.1016/j.bdr.2016.05.002

Salakhutdinov, R., & Hinton, G. E. (2009). Deep boltzmann machines. In *International Conference on, Artificial Intelligence and Statistics.* JMLR.org.

Salehi, M., & Boukerche, A. (2017, July). A Novel Packet Salvaging Model to Improve the Security of Opportunistic Routing Protocols. *Computer Networks*, *122*(20), 163–178. doi:10.1016/j.comnet.2017.04.019

Salehi, M., Darehshoorzadeh, A., & Boukerche, A. (2015). On the Effect of Black-hole Attack on Opportunistic Routing Protocols. *Proceedings of the 12th ACM Symposium on Performance Evaluation of Wireless Ad Hoc, Sensor, and Ubiquitous Networks*, 93-100. 10.1145/2810379.2810386

Sanai, D. (2002). *Detection of Promiscuous Nodes Using ARP Packets.* Retrieved from http://www. securityfriday. com

Sathiyavathi, R. (2015). A Survey: Big Data Analytics on Healthcare System. *Contemporary Engineering Sciences*, *8*(3), 121–125. doi:10.12988/ces.2015.412255

Saupe. (1995). Accelerating Fractal Image Compression by Multi-Dimensional Nearest Neighbor Search. *Proceedings DCC'95 Data Compression Conference.*

Saupe, D., & Ruhl, M. (1996). Evolutionary fractal image compression. *IEEE Int. Conf. Image Processing, 1*, 129–132. 10.1109/ICIP.1996.559449

Schierholt, K., & Dagli, C. H. (1996). Stock market prediction using different neural network classification architectures. *IEEE/IAFE Conference on Computational Intelligence for Financial Engineering*, 72–78. 10.1109/CIFER.1996.501826

Schmidhuber, J. (2015). Deep learning in neural networks: An overview. *Neural Networks*, *61*, 85–117. doi:10.1016/j.neunet.2014.09.003 PMID:25462637

Scholkopf, B., & Smola, A. J. (2001). *Learning with kernels: support vector machines, regularization, optimization, and beyond.* MIT Press. 10.1017/CBO9781107415324.004

Scholl, I., Aach, T., Deserno, T. M., & Kuhlen, T. (2011). Challenges of medical image processing. *Computer Science Research Development*, *26*(1-2), 5–13. doi:10.100700450-010-0146-9

Schut, M. (2007). *Scientific Handbook for Simulation of Collective Intelligence.* Available under Creative Commons License.

Scridon, M. A. (2008). Understanding customers-profiling and segmentation. *Management & Marketing-Craiova*, (1), 175-184.

Sebastiani, F. (2002). Machine learning in automated text categorization. *ACM Computing Surveys*, *34*(1), 1–47. doi:10.1145/505282.505283

Seibert, J. A. (2010). *Modalities and data acquisition in Practical Imaging Informatics*. New York: Springer.

Seide, F., Li, G., & Yu, D. (2011). Conversational speech transcription using context-dependent deep neural networks. In *INTERSPEECH* (pp. 437–440). ISCA.

Shalev-Shwartz, S. (2012). Online learning and online convex optimization. *Foundations and Trends® in Machine Learning, 4*(2), 107-194.

Sharma, A. K. (2011). A Comparative Study of Classification Algorithms for Spam Email Data Analysis. IJCSE, 3(5).

Shatnawi, M. K. A. (2013). Stock Price Prediction Using K -Nearest Neighbor (k NN) Algorithm. *International Journal of Business Human Technology, 3*(3), 32–44.

Shemberko, L., & Sliva, A. (2012). Philosophical information in the INION databases on social sciences and humanities. *Scientific and Technical Information Processing, 39*(4), 187–198. doi:10.3103/S014768821204003X

Shevade, S. K., Keerthi, S. S., Bhattacharyya, C., & Murthy, K. R. K. (2000). Improvements to the SMO algorithm for SVM regression. *IEEE Transactions on Neural Networks, 11*(5), 1188–1193. doi:10.1109/72.870050 PMID:18249845

Shin, H., Yen, M., Tseng, C., & Liu, H. (2011). Fast data access and energy-efficient protocol for wireless data broadcast. *Wireless Communications and Mobile Computing, 12*(16), 1429–1441. doi:10.1002/wcm.1076

Shmueli, G. (2017). Research Dilemmas with Behavioral Big Data. *Big Data, 5*(2), 98–119. doi:10.1089/big.2016.0043 PMID:28632441

Shoaib, M., & Maurya, A. K. (2014, August). URL ordering based performance evaluation of Web crawler. In *Advances in Engineering and Technology Research (ICAETR), 2014 International Conference on* (pp. 1-7). IEEE. 10.1109/ICAETR.2014.7012962

Shuijing, H. (2016). Big Data Analytics: Key Technologies and Challenges. *Proc. Int. Conf. on Robots & Intelligent Systems*, 141-145. 10.1109/ICRIS.2016.30

Shvachko, K., Kuang, H., Radia, S., & Chansler, R. (2010). The Hadoop distributed file system. *Proceedings of the IEEE 26th Symposium on Mass Storage Systems and Technologies (MSST '10)*, 1–6.

Shvachko, K., Kuang, H., Radia, S., & Chansler, R. (2010). The Hadoop distributed file system. *Proceedings of the IEEE 26th Symposium on Mass Storage Systems and Technologies*, 1-6.

Shyu, M. L., Haruechaiyasak, C., & Chen, S. C. (2006). Mining user access patterns with traversal constraint for predicting web page requests. *Knowledge and Information Systems, 10*(4), 515–528. doi:10.100710115-006-0004-z

Signorello, S., Palattella, M. R., & Grieco, L. A. (2016). *Security Challenges in Future NDN-Enabled VANETs, IEEE Trustcom, BigDataSE*. ISPA.

Singh. (2014). Video Steganography Text Hiding In Video By LSB Substitution. *International Journal of Engineering Research and Applications, 4,* 105-108.

Sinha, K., & Belkin, M. (2009). Semi-supervised learning using sparse eigen function bases. In Advances in Neural Information Processing Systems (pp. 1687-1695). Academic Press.

Sisodia, D., & Verma, S. (2012). Web Usage Pattern Analysis Through Web Logs: A Review. *IEEE 9th International Joint Conference on Computer Science and Software Engineering (JCSSE 2012)*, 49–53. 10.1109/JCSSE.2012.6261924

Sisodia, D. S. (2017). Augmented Session Similarity-Based Framework for Measuring Web User Concern from Web Server Logs. *International Journal on Advanced Science Engineering and Information Technology*, 7(3), 1007–1013. doi:10.18517/ijaseit.7.3.1563

Sisodia, D. S., Verma, S., & Vyas, O. (2016a). A Discounted Fuzzy Relational Clustering of Web Users ' Using Intuitive Augmented Sessions Dissimilarity Metric. *IEEE Access: Practical Innovations, Open Solutions*, 4(1), 2883–2993.

Sisodia, D. S., Verma, S., & Vyas, O. P. (2015a). A Comparative Analysis of Browsing Behavior of Human Visitors and Automatic Software Agents. *American Journal of Systems and Software*, 3(2), 31–35. doi:10.12691/ajss-3-2-1

Sisodia, D. S., Verma, S., & Vyas, O. P. (2015b). Agglomerative Approach for Identification and Elimination of Web Robots from Web Server Logs to Extract Knowledge about Actual Visitors. *Journal of Data Analysis and Information Processing*, 3(2), 1–10. doi:10.4236/jdaip.2015.31001

Sisodia, D. S., Verma, S., & Vyas, O. P. (2016b). Augmented Intuitive Dissimilarity Metric for Clustering Of Web User Sessions. *Journal of Information Science*, 43(4), 480–491. doi:10.1177/0165551516648259

Sisodia, D. S., Verma, S., & Vyas, O. P. (2016c). Performance Evaluation of an Augmented Session Dissimilarity Matrix of Web User Sessions Using Relational Fuzzy C-means clustering. *International Journal of Applied Engineering and Research*, 11(9), 6497–6503.

Sisodia, D. S., Verma, S., & Vyas, O. P. (2016d). Quantitative Evaluation of Web User Session Dissimilarity measures using medoids based Relational Fuzzy clustering. *Indian Journal of Science and Technology*, 9(28), 1–9. doi:10.17485/ijst/2016/v9i28/89455

Siuly, S., & Zhang, Y. (2016). Medical Big Data: Neurological Diseases Diagnosis Through Medical Data Analysis. *Data Science and Engineering*, 1(2), 54–64. doi:10.100741019-016-0011-3

Sizov, I. (2016). Big data – big data in business. *Economy Business, Computer Science*, (3): 8–23. doi:10.19075/2500-2074-2016-3-8-23

Skrzynski, P., Szuba, T., & Szydło, S. (2011). Collective intelligence approach to measuring invisible hand of the market. *Proceedings of the 3rd international conference on computational collective intelligence: technologies and applications, ICCCI'11, 2*, 435-444. 10.1007/978-3-642-23938-0_44

Smola, A., & Schölkopf, B. (2004). A tutorial on support vector regression. *Statistics and Computing*, 14(3), 199–222. doi:10.1023/B:STCO.0000035301.49549.88

Sobhy, D., El-Sonbaty, Y., & Abou Elnasr, M. (2012). MedCloud: healthcare cloud computing system. *Proceedings of the International Conference for Internet Technology and Secured Transactions*, 161–166.

Socher, R., Huang, E. H., Pennin, J., Manning, C. D., & Ng, A. (2011). Dynamic pooling and unfolding recursive auto encoders for paraphrase detection. In Advances in Neural Information Processing Systems. Curran Associates, Inc.

Soranamageswari, M., & Meena, C. (2011). A Novel Approach towards Image Spam Classification. *International Journal of Computer Theory and Engineering*, 3(1).

Spangler, R. (2003). *Packet sniffer detection with antisniff*. University of Wisconsin Whitewater, Department of Computer and Network Administration.

Spark, A. (2017). *Spark Research*. Retrieved May 2nd, 2017 fromhttps://spark.apache.org/research.html

Spiliopoulou, M. (2000). Web usage mining for Website evaluation. *Communications of the ACM*, 43(8), 127–134. doi:10.1145/345124.345167

Spiliopoulou, M., Mobasher, B., Berendt, B., & Nakagawa, M. (2003). A Framework for the Evaluation of Session Reconstruction Heuristics in Web-Usage Analysis. *INFORMS Journal on Computing*, *15*(2), 171–190. doi:10.1287/ijoc.15.2.171.14445

Srivastava, N., & Salakhutdinov, R. R. (2012). Multimodal learning with deep boltzmann machines. In Advances in neural information processing systems (pp. 2222-2230). Academic Press.

Srivastava, T., Desikan, P., & Kumar, V. (2005). Web mining – concepts, applications and research directions. In W. Chu & T. Young Lin (Eds.), *Foundations and Advances in Data Mining. Studies in Fuzziness and Soft Computing* (Vol. 180). Berlin: Springer. doi:10.1007/11362197_10

StockCharts: Simply the Web's Best Financial Charts. (n.d.). Retrieved November 21, 2015, from http://stockcharts.com/

Street & Kim. (2001). A streaming ensemble algorithm(SEA) for large-scale classification. *KDD*, 377–382.

Studer, A., Bai, F., Bellur, B., & Perrig, A. (2009). Flexible, extensible, and efficient VANET authentication. *Journal of Communications and Networks (Seoul)*, *11*(6), 574–588. doi:10.1109/JCN.2009.6388411

Sugiyama, M., & Kawanabe, M. (2012). *Machine learning in non-stationary environments: Introduction to covariate shift adaptation*. MIT Press. doi:10.7551/mitpress/9780262017091.001.0001

Sun, J., & Reddy, C. K. (2013). *Big Data Analytics for Healthcare*. IBM. Available at: https://www.siam.org/meetings/sdm13/sun.pdf

Surowiecki, J. (2004). *The Wisdom of the Crowds*. London: Random House.

Sweet, L., & Moulaison, H. (2013). Electronic Health Records Data and Metadata: Challenges for Big Data in the United States. *Big Data*, *1*(4), 245–251. doi:10.1089/big.2013.0023 PMID:27447257

Swetha, V., Prajith, V., & Kshema, V. (2015). Data Hiding Using Video Steganography-A Survey. *International Journal of Computer Science & Engineering Technology*, *5*, 206–213.

Szuba, T., Polanski, P., Schab, P., & Wielicki, P. (2011). On Efficiency of Collective Intelligence Phenomena. *Transactions on Computational Collective Intelligence*, *3*, 50-73.

Tahooni, A., Darehshoorzadeh, A., & Boukerche, A. (2014). Mobility-based Opportunistic Routing for Mobile Ad-Hoc Networks. *Proceedings of the 11th ACM symposium on Performance evaluation of wireless ad hoc, sensor, and ubiquitous networks*, 9-16. 10.1145/2653481.2653485

Tan & Sherwood. (2005). A High Throughput String Matching Architecture for Intrusion Detection and Prevention. *Proceedings of the 32nd Annual International Symposium on Computer Architecture*.

Tang, L., & Liu, H. (2009a). Scalable learning of collective behavior based on sparse social dimensions. *Proceedings of the 18th ACM conference on Information and knowledge management (CIKM '09)*, 1107-1116. 10.1145/1645953.1646094

Tang, L., & Liu, H. (2009b). Relational learning via latent social dimensions. *Proceedings of the 15th ACM SIGKDD International Conference on Knowledge Discovery and Data Mining (KDD '09)*, 817-826. 10.1145/1557019.1557109

Tang, L., & Liu, H. (2010). Toward predicting collective behavior via social dimension extraction. *IEEE Intelligent Systems*, *25*(4), 19–25. doi:10.1109/MIS.2010.36

Tang, L., Wang, X., & Liu, H. (2012a). Scalable learning of collective behavior. *IEEE Transactions on Knowledge and Data Engineering*, *24*(6), 1080–1091. doi:10.1109/TKDE.2011.38

Tanimoto, H. O., & Kimoto, T. (1996). A new fractal image coding scheme employing blocks of variable shapes. *IEEE Int. Conf. Image Processing, 1*, 137–140. 10.1109/ICIP.1996.559452

Tan, P. N., & Kumar, V. (2002). Discovery of web robot sessions based on their navigational patterns. *Data Mining and Knowledge Discovery, 6*(1), 9–35. doi:10.1023/A:1013228602957

Tan, T. Z., Quek, C., & Ng, G. S. (2004). Brain-inspired Genetic Complementary Learning for Stock Market Prediction. pdf. *IEEE Congress on Evolutionary Computation*, 2653–2660.

Teunissen, P. J. G., & Montenbruck, O. (2017). *Springer Handbook of Global Navigation Satellite Systems*. Springer International Publishing. doi:10.1007/978-3-319-42928-1

Texter, K., Waymach, R., Kavanagh, P., O'Brien, J., Talbot, B., Brandt, S., & Gardner, E. (2017). Identification of pyrolysis products of the new psychoactive substance 2-amino-1-(4-bromo-2,5-dimethoxyphenyl)ethanone hydrochloride (bk-2C-B) and its iodo analog bk-2C-I. *Drug Testing and Analysis*. doi:10.1002/dta.2200 PMID:28371351

Thara, D. K., Premasudha, B. G., Ram, V. R., & Suma, R. (2016). Impact of Big Data in Healthcare. *Proceedings of the 2nd International Conference on Contemporary Computing and Informatics*, 729-735.

Thara, D. K., Premasudha, B. G., Ram, V. R., & Suma, R. (2016). Impact of big data in healthcare: A survey. *2nd International Conference on Contemporary Computing and Informatics (IC3I)*, 729-735. 10.1109/IC3I.2016.7918057

The Four V's of Big Data. (2017). *IBM Big Data & Analytics Hub*. Retrieved 10 June 2017, from http://www.ibmbigdatahub.com/infographic/four-vs-big-data

The Spyder Project Contributors. (2017). *Spyder 3.1.4*. Retrieved on 24th April 2017 from https://pypi.python.org/pypi/spyder

Tiwari, V., & Thakur, R. S. (2016). Pattern Warehouse: Context Based Modeling and Quality Issues, National Academy of Sciences, India Section A: Physical Sciences, 85(3), 1-15.

Tiwari, V., & Thakur, R. S. (2016). Pattern Warehouse: Context Based Modeling and Quality Issues. National Academy of Sciences, India Section A: Physical Sciences, 85(3), 1-15.

Tiwari, V., & Thakur, R. S. (2016). Pattern Warehouse: Context Based Modeling and Quality Issues. *Proceedings of the National Academy of Sciences, India Section A: Physical Sciences, 86*(3), 417-431.

Tiwari, V., & Thakur, R.S. (2015). P2MS- A Phase-Wise Pattern Management System for Pattern Warehouse. *Int. J. of Data Mining, Modeling and Management, 7*(4), 331-350.

Tiwari, V., & Thakur, R.S. (in press). Towards Elementary Algebra for On-Line Knowledge Processing of Pattern Cube. In *National Academy Science Letters (NASL)*. Springer.

Tiwari, V., & Thakur, R.S. (in press). Towards Elementary Algebra for On-Line Knowledge Processing of Pattern Cube. *National Academy Science Letters, 40*.

Tiwari, V., Thakur, R. S., Tiwari, B., & Choube, M. (in press). Optimization of EHR data flow towards healthcare analytics. In *International Conference on Recent Advancement in Computer and Communication (IC-RAC-2017)*. Springer.

Tiwari, V., Tiwari, V., Gupta, S., & Tiwari, R. (2010). Association rule mining: a graph based approach for mining frequent itemsets. *International Conference on Networking and Information Technology (ICNIT)*, 309-313. 10.1109/ICNIT.2010.5508505

Top 10 Big Data Challenges – A Serious Look at 10 Big Data V's | MapR. (2017). Retrieved 26 June 2017, from https://mapr.com/blog/top-10-big-data-challenges-serious-look-10-big-data-vs/

Top 10 Big Data Challenges – A Serious Look at 10 Big Data V's | MapR. (2017). Retrieved 27 May 2017, from https://mapr.com/blog/top-10-big-data-challenges-serious-look-10-big-data-vs/

Trabelsi, Z., Rahmani, H., Kaouech, K., & Frikha, M. (2004). Malicious Sniffing System Detection Platform. In *Proceedings of the 2004 International Symposium on Applications and the Internet*. IEEE Computer Society. 10.1109/SAINT.2004.1266117

Trends, S. P., Chowdhury, S. G., Routh, S., & Chakrabarti, S. (2014). News Analytics and Sentiment Analysis to Predict. *International Journal of Computer Science and Information Technologies*, *5*(3), 3595–3604.

Triantafyllidis, A. K., Velardo, C., Salvi, D., Shah, S. A., Koutkias, V. G., & Tarassenko, L. (2015). A Survey of Mobile Phone Sensing, Self-reporting and Social Sharing for Pervasive Healthcare. *IEEE Journal of Biomedical and Health Informatics*. doi:10.1109/JBHI.2015.2483902 PMID:26441432

Tsai, Lai, Chao, & Vasilakos. (2015). Big data analytics: a survey. *Journal of Big Data*.

Tsetoura, A. (2013). Property Protection as a Limit to Deteriorating Social Security Protection. *European Journal of Social Security*, *15*(1), 55–78. doi:10.1177/138826271301500105

Tsytsarau, M., & Palpanas, T. (2012). Survey on mining subjective data on the web. *Data Mining and Knowledge Discovery*, *24*(3), 478–514. doi:10.100710618-011-0238-6

Tüfekci, P. (2016). Classification-based prediction models for stock price index movement. *Intelligent Data Analysis*, *20*(2), 357–376. doi:10.3233/IDA-160809

Tzeng, S. F., Horng, S. J., Li, T., Wang, X., Huang, P. H., & Khan, M. K. (2017). Enhancing Security and Privacy for Identity-Based Batch Verification Scheme in VANETs. *IEEE Transactions on Vehicular Technology*, *66*(4), 3235–3248. doi:10.1109/TVT.2015.2406877

UAD. (2014). *User Agents Database*. Retrieved February 20, 2014, from http://www.user-agents.org/index.shtml

Upadhyay, A., & Kashyap, R. (2016). Fast Segmentation Methods for Medical Images. *International Journal of Computers and Applications*, *156*(3), 18–23. doi:10.5120/ijca2016912399

Vakali, A., Pokorný, J., & Dalamagas, T. (2004). An overview of web data clustering practices. In *Current Trends in Database WebKdd* (pp. 597–606). Springer Berlin Heidelberg. doi:10.1007/978-3-540-30192-9_59

Vanhoucke, V., Senior, A., & Mao, M. Z. (2011). Improving the speed of neural networks on CPUs. In *Proc. Deep Learning and Unsupervised Feature Learning NIPS Workshop* (*Vol. 1*, p. 4). Academic Press.

Villegas-Quezada, C., & Climent, J. (2008). Holistic face recognition using multivariate approximation, genetic algorithms and adaboost classifier: Preliminary results. *World Academy of Science, Engineering and Technology*, *44*, 802–806.

Vinothini, S., & Subha, T. (2015). An Efficient Crl Authentication Scheme For Vehicular Communications. *International Conference on Computing and Communications Technologies*, 282 – 285. 10.1109/ICCCT2.2015.7292761

Virmani, D., Arora, P., & Kulkarni, P. (2017). *Cross domain analyzer to acquire review proficiency in big data*. ICT Express. doi:10.1016/j.icte.2017.04.004

Waghmode, R., Gonsalves, R., & Ambawade, D. (2016). Security enhancement in group based authentication for VANET. *IEEE International Conference on Recent Trends in Electronics, Information and Communication Technology*. 10.1109/RTEICT.2016.7808069

Wah, Y., & Wong, D. W. (2009). Scalable Attribute-Value Extraction from Semi-Structured Text, *ICDM Workshop on Large-scale Data Mining: Theory and Applications*.

Wang, S., Schäfer, R., & Guhr, T. (2015). *Price response in correlated financial markets: empirical results.* arXiv Preprint arXiv:1510.03205

Wang, F., Ercegovac, V., & Mahmood, T. S. (2010). Large-scale multimodal mining for healthcare with MapReduce. *Proceedings of the 1st ACM International Health Informatics Symposium*, 479–483. 10.1145/1882992.1883067

Wang, H., Fan, W., Philip, S. Yu., & Han, J. (2003). Mining concept-drifting data streams using ensemble classifiers. *KDD: Proceedings / International Conference on Knowledge Discovery & Data Mining. International Conference on Knowledge Discovery & Data Mining*, 226–235.

Wang, J., & Shen, X. (2007). Large margin semi-supervised learning. *Journal of Machine Learning Research*, 8(Aug), 1867–1891.

Wang, Q., Ma, J., Wang, X., & Zhao, F. (2017). Image watermarking algorithm based on grey relational analysis and singular value decomposition in wavelet domain. *Proceedings of 2017 International Conference on Grey Systems and Intelligent Services (GSIS)*, 94-98. 10.1109/GSIS.2017.8077676

Wan, Y., & Gao, Q. (2015, November). An ensemble sentiment classification system of Twitter data for airline services analysis. In *Data Mining Workshop (ICDMW), 2015 IEEE International Conference on* (pp. 1318-1325). IEEE. 10.1109/ICDMW.2015.7

Waoo, N., Kashyap, R., & Jaiswal, A. (2010). DNA Nano array analysis using hierarchical quality threshold clustering. In The 2nd IEEE International Conference on Information Management and Engineering (ICIME), 2010 (pp. 81-85). IEEE. doi:10.1109/ICIME.2010.5477579

Waoo, N., Kashyap, R., & Jaiswal, A. (2010, April). DNA Nano array analysis using hierarchical quality threshold clustering. In *The 2nd IEEE International Conference on Information Management and Engineering (ICIME), 2010* (pp. 81-85). IEEE.10.1109/ICIME.2010.5477579

Watkins, J., & Jennifer, H. (2007). Prediction Markets as an Aggregation Mechanism for Collective Intelligence. *Proceedings of 4th UCLA Lake Arrowhead Conference Human Complex Systems*, 1-10. Retrieved from: http://escholarship.org/uc/item/8mg0p0zc

Watkins, J., & Rodriguez, M. (2008). A Survey of Web-Based Collective Decision Making Systems. In Evolution of the Web in Artificial Intelligence Environments, ser. Studies in Computational Intelligence. Springer-Verlag. doi:10.1007/978-3-540-79140-9_11

Web Log Data. (1995). Retrieved from http://ita.ee.lbl.gov/html/contrib/NASA-HTTP.html

Wein, C. J., & Blake, I. F. (1996). On the performance of fractal compression with clustering. *IEEE Transactions on Image Processing*, 5(3), 522–526. doi:10.1109/83.491325 PMID:18285137

Weistead, S. (2005). Fractal and Wavelet Image Compression Technique. PHI.

Weston, J., Ratle, F., Mobahi, H., & Collobert, R. (2012). Deep learning via semi-supervised embedding. In *Neural Networks: Tricks of the Trade* (pp. 639–655). Springer Berlin Heidelberg. doi:10.1007/978-3-642-35289-8_34

White, R. W., & Drucker, S. M. (2007). Investigating behavioral variability in web search. In *Proceedings of the 16th international conference on World Wide Web (WWW '07)* (pp. 21–30). Academic Press. 10.1145/1242572.1242576

Wi, H., Oh, S., Mun, J., & Jung, M. (2009). A team formation model based on knowledge and collaboration. *Expert Systems with Applications*, 36(5), 9121–9134. doi:10.1016/j.eswa.2008.12.031

Wilems. (2016). *Pandas Tutorial: DataFrames in Python*. Retrieved October 21st, 2016 in Python from https://www. datacamp.com/community/tutorials/pandas-tutorial-dataframe-python

Wohlberg, B., & Jager, G. D. (1999). A review of fractal image coding literature. *IEEE Transactions on Image Processing*, *8*(12), 1716–1729. doi:10.1109/83.806618 PMID:18267449

WRD. (2014). *Web Robots Database*. Retrieved February 20, 2014, from http://www.robotstxt.org/db.html

Wu. (2009). Behavior-based spam detection using a hybrid method of rule-based techniques and neural networks. Expert Systems with Applications, 36(3), 4321–4330.

Wuthrich, B., Cho, V., Leung, S., Permunetilleke, D., Sankaran, K., & Zhang, J. (1998). Daily stock market forecast from textual web data. *Proceedings of IEEE International Conference on Systems, Man, and Cybernetics (SMC'98)*, 3, 1–6. 10.1109/ICSMC.1998.725072

Wu, X., & Zhang, S. (2003). Synthesizing High-Frequency Rules from Different Data Sources. *IEEE Transactions on Knowledge and Data Engineering*, *15*(2), 353–367.

Wu, X., Zhu, X., Wu, G. Q., & Ding, W. (2014). Data Mining with Big data. *IEEE Transactions on Knowledge and Data Engineering*, *26*(1), 97–107. doi:10.1109/TKDE.2013.109

Xianghua, F., Guo, L., Yanyan, G., & Zhiqiang, W. (2013). Multi-aspect sentiment analysis for Chinese online social reviews based on topic modeling and HowNet lexicon. *Knowledge-Based Systems*, *37*, 186–195. doi:10.1016/j.knosys.2012.08.003

Xiang, W., Wang, G., Pickering, M., & Zhang, Y. (2016). Big video data for light-field-based 3D telemedicine. *IEEE Network*, *30*(3), 30–38. doi:10.1109/MNET.2016.7474341

Xiao, J., & Zhang, Y. (2001). Clustering of web users using session-based similarity measures. *International Conference on Computer Networks and Mobile Computing*, 223–228. 10.1109/ICCNMC.2001.962600

Xing-yuan, W., Fan-ping, L., & Shu-guo, W. (2009, November). Fractal image compression based on spatial correlation and hybrid genetic algorithm. *Journal of Visual Communication and Image Representation*, *20*(8), 505–510. doi:10.1016/j.jvcir.2009.07.002

Xu, Jiang, Wang, Yuan, & Ren. (2014). *Information Security in Big Data: Privacy and Data Mining*. IEEE. DOI 10.1109/Access.2014.2362522

Xu, K., Guo, X., Li, J., Lau, R. Y., & Liao, S. S. (2012). Discovering target groups in social networking sites: An effective method for maximizing joint influential power. *Electronic Commerce Research and Applications*, *11*(4), 318–334. doi:10.1016/j.elerap.2012.01.002

Yadav, V., Verma, M., & Kaushik, V. D. (2015, October). Big data analytics for health systems. In *Green Computing and Internet of Things (ICGCIoT), 2015 International Conference on* (pp. 253-258). IEEE. 10.1109/ICGCIoT.2015.7380468

Yadav, S., Tiwari, V., & Tiwari, B. (2016, March). Privacy Preserving Data Mining With Abridge Time Using Vertical Partition Decision Tree. In *Proceedings of the ACM Symposium on Women in Research 2016* (pp. 158-164). ACM. 10.1145/2909067.2909097

Yang, C.F., Ju, Y.H., Hsieh, C.Y., Lin, C.Y., Tsai, M.H., & Chang, H.L. (2017). iParking – a real-time parking space monitoring and guiding system. *Vehicular Communications*.

Yang, Z. C. K., Yeo, S., Lee, B.S., & Boleng, J. (2009). Position based Opportunistic Routing for Robust Data Delivery in MANETs. *Proceedings of the 28th IEEE conference on Global telecommunications*, 1325-1330. 10.1109/GLO-COM.2009.5425351

Yang, H., Liu, J., Sui, J., Pearlson, G., & Calhoun, V. D. (2010). A Hybrid Machine Learning Method for Fusing fMRI and Genetic Data: Combining both Improves Classification of Schizophrenia. *Frontiers in Human Neuroscience, 4*, 192. doi:10.3389/fnhum.2010.00192 PubMed

Yang, Z., & Wang, J. (2015). Differential effects of social influence sources on self-reported music piracy. *Decision Support Systems, 69*, 70–81. doi:10.1016/j.dss.2014.11.007

Yee Liau, B., & Pei Tan, P. (2014). Gaining customer knowledge in low cost airlines through text mining. *Industrial Management & Data Systems, 114*(9), 1344–1359. doi:10.1108/IMDS-07-2014-0225

Ye, Q., Zhang, Z., & Law, R. (2009). Sentiment classification of online reviews to travel destinations by supervised machine learning approaches. *Expert Systems with Applications, 36*(3), 6527–6535. doi:10.1016/j.eswa.2008.07.035

Yoon, Y., & Swales, G. S. (1991). Predicting stock price performance: a neural network approach. *Proceedings of the Twenty-Fourth Annual Hawaii International Conference on System Sciences*, 156–162. 10.1109/HICSS.1991.184055

Yudong, Z., & Lenan, W. (2009). Stock market prediction of S&P 500 via combination of improved BCO approach and BP neural network. *Expert Systems with Applications, 36*(5), 8849–8854. doi:10.1016/j.eswa.2008.11.028

Yuen, M.-C., King, I., & Leung, K.-S. (2011). A Survey of Crowdsourcing Systems. *Proceedings of the 3rd IEEE International Conference on Social Computing (SocialCom-11)*, 766-773.

Yu, J. X., Ou, Y., Zhang, C., & Zhang, S. (2005). Identifying interesting visitors through weblog classification. *IEEE Intelligent Systems, 20*(3), 55–60. doi:10.1109/MIS.2005.47

Yu, L. Q., & Rong, F. S. (2010). Stock Market Forecasting Research Based on Neural Network and Pattern Matching. *International Conference on E-Business and E-Government*, 1940–1943. 10.1109/ICEE.2010.490

Yu, L., Chen, H., Wang, S., & Lai, K. K. (2009). Evolving Least Squares Support Vector Machinesfor Stock Market Trend Mining. *IEEE Transactions on Evolutionary Computation, 13*(1), 87–102. doi:10.1109/TEVC.2008.928176

Zaharia, M., Chowdhury, M., Franklin, M. J., Shenker, S., & Stoica, I. (n.d.). Spark: Cluster Computing with Working Sets (PDF). *USENIX Workshop on Hot Topics in Cloud Computing (HotCloud)*.

Zdravko, M., & Daniel, T. L. (2007). *Data mining the Web, Uncovering patterns in Web content, structure, and usage.* John Wiley & sons Inc.

Zhang, D., & Zhou, L. (2004). Discovering Golden Nuggets: Data Mining in Financial Application. *IEEE Transactions on Systems, Man and Cybernetics. Part C, Applications and Reviews, 34*(4), 513–522. doi:10.1109/TSMCC.2004.829279

Zhang, J. (2016). High-performance data processing for image and data fusion. *International Journal of Image and Data Fusion, 7*(1), 1–2. doi:10.1080/19479832.2016.1122697

Zhang, J., Chen, C., & Cohen, R. (2010). *A Scalable and Effective Trust-Based Framework for Vehicular Ad-Hoc Networks.* Advances in Trust Management.

Zhang, X., Hu, Y., Xie, K., Wang, S., Ngai, E. W. T., & Liu, M. (2014). A causal feature selection algorithm for stock prediction modeling. *Neurocomputing, 142*, 48–59. doi:10.1016/j.neucom.2014.01.057

Zheng, T., Cao, L., He, Q., & Jin, G. (2014). Full-range in-plane rotation measurement for image recognition with hybrid digital-optical correlator. *Optical Engineering (Redondo Beach, Calif.), 53*(1).

Zheng, X., Zeng, D., & Wang, F.-Y. (2015). Social balance in signed networks. *Information Systems Frontiers, 17*(5), 1077–1095. doi:10.100710796-014-9483-8

Zhong, Z. (2011). Speed Up Statistical Spam Filter by Approximation. *IEEE Transaction on Computers, 60*(1), 120 – 134.

Zhongyi, L., Tong, Z., Wei, Y., & Xiaoming, L. (2009). *GOSR: Geographical Opportunistic Source Routing for VANETs. In Mobile Computing and Communications Review* (pp. 48–51). ACM SIGMOBILE.

Zhou, M., & Wei, H. (2006). Face verification using gabor wavelets and AdaBoost. *Proceedings of the 18th International Conference on Pattern Recognition (ICPR '06), 1*, 404–407. 10.1109/ICPR.2006.536

Zhou, X. C., Shen, H. B., Huang, Z. Y., & Li, G. J. (2012). Largemargin classification for combating disguise attacks on spam filters. *Journal of Zhejiang University-Science C, 13*(3), 187–195. doi:10.1631/jzus.C1100259

Zhu, L., Wang, X., & Lim, A. O. (2011). SMSS: Symmetric-Masquerade Security Scheme for VANETs. *10th International Symposium on Autonomous Decentralized Systems (ISADS).*

Zliobaite. (2010). *Adaptive training set formation* (Ph.D thesis). Vilnius University.

About the Contributors

Vivek Tiwari is from India He is the recipient of Young scientist award by Govt. by the MPCST, Govt. of M.P., India. He has published more than 25 research papers and book chapters in the areas of data mining, data warehousing, pattern warehousing, distributed computing and cloud computing in leading international journals (Springer, Inderscience, Elsevier, ACM and IGI-Global) indexed by Science Citation Index (SCI) and conferences (IEEE and ACM). He is Editors-in-chief of book "Handbook of Research on Pattern and Data Analysis in Healthcare Settings" under the series of Advances in Data Mining & Database Management (ADMDM), published by IGI-Global, USA. A research project "Aakash for Education" of cost 5 lac funded by MHRD, India is in his credit. He has been invited from various universities of India as keynote speaker/expert/visiting/guest faculty. He has given their services for various conferences under the umbrella of Springer, ACM, IEEE. He is an active member of the CSI, IAENG and IACSIT and regular reviewer of various international journals including Inderscience and IGI-Global.

Ramjeevan Singh Thakur received his BSc from Sagar University in 1995, MCA from SATI Vidisha in 1999 and a PhD degree from RGPV, Bhopal in 2008 in Computer Science and Applications. He worked as an Assistant Professor in RGPV Technical University, Bhopal from July 2000 to July 2007. After then, he joined NIT, Trichy from July 2007 to June 2010. Currently, he is an Associate Professor in Maulana Azad National Institute of Technology, Bhopal, India. His research interests include data/document warehousing, and data/text mining. He is a member of the IAENG, IACSIT and CSI.

Basant Tiwari is currently serving as Assistant Professor at Hawassa University Institute of Technology, Ethiopia in Department of Computer Science. He has rich experience in teaching undergraduate and postgraduate classes. He has many International and National publications to his credit in conferences and journals. He is also attended many National & International Conferences/ Workshops/ Seminars/ Symposiums etc. in all over India and Abroad. His current area of research is "Pervasive Healthcare and Remote Medical Care". He is a Senior Member of IEEE, Senior Member of ACM, CSI and IACSIT. Currently, he has honored as Bhopal Representative in IEEE M.P. Sub-section, Treasurer in ACM Udaipur Chapter and Secretary in CSI Bhopal chapter. Prof. Basant Tiwari has organized various National and International conferences and delivered invited talks and also chaired the technical sessions. He is the reviewer of various reputed International journals and Books. He did his Ph. D. from, Devi Ahilya University, Indore.

***

Mohd Vasim Ahamad has completed his M.Tech in Computer Science and Engineering (Software Engineering) from Department of Computer Engineering, Zakir Husain College of Engineering and Technology, AMU Aligarh in 2015. He has professional experience of 1.5 years as a Software Engineer. Currently, he is with Computer Engineering Section, University Women's Polytechnic, Aligarh Muslim University. His areas of expertise are Data Mining, Big Data Analytics and Machine Learning.

Gaganmeet Kaur Awal is currently pursuing Ph.D. (Computer Science) from School of Computer and Systems Sciences, Jawaharlal Nehru University (JNU), New Delhi, India. She has been awarded prestigious DST Inspire Fellowship from Ministry of Science and Technology, Govt. of India for being the first rank holder in the university. She received her M.Tech degree in Computer Science and Technology from JNU, in 2013 and her B.Tech degree in Computer Science and Engineering from Guru Gobind Singh Indraprastha University, New Delhi, India, in 2011. Her current research interests include Social Computing, Collective Intelligence, Machine Learning, and Computational Web Intelligence.

Syed Basha is a research scholar at VIT University. His research areas are Text Mining and BigData Predictive Analytics.

K. K. Bharadwaj is currently a professor in the School of Computer & Systems Sciences, Jawaharlal Nehru University (JNU), New Delhi, India. He joined JNU in 1985 as an Associate Professor and since 1990 he is full Professor at JNU. Prior to JNU he has been a Faculty in the Computer Science Department, BITS, Pilani (Rajasthan), India. He received his M.Sc. degree in Mathematics from the University of Udaipur (Rajasthan), India and Ph.D. degree in Computer Science from the Indian Institute of Technology (IIT), Kanpur, India. He has published widely in International journals and International conference proceedings. His current research interests include Machine Learning, Intelligent Systems, Knowledge Discovery in Databases (KDD), and Computational Web Intelligence.

Debasis Das received his Ph.D in Computer Science and Engineering from Indian Institute of Technology (IIT) Patna, Bihar, India. His thesis work was on Vehicular Ad-hoc Networks in (VANET). He received his M. Tech in Computer Science and Engineering degree from School of Computer Engineering, KIIT University, Bhubaneswar, Orissa, India. He joined BITS Pilani, K. K. Birla Goa Campus in 2016 and before joining BITS, he was working as an Assistant Professor in NIIT University, India. His research interests include Computer Networks, Vehicular Network, Cloud Computing, Algorithm, Network Security and Cellular Automata.

Pratima Gautam has published research papers, and book chapters in international journals and conferences like Springer, Inderscience, Elsevier, ACM and IGI-Global indexed by Science Citation Index (SCI) and Scopus (Elsevier). Areas of interest are image processing, pattern recognition and machine learning.

Misbahul Haque received his B.Tech. and M.Tech. degree from ZHCET, Aligarh Muslim University. His area of research interest is Social Networks, Mobile Ad-Hoc Networks, and Big Data. He is currently working as a faculty in the Department of Computer Engineering, Aligarh Muslim University.

Mohd Imran is currently with the department of computer engineering, Faculty of Engineering & Technology, Aligarh Muslim University. He received his master degree from AMU in 2015 with Hons. His areas of expertise are Networking, Multimedia Technology, and Mining.

Vijayalakshmi Kakulapati is Professor in the Department of Information Technology and having around 24 years of industry and teaching experience. Her area of research includes theoretical and practical information retrieval problems, as well as machine learning applied to large scale textual applications. Her research focused on retrieval models, query/document representations, term weighting, term proximity models, and learning to rank (machine learned ranking functions). She has always interested in expanding the breadth and the depth of research into other related areas or fields of study. She has passionate about seeing her research applied to real world problems, especially those dealing with large, complex data sets. Along these lines, she is working with evaluating and designing novel search algorithms for web search, summarization. Currently she is working with big data, Internet of Things, Data Science and Health informatics. She is having more than 40+ publications in National, International Journals and conferences.

Ramgopal Kashyap has published research papers in International journals and conferences in the Scopus indexed journal. He has Reviewed Research Papers in the Science Citation Index Expanded and Editorial Board Member of International Journal on Cryptography and Information Security, Publisher Wireilla Scientific Publications, New South Wales, Australia. Ramgopal Kashyap has reviewed more than 300 research papers in the 70 international journals and conferences and Programme committee member of the IEEE, Springer international conferences and journals held in countries: Czech Republic, Switzerland, UAE, Australia, Hungary, Poland, Taiwan, Denmark, India, USA, UK, Austria, and Turkey. He has written many book chapters published by IGI Global, USA. His areas of Research are Digital Image Processing, Pattern Recognition, Machine Learning, Medical Image Segmentation, and Medical Image Analysis.

Sreeram Kattamuri is a researcher and his area of interest is Intrusion Detection, python programming.

Arvind Kourav is working as an Associate Professor in Bhopal Institute of Technology & Science Bhopal (MP). Arvind Kourav received a BE in 2003 in Electronics & Telecommunication Engineering, MTech in 2008 in Digital Communication and a PhD in 2015 in Image Processing. Research field is digital Image Processing.

Vinod Kumar is a PhD Research Scholar in the Department of Computer Applications, Maulana Azad National Institute of Technology, Bhopal (M.P.) INDIA. He is doing research in the field of Big Data and web mining Tools and Techniques.

Dasari Naga Raju is working as Associate Professor in the Department of Computer Science and Engineering, SVCET(Autonomous), Chittoor. His research areas include cloud computing, Big Data and MANETs.

Lingamallu Naga Srinivasu is working as an assistant professor in Kallam Haranadha Reddy Institute of Technology.

Rajit Nair is pursuing a Ph.D. from NIT Bhopal. Rajit has a total 11 years of teaching experience. Research areas are Big Data, Machine Learning & Data Mining. Rajit has presented many research papers in national & international conferences. More than six papers are published in reputed journals.

Albert Piersson holds MSc in Magnetic Resonance Imaging (MRI) from the Anglia Ruskin University, UK. He is an Assistant lecturer at the Department of Imaging Technology and Sonography, University of Cape Coast, Ghana. Albert Piersson is also a Diagnostic Radiographer with an extensive clinical experience which spans over 12 years in a wide range of diagnostic imaging modalities which include General Radiography, fluoroscopy, Computed Tomography (CT), Magnetic Resonance Imaging (MRI), and General Ultrasound. He has published in Elsevier peer-reviewed journals, and have presented at scientific conferences both locally and internationally. His research area include MRI, Neuroimaging, Pica, and Geophagia.

Dharmendra Singh Rajput is working as Associate Professor in the Department of Software and Systems Engineering, School of Information Technology and Engineering, VIT University. His research areas are Data Mining and Big Data Predictive Analytics.

Dasari Raju is working as Associate Professor in the Department of Computer Science and Engineering, SVCET(Autonomous), Chittoor. His research areas include cloud computing, Big Data and MANETs.

Kolakaluri Rao is working as an associate professor in Kallam Haranadha Reddy Institute of Technology and presently pursuing a PhD in JNTU-H, Hyderabad, A.P, India.

T. Reddy is working as Professor and Head in the Department of Computer Science and Engineering, SVCET(Autonomous), Chittoor. His research areas are Data Mining and Big Data Predictive Analytics.

Pallam Setty S. is professor in Andhra University.

Shabina Sayed received an Mtech in computer engineering from Makes Patel School of Technical Education and has 13 years of teaching experience in Sabot Siddik College of Engineering. Personally interested in data base related subject. Doing specialization in data stream mining. Dream is to open research laboratory.

Shilpi Sharma has twelve years' experience in the field of teaching and area of expertise is digital image processing.

Mohd Shoaib is currently working in Department of Computer Engineering, Zakir Husain College of Engineering and Technology, Aligarh Muslim University. He has over five years of experience in academics. His current research interests are Web Mining, Parallel Computing and Software Engineering.

Dilip Singh Sisodia received the Bachelor of Engineering and Master of Technology degrees respectively in computer science & engineering and information technology (with specialization in artificial intelligence) from the Rajiv Gandhi Technological University, Bhopal, India. He received the Ph.D. degree in computer science and engineering from the National Institute of Technology Raipur, India. Dr. Sisodia is an assistant professor with the department of computer science engineering, National Institute of Technology Raipur. He has over thirteen years of experience of various reputed institutes in the field of academics & research. He has published over 45 referred articles in SCI/ Scopus journals and conferences and also served as a reviewer for several international journals, and conferences. His current research interests include web usage mining, Machine learning, and computational intelligence. Dr. Sisodia is actively associated with various professional societies including IEEE, ACM, CSI, IETE, IE (India) etc.

Vimal Tiwari works as an Assistant Professor in Bhopal Institute of Technology Bhopal (MP). Research field is Data Mining & Digital Image Processing. Vimal Tiwari received a BE in 2006 in Computer Science & Engineering and an MTech in 2013 in Computer Science & Engineering.

Harsha Vasudev is a Ph. D student.

Index

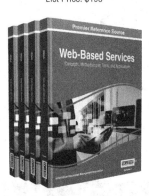
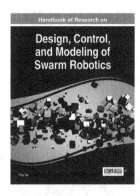

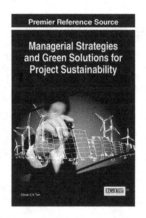

Printed in the United States
By Bookmasters